The

Italian Lakes

written and researched by

Matthew Teller and Lucy Ratcliffe

ROUGH
GUIDES

NEW YORK · LONDON · DELHI

www.roughguides.com

Contents

Lake cuisine colour
section following p.112

Gardens of the lakes
colour section
following p.240

◀◀ Lake Garda ◀ Isola Bella, Lake Maggiore

Venice

N

Passo del Brennero

Trento

Riva del Garda
Torbole
Malcesine
Limone sul Garda
Torri del Benaco
Gargnano
Riviera
Gardone
Salò
Idro
Bagolino
Capo di Ponte
Edolo
Breno
Tirano
Clusone
Lovere
Monte Isola
Sarnico
Iseo
Breno
Sóndrio
San Pellegrino
Bergamo
Bergamo-Orio al Serio
Treviglio
Caravaggio
Lecco
Colico
Gravedona
Menaggio
Tremezzo
Varenna
Bellagio
Como
Varese
Porto Ceresio
Lugano
Lugano-Agno
Locarno
Ascona
Cannobio
Luino
Laveno
Porto Ceresio
Verbania
Stresa
Gravellona
Orta
San Giulio
Arona
Domodossola
Novara
Vigévano
Certosa di Pavia
Pavia
Milan-Linate
Milan-Malpensa
Milan
Lodi
Crema
Lodi
Cremona

Verona
Verona-Villafranca
Peschiera del Garda
Sirmione
Bardolino
Desenzano del Garda
Brescia
Brescia-Montichiari
Mantova

SWITZERLAND

Passo del San Gottardo
St Moritz
Chiavenna
Bellinzona

Passo del Sempione
Turin
Genoa
Genoa
Piacenza
Piacenza
Cremona
Parma
Modena

Lake Garda
Lake Como
Lake Iseo
River Adige
River Mincio
River Oglio
River Adda
River Po
River Ticino

A22
A4
A21
A1
A9
N2
A8
A26

20 km
0

Metres
3000
2000
1500
1000
500
200
100
0

4

Introduction to the

Italian Lakes

One can't describe the beauty of the Italian lakes, nor would one try if one could.

Henry James

The Italian Lakes are a little slice of paradise. Generations of travellers from the north, descending wearily from the chilly Alpine passes, have come into this Mediterranean vision of figs and palms, bougainvillea and lemon blossom, and, like Henry James, been lost for words. Elegant ribbons of blue water stretch out ahead, folded into the sun-baked foothills; after the rigours of the high Alps, the abundance of fine food and wine must have been a revelation. Warming, awe-inspiring and graced with natural beauty, the lakes are still a place to draw breath and wonder.

 These days, of course, mass tourism has found the lakes, and the shoreside roads that link every town can be as packed as the ferries that chug to and fro. But the chief reason to visit the area – its spectacular landscapes – remains compelling, and there are plenty of ways to avoid the crowds.

The lakes – deep, slender fjords gouged by glaciers – are sublime. All are oriented north-south, ringed by characterful old villages often wedged onto narrow beaches between rugged cliffs and the water. And those classic lakes images of flower-bedecked balconies, Baroque gardens and splendid waterside villas can be found here in abundance.

Long a stop on the Grand Tour, the lakes and their nearby cities hold some of the grandest of Europe's grand hotels, yet throughout the region there also

Two of the major Italian lakes – Maggiore and Lugano – straddle the Swiss frontier, with shorelines in two countries. Although the title of this book is *The Rough Guide to the Italian Lakes*, you'll nonetheless find full coverage of attractions and travel practicalities on both sides of the border.

Fact file

• There are **seven** major lakes occupying the southern foothills of the Alps – from west to east: Orta, Maggiore, Lugano, Como, Iseo, Idro and Garda.

• The area takes in four Italian administrative regions – **Piemonte**, **Lombardia** (Lombardy), **Trentino** and **Veneto** – as well as part of the Swiss canton of **Ticino**.

• Lake Garda is the **largest** lake in Italy, at 52km long and 17km wide. Lake Maggiore is the **longest**, at 66km. Lake Idro is the **highest** of Italy's major lakes, at 368m above sea level.

• **Milan** is the nearest city to the lakes, with a population of 1.3 million. Several large towns fall within the Lakes area, including Verona (260,000), Brescia (200,000), Bergamo (120,000), Como and Varese (both 80,000), and Pavia and Cremona (both 70,000).

• This is a **wealthy** region, with small, family-run companies widespread. Light industry – including traditional manufacturing, such as silk-making around Como and furniture-making in the Brianza region – contributes significantly to Italy's GDP.

• Italian is the official **language** on both sides of the international border here, but the region has almost as many dialects as it has communities. These have their roots in the history of the region and often include words drawn from past French, Austrian and Spanish occupiers.

◄ Galleria Vittorio Emanuele II, Milan

runs a vein of genial, low-key hospitality that has produced countless attractive little family-run establishments offering simpler, cosier comforts.

Dotted around and between the lakes are some of Italy's finest art cities. Milan is pre-eminent, while Verona, Bergamo, Mantova and others display – in their architecture as well as their art – a civilized, urban vision that stands in marked contrast to the wild, largely rural character of the lakeside hinterlands. Italy only became a unified state in 1861 and, as a result, people often feel more loyalty to their home town than to the nation as a whole – a feeling manifest in the multitude of cuisines, dialects and outlooks that span the region.

Where to go

Milan needs little introduction – the undisputed "capital" of the north, and richest city of Italy's richest region, Lombardy. Its pilgrimage status is four-fold. Art – pay homage to Leonardo da Vinci's iconic **Last Supper**. Architecture – explore the spectacular **Duomo** inside and out. Music – sample opera at the world-famous **La Scala**. Shopping – this is one of the world's **fashion** capitals. Stylish, sophisticated and good-looking, Milan embodies Italian chic.

The opulent **Certosa di Pavia** monastery, set amid the rice fields south of the city, stands as a monument to Milan's Renaissance rulers.

The lakes are ranged in formation north of Milan, interleaved between the Prealpine foothills. The westernmost is **Lake Orta**, a pretty little wedge of blue water that holds one of the loveliest of all the region's medieval villages – **Orta San Giulio**.

The longest of the lakes – **Lake Maggiore** – lies draped between high ridges of green mountainside. The resorts of **Stresa** and **Pallanza** face idyllic islets crowned with palaces and Baroque gardens. North are genteel **Cánnero** and **Cannóbio**, while, across the border, the Swiss neighbours of **Locarno** and **Ascona** are two of Maggiore's most alluring destinations.

Milan is the undisputed "capital" of the north.

Varese is the region's most underrated city. Penetrate its industrial suburbs and you find a core of cobbled piazzas and stylish boutiques, made unmissable by the superb gallery of contemporary art at **Villa Panza**.

Nearby **Lake Lugano** lies mostly in Switzerland. Wilder than its neighbours, with long stretches of forested shoreline that plunge directly into the water, it offers a sense of seclusion lacking elsewhere. Cosmopolitan **Lugano** basks on a sunny, south-facing bay, cogwheel trains climb the nearby peak of **Monte Generoso**, while further north rise the fortifications of **Bellinzona**.

▶ Riva del Garda, Lake Garda

Rocca Scaligera, Sirmione, Lake Garda

The forked **Lake Como** is one of the best-known holiday destinations in Italy, offering, in waterfront villages such as **Bellagio** and **Varenna**, the classic images of the lakes. **Como** itself is a dignified old silk town with a magnificent cathedral, while behind **Menaggio** coil scenic mountain footpaths.

The hill-town of **Bergamo** rises from the plain northeast of Milan. Its Gothic-medieval upper town, characterized by cobbled alleys winding between high-fronted palazzi, is a foodie's delight, packed with fine restaurants, while the **Accademia Carrara** is Lombardy's most prestigious gallery outside Milan.

A little east is **Brescia**, a hard-working, business-minded city which boasts fine Roman ruins as well as, nearby, the squiggle of **Lake Iseo**. To the south stands the old violin-making town of **Cremona**.

Marking the eastern limit of Lombardy is Italy's largest and most famous lake: **Lake Garda**. The southern shores are flat or gently rolling; highlights here include busy **Sirmione**, on its long peninsula.

> **The lakes – deep, slender fjords gouged by glaciers – are sublime.**

To the east, a string of old Venetian ports includes gentle **Garda** and little-visited **Torri del Benaco**. The western shore has more classic lake imagery – exotic flower gardens, palm-shaded promenades and fine Art Nouveau villas crowding the waterfront around **Salò** and **Gardone Riviera**.

In the north, Lake Garda's shores are hemmed in by sheer, parallel mountains: the dramatic scenery here takes your breath away. **Gargnano** village – beloved of D.H. Lawrence – is a highlight on the trip north past **Limone** to the splendid, once-Austrian resort of **Riva del Garda** at the head of the lake. As well as a sense of history, Riva, and its neighbour, **Torbole**, have watersports aplenty, and there are good walks on the crest of **Monte Baldo** nearby, above **Malcésine**.

A little east of Lake Garda stands **Verona**, a laid-back, easy-going city with, at its core, the near-perfectly preserved Roman **Arena**, scene of a famous summer opera festival. Roaming Verona's alleys, dipping into the local taverns and restaurants, is a rare pleasure.

Just to the south, the dignified old town of **Mantova** (Mantua in English) makes a compelling side-trip. The Renaissance frescoes in its **Palazzo Ducale** and **Palazzo Te**, not to mention boat trips across its three, lotus-fringed lakes, are a fitting climax to a trip across the region.

▶ Café society, Verona

When to go

The best months to visit are **June** and, especially, **September**. At these times, visitor numbers are below their peak, but the weather is lovely: sunshine pouring from blue skies, temperatures that are toasty but not scorching and magically clear, cool evenings.

The hottest months, **July** and **August**, are when the lakes are at their most crowded: weekends in particular can see roads jam-packed with traffic. The cities, especially Milan, can be sweltering, with temperatures topping 35°C

The lakes in Latin

On maps and in tourist brochures, you'll notice that the lakes are often referred to by their old **Latin** names. These titles – which are also much used by writers and poets – evoke a sense of pride in local culture and history, forming a linguistic link between the present and the distant past. For this reason, politicians also love them: when the Province of Novara was reorganized in the 1990s, the new province which resulted, covering territory around lakes Maggiore and Orta, was named "Verbano-Cusio-Ossola", deliberately playing on the Latin appellations.

For all practical purposes, though, these names are a curiosity: they are rarely used without their modern equivalents – and never on road signs.

Lake Orta	= "Cusio"	Lake Iseo	= "Sebino"
Lake Maggiore	= "Verbano"	Lake Idro	= "Eridio"
Lake Lugano	= "Ceresio"	Lake Garda	= "Benaco"
Lake Como	= "Lario"		

for days on end. Spectacular – but shortlived – thunderstorms are common in the region in late August.

Italians take the first two or three weeks of August as their annual holiday; this means the urban centres – Milan, Verona, Bergamo – can feel somewhat artificial, as the only people around are foreign tourists. Many restaurants, bars and shops close altogether. In this, the Swiss are more flexible: head across to Lugano or Locarno in August and you'll find that life continues more or less as normal.

The season on the lakes runs from **Easter** to **October**. Outside these months you'll find that tourism shuts down: many hotels and restaurants close for the winter, ferry services are reduced or halted and attractions open for shorter hours, if at all. Skies are often grey, with chill winds sweeping down

▲ Menaggio, Lake Como

from the peaks. Nonetheless, the lakes retain their romance – morning mist hangs on the waters, snow carpets the lakeside ridges. With prices low and few tourists around, winter can be a great time to visit.

Climate

The chart shows average minimum and maximum temperatures, followed by the average number of rainy days in the month (d) and the average number of sunshine hours per day (hr).

	Como & Lugano	Milan & Bergamo	Verona & Lake Garda
Jan	0–6°C 6d / 4hr	-1–5°C 7d / 2hr	-2–5°C 7d / 3hr
Feb	1–7°C 7d / 5hr	1–8°C 5d / 3hr	0–9°C 6d / 4hr
Mar	4–11°C 8d / 5hr	5–13°C 7d / 5hr	3–13°C 7d / 5hr
Apr	7–15°C 10d / 6hr	9–18°C 9d / 6hr	7–17°C 9d / 5hr
May	11–19°C 14d / 6hr	13–23°C 10d / 7hr	11–22°C 9d / 7hr
Jun	14–23°C 11d / 7hr	17–28°C 7d / 8hr	15–26°C 8d / 8hr
Jul	16–25°C 9d / 8hr	19–31°C 5d / 9hr	18–29°C 6d / 9hr
Aug	16–24°C 10d / 7hr	19–29°C 5d / 8hr	17–28°C 6d / 8hr
Sep	13–21°C 8d / 6hr	15–24°C 6d / 6hr	14–24°C 5d / 6hr
Oct	9–15°C 8d / 5hr	10–17°C 8d / 4hr	8–18°C 7d / 5hr
Nov	4–10°C 8d / 4hr	5–10°C 8d / 2hr	3–11°C 8d / 3hr
Dec	1–7°C 6d / 4hr	1–6°C 7d / 2hr	-1–6°C 6d / 3hr

15

things not to miss

It's not possible to see everything that the Italian Lakes have to offer in one trip – and we don't suggest you try. What follows is a selective and subjective taste of the region's highlights: great places to visit, top attractions and scenic journeys. They're arranged in five colour-coded categories to help you find the very best things to see, do and experience. All entries have a page reference to take you straight into the Guide, where you can find out more.

01 **Orta San Giulio** Page **150** • Perhaps the most alluring of all Italian lake villages – characterful, good-looking and fronting the beautiful islet of Isola San Giulio.

04 Bergamo Alta
Page **230** • The tower of Santa Maria Maggiore rises high above Bergamo's picturesque Città Alta, or upper town.

02 Watersports, Lake Garda
Page **294** • Riva del Garda and its neighbour, Torbole, are renowned for their watersports, set against a mountain backdrop.

05 Lago Maggiore Express
Page **130** • A varied and beautiful circular journey by boat and train from Lake Maggiore; pictured is Intragna, a mountain village on the spectacular Centovalli line.

06 Mantova
Page **327** • One of Renaissance Italy's most prominent city-states, boasting a vast Palazzo Ducale and Giulio Romano's eye-catching frescoes in the Palazzo Te (including the Sala di Amore e Psiche, pictured).

03 Shopping in Milan
Page **100** • From slick designer boutiques to bargain-basement factory outlets, Milan is one of the world's best shopping destinations.

07 **Four Lakes Drive** Page **284** • A scenic full-day drive on a looping route through Alpine landscapes above Lake Garda; pictured is Bagolino, above Lake Idro.

08 **The Last Supper** Page **97** • Book well in advance to see Leonardo da Vinci's masterpiece, tucked away on a refectory wall in Milan.

09 **Certosa di Pavia** Page **116** • This beautiful Carthusian monastery, just south of Milan, offers a respite from the city's worldly pleasures.

10 **Bellinzona's castles** Page **219** • This chain of superbly preserved medieval fortifications strung across the upper Ticino valley now forms a UNESCO World Heritage Site.

12 **Brescia** Page **243** • Venerable Lombard city with fine galleries, restaurants and the uniquely well-preserved circular Duomo Vecchio.

11 **Roof of Milan's Duomo** Page **79** • Stroll among the marble spires on top of the city's colossal cathedral.

14 **Monte Generoso** Page **215** • A rugged chunk of mountain perched above Lake Lugano, reached by cogwheel railway, which offers stiff hiking trails and sensational views over the lakes, clear right across to Milan.

13 **Lake Como** Page **176** • Take a ferry across the idyllic Centro Lago, between the lakeside villages of Bellagio, Menaggio and Varenna.

15 **Opera in Verona** Page **314** • Of the many reasons to visit the city of Romeo and Juliet, Verona's world-famous summer opera season, staged in the huge Roman arena, is perhaps the most compelling.

Basics

Basics

Getting there

The Italian Lakes region is well-connected with airports all around the world. Intercontinental flights head for Milan's Malpensa, which also serves many European routings, as does Milan's other airport, Linate. The smaller airports at Bergamo, Brescia, Verona, and Lugano in Switzerland are also within striking distance of Milan and the lakes. Travelling by train, car or even bus from the UK is a viable, greener, more leisurely option, though not competitive in terms of price.

The availability of flights and prices depends on when you travel. It's invariably cheaper to fly midweek; flights at the beginning and end of the week are in demand from business-people and holiday-makers alike. Easter, public holidays and the beginning and end of August see airports at their busiest. Flights to the region are also booked up well in advance around Milan's fashion and design shows in January, April and September, while in August most people choose to avoid the humid heat of the city and so flights can be easier to come by. As always, the best advice is to reserve your flight as far ahead as possible: good-value last-minute tickets are rare.

The **internet** is the best place to start looking for flights, but don't ignore **specialist agents** either: many offer youth fares and a range of other travel-related services such as insurance, car rentals, tours and the like. Italy is also a common stop on European and worldwide **tours**, and you should have no problem including the region in a tailor-made itinerary if off-the-peg tickets are not suitable.

Flights from the UK and Ireland

The fastest and most economical way of reaching the Italian Lakes is by air. It takes just under two hours to fly from southern England to the heart of the region, and good bus, train and road routes ensure swift onward transport. If you're planning to tour the area, consider flying into one airport and out of another.

Airports and routes

It's worth spending a moment establishing which is the most **convenient** of the region's numerous airports for your holiday, so that you can cut down travelling time when you arrive. Milan has two airports, both of which receive regular flights from the UK and Ireland. **Malpensa** (MXP), 45km northwest of the city, is just 15km from the southern tip of Lake Maggiore and convenient for lakes Orta and Como, too. **Linate** (LIN), 7km east of the city, is your best bet if you're starting or ending your trip in Milan itself. **Orio al Serio** (BGY), just outside Bergamo, is also billed as Milan, but is a good hour's drive from the city centre. It is, however, conveniently located halfway between lakes Como and Garda, near the smaller Lake Iseo. **Brescia-Montichiari** (VBS) airport, confusingly otherwise known as "Verona (Brescia)" airport and "Gabriele d'Annunzio" airport, is 20km southeast of Brescia, just 12km from Lake Garda, though it's actually quite a long way out of Verona – 52km southwest. Much closer to Verona itself is **Verona-Villafranca** (VRN), also called "Valerio Catullo". Venice and Turin are outside the scope of this book, but their airports (Turin and both Venice Marco Polo and Venice Treviso) are under an hour away from the western and eastern lakes respectively. In Switzerland, the small **Lugano-Agno** (LUG) airport is ten minutes from the town centre and convenient for lakes Maggiore and Como, as well as Lake Lugano itself.

The table on p.20 shows the distance from the different airports to a main town on each of the lakes. Distances have been worked out along major roads and the estimated times based on travelling at a steady 100km per hour. Tolls vary depending on the route but are always inexpensive. At the time of writing, for example, the 58km from Linate to

Arrival airport/ final destination	Stresa (Lake Maggiore)	Lugano (Lake Lugano)	Milan city centre	Como (Lake Como)	Bergamo city centre	Sirmione (Lake Garda)	Verona city centre
Milan-Malpensa (MXP)	45km (30min)	65km (45min)	48km (35min)	43km (30min)	72km (55min)	150km (1hr 40min)	178km (2hr)
Milan-Linate (LIN)	100km (1hr 10min)	87km (1hr)	7km (20min)	65km (45min)	45km (30min)	124km (1hr 25min)	152km (1hr 45min)
Lugano-Agno (LUG)	90km (1hr 45min)	4km (10min)	86km (1hr)	25km (15min)	95km (1hr 15min)	185km (2hr)	215km (2hr 25min)
Bergamo-Orio al Serio (BGY)	124km (1hr 25min)	112km (1hr 15min)	40km (30min)	88km (1hr)	5km (15min)	81km (55min)	108km (1hr 15min)
Brescia-Montichiari (VBS)	186km (2hr)	172km (1hr 55min)	105km (1hr 15min)	150km (1hr 40min)	66km (45min)	22km (15min)	50km (35min)
Verona-Villafranca (VRN)	242km (2hr 40min)	230km (2hr 35min)	155km (1hr 45min)	206km (2hr 15min)	122km (1hr 25min)	42km (30min)	13km (10min)

Como cost €4.50, while the 150-kilometre journey from Malpensa to Sirmione on Lake Garda was €7.80.

The **no-frills airlines**, such as easyJet and Ryanair, fly regularly from London and many regional airports to Orio al Serio, Brescia-Montichiari, Milan, Venice Treviso and Turin. Of the major **full-service carriers** covering the region, British Airways offers the most choice while Alitalia flies to Milan from the UK. SWISS has daily flights to Lugano-Agno (via Zurich).

From the Irish Republic, Aer Lingus and Alitalia have services to Milan and Ryanair flies from Shannon to Bergamo-Orio al Serio.

Tickets and prices

All airlines have a **ticketless system** – when booking your flight you are simply given a reference number to check in with at the airport. If you book far enough in advance on the **no-frills airlines**, or bag one of their frequent special offers, you can get tickets for less than £50 return (including taxes) for an off-peak flight. The cheapest **full-service** tickets normally cost around £120–160 (including taxes) to Milan or Verona for a return fare in low season; be prepared to pay £250–350 in high season, when the cheaper seats get booked up months in advance.

It is possible to find deals for around €100 for direct return flights **from Ireland** if you book early, but prices are usually significantly higher (€300–500). It might make more sense to pick up an inexpensive flight to England or the Continent and get a connecting flight from there.

Flights from the US and Canada

Delta Air Lines fly the widest choice of routes between the **US** and Italy, with daily direct flights to Milan from New York, Atlanta, Chicago and Boston. In addition, many European carriers fly to Milan (via their capitals or via Rome) from major US and Canadian cities.

The **fares** don't vary much so you can usually base your choice on flight timings, routes, gateway cities, ticket restrictions and even the airline's reputation for comfort and service. Flight time is around nine hours from New York, Boston and the eastern Canadian cities, twelve hours from Chicago and fifteen hours from Los Angeles. The cheapest **return fares** to Milan, travelling midweek in low season, start at around $800 from New York or Boston, rising to about $1000 during the summer. Add another $150–300 for flights from LA, Miami and Chicago. Numerous airlines, including Air Canada and United, have flights from **Toronto** via Rome to Milan for a low-season fare of around Can$1000 midweek, increasing to around $2500 in high season without taxes.

Flights from Australia and New Zealand

There are no direct flights to Italy from Australia or New Zealand, but there are some good deals to be had which include **stopovers** in East Asia or European airline hubs. **Return fares** to Milan from the main cities in **Australia** cost A$1500–1850 in low season, and A$1700–2500 in high season. Fares to Milan from **New Zealand** cost from NZ$1900 low season to NZ$3500 high season. It's also worth considering flying to one of the European hubs like London or Berlin and looking for a low-cost flight from there.

Airlines

Aer Lingus UK ☎0870/876 5000, Ireland ☎0818/365 000; ⊛www.aerlingus.com.
Air Canada Canada ☎1-888/247-2262, ⊛www.aircanada.ca.
Air France US ☎1-800/237-2747, Canada ☎1-800/667-2747; ⊛www.airfrance.com.
Air One Outside Italy ☎+39 0648.88.0069, US 1-888-9-FLY-AIR1; ⊛www.flyairone.it.
Alitalia UK ☎08714/241 424, Ireland ☎01/677 5171, US ☎1-800/223-5730, Canada ☎1-800/361-8336; ⊛www.alitalia.com.
American Airlines US ☎1-800/433-7300, ⊛www.aa.com.
Austrian Airlines US ☎1-800/843-0002, ⊛www.aua.com.
British Airways UK ☎0844/493 0777, Ireland ☎1890/626 747, US ☎1-800/247-9297, Australia ☎1300/767 177, New Zealand ☎09/966 9777; ⊛www.ba.com.
Cathay Pacific Australia ☎13 17 47, New Zealand ☎0800/800 454; ⊛www.cathaypacific.com.
Continental Airlines US ☎1-800/231-0856, ⊛www.continental.com.
Delta Air Lines US ☎1-800/231-0856, ⊛www.delta.com.
easyJet UK ☎0905/821 0905 (65p per min), ⊛www.easyjet.com.
Iberia US ☎1-800/772-4642, ⊛www.iberia.com.
Japan Airlines Australia ☎1300/525 287, New Zealand ☎0800/525 747; ⊛www.jal.com.

KLM Australia ☎1300/303 747, New Zealand ☎09/309 1782; ⊛www.klm.com.
Lufthansa US ☎1-800/645-3880, Canada ☎1-800/563-5954, Australia ☎1300/655 727, New Zealand ☎09/303 1529; ⊛www.lufthansa.com.
Malaysia Airlines Australia ☎13 26 27, New Zealand ☎09/373 2741; ⊛www.malaysia-airlines.com.
Northwest US ☎1-800/225-2525, ⊛www.nwa.com.
Qantas Australia ☎13 13 13, New Zealand ☎0800/808 767; ⊛www.qantas.com.au.
Ryanair UK ☎0906/270 5656 (25p per min), Ireland ☎1530/787 787 (33c per min); ⊛www.ryanair.com.
SAS (Scandinavian Airlines) US ☎1-800/221-2350, ⊛www.scandinavian.net.
Singapore Airlines Australia ☎13 10 11, New Zealand ☎09/303 2129; ⊛www.singaporeair.com.
Sri Lankan Airlines Australia ☎02/9244 2234, New Zealand ☎09/308 3353; ⊛www.srilankan.aero.
SWISS UK ☎0845/601 0956, Ireland ☎01/806 7430, US ☎1-877/359-7947; ⊛www.swiss.com.
Thai Airways Australia ☎1300/651 960, New Zealand ☎09/377 3886; ⊛www.thaiair.com.

Travel agents and online booking

Air Brokers International US & Canada ☎1-800/883-3273, ⊛www.airbrokers.com. Consolidator and specialist in round-the-world tickets.
CIT Australia ☎1300/361 500, ⊛www.cittravel.com.au. Italian specialists, with packages to Milan, as well as the lakes.
Educational Travel Center US & Canada ☎1-800/747-5551 or 608/256-5551, ⊛www.edtrav.com. Student/youth discount agent.
Flight Centres Australia ☎13 31 33, New Zealand ☎09/358 4310; ⊛www.flightcentre.com.au. Discount international airfares and holiday packages.
Joe Walsh Tours Eire ☎01/241 0800, ⊛www.joewalshtours.ie. General budget fares agent.
North South Travel UK ☎01245/608 291, ⊛www.northsouthtravel.co.uk. Friendly, competitive travel agency whose profits are used to promote sustainable tourism.
Premier Travel Eire ☎028/7126 3333, ⊛www.premiertravel.uk.com. Discount flight specialists with hotel, insurance and car-rental deals.
Travel Cuts Canada US & Canada ☎1-866/246-9762, ⊛www.travelcuts.com. Canadian student-travel organization.
Worldtek Travel US & Canada ☎1-800/243-1723, ⊛www.worldtek.com. Discount travel agency for worldwide travel.

Ⓦ **www.cheapflights.co.uk/www**
.cheaptickets.com Flight deals, travel agents, plus links to other travel sites.

Ⓦ **www.etn.nl/discount.htm** A US hub of consolidator and discount agent web links.

Ⓦ **www.expedia.co.uk** (UK), Ⓦ **www.expedia**
.com (US), Ⓦ **www.expedia.ca** (Canada) Discount airfares, all-airline search engine and daily deals.

Ⓦ **www.flyaow.com** US online air travel info and reservations site.

Ⓦ **www.hotwire.com** Last-minute savings of up to forty percent on regular published US fares.

Ⓦ **www.kayak.com** Award-winning travel search engine with a clear easy-to-use format.

Ⓦ **www.lastminute.com** Offers good last-minute holiday-package and flight-only deals.

Ⓦ **www.opodo.co.uk** Reliable source of low airfares from the UK, run by nine major European airlines.

Ⓦ **www.orbitz.com** Comprehensive North American web travel source, with the usual flight, car rental and hotel deals, as well as excellent follow-up customer service.

Ⓦ **www.priceline.com** Name-your-own-price website that has deals at around forty percent off standard fares.

Ⓦ **www.travelocity.co.uk** (UK), Ⓦ **www**
.travelocity.com (US), Ⓦ **www.travelocity.ca**
(Canada), Ⓦ **www.travelocity.com.au** (Australia),
Ⓦ **www.travelocity.co.nz** (New Zealand)

Destination guides plus best deals for car rental, accommodation and air fares.

Packages and organized tours

Package tours may not sound like your kind of travel, but don't dismiss the idea out of hand. In addition to the fully escorted variety, many agents can put together very flexible deals, sometimes amounting to no more than a flight plus car and accommodation. If you're planning a trip geared around special interests, such packages can sometimes work out cheaper – and are certainly less hassle – than the same arrangements made on arrival.

An increasing number of operators organize **specialist holidays**, such as walking tours, art and architecture trips, and Italian food and wine jaunts, as well as short breaks to coincide with opera festivals and even football matches. However, they don't come cheap: accommodation, food, local transport and the services of a guide are nearly always included. Prices vary widely, so check what you are getting for your money (many don't include the cost of the airfare).

Fly less – stay longer! Travel and climate change

Climate change is perhaps the single biggest issue facing our planet. It is caused by a build-up in the atmosphere of carbon dioxide and other greenhouse gases, which are emitted by many sources – including planes. Already, **flights** account for 3–4 percent of human-induced global warming: that figure may sound small, but it is rising year on year and threatens to counteract the progress made by reducing greenhouse emissions in other areas.

Rough Guides regard travel as a **global benefit**, and feel strongly that the advantages to developing economies are important, as are the opportunities for greater contact and awareness among peoples. But we also believe in travelling responsibly, which includes giving thought to how often we fly and what we can do to redress any harm that our trips may create.

We can travel less or simply reduce the amount we travel by air (taking fewer trips and staying longer, or taking the train if there is one); we can avoid night flights (which are more damaging); and we can make the trips we do take "climate neutral" via a carbon-offset scheme. **Offset schemes** run by climatecare.org, carbon neutral.com and others allow you to "neutralize" the greenhouse gases that you are responsible for releasing. Their websites have simple calculators that let you work out the impact of any flight – as does our own. Once that's done, you can pay to fund projects that will reduce future emissions by an equivalent amount. Please take the time to visit our website and make your trip climate neutral, or get a copy of our *Climate Change* book for more detail on the subject.

www.roughguides.com/climatechange

There's also a plethora of operators selling **short-break deals**, especially to Milan and Verona: for these, reckon on spending upwards of £250 per person for three nights in Milan in a three-star hotel during low season and upwards of £300 between April and October, though special offers can sometimes cut prices drastically, especially for late bookings.

If you want to rent a car in Italy, check with tour operators, airlines and flight agents before you leave, as some **fly-drive** deals work out very cheaply. See p.28 for more on car rental.

Tour operators in the UK and Ireland

Arblaster & Clarke ☎01730/263 111, ⓦwww.arblasterandclarke.com. Upmarket outfit which organizes three-day opera and wine-tasting breaks.

Citalia ☎0871/200 2004, ⓦwww.citalia.co.uk. Hotel packages around the main lakes plus tailor-made itineraries, city breaks in Milan and Verona, and car rental.

Crystal Holidays ☎0871/231 5661, ⓦwww .crystalholidays.co.uk. Hotel packages on the lakes, and in Milan and Verona, plus opera breaks in Verona in Aug.

Exodus UK ☎0845/863 9600, ⓦwww.exodus .co.uk. Activity holidays, including an eight-day walking tour of Lake Garda.

Italian Connection ☎01424/728 900, ⓦwww .italian-connection.co.uk. Tailor-made holidays throughout the region, including accommodation and car rental.

Martin Randall Travel ☎020/8742 3355, ⓦwww.martinrandall.com. Small-group cultural holidays led by experts on art, archeology or music. At the time of writing, they were offering tours of lakeside gardens and Verona opera.

Saga Holidays ☎0800/096 0074, ⓦwww .sagaholidays.com. Tours of the lakes aimed at people who are 50 and over.

Tour operators in North America

Adventures Abroad ☎1-800/665-3998, ⓦwww .adventures-abroad.com. Small-group tours including a two-week "Lakes and Mountains" trip.

Backroads ☎1-800/462-2848 or 510/527-1555, ⓦwww.backroads.com. Cooking, cycling and hiking holidays, including around Lake Como.

Butterfield & Robinson ☎1-800/678-11477, ⓦwww.butterfield.com. Escorted cycling and walking tours in Italy, featuring a trip to Lake Garda, staying in top-notch hotels.

Central Holidays ☎1-800/539-7098, ⓦwww .CentralHolidays.com. Wide range of independent and escorted tours plus city breaks, including a five-day fly-drive trip to the main lakes.

CIT ☎1-800/387-0711, ⓦwww.cittours -canada.com. Well-organized coach and rail tours, including Milan, Bergamo, Verona and the lakes, plus advice for independent travellers on hotels and car rental.

Classic Journeys ☎1-800/200-3887, ⓦwww .classicjourneys.com. Gentle hikes around lakes Maggiore, Lugano and Como.

Country Walkers ☎1-800/464-9255, ⓦwww .countrywalkers.com. Small-group walking tours around the lakes with local guides.

Europe Through the Back Door ☎425/771-8303, ⓦwww.ricksteves.com. The cult traveller Rick Steves offers an informative website to help with planning independent trips and also offers a range of tours, including Milan and the lakes region.

Italian Connection ☎1-800/462-7911, ⓦwww .italian-connection.com. Hiking and gourmet holidays that take in the western lakes.

Mountain Travel–Sobek ☎1-888/831-7526, ⓦwww.mtsobek.com. Hiking tours around the Italian Lakes.

Tour operators in Australia and New Zealand

Adventure Travel Company New Zealand ☎09/355 9135, ⓦwww.adventuretravel.co.nz. Hotels and car rental, plus walking and cycling tours in the Italian Lakes.

Walkabout Gourmet Adventures Australia ☎02/9871 5526, ⓦwww.walkaboutgourmet.com. Classy food, wine and walking tours that take in both Swiss and Italian lakes.

By rail from the UK

Travelling **by train** to Italy won't save you money, but it can be an enjoyable and leisurely way of getting to the country and you can stop off in other parts of Europe on the way. The choice of routes and fares is hugely complex, but most trains pass through Paris and head south through Switzerland towards Milan. A return ticket to Milan, using Eurostar and the high-speed TGV through France, starts at £180 and takes around eleven hours. Booking ninety days or more in advance will give you more choice of services and you should bag any special offers that are going. Using slower trains won't cut the cost very significantly and neither will the cross-Channel ferry route, which is now barely used and accordingly badly timetabled. Bear in mind that if you travel via Paris on Eurostar you have to change stations, which means lugging your bags on the metro from the Gare du Nord to the Gare de Lyon. Details on the options for international rail routes are reliably explained on the wonderful website ⓦ www.seat61.com

Rail contacts in the UK

Eurostar ⓣ 0870/518 6186, ⓦ www.eurostar .com.

Rail Choice ⓣ 0870/165 7300, ⓦ www.railchoice .co.uk. Helpful UK-based company offering Eurostar tickets and InterRail and Trenitalia passes, all available to buy through their website.

Rail Europe ⓣ 08448/484 064, ⓦ www .raileurope.co.uk. Informative agent selling tickets for rail journeys to Italy, with discounted fares for under-26s. Also agents for InterRail and Eurostar.

Simply Rail ⓣ 0870/084 1414, ⓦ www.simplyrail .com. Friendly company offering a wide variety of rail options including Eurostar, international sleepers and ferry crossings.

By bus from the UK and Ireland

The days when **bus travel** was the cheapest way of getting to Italy have long gone and it's difficult to see why anyone would choose to get there this way. National Express Eurolines have direct services **from London** to Milan and Turin, with less frequent services to Brescia and Verona, all for around £100 return (mid-season). They have occasional bargain offers for tickets booked a week or more in advance and there is a ten-percent discount for passengers under 26 or over 60. The Milan service departs four times a week and takes 23 hours; the journeys to Turin and Verona take a similar length of time but departures are a little less frequent. Eurolines also has a regular service **from Dublin**, Cork, Limerick and Belfast to London, from where you can get a connection to Italy.

Bus contacts in the UK and Ireland

Eurolines UK ⓣ 08705/143219, ⓦ www.eurolines .co.uk. Tickets can also be purchased from any National Express agent: ⓣ 0870/580 8080, ⓦ www .nationalexpress.co.uk.

By car from the UK and Ireland

There's no one fixed route to Italy if you're travelling with **your own vehicle**. The best cross-Channel route will depend on your starting point, but any travel agent can provide up-to-date ferry schedules and make advance bookings – essential for high season. As regards **routes** from northern France, the Alpine route via Germany and Switzerland entering Italy at Chiasso by Lake Como is the shortest as the crow flies. Alternatively, you could push down further into France and then cross the Alps at the Mont Blanc tunnel to Courmayeur and the A5, or at Fréjus from where the A32 heads to Turin and from there the A4 continues into Lombardy. See ⓦ www.bls.ch for details of the car-carrying trains **under the Alps** from Kandersteg (near Bern) to Iselle (near Domodossola), through the Lötschberg Tunnel and the Simplon Tunnel.

Remember that **motorways** in France, Switzerland and Germany – not to mention Italy – are toll roads, so you'll need to factor these in when calculating costs; €50, for example, should cover a trip from the UK to Lake Como. In France and Italy you get a ticket when you join the motorway and pay when you exit, while in Switzerland you need a vignette which you display in your windscreen, granting the right to drive anywhere on the Swiss motorway network for up to a year; this costs Fr.40, buyable from customs officials as you enter the country.

Eurotunnel runs shuttle trains for vehicles between Folkestone and Coquelles, near Calais, via the **Channel Tunnel**. You can just turn up and go, though booking is advisable. Boarding is quick and easy – there are up to four departures per hour (one per hour midnight–6am) – and the journey takes a smooth, hassle-free 35–45 minutes. **Fares** vary a lot; travelling between 10pm and 6am can cut costs, while travelling at weekends, or in July and August, adds a premium. A two-week return in the peak summer period can be £150–180 per car, though last-minute fares are likely to be much higher.

There are several excellent online **route-planning services** which calculate not only the best route but also toll booth and petrol prices, as well as conveniently listing service stations; both the AA and RAC sites are good, but the quickest and easiest to use is the Michelin service (ⓦ www.viamichelin .co.uk).

Cross-Channel companies

For an up-to-date list of ferry companies and their routes, check ⓦ www.seaview.co.uk.
Brittany Ferries UK ⓣ 0871/244 0744, ⓦ www .brittanyferries.co.uk. Poole to Cherbourg; Portsmouth to Cherbourg, Caen and St Malo; Plymouth to Roscoff (March–Nov/Dec).
Eurotunnel UK ⓣ 0870/535 3535, ⓦ www .eurotunnel.com. Folkestone to Calais.

Irish Ferries GB ⓣ 0870/517 1717, Ireland ⓣ 0181/300 400, ⓦ www.irishferries.com. Rosslare to Cherbourg and Roscoff (March–Sept).
Norfolkline ⓣ 0844 847/5000, ⓦ www .norfolkline.com. Dover to Dunkerque.
P&O Ferries UK ⓣ 0870/598 0333, ⓦ www .poferries.com. Dover to Calais.
Sea France ⓣ 08716/645 645, ⓦ www.seafrance .com. Dover to Calais.
Speedferries ⓣ 08716/000 7456, ⓦ www .speedferries.com. Dover to Boulogne.
Transmanche ⓣ 0800/917/1201, ⓦ www .transmancheferries.com. Newhaven to Dieppe and Rosslare, Portsmouth and Newhaven to Le Havre.

Getting around

Whether you choose to spend your lakes holiday taking ferries from one village to another or wish to venture further afield, you'll have plenty of modes of transport to choose from. Public transport is comprehensive, with ferries, buses and trains covering the region, and prices are low. Naturally, you'll have more flexibility with your own transport, allowing you to travel at your own pace and to out-of-the-way places. Roads are good throughout the region, although they do get very crowded on summer weekends and public holidays.

All the lakes are crisscrossed by regular **ferry services** throughout the year, with car-ferries traversing the middle of the three big lakes. Trains link the larger towns away from the lakes. Milan is the main hub, while buses connect smaller centres and trace the lakeside roads to serve the waterfront villages. This is also motorbike and cycle territory, so if you're happier on two wheels you certainly won't be alone.

We've detailed train, bus and ferry frequencies in the "Travel details" sections at the end of each chapter of the Guide: note that these refer to regular working-day schedules (ie Mon to Sat); services can be much reduced or even nonexistent on Sundays. Bus and train timetables are also affected by school holidays and some services don't run at all during August.

In Italy

Public transport in Italy is good value for money and efficient. Most Italians still choose to use their own vehicles, however, and you may want to follow suit if you wish to explore beyond the lakes themselves.

By car

Italy is a car-loving nation and its population spends an awful lot of money on new vehicles and takes every possible opportunity to use them. The result is busy roads full of new – or newish – cars travelling at high speeds. The **road network**, though, is generally good, with a comprehensive motorway (*autostrada*) system running the length and breadth of the region. The best plan is to avoid driving on public holidays or

Friday and Sunday nights in summer when nature-starved townsfolk head for the lakes and mountains – and back again. Town centres should be avoided as much as possible, too, as congestion, a proliferation of one-way systems and confusing signage can make them a headache. The centres of many of the lake villages are closed to traffic, although access is usually allowed if you have a hotel reservation. Driving in Milan and on its notorious *Tangenziale* (ring road) is best avoided whenever possible, but especially during the morning and evening rush hours (7–9am & 5–8pm).

To try and combat the pollution problems of some of Italy's big towns, **No-Car Days** are becoming increasingly common. On these designated days, between the allotted hours, only authorized cars are allowed to circulate. On Sundays this will usually mean just public transport and taxis. When pollution levels get particularly high (often in Jan and Sept), authorization is by number plate, with odd and even numbers being allowed on the roads on different weekdays. Ask at your hotel or local tourist office for the latest information, or, if your Italian is up to it, look in local papers or online. In some towns – most notably Bergamo's Città Alta – the *centro storico* is closed every Sunday and you'll need to use the well-organized public transport instead.

Rules of the road

Rules of the road are straightforward. Drive on the right; observe the speed limits – 50kph in built-up areas, 110kph on dual carriageways and 130kph on motorways (for camper vans, these limits are 50kph, 80kph

Crossing the road

Don't assume that as a **pedestrian** you're safe in Italy; even on crossings with traffic lights you can be subject to some close calls. Drivers will not automatically stop at pedestrian crossings. Look both ways before crossing the road – even when there's a green light for you, as it will probably also be giving the go-ahead to a line of traffic.

and 100kph respectively); and don't drink and drive. Police checkpoints are relatively common in holiday areas and speed cameras are popping up everywhere. Similarly, cameras record any unauthorized vehicles entering the "Zona Traffico Limitato" areas of old towns and the consequent fines are high. Drivers also need to have their dipped headlights on when using any road outside a built-up area and carry a warning triangle and a fluorescent jacket, in case of breakdown.

As regards **documentation**, if you're bringing your own car, as well as current insurance, you need a valid driving licence and an international driving permit if you're a non-EU licence holder. If you hold a UK pre-1991 driving licence you'll need an international driving permit or to update your licence to a photocard version. It's compulsory to carry your car documents (not photocopies) and passport while you're driving, and you can be fined on the spot if you cannot present them when stopped by the police – not an uncommon occurrence. For more information, consult ⓦ www.theaa.com.

Signage and fuel

Confusingly for UK visitors, motorway **signage** is on a green background and main-road information on blue. In most cases you'd do best to have a map rather than just follow signs, as they can be, at best, erratic and, at worst, indecipherable. Abbreviations are common, so if you get a few of the main ones under your belt, navigating will be a whole lot easier: MI is Milan, BG Bergamo, BS Brescia, VR Verona, TO Turin and CH Switzerland. Motorways are often more prominently named by their start and finish points on some signs than by their A-number – for example, the signs to "GENOVA-GRAVELLONA T." are in fact indicating the A26 which leads to Lake Maggiore. To be properly prepared, check the end point of the motorway in the direction you're going before you head off.

Another common sight that can leave visitors perplexed is **flashing traffic lights** at crossroads. This happens in locations where the lights are needed for traffic control during the day, but where there is not enough night-time traffic to warrant continued control. The lights basically serve to alert you to a junction; they do not give anyone the right of way, you just have to look and go when it's clear.

During your holiday you will no doubt encounter a route or two undergoing **roadworks**. Slow down and follow the temporary yellow road lines. Whenever possible try and work out any temporary signs too – motorway exits, for example, are frequently closed (*chiuso*) if they are affected by works, but this will be well signed for up to 100km beforehand.

Most **petrol stations** give you the choice of self-service (*Fai da te*), or, for a few cents more per litre, someone will fill the tank and usually wipe down the windscreen while they're at it. Petrol stations often have the same working hours as shops, which means they'll be closed for a couple of hours at midday, will shut up shop at around 7pm and are likely to be closed on Sundays. Outside these times many have a self-service facility payable into a machine between the pumps by bank note or, more rarely, credit card; these are often not well advertised so you might need to go onto the forecourt to check. It's worth bearing in mind that petrol is considerably **cheaper in Switzerland**. Unsurprisingly, there are hardly any petrol stations within about 20km of the border on the Italian side, so, do as the locals do, and pop over the border (don't forget you might need your passport). Or, alternatively, if you're visiting Swiss lakes and mountains be sure to fill your tank while you're there.

Lakeside driving

Most of the **roads around the lakes** are narrow and you'll often find yourself fast up against the mountainside with the lake on the other side just a few metres away. Some of the roads give stunning views across the water; others, hemmed in by campsites, Baroque palaces or lemon groves, keep you tantalizingly just out of sight of the lake. The roads at the southern end of the lakes, nearer the major urban centres, can get very busy in summer; you could find yourself in gridlock for several miles on a sunny Sunday afternoon.

The roads along some parts of the lakes are cut into the mountains with single-bore tunnels or *gallerie*, with one lane in each direction and no central divider. Beware of driving with sunglasses on, as you can be plunged from sunshine into scary blackness with little warning.

Motorway driving

All **motorways** (*autostrade*) are toll-roads. Take a ticket as you come on and pay on exit; the amount due is flashed up on a screen in front of you. Paying by cash is the most straightforward option – booths are marked "cash/contanti" and colour-coded white. To pay by credit card follow the "Viacard" sign (colour-coded blue). Avoid the Telepass lane (colour-coded yellow), which is for drivers holding post-paid electronic cards. Be alert as you get into lane as traffic zigzags in and out at high speed to get pole position at the shortest-looking queue. Since other roads can be frustratingly slow and heaving with freight traffic, the very reasonable tolls are well worth it over long distances, but be prepared for queues at exits at peak times.

You're most likely to use the A4 Turin–Venice motorway, which travels south of the lakes and skirts Milan to the north. Running north, the A8 and A9 head out from Milan to Varese and Lake Como respectively, while

---

Motorways in the lakes region

A4 "Torino–Venezia/Trieste" – runs Turin–Milan–Bergamo–Brescia–Verona–Venice.
A8 "Milano–Varese" – runs Milan–Varese.
A9 "Lainate–Chiasso" – runs Milan–Como–Switzerland (Lugano).
A21 "Torino–Brescia" – connects Cremona to Brescia.
A22 "Modena–Brennero" – connects Mantova, Verona & Lake Garda's east shore.
A26 "Genova–Gravellona Toce" – runs up the west side of Lake Maggiore, and on to Domodossola (signposted for the "Passo del Sempione").

the A21 and A22 feed traffic south to Cremona and Mantova. Milan's ring road – the Tangenziale – is divided into the A50 Tangenziale Ovest (west, which also covers the southern part) and the A51 Tangenziale Est (the eastern part); the A4 comprises the northern stretch.

Italian motorway driving is aggressive, with excessive speeds and tailgating all too common. The inside lane is often taken by large freight vehicles (part of Italy's severe pollution problem comes from the fact that so much commercial traffic uses the road rather than the rail system), while the outside lane frequently resembles a Formula One testing track. Your best bet is to drive within the speed limit, observe all the rules and be alert to juggernauts or Mercedes swinging out in front of you without any warning.

Parking

Parking can be a problem. On the lakes, most towns and villages have pay-and-display areas just outside the centre, but these can get very full during high season. Parking at night is easier than during the day, but check the signs to make sure you're not parked in a street that turns into a market in the morning or on the one day of the week when it's cleaned in the small hours; otherwise you're likely to be towed.

Parking attendants are especially active in tourist areas and if you get fed up with driving around and settle for a space in a *zona di rimozione* (tow-away zone), don't expect your car to be there when you get back. In **Milan**, don't be surprised to see parking just about anywhere, notably on pavements, seemingly working tram lines and bus stops, but you'd be unwise to follow suit.

Towns generally operate a colour-coded parking scheme: **blue-zone** parking spaces (delineated by a blue line) usually have a maximum stay of one or two hours; they cost around €1 per hour (pay at meters, attendants wearing authorizing badges or buy scratch-cards from local tobacconists), but are sometimes free at lunchtimes, after 8pm and on Sundays. Much coveted **white-zone** spaces (white lines) are free, while **yellow-zone** areas (yellow lines) are reserved for residents.

Breakdown and safety

If your vehicle **breaks down**, dial ☎116 and tell the operator where you are, the type of car you're in, and your registration number: the nearest office of the Automobile Club d'Italia (ACI) will send someone out to fix your car – although it's not a free service and can work out very expensive if you need a tow. For this reason, if you're bringing your own vehicle you might consider arranging cover with a motoring organization in your home country before you leave. Any ACI office in Italy can tell you where to get **spare parts** for your particular car.

Never leave anything visible in the car when you're not using it. Thefts are particularly common at motorway service areas and in tourist centres.

Car rental

Car rental in Italy is pricey, especially in high season, at around £175/US$300 per week for a small hatchback, with unlimited mileage if booked in advance. The major chains have offices in all the larger towns and the airports, as well as Milan's Stazione Centrale; addresses are detailed in the "Listings" sections at the end of town accounts throughout the Guide. Generally the best deals are to be had by arranging things in advance, through one of the agents listed below or with specialist tour operators when you book your flight or holiday. You need to be over 21 to rent a car in Italy and will need a credit card with enough available funds to act as a deposit when picking up your vehicle.

If you're planning to head into Switzerland on your trip – to go round the top of Lake Maggiore, say, or spend a day or two around Lugano or Bellinzona – you should always check the rules with your rental company in advance. Switzerland is not in the EU, although it's surrounded by EU countries. Border controls, especially at heavily used crossing points, can lead to long lines of traffic, even though regulations are a formality and searches are very infrequent. However, you'd do well to be certain before you depart that you're not going to inadvertently break customs regulations or passport/visa requirements on your way back in.

Car-rental agencies

Avis UK ☏ 08700/100 287, @ www.avis.co.uk;
Ireland ☏ 353 214211 111, @ www.avis.ie; US
& Canada ☏ 1-800/331-1084, @ www.avis.com;
Australia ☏ 13 63 33, @ www.avis.com.au; NZ
☏ 0800/655 111, @ www.avis.co.nz.
Budget UK ☏ 0844/581 9998, @ www.budget.co
.uk; Ireland ☏ 09/0662 7711, @ www.budget.ie;
US ☏ 1-800/527-0700, @ www.budget.com;
Australia ☏ 1300/362 848, @ www.budget.com.au;
NZ ☏ 0800/283 438, @ www.budget.co.nz.
Europcar UK ☏ 0870/607 5000, Ireland ☏ 01/614
2800, US & Canada ☏ 1-877/940 6900, Australia
☏ 1300 131 390; @ www.europcar.com.
Hertz UK ☏ 0870/848 8848, @ www.hertz.co.uk;
Ireland ☏ 01/676 7476, @ www.hertz.ie;
US ☏ 1-800/654-3131, Canada ☏ 1-800/263-
0600; @ www.hertz.com; Australia ☏ 13 30
39, @ www.hertz.com.au; NZ ☏ 0800/654 321,
@ www.hertz.co.nz.
National UK ☏ 0870/400 4581, @ www
.nationalcar.co.uk; US ☏ 1-800/227-7368, @ www
.nationalcar.com; Australia ☏ 1300/13 13 13 90,
@ www.nationalcar.com.au; NZ ☏ 0800/800 115,
@ www.nationalcar.co.nz.
Sixt UK ☏ 08701/567567, Eire ☏ 01/844 4199;
@ www.sixt.com.
Thrifty UK ☏ 01494/751 500, @ www.thrifty.co.uk;
Ireland ☏ 1800/515 800, @ www.thrifty.ie;
US ☏ 1-800/847-4389, @ www.thrifty.com;
Australia ☏ 1300/367 227, @ www.thrifty.com.au;
NZ ☏ 0800/73 70 70, @ www.thrifty.co.nz.

Camper van rental

Camper van or mobile-home holidays
are becoming increasingly popular in Italy
and the rental market is opening up to
meet the demand. To add to the obvious
convenience of this type of holiday, facilities in campsites are usually dependable
(see p.36), and more and more resorts
have created free camper van parking
areas (*sosta camper*). The following are just
a selection of the companies offering new
(or newish) vehicles for rent. Prices are
usually around €1500 for a two-berth
vehicle for a week in high season, with
unlimited mileage.
Blu rent ☏ 39/0171 601 702, @ www.blurent.com.
Website in English available.
Comocaravan ☏ 39/031 521 215, @ www
.comocaravan.it
Maggiore ☏ 39/840 008 840, @ www
.maggiorecamperrent.it

Motoring organizations

Australia AAA ☏ 02/6247 7311, @ www.aaa
.asn.au.
Canada CAA ☏ 613/247-0117, @ www.caa.ca.
Ireland AA ☏ 01/617 9999, @ www.aaireland.ie.
Italy TCI ☏ 02.852.6304, @ www.touringclub.it.
New Zealand AA ☏ 0800/500 444, @ www.nzaa
.co.nz.
UK AA ☏ 0870/600 0371, @ www.theaa.co.uk;
RAC ☏ 0800/550 055, @ www.rac.co.uk.
US AAA ☏ 1-800/222-4357, @ www.aaa.com.

By rail

The **railway network** around Lombardy is
good, especially if you want to travel
between the provincial towns. It is not so
comprehensive, however, when it comes to
the lakes, where railway lines often serve
one shoreline only. Milan is naturally the
hub of the system and you may find it
quicker to head into the city and then out
again rather than fiddle around with
connections at smaller stations. Services
are usually on time, efficient and good value
for money.

The majority of trains are run by the state-
run Ferrovie dello Stato (FS) under the brand
name **Trenitalia**, but there are also a few
other companies operating services in the
region, for example the **Ferrovia Vigezzina**
(@ www.vigezzina.com), which operates the
Domodossola to Locarno route, and the
Ferrovie Nord Milano (@ www.lenord.it),
which runs many services around Varese,
Lake Maggiore, Como, and from Brescia
past Lake Iseo, as well as operating the
Malpensa Express from Malpensa airport
into Milan.

Standards of trains and carriages vary. At
the top of the range are the **Pendolino**
(CiS), a trans-Alpine service between Italy
and Switzerland with very smart trains; the
Eurostar Italia (ES), which runs between
major cities, is slightly faster and more
efficient than the **Intercity** (IC); and the
Eurocity trains that connect Milan with
centres such as Paris, Vienna, Hamburg
and Barcelona. Reservations are usually
required for all of these services and a
supplement in the region of thirty percent of
the ordinary fare is payable. Make sure you
pay your supplement before getting on
board, otherwise you'll have to cough up a

Timetable reading

On timetables – and parking signs too – *Lavorativo* or **feriale** is the word for the Monday to Saturday service, represented by two crossed hammers; and festivo means that a train runs only on Sundays and holidays, symbolized by a Christian cross. Also pay attention to the **timetable notes**, specifying the dates between which some services run (*Si effetua dal ... al ...*), or whether a service is seasonal (*periodico*, denoted by a vertical squiggle).

Some other common terms on timetables are:

escluso sabato – not including Saturdays
si effettua fino all' ... – running until
si effettua dal ... – starting from
giornalmente – daily
prenotazione obbligatoria – compulsory reservation
estivo – summer
invernale – winter
Fer5 – Monday to Friday
Fer6 – Monday to Saturday

far bigger surcharge to the conductor. **Diretto**, **Espresso** and **Interregionale** trains are the common-or-garden long-distance expresses, calling only at larger stations. Although reservations are not required for these trains, it's worth booking seats, especially in summer, when they can get very crowded. **Reservations** can be made at any major train station or travel agent in Italy or via Italian State Railways agents in the UK (see p.24). Lastly, there are the **Regionale** services, which stop just about everywhere.

For **information** on the above trains call ☏064 4101 or visit the Trenitalia website at ⓦ www.trenitalia.com.

Timetables and fares

Timings and route information for the Trenitalia network are posted up at train stations, and we give a rough idea of frequencies and journey times in the "Travel details" sections at the end of each chapter. If you're travelling extensively it would be

worth investing in a copy of the twice-yearly *Orario delle ferrovie* (€3.50), the timetable for the main rail routes, on sale at most newspaper stands.

Fares are inexpensive, calculated by the kilometre and easy to work out for each journey. The timetables give the prices per kilometre, but as a rough guide, a second-class one-way fare from Milan to Verona currently costs about €12 by Intercity and Eurostar, €6 on Interregionale. **Children** aged 4–12 qualify for a fifty percent discount on all journeys, and children under 4 (not occupying a seat) travel free.

All stations have yellow validating machines in which passengers must stamp their ticket before embarking on their journey. Look out for them as you come onto the platform: if you fail to **validate your ticket** you'll be given an on-the-spot-fine. Return tickets are valid within two months of the outward journey, but as two one-way tickets cost the same it's hardly worth bothering.

ⓦ**www.trasporti.regione.lombardia.it** (click on "orari e informazioni") is a very useful site combining timetables for different forms of public transport in Lombardy. Type in your start point and destination and the site will come up with different options, including bus, train, cable car and ferry connections. The down side is that it sticks strictly to the administrative region of Lombardy and so the eastern shore of Lake Garda and the western shore of Lake Maggiore and Lake Orta are not included.

Rail passes

A **rail pass** is only really worth considering if you plan to travel extensively around Italy or are visiting the country as part of a wider tour of Europe. A **Trenitalia** pass (Ⓦ www.trenitalia.com) or an Italy-only InterRail or Eurail pass might be worth your while if you are planning to cover a lot of Italian ground. Otherwise, the Europe-wide **InterRail** pass (Ⓦ www.interrail.net) is available to European citizens for travelling around a chosen combination of countries in Europe, including Italy. And for non-EU citizens, **Eurail** passes (Ⓦ www.eurail.com) give unlimited travel in Europe including the Trenitalia network. With any of these passes you will be liable for supplements of €12 per journey on the faster trains.

By bus

The train lines are complemented by regular **bus services** (*autobus* or *pullman*), which run up and down the lake shores and link towns and villages across the region. Remember, however, that in out-of-the-way villages schedules can be sketchy and are drastically reduced – sometimes nonexistent – at weekends, especially on Sundays. On lakes Maggiore and Garda the situation is slightly complicated by the fact that the shorelines lie in different regions and so tourist offices will not necessarily have information on the bus routes on the other side.

Timetables are usually displayed by the stop, or details can be picked up from tourist offices. There is no national bus company; dozens of private companies cover the lakes area. Buy **tickets** immediately before you travel from the bus station ticket office, or on the bus itself. If you want to get off, ask *"posso scendere?"*; "the next stop" is *"la prossima fermata"*. The details of the whereabouts of **bus terminals** (*autostazione*) are detailed in the text, although they are often within walking distance of the train station. In smaller towns and villages, most buses pull in at the central piazza or on the main road just outside the centre.

City buses are always cheap, usually costing a flat fare of around €1. **Tickets** are available from a variety of sources, commonly newsagents and tobacconists, but also from anywhere displaying a sticker saying "tickets" or *"biglietti"*, including many campsite shops and hotel front desks. Once on board, you must register your ticket in the machine at the back of the bus. The whole system is based on trust, though in most cities checks for fare-dodging are regularly made, and hefty spot-fines are levied against offenders.

By ferry

The three biggest lakes are all well served by **ferries,** which zigzag from shore to shore, docking at jetties that are usually conveniently positioned on the main lakeside piazzas or in the centre of the larger towns' promenades. Some of the regular boats are pretty slow; if you're in a hurry, you can pay extra for a hydrofoil.

Car ferries also operate on Lake Maggiore (Intra–Laveno), Lake Como (Cadenabbia–Menaggio–Bellagio–Varenna) and Lake Garda (Maderno–Torri del Benaco and Limone–Malcesine). These can be a good way to minimize driving along slow, traffic-congested lakeside roads.

Timetables and fares are available at all tourist offices and the ticket booths on the jetties themselves. Prices vary from lake to lake, but fares are relatively inexpensive; Como to Bellagio, for example, is €7.90 one-way. There are some discounts for EU citizens over 65 and for children; details of passes are given in the relevant chapters.

For full up-to-date schedules and prices, check Ⓦ www.navigazionelaghi.it, which covers the services on lakes Maggiore, Como and Garda; Ⓦ www.lakelugano.ch for Lake Lugano; and Ⓦ www.navigazionelagoiseo.it for Lake Iseo.

By bicycle and motorbike

Cycling is a very popular sport and mode of transport in northern Italy. If you're intending to do a fair amount of touring by bike you could think about bringing your own machine from home – most flights take cycles (double-check the conditions with your carrier before you purchase a ticket). Alternatively, you could rent a bike on the ground; bikes are often available by the hour for around €3 in towns and lake resorts. The flat topography of the Bassa Padana around

Mantova is perfect cycling territory and the paths along the rice fields make ideal cycle tracks (see p.327 for more information). Many local tourist authorities have leaflets detailing recommended routes.

The serious cyclist might consider staying at one of a chain of hotels that cater specifically for cycling enthusiasts. Each hotel has a secure room for your bike, a maintenance workshop, overnight laundry facilities, suggested itineraries and group-tour possibilities, a doctor at hand and even a special cyclists' diet. At the time of writing there were two affiliated hotels in the lakes region; contact ☎39/0541 307 531, ⓦwww.italy bikehotels.it for further information and a list of hotels.

An alternative is to tour by **motorbike** (*moto*), and there are several professional outfits in Milan where you can rent by the day or the week. Crash helmets are compulsory, and police rigorously enforce this rule. In Milan, you could copy the locals and scoot around on a **moped** (*motorino*); see p.73.

In Switzerland

The efficiency of the massively comprehensive Swiss public transport system remains one of the wonders of the modern world. You can get anywhere you want quickly, easily and relatively cheaply, and it's clean, safe and pleasant. Services always depart on the dot, and train timetables are well integrated with those of the ferries and postbuses, which operate on routes not covered by rail, including the more remote villages and valleys. Cyclists are well served by the Swiss instinct for encouraging green thinking in all things.

Trains in Switzerland

Swiss Federal Railways, or **FFS** (*Ferrovie federali svizzere*), maintains a modern, integrated, ecologically sound transport system and travelling by train in Switzerland is invariably comfortable and hassle-free. There's a confusing array of different **Swiss travel passes** and you'll need to do your sums carefully to see if they're worth your while. Full details are online at ⓦwww.rail.ch, where there is also a complete timetable with English-language information on connection

timings, platform numbers and even the kind of refreshments available on board. Alternatively, most main stations keep a public copy to consult.

Just about the only people you'll see lugging suitcases or rucksacks through train compartments in Switzerland are foreigners. Many Swiss register their heavy bags at the station baggage counter before boarding (per item: same-day service Fr.20/€13; next-day service Fr.10/€6.50; ⓦwww.rail.ch /baggage). This is a great service to take advantage of if you want to move on during the day but don't fancy carting your gear from locker to locker.

Buses and boats in Switzerland

Backing up the train network is a yet more comprehensive system of **buses**, which get to every single village and hamlet in the country. In addition, all Swiss travel passes are valid for travel on buses as well as trains. Bus stations are nearly always located in the forecourt of train stations. Even more handily, the bus and train **timetables** are coordinated, ensuring watertight connections from one to the other.

Boats on Lake Maggiore (see p.124) run smoothly from Italian waters to Swiss, while details of the service on Lake Lugano – which lies mostly in Switzerland – are given on p.211.

Driving in Switzerland

Switzerland's road network is comprehensive and well planned. However, Swiss transport policy means that **cars** are slowly being given the squeeze, with tough city parking regulations and strict law enforcement.

The minimum driving age is 18, international licences are recognized for one year's driving in Switzerland and, as across Europe, **third-party insurance** is compulsory. It's obligatory to carry both a red warning triangle and the registration documents of the vehicle. If you intend driving on Swiss **motorways**, you have to stick a **vignette** inside your windscreen. These cost Fr.40/€25 for any vehicle up to 3.5 tonnes, are bought most easily from the customs officials when you first cross the border (also at post offices and petrol stations), and remain valid until January 31 of the following year. Trailers or caravans must have their own, separate vignette. Getting caught without one lays you open to a significant fine. However, it's quite easy to avoid motorways altogether and stick to ordinary main roads, which are free and – outside urban centres at least – reasonably fast.

Switzerland drives on the **right**, **seatbelts** are compulsory for all, and penalties for **drink-driving** are tough (one glass of beer has you on the limit). **Speed limits** are 120kph on motorways, 80kph on main roads and 50kph in urban areas. Like Italy, Swiss motorways are **signed in green**, while main roads are signed in blue; it's common to see a green sign and a blue sign to the same place pointing in opposite directions. At junctions, yellow diamonds painted on the road show who has **priority**; if in doubt, always let trams and buses go first, and give way to traffic coming from your right. On gradients, vehicles heading **uphill** have priority over those coming down; some narrow mountain tracks have controlled times for ascent and descent.

Parking

Parking in Switzerland is hellish, and can be very limited and prohibitively expensive. In cities, full car parks will quite often harbour queues of cars, their engines off, drivers waiting – sometimes for over an hour – for the next person to finish their shopping and so liberate a space.

Onstreet parking and open **car parks** are colour-coded. Spaces delineated with white lines – the **White Zone** – are the most common, time-limited places controlled either by individual meters or, more usually, a prominently marked central pay-point or *Parchimetro collettivo*, taking coins only. Outside the hours posted on the pay-point, and where there isn't a machine at all (in a small village, say), White Zone spaces are free, unless there's a sign reserving them. You can park in **Blue Zone** spaces if you have a special parking disc (available for free from tourist offices, police stations and banks, and generally supplied in the glove box of rental cars). Spin the wheel round to show your time of arrival

and leave it on your dashboard: this gives you ninety minutes' free parking if you arrive between 8am and 11.30am or between 1.30pm and 6pm. Between 11.30am and 1.30pm doesn't count so you're safe until 2.30pm; if you arrive after 6pm, you're OK until 9am next day. Rarer **Red Zone** spaces are free for up to fifteen hours, as long as you display the disc. Spaces marked in **yellow** indicate private parking for, say, staff of a nearby company or perhaps guests of a local hotel; the only way to know is to ask. Illegal parking of any kind is much less tolerated in Switzerland than in Italy, and fines for minor transgressions are common.

Car rental

Car rental in Switzerland can be nastily expensive. You can significantly cut costs by renting in advance from the big international agencies (see p.29); they all cover Switzerland, with offices in all major towns, most minor ones, and at all airports. **One-way rentals** are simple to arrange, although they may attract a handling fee. Remember to check that there are no restrictions to taking the car across international borders if you're intending to head for Italy; remember, too, to have your passport, and visa if necessary, at the ready for the border crossings.

Cycling and mountain-biking in Switzerland

If you're arriving in Switzerland with **your own bike**, you have to buy a **vignette** from post offices for around Fr.5/€3, which covers road tax and third-party insurance for a year. There are various methods of transporting your bike on public transport; check the national railway website (Ⓦ www.rail.ch) for more information. Alternatively, there are two well-organized nationwide **bike rental** systems. New seven-gear country bike or quality 21-gear mountain bikes are available from Rent-A-Bike (Ⓦ www.rentabike.ch) located at most Swiss train stations (look for *bici da noleggiare*). If there's no dedicated bike office, you can normally rent from left-luggage counters. **Prices** are Fr.20/€13 for a half-day (the cut-off time is 12.30pm) or Fr.28/€18 for a full day. The popular option of one-way rental (for a full day or more) attracts a Fr.6/€4 surcharge; you must let staff know where and when you intend to drop the bike off when you rent. Kids' bikes and seats for children which you can attach to an adult's bike are also available. Station bike rental is massively popular, especially throughout the summer months, and if you're planning to rent you should always **reserve** as far as possible in advance (normally, a day or two is OK). Look for the bike-train leaflet at stations, which has a list of stations, phone numbers and the number of rental bikes at each one.

Accommodation

Whether you prefer to stay in a nineteenth-century villa, a modern hotel designed by one of Europe's top architects, a sixteenth-century farmhouse, or under canvas, you'll be spoilt for choice.

While never especially cheap, tourist accommodation in Italy is strictly regulated; hotels and campsites are star rated and required to post their prices up clearly. Booking ahead is more than advisable, especially during July and August. Although some tourist offices will help you find a room if you turn up on spec, others will just hand you a photocopy of all the options and expect you to sort yourself out. Advance reservations can be made through online agents like ⓦ www.venere.it or with travel agents, but we've given contact details throughout the Guide if you want to reserve directly. Make sure you get confirmation of the booking by fax or email – in the cities it's not uncommon to arrive and find all knowledge of your booking is denied. The phrases on p.361 will help you get over any language barrier, although English is commonly spoken. For details on accommodation in Switzerland, see box on p.36. Note that some hotels may ask you to email or fax credit card details to secure a booking.

Hotels

Hotels in Italy come tagged with a confusing variety of names, and, although the differences are minimal these days, you will still find various terms used for what are basically private hotel facilities. A **locanda** was historically the most basic option, although these days the word is often used by boutique

hotels and the like to conjure up images of simple, traditional hospitality. **Pensione**, **albergo** or **hotel** are all commonly used and more or less interchangeable. **Prices** vary greatly between the cities and tourist hot spots and the more rural areas. The official star system is based on facilities (TV in rooms, swimming pool, and so on) rather than character or comfort.

In season on the lakes it's not unusual to have to stay for a minimum of three nights, and many proprietors will add the price of **breakfast** to your bill whether you want it or not; try to ask for accommodation only – you can always eat more cheaply – and often better – in a bar. Be warned, too, that some places will also insist on **half** or **full board** during the summer although, on the whole, besides the top-end hotels, the quality can be disappointing and not worth the saving. Note that people travelling alone may sometimes be clobbered for the price of a double room even when they only need a single, though it can also work the other way round – if all their **single rooms** are taken, a hotelier may well put you in a double room but only charge the single rate.

Hostels, convents and monasteries

There are several **hostels** in the lakes area providing decent accommodation at

Accommodation price codes

Hotels in this guide have been categorized according to the price codes outlined below. They represent the **least expensive rates for a double room in high season** (generally June–Sept). The conversion (in brackets) from euros to Swiss francs is approximate. Our guide below to the standard of accommodation you can expect in each price category holds good for hotels throughout the region, apart from Milan, where you get less for your money; a hotel in price category 6 in Milan, for example, would probably be the equivalent of a hotel in category 5 elsewhere in the region.

❶ under €50 (Fr.80). One-star hotels, usually with a mixture of rooms with both shared and private facilities and in most cases comfortable enough for a shortish stay. Double rooms at hostels – where they exist – also fall into this category.

❷ €51–75 (Fr.81–120). Better-quality one-star hotels, and the bulk of two-star hotels, most offering rooms with private facilities. You'll sometimes have a TV and phone at this price, too.

❸ €76–100 (Fr.121–160). This price will get you a room in a two-star, or even a three-star hotel, almost always with private bath or shower, phone and TV.

❹ €101–125 (Fr.161–200). This will buy you solid three-star quality anywhere in the region – rooms that are pleasant to spend time in, reasonably well fitted-out, perhaps with a view, certainly with private bathroom, TV and phone.

❺ €126–150 (Fr.201–240). These are places on the border between three and four stars. This may include international chain hotels that are passable in terms of facilities and service – you'll be paying partly for the name – as well as small, well-cared-for family hotels, perhaps in historic buildings or prime locations.

❻ €151–200 (Fr.241–320). Usually a moderate four-star; expect high standards in the rooms – special bathrooms, king-sized beds, wireless internet – and a range of public facilities, perhaps including a pool or restaurant.

❼ €201–250 (Fr.321–400). These are special hotels, either by virtue of their location or facilities – generally at the upper end of the four-star category, although some five-star hotels will offer rooms at these prices. Expect hi-tech bathrooms, a choice of restaurants, and perhaps a spa or pool.

❽ €251–300 (Fr.401–485). Serious five-star quality. Service should be impeccable, facilities wide-ranging and displaying outstanding attention to detail. We've only recommended somewhere in this category if it is really special, if it enjoys a wonderful location, a superb site or building, or if the service and food are just too good to miss.

❾ Over €301 (Fr.486). The sky's-the-limit category, populated by a select few of the most celebrated hotels in northern Italy and southern Switzerland.

economical prices. For two people travelling together they don't always represent a massive saving on the cheapest double hotel room, however, but if you're on your own – or with a family – hostels can work out a lot cheaper. Many have facilities such as inexpensive restaurants and self-catering kitchens that enable you to cut costs even further and, in general, they are more sociable.

Virtually all of the Italian hostels are members of the official **Hostelling International** (HI; ⓦwww.hihostels.com) and charge around €15 per night for a dormitory bed. Strictly speaking you need to be a member of that organization in order to use

them – you can join through your home country's hostelling organization. You need to reserve well ahead in the summer months, most efficiently by using HI's Booking Network which, for a small fee, enables you to book (including online) from your home country up to six months in advance.

A new online agency, Monastery Stays (ⓦwww.monasterystays.com), offers a centralized booking service for numerous **convents** and **monasteries** around the region. There are no restrictions on age, sex or faith in the establishments they cover, all rooms have private bathrooms and few places have early curfews.

Camping

Camping is popular in Italy and there are hundreds of sites around the lakes and in the surrounding mountains catering for Italians and holidaying Europeans alike. Mobile homes have become popular in recent years and most campsites offer space for these as well as tents (see p.29 for rental details); some of the larger sites also offer space for accommodation in chalets or caravans. Camping grounds are generally open April to September. The majority are well equipped and often have swimming pools, games areas and usually a bar and small supermarket. Sites are graded with a star rating system, which, as with hotels, refers to facilities available rather than standard of upkeep. In high season on the lakes you can expect to pay a daily rate of €7–12 per person plus €5–15 per tent or caravan and €5 per vehicle.

We have listed some campsites in the Guide; otherwise local tourist offices have details of nearby sites, and the exhaustive Italian camping website, ⓦwww.camping .it, has information and booking facilities by region.

Villas and apartments

If you fancy lazing away your holiday on a lakeside in your own space, you should consider renting a **villa** for a week or two. Often enjoying marvellous lakefront locations, they can prove a cost-effective way of putting up a family or a group of friends. Rented **apartments** are becoming an increasingly popular way of experiencing Italy's towns and cities, too. Available for anything from a couple of nights to a month or so, they are usually equipped for self-catering and there's nothing like shopping for supplies in a local market to make you feel part of Italian daily life, even on a short break.

As well as the specialist companies below, tour operators who rent villas, either on their own or in conjunction with a flight or fly-drive package, are detailed on p.23.

Villa and apartment companies

Autoplan Holidays UK ☏01543 257777, ⓦwww .autoplanhols.co.uk. Small company offering apartments and villas on the lakes, including Ledro.
Cottages to Castles UK ☏01622/775 236, ⓦwww.cottagestocastles.com. Property rental company with a few apartments in the lakes area.

Accommodation in Switzerland

Accommodation in Switzerland is of a universally high standard: hotels are famous for having some of the best service in the world, rented accommodation and campsites are usually spotless and, although perhaps a little pricey by European standards, establishments are invariably conscientiously run and hospitable. Tourist offices always have lists of hotels, hostels, campsites and apartments in their area, and outside office hours they normally have a display board on the street with details of the local hotels, often with a courtesy phone.

Most **hotels** in the country (and some hostels) are regulated by the Swiss Hotel Association which awards stars (between zero and five) according to strict guidelines on everything from room size to the presence or absence of bubble bath. ⓦwww.swisshotels.com has the full listing and – more significantly – plenty of last-minute offers for cut-price multi-night deals. As well as the youth **hostels** that are part of the Hostelling International network (ⓦwww.youthhostel.ch), Switzerland has a rival group of independent hostels that work together as the Swiss Backpacker umbrella organization (ⓦwww.backpacker.ch). Often less institutional than the competition, these lively places don't require membership and are usually located in prime positions. When it comes to **camping**, prices are reasonable at Fr.6–8 per person, plus Fr.8–12 for a tent; booking ahead is recommended at all times of the year.

The **price codes** given on p.35 also apply to Switzerland. Swiss hotels listed in this book will happily accept euros as payment for accommodation, but the euro price will always be converted, according to that day's exchange rate, from the quoted price in Swiss francs.

Interhome UK ☎020/8891 1294, ⓦwww
.interhome.co.uk. Swiss company renting apartments
and villas in the lakes region at competitive prices.
Italian Breaks UK ☎020/8666 0407, ⓦwww
.italianbreaks.com. Lovely selection of lakeside villas,
many with pools and great views.
Italian Life UK ☎0800/085.7732, ⓦwww
.italianlife.co.uk. Database of properties featuring
apartments around Lake Garda.
Owners' Syndicate ☎020/7401 1086, ⓦwww
.ownerssyndicate.co.uk. Various properties on the
three main lakes.
Rentxpress ITALY ☎39/028 053 151, ⓦwww
.rentxpress.com. English-speaking company with
apartments for rent in Milan.
Unusual villa rentals US ☎804-288-2823,
ⓦwww.Unusualvillarentals.com. US company
offering some spectacular properties on Lake Como.

Agriturismo and bed and breakfast

The **agriturismo** scheme has grown considerably in recent years and enables farmers to
rent out converted barns and farm buildings to
tourists – and, increasingly, city-bound Italians
– through a centralized booking agency. The
lakes region has a good selection of options;
the agricultural area to the south, particularly
around Mantova and Cremona, is perhaps the
best hunting ground, as more and more
cascine and rice-growing estates diversify.
Some establishments offer self-contained
apartments, others have rooms with or without
en-suite bathrooms; rates start at around €80
per night for self-contained places with two
beds. There's often a wide range of activities
on offer, such as horseriding, fishing and
cycling, plus escorted walks and excursions.
For a full list of properties, consult ⓦwww
.agriturist.com, or one of the many publications about farmhouse holidays/agriturismo
that are on sale at airports, newsstands and
bookshops in Italy, or at any good travel
bookshop before you leave home.

Bed and breakfast schemes are a
relatively new arrival; the best ones are a
good way to get a flavour of Italian home life,
though they're not necessarily cheaper than
an inexpensive hotel, and they rarely accept
credit cards. For a comprehensive list of
B&Bs check the BBItalia ⓦwww.bbitalia.it
website or the links at ⓦwww.terranostra.it,
organized by region.

Eating and drinking

The importance Italians attach to food and drink makes any holiday in the country a
treat. Although you should be sure to try local specialities (see *Lake cuisine* colour
section), the sheer variety of Italian cooking should mean there's something for most
tastes. The region is also a treasure-trove for wine lovers, with Franciacorta, Valpolicella and the lesser-known Valtellina vineyards all within easy reach of the lakes.

Types of restaurants

Full meals are generally served in either a
trattoria or a *ristorante*. Traditionally, a **trattoria**
is a cheaper and more basic purveyor of
homestyle cooking (*cucina casalinga*), while a
ristorante is more upmarket, though the two
names are often interchangeable. Other types
of eating places include those that bill
themselves as everything – trattoria-ristorante-
pizzeria – and perform no function very well,
serving mediocre food that you could get
at better prices elsewhere. **Osterie** are
common too, basically an old-fashioned
restaurant or inn-like place specializing in
home cooking, though some upmarket places
with pretensions to established antiquity
borrow the name. In all mid-range establishments, pasta dishes go for €5–10, while the
main fish or meat courses will normally cost
between €10 and €15.

No smoking

It is illegal in Italy (and the Swiss canton of Ticino) to smoke in restaurants or bars. Any establishment that wants to allow smoking has to follow very stringent rules for isolating a separate room – including doors and special air-conditioning. Needless to say, this is beyond the pocket of most places and so the majority remain no-smoking throughout. Conversely, the pavement outside has become a popular gathering-point for smokers.

Italy is a latecomer to the boom in non-indigenous eating, partly owing to its lack of any substantial colonial legacy but also because of the innate chauvinism of Italian eating habits. The exceptions are the Chinese restaurants that crop up in every town, the ubiquitous burger bars, and the growing numbers of Japanese and North African restaurants in larger towns. Milan is the largest, most cosmopolitan city in the region and is very proud of its "fusion" cooking, ostensibly pan-Pacific flavours, usually served in restaurants with minimalist Asian decor.

Understanding the menu

Perhaps the most striking thing about eating in Italy is how deeply embedded in the culture it really is. Food is celebrated with gusto: **traditional meals** tend to consist of many courses and can seem to last forever, starting with an antipasto, followed by a risotto or a pasta dish, leading on to a fish or meat course, cheese, and finished with fresh fruit and coffee. Even everyday meals are a scaled-down version of the full-blown affair.

Traditionally, **lunch** (*pranzo*) and dinner (*cena*) start with **antipasto** (literally "before the meal"), a course consisting of various cold cuts of meat, seafood and cold vegetable dishes, generally costing €5–10. Some places offer self-service antipasto buffets. The next course, the **primo**, consists of a soup, risotto or pasta dish, and is followed by the **secondo** – the meat or fish course, usually served alone, except for perhaps a wedge of lemon or tomato. Watch out when ordering fish, which will either be served whole or by weight – 250g is usually plenty for one person – or ask to have a look at the fish before it's cooked. Note that by law, any ingredients that have been frozen need to be marked (usually with an asterisk)

on the menu; you might decide that it's better to try the local fish rather than one flown in from the South Atlantic, for example. Vegetables or salads – **contorni** – are ordered and served separately, and there often won't be much choice: potatoes will usually come as fries (*patate fritte*), but you can also find boiled (*lesse*) or roast (*arrostite*) potatoes, while salads are either green (*verde*) or mixed (*mista*) and vegetables (*verdure*) usually come very well boiled. Afterwards, you nearly always get a choice of fresh local fruit (*frutta*) and a selection of **desserts** (*dolci*) – sometimes just ice cream or *macedonia* (fresh fruit salad), but often home-made items, like apple or pear cake (*torta di mela/pera*) or *tiramisù*. **Cheeses** (*formaggi*) are always worth a shot if you have any room left; ask to try a selection of local varieties.

You will need quite an appetite to tackle all these courses and if your stomach – or wallet – isn't up to it, it's perfectly acceptable to have less. If you're not sure of the size of the portions, start with a pasta or rice dish and ask to order the *secondo* when you've finished the first. And, although it's not a very Italian thing to do, don't feel shy about just having just an *antipasto* and a *primo*; they're probably the best way of trying local specialities anyway. If there's no menu, the verbal list of what's available can be bewildering; if you don't understand, just ask for what you want – if it's something simple they can usually rustle it up. Everywhere will have pasta with tomato sauce (*pomodoro*) or meat sauce (*al ragù*).

At the end of the meal ask for the **bill** (*il conto*); bear in mind that almost everywhere you'll pay a cover charge (*coperto*) of €1–5 a head. In many trattorias the bill amounts to little more than an illegible scrap of paper; if you want to check it, ask for a **receipt** (*ricevuta*). In more expensive places, service (*servizio*) will often be added on top of the cover charge, generally about ten percent. If service isn't included it's common just to leave a few coins as a **tip** unless you're particularly pleased with the service, in which case, leave up to ten percent.

There's a detailed **menu reader** of Italian terms starting on p.362. See the *Lake cuisine* colour section for information on **local specialities**.

Breakfast and ice cream

Most Italians start their day in a bar, their **breakfast** (*prima colazione*) consisting of a coffee and a brioche or *cornetto* – a croissant often filled with jam, custard or chocolate, which you usually help yourself to from the counter and eat standing at the bar. It will cost between €1.30 and €1.60. Breakfast in a hotel can be a limp affair of watery coffee, bread and processed meats, often not worth the price.

Italian **ice cream** (*gelato*) is justifiably famous and a cone (*un cono*) is an indispensable accessory to the evening *passeggiata*. Most bars have a fairly good selection, but for real choice go to a **gelateria**, where the range is a tribute to the Italian imagination and flair for display. There's no problem locating the finest *gelateria* in town – it's the one that draws the crowds – and we've noted the really special places throughout the Guide. If in doubt, go for the places that make their own ice cream, denoted by the signs "Produzione Propria" outside. There's usually a veritable cornucopia of flavours ranging from those regarded as the classics – like lemon (*limone*) and pistachio (*pistacchio*) – through staples including *stracciatella* (vanilla with chocolate chips), strawberry (*fragola*) and *fiordilatte* (similar to vanilla), to

house specialities that might include cinnamon (*cannella*), chocolate with chilli pepper (cioccolato con peperoncino) or even pumpkin (*zucca*).

Pizza and snacks

Pizza is now a worldwide phenomenon, but Italy remains the best place to eat it. When good, the creations served up here are wholly different from the soggy concoctions that have taken over the international fast-food market, though it has to be said that some of the joints in the lakeside villages feel they can fob off undiscerning tourists with deeply inferior versions. For a quality pizza opt for somewhere with a wood-fired oven (*forno a legna*) rather than an electric one, so that the pizzas arrive blasted and bubbling on the surface and with a distinctive charcoal taste. This adherence to tradition means that it's unusual to find a good pizzeria open at lunchtime; it takes hours for a wood-fired oven to heat up to the necessary temperature. In Italy pizza usually comes thin and flat, not deep-pan, and the choice of toppings is fairly limited, with none of the dubious pineapple and sweetcorn variations.

Pizzerias range from a stand-up counter selling slices to a fully fledged sit-down restaurant, and on the whole they don't sell much else besides pizza, soft drinks and beer. A basic cheese and tomato *margherita* costs around €6, a fancier variety €6–10, and it's quite acceptable to cut it into slices and eat it with your fingers. Consult our food glossary (see p.363) for the different kinds of pizza.

For a lunchtime snack **sandwiches** (panini) can be pretty substantial, a bread stick or roll packed with any number of fillings. A sandwich bar (*paninoteca*) in larger towns and cities, and in smaller places a grocer's

Slow Food

The very Italian appreciation of good-quality local products led to the development of the Slow Food movement (@ www.slowfood.com) in 1986. An organization with increasing recognition worldwide, it seeks to encourage high-quality gastronomic production and the protection of traditional cuisine in the face of the "aggressive advance of food and cultural standardization". Two excellent publications listing establishments that adhere to the ethos, *Osterie d'Italia* and *Vini d'Italia*, are on sale in most Italian bookshops.

Vegetarians and vegans

Although your diet will probably be based around pasta, Italy isn't a bad country to travel in if you're a **vegetarian**. As well as the ubiquitous tomato sauce there are numerous other pasta sauces without meat, some superb vegetable antipasti and, if you eat fish and seafood, you should have no problem at all. Salads, too, are fresh and good. The only real difficulty is one of comprehension: outside the cities and resorts Italians don't really understand someone not eating meat, and stating the obvious doesn't always get the point across. Saying you're a vegetarian (*Sono vegetariano/a*) and asking if a dish has meat in it (*c'è carne dentro?*) might still turn up a poultry or prosciutto dish. Asking for it *"senza carne e pesce"* should make things sufficiently clear. **Vegans** will have a much harder time, though pizzas without cheese (*marinara* – nothing to do with fish – is a common option) are a good standby, vegetable soup (*minestrone*) is usually just that, and the fruit is excellent.

shop (*alimentari*) will normally make you up whatever you want. Bars may also offer *tramezzini*, ready-made sliced white bread with mixed fillings. Toasted sandwiches (*toast*) are common, too: in a *paninoteca* you can get whatever you want toasted; in ordinary bars it's more likely to be a variation on cheese or ham with tomato.

Other sources of quick **snacks** are **markets**, where fresh, flavoursome produce is sold, often including cheese, cold meats, spit-roast chicken and *arancini* (deep-fried balls of rice with meat (*rosso*) or butter and cheese (*bianco*) filling. **Bread shops** (*panetterie*) often serve slices of pizza or *focacce* (bread with oil and salt topped with rosemary, olives or tomato). **Supermarkets**, also, are an obvious stop for a picnic lunch: the major chains Esselunga, Carrefour and Auchan, are on the outskirts of larger towns, while GS, Unes! and Sma are often in the centre.

In recent years the very civilized habit of having a few nibbles with your late-afternoon **aperitivo** (aperitif) has taken on a whole new meaning. In the 1990s some bars began to supplement the usual olives and things on cocktail sticks with cold pasta salads and quiches to attract more customers. Before long the trend had spread and bars now groan with cold buffets at what has become known as "happy hour" – although it typically lasts from 6pm until 9pm. As with most things in these parts, the fad started in Milan, but the waves have spread outwards and bars throughout the region these days offer a fine variety of finger food to accompany your *prosecco*. If you've had a large lunch, a discreet plateful or two may be all you feel

like for an evening meal – and it's available for just the price of a drink.

Drinking

A mezzo caraffa (half-litre carafe) may be a standard accompaniment to any meal but there's not a great emphasis on dedicated **drinking** in Italy. You'll rarely see drunks in public, young people don't devote their nights to getting wasted, and women especially are frowned upon if they're seen to be overindulging. Nonetheless there's a wide choice of alcoholic drinks available, often at low prices; soft drinks come in multifarious hues; and there's also mineral water and crushed-ice drinks – you'll certainly never be stuck if you want to slake your thirst.

Where to drink

Traditional **bars** are less social centres than functional places – brightly lit places, with a bar, a Gaggia coffee machine and a picture of the local football team on the wall. This is the place to come for a coffee in the morning, a quick beer or a cup of tea in the afternoon – people don't generally idle away evenings in bars; indeed it's often difficult to find this kind of bar open much after 8pm. It's cheapest to drink standing at the counter, in which case you usually pay first at the cash desk (*la cassa*), present your receipt (*scontrino*) to the barperson and give your order. There's always a list of prices (*listino prezzi*) behind the bar. If there's waiter service, just sit where you like, though bear in mind that to do this will cost up to twice as much as positioning yourself at the bar, especially if you sit outside (*fuori*) – the difference is shown on the price list as *tavolo* (table).

The larger resorts and towns offer a much greater variety of places to sit and drink in the evening, sometimes with live music or DJs. The more energetic or late-opening of these have taken to calling themselves **pubs**, a spill-over from the outrageous success of Irish pubs, at least one of which you'll find, packed to the rafters, in almost every small town. Beer, particularly in its draught form, *alla spina*, has become fashionable in recent years. Real enthusiasts of the grape should head for an **enoteca**, though many of these are as much restaurants as bars, as well as being a good place to buy a few bottles of the local brew.

Coffee, tea and soft drinks

One of the most distinctive smells in an Italian street is that of fresh **coffee**. The basic choice is either small and black (*espresso*, or just *caffè*), which costs around €1 a cup, or white and frothy (*cappuccino*, for about €1.30), but there are scores of variations. If you want your espresso a little longer and weaker, ask for a *caffè lungo* or, for an espresso with hot water added to make it more like a filter coffee, an *Americano*; with a drop of milk is *caffè macchiato*; very milky is *latte macchiato or caffè latte* (ordering just a "*latte*" Starbucks-style will get you a glass of milk). Coffee with a shot of alcohol – and you can ask for just about anything – is *caffè corretto*. Many places also sell decaffeinated coffee (*decaffeinato*); while in summer you might want to have your coffee on ice (*Caffè freddo*).

If you don't like coffee, there's always **tea**. In summer you can drink this cold too (*tè freddo*) – excellent for taking the heat off. Hot tea (*tè*) comes with lemon (*con limone*) unless you ask for milk (*con latte*). Milk itself is drunk hot as often as cold, or you can get it as a milk shake – *frappé* or *frullati*. A small selection of herbal teas (*infusioni*) are generally available: camomile (*camomilla*) and peppermint (*infuso di menta*) are the most common.

There are various **soft drinks** (*analcolici*) to choose from. Slightly fizzy, bitter drinks like San Bittèr or Crodino are common, especially at *aperitivo* time. A **spremuta** is a fresh fruit juice, squeezed at the bar, usually orange, lemon or grapefruit. There are also crushed-ice *granite*, offered in several flavours and available with or without ice cream on top. Otherwise there's the usual range of fizzy drinks and concentrated juices. Coke is as prevalent as it is everywhere, though the diet or light versions less so; the home-grown Italian version, Chinotto, is less sweet. **Tap water** (*acqua del rubinetto*) is quite drinkable, and you won't pay for a glass in a bar, though Italians prefer **mineral water** (*acqua minerale*) and drink more of it than any other country in Europe. It can be drunk either still (*senza gas* or *naturale*) or sparkling (*con gas* or *frizzante*).

Beer and spirits

Beer (*birra*) is always a lager-type brew which usually comes in one-third or two-third litre bottles, or on tap (*alla spina*), measure for measure more expensive than the bottled variety. A small beer is a *piccola* (20cl or 25cl), a larger one (usually 40cl) a *media*. The cheapest and most common brands are the Italian Moretti, Peroni and Dreher, all of which are very drinkable; if this is what you want, either state the brand name or ask for *birra nazionale* or *birra chiara* – otherwise you could end up with a more expensive imported beer. You may also come across darker beers (*birra nera* or *birra rossa*), which have a sweeter, maltier taste and in appearance resemble stout or bitter.

All the usual **spirits** are on sale and known mostly by their generic names. The home-grown Italian firewater is **grappa**, originally from Bassano di Grappa in the Veneto but now available just about everywhere. It's made from the leftovers from the winemaking process (skins, stalks and the like) and is just the thing on a cool evening.

You'll also find **fortified wines** like Martini, Cinzano and Campari; ask for a Campari-soda and you'll get a ready-mixed version from a little bottle, Campari Bitter is a shot of Campari with soda. You might also try Cynar – an artichoke-based sherry often drunk as an aperitif with water. There's also a daunting selection of **liqueurs**. Amaro is a bitter after-dinner drink or *digestivo*, Amaretto much sweeter with a strong taste of almond, Sambuca a sticky-sweet aniseed concoction, traditionally served with a coffee bean in it and set on fire (though, increasingly, this is something put on to impress tourists). A shot of clear grappa is a common accompaniment to a coffee and can range from a warming palate cleanser to throat-burning firewater, while another sweet alternative, originally from Sorrento, is *Limoncello* or *limoncino*, a lemon-based liqueur best drunk in a frozen vase-shaped glass. Strega is another drink you'll see behind every bar, yellow, herb-and-saffron based stuff in tall, elongated bottles: about as sweet as it looks but not unpleasant.

Wine

The labelling of **Italian wine** is confusing: there is no established system and there is often little geographical and varietal information to help you identify where a wine is from or what it is like. **The Denominazione d'Origine Controllata** (DOC) system was introduced in the 1960s as a way of guaranteeing the quality but it quickly became a mixed blessing. Though it's undoubtedly true that the DOC and DOCG system helped lift standards of Italian wines, the laws have come under fire from both growers and critics for their rigidity, constraints and anomalies. They leave no room for the experimentation and modern methods that northern Italy, for one, specializes in. Denomination zones are set by governmental decree specifying where a certain named wine may be made, what grape varieties may be used, the maximum yield of grapes per hectare and for how long the wine should be aged. The **Denominazione d'Origine Controllata e Garantita** (DOCG) was established in the 1980s as one step up: wines sold under this label not only have to conform to the ordinary DOC laws, but are also tested by government-appointed inspectors. Increasingly, producers eager to experiment began to disregard the regulations and make new wines that were sometimes among Italy's best, though they were officially labelled only table wine (*da tavola*). The **Indicazione**

Geografica Tipica (IGT) was introduced in 1992 to enable producers to use geographical names and grape varieties on labels to help describe their wines – something that has benefited the less traditional producers in particular.

The hillsides around the lakes are spread with vineyards producing the kind of decent, ordinary stuff you'll find as house wine in the region's restaurants. These include the Merlot reds from the Sottoceneri, around Lugano, and Valcalepio and Scanzo from the Bergamasc valleys, which are often served by the *carafa* – available in quarter (*quarto*), half (*mezzo*) and litre (*un litro*) measures.

There are also some internationally celebrated wine-producing areas around the lakes and it's worth trying a bottle or two of these very affordable local gems. The world-class sparkling wine produced in the hills of the **Franciacorta** between Bergamo and Brescia has made its name in recent years using the *metodo classico* of the French Champagne region. Although the elegant, bubbly Cuvée (Cà del Bosco and Bellavista are two of the best) is the most renowned product of this area, velvety reds and well-perfumed whites are also worth trying (usually labelled Terre di Franciacorta). For a very different type of sparkling wine, try the slightly fizzy red Bonarda from the little-known **Oltropò Pavese** region, across the Po River south of Pavia.

In the east of the lakes region, around the southern and eastern shores of **Lake Garda**, light reds and aromatic whites admirably accompany local lake fish and risottos; Bardolino and Bianco di Custoza are names to look out for, along with the DOC labels of Garda Classico, Lugana and San Martino della Battaglia. Recioto di Soave and Soave Superiore from around Verona are some of the oldest types of wine hereabouts with evidence of their cultivation dating back to the fifth century. The wine's deep yellow colour and honey bouquet make the perfect partner for a slice of local *pandoro*. The **Valpolicella** district, north of Verona, produces some of northern Italy's best-known red wines.

On the south-facing mountain slopes in the north of Lombardy, the **Valtellina Superiore** (divided into the different geographic zones of Sassella, Inferno, Grumello and Valgella) cultivates the Nebbiola grape (known here as Chiavennasca), creating strong red wines with a characteristic perfume that perfectly complements the mountain meats and salamis of the area.

The media

The decentralized press of Italy and Switzerland serves to emphasize the strength of regionalism in the countries. Local TV is popular, too, in the light of little competition from the national channels. If you know where to look, journalistic standards can be high.

Newspapers

The **Italian press** is largely regionally based, with just a few newspapers available across the country. The centre-left *La Repubblica* (Ⓦ www.repubblica.it) and authoritative *Corriere della Sera* (Ⓦ www.corriere.it) are the two most widely read, published nationwide with local supplements, but originating in Milan. *La Stampa* (Ⓦ www.lastampa.it), the daily of Turin, is a rather stuffy, establishment broadsheet. Most people's choice of reading matter, however, bears witness to how intensely regionalist Italy remains; the majority buy their local rag – like *L'Eco di Bergamo* or *Il Corriere di Como*, for example – rather than bother with anything more universal in outlook. Many of the imprints you see on newsstands are the official mouthpieces for political parties: *L'Unità* was the party organ of the former Communist Party, while *La Padania* is the press of the right-wing, regionalist Lega Nord party. The traditionally radical *Il Manifesto* has always been regarded as one of the most serious and influential sources of Italian journalism. Perhaps the most avidly read newspapers of all, however, are the specialist sports papers, most notably the *Corriere dello Sport* and the pink *Gazzetta dello Sport* (Ⓦ www.gazzetta.it) – both essential reading if you want an insight into the Italian football scene.

One-man band

In an independent survey of 193 nations conducted in 2006 by the non-profit organization Freedom House, Italy ranked below Bolivia and Bulgaria and on a par with Botswana in terms of press freedom. Prime Minister Silvio Berlusconi's personal influence over six of the seven national TV channels (La 7 is the only exception) is often seen as causing a conflict of interests. His Milan-based media corporation, Mediaset, is owner of the commercial channels Italia 1, Rete 4 and Canale 5 and, as leader of a coalition with an overwhelming majority in both chambers of parliament, he has significant influence on the national TV and radio channels (RAI). Nor is his control restricted to broadcasting: his empire extends to the country's main magazine and book publishers, Mondadori, and his brother Paolo runs one of the few national newspapers, *Il Giornale*. Perhaps the most extraordinary fact, however, is that when Berlusconi was returned to power in 2008 there remained no legislative curbs on the role of politician and media mogul.

Switzerland has a ton of **newspapers** – more than 200 nationwide – but again almost without exception they're parochial local news-sheets, reporting cantonal and municipal affairs in some detail, but relegating the rest of Switzerland, let alone the world, to a few inside columns. Zürich's *Neue Zürcher Zeitung*, or *NZZ* (✆www.nzz .ch), is the best known of Swiss newspapers. Conservative and highbrow in the extreme, it nonetheless has gained its reputation by reporting Swiss and world events with scrupulously high journalistic standards. The local Italian-language *Corriere del Ticino* (✆www.cdt.ch) and German-language *Tessiner Zeitung* (✆www.tessinerzeitung.ch) are provincial small-fry in comparison.

English-language newspapers can be found for around three times their home cover price in all the larger towns and most of the more established resorts. There are several English-language publications available; we've listed them in the Guide chapters when they are particularly worth seeking out.

TV and radio

Italian TV is appalling, with ghastly quiz shows, mindless variety programmes and cathartic chat-shows squeezed in between countless artless advertisements. Of the three national channels, RAI 1, 2 and 3, RAI 3 has the odd worthwhile programme, although the intelligent, satirical shows are often indecipherable to foreigners who have anything less than an encyclopedic knowledge of Italian politics from the last fifty years. **Swiss television** is similarly undemanding with a diet of game shows,

made-for-TV movies (dubbed) and lots of local news and local-interest programming. There are at least six national terrestrial stations including two channels from Televisione Svizzera Italiana (TSI), plus plenty of local stations for each area. **Satellite television** is widely distributed across the region, and hotels with three stars and above usually offer a mix of BBC World, CNN, and French-, German- and Spanish-language news channels, as well as MTV and Eurosport.

Radio is highly deregulated in Italy, with the FM waves crowded to the extent that you continually pick up new stations whether you want to or not – with the Catholic Radio Maria popping up with an uncanny frequency. On the whole the RAI stations are again the more professional – though even with them daytime listening is virtually undiluted Euro-pop. For intelligent discussion programmes try Radio Popolare (FM 107.6), or, alternatively, in and around Milan and Varese, Lifegate Radio (FM 105.1, 105.2 or 88.7) is worth a listen. It started life as an alternative to the commercial stations with no talking (not even credits for the songs they play), but adverts are steadily creeping in, albeit for fair-trade and zero-impact goods and services. Each language area of **Switzerland** has three regional **radio stations**, one channel devoted to each of news, classical music and popular music (see ✆www.srg.ch), as well as a fistful of community stations.

For **world service** stations check the following websites for details of their global frequencies: **BBC** ✆www.bbcworldservice .com, **Radio Canada** ✆www.rcinet.ca and **Voice of America** ✆www.voa.gov.

Festivals and special events

Although religion is rarely at the forefront of celebrations in the north of Italy, the origins of many festivities lie in the Church calendar. Epiphany, Carnival, Easter and Christmas, as well as local patron saints' days, are all a good excuse to break the daily routine. The lakes region is also well blessed with music festivals and events, including several good jazz festivals, lakeside classical music concerts, and the world-famous opera seasons in both Verona and Milan. Last, but by no means least in terms of the economy of the region, are Milan's big fashion and design fairs, which draw fashionistas and design gurus from around the world.

Notable festivals in honour of local saints include **Santa Lucia** (Dec 13), which is particularly celebrated around Bergamo and Brescia and sees the setting up of handicraft stalls and local produce markets. A street fair is also central to celebrations of the patron saint of Milan, **Sant'Ambrogio** on December 7, when the *Oh bej, Oh bej!* stalls of handicrafts, antiques and Christmas gifts fill the streets around the saint's eponymous church. Recently there's been a revival of interest in **Carnival** (*Carnevale*), the last fling before Lent. One of the best places to witness Carnival celebrations is the village of Bagolino above Lake Idro: locals dress up in traditional costume and there is much music-making and dancing.

Food-inspired *feste* are lower-key, but no less enjoyable, affairs, usually celebrating the local speciality of the region to the accompaniment of dancing, music from a local band and noisy fireworks at the end of the evening. There are literally hundreds of food festivals,

sometimes advertised as **sagre** – most are modest affairs, primarily aimed at locals and little publicized, but look in the local papers or ask at the tourist office during summer and autumn and you're bound to find something going on.

One other type of festival to keep an eye out for are the summer **political** shindigs, like the Festa de l'Unità, usually taking place in the evenings and advertised by posters all over the region. Begun initially to recruit members to the different political parties, they have become something akin to a village fete but with a healthy Italian twist. The food tents are a great way to try tasty local dishes washed down with a cup of wine. There's usually bingo going on in one corner, the sort of dancing that will make teenagers cringe and the odd coconut shy or two. In larger towns these have become more sophisticated affairs with big-name national bands playing.

Efficient as ever, Switzerland Tourism maintains an encyclopedic events calendar at ⓦwww.myswitzerland.com, detailing hundreds of pageants big and small, while the Italian Tourist Board have a slightly temperamental search engine organized by region on their site ⓦwww.enit.it.

We've put together a selection of festivals and special events held throughout the year in towns and cities across the lakes region - see overleaf for details.

Calendar of festivals and special events

There are literally hundreds of local festivals around the lakes and sometimes the best ones are those that you come across unexpectedly. Below are some of the highlights, but note that **dates change** from year to year, so it's best to contact the local tourist office for specific details.

January

6 Milan *Epifania* Costumed parade of the Three Kings from the Duomo to Sant'Eustorgio, the resting place of the bones of the Magi. Across the region, *La Befana*, the good witch, who brings toys and sweets to children who've been good and coal to those who haven't, is celebrated.

17 Mantova *San'Antonio* Human chess game, stalls and street celebrations.

February

Milan *Carnevale Ambrosiano* The city's patron saint is celebrated with children's fancy-dress processions and religious services, and the traditional biscuits, *chiacchiere*, are available in the city's *pasticcerie*.

Carnevale Carnival festivities across the region, especially lively at Lecco and Bagolino, which celebrate with processions, floats and traditional dancing.

Verona *Baccanale del Gnoco* (Gnocchi Festival), at the end of Carnival. Parades and floats around the San Zeno neighbourhood led by the newly voted King Gnoco.

15 Brescia *SS Faustino and Giovita* Fireworks, food stalls and music to celebrate the city's patron saint's day.

Last week Milan Spring Fashion Week, presenting the summer's must-have clothes.

March

8 *Festa della Donna* International Women's Day, on which women are given bunches of mimosa.

Third week Milan *Salone Internazionale del Mobile* The world's designers come to check out the latest in furnishing and design throughout the city.

Last Thurs Verona *Vinitalia* Wine enthusiasts from around the world converge to try each other's wares.

April

20 Como Light and illumination displays honouring Volta's presentation to the Royal Society in London in 1800 of a device to produce energy.

Third Sun Milan *Mercato dei Fiori* Milan's canal district is strewn with blooms.

Fourth week Pavia *Le Grande Feria di Pavia Sapori* Typical Pavian food, wine and handicrafts on display throughout town.

May

Second week Brescia *Mille Miglia* Vintage cars set off on their 1600-kilometre race around the country.

Last Sun All Italy *International Wine Day* Wine estates open their cellars to the public.

June

First Sun Milan *Festa sui Navigli* Boat race, food and craft stalls in Milan's canal district.

15 Valeggio sul Mincio, Verona *Tortelloni Festival* This attractive small village, with its numerous restaurants, draws lovers of pumpkin ravioli, and this weekend sees the speciality at its best.

Second half Bellinzona *Piazza Blues* Free open-air jazz festival.

Third Sun Menaggio, Lake Como Annual fish fry-up.

Third Sun Milan *Sagra di San Cristoforo* Candle-lit boat parade with fireworks, dancing and music along the canals.

Fourth Fri Verona The opera season starts in the Roman arena; ⓦwww.arena.it.

July

All month Clusone *Clusone Jazz* Twenty-year-old festival attracting some big names to this quiet little town near Lake Iseo.

First half Lugano *Estival Jazz* Free jazz festival held alfresco in the main squares in Lugano.

15 Cremona *Palio dell'oca* Inter-district rivalry fuels this goose race, plus there are processions with floats, and lots of local produce on offer.

August

15 Laveno, Lake Maggiore *Illuminated Boat Race* Held in Laveno, but the lights and fireworks are clearly visible from the other side of the lake around Stresa.

September

First week Monza, Milan Italian Formula One Grand Prix.

12 Verona Street entertainment and general partying to celebrate the birthday of the town's most famous lover, Juliet.

21 Varenna, Lake Como Polenta and fish festival.

Last week Lake Como Ancient rivalries are played out in the gondola race between Lecco, Varenna and Bellagio.

Last Sun Desenzano del Garda, Lake Garda Autumn festival that sees the village alive with street entertainment and local food and wine.

Last week Milan Autumn Fashion Week. The fashionistas hit town again, and the traffic comes to a stand-still.

October

Fourth weekend Cremona Torrone Festival. Nougat is celebrated in the town that claims to have invented it.

December

All month Riva del Garda, Lake Garda Each of the town's piazzas is decorated on the theme of a fairytale; ⓦwww.nottedifiaba.it.

All month Arco, Lake Garda Celebrations of the Austrian connection with the village focus on a Christmas market.

Second week Verona Christmas market in Piazza Bra.

7 Milan *Oh Bej, Oh Bej!* The city's patron saint, Sant'Ambrogio, is celebrated with a huge street market around his church and a day off work and school for all.

13 Bergamo, Brescia and Cremona *Santa Lucia* Children are given presents and sweets, and there are candlelit processions.

First week Milan Opera season starts with an all-star opening night at La Scala.

Sports and outdoor pursuits

The Italian Lakes region and the Ticino district of Switzerland provide opportunities for activities ranging from swimming, sailing and windsurfing to exploring the surrounding mountains on foot, bike, or even hang-glider. Spectator sports are popular in Italy, especially the hallowed *calcio* (football), and there is undying national passion for frenetic motor and cycle races.

Sport

Calcio, or football, is the national sport, followed fanatically by millions of Italians, and if you're at all interested in the game, it would be a shame to leave the country without attending a *partita* or football match. The **season** starts around the middle of August, and finishes in June. **Il campionato** is split into four principal divisions with the twenty teams in the Serie A being the most prestigious. Matches are normally played on Sunday afternoons, although Saturday, Sunday-evening and Monday games are becoming more common, too. The top-flight sides in this part of the country are Milan's two teams, Milan and Inter, both of which have consolidated their positions near the top of Serie A in recent years and who usually spend the season vying for top place with Turin's Juventus. At the other end of the table, Bergamo's main team Atalanta, Brescia and Verona can usually be found hovering between relegation or promotion between Serie A and B. See ⓦwww .lega-calcio.it for results, a calendar of events and English links to the official team websites.

Inevitably **tickets** for Serie A matches are not cheap, starting at about €15 for "Curva" seats where the *tifosi* or serious fans go, rising to €40–50 for "Tribuna" seats along the side of the pitch, and anything up to €100 for the more comfortable "Poltroncina" cushioned seats in the centre of the Tribuna. Once at the football match, get into the atmosphere of the occasion by knocking back *borghetti* – little vials of cold coffee with a drop of spirit added.

The chosen sport after football in northern Italy is **cycling**. Popular as a participatory and spectator sport alike, at weekends especially, you'll often see a club group out, dressed in bright team kit, whirring along on their slender machines taking the hairpin bends of the pre-Alps at death-defying speeds. The annual Giro d'Italia, in the second half of May, is a prestigious event that attracts scores of international participants each year, closing down roads and finishing in Milan. It has a long history and the region is very proud that several local boys, brought up on the punishing pre-Alp roads, have been winners of the pink jersey; the latest of these – Simone Savoldelli – is from the Val Seriana in Bergamo.

In a country that has produced Ferrari, Maserati, Alfa Romeo and Fiat, it should come as no surprise that **motor racing** gives Italians such a buzz. The **Formula One** track at Monza, near Milan, holds the Italian Grand Prix in June every year and numerous companies organize packages that include flights, entrance tickets and accommodation.

Basketball is a surprisingly popular sport in Italy. It was introduced from the United States after World War II and most cities now have a team. Italy is now ranked among the foremost basketball teams in the world. For more details on fixtures and the leagues, see ⓦwww.eurobasket.com/ita.

Outdoor pursuits

Lake Garda is the best option for **watersports**: Torbole is famous for windsurfing but is also well organized for kayaking, dinghy sailing and waterskiing on the lake, and canyoning excursions in the mountains behind. Full details are on p.294. Gargnano, also on Lake Garda, holds the annual Centomiglia **sailing** race at the beginning of September, and sailing is similarly popular on the other lakes, with many outlets – such as at Sarnico on Lake Iseo, Dongo on Lake Como and Cánnero on Lake Maggiore – offering boats, boards and gear for rental, with and without tuition.

The hills and mountains above all the lakes make perfect **walking** and **mountain-bike** country: tour operators offer many independent or escorted tours throughout the region, but it's just as easy to strike out alone. Tourist offices in most locations keep details of walks in the vicinity, while those in popular walking areas – such as Menaggio on Lake Como or Cannobio on Lake Maggiore – stock hiking maps and detailed route descriptions, and can advise on particular trails to follow. The tourist offices in Ascona and Locarno keep loads of resources for walkers, including details of circular trails between stations on the Centovalli railway nearby. Several high peaks in the area are easily reached by public transport, including Monte Baldo above Malcesine (Lake Garda), Monte Generoso above Lugano (Lake Lugano) and the Mottarone above Stresa (Lake Maggiore); when skies are clear, taking the train or cable car up in order to follow trails around their summits can offer breathtaking panoramic views. The Mottarone in particular has some excellent mountain-bike routes.

By contrast, the flatter lands to the south of the region, around Mantova, Cremona and Pavia, are perfect for leisurely **cycle rides** or strolls. Tourist offices in all three cities keep details: one especially good route is the full-day bike ride between Peschiera del Garda and Mantova, following the River Mincio all the way.

Horseriding (*maneggio*) is becoming increasingly popular in rural areas and most tourist offices have lists of local stables. Many *agriturismi* also have riding facilities and sometimes offer daily or weekly treks and night rides. Note that Italians rarely wear or provide riding hats.

In the winter months, it's possible to spend a day **skiing** or **snowboarding**. Resorts in this area (universally small, with limited facilities) are found chiefly above Bergamo – and thus are often crammed with weekending Milanese – as well as the much more remote high valleys above Locarno; small pistes are also created on slopes such as Monte Tamaro above Lugano, Monte Baldo above Malcesine and in the side-valleys of the Val Camonica and Val Sabbia above Brescia. Though great for a few hours of fun, these resorts can't match the snow cover, facilities and ambience of the major winter-sports centres of Piemonte, Trentino and Switzerland. There is information in English on Italian resorts and conditions at Ⓦ www.skiinfo.it. For details of skiing in Ticino, check Ⓦ www .ticino.ch.

Travelling with children

Children are adored in Italy and will be made a fuss of in the street, and welcomed and catered for in bars and restaurants. Hotels normally charge around thirty percent extra to put a bed or cot in your room, though kids pay less on trains and can generally expect discounts for museum entry: prices vary, but 11–18-year-olds are usually admitted at half price on production of some form of ID (although sometimes this applies only to EU citizens). Under-11s – or sometimes only under-6s – have free entry.

Supplies for **babies** and small children are pricey: nappies and milk formula can cost up to three times as much as in other parts of Europe. Discreet breastfeeding is widely accepted – even smiled upon – but nappy changing facilities are few and far between. Branches of the children's clothes and accessories chain Prenatal have changing facilities and a feeding area, but otherwise you may find you have to be creative. It is rare to find any facilities in stations, department stores or public toilets, although that said, people will usually go out of their way to help you.

For **older children**, most towns and villages have central playgrounds, while the theme parks of Gardaland (ⓦwww.gardaland.it) and Caneva World (ⓦwww.canevaworld.it) will no doubt entertain. Once you're on the lakes, there is plenty to keep children of all ages occupied, from pedaloes to windsurfing and from paddling to dinghy-sailing.

The only **hazards** when travelling with children to the lakes are the heat and sun. Very-high-factor suncreams are quite difficult to find, although pharmacies usually sell sunblock. Bonnets or straw hats are plentiful in local markets. Take advantage of the periods of less intense sun – mornings and evenings – for travelling, and use the quiet of siesta-time to recover flagging energy. The rhythms of the southern climate soon modify established patterns, and you'll find it more natural carrying on later into the night, past normal bedtimes.

Internet resources

ⓦ**www.italyfamilyhotels.it** An organization of hotels across Italy geared up with facilities from cots and bottle warmers in rooms to baby sitters, play areas and special menus. New hotels are constantly joining and at the time of writing there was one close to Lake Garda.

ⓦ**www.travelforkids.com** Advice on planning holidays with children and tips on child-friendly tourist sights and activities, region by region.

Travel With Your Children 40 Fifth Ave, New York, NY 10011 ☎212/477 5524 or 1-888/822-4388. Publishes a regular newsletter, *Family Travel Times* (ⓦwww.familytraveltimes.com), as well as a series of books on travel with children.

Holidays With Kids ⓦwww.holidayswithkids .com.au. The website of the popular *Holidays With Kids* magazine, this site lists kid-friendly destinations and accommodation as well as providing advice to frazzled parents. You can book tours and holidays here, too.

Travel essentials

Costs

The north of Italy has always been fairly expensive, with **prices** in line with northern Europe rather than the Mediterranean south. In recent years, inflation caused by the introduction of the euro and a wavering economy have conspired to increase prices still further. Public transport and entrance to sights is usually relatively inexpensive, but restaurant and hotel prices are not much lower than in the UK or parts of the US.

Prices in the **Swiss Ticino** are similar to those in northern Italy, and the banking infrastructure works along the same lines, so the advice below for carrying and exchanging money is also relevant once you cross the border; remember that Switzerland is not in the Eurozone, although it will accept euros as payment.

Full-time students are entitled to special **discounts** on museum and gallery entrance in Italy as long as they have recognized ID cards. University photo ID might open some doors, but they are not as readily accepted as the **International Student ID Card** (ISIC; Ⓦ www.isiccard.com), which also entitles the bearer to some discounts on accommodation, entertainment and even language courses in Milan – check the Ⓦ www.istcnet .org site for detailed information. At some tourist sights, **children** under 12 are allowed in free. On public transport children under 1m tall (city trams and buses have an official mark on the wall to show the level) can travel free, At the other end of the scale, European citizens who are **over 60** – or sometimes 65 – are often allowed into sights at a reduced rate. It's always worth carrying proof of your age and asking – "*C'è sconto per gli anziani?*"

Crime and personal safety

Both Italy and Switzerland are safe countries and you should feel comfortable walking around town centres and resorts, even in the evening. That said, in the bigger towns, like Milan and Verona, tourists can be targeted by pickpockets: crowded streets or markets, big train stations and busy tourist areas are the places to be on your guard: don't flash anything of value, keep a firm hand on your camera, and carry shoulderbags, as Italian women do, slung across your body.

Keep an eye out for two or three people begging together, often with an infant or small child in tow; they will usually have a piece of cardboard explaining their predicament which will be adroitly used to cover one of them whipping away your valuables. On the whole, it's common sense to avoid badly lit areas completely at night. Confronted with a robber, your best bet is to submit meekly. If driving, never leave anything valuable in your vehicle, and try to park on well-lit, well-used streets or in garages with custodians. Motorway service stations have a particularly high rate of petty crime, so make sure you always leave your vehicle locked with all valuables out of sight.

If the worst happens, you'll be forced to have some dealings with the **police.** In **Italy** these come in many forms: the **Vigili Urbani,** with their white pith helmets and natty gloves, are mainly concerned with directing traffic and issuing parking fines, whereas the **Polizia Stradale** patrol the motorways. You may, however, have dealings with the **Carabinieri**, in their military-style uniforms and white shoulderbelts, who deal with general crime, public order and drug control. These are the ones Italians are most rude about, but a lot of jokes concerning their supposed stupidity stem from the usual north–south prejudice. The Carabinieri tend to come from southern Italy – joining the police is one way to escape the poverty trap – and they are posted away from home so as to be well out of the sphere of influence of their families. The **Polizia Statale**, the other general crime-fighting force, enjoy a fierce rivalry with the Carabinieri and are the ones you'll perhaps have most chance of coming into contact with, since **thefts** should be reported to them. You'll find the address of the **questura** or police station in the local telephone directory (in smaller places it may be just a local *commissariato*); alternatively ask your hotel or the tourist office for details. The *questura* is where you go to get a *denuncia*, the official report of anything that's been lost or stolen that you will need for any insurance claim; take a book and be prepared for a long wait.

By contrast with Italy, **Switzerland** has only one small force of plain-clothes federal police (*polizia*), as most police duties are managed by the cantonal authorities. Ticino's **Polizia Cantonale** has its own website ⓦwww.polizia.ti.ch – with contact details for every local police station.

Electricity

The supply is 220V, though anything requiring 240V will work. Most plugs have two round pins, though you'll find the older three-pin plug in some places: a multi plug adapter is very useful.

Entry requirements

British, Irish and other EU citizens can enter Italy on production of a valid passport, although if you're planning to work or stay for a while a *permesso di soggiorno* (resident's permit) is required. Citizens of the United States, Canada, Australia and New Zealand need only a valid passport, too, but are limited to stays of three months. Likewise, EU nationals and citizens of the US, Canada, Australia and New Zealand need only a valid passport to visit Switzerland, where stays are limited for all to a maximum of three months. Other nationals should consult the relevant embassy about visa requirements.

In Italy, you're legally required to register with the police within three days of entering the country, though if you're staying at a hotel this will be done for you and, even if it isn't, most police officers would be amazed at any attempt to register yourself down at the local station while on holiday. However, if you're going to be staying around for a while, you'd be advised to comply.

Italian embassies and consulates abroad

Australia Embassy: 12 Grey St, Deakin, Canberra, ACT 2600 ☎02/6273 3333, ⓦwww.ambcanberra .esteri.it. Consulates in Melbourne ☎03/9867 5744, Sydney ☎02/9392 7900, Adelaide ☎08/8337 0777, Brisbane ☎07/3229 8944.

Canada Embassy: 275 Slater St, Ottawa, ON, K1P 5H9 ☎613/232-2401, ⓦwww.ambottawa.esteri .it. Consulates in Montréal ☎514/849-8351 and Toronto ☎416/977-1566.

Ireland Embassy: 63–65 Northumberland Rd, Dublin 4 ☎01/660 1744; ⓦwww.ambdublino .esteri.it.

New Zealand Embassy: 34–38 Grant Rd, PO Box 463, Thorndon, Wellington ☎04/473-5339, ⓦwww.ambwellington.esteri.it.

South Africa Embassy: 796 George Ave, Arcadia 0083, Pretoria ☎012/423 0000, ⓦwww .ambpretoria.esteri.it.

UK Embassy: 14 Three King's Yard, London W1Y 2EH ☎020/7312 2200, ⓦwww.amblondra.esteri.it. Consulate in Manchester ☎0161/236 9024.

US Embassy: 3000 Whitehaven St NW, Washington DC 20008 ☎202/612-4400, ⓦwww .ambwashingtondc.esteri.it/. Consulates in Boston ☎617/722-9201, Chicago ☎312/467-1550, New York ☎212/737-9100, San Francisco ☎415/931-4924 and other cities nationwide.

Swiss embassies and consulates abroad

Full listing at ⓦwww.eda.admin.ch.

Australia Embassy 7 Melbourne Ave, Forrest, ACT 2603 ☎02/6273 3977.

Canada Embassy 5 Marlborough Ave, Ottawa, ON K1N 8E6 ☎613/235-1837, ⓦwww.eda.admin .ch/canada.

Ireland Embassy 6 Ailesbury Rd, Ballsbridge, Dublin 4 ☎01/218 6382, ⓦwww.swissembassy.ie.

New Zealand Embassy 22 Panama St, Wellington ☎04/472 1593.

UK Embassy 16–18 Montague Place, London W1H 2BQ ☎020/7616 6000, ⓦwww.swissembassy .org.uk.

US Embassy 2900 Cathedral Ave NW, Washington DC 20008 ☎202/745-7900, ⓦwww.swissemb.org.

Health

As a member of the European Union, Italy has free reciprocal **health agreements** with other member states. EU citizens are entitled to free treatment within Italy's public health-care system on production of a **European Health Insurance Card** (EHIC), which British citizens can obtain by picking up a form at the post office, calling ☎0845/606 2030, or applying online at ⓦwww.dh.gov.uk. Allow up to 21 days for delivery. The EHIC is free of charge and valid for at least three years, and it basically entitles you to the same treatment as an Italian. The Australian Medicare system also has a reciprocal health-care arrangement with Italy.

Vaccinations are not required, and neither Italy – nor neighbouring Switzerland – present any more **health worries** than anywhere else in Europe. In Italy, although the water is safe to drink, most Italians drink bottled water, in some areas because there is a very high limescale content in the supply but, more often than not, simply out of habit. Public water fountains (usually button- or tap-operated) in squares and city streets are common, though look out for *acqua non potabile* signs, indicating that the water is unsafe to drink.

It's wise to take high-factor suntan lotion to protect against sunburn – the gentle breezes on the lakes and in the mountains can make the strength of the sun deceptive. Mosquitoes can be a problem between June and October, especially in Milan and the southern parts of the lakes, so you might want to pack insect repellent, sprays and/or plug-ins.

In Italy

If you do become ill, your first port of call should be a **pharmacy** (*farmacia*). Italian pharmacists are well qualified to give you advice on minor ailments and can dispense many medicines that need prescriptions in other countries. There's generally at least one pharmacy open all night in the bigger towns. A rota system operates and you should find the address of the one currently open on any *farmacia* door or listed in the local paper.

If your condition is more **serious** or you're involved in an **accident**, head for the *pronto soccorso* (accident and emergency department) of the nearest hospital or, in extreme cases, phone ☎118 and ask for *ospedale* or

Emergencies

For help in an **emergency**, call one of the following national emergency telephone numbers:

Italy
☎112 **Police** (Carabinieri)
☎113 **Local police** (Polizia Statale)
☎115 **Fire brigade** (Vigili del Fuoco)
☎116 **Roadside assistance** (Soccorso Stradale)
☎118 **Ambulance** (Ambulanza)

Switzerland
☎117 **Police**
☎118 **Fire, ambulance and accidents**
☎140 **Roadside assistance**

ambulanza. Casualty departments are organized according to the triage system, which means that you will be seen whatever your condition, but more serious cases will be treated first. You may be charged for the service if the hospital staff feel that your condition was not really urgent, but this is still the quickest and mot effective way of getting the best treatment: the fee will usually be around €30. Whenever possible, make sure you take your passport with you and your European Health Insurance Card, if you're eligible, to enable you to get prescriptions for medicines at the local rate (about ten percent of the full price). If at all possible, try to avoid going to the **dentist** (*dentista*) while you're in Italy or Switzerland. These aren't covered by the health service, and for the smallest problem you'll pay through the teeth. If it's an emergency that really can't wait until you get home, visit *pronto soccorso* in the big towns or take local advice in the smaller ones.

In Switzerland

Although Switzerland isn't a member of the EU, citizens of European member states are entitled to **emergency health care** in the country under the same terms as Swiss residents. This effectively means that, on production of an EHIC, the care will be subsidized but you will have to contribute to the costs: for example, there is a small charge for bed and board if you have to stay in hospital, although medical treatment is free. If you need an ambulance, you will be required to pay fifty percent of the cost (as local residents do) and there is usually a small standard charge for any prescribed drugs.

Insurance

Even though EU health care privileges apply in Italy, you'd do well to take out an **insurance policy** before travelling to cover against theft, loss, illness or injury. A typical policy usually provides cover for the loss of baggage, tickets and – up to a certain limit – cash or cheques, as well as cancellation or curtailment of your journey. Most policies exclude so-called dangerous sports unless an extra premium is paid; around the lakes this can mean scuba diving, windsurfing and trekking. Many policies can be chopped and changed to exclude coverage you don't need – for example, sickness and accident benefits can often be excluded or included at will. If you do take medical coverage, ascertain whether benefits will be paid as treatment proceeds or only after your return home, and whether there is a 24-hour medical emergency number. When securing baggage cover, make sure that the per-article limit – typically under £500 – will cover your most valuable possession. If you need to make a claim, you should keep receipts for medicines and medical treatment, and in the event you have anything stolen, you must obtain an official statement from the police (*polizia* or *carabinieri*).

Rough Guides has teamed up with Columbus Direct to offer you **travel insurance** that can be tailored to suit your needs. Products include a low-cost **backpacker option** for long stays; a **short-break option** for city getaways; a typical **holiday package option**; and others. There are also annual **multi-trip policies** for those who travel regularly. Different sports and activities (such as trekking and skiing) can usually be covered if required. See our website (ⓦwww.roughguides.com /website/shop) for eligibility and purchasing options. Alternatively, UK residents should call ☏0870/033 9988; Australians,

☏1300/669 999 and New Zealanders, ☏0800/55 9911. All other nationalities should call ☏+44 870/890 2843.

Mail

Post office (ⓦwww.poste.it) opening hours in Italy are usually Monday–Saturday 8.30am–1pm, and it pays to get there early, as large queues invariably form around mid-morning. Unless you need registered post (*raccomandata*) or have parcels to send though, you won't need to waste your holiday time in post office queues. Stamps (*francobolli*) are sold in *tabacchi*, too, as well as in some gift shops in tourist resorts; they will often also weigh your letter. If your letter is urgent make sure you mark it "posta priori-taria"; this service is included in the basic price of €0.60 to anywhere in Europe, including Italy. Sending a standard-sized envelope or a postcard costs €0.85 to the US and €1 to Australia and New Zealand.

Post offices (☏0800/888 777, ⓦwww .post.ch) in Switzerland are generally open Monday to Friday 7.30am–noon and 1.30–6.30pm, and Saturday 8–11am, although watch out for slight regional varia-tions and restricted hours in smaller branches. Sending a postcard or a 20g letter costs Fr.1.20 to Europe, Fr.1.40 worldwide.

Maps

The **town plans** throughout the Guide should be fine for most purposes, and practically all tourist offices give out maps of their local area for free. The clearest and best-value **road maps** for Italy are produced by Touring Club Italiano (TCI). The fold-up 1:200,000 scale map of Lombardy is excellent and includes the neighbouring areas of Piemonte, Veneto and Switzerland covered in this guide. If you prefer an atlas format, go for their *Atlante Stradale d'Italia* (*Nord*) on the same scale; this covers every-where in the country north of Florence and features profiles of the motorways, including the facilities at individual service stations. For **hiking** you'll need at least a scale of 1:50,000. Studio FMB and the TCI cover the major mountain areas of northern Italy to this scale. Both the Istituto Geografico Centrale and Kompass series cover the area with more detailed 1:25,000 maps.

For Switzerland, the most respected commercial series is that published by the Federal Office of Topography (Ⓦ www .swisstopo.ch). They do a full range starting at 1:1 million, detailed 1:100,000 regional maps and 1:50,000 or 1:25,000 hikers' maps, as well as specialist maps on different scales highlighting cycling and inline-skating routes, ski runs, historic sites, vineyards, cultural attractions and more.

Money

Italy's currency is the euro (€), which is split into 100 cents. The currency in Switzerland is the Swiss franc (franco svizzero). The most common abbreviation is "Fr" – but you may also see "fr", "sFr", "Sfr", "SF", "FS", or the official bank abbreviation "CHF". Each franc is divided into 100; these are called *centesimi* (also c) in the Italian-speaking areas covered by this guide. This being border territory, however, you can pay for just about every-thing in the Ticino in euros (cash or card). All hotels advertise rates in francs and euros (check closely which column you're referring to), as do the boat companies and even restaurants and shops. Note that the euro equivalent price is always worked out when you buy according to the daily CHF–EUR exchange rate, so it can vary slightly from the advertised figure.

Banking hours are normally Monday to Friday mornings from 8.30am until 1.30pm, and for an hour in the afternoon (usually between 2.30pm & 4pm). There are local variations on this and banks are usually open only in the morning on the day before a public holiday. Although it's a good idea to have some **cash** when you first arrive, one of the easiest ways of accessing funds while you're abroad is with your **debit card** direct from an ATM cash machine (*bancomat*). While the flat transaction fee is usually quite small, most cards can only issue a maximum of €250 per day; check with your bank before you leave home to make sure your card is set up to work abroad, as some banks have an increased security system that means your card will not work abroad unless you have informed them that you are travelling. Debit cards from the UK can be used to purchase goods in shops, with verifi-cation by PIN number at the checkout.

Credit cards can also be used in ATMs with a PIN number that's designed to be used overseas but remember that cash advances on credit cards are treated as loans with interest accruing daily from the date of withdrawal, and there may be a transaction fee on top of this. Note that payment by card (*carta*) is not as prevalent as in the UK and US; many budget hotels aren't set up to take cards, and even some upmarket restaurants insist on cash, although you shouldn't have too many problems in the main tourist centres. Master-Card, Visa and American Express are the most widely accepted cards in Italy and Switzerland.

A safe alternative to cash and cards are **traveller's cheques**, available from any bank or post office in the UK. Most American and Canadian banks sell American Express cheques, and they're widely accepted; your local bank will probably also sell one or more of the other brands, sometimes waiving the commission if you have an account there. Alternatively, check the American Express Ⓦ www.americanexpress.com, Thomas Cook Ⓦ www.thomascook.com or Visa Ⓦ www.visa.com websites direct. Make sure you keep the purchase agreement and a record of cheque serial numbers safe and separate from the cheques themselves. In the event that cheques are lost or stolen, the issuing company will expect you to report the loss forthwith to their office in Italy; most companies claim to replace lost or stolen cheques within 24 hours.

Opening hours

In Italy most shops and businesses open Monday to Saturday from around 9am until 1pm, and from about 3/4pm until 6/7pm, though some places still close on Saturday afternoons and Monday mornings. Tradition-ally, everything except bars and restaurants closes on Sunday, though *pasticcerie* are open in the mornings; while in Milan and tourist areas, Sunday shopping is becoming more common and around Christmas time, in particular, there are extended openings. **Opening hours** for state-run **museums** are generally Tuesday to Saturday 9am until 7pm, and Sunday 9am until 1pm. Most other museums roughly follow this pattern too,

Closed on Mondays

Most museums and sights are closed on Mondays; see the relevant sections in the Guide for more specific details.

although they are more likely to close for a couple of hours in the afternoon, and have shorter opening times in winter. The majority of churches open in the early morning, around 7 or 8am for Mass, and close around noon, opening up again at 4pm and closing at 7 or 8pm. The rules for visiting **churches** are strictly enforced everywhere: **dress modestly**, which means no shorts (not even Bermuda-length ones) for men or women, and covered shoulders for women, and try to avoid wandering around during a service.

Shop opening hours in Switzerland are customarily Monday to Saturday 9am–5.30/6pm some places then take Monday morning off. Quiet Sundays are sacrosanct. **Cafés** that serve full meals (which is most of them) will only do so at the customary mealtimes: roughly noon to 2pm and 6 to 10pm. Outside those hours, you'll generally be able to find only snacks. Closing times of all establishments are regulated by each individual municipality: Lugano, for example, shuts up shop at midnight. All places can stay open an hour later than normal on Friday and Saturday nights.

Phones

Public telephones, run by **Telecom Italia**, come in various forms, usually with clear instructions in English. Coin-operated machines are increasingly hard to find so you will probably have to buy a **telephone card** (*carta* or *scheda telefonica*), available from *tabacchi* and newsstands. **Telephone numbers** change with amazing frequency in Italy and codes are now an integral part of the number and always need to be dialled, regardless of whether or not you are in the zone you are telephoning. All telephone numbers listed in the Guide include the relevant code. Numbers beginning ☎800 are free, ☎170 will get you through to an English-speaking operator, ☎176 to international directory enquiries.

Phone tariffs are among the most expensive in Europe, especially if you're calling long-distance or internationally. You can cut costs hugely by buying a **phone card** – on sale for upwards of €5 from newspaper stands; you don't insert it into the phone but dial a central freephone number and then a pin code given on the reverse of the card. For example, the EDICARD, available for €5, €10, €20, from anywhere with a SISAL terminal (the machines used for lottery tickets): €5 will buy you around 350 minutes to the UK or US. Telecom Italia have a similar card called WELCOME but it's not as good value.

Mobile/cell phones in Italy and Switzerland work on the GSM European standard, usually compatible with phones from the UK, the rest of Europe, Australia and New Zealand, but not the US and Canada, which use a different system. You'll hardly ever see an Italian without their *telefonino*, but if you want to join them make sure you have made the necessary "roaming" arrangements before you leave home – check with your service provider for details.

Public holidays

It is worth trying to avoid travelling on the eve of a national holiday, as roads and public transport are usually packed. On the country's official national holidays, everything closes down – including many museums – although bars and restaurants are likely to stay open in resorts. If a holiday falls on a Tuesday or Thursday, it is common for people to take the Monday or Friday as a ponte – or bridge – and so enjoy a long weekend. In August, particularly during the weeks either side of *Ferragosto* (Aug 15), most townsfolk flee to the coast, lakes or mountains, leaving many towns half-deserted, with shops, bars and restaurants closed and a reduced public transport service. Meanwhile, the lakeside villages fill up with the townies, and the routes around the lakes reach near-saturation point.

The following dates are holidays in both Italy and Switzerland, unless otherwise stated.

January 1 *Primo dell'anno*; New Year's Day.
January 6 *Epifania*; Epiphany.
Pasquetta Easter Monday.

Calling home from Italy

UK and Northern Ireland Dial 00 44
Republic of Ireland Dial 00 353
US and Canada Dial 00 1
Australia Dial 00 61
New Zealand Dial 00 64

Calling Italy and Switzerland from abroad

To call from abroad, dial your international access code (00 from the UK, Ireland & New Zealand, 011 from the US & Canada, 0011 from Australia), followed by **39** for Italy, then the area code and number **including the initial zero**. For Switzerland you need the international access code followed by by **41** for Switzerland, followed by the local number **excluding the initial zero**.

April 25 *Giorno della Liberazione*; Liberation Day, in Italy only.
May 1 *Festa dei Lavoratori*; Labour Day.
June 2 *Festa della Repubblica*; Republic Day, in Italy only.
August 1 *Festa nazionale*; Swiss National Day, in Switzerland only.
August 15 *Ferragosto*; Assumption of the Blessed Virgin Mary.
November 1 *Ognissanti*; All Souls Day.
December 8 *Immacolata*; Immaculate Conception of the Blessed Virgin Mary.
December 25 *Natale*; Christmas.
December 26 *Santo Stefano*; St Stephen's Day.

Time

Italy and Switzerland are always one hour ahead of Britain, seven hours ahead of US Eastern Standard Time and ten hours ahead of Pacific Standard Time.

Tipping

Service is generally included on restaurant bills in Italy, but if not, a couple of euros will suffice. You only need to tip taxi drivers, concierge and so on, if they have been particularly helpful. In Switzerland, all bar, restaurant and hotel bills are calculated with fifteen percent service included: tipping is officially abolished. Nonetheless, unless service was truly diabolical, everyone rounds things up at least to the nearest franc; in restaurants, it's common to add a few francs.

Toilets

Public facilities have improved around tourist sites in recent years, although the main options remain train and bus stations, or nipping into a bar or café for the loo followed by a quick drink. In stations and motorway services there might be an attendant who should keep the facilities stocked with paper (*carta*) and will expect a tip of a few cents. Most places are relatively clean, though hole-in-the-floor versions are still common for public toilets and it's advisable not to be without your own toilet roll. By law, basins in public places in Italy have to be designed so that you don't need to touch the taps: in modern bathrooms this requires waving your hands under the tap to start the flow; in older ones there is usually a foot pedal.

Tourist information

There is no shortage of information on the lakes region. The national tourist offices are an obvious starting point. Their websites – ⓦwww.enit.it for Italy and ⓦwww.My Switzerland.com for Switzerland – hold a wealth of information, and once you're on the ground, you'll find plenty of brochures, maps and leaflets at tourist offices throughout the district. There are hundreds of other **websites**, covering every aspect of Italian and Swiss life; we've listed some of the best general sites with English-language sections below. Other, more specific, ones are listed elsewhere in the relevant parts of Basics or throughout the Guide chapters.

Italian tourist offices

Most towns and villages have a **tourist office** and there are branches at the major airports and stations. They vary in degrees of usefulness (and helpfulness), but usually provide at least a town plan and local listings guide. In smaller villages there is sometimes a "Pro Loco" office (representing a consortium of local businesses) that has much the same kind of information, but the staff are unlikely to speak English.

Opening hours vary: offices in larger cities and resorts are likely to be open Monday to Saturday 9am to 1pm and 4 to 7pm – and sometimes on Sunday mornings – while smaller offices may open weekdays only. In peak season, however, many offices will stay open over lunch. Pro Loco times are notoriously erratic – some open for only a couple of hours a day, even in summer. Some of the lake resorts have information boards outside the offices, which can be helpful if you need numbers or directions when everything is closed.

General site: ⓦwww.enit.it.

Australia ☎02/9962 1666, ⓦitaliantourism .com.au

Canada ☎416/925 4882, ⓦwww .italiantourism.com.

Ireland ☎01/660 1744, ⓦwww.italianembassy.ie.

New Zealand ☎04/473 5339, ⓦwww.italy -embassy.org.nz.

UK ☎020/7408 1254, ⓦwww.italiantouristboard .co.uk.

Useful websites

Regional tourist sites

Lake Orta & Lake Maggiore (west) ⓦwww.distrettolaghi.it

Lake Maggiore (east shore) & Varese ⓦwww.turismo.provincia.varese.it

Lake Maggiore (north shore) ⓦwww.maggiore.ch

Lake Lugano ⓦwww.lugano-tourism.ch

Milan ⓦwww.milanoinfotourist.com

Lake Como (west leg) ⓦwww.lakecomo.com

Lake Como (east leg) ⓦwww.turismo.provincia.lecco.it

Bergamo ⓦwww.provincia.bergamo.it/turismo

Brescia ⓦwww.bresciaturism.it

Lake Garda ⓦwww.visitgarda.com

Verona ⓦwww.tourism.verona.it

Mantova ⓦwww.turismo.mantova.it

Cremona ⓦwww.aptcremona.it

Italy – general sites

ⓦ**www.corriere.it** Online version of the Milan daily with some interesting general articles translated into English and a regularly updated weather forecast.

ⓦ**www.italianlakes.com** An attractive site run by an expat American couple that's full of helpful tips and resources.

ⓦ**www.italymag.co.uk** Aimed at expats, with articles on life in Italy plus some good links and a forum for posting queries.

ⓦ**www.paginegialle.it** Italian *Yellow Pages* online.

ⓦ**www.parks.it** Good, detailed info on national and regional parks, plus some wildlife information.

Switzerland – general sites

ⓦ**www.directories.ch** Search the Swiss phonebook and *Yellow Pages*.

ⓦ**www.museums.ch** Catalogue and description of all museums nationwide.

ⓦ**www.swissembassy.org.uk** Engaging information in English about the country and its politics put together by the Swiss Embassy in London.

ⓦ**www.swissinfo.org** Useful news site reporting on all things Swiss.

ⓦ**www.ticino.ch** Vast array of useful stuff on Ticino canton.

US New York ☎ 212/245 4822, Chicago ☎ 312/644 0996, Los Angeles ☎ 310/820-1898; ⓦwww .italiantourism.com.

Switzerland Tourism offices

The efficient **Switzerland Tourism** is only too happy to supply you with exhaustive information on all things Swiss; its partner **Ticino Tourism** (ⓦwww.ticino.ch) covers Italian-speaking Switzerland. All towns, and a sizeable number of villages have a tourist office (*Ente Turistico*), where staff speak at least some English and are scrupulously helpful.

From April to October tourist offices are usually **open** Mon–Sat 9am–6pm, Sun 9am–3pm, although some may close a little earlier. Out of season they are likely to shut up shop between noon and 2pm and all day on Sundays.

General site: ⓦwww.MySwitzerland.com.
UK & Ireland ☎ 00800/100 200 30.
US & Canada Toll-free from US ☎ 1-877/ SWITZERLAND, toll-free from Canada ☎ 011800/100 200 30.
Other countries Either call ☎ +4144/288 1111 or use the international toll-free number ☎ +800/100 200 30 (add your international prefix: 0011 from Australia, 00 from New Zealand, etc).

Travellers with disabilities

Italy isn't generally geared towards disabled travellers, though people are helpful enough and progress is gradually being made in the areas of accessible accommodation, transport and public buildings. In Switzerland, on the other hand, you'll find most tourist facilities have been designed with everybody, not just the able-bodied, in mind and there's a wealth of information to help you plan your trip.

Public transport can be challenging in Italy, although low-level buses are gradually being introduced and some trains have disabled facilities. There are several appropriate accommodation options in most lake resorts; you might want to rope the local tourist office in to give you a hand with finding the most suitable. Spacious, specially designed toilets are becoming increasingly common in bars, restaurants and hotels as new legislation takes force. The cobbled streets in old town and village centres can present their own problems as can access to sights, including galleries and museums. Even in the bigger cities – like Milan and Verona – high kerbs, ad hoc parking and constant building works can make life difficult for those in wheelchairs and the partially sighted. On the plus side, some of the lake resorts, particularly on Lake Maggiore, have been a favourite with senior citizens for decades and so some hotels and restaurants have slightly better facilities for those with reduced mobility.

Switzerland Tourism (see opposite for worldwide contacts) publishes a very useful hotel guide specifically for visitors with disabilities, listing and assessing hotels around the country according to their access for people with limited mobility or in wheelchairs. If you contact the "Call Center Handicap" team (see below) of Swiss Federal Railways at least two hours before you want to travel, giving them your full name, phone number, date of travel, desired departure and arrival times, and the nature of your disability, they can arrange for people to help you on and off the train and access the "Mobilifts" at most stations; this is a free service. All fast trains (single- and double-decker), and most regional trains have spaces within second-class carriages to park wheelchairs, identified by a wheelchair pictogram. Boats are generally easy to board and often have facilities such as disabled toilets; and private narrow-gauge train companies including FART (the Centovalli line from Locarno) are converting carriages for passengers with disabilities. The Call Center Handicap office has full details.

Contacts for travellers with disabilities

Access-Able ⓦwww.access-able.com. Online resource for US travellers with disabilities.
Accessible Italy Italy ☎ +39.378.941.108, ⓦwww.accessibleitaly.com. Italian operation offering organized tours and tailor-made trips to foreigners.
Accessible Journeys 35 W Sellers Ave, Ridley Park, PA 19078, US ☎ 1-800/846-4537, ⓦwww .disabilitytravel.com. Travel tips and programmes for groups or individual travellers from the US, including an Italian Lakes tour.
Call Center Handicap Mobil Services Handicap, Bahnhofplatz 1, CH-3900 Brig, Switzerland

⊤0800 007 102 or +41 51 225 7150, ⓔmobil @sbb.ch. Part of the Passenger Division of SBB. Gives full details of accessibility on all forms of public transport, and makes arrangements for travel anywhere in Switzerland.

Disabled Persons Assembly 4/173–175 Victoria St, Wellington, New Zealand ⊤04/801 9100. NZ resource centre with lists of travel agencies and tour operators for people with disabilities.

Holiday Care 2nd floor, Imperial Building, Victoria Rd, Horley, Surrey RH6 7PZ, UK ⊤01293/774 535, Minicom ⊤01293/776 943, ⓦwww.holidaycare .org.uk. Provides free lists of accessible accommodation outside the UK and information on financial help for holidays.

Irish Wheelchair Association Blackheath Drive, Clontarf, Dublin 3, Eire ⊤01/833 8241, ⓦiwa.ie. Useful information for wheelchair users about travelling abroad.

Mobility International Switzerland (MIS) ⓦwww.mis-ch.ch. Loads of useful information and links for visitors to Italy.

NICAN ⓦwww.ncan.com.au. Australian website including information about the Qantas Carers Concession card.

Society for the Advancement of Travelers with Handicaps (SATH) 347 5th Ave, New York, NY 10016, US ⊤212/447-7284, ⓦwww.sath.org. Information on the accessibility of specific airlines and advice on travelling with certain conditions.

Guide

Guide

1

Milan

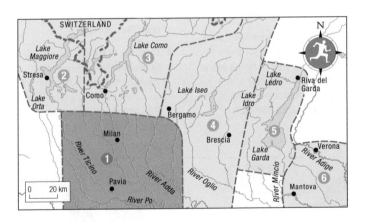

CHAPTER 1 # Highlights

✱ **Roof of Milan's Duomo**
Wander amid the tracery of
the world's largest Gothic
cathedral and enjoy views of
the city and the mountains
beyond. See p.79

✱ **La Scala** A night at the home
of the Golden Age of Italian
opera is simply unforgettable.
See p.81

✱ **Pinacoteca di Brera** This
venerable art gallery, opened
in 1809, holds a peerless
collection of northern Italian
masterpieces. See p.86

✱ **The Last Supper** Leonardo
da Vinci's mural for the
refectory wall of Santa Maria
delle Grazie is one of the
greatest masterpieces of the
Renaissance. See p.97

✱ **Sant'Ambrogio** This beautiful
church dedicated to the
city's patron saint provided
the prototype for many of
the region's Romanesque
basilicas. See p.99

✱ **Shopping in Milan** Whether
looking for top-label chic or
bargain designer threads, you'll
be spoilt for choice in Italy's
fashion capital. See p.100

✱ **Aperitivo** Unwind with Milan's
signature drink – Campari
– and a plate of nibbles during
the city's extended happy
hour. See p.105

✱ **Certosa di Pavia** Rising out
of the rice fields near Pavia,
this Carthusian monastery is a
wonderful fusion of Gothic and
Renaissance architecture.
See p.116

▲ Sant'Ambrogio

Milan

ILAN stands at the foot of the Alps, amid Lombardy's rich agricultural plains, guarding the route south from central Europe to Rome. Linked with the western lakes and the Adriatic Sea by a network of canals and tributaries that feed the mighty River Po, the Lombard capital enjoys a strategic location and since its Celtic beginnings has been a hub of trade and business, as well as an important political centre.

Milan is the working face of Italy. The small factories that kick-started the city's economy in the 1950s have moved on now, but multi-million-euro service industries have taken their place. The home of the country's Stock Exchange and banks, and the centre of Italian broadcasting, publishing and marketing, twenty-first-century Milan has in many ways more of a claim to be Italy's capital city than Rome. Indeed, there's a long-standing antipathy between the two cities, with the Milanese often insinuating that the Romans are lazy and corrupt.

But, although Milan may be closer in distance – and attitude – to London than Palermo, its habits are still very much Italian. The Milanese take food just as seriously as anywhere else in the country, and the city continues to empty to the coast and mountains every weekend and for most of August. Its visitor attractions couldn't be more Italian either – a monumental cathedral, works of art by the masters of the Renaissance, plus ultra-chic boutiques selling the world's most stylish clothes.

Milan's rich history has bequeathed it a wealth of art and monuments, not least its spectacular **Duomo**, some splendid **ancient churches**, the medieval **Castello Sforzesco** and the world-famous **La Scala** opera house. Chief among its artistic treasures and justifying a visit alone is Leonardo da Vinci's masterpiece of Renaissance art, **The Last Supper**, hidden away on a monastery wall in the church of **Santa Maria delle Grazie**. More superlative artworks by the likes of Mantegna, Veronese and Tintoretto can be seen at the city's premier art gallery, the **Pinacoteca di Brera**.

Milan's other major draw is **shopping**. The second half of the twentieth century saw Milan become a catwalk for the world's top **fashion** designers; the city proudly hosts all the main international labels – and many of the smaller ones, too. But Milanese shopping is not just about fashion: since the 1950s the city has been home to the most important **design** and manufacturing companies in the world, and the **Salone del Mobile** every spring spawns a city-wide showcase for the latest in design and invention.

Milan's high proportion of beautiful people – from fashionistas and their wealthy clients to would-be models and *veline* (scantily dressed TV presenters) – means that it's difficult to be overdressed. This is a place where appearance counts and the Italian obsession with **la bella figura**, or looking good, is honed

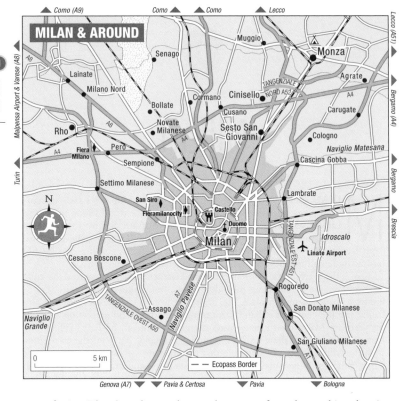

to perfection. There's no better place to do a spot of people-watching than in the city's bars, especially at **aperitivo** time, an extended happy hour that's become something of an institution.

If you begin to tire of the city or want to slow down a gear or two, head for nearby **Pavia**, a comfortable provincial town on the River Ticino that once held the hunting lodge and summer residence of the Sforza family. Close by is the stunning **Certosa**, the Carthusian monastery that Gian Galeazzo Visconti founded as his mausoleum.

Some history

Milan first stepped into the historical limelight in the fourth century when Emperor Constantine issued the **Edict of Milan** here, granting Christians throughout the Roman Empire the freedom to worship for the first time. The city, under its charismatic bishop, Ambrogio (Ambrose), swiftly became a major centre of Christianity – many of today's churches stand on the sites, or even retain parts, of fourth-century predecessors.

Medieval Milan rose to prominence under the ruthless regime of the Visconti dynasty, who founded what is still the city's most recognized building, the florid late-Gothic **Duomo**, and built the first, heavily fortified nucleus of the **Castello** – which, under their successors, the Sforza, was extended to house what became one of the most luxurious courts of the Renaissance. This was a period of much building and rebuilding, notably under the last Sforza, Lodovico, who employed the architect **Bramante** to improve the city's churches. He also commissioned **Leonardo da Vinci** to paint *The Last Supper* and design war-machines to aid him in his struggles with foreign powers and other Italian states. Leonardo's inventions didn't prevent Milan falling to the French in 1499, marking the beginning of almost four centuries of foreign rule. Two hundred years of Spanish dominance – beginning in the mid-sixteenth century – were mainly characterized by high taxes, plague and the construction of a new defensive wall around the city. Later, the Austrian Habsburgs took control; their major legacies were the **Teatro della Scala** and the **Brera** art gallery, which, during Milan's short spell under Napoleon, was filled with paintings looted from churches and private collections and opened to the public.

Mussolini made his mark on the city, too. Arrive by train and you emerge into the massive white megalith of the Stazione Centrale built on the dictator's orders; while the town council offices are housed in the pompous **Arengario** from which he would address crowds gathered in Piazza Duomo. And it was on the insalubrious roundabout of **Piazzale Loreto** that the dead dictator was strung up for display to the baying mob as proof of his demise in April 1945.

The city's postwar development was characterized by the boom periods of the 1950s and 1980s. The industry that launched the so-called "miracle of Milan" in the 1950s led to the construction of the hundreds of small factories and the infamous dreary **suburbs** that still encircle the city today. Most of the factories stopped production during the last few decades, and the city's wealth now comes from banking and its position at the top of the world's **fashion** and **design** industries.

Politically, too, Milan has been at the centre of Italy's postwar history. A bomb in Piazza Fontana in 1969 that killed sixteen people signalled the beginning of the dark and bloody period in the country's history known as the **Anni di piombi**, when murky secret-service goings-on led to over one hundred deaths from bomb attacks. In the 1980s, the corruption and political scandals of the Craxi period once again focused attention on Milan, the centre of the country's institutional corruption, gaining it the nickname **Tangentopoli** or "Bribesville". The subsequent dismantling of the existing political system paved the way for the birth and rapid success of Forza Italia, the political party founded by the self-promoting media magnate **Silvio Berlusconi**, which has ruled the country for longer than any other postwar government. Berlusconi is Milan born and bred and has his financial and power base in the media and publishing companies of the city – not to mention being owner of the football team, AC Milan.

Arrival

Milan has two main **airports** – Malpensa and Linate – both used by domestic and international traffic. It is also within easy reach of several smaller terminals: Bergamo-Orio al Serio (see p.227) is the best connected and the most convenient, while Brescia-Montichiari (see p.245) is a couple of hours' drive away. For more on airports in the lakes region, see p.19.

Malpensa (Ⓦ www.sea-aeroportimilano.it), 50km northwest of the city near Lake Maggiore, is connected by direct **bus** with the Stazione Centrale, Milan's main train station (every 20min 4.25am–11.15pm; 1hr; €7), and by a fast **train**, the Malpensa Express, with Milano Nord (every 30min 4.20am–11.27pm; 50min; Ⓣ 199.151.152, Ⓦ www.malpensaexpress.it; early-morning and evening services are replaced by a bus from Via Leopardi, just to the left of the station as you face it). Tickets cost €11 if bought beforehand, more if purchased on the

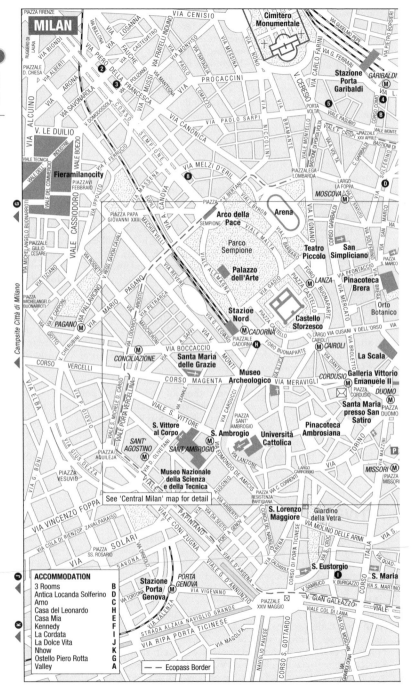

MILAN

Camposite Citta di Milano

ACCOMMODATION

3 Rooms	B
Antica Locanda Solferino	D
Arno	C
Casa del Leonardo	H
Casa Mia	E
Kennedy	F
La Cordata	I
La Dolce Vita	J
Nhow	K
Ostello Piero Rotta	G
Valley	A

– – – Ecopass Border

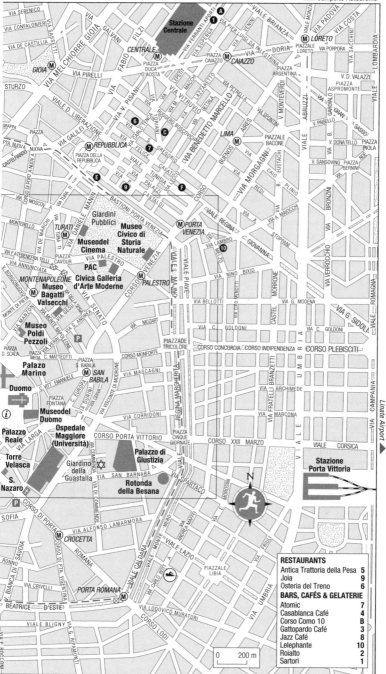

RESTAURANTS

Antica Trattoria della Pesa	5
Joia	9
Osteria del Treno	6

BARS, CAFÉS & GELATERIE

Atomic	7
Casablanca Café	4
Corso Como 10	B
Gattopardo Café	3
Jazz Café	8
Lelephante	10
Roialto	2
Sartori	1

train. Both the Stazione Centrale and Milano Nord are connected with the city's metro system: the stations are called Centrale F.S. and Cadorna respectively. A **taxi** from Malpensa to the centre takes about forty minutes and costs around €80 when the traffic is not too heavy.

Regular privately run buses also link Malpensa to several of the **regional towns** around the lakes. Tickets are available from the Airport 2000 desk in the airport or on the buses themselves: Arona, Stresa and Verbania (5 daily; must be reserved by midday the day before travelling, 48hr in advance for weekends and public holidays; ☎0323.552.172, ⊛www.safduemila.com; €11.50; Terminal 1). Gallarate train station, linked to Malpensa airport 5km away by regular local bus services, is on the main train line from Milan to Lake Maggiore (including Arona, Stresa and Intra), as well as the Varese branch line.

Milan's other airport, **Linate** (⊛www.sea-aeroportimilano.it), is just 7km east of the city centre: airport buses connect it with the Piazza Luigi di Savoia, on the east side of Stazione Centrale (every 20min 5.40am–9.30pm; 20min; €2; buy ticket on board). Ordinary ATM urban transport **buses** (#73) also run every ten minutes from 5.30am until around midnight between Linate and the city centre, just south of Piazza San Babila (M1) on Corso Europa, and they don't take much longer; tickets cost the usual €1 and should be bought before you get on the bus from the airport newsagent, or, if you have change, from the ticket machine at the bus stop. A **taxi** to the centre will cost around €30. There's also a twice-daily connecting bus service between Linate and Malpensa, a 75-minute journey.

Most international and domestic **trains** pull in at the monumental **Stazione Centrale**, northeast of the city centre on Piazza Duca d'Aosta, at the hub of the metro network on lines M2 and M3. Other services, especially those from stations in the Milan region – Bergamo, Pavia, Como and the other western lakes – terminate at smaller stations around the city: **Garibaldi**, **Lambrate**, **Porta Genova** and **Milano Nord**, all on M2 (the metro stop for Milano Nord is "Cadorna"), although these often also stop at Stazione Centrale.

All international and long-distance **buses**, and many regional buses, arrive at and depart from the bus station in front of the Porta Garibaldi train station (M2), where you can get information and buy tickets from the Autostradale/ Eurolines bus office (☎02.3391.0794; Mon–Fri 9am–6.30pm).

If you're arriving by **car**, try to time your arrival to avoid the morning and evening rush hours (approximately 7.30–10am & 4.30–7pm) when Milan's ring road, the infamous Tangenziale, is often grid-locked. Signage is copious, if not always very clear, and the ring road links onto the autostradas for Bergamo, Brescia, Verona and Lake Garda (A4), Varese and Lake Maggiore (A8), Lake Como (A9) and the "Autostrada del Sole" (A1) for Cremona and Mantova. See p.72 for information about the Ecopass zone and advice on parking in Milan.

Information

Milan has two **tourist offices**, plus smaller branches at Malpensa and Linate airports (daily 9am–4pm). The main city-centre office is at Piazza Duomo 19/A, on the north side of the square, underground in an old day hotel (Mon–Sat 8.45am–1pm & 2–6pm, Sun 9am–1pm & 2–5pm; ☎02.7740.4343, ⊛www .milanoinfotourist.com); it has tour- and concert-booking desks and literature on the city and around. There's another smaller office in the Stazione Centrale, although, at the time of writing, its future location was unclear due to the station refurbishment (Mon–Sat 9am–6pm Sun 9am–1pm & 2–5pm; ☎02.7740.4318). The station office will phone ahead to make free hotel reservations for you if you're stuck and has a reduced selection of leaflets and city maps.

For English-language **listings**, *Milano Mese*, a monthly booklet published by the tourist office, is good on exhibitions, while *Hello Milano* (🌐www.hellomilano.it), available free in hotel lobbies and the city-centre tourist office, gives comprehensive monthly rundowns of cultural events and is best for up-to-date opening hours of the major sights. The supplements in *Corriere della Sera* on Wednesdays, and *La Repubblica* on Thursdays, are also valuable sources of listings – in Italian.

Getting around

Milan's street-plan resembles a spider's web, with roads radiating out from the central Piazza Duomo. The bulk of the city is encircled by two concentric ring roads following the medieval and Spanish walls of the city, while the suburbs and industrial estates spill out towards a third ring, the Tangenziale, which links the main autostradas. The city centre is just about compact enough to explore on foot and you'll probably only want to use the easy-to-master **public transport** system when you're flagging or going out of the way. The network of trams, buses and metro is cheap and, on the whole, efficient, although wildcat strikes are frequent on the metro.

By public transport

The orange ATM **map** (*Pianta dei Trasporti Pubblici*; €3), available from newspaper kiosks in Stazione Centrale, Duomo, Cadorna and Garibaldi metro stations, is invaluable, as it shows the routes and numbers of all buses and trams, as well as the metro system. The fast, if gloomy, metro is good for crossing the city quickly, while the well-organized bus and tram routes are more pleasant for short hops. Most **bus** and **tram** stops display the route and direction of travel, and the front of each metro train shows the station at the end of the line. The **metro** is made up of four lines, the red MM1, green MM2, yellow MM3, and blue *passante ferroviario*; the four main intersections are Stazione Centrale,

Duomo, Cadorna (Milano Nord) and Loreto (see map, p.71). Buses, trams and the metro run from around 6am to midnight, after which **nightbuses** take over, following the metro routes until 1am. For all **public transport enquiries** (ⓦwww.atm-mi.it) the information offices at the Duomo or Stazione Centrale metro stations are helpful, and have English-speaking staff.

Tickets, valid for 75 minutes, cost €1 and can be used for one metro trip and as many bus and tram rides as you want. They are on sale at tobacconists, bars and at the metro station newsagents; most outlets close at 8pm, so it's best to buy a few tickets in advance if you intend to use public transport after this time, or get a carnet of ten for €9.20. Some stations have automatic ticket machines, although only the newer ones give change. You can also buy a one-day (€3) or two-day **pass** (€5.50) from the Stazione Centrale or Duomo metro stations. Remember to validate your ticket in the orange machines when you enter the metro and board buses and trams, as inspections are common.

By taxi and car

Taxis don't cruise the streets, so don't bother trying to flag one down. Your best bet is to phone one of the following numbers (operators speak English): ⓣ02.6767, 02.4040 or 02.8585, say where you are and the operator will check how long before a cab can get to you (usually under 5min) and then give you a code to quote to the driver. Alternatively, there are a number of taxi ranks around town – including in Piazza Duomo, Largo Cairoli, Piazza San Babila and Stazione Centrale. All cabs are metered and prices are reasonable, although in the daytime Milan's traffic-logged streets can quickly start to push fares up.

Driving your own car in the city is best avoided: the streets are congested and **parking** nigh on impossible in the evenings and on Saturdays. If you do bring a car, you need to know that the **Ecopass** – a recent initiative to cut pollution and congestion in the city centre – is in force (Mon–Fri 7am–7pm) in the area within the Cerchia de Bastione (see map, p.74). The pass must be bought on the day of entry or up to midnight of the day afterwards and the fee is worked out on a sliding scale depending on your engine type. Payments can be made at authorised newsagents and tobacconists, through Intesa-SanPaolo ATMs, or, in English, by freephone (ⓣ800.437.437) or online (ⓦwww.comune.milano.it/ecopass). If your hotel is within the Ecopass area, ask reception if they have any special provision for guests.

For **parking** you're probably best off heading for one of the numerous **central car parks**, costing around €2.50 per hour, less if you stay longer than four hours. Central options include Autosilo Diaz, Piazza Diaz 6, just south of Piazza Duomo; Garage Traversi, on Via Bagutta, close to Piazza San Babila; Parking Majno, on Viale Majno and Garage Venezia, Corso Venezia 11, both near Porta Venezia. Alternatively, for short stays of two hours or less, it's worth getting the useful **SostaMilano** scratch-card, which is valid in parking spaces marked with blue paint: cards are available from bars, newspaper kiosks and bibbed car-park attendants; you have to scratch off the date and time of arrival and display the card in your windscreen. Prices vary from zone to zone but are displayed on the sign. Parking in prohibited zones is not worth it; you'll be fined if caught and have your car impounded by the police.

By bike

Although Milan's streets are congested and the atmosphere can be so smoggy that traffic police have to wear masks, **cycling** is a pleasant way of exploring the city. The terrain is flat, there is little of the aggression that you see on the streets of London or New York, and it is easy to head off down a quiet side-road and get away from it all. What's more, you'll feel like a local: nearly everyone cycles, from pensioners with dogs in baskets or umbrellas (or both) to parents with children on board. Several hotels offer bicycles as part of their facilities, or, alternatively, they can be rented by the hour, day or week from the companies below. The price starts at around €11 per day and you'll need a passport or ID card and often a credit card, as well. If you fancy something a little more powerful, you could rent a **scooter**; you have to be 18 or over and will need to rent a helmet, too.

Bike rental outlets

AWS Via Ponte Seveso 33 ☎02.6707 2145, ⓦ www.awsbici.com. City and mountain bikes.
Biancoblu Via Gallarate 33 ☎02.308.2430, ⓦ www.biancoblu.com. Motorbikes and scooters.

Motorcycle tours and rentals Via del Ricordo 31 ☎02.2720.2556, ⓦ www.mototouring.com. Scooters and motorbikes.
La Stazione next to San Donato Milanese metro station ☎02.5560.3730, ⓦ www.lastazionedelle biciclette.com. Bicycle store, rental and repair shop.

Tours

The central tourist office has information and sells tickets for various English-speaking tours. The Gran Tour di Milano is a coach and walking tour that includes entrance to the castle, La Scala museum and *The Last Supper* (daily 9.30am & 2.30pm; €50; ⓦ www.zaniviaggi.it); advance booking highly recommended. Alternatively, there's a hop-on hop-off **bus tour** (daily every 30min 9.30am–5.45pm; €20 for 24hr, multi-language headphone commentaries included) with two different routes around central Milan in an open-top bus. Canal boat cruises along the Navigli (see p.94) are organized periodically in summer. For tours of San Siro stadium, see p.104.

Accommodation

Much of Milan's **accommodation** is geared towards people travelling on business and, as a result, prices are high, rooms can be characterless and many hotels are booked up all year round. You'd be wise to reserve ahead, especially during the spring (mid-Feb) and autumn (end Sept) fashion weeks and during the Salone del Mobile in April. Hotel prices can more then double during these periods. In August, on the other hand, visitors are so scarce that some hotels shut up shop for the month and those that don't might be prepared to negotiate over prices.

The **hotels** below have been divided into three areas – the Station area, covering places within a twenty-minute walk of the Stazione Centrale, and districts north and south of Piazza Duomo. None of our recommendations are more than a half-hour stroll from the cathedral and they are all relatively well served by public transport. The area around Stazione Centrale, and across to Porta Venezia, is home to a good proportion of the city's cheaper hotels, and although many cater to the area's considerable red-light trade, you should be fine at any of the carefully chosen places below. As you go towards the centre, prices rise, but there are still a number of good deals to be had in some of the side streets off the city's main thoroughfares.

As many of the mid-range hotels are rather dingy you may want to look into the range of **bed and breakfast** accommodation that's opened in recent years. As well as the establishments listed on ⓦ www.bed-and-breakfast.it, the stylish, well-run

CENTRAL MILAN

ACCOMMODATION

Antica Locanda dei Mercanti	G
Antica Locanda Leonardo	I
Ariston	L
Bulgari	D
Cavour	C
Euro	B
Foresteria Monforte	H
London	F
Mercure Milano	A
Palazzo Stelline	J
Rovello	E
Town House Galleria	K

BARS, CAFÉS & GELATERIE

Bar Bianco	5
Bar Jamaica	12
Bar Magenta	19
Bhangrabar	1
Café Design	11
Cafeteria Duomo	21
Caffè Miani	20
Chocolat	16
Cova	15
Diana Garden	7
Grom	17
Just Cavelli Café	9
Lelephante	8
Luini	18
Panino Panini	22

RESTAURANTS

Da Claudio	14
Da Pino	23
La Latteria	4
La Libera	2
Oskar	3
Palazzo Stelline	6
Pizza OK	
Taverna Morigi	24
Torre di Pisa	13
Trattoria Milanese	25
Vecchia Latteria	26
Warsa	10

0 — 200 m

--- Ecopass Border

rooms at *Foresteria Monforte* (☎340.237.0272, ⓦwww.foresteriamonforte.it; ❹) come highly recommended, while *La Casa di Leonardo* is a central choice with an attractive sister option boasting a garden in *La Dolce Vita* (both ☎347.377.3044, ⓦwww.ladolcevite.net; ❸); alternatively, if money is no option, head for the design-tastic *3 Rooms* at Corso Como 10 (☎02.626.163, ⓦwww.3rooms -10corsocomo.com; ❾). The English-speaking outfit Rentxpress (☎02.805.3151, ⓦwww.rentxpress.com) also has a selection of **apartments** to rent throughout the city which can make an economical alternative for a small group or family.

Stazione Centrale and around

Arno Via Lazzaretto 17 ☎&ⓕ02.670.5509, ⓦwww.hotelarno.com. The clean, simple rooms at this friendly pensione have recently been refurbished and there's usually room at the sister *Hotel Eva* (ⓦwww.hotelevamilano.com) across the corridor when things get full. Most rooms are en suite, some have a/c and there's free internet access for guests. M Centrale FS or Pta Venezia. ❷

Casa Mia Viale Vittorio Veneto 30 ☎02.657.5249, ⓦwww.casamiahotel.it. A spotless if slightly dowdy hotel with quiet en-suite rooms, just across from the Giardini Pubblici. All rooms have a/c and internet and breakfast included. M Repubblica. ❸

Euro Via Sirtori 24 ☎02.3040.4010, ⓦwww.eurohotelmilano.it. Very good value a/c rooms with parquet floors are offered in this well-located hotel. There's also a small gym, a patio for alfresco breakfast and cheaper – but still pleasant – rooms available without a/c if you're budget is tighter. ❷–❸

Kennedy Viale Tunisia 6, 6th floor ☎02.2940.0934, ⓦwww.kennedyhotel.it. A well-organized, friendly one star with bright, simple rooms, some of which are en suite. Some rooms even have their own balconies overlooking the rooftops. M Repubblica or Pta Venezia. ❷

Mercure Milano Porta Venezia 1 ☎02.2940.0937, ⓦwww.mercure.com. One of the city's several branches of this French hotel chain offering very pleasant, comfortable rooms in a convenient location right on Porta Venezia. M Pta Venezia. ❻

Valley Via Soperga 19 ☎02.669.2777, ⓦwww .hotelvalley.it. Two-minutes' walk north of the Stazione Centrale, this simple little spot is a good choice if you're catching an early train or arriving late at night. Most rooms are en suite and those at the back are pleasant and airy. M Centrale FS. ❷

North of Piazza Duomo

Antica Locanda Leonardo Corso Magenta 78 ☎02.4801.4197, ⓦwww.anticalocandaleonardo .com. Just steps away from *The Last Supper*, this discreet three star offers light airy rooms, some overlooking a pretty internal garden. M Cadorna. ❺

Antica Locanda dei Mercanti Via San Tomaso 6 ☎02.805.4080, ⓦwww.locanda .it. Tucked away near the castle, this quietly elegant *locanda* offers individually decorated rooms; two even have their own roof terraces. Breakfast (not included) is served in the rooms. The *Alle Meraviglie* (ⓦwww.allemeraviglie.it) next door, at no. 8, is run by the same people with similarly bright, tastefully decorated rooms. M Cairoli. ❻

Antica Locanda Solferino Via Castelfidardo 2 ☎02.657.0129, ⓦwww.anticalocandasolferino.it. A nineteenth-century *palazzo* crammed full of antique furnishings in the side streets of Brera. The intimate atmosphere has been popular with actors, singers and other celebs for several generations. M Moscova. ❻

Bulgari Via Fratelli Gabba 7b ☎02.058.051, ⓦwww.bulgarihotels.com. In a hidden corner of Brera, the city's top hotel has all the style you could wish for on a trip to Milan and none of the attitude you might expect. Staff are charming, facilities impeccable, and the bar terrace and garden are an absolute treat. Rooms start at around €350 per night depending on special offers. M Montenapoleone. ❾

Cavour Via Fatebenefratelli 21 ☎02.620.001, ⓦwww.hotelcavour.it. A business-oriented hotel in a great position between the Giardini Pubblici and the Quadrilatero d'Oro. Service is well judged, and the comfortable, soundproofed rooms are good value. M Montenapoleone or Turati. ❻

London Via Rovello 3 ☎02.7202.0166, ⓦwww .hotellondonmilano.com. A plain, family-run hotel in a good central position. There's a choice of singles and doubles with or without en-suite shower; the decor is unexciting but all rooms have a/c. M Cairoli. ❺

Palazzo delle Stelline Corso Magenta 61 ☎02.481.8431, ⓦwww.hotelpalazzostelline.it. Plain but pleasant rooms are set around the attractive courtyard of a renovated seventeenth-century convent opposite Santa Maria delle Grazie. The complex has an appealing garden where Leonardo da Vinci supposedly tended the vines while working on *The Last Supper*. M Cadorna. ❺

Rovello Via Rovello 18a ☎02.8646.4654, ⓦwww .hotel-rovello.it. Close to Castello Sforzesco, the spacious rooms at this well-located hotel are en suite and a/c. You're paying for the location but rates may be negotiable in summer. Breakfast included. **Town House Galleria** Via Silvio Pellico, 8 ☎02.8905.8297, ⓦwww.townhousegalleria.it. Aiming to outdo the world's most exclusive hotels, Milan's newest top-end option offers the last word in elegance plum in the centre of the city with rooms overlooking the Galleria Vittorio Emanuele. The seven-star atmosphere is friendly and discreet and your private butler ensures that nothing is too much trouble. Rooms start at €800. M. Duomo. ❾

South of Piazza Duomo

Ariston Largo Carobbio 2 ☎02.7200.0556, ⓦwww.aristonhotel.com. The best thing about this pleasant modern hotel is its position – within walking distance of the Duomo and the Navigli – and the free bicycles. Rooms are a little cramped, but all are en suite and there's a decent breakfast included in the price. M Duomo, then tram #2, #3 or #14. ❺

Nhow Via Tortona 35 ☎02.489.8861, ⓦwww.nhow-hotels.com. A 246-room hotel to the south of the centre in the up-and-coming Porta Genova district. This spacious design-fest is aimed at those coming to town on business – albeit the fashion business – but the weekend offers can be worthwhile and the colours, textures and contemporary feel are streets away from Milan's usual unimaginative offerings. M. Porta Genova. ❻

Hostels and campsites

Autodromo Parco di Monza, Monza ☎039.387.771, ⓦwww.monzanet.it. A leafy campsite in the old royal hunting ground near the renowned Formula One circuit, north of Milan. Trains run from Stazione Centrale to the attractive satellite town of Monza, from where it's a short bus ride from the station. Open from early May to the end of Sept only.

Città di Milano Via G. Airaghi 61 ☎02.4820.7017, ⓦwww.campingmilano.it. Next to an aquapark and the nearest campsite to the centre, but still a metro trip and a bus ride away. M1 to De Angeli, then bus #72. Open all year.

La Cordata Via Burigozzo 11, off Corso Italia ☎02.5831.4675, ⓦwww.lacordata.it. Clean, basic and in a very good central location, this is Milan's best hostel option by far. Bunks are in single-sex, 6-, 10- or 16-bed dorms from €21 per night with sheets; each dorm has its own shower room. Alternatively, there are spacious twin rooms for €70 per night. There's also a large kitchen, internet access and a communal TV room for residents' use. M Missori, or 4 stops on tram #15 from Piazza Fontana by the Duomo.

Ostello Piero Rotta Viale Salmoiraghi 1, on the corner of Via Martino Bassi ☎02.3926.7095. An HI hostel with an institutional feel, inconveniently out in the insalubrious northwest suburbs near the San Siro stadium. MM1 to QT8, then a couple of hundred metres straight ahead and the hostel is on your right. €19 including breakfast.

The City

Milan's reputation for being ugly and industrial is mainly unfounded. True, the postwar suburbs are not attractive places, but the centre is a collage of architectural styles displaying the city's history in a comfortably wanderable maze

Hidden Milan

Much of the best that Milan has to offer is hidden away from view behind imposing facades and heavy doors. If you get a chance, sneak a look behind a door that's been left ajar and you might catch a glimpse of a wonderful garden or a courtyard full of flowers. The city also harbours some peaceful corners, listed below, where you can relax with a book or a sandwich and recharge your batteries before continuing your sightseeing.

Roof of the Duomo; see p.79
Giardino Botanico; see p.86
Giardini della Villa Reale; see p.89
Ospedale Maggiore; see p.91
Rotonda della Besana; see p.91
Bramante courtyard, Santa Maria delle Grazie; see p.97
Palazzo Stelline; see p.105

of pedestrianized routes and side streets, although Allied bombing raids in the summer of 1943 more or less put paid to what the nineteenth century and Fascist town planners had left of the medieval centre. Bomb damage still riddles the city, as many sites were issued with preservation orders limiting what could be built, while the 1950s and 1960s saw the construction of rather too many unimaginative office blocks. Beside them, however, lie Roman remains, medieval piazzas and Neoclassical palaces, not to mention the city's ancient canals.

We have divided the centre up into areas radiating out from the obvious focal point of Piazza Duomo, which as well as hosting the city's iconic **Duomo** leads on to the elegant **Galleria Vittorio Emanuele** and the Piazza della Scala, home to the world-famous **opera house**. Heading northwest along the shopping street of Via Dante takes you to the imperious **Castello Sforzesco** and the extensive **Parco Sempione** beyond. North, the well-heeled neighbourhoods of **Moscova** and **Brera** are the stomping ground of Milan's most style-conscious citizens. Here you'll find the fine art collection of the **Pinacoteca di Brera** and the so-called **Quadrilatero d'Oro** (golden quadrangle), a concentration of top designer fashion boutiques. Slightly further north is Milan's most pleasant park, the **Giardini Pubblici**. Southeast of the Duomo is one of Milan's studenty areas, home to the city's medieval hospital, the **Ospedale Maggiore**, and the burial ground of the **Rotonda del Besana**. Southwest, the shopping streets of Via Torino take you to the **Ticinese** district, a focal point at *aperitivo* time, and home to a couple of the city's most beautiful ancient churches. Continuing south on to the **Navigli** leads to the bar and restaurant area around the city's remaining canals. West of the cathedral stands the church of **Santa Maria delle Grazie** and the adjacent refectory building, holding Leonardo da Vinci's *The Last Supper*. There's more Leonardo at the **Museo Nazionale della Scienza e della Tecnologia**, while the basilica of Milan's Christian father **Sant'Ambrogio** is a couple of blocks away.

Piazza del Duomo and around

The hub of the city is **Piazza del Duomo**, a large, mostly pedestrianized square that's rarely quiet at any time of day, lorded over by the exaggerated spires of the **Duomo**, Milan's cathedral. Milanese hurry out of the metro station deftly avoiding the buskers and ice-cream vendors; harassed tour guides gather together their flocks; loafers meet for a chat; and elegant women stiletto-click across the square.

The piazza was given its present form in 1860 when medieval buildings were demolished to allow grander, unobstructed views of the cathedral and the **Galleria Vittorio Emanuele II** was constructed to link the piazza with the showy new opera theatre, **La Scala**. Roads fan out from the piazza like bicycle spokes, taking you within a few steps to a number of worthwhile sights, including Bramante's first work in Milan, the ingeniously designed **Santa Maria presso San Satiro**; a handful of important paintings at the **Pinacoteca Ambrosiana**; and the unassuming **Piazza Mercanti**, the centre of the medieval city.

The Duomo

The **Duomo** is the world's largest Gothic cathedral and the third-largest Roman Catholic church in the world – after St Peter's in Rome and Seville's cathedral. It was begun in 1386 under the Viscontis, but not completed until nearly five centuries later, when the finishing touches to the facade were finally added in 1813. Many of the masters of their day worked on its construction: Milanese architects and craftsmen such as the Solari clan, Giovanni Antonio

▲ The roof of the Duomo

Amadeo and Pellegrino Tibaldi, as well as outsiders like Filarete and Martino Bassi. Understandably, it is characterized by a hotchpotch of styles that range from Gothic to Classical. From the **outside** at least, it's an incredible building, notable as much for its strange confection of Baroque and Gothic decoration, including 3500-odd statues, as its sheer size. The marble, chosen by the Viscontis in preference to the usual material of brick, was brought on specially built canals from the quarries of Candoglia, near Lake Maggiore, and continues to be used in renovation today. A seven-year-long facelift was completed in 2008, having repaired the damage done by centuries of smoke and pollution and leaving the cathedral resplendent once more.

The **interior** of the Duomo is striking for its size and atmosphere. The five aisles are separated by 52 towering piers (one for each week of the year), while a green, almost subterranean half-light filters through the stained-glass windows, lending the marble columns a bone-like hue that led the French writer Suarés to compare the interior to "the hollow of a colossal beast".

By the entrance, the narrow brass strip embedded in the pavement with the signs of the zodiac alongside is Europe's largest **sundial**, laid out in 1786. A beam of light still falls on it through a hole in the ceiling, though changes in the Earth's rotation mean that it's no longer accurate. To the left of the entrance you'll find the archeological remains of a fourth-century **Battistero Paleocristiano** (daily 9.30am–5.15pm; €2), where the city's patron saint Sant'Ambrogio baptized St Augustine in 387 AD. Augustine had arrived in Milan three years earlier with his illegitimate son, and after sampling various religions, including paganism, was eventually converted to Christianity by Ambrose, then the city's bishop. The remains of the baptistry were discovered during excavations for a bomb shelter in the 1940s, and more was unearthed later during work for the metro system in the 1950s, also revealing the foundations for the fourth-century basilica of Santa Tecla and some first-century Roman baths.

At the far end of the church, suspended high above the chancel, a large crucifix contains the most important of the Duomo's holy relics – **a nail from Christ's cross**, which was crafted into the bit for the bridle of Emperor Constantine's horse. The cross is lowered once a year, on September 14, the Feast of the Cross, by a device invented by Leonardo da Vinci. Close by, beneath the presbytery, is the **Scurolo di San Carlo** (daily 9am–noon & 2.30–6pm; €1), an octagonal crypt housing the remains of San Carlo Borromeo, the zealous sixteenth-century cardinal who was canonized for his unflinching work among the poor of the city, especially during the Plague of 1630, and whose reforms antagonized the higher echelons of the corrupt Church. He lies here in a glass coffin, clothed, bejewelled, masked and gloved, wearing a gold crown attributed to Cellini.

Borromeo was also responsible for the large altar in the north transept, erected in order to close off a door that was used by locals as a shortcut to the market. Adjacent to Borromeo's resting-place, the **treasury** (€3) features extravagant silver-work, Byzantine ivory carvings and heavily embroidered vestments. Nearby is the Duomo's most surprising exhibit: British artist Mark Wallinger's haunting video installation **Via Dolorosa**, commissioned by the diocese of Milan in a bold attempt to resurrect the role of the Church as a patron of the arts. A large screen shows the last eighteen minutes of Zeffirelli's *Jesus of Nazareth*, with ninety percent of the image blacked out, leaving just a narrow frame visible round the sides.

To the right of the chancel, by the door to the Palazzo Reale, the sixteenth-century statue of St Bartholomew, with his flayed skin thrown like a toga over his shoulder, is one of the church's more gruesome statues, with veins, muscles and bones sculpted with anatomical accuracy, the draped skin retaining the form of knee, foot, toes and toenails.

The roof of the Duomo

Outside again, from the northwest end of the cathedral you can get to the **Duomo roof** (daily: mid-Feb to mid-Nov 9am–5.45pm; rest of year 9am–4.15pm; €5 to walk, €7 for the elevator), one of the highlights of the city. Here you can stroll around the rooftop forest of tracery, pinnacles and statues while enjoying fine views of the city and, on clear days, even the Alps. The lacy marble of the central spire is crowned by a gilded statue of the Madonna, or **Madonnina**. The 4.16-metre-high statue has become a symbol of the city – a kind of guardian – inspiring numerous popular songs and ballads. When the Pirelli Tower, near the station, usurped the cathedral's position as the tallest building in town in the late 1950s, the city's clergy insisted on a replica of the Madonnina being placed on top in order to ensure the well-being of Milan.

Santa Maria presso San Satiro

South of the Piazza del Duomo, tucked away off the busy shopping street of Via Torino is the charming church of **Santa Maria presso San Satiro** (daily 8–11am & 3.30–6.30pm), a study in ingenuity by Milan's foremost Renaissance architect, Bramante, in 1478. It was built up against (*presso*) the ninth-century chapel of San Satiro to celebrate a miracle when the Virgin painted on the outside wall of the chapel was knifed and supposedly started bleeding. The site was originally to have been larger, but there were problems acquiring the land of present-day Via Falcone behind. Undeterred, Bramante continued with a Greek-cross plan and solved the space problem by falsifying the perspective with the wonderful trompe l'oeil apse on the back wall. The fresco in the lunette above the altar records the story of the vandalizing of the Madonna. The octagonal chapel of San Satiro stands to the left of the altar and includes traces of Byzantine frescoes in the niches round the sides. Bramante's plans for the facade were never realized and the current one dates from the nineteenth century.

Pinacoteca Ambrosiana

Five-minutes' walk west, just off Via Torino at Piazza Pio 2, lies the **Pinacoteca Ambrosiana** (Tues–Sun 10am–5.30pm; €8; Ⓦwww.ambrosiana.it), founded by another member of the Borromeo family, Cardinal Federico Borromeo, in the early seventeenth century. In the face of Protestant reforms, the Cardinal was concerned to defend Catholic traditions not only through doctrine and liturgy, but also by educating the faithful about their Catholic origins. To this end he set about collecting ancient manuscripts, assembling one of the largest libraries in Europe (Mon–Fri 9.30am–5pm). The main draw, however, is his art collection, and though it includes many mediocre works of the Lombard school, there are some real gems, such as a rare painting by Leonardo da Vinci, *Portrait of a Musician*, a cartoon by Raphael for the School of Athens fresco in the Vatican, and a Caravaggio, *Basket of Fruit*, considered to be Italy's first-ever still life. Borromeo had met Caravaggio in Rome, where he had also become acquainted with Jan Brueghel, who was teaching at the Accademia di San Luca in 1593. The Cardinal was obviously taken with Flemish painting, building up a collection of works by Brueghel the Elder and Paul Brill, the highlights of which are the fantastical landscapes of *Allegory of Water* and *Allegory of Fire* by Jan Brueghel. The huge museum has been continually added to since the Cardinal's death and now also contains a collection of objects and artefacts to complement the art. The prize for the quirkiest exhibit is shared between a pair of white gloves that Napoleon reputedly wore when he met his Waterloo, and a lock of Lucrezia Borgia's hair – displayed for safe-keeping in a glass phial ever since Byron (having decided that her hair was the most beautiful he had ever seen) extracted a strand as a keepsake from the library downstairs, where it used to be kept unprotected.

Piazza dei Mercanti

Just off Piazza del Duomo to the northwest stands **Piazza dei Mercanti**, once the commercial centre of medieval Milan and now an almost forgotten corner of the city. Surrounded by medieval palaces, once the seats of guilds, the square was the city's financial hub until the turn of the twentieth century, when the Borsa or Stock Exchange – then housed in the sixteenth-century **Palazzo dei Giureconsulti** on Via Mercanti – was moved north to a new building in Piazza degli Affari. The square is dominated by the **Palazzo della Ragione**, built in the early thirteenth century to a common European model: on the first floor was the **Broletto** – or town hall – which was used for council meetings and tribunals, while markets were held under the porticoes below. The uppermost storey is an eighteenth-century addition built to house the city's notary archive. The stone relief on the façade above the arcade shows the forlorn-looking figure on a horse of Oldrado di Tressano, the mayor who commissioned the building in 1228. These days the Broletto is occasionally used for temporary exhibitions, while the arcades below often shelter small markets or fair-trade stalls. Opposite, the **Loggia degli Orsi**, built in 1316, was where council proclamations were made and sentences announced. The building is striped in black and white marble and decorated with the coats of arms of the various districts of Milan – just about visible beneath the grime left by Milanese smog.

Galleria Vittorio Emanuele II

Almost as famous a Milanese sight as the Duomo is the gaudily opulent **Galleria Vittorio Emanuele II**, to the north of the cathedral. This nineteenth-century equivalent of a shopping mall was such a success that the model was copied in Rome, Turin and Naples. Intended as a covered walkway between the Piazza del Duomo and Piazza della Scala, the cruciform glass-domed arcade was designed in 1865 by Giuseppe Mengoni, who died when he fell from the roof a few days before the inaugural ceremony, also leaving his remodelling of the Piazza del Duomo incomplete. The circular mosaic beneath the glass cupola is composed of the symbols that made up the cities of the newly unified Italy: Romulus and Remus for Rome, a fleur-de-lys for Florence, the white shield with a red cross for Milan and a bull for Turin – it's considered good luck to spin round three times on the bull's testicles, hence the indentation in the floor.

Nicknamed the "salotto" – or drawing room – of Milan, the Galleria was once the focal point for parading Milanese on their *passeggiata*. These days, visitors rather than locals are more likely to swallow the extortionate prices at the gallery's cafés, which include the historic *Zucca*, with its glorious 1920s tiled interior at one end, and the newer, stylish *Gucci Café* – the label's first foray into catering – at the other. Shops, too, are aimed at visitors to the city, with top designer labels jostling next to pricey souvenir outlets. Somehow, however, the Galleria still manages to retain its original dignity, helped along by quietly elegant boutiques selling handmade leather gloves or carefully turned hats, and the handsome ninety-year-old Prada store in the centre.

Teatro alla Scala

The main branch of Galleria Vittorio Emanuele leads through to Piazza della Scala fronted by the rather plain Neoclassical façade of the world-famous **Teatro alla Scala** opera house, popularly known as La Scala (Ⓦ www.teatroallascala.org). The theatre was commissioned by Empress Maria Theresia of Austria from the architect Piermarini and built on the site of the burnt-down church of Maria della Scala. It opened in 1778 with the opera *Europa Riconsciuta* by Antonio Salieri – a well-known name in his own right then, though more famous now (thanks to Peter Schaffer's play and movie *Amadeus*) for his rivalry with Mozart than for his music. Many of the leading names in Italian opera had their major works premiered here, including Bellini, Donizetti and Rossini, but it is Giuseppe Verdi who is most closely associated with the opera house and whose fame was consolidated in 1842 with the first performance of *Nabucco* and its perfectly timed patriotic sentiments.

As the heyday of Italian *opera seria* petered out with Puccini's *Turandot*, the early years of the twentieth century saw foreign composers welcomed to

La Scala for the first time. The post-World War II period in particular saw a breathtaking roll call of top composers and musical performers: Schoenberg, Lucio Berio, Rudolf Nureyev and Maria Callas all had close relationships with the theatre. Perhaps the most influential conductor of all time, Toscanini, devoted more than fifty years to the theatre and led the orchestra when the opera house reopened in 1946 after being bombed out. These days, however, La Scala is a bit at sea: no quality Italian composers have emerged for over eighty years, the theatre is plagued by internal political problems and the repertoire has become a touch predictable, presenting too many museum pieces rather than the groundbreaking productions for which it was famous.

In 2004, after three years of refurbishment, La Scala reopened for the third time, once again with Salieri's opera, which had lain unperformed since 1778. The latest improvements include the extension of the backstage area, with the addition of a new flytower and administration areas by the Swiss architect Mario Botta and a facelift for the inside. The acoustics have been reworked, while the opulent gilt-and-velvet auditorium, with its immense central chandelier and gilded tiers of boxes, remains unaltered.

La Scala is still, to a great extent, the social and cultural centre of Milan's elite, and although protests in the 1960s led to a more open official policy on the arts in Milan, unusually for opera-going in Italy it remains as exclusive a venue as it ever was. Every year on the opening night – 7 December, the festival of Milan's patron saint, Sant'Ambrogio – when fur coats and dinner jackets are out in force, there are demonstrations from political and social groups, ranging from animal rights' campaigners to local factory workers complaining about redundancies. **Tickets** (see p.110) can be hard to come by, but there are numerous avenues to try.

Tucked in next door to La Scala is the theatre's small **museum** (daily 9am–12.30pm & 1.30–5pm; €5), featuring costumes, sets, composers' death masks, plaster casts of conductors' hands and a rugged statue of Puccini in a capacious overcoat. A visit to the auditorium is included in the ticket, providing there is no rehearsal taking place; times when the auditorium is empty are listed daily outside the entrance to the museum. Down in the south of the city, near Porta Genova, the **costume and scenery workshop** offers guided visits (see p.96).

As part of the opera house refurbishment, a formal – and overpriced – **restaurant** has been opened next to the museum; you'd do better to head across the side road to the Trussardi building just opposite and snack at the stylish ground-floor café or treat yourself at the superior restaurant upstairs.

The Castello Sforzesco and around

At the northwestern end of the pedestrianized Via Dante, which leads from Piazza del Duomo, **Castello Sforzesco** rises imperiously from the traffic roundabout of Foro Buonaparte, a road laid out by Napoleon in self-tribute. He had a vision of a grand new centre for an Italian capital, built along Roman lines, but he only got as far as constructing an arena, a triumphal arch and these two semicircular roads before he lost Milan to the Austrians a few years later. The arena and triumphal arch still stand half-forgotten behind the castle on the edges of the **Parco Sempione**, the city centre's largest area of greenery.

The Castello Sforzesco

The red-brick **Castello Sforzesco** (Ⓦ www.milanocastello.it), with its crenel-lated towers and fortified walls, is one of Milan's most striking landmarks. Begun by the Viscontis in 1368, it was destroyed by rebellious mobs in 1447 and rebuilt by the Viscontis' successors, the Sforzas. Under Lodovico Sforza the court became one of the most powerful, luxurious and cultured of the Renaissance, renowned for its ostentatious wealth and court artists, such as Leonardo and Bramante. Lodovico's days of glory came to an end when Milan was invaded by the French in 1499, and from then until the end of the nineteenth century the castle was used as a barracks by successive occupying armies. Just over a century ago it was converted into a series of museums to house municipal collections, the highlight of which is Michelangelo's last unfinished work, the *Rondanini Pietà*. Note that ongoing restoration means that parts of the complex may be closed during your visit.

The buildings are grouped around three courtyards: through the Filarete Tower (rebuilt in 1905, having been destroyed in the sixteenth century by an explosion of gunpowder) you enter the larger of the three, the dusty-looking parade ground, with a good bookshop to your left. It is not until you're through the gateway opposite that you begin to get the sense of a Renaissance castle: this is the Corte Ducale, which formed the centre of the residential quarters and is now the home of the castle's museums. The Rocchetta, to your left, was the most secure part of the fortress and is used for temporary exhibitions. The gateway ahead leads to the Parco Sempione, once the castle's garden and hunting grounds and now the city's largest park.

The museums

The ticket office (Tues–Sun 9am–5.30pm; combined ticket €3) is on your right as you enter the Corte Ducale and gives access to the **Museo d'Arte Antica** (Museum of Ancient Art), a succession of rooms containing an extensive collection of artefacts, including mosaics, bas-reliefs and column fragments, saved from the city's churches and archeological excavations. More interesting than these, though, are the castle rooms themselves, especially the **Sala delle Asse**, designed by Leonardo da Vinci; his black-and-white preparatory sketches were discovered in the 1950s during the elegant reorganization of the museums by the architecture studio BBPR (see p.89) and can be seen on the walls. After some rather dull armoury you reach the museum's star exhibit: Michelangelo's **Rondanini Pietà**, which the artist worked on for the last nine years of his life. It's an unfinished but oddly powerful work; much of the marble is unpolished and a third arm, indicating a change of position for Christ's body, hangs limply from a block of stone to his right.

Upstairs, the **Museo delle Arti Decorative** (Museum of Decorative Arts) holds exhibits of furniture and decorative arts through the ages, including fascinating early works by the great Milanese designer, Gio Ponti, which show his evolution from the elegant lines of the Domus Nova dining suite in the 1920s to the modern design classic of the Superleggera chair.

Beginning in the Torre Falconiere (the falconry tower) next door, is the castle's **art collection** containing numerous paintings by Lombard artists, such as Foppa and Bramantino, as well as Venetian works, including some Canalettos. The best are all grouped together in Room XIII and include Antonello da Messina's *Saint Benedict*, originally part of a five-piece polyptych, of which the central painting, a *Madonna and Child*, and the left-hand panel, *Saint John the Baptist*, are in the Uffizi Gallery in Florence. The Duke of Milan, Galeazza Maria Sforza, had tried to engage Antonello as his court portrait painter, but he preferred to stay and complete his masterpiece in the church of San Cassiano in Venice. In his *Saint Benedict* the artist shows his talent as a portraitist, bestowing this formal, stylized figure with a truly human face. Nearby are Giovanni Bellini's touching *Madonna and Child* and Mantegna's decorative *Madonna in Glory and Saints*, both minor works by the artists on subjects they returned to on several occasions.

Across the courtyard, in the castle cellars are two small, rather eclectic collections. The **Egyptian collection** has impressive displays of mummies, sarcophagi and papyrus fragments from *The Book of the Dead*, while the deftly lit **prehistoric collection** consists of an assortment of finds from the Iron Age burial grounds of the Golasecca civilization, south of Lake Maggiore.

The Parco Sempione

The **Parco Sempione** was laid out in the castle's old hunting grounds and orchards. It can make a refreshing break from the city's traffic-choked roads, but it does have its sleazy side and you might feel more comfortable visiting when the locals do – at the weekend or early summer evenings. That said, there are several sights within the park itself, the most interesting of which is the Palazzo dell'Arte or **Triennale** (Tues–Sun 10.30am–8.30pm; Ⓦ www.triennale .it), on the western reaches, at Viale Emilio Alemagna 6. Designed by Giovanni Muzio in 1931, the building played a pivotal role in the development of Milan's importance in the world of design, providing a permanent home to the tri-annual design exhibition held here since the 1930s. The majestic lines of the building and its light airy interior are reason enough for a visit, but the *palazzo* also holds the **Triennale Design Museum** (same opening hr) and other good-quality temporary exhibitions of design, architecture and contemporary art. There's a great café-bar, *Design* (see p.105), which overflows downstairs into the park in the summer. The Triennale is also the place to reserve entrance to one of the city's little-visited gems, **Studio Museo Achille Castiglioni** (Tues–Sat 10am–1pm; free guided tours 10am, 11am & noon; included in the price of the Triennale Design Museum), just outside the park at Piazza Castello 27. The utterly beguiling studio of one of Milan's best-known industrial designers is stuffed with found objects, plans and sketches as well as prototypes of some of his most famous works; the guided tours are often given by his wife or daughter.

Just behind the Palazzo dell'Arte stands the **Torre Branca** (Wed 10.30am–12.30pm & 4–6.30pm, Sat 10.30am–1pm, 3–6.30pm & 8.30pm–midnight, Sun 10.30am–2pm & 2.30–7pm; €3, free Wed for senior citizens), designed by Gio Ponti on the occasion of the fifth Triennale in 1933. An elevator takes you up the outside to the top of the tower, 108m high and from where, on a clear day, there are vertiginous views across Milan to the Alps to the north and the Apennines to the south. The base of the tower is the venue for one of Milan's signature bars, *Just Cavelli Café* (see p.109), which struts into full gear on summer evenings.

The northern end of the park is topped by what was intended by Napoleon and his urban planners to be a triumphal arch to mark the road from Milan to Paris. It was finally finished by the Austrians thirty years later in 1838, and renamed the **Arco della Pace**, the Arch of Peace, once the chariot had been turned round to face Milan rather than Paris. A little round to the east is another monument to Napoleon's imperial aspirations in the **Arena Civica**, a Colosseum-inspired area where mock chariot races and naval battles were held. These days it's used for sports events and the odd summer pop concert. Next door, the recently refurbished **Aquario Civico** (Tues–Sun 9am–1pm & 2–5.30pm; free; Ⓦ www.verdeacqua.eu), is a pretty Liberty building with a small collection of tanks that will keep children entertained for a spell.

Brera, Moscova, the Quadrilatero d'Oro and the Giardini Pubblici

Elegant Via Manzoni sets the tone for the neighbourhoods north of the Piazza Duomo. Patrician *palazzi* line the Roman thoroughfare north from La Scala to **Porta Nuova**, one of the medieval entrances to the city. Named after the nineteenth-century author who lived and died in a house just off the street, Via Manzoni forms one side of the **Quadrilatero d'Oro**, the centre of Milan's fashion district. Nestled in among the *haute couture* houses are two eclectic museums, the **Museo Poldi Pezzoli** and the **Museo Bagatti Valsecchi**, legacies of the nineteenth-century mania for collecting.

To the northeast, the medieval streets of the **Brera** district lead to the renowned **Pinacoteca Brera**, while the neighbouring district, **Moscova**, is full of boutiques, bars and restaurants, popular with an image-conscious, stylish crowd. Further north, at the top of Piazza Cavour, on the northern side of Porta Nuova, lie the **Giardini Pubblici**, Milan's most attractive park and home to the city's contemporary art gallery.

Via Manzoni and the Museo Poldi Pezzoli

Many of the aristocratic houses of **Via Manzoni** have become banks, museums and hotels; one of them, the opulent *Grand Hotel et de Milan*, was where the composer Giuseppe Verdi lived for the last twenty years of his life and died. Another of the *palazzi* worth seeking out is at no. 12, where the **Museo Poldi Pezzoli** (Tues–Sun 10am–6pm; €8; ⓦ www.museopoldipezzoli.it) houses an extensive collection of artefacts assembled in the nineteenth century by the collector Gian Giacomo Poldi Pezzoli. Much of the house was destroyed by Allied bombs and only Gian Giacomo's study was left unscathed; the reconstruction is somewhat soulless in places, but the early twentieth-century photographs of the original in each room help evoke the atmosphere of the past. There's a lot to take in, with room upon room of timepieces, archeological remains, Venetian glassware and jewellery, but dipping in where you fancy, you can become entranced by individual pieces – exquisite Lombard embroidery, for example, or a seventeenth-century carved ivory chest. The Salone Dorato upstairs contains a number of striking paintings, including a portrait of a portly *San Nicola da Tolentino* by Piero della Francesca, part of an altarpiece on which he worked intermittently for fifteen years. St Nicholas looks across at two works by Botticelli, one a gentle *Madonna del Libro*, the other a mesmerizing *Deposition*, painted towards the end of his life in response to the monk Savonarola's crusade against his earlier, more humanistic canvases. Also in the room is the museum's best-known painting, *Portrait of a Young Woman* by Pollaiuolo, whose anatomical studies are evidenced in the subtle suggestion of bone structure beneath the skin of this ideal Renaissance woman.

The Quadrilatero d'Oro and the Museo Bagatti Valsecchi

Bordered by Via Manzoni to the west and **Via Montenapoleone**, Via Sant'Andrea and **Via della Spiga** on the other sides, the so-called **Quadrilatero d'Oro** (Golden Quadrangle) is home to the shops of all the big international and Italian fashion names, along with design studios and contemporary art galleries. This is Milan in its element and the area is well worth a wander if only to see the city's better-heeled residents in their favourite habitat.

In a house linking Via Santo Spirito with Via Gesù 5, just off Via Montenapoleone, is the **Museo Bagatti Valsecchi** (Tues–Sun 1–5.45pm; €8;

Ⓦ www.museobagattivalsecchi.org), an absorbing private museum affording an intriguing insight into the tastes of the Bagatti Valsecchi brothers, Giuseppe and Fausto. Taking the nineteenth-century fashion for collecting to an extreme, they built a Renaissance-style home, inspired by the Palazzo Ducale in Mantova, in which to house their Renaissance collections. Nineteenth-century reproductions were artfully executed to integrate harmoniously with the original Renaissance tapestries, furniture and other works of art that decorated the premises.

The brothers lived in separate apartments sharing the drawing room, dining room and a gallery of weapons and armour. All the rooms are richly decorated with carved fireplaces, painted ceilings and heavy wall-hangings and paintings. The fireplace in the drawing room perfectly illustrates the brothers' eclectic approach to decoration: the main surround is sixteenth-century Venetian, the frescoes in the middle are from Cremona, while the whole ensemble is topped off with the Bagatti Valsecchi coat-of-arms. Modern conveniences were incorporated into the house but not allowed to ruin the harmony, so the shower in the bathroom is disguised in a niche, and the piano, which had not yet been invented in the sixteenth century, is discreetly incorporated within a cabinet. Among the miscellany of paintings, ceramics, armoury, ironwork and musical instruments are touching domestic details like the nursery furniture for Giuseppe's children.

Brera

Due north of Via Manzoni, **Via Brera** runs through the centre of the city's over-hyped arty quarter. This is home to Milan's most famous art gallery, the **Pinacoteca di Brera**, part of a cultural complex founded in the eighteenth century, under the patronage of Empress Maria Theresia of Austria, and including a Fine Arts Academy, an observatory and a botanical garden. There was a time when this area was a hotbed of artistic talent: in the 1960s, *Bar Jamaica*, on Via Brera, was the haunt of Piero Manzoni and other members of the Milan branch of the *Arte Povera* movement, but these days you're more likely to meet the expat Americans or wealthy Milanese teenagers who frequent the bars and pavement cafés in this part of town. The students from the Accademia di Belle Arti help to provide a touch of colour to the neighbourhood in the daytime, but bohemianism is not a style that the Milanese take to with ease. In the evening the pedestrian streets are lined with fortune-tellers, portrait painters and more fake Gucci and D&G goods than you could shake a handbag at.

Hidden behind the Pinacoteca, the delightful **Giardino Botanico** (entrance through the ground floor of the Accademia di Belle Arti or from Via Chiari Oscuri to the side; free; Mon–Sat 9am–12.30pm) has been opened to the public in recent years and provides a wonderful bolt-hole if you want a break from pounding the cobbled pavements. No more than about an acre in size, the gardens were founded in 1774 by the Empress Maria Theresia of Austria to teach botany to the students of the nearby science colleges and are still used today by the college students. One part of the gardens is given over to flower beds and floral experiments, while the other consists of an attractive patch of grass shaded by trees, including a giant *Ginkgo biloba*, apparently the largest in the world and dating back to the opening of the gardens.

Pinacoteca di Brera

The Brera district gives its name to Milan's prestigious art gallery, the **Pinacoteca di Brera** at Via Brera 28 (Tues–Sun 8.30am–7.15pm; €5; Ⓦ www.brera .beniculturali.it), the most important collection of North Italian art anywhere.

Originally consisting of plaster casts and drawings put together as a study aid for students from the Fine Arts academy, the collection was added to by works looted from the churches and aristocratic collections of French-occupied Italy when Napoleon decided to make it a public museum. Opened in 1809, the **collection** has gradually grown over the years, to the extent that plans are now being discussed to extend the gallery to the nearby Palazzo Citterio.

It's a fine gallery – well-organized, in chronological order, with good explanatory notes – but it's also large, and your visit will probably be more enjoyable if you're selective. There's a good audioguide available (€3.50), although it does rather gallop through the highlights.

Exiting the three rooms of early medieval works brings you face to face with the stunningly powerful *The Dead Christ* (Room VI), a painting by Andrea Mantegna, the court artist in fifteenth-century Mantova responsible for the Camera degli Sposi (see p.333). It's an ingenious composition – Christ, lying on a wooden slab being prepared for burial, viewed from the wrinkled and pierced soles of his feet upwards. We are drawn into the scene not just by the foreshortening technique but by Christ's serene expression and the realism in the colouring and details of his wounds. One of Mantegna's sons had died around the time he was working on this painting and it seems that the desolation in the women's faces and the powerful sense of bereavement emanating from the work were autobiographical. In the same room, the *Pietà* by Mantegna's brother-in-law, Giovanni Gentile, is another beautifully balanced work of grief and pain that has been deemed "one of the most moving paintings in the history of art".

Next door in Room VIII, the impressive *St Mark Preaching in St Euphemia Square* introduces an exotic note, the square bustling with turbaned men, veiled women, camels and even a giraffe. Gentile Bellini, who had lived and worked in Constantinople for several years, died before the painting was complete, so it was finished off by his brother Giovanni for the Scuola Grande di San Marco in Venice. Another theatrical work hanging nearby is Paolo Veronese's depiction of *Supper in the House of Simon* (Room IX); it got him into trouble with the Inquisition, who considered the introduction of frolicking animals and unruly kids unsuitable subject matter for a religious painting. Tintoretto's *Pietà* (Room IX) was more starkly in tune with requirements of the time, a scene of intense concentration and grief over Christ's body, painted in the 1560s. Nearby in the same room is another Tintoretto, painted around the same time and one of the highlights of Venetian Renaissance painting: *The Finding of the Body of Saint Mark in Alexandria* shows the moment when the frantic search for the saint's body is interrupted by the appearance of Saint Mark himself, on the left of the picture, to identify his own corpse. The dramatic use of perspective – with the tombs disappearing into the background – coupled with mystical use of light and shadow create a truly operatic ensemble.

Works by Lombard masters showing the transition from medieval to Renaissance art take you through to a number of rooms featuring artists from Le Marche and Emilia Romagna. You might want to skip through these, saving yourself for Room XXIV, the pride of the Brera collection, containing three paintings ranked among the highest expression of Renaissance culture in art. Piero della Francesca's haunting *Madonna and Child with Angels, SS and Federigo da Montefeltro* (Room XXIV) is the most arresting, with its stylized composition and geometric harmony. Kneeling on the right is the commissioner of the painting, the powerful Duke of Urbino in a full suit of armour reflecting the light from an open window just out of the picture. The painting is full of symbolism, such as the ostrich egg suspended above the Virgin, an image of fertility and also the Montefeltro family emblem. On the wall opposite,

Christ at the Column is the only known painting by the architect Bramante, painted for the Chiaravalle monastery to the south of the city. The resemblance between the architectural detail of the painting and the very similar motifs used by the architect in Santa Maria presso San Satiro (see p.80) is striking. Take a look, too, at Raphael's altarpiece, the *Marriage of the Virgin* (Room XXIV; under restoration at the time of writing), whose lucid, languid Renaissance mood stands in sharp contrast to the grim realism of Caravaggio's deeply human *Supper at Emmaus* (Room XXIX), set in a dark tavern. Less well known but equally naturalistic are the paintings of Lombardy's brilliant eighteenth-century realist, Ceruti – known as Il Pitochetto (The Little Beggar) for his unfashionable sympathy with the poor, who stare out with reproachful dignity from his canvases (Room XXXVI). As his main champion, Roberto Longhi, said, his figures are "dangerously larger than life", not easily transformed into "gay drawing room ornaments", a description that could easily apply to the Canalettos and Crespis on the surrounding walls. Francesco Hayez's Romantic-era *The Kiss* (Room XXXVII) is one of the most reproduced of the gallery's paintings, but the artist's fine portrait of the writer Alessandro Manzoni, in the same room, is far less saccharine. The collection ends with the unfinished *Fuimaria* (Room XXXVII) by Giuseppe Pelizza da Volpedo, a composition showing the emerging people-power of the time and the artist's socialist ideals – themes that he developed for *the Fourth Estate* in the Museo dell'Ottocento (see below), adopted as an emblem of the power of the populace.

There is also a small collection of modern work from the Jesi donation on display in Room X, which is particularly strong on the Futurists but includes paintings by Morandi, Modigliani, De Chirico and Carrà, as well as abstract sculpture by Marino Marini and Medardo Rosso.

Moscova

The style bars and traditional trattorias continue north of Brera through the neighbourhood of **Moscova**, renowned as the haunt of journalists – the offices of the *Corriere della Sera* are located here. A good area for shopping and window browsing, the local delicatessens and small boutiques of Corso Garibaldi, Via Solferino and Via San Marco lead up to the bastion of Piazza XXV Aprile which marks the northern extent of the Spanish walls and the beginning of **Corso Como**, a trendy street full of bars, clubs and stylish shops that, in turn, gives onto the train and bus station of Porto Garibaldi.

Set back from Corso Garibaldi, austere **San Simpliciano** is one of the four churches founded on the outskirts of Milan by Sant'Ambrogio in the fourth century. Much restored and with a nineteenth-century facade, it contains the remains of Sant'Ambrogio's successor San Simpliciano and those of three martyrs who were instrumental in the city's victory over Barbarossa at the Battle of Legnone in 1176. The legendary moment when the spirits of the martyrs in the form of three white doves flew from the church to bless the Carroccio (the battle cart and symbol of Milan) is recalled in the stained-glass windows of the facade.

The Giardini Pubblici and its art galleries

The **Giardini Pubblici**, designed by Piermarini shortly after he completed La Scala, stretch from Piazza Cavour over to Porta Venezia. Re-landscaped in the nineteenth century to give it a more rustic look, the park, with its shady avenues and small lake, is ideal for a break from the busy streets.

Across the road from the park, housed in Napoleon's former town residence, the **Villa Belgiojoso Bonaparte** or Villa Reale, is the rather ordinary **Museo dell'Ottocento** at Via Palestro 16 (Tues–Sun 9am–1pm & 2–5.30pm; free;

@www.villabelgiojosobonaparte.it). The mosaic-lined ballroom is worth a glance but otherwise you might want to skip through the unexciting collection of nineteenth-century Italian art and sculpture to the striking canvas of the *Fourth Estate* by Giuseppe Pelizza da Volpedo.

In the grounds, the **Padiglione d'Arte Contemporanea** or PAC (Tues–Sun 9.30am–7.30pm, Thurs closes 10.30pm; €6; @www.comune.milano.it/pac) is a venue for good, temporary exhibitions of contemporary art. The elegant, luminous spaces of the pavilion were designed by the architect Ignazio Gardella and opened in 1979 only to be destroyed in July 1993 by a Mafia bomb that killed five people; the bomb was actually intended for journalists at the Palazzo dei Giornali in nearby Piazza Cavour. The pavilion was reconstructed, again by Gardella, and reopened in 1996.

Behind the art galleries, the **Giardini della Villa Reale** offer an urban oasis reserved for those with children under 13. With a small area of swings, lawns, shady trees and a little pond with ducks and giant carp, it makes a perfect bolt-hole.

Southeast from Piazza Duomo

The area southeast from Piazza Duomo is characterized by a jumble of architectural styles typical of Milan's city centre. Medieval streets give way to 1930s and post-World War II constructions, the most striking example of which is the 1950s **Torre Velasca**, which guards the start of the Roman road from Milan to Rome. The streets are populated by a comfortable mix of students from the Arts faculties of Milan's university, lawyers from the Palazzo di Giustizia and medical professionals from the city's university hospital. The area's biggest draw is the medieval hospital, the **Ospedale Maggiore**, which was rebuilt after being destroyed by World War II bombs, as was **San Nazaro Maggiore**, one of Milan's original Christian basilicas. Nearby, the cemetery chapel of the **Rotonda della Besana** has taken to its secular role with dignity, providing an attractive backdrop for interesting temporary exhibitions.

Torre Velasca

Directly south of the Duomo, just off Corso Porta Romana, Piazza Velasca holds one of the city's most iconic twentieth-century buildings, the **Torre Velasca**. At 105m high, the Brutalist structure towers above the city, inspiring loathing and admiration in equal measure. It was built between 1956 and 1958 by the studio BBPR – the "R" of which was Ernesto Rogers, a close relative of the British architect Richard Rogers, who used to work in the studio in university holidays. The top-heavy structure was an ingenious way of wangling more real estate out of a narrow plot and strict planning rules, but it was also an elegant reference to the medieval towers that characterize the cityscape of so many Italian towns. Just as these domestic fortresses housed businesses, warehouses and shops on the lower floors and homes on the upper floors, so Torre Velasca is a mixed-use block, with offices in the narrower part of the tower and residential accommodation in the overhanging section above.

San Nazaro Maggiore

East of the Torre Velasca lies Corso di Porta Romana, the beginning of the ancient Roman road to Rome. Follow this for a few blocks and you come to the church of **San Nazaro Maggiore**. One of the four churches founded in the fourth century by Sant'Ambrogio outside the city walls, it was rebuilt several times after being destroyed by fires and World War II bombs. Its most notable feature is the octagonal chapel designed by Bramantino for the treacherous

▲ Torre Velasca

condottiere Giangiacomo Trivulzio, who led the French attack on Milan to spite his rival Lodovico Sforza and was rewarded by being made the city's French governor. Not one to be relegated to the sidelines, Giangiacomo had his *cappella* built as a vestibule rather than as the more usual side-chapel, so that everyone had to pass through it on their way into the church. His tomb is contained in a niche of the chapel, along with other family members, and the epitaph, written by Giangiacomo himself, reads: "He who never rested now rests: silence."

Ospedale Maggiore (Ca' Grande)

Behind San Nazaro stands the **Ospedale Maggiore**, built by Francesco Sforza in the mid-fifteenth century. Used as a hospital until 1939, today the building houses the offices of the university hospital and several faculties. The Ospedale Maggiore united all Milan's smaller hospitals and charitable institutions on one site, hence the name Ca' Grande, or Big House. Opened at the same time as the Lazaretto, the plague hospital established outside the walls near the current Porta Venezia, the huge Ospedale was an attempt to control the outbreaks of the deadly disease and improve the city's health services. In a thoroughly modern design by the Florentine architect Filarete, a series of courtyards – eight in all – provided separate wings for men and women.

Over the years, local architects adapted and altered Filarete's original design, creating a mix of styles. The right side of the wide facade shows the original fifteenth-century brickwork with Lombard terracotta decorations, while to the left, the style is Neoclassical. Inside, in the main courtyard, Filarete's Renaissance arcade survives, with the additions of a Baroque loggia and stone busts. All but razed to the ground by Allied bombs in World War II, the court-yards to the right were reconstructed using original plans and masonry, and now make a pleasant spot to rest.

Rotonda della Besana

Behind the Ospedale Maggiore, the **Giardino delle Guastalla**, laid out in 1555, leads through to Milan's main synagogue. Four blocks east, past the monolithic Palazzo di Giustizia law courts and the city's main hospital, stands the peaceful **Rotonda della Besana**, the Ospedale Maggiore's cemetery, opened in 1695 and designed by Francesco Raffagno. At the centre, the Greek-cross chapel of San Michele ai Nuovi Sepolcri, built in 1713, was turned into the hospital laundry in the early nineteenth century. Now deconsecrated, the tranquil space is used for temporary exhibitions, while the surrounding grass and cool arcaded porticoes make a perfect spot for a picnic.

Southwest of the centre: the Ticinese and Navigli

Past the chain stores of Via Torino, leading southwest away from the Duomo, the city takes on a different, slightly more alternative air. The main thoroughfare of the **Ticinese** district, the Corso Porta Ticinese, has become a focus for young fashion and is lined with small boutiques and bars. The area really comes into its own at *aperitivo* time, especially during summer when people spill onto the pedestrian streets from the numerous bars and cafés. The neighbourhood also boasts two of Milan's most important churches, **San Lorenzo alle Colonne** and **Sant'Eustorgio**.

Flanking two of the city's remaining **canals** just to the south, the streets of the **Navigli** quarter feel a long way from the city centre, the ex-industrial spaces and workers' accommodation much sought after these days by the city's would-be bohemians. It's a strange area, much lauded by tourist brochures, but scruffy and often disappointing in the harsh light of day. The best time to visit is in the evening when the quarter's many restaurants and bars come alive, although the monthly Sunday **antiques market** also brings a lively focus to the waterways.

The Ticinese district

The **Ticinese district** has always played an important role in the history of the city. It was here just outside the walls that in Roman times a giant amphitheatre was built, as well as some of the first paleo-Christian places of worship. In the Middle Ages this was one of the main gateways into the city from the important town of Pavia and the monastic complexes scattered across the Po plain to the south. Later, when the canals were at the height of their trading success, goods were brought through the Porta Ticinese to the city centre. These days most people come here for the bars or shops, while the churches of **San Lorenzo alle Colonne** and **Sant'Eustorgio** are among the most rewarding sights in the city.

San Lorenzo alle Colonne and around

Towards the northern end of Corso Ticinese stands **San Lorenzo alle Colonne**, considered by Leonardo da Vinci to be the most beautiful church in Milan. It is indeed a graceful building with a quiet dignity, somewhat at odds with the skateboarding and partying that goes on in the piazza outside. One of the four churches founded by Sant'Ambrogio in the city in the fourth century, it was the largest centrally planned church in the western Roman Empire, built with masonry salvaged from various Roman buildings, most notably the amphitheatre. The sixteen Corinthian columns outside – **the Colonne di San Lorenzo** – were probably scavenged from a bath or temple complex and placed here as a portico to the church in the fourth century. The current building is a sixteenth-century renovation of an eleventh-century church, which in turn replaced the original after several fires. Inside, the octagonal plan – a sixteenth-century remodelling of the original square – gives the church an intimate feel, while the light streaming down from the four large windows in the dome makes a refreshing change from the penumbra of the city's sombre medieval places of worship.

To the right of the altar, the **Cappella di San Aquilino** (daily 7.30am–6pm; €2, combined ticket with Cappella Portinari & Museo Diocesano €9.50) was probably built as an imperial mausoleum in the fourth century. The lunettes in the Roman octagonal room hold beautiful fourth-century mosaics, which would originally have covered all the walls, while beneath the relics of San Aquilino steps lead down to what is left of the original foundations, a jigsaw of fragments of Roman architecture.

Behind San Lorenzo, shady **Piazza della Vetra** was a site for public executions until the mid-nineteenth century and the park here makes a good spot for a breather. It also allows fabulous views of the back of San Lorenzo, showing the mishmash of building styles that make up the basilica.

Sant'Eustorgio

Heading south through the Parco della Vetra, or straight down Corso Ticinese, you come to **Sant'Eustorgio**, another fourth-century church, built to house the bones of the Magi, said to have been brought here by Sant'Ambrogio. It was rebuilt in the eleventh century, and in the twelfth century was virtually destroyed by Barbarossa, who seized the Magi's bones and deposited them in Cologne cathedral. Some of the bones were returned in 1903 and are kept in a Roman sarcophagus tucked away in the right transept. Every year at Epiphany (6 Jan) the bones are taken to the Duomo and paraded back to the church by men dressed in slightly pantomime-like satin costumes of the Three Kings.

The simple Romanesque nave and the medieval and Renaissance private chapels jostling for position on the right of the church are only half the story. The primary reason for visiting Sant'Eustorgio is to see the **Portinari chapel**, accessed round to the left of the main entrance (Tues–Sun 10am–6pm; €6, combined ticket with Cappella di San Aquilino & Museo Diocesano €9.50). En route, you can dip down under the nave to see remnants from the Roman burial ground that the church was built on, including several surprisingly

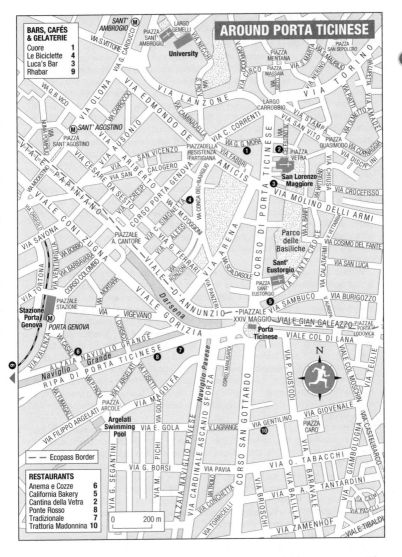

AROUND PORTA TICINESE

BARS, CAFÉS & GELATERIE

Cuore	1
Le Biciclette	4
Luca's Bar	3
Rhabar	9

RESTAURANTS

Anema e Cozze	6
California Bakery	5
Cantina della Vetra	2
Ponte Rosso	8
Tradizionale	7
Trattoria Madonnina	10

— — Ecopass Border

0   200 m

well-preserved funeral monuments, tombs and the odd bone or two. The dignified sacristy offers an impressive collection of reliquaries from different periods: note San Carlo Borromeo's shirt rolled up in one and the many B-movie-like paintings of St Peter the Martyr's untimely end.

The beautiful Portinari chapel consciously recalls Brunelleschi's San Lorenzo in Florence, with two domed rooms, the smaller one housing the altar. It has been credited with being Milan's first real Renaissance building because of its simple geometric design. The mixture of Lombard terracotta sculpture and Florentine monochromatic simplicity makes for an enchanting fusion of styles. It was commissioned from the Florentine architect Michelozzi in the 1460s by

Canals play an important part in the history of Milan and hold a special place in the hearts of the Milanese. Comparisons with Amsterdam and Venice seem improbable these days, but less than fifty years ago the city was still a viable port and only one hundred years ago, several of the main arteries – including Via Senato and Via San Marco – were busy waterways. Rivers and canals still run under much of Milan and there are ghostly reminders in the names of streets and alleyways, such as the Conca del Naviglio (canal basin) in the south, the Tombone di San Marco (St Mark's lock) in Brera and Via Laghetto (the pool or wharf where the Duomo building materials arrived by canal), near the Ospedale Maggiore. There is much talk of uncovering the city's old canals as a nostalgic nod to the time when Milan was a great military and manufacturing power, although in reality it is little more than political posturing.

The first section of the **canal system** was started in the eleventh century and was gradually developed and added to over the centuries to enable Milan to become one of the most important ports in the country, despite its inland position. The process of covering over the canals began in the 1930s to make way for the city's trams and trolley buses. By the mid-1970s, only the Naviglio Grande and the Naviglio Pavese, to the south of the city, were left in the centre; the last working boat plied the waters in 1977.

Milan is surrounded by rivers and it was only logical for the city's powers to want to harness these natural resources for both trade and military purposes. In the twelfth century, the first canals connected irrigation channels and the various defensive moats of the city. Later, in 1386, the Naviglio Grande was opened, linking the city to the River Ticino and thus Lake Maggiore and Switzerland. It was Gian Galeazzo Visconti, however, who was really responsible for the development of the system. Looking for a way to transport the building materials for the Duomo, especially marble from Lake Maggiore, he invited proposals for solving the different logistical problems involved: Leonardo da Vinci is said to have had a hand in the invention of a system of locks developed to compensate for the different water levels of the canals. During the building of the cathedral, boats carrying construction materials – marked with "AUF" for "ad usum fabricae" – had precedence over all other water traffic.

Different rivers and canals were added to the system over the centuries, with the Spanish developing the Darsena to the south in 1603 and Napoleon's regime finally managing to make the Naviglio Pavese navigable all the way to Pavia and down to the Po, and so to the sea. During the industrial revolution at the end of the nineteenth century, raw materials such as coal, iron and silk were brought into the city, and handmade finished products transported out with an ease that ensured Milan's commercial and economic domination of the region. In the 1950s, desperately needed materials were floated in for reconstructing the badly bombed city and it wasn't until the 1970s that the remaining canals finally fell into disuse.

The canals were not just reserved for business. Ruling families used the extensive network of waterways to visit one another and journey between their summer and winter residences. Prospero and Miranda escaped along the Navigli in *The Tempest*, and they were still being used by visitors on the Grand Tour in the eighteenth century; Goethe, for example, describes the discomfort and hazards of journeying by canal.

The best way to explore the canals these days is to don a pair of walking shoes or rent a bike (see p.73), pack some mosquito block, and head off down the towpaths into the paddy fields of Lombardy. Alternatively, you could take a relaxing boat trip; these run between April and mid-September when the canals are not being dredged or cleaned. For more information ask at the tourist office, call the Information line on ☎02.3322.7336 or check ⊛www.navigliolombardi.it and ⊛www .amicideinavigli.org.

▲ San Lorenzo alle Colonne

one Pigello Portinari, an agent of the Medici bank, to house the remains of St Peter the Martyr. Peter, one of Catholicism's less attractive saints, was excommunicated for allegedly entertaining women in his cell, then cleared of the charge and given a job as an Inquisitor. His death was particularly nasty – he was axed in the head by a member of the Cathar sect that he was persecuting near Lake Como – but the martyrdom led to almost immediate canonization and the dubious honour of being deemed Patron of Inquisitors. St Peter the Martyr's wildly elaborate tomb is crowded with reliefs showing scenes of his various miracles and supported by statues of the eight *Virtues*. The wonderful frescoes on the walls and ceiling are attributed to Foppa; the gold-cloaked figure half hiding from the scene in the right-hand lunette of the right wall is said to be a self-portrait. The rainbow-coloured scales on the dome above the gaily dancing angels lead up to the Portinari coat-of-arms in the lantern directly above the spot where the banker is buried.

The church was part of a large complex belonging to the Dominican order – the entrance to the Portinari chapel is through one of the courtyards – part of which is now the home of the **Museo Diocesano** (Tues–Sun 10am–6pm; €8, Tues €4, combined ticket with Cappella Portinari & Cappella di San Aquilino €12; Ⓦwww.museodiocesano.it), a mixed bag of religious paintings taken from Milan's churches. However, as most of the city's quality ecclesiastical art and artefacts are in the Pinacoteca Brera and the Castle collection rather than here, you're better off visiting when one of the quality temporary exhibitions interests you.

The Navigli

The southern end of Corso di Porta Ticinese is guarded by the nineteenth-century **Arco di Porta Ticinese**, an Ionic-style gateway, on the site of a medieval entrance to the city, built to celebrate Napoleon's victory at Marengo. It marks the beginning of the canal – or **Navigli** – neighbourhood, once a bustling industrial area and these days a focus for the nightlife of the city. Alongside, the forlorn-looking **Darsena**, or Basin, was the busiest part of the city's canal system (see opposite), the main dock area for goods entering and leaving the city. This unloved body of stagnant water has been promised a new lease of life by an international architectural competition, which will remodel the basin and link it with newly created parks and bridges. This will hopefully spur the way for investment in the rest of the canal area, which although full of lively restaurants, bars and clubs in the evenings, promises much more than it currently offers to daytime visitors.

South from the Darsena, the **Naviglio Grande** and the **Naviglio Pavese**, respectively the first and last of the city's canals to be completed, lead into the plains of Lombardy. Although the bohemian atmosphere of the area is somewhat over-hyped, it certainly shows a different side to Milan; this was Milan with its sleeves rolled up, the working city at its grittiest. Some of the warehouses and traditional tenement blocks, or *case ringhere*, have been refurbished and become prime real estate, although you'll still find plenty of unreconstructed corners too. Some craftsmen and artists have moved in and although the overpriced craft and antique shops won't hold your attention for long, a wander round the streets popping into open courtyards will give you a feel of the neighbourhood. One of the few specific sights is the prettified **Vicolo dei Lavandai**, or Washerwomen's Alleyway, near the beginning of the Naviglio Grande, where washerwomen scrubbed smalls in the murky canal waters.

A good time to visit is the last Sunday of the month (closed July & Aug) when the canals host the lively **Mercato dell'Antiquariato**, offering a mixture of bric-a-brac, appealing tat and genuine antiques; the further south down the canals you go, the more interesting the merchandise. During the first two weeks of June, a series of festivals keeps the waterways busy, culminating in the celebrations for the patron saint of travellers and boatmen, **San Cristoforo**, at the church dedicated to him on the Naviglio Grande.

Five-minutes' walk west from the Naviglio Grande is **Porta Genova**, the station for Milan's southern outskirts. It is also the name given to one of Milan's up-and-coming areas, another ex-industrial district that is slowly being regenerated. Across the tracks from the train station, disused warehouses and factories are being reclaimed by photographers, fashion houses and designers. Giorgio Armani has an exhibition space and workshops here, as does Prada. And round the corner at Via Bergognone 34, the old Ansaldo tram and train factory now houses **La Scala's scenery and costume department** (Tues & Thurs guided tours 3pm; €5; booking essential ☏02.4335.3521); there are plans for it to be further developed by the British architect David Chipperfield to include an ethnographic museum and cultural centre.

Santa Maria delle Grazie, Sant'Ambrogio and around

To the south of the Castello Sforzesco, beyond the busy streets of the financial district, skirted by Corso Magenta, are some of Milan's richest cultural pickings. Nineteenth-century *palazzi* and smart residential blocks have replaced the religious communities that once populated the area and it's their treasures that really bring visitors into this part of town. The church of **Santa Maria delle Grazie** is famous for the mural of **The Last Supper** by Leonardo da Vinci painted on the refectory wall of the adjacent Dominican monastery. There are more works by da Vinci at the **Museo Nazionale della Scienza e della Tecnica** where displays bring to life the engineering projects of the fifteenth-century genius. Nearby is one of the city's most enchanting churches, that of Milan's patron saint **Sant'Ambrogio** – an important prototype of Lombard Romanesque architecture.

Santa Maria delle Grazie and around

The beautiful terracotta-and-brick church of **Santa Maria delle Grazie** was first built in Gothic style by the fifteenth-century architect Guiniforte Solari. It was part of the Dominican monastery that headed the Inquisition for over one hundred years in the late-fifteenth and sixteenth centuries. Ludovico Sforza set about making changes to the complex, conceiving the church as a grand dynastic mausoleum. Included in these improvements was a painting for the wall of the monks' refectory, which has become one of the world's most famous works of art, Leonardo da Vinci's **The Last Supper**.

A disatisfied Lodovico Sforza, who wanted a funerary chapel for his wife, Beatrice d'Este, had the church partially rebuilt by Bramante, who tore down Solari's chancel and replaced it with a massive dome supported by an airy Renaissance cube. Lodovico also intended to replace the nave and facade, but was unable to do so before Milan fell to the French, leaving an odd combination of styles – Solari's Gothic vaults, decorated in powdery blues, reds and ochre, illuminated by the light that floods through the windows of Bramante's dome. A side door leads into Bramante's cool and tranquil cloisters, from which there's a good view of the sixteen-sided drum the architect placed around his dome.

The Last Supper

Leonardo's *The Last Supper* – signposted **Cenacolo Vinciano** – is one of the world's great paintings and most resonant images. However, art of this magnitude doesn't come easy: visits must be booked at least a week in advance, more like a month or three in summer and for weekends (reservations Mon–Fri 9am–6pm, Sat 9am–2pm on ℡02.8942.1146 or via the website ⓦwww.cenacolovinciano.org; viewing Tues–Sun 8.15am–6.45pm; €6.50, plus €1.50 obligatory booking fee). If it's fully booked when you ring, try asking about cancellations: people don't always turn up for the early-morning slots so it might be worth chancing your luck and enquiring at the desk. Alternatively, try the city tours listed on p.73, where entrance to view the painting is included. At your allotted hour, once you've passed through a series of air-filtering systems along the rebuilt sides of what was the monastery's largest courtyard, your fifteen-minute slot face-to-face with the masterpiece begins.

Henry James likened the painting to an "illustrious invalid" that people visited with "leave-taking sighs and almost death-bed or tip-toe precautions"; certainly it's hard, when you visit the fragile painting, not to feel that it's the last time you'll see it. A twenty-year restoration process recently re-established the original colours using contemporary descriptions and copies, but that the work survived at all is something of a miracle. Leonardo's decision to use oil paint rather than the more usual faster-drying – and longer-lasting – fresco technique with watercolours led to the painting disintegrating within five years of its completion. A couple of centuries later Napoleonic troops billeted here used the wall for target practice. And, in 1943, an Allied bomb destroyed the building, amazingly leaving only *The Last Supper*'s wall standing.

A Last Supper was a conventional theme for refectory walls, but Leonardo's decision to capture the moment when Christ announces that one of his disciples will betray him imbues the work with an unprecedented sense of drama. The composition is divided into four groups with Christ as the calm central focus. The serenity of the landscape behind echoes his peace of mind while it also provides his figure with the luminosity that allowed Leonardo to dispense with the traditional halo with which Christ was usually portrayed. The decision to set the table at the front of the composition draws us into the scene, and the trestle table, simple tablecloth tied to the table at the corners and crockery are said to have been the same as those used by the monks, thus emphasizing that this was just an extension of the refectory itself. The use of perspective adds a depth and realism to the painting unseen in previous versions of the theme, while the architectural angles draw our eyes up to the coats-of-arms of the Sforza family – and patrons – above.

Leonardo spent two years on the mural, wandering the streets of Milan searching for and sketching models. When the monks complained that the face of Judas was still unfinished, Leonardo replied that he had been searching for over a year among the city's criminals for a sufficiently evil face, and that if he didn't find one he would use the face of the prior. Whether or not Judas's face is modelled on the prior's is unrecorded, but Leonardo's Judas does seem, as Vasari wrote, "the very embodiment of treachery and inhumanity".

Goethe commented on how very Italian the painting was in that so much is said through the expressions of the characters' hands; the group of Matthew, Thaddaeus and Simon on the far right of the mural could be discussing a football match or the latest government scandal in any bar in Italy today. The only disciple not gesticulating or protesting in some way is the recoiling Judas, who has one hand clenched, while a bread roll has just dropped dramatically out of the other. Christ is calmly reaching out to share his bread with him while his other hand falls open in a gesture of sacrifice.

If you feel you need any confirmation of the emotional tenor or accomplishment of the painting, take a look at the contemporary *Crucifixion* by Montorfano on the wall at the other end of the refectory: not a bad fresco in itself, but destined always to pale into mediocrity beside da Vinci's masterpiece.

Museo Archeologico and around

The **Museo Archeologico**, in the ex-Monastero Maggiore at Corso Magenta 15 (Tues–Sun 9am–1pm & 2–5.30pm; €2, free on Fri afternoon), is worth a quick visit if you wish to delve deeper into the city's Roman heritage. The displays of glass phials, kitchen utensils and jewellery from Roman Milan are compelling, and though there's a scarcity of larger objects, you can see a colossal stone head of Jove, found near the castle, a carved torso of Hercules and a smattering of mosaic pavements unearthed around the city.

East from the museum, Via Brisa runs alongside the ruins of the imperial palace of the Roman Emperor Maximian unearthed after World War II bombing. South of here towards Via Torino, the medieval plan of the streets belies the Roman origins of the neighbourhood, where remnants of ancient mosaics and masonry are incorporated into the current buildings. Here stood a bath complex, the arena and the huge circus, the only traces of which are the rather forlorn-looking foundations at the corner of Via Circo and Via Cappuccio.

Museo Nazionale della Scienza e della Tecnica

A couple of blocks south of Santa Maria delle Grazie, at Via S. Vittore 21, the **Museo Nazionale della Scienza e della Tecnica** (Tues–Fri 9.30am–5pm, Sat & Sun 9.30am–6.30pm; €8; Ⓦwww.museoscienza.org) is housed in the sixteenth-century Olivetan monastery of San Vittore. This is a wet-weather museum with a huge miscellany of exhibits of varying quality; school-age children, in particular, are likely to enjoy exploring the labyrinth of displays spanning molecular science to early Vespas, taking in astronomy, telecommunications, the history of the car, musical instruments and much more on the way. The collection even includes several hangars housing steam engines, a submarine, aeroplanes, and a full-sized galleon from 1850. Labelling is erratic;

there are some good English-language translations on the more recent exhibits and faded Italian-only notes on others.

The **Leonardo da Vinci gallery** on the first floor contains sketches and models of many of his inventions, as well as reconstructions of some of his wackier contraptions, including the famous flying machine and an automatic weaving machine. It is a dry, no-nonsense display dating from the 1950s, but it offers an insight into the prodigious mind of this most Renaissance of men.

The slightly down-at-heel **bar** and canteen offer a passable lunch, with seating outside in one of the attractive cloisters, or you can bring your own picnic and sit in the pleasant gardens among the locomotives. Weekends see the museum buzzing with children involved in the numerous free organized **activities** that are on offer – from ceramics courses to making plastic. Most are run in Italian but it's always worth enquiring to see what's on offer – and ideally you should book a day or two in advance.

Sant'Ambrogio

On the other side of Via Carducci, the church of **Sant'Ambrogio** (Mon–Sat 7.30am–12.30pm & 2.30–9pm, Sun 7.30am–1pm & 3–8pm) was founded in the fourth century by Milan's patron saint. St Ambrose, as he's known in English, is even today an important name in the city: the Milanese refer to themselves as Ambrosiani, have named a chain of banks after him, and celebrate his feast day, December 7, with the opening of the Scala season and a big street market around the church. Ambrose's remains still lie in the church's crypt, but there's nothing left of the original church in which his most famous convert, St Augustine, first heard him preach.

The present twelfth-century church, the blueprint for many of Lombardy's Romanesque basilicas, is, however, one of the city's loveliest, reached through a colonnaded quadrangle with column capitals carved with rearing horses, contorted dragons and an assortment of bizarre predators. Inside, to the left of the nave, a freestanding Byzantine pillar is topped with a "magic" bronze serpent, flicked into a loop and symbolizing Aaron's rod – an ancient tradition held that on the Day of Judgement it would crawl back to the Valley of Jesophat. Look, too, at the pulpit, a superb piece of Romanesque carving decorated with reliefs of wild animals and the occasional human, most of whom are intent upon devouring one another. There are older relics further down the nave, notably the ciborium, reliefed with the figures of saints Gervasius and Protasius – martyred Roman soldiers whose clothed bodies flank that of St Ambrose in the crypt. A nineteenth-century autopsy revealed that they had been killed by having their throats cut. Similar investigations into St Ambrose's remains restored the reputation of the anonymous fifth-century artist responsible for the mosaic portrait of the saint in the Cappella di San Vittorio in Ciel d'Oro (to the right of the sacristy). Until then it was assumed that Ambrose owed his crooked face to a slip of the artist's hand, but the examination of his skull revealed an abnormally deep-set tooth, suggesting that his face would indeed have been slightly deformed.

Outside (entrance to the left of the choir) is Bramante's unfinished **Cortile della Canonica**. The side that Bramante did complete, a novel concoction incorporating knobbly "tree trunk" columns and a triumphal arch, was shattered by a bomb in World War II and reconstructed from the fragments; the second side was added only in 1955. The adjacent Benedictine monastery that the Sforza family commissioned Bramante to restructure has housed the **Università Cattolica** since the 1920s.

Shopping

Milan is synonymous with **shopping**: whether you're here to indulge in the ultimate consumer experience or want to bag a designer bargain, there are few places on earth with more to offer. The city's reputation as a **fashion** Mecca means you can find boutiques from all the world's top clothes and accessories designers within a hop, skip and a high-heeled teeter from each other. If your pockets are not quite deep enough, you could always rummage through last season's leftovers at the many factory stores around town, or check out the city's wide range of medium- and budget-range clothes shops. Milan also excels in furniture and **design**, with showrooms from the world's top companies, plus a handful of shops offering a selection of brands and labels under one roof.

Most shops **open** Tuesday to Saturday 10am to 12.30pm and 3.30 to 7pm plus Monday afternoons, although some larger places stay open at lunchtime and on Sunday afternoons. Opening hours for in-house cafés vary, but in general they follow the store hours, and prices are in line with the rest of the city's watering holes. There are official dates for **sales**, set by the town council a week or two in advance, so all shops make their reductions at the same time. The summer sale usually lasts from early July through August, while the winter one starts around the second week of January and lasts for a month; as always bargains are best on the first day – when there are big crowds and queues – or at the tail end, when shops are desperate to get rid of stock.

Fashion

Twice a year Milan is brought to a standstill by the world's fashionistas who flock to show and be shown the latest collections in the spring and autumn fashion shows which occupy every possible venue across town. Milan has been associated with top-end fashion since the 1970s, when local designers broke with the staid atmosphere of Italy's traditional fashion home at the Palazzo Pitti

▲ Shopping

in Florence. It was during the 1980s, however, that the worldwide thirst for **designer labels** consolidated the international reputations of home-grown talent such as Armani, Gucci, Prada, Versace and Dolce & Gabbana.

The top-name fashion stores are mainly concentrated in three areas. The "**Quadrilatero d'Oro**" – Via Montenapoleone, Via della Spiga and around – is the place for Versace, Prada et al and the shop assistants here could win awards for condescension. **Corso di Porta Ticinese** houses the funkier, more youth-oriented shops, with a handful of interesting, independent stores, as well as international names like Diesel, Carhartt and Stussy. If your budget is smaller, head to **Corso Vittorio Emanuele, Via Torino** or **Corso Buenos Aires** for large branches of Italian middle-range chainstores, including Max Mara, Benetton and Stefanel, plus international high-street giants H&M and Zara.

Designer stores

The following is just a taster of some of the best top-label shopping Milan has to offer. These days the store itself is almost as important as the clothes: it can be sleek, funky, elegant, kitsch – everything the collections can be, although, of course, a good showroom will never overshadow its merchandise. The concept of a shop is being extended further and further: in-house cafés are springing up, as are exhibition spaces, spas, barbers, even gyms. It's worth popping your head round any door that takes your fancy, as there's often so much more inside than you'd guess from the window.

If you're a little daunted by the full collections or simply don't have the time or energy to visit all the showrooms, help is at hand. Right in the heart of the Quadrilatero there are a couple of shops offering a selection of the best of the season from various top designers. Banner, at Via Sant'Andrea 8, offers garments by international avant-garde labels, including Junya Watanabe and Yohji Yamamoto and Viktor & Rolf, in a store designed by the ubiquitous Milanese architect Gae Aulenti, while Gio Moretti, at Via della Spiga 4, offers slightly more mainstream names like Jil Sander, John Paul Gaultier and DKNY. Alternatively, the revamped Rinascente, at Piazza Duomo 14, is a swish experience these days offering a host of international designers displayed in a shopper-friendly layout.

Dolce & Gabbana Menswear, Corso Venezia 15, Womenswear, Via della Spiga 26. D&G trendy line including D&G junior at Corso Venezia 7. Go through to the courtyard on the ground floor of the eighteenth-century palace at Corso Venezia 15 to find a space dedicated to enhancing your shopping experience. There's an old-fashioned barber's, a small beautican's or "grooming centre" and the oh-so-stylish *Bar Martini*, popular with beautiful people of all nationalities.

Gianfranco Ferré Via Sant'Andrea 15. The sculptural designs of this master of couture are mirrored by the decor of his new boutique with its stunning red-resin wall, but it is the adjoining day-spa that makes it really special. Mon–Fri 10am–10pm, Sat 10am–9pm, Sun 11am–6pm.

Gianni Versace Via Montenapoleone 11. Unusually for Versace, this store, spread over five storeys, is nothing if not understated. The clean lines provide a perfect backdrop for the luxurious ostentation of

the clothes, shoes and accessories in glinting gold and swirling colours.

Giorgio Armani Via Manzoni 31. This temple to all things Giorgio is more a mini-shopping centre than a shop. There are boutiques for all his ranges – women's- and menswear, furnishings and houseware – accompanied by *Armani Café*, a relaxed pavement café, and *Nobu*, a pricey, hi-tech Japanese restaurant that's been one of *the* places in town to be seen for years. With a book corner selling design and coffee-table books, a florists' and a chocolate counter offering monogrammed sugary confections, you really won't need to spend your money anywhere else in town.

Gucci Via Montenapoleone 5–7 & Galleria Vittorio Emanuele II. Every desirable fashion item imaginable is available in the warren of sleek show rooms in Montenapoleone, while the newer store in the Galleria Vittorio Emanuele II has the *Gucci café*, where you can get a freshly squeezed fruit juice or a coffee accompanied by an exquisite chocolate –

sporting the famous GG symbol, of course – all in an atmosphere of elegant minimalism.

Just Cavalli Boutique Via della Spiga 30. The ultimate in bling. Cavalli's leopardskin-clad clientele will feel wonderfully at home in the white-cloud lift or shimmering up and down the giant central staircase. The *pièce de résistance*, however, is down in the café, *Just Cavalli Food*, where a saltwater aquarium swims with brightly coloured tropical fish.

Prada Galleria Vittorio Emanuele II. The original Prada store, dating from 1913, stands on a side corner in the centre of the Galleria Vittorio Emanuele II. Much of the elegant interior is original, including the monochrome marble floor and the polished wood display cabinets, but the best bit is

the central staircase swirling down past the leather goods to the men's and women's collections in the basement. Accessories, including shoes: Via della Spiga 18. Menswear: Via Montenapoleone 6. Women: Via Montenapoleone 8. Sportswear: Via Sant'Andrea 21.

Trussardi Via Sant'Andrea 3–7. A spacious boutique spread across three floors. The uber-chic *Trussardi-Marino Alla Scala café* occupies the ground floor, with a huge video-wall to keep you entertained while you sip your coffee. On the floor above the soft leather bags and crisp home lines is the formal but well-priced restaurant, and one floor higher still is a gallery space that's worth checking out for contemporary art and fashion exhibitions. Accessories and home collection: Piazza della Scala 5.

Factory stores

There's a selection of outlets or **factory stores** in and around Milan for designer labels at affordable prices. A couple of these are centrally located: the multi-label D-Magazine, Via Montenapoleone 26; the hard-to-find Basement, entered through the door to the left of no. 15 on Via Senato, with bargains from all the top labels; and Diffusione Tessile, Galleria San Carlo 6 near the Duomo, offering discounts on the Max Mara brands. Others demand more of a hike, although the savings are higher: the grande dame of Milan's outlet stores is Il Salvagente, at Via Bronzetti 16, fifteen minutes east of San Babila by bus (#54 & #61), where, with a little rummaging, you can bag a designer label for around a third of its original price.

Design and furniture

To pick up Gio Ponti, Castiglione, or Alessi **designer furniture**, make for the broad streets off San Babila: Corso Europa, Via Durini, Corso Venezia and Corso Monforte are home to the furniture and lighting showrooms that made Milan the design capital of the world in the 1950s.

For a more relaxed, but very Milanese, shopping experience, try a **concept store** that sells a bit of everything: High Tech, at Pizza XXV Aprile 12, is great for getting lost among designer, imitation and ethnic knick-knacks; while 10 Corso Como is an institution selling a few perfectly chosen design and fashion objects, as well as books and music, with a café and art gallery, too. The basement of the Rinascente department store, at Piazza Duomo 14, offers an array of the best design pieces from around the world with an emphasis on Italian creations.

Alessi Corso Matteoti 9 ⓦ www.alessi.com. A whole store full of Alessi's colourful and entertaining objects for the home.

Artemide Corso Monforte 19 ⓦ www.artemide .com. This company, largely responsible for Italy's international reputation for lighting design, has a showroom exhibiting all their lines, from the classics such as De Lucchi's Tolomeo and Richard Sapper's Tizio, to the season's latest.

B&B Italia Via Durini 14 ⓦ www.bebitalia.it. International name that specializes in stylish contemporary furniture by big names in Italian modern design.

Cassina Via Durini 16 ⓦ www.cassina.it. The showroom of this legendary Milanese company, which worked with all the greats in Italian design in the 1950s, is always worth a visit for both new designs and their range of twentieth-century design classics including Eames, De Stijl and Rennie Mackintosh chairs.

De Padova Corso Venezia 14 ⓦ www.depadova.it. Two floors of elegant own-brand furniture and houseware artfully displayed in a stylish showroom. Their collections are designed by big names including Vico Magestretti and Patricia Urquiola.

Driade Via Manzoni 30 ⓦ www.driade.com.
A wonderful multi-brand store with their own
designs, as well as work by designers like Ron
Arad and Philippe Starck. The collection includes

furniture, tableware, kitchen and bathroom
accessories, but the real treat here is the
showroom housed in an elegant nineteenth-
century *palazzo*.

Books

The English Bookshop Via Mascheroni 12
ⓣ02.469.4468. Chaotic collection of new and
used English books, with well-informed advice
on hand.
Feltrinelli International Piazza Cavour 1.The best
selection of English-language guidebooks in the
city, plus a reasonable choice of literature, poetry
and nonfiction in English, Spanish and French.
Fnac Via Torino, cnr Via della Palla. French chain
selling a decent selection of books – including

some English-language – and music, in a very
browseable display.
Libreria Milanese Via Meravigli 18. Bookshop and
publishers specializing in all things Milanese, from
cooking to history, encompassing photography and
folklore on the way. Most rewarding if you have some
level of proficiency in Italian, or the Milanese dialect.
Punto Touring Corso Italia 10. The city's best
collection of Italian guidebooks, with good sections
on cycling and hiking, plus maps to all scales.

Food and drink

Cotti Via Solferino 42. A treasure-trove of wines
and liqueurs from across the country is accompanied by an array of gourmet treats – both sweet
and savoury.
Cova Via Montenapoleone 8. Banks of irresistible
cakes and confectionery are on offer at this famous
tearoom dating back to the Napoleonic era.
Il Salumaio Via Montenapoleone 12. The selection
of savoury delicacies and handmade pasta are to

die for in this smart delicatessen, with a café and
tables outside in the courtyard.
Peck Via Spadari 7–9. Three floors of top-priced
Italian delicacies, from olive oil and home-made
chocolate to mouthwatering prosciutto, cheeses,
and an impressive wine cellar. There's also a café
on the first floor and a swish cocktail bar and
restaurant round the corner at Via Cantù 3.

Markets

Fiera di Sinigallia Via Valenza. The hugely popular
Saturday-morning fleamarket has been moved
temporarily from the Darsena to this site by Porta
Genova station while the Darsena is regenerated.
Anything and everything from Tupperware to
designer-knitwear seconds.
Mercato Antiquariato di Brera Via Fiori Chiari.
On the third Sun of the month, this upbeat
market along the main pedestrianized road
makes a good focus for a wander around the
area. Closed July & Aug.

Mercato Communale Piazza Wagner. The city's
main fresh-food market has had a makeover and is
now, once again, the place to head for a glorious
array of picnic supplies or take-home food gifts.
Closed Sun & Mon pm.
Mercatone dell'Antiquariato Naviglio Grande.
Lining the canal-side on the last Sun of the month,
this fun market has a vast array of knick-knacks
on offer, though genuine bargains are rare. Closed
July & Aug.

Sport

Really there's just one spectator sport that you'd come to Milan for and that's
football. Home to two of the country's top teams, San Siro stadium is a big
draw for anyone even vaguely interested in the beautiful game.

If you want to work off some of those pasta calories while you're in town,
your best bets are **jogging**, cycling or swimming. Although the city centre's
green spaces are not vast, the Parco Sempione or a couple of laps of the Giardini
Pubblici should suffice for an early-morning run. **Cycling** is a very popular way

of getting around the city (see p.72). There are a couple of conveniently located indoor **swimming** pools, and in summer the open-air pools offer a way of keeping cool and doing some exercise at the same time.

Football

Milan has two rival football teams – **Inter Milan** and **AC Milan** – which share the G. Meazza or San Siro stadium, playing on alternate Sundays. In 1899 AC (Associazione Calcio or Football Association) Milan was founded by players from the Milan Cricket and Football Club. Eight years later, a splinter group broke away to form Inter in reaction to a ruling banning foreigners playing in the championships. Inter – or the Internationals – were traditionally supported by the middle classes, while AC Milan, with its socialist red stripe, claimed the loyalty of the city's working class. This distinction was blown apart in the mid-1980s when the ardent capitalist Silvio Berlusconi bought the ailing AC and revived its fortunes, leaving many an AC fan with a moral quandary. Recent years have seen the two clubs vying for top positions in Serie A and their twice-yearly derbies are a highlight of the city's calendar and well worth experiencing live.

There are hourly guided **tours** around the G. Meazza stadium, at Via Piccolomini 5 (T 02.404.2432, W www.sansirotour.com; M Lotto, then a longish walk; Mon–Sat 10am–5pm from Gate 21; €12.50), including a visit to the clubs' museum. Match tickets can be bought here. Other ticket outlets are New Milan Point, in Piazza San Fedele (T 02.4548.6224) for AC Milan games (W www.acmilan.it); and for Inter games (W www.inter.it) Feltrinelli Books and Music, Piazza Piemonte 2 (Mon–Sat 11am–2.30pm & 3.30–7pm), and at Banca Popolare di Milano branches or online (T 800.001.908).

Swimming

In the wintertime there are three main options for a **swim**: the Olympic-sized Piscina Cozzi (T 02.659.9703; M Repubblica/M Porta Venezia), at Viale Tunisia 35, near to the Stazione Centrale; Piscina Solari (T 02.469.5278; M S Agostino), at Via Montevideo 20, to the south of the city; and the Lido di Milano (T 02.392.791 or 02.66.100; M Lotto), which has both indoor and open-air pools, out to the west.

From June to mid-September, however, swimming becomes less exercise and more a way of cooling down. The 1930s-built neighbourhood, **open-air pools**, with their sunbathing areas, playgrounds and late-night bars, can get very crowded, especially during weekends and late afternoon, but are a great place to wash away the muggy heat of the Milanese summer. Among the nicest are Argelati, at Via Segantini 6 (T 02.5810.0012; Pta Genova), by the Navigli and Romano in Città Studi, at Via Ampère 20 (T 02.7060.0224; M Piola). Prices are €5 during the week and €5.50 at weekends; for more information see W www.milanosport.it.

Eating and drinking

Milan may seem to live at a faster pace than much of Italy but it takes its food just as seriously. There are **restaurants** and **cafés** to suit every pocket and more choice of types of cuisine than you'll find pretty much anywhere else in the country. Whether you're looking for a neighbourhood trattoria, want to watch models pick at their salads or fancy well-priced ethnic food, Milan has it all.

If you don't fancy a sit-down meal, make the most of the Milanese custom of **aperitivo** (see box below) to curb your hunger.

Lunch and snacks

Weekday lunchtime is an ideal time to sample good-value cuisine: unprepossessing-looking bars throughout the city centre serve tasty pasta dishes or **set menus** at modest prices to local office workers. As well as the options below, your best bet is to look for establishments with queues between 12.30pm and 1.30pm. Unless otherwise stated, the restaurants on p.106 also serve at lunchtime.

For real low-budget eating, there are **street markets** every day, except Sunday, scattered throughout the city, selling all the cheese, salami and fruit you need for a picnic lunch; a complete list is given daily in the *Corriere della Sera* under "Mercati". Alternatively, the *mercato comunale* in Piazza Wagner has similar fresh produce to the street markets, but under one, large colourful roof. The handiest **supermarkets** are Standa at Via Torino 37, near the Duomo, Esselunga at Viale Piave 38, near Porta Venezia, and the over-priced Centro Commerciale in the Stazione Centrale (daily 5.30am–midnight).

Café Design La Triennale, Viale Alemagne 6 ☏02.875.441. Many of the chairs are design classics in this bright, spacious café, with huge picture windows overlooking the Parco Sempione. There's a good lunchtime menu (noon–2.30pm) and snacks throughout the day. M Cadorna. Closed Mon.

Cafeteria Duomo Top floor, La Rinascente, Via San Raffaele 2. A recent refurb finally allows you to enjoy one of the best views in town with a plate of nibbles or a full-blown meal to match. The space is divided between the city's best breadmakers, mozzarella specialists, sushi chefs, experts in Milanese cooking and chocolatiers to provide a gourmet pick-and-mix to please any tastes. Choose a table on the terrace outside and you can almost reach over and feed the gargoyles on the Duomo roof. M Duomo.

Da Claudio Via Ponte Vetrero 16. Mouth-wateringly fresh sashimi and shellfish served at the central bar amid the bustle of this traditional fishmongers on the edge of Brera. M Cairoli or Lanza. Lunch (noon–2pm) and *aperitivo*-time only. Closed Sun & Mon.

Da Pino Via Cerva 14 ☏02.7600.0532. A friendly neighbourhood bar that offers a quality lunchtime menu of Lombardy specialities aimed at local office workers. Be sure to ring for a table before you go. M San Babila. Mon–Sat noon–3pm; closed Sun.

Luini Via S. Radegonda 16. A city institution that's been serving *panzerotti* (deep-fried mini-calzone) round the corner from the Duomo for over a hundred and fifty years; be prepared to queue. There are a couple of benches in nearby Piazza San Fedele if you want to eat sitting down. M Duomo. Closed Sun.

Palazzo Stelline Corso Magenta 61. The sunny terrace of this bar – in the convent where Leonardo stayed while painting *The Last Supper* – is the perfect spot to reflect on his nearby masterpiece over a salad or toasted panino (daily 9am–10pm). If you fancy something a little more filling, head into

Un aperitivo

An Italian custom that has been honed to a fine art in Milan is the **aperitivo**, or pre-dinner drink. Between 6 and 9pm the city unwinds over a drink and a bite to eat. As well as another opportunity to preen and pose, *aperitivo*-time – or happy hour as it is also called – is a boon for budget travellers: counters often groan under the weight of hot and cold food, all of which is included in the price of your drink (somewhere between €3 & €10, depending on the establishment). Take a plate and help yourself, although if you're really planning to fill up, it'll go down better if you go back several times rather than piling your plate high. If you choose your venue wisely you won't need to spend another penny on food all night. Most *aperitivo* bars evolve as the evening goes on: the lights dim, the volume of the music increases and you can settle in for the night.

For *aperitivo* bar listings, see pp.108–109.

the basement to the self-service restaurant *buonappetito!*, with its wonderful array of cold and hot dishes. Mon–Fri noon–2.15pm. M Cadorna.

Panino Panini Via Beccaria 1. A dizzying selection of sandwiches just off Piazza Duomo,

with outside seating year round. M Duomo. Closed Sun.

Vecchia Latteria Via dell'Unione 6. Delicious vegetarian dishes in a tiny neighbourhood café just off Via Torino. M Duomo. Closed Sun.

Cafés & gelaterie

Milan has traditional cafés and salons de thé galore; bourgeois, staid and very comfortable, they serve morning coffee, lunchtime snacks and afternoon tea. We've listed a selection of the best below, as well as some of the city's most famous ice-cream parlours, or **gelaterie**. For bars and cafés that are more popular for evening drinks, see the listings on p.108.

Caffè Miani Piazza Duomo 21. Opened with the *Galleria* in 1867, *Caffè Miani*, also known as *Zucca in Galleria* and *Camparino*, was where David Campari invented Milan's famous sticky red drink. These days it's both expensive and touristy, but the price of a coffee standing at the tiled bar is easier to swallow. Closed Wed.

Chocolat Via Boccaccio 9. Down the side of Milano Nord station, this small, modern bar, with comfy sofas, offers a selection of thirty different chocolate-flavoured ice creams plus some refreshing fruit ones, too; there's hot chocolate to die for in winter. Closed Sun am.

Cova Via Montenapoleone 8. *Fin-de-siècle* surroundings set the scene for this elegant tearoom

dating from the Napoleonic era. Discreet service and starched linen accompany the mouthwatering chocolate delicacies, although naturally they don't come cheap.

Grom Via Santa Margherita 16. Practically opposite La Scala the central branch of this specialist ice-cream chain serves up traditional flavours using top-quality organic ingredients.

Sartori Piazza Luigi di Savoia. Legendary kiosk up against one side of the Stazione Centrale (by the airport buses), serving some of the city's best ice cream, including avocado and lychee flavours. Closed Thurs.

Restaurants

Predictably, the **centre** of Milan has numerous pricey, expense-account establishments, but usually, just round the corner, there is somewhere more atmospheric or better value. To the south of the centre, the area around the **Ticinese** and **Navigli** is full of restaurants and cafés but you should choose carefully as this is a touristy area and quality is not always a priority. The districts of **Brera** and **Moscova** are also popular in the evening, so we've included a few of the better establishments here, as well as several bargain places around the budget hotels near the **Stazione Centrale** and **Porta Venezia**.

North of Piazza Duomo

Antica Trattoria della Pesa Viale Pasubio 10 ☎02.6566.741. Just west of Corso Como, this elegant trattoria serves up well-presented Lombard classics in a very friendly atmosphere. Step in from Milan's inclement weather and choose home-made pasta, creamy risotto, or a filling *cassoeula*. M Moscova or Pta Garibaldi. Closed Sun.

Joia Via P. Castaldi 18, ☎02.2952.2124. Well-established foodie haven serving highly imaginative combinations of vegetables and fish. The lunchtime menu is good value, but dinner can cost around €70 per person. M Pta Venezia. Closed Sat lunch, Sun & Aug.

La Latteria Via San Marco 24 ☎02.659.7653. This former dairy shop has been converted into a cosy trattoria that's a favourite with the designer folk of the area. Delicious home-made pastas and roast meats are served up by the owner; reckon on around €15 for a main course. M Moscova. Closed Sat & Sun & Aug.

La Libera Via Palermo 21 ☎02.8646.2773 Convivial wood-panelled trattoria serving excellent dishes that combine the traditional with the more unusual. The pumpkin risotto (€12) melts in your mouth while the tropical fruit of the speciality *insalata esotica* is perfectly complemented by the good range of house beers. M Moscova.

L'Osteria del Treno Via San Gregorio 46–48
ⓣ 02.670.0479. The welcome couldn't be friendlier at this converted railworkers' canteen. Many diners opt for the delicious house platters of cold meats or cheese (€12), although the pasta dishes are recommended, too. M Repubblica. Closed all day Sat & Sun eve.

Oskar Via Palazzi 4. A popular restaurant with bags of local atmosphere, serving fantastic-value pasta dishes (€8 a plate) in huge portions. Don't be put off by the voluble owner or the Mussolini memorabilia in the corners. M Pta Venezia. Closed Sun.

Pizza OK Via Lambro 15. Very busy pizzeria that serves some of the best – and biggest – pizzas in town. Huge choice of toppings and good prices that start at €4 for a margherita. M Pta Venezia. Open until 12.30am. Closed Sun lunch.

Torre di Pisa Via Fiori Chiari 21 ⓣ 02.874.877. An authentic Tuscan restaurant offering delicious antipasti for around €9 and great cuts of meat – sold by weight – in the very heart of pedestrian Brera. M Lanza. Closed Sat lunch & Sun.

Warsa Via Melzo 16 ⓣ 02.201.607. An Eritrean restaurant in among the shops and bars of Milan's African community, serving very tasty bargain-priced food; good variety of vegetarian dishes, as well as various meat options. Count on around €15 for a full meal. M Pta Venezia. Closed Wed.

South of Piazza Duomo

Anema e Cozze Via Casale 7
ⓣ 02.837.5459. This bright, lively Neapolitan spot sitting plump on a corner of the Naviglio Grande is a good choice for tasty, informal meals. The pizzas are crispy, the seafood fresh and the flavoursome salads make a pleasant change from pasta; expect to pay around €30 per person. Sister restaurants at Via Palermo 15 (ⓣ 02.8646.1646) and Via Orseolo 1 (ⓣ 02.36576140) are equally recommended. M Pta Genova.

California Bakery Piazza Sant'Eustorgio 4
ⓣ 02.3981.1517. The leafy terrace tucked in beside Sant'Eustorgio church is a splendid spot to enjoy the delicious savouries and mouth-watering

cakes served in this very pleasant joint. More San Fran than Milan but pleasant outside eating is tricky to find in this city. Tram #3. Closed Mon.

Cantina della Vetra Via Pio IV ⓣ 02.8940.3843. Just behind San Lorenzo, this agreeable restaurant, with big windows onto the park, serves up flavoursome good-value cooking. Primi, such as pappardelle with saffron and courgette flowers or the speciality gnocchi fritti, cost €10, while the meat dishes range from €10 to €15. M Pta Genova FS. Closed Sat lunch & Sun eve.

Ponte Rosso Ripa di Porte Ticinese 23 ⓣ 02.837. 3132. One of the best spots in the canal area for a tasty, relaxed meal of local flavours. A full meal without wine costs around €35, including one of the delicious home-made desserts. M Pta Genova FS. Closed Mon lunch & Sun.

Taverna Morigi Via Morigi 8 ⓣ 02.8645.0880. Daily specials are chalked up on the board in this 1920s osteria with a fine wine list. The good, no-nonsense home cooking, served to a loyal clientele, includes fresh pasta but the platters of cold meats and cheeses are particularly popular. M Duomo. Closed Mon.

Tradizionale Ripa de Porta Ticinese 7
ⓣ 02.839.5133. Tasty pizzas and yummy fish dishes are on offer in the rustic atmosphere of this popular canal-side joint. There's another branch at Via de Amicis 26. M Pta Genova FS.

Trattoria Madonina Via Gentilino
ⓣ 02.8940.9089. On a warm evening the little garden makes this gem near the Navigli hard to beat. The atmosphere is relaxed and the cooking simple with the emphasis on Milanese dishes – *bollito con salsa verde*, *cotoletta* etc – for around €10 a main course. Booking essential. Tram #3 or #15. Closed Sun & Mon–Wed eve.

Trattoria Milanese Via Santa Marta 11
ⓣ 02.8645.1991. An elegant, well-priced neighbourhood restaurant in the labyrinth of ancient streets 10min walk west of the Duomo. Understandably, risotto and *osso buco* take pride of place among all that's best of Milanese cooking (main courses weigh in at around €15). M Duomo. Closed Tues.

Nightlife

Milan is renowned as having some of the best nightlife in Italy. Although hardly cutting-edge, it's a diverse scene that offers something for just about everyone. There are plenty of places catering for those who want to see and be seen but there are also laid-back joints where the music and company are just as important.

Milan's **nightlife** traditionally centres on three main areas: the designer-label streets around Corso Como and south around Via Brera; the Porta Venezia area, with its more relaxed, alternative scene; and the canal-side Navigli and the adjacent Ticinese quarter, south of the city, where a more mixed clientele enjoys the lively bars, restaurants and nightclubs, some hosting regular live bands. Recently, however, a fourth neighbourhood, Corso Sempione, has been attracting new bars and clubs, and, from *aperitivo*-time onwards, this is one of *the* spots to head for. Milan's relatively small size and car and scooter culture mean that people are happy to drive to places out of the centre, so some of the more popular bars and clubs that we recommend below may require a bus or a quick taxi ride.

If you need an antidote to the expensive designer side of Milan's nightlife, check out the very healthy alternative scene, which revolves around the city's many **Centri Sociali**. Born out of the student protests of the late 1960s, these centres are essentially squatted buildings, where committees organize cheap, sometimes free, entertainment, such as concerts and film showings. They also contain bars and – often good – vegetarian restaurants, and are an established part of the social scene, even sometimes receiving local funding. Check out the flagship *Leoncavallo*, at Via Watteau 7 (℡02.670.5621, ⊛www.leoncavallo.org), or look in the listings section of the newspaper *Il Manifesto* for other *centri*.

Bars

Many **bars** metamorphose, as the day – and night – progresses, serving coffee and food in the day and becoming clubs in all but name and entry charge later in the evening. Most of the following bars open at around 11am and don't close their doors until 2am at the earliest. They are at their busiest from *aperitivo*-time onwards. For a truly Milanese experience, don't forget to check out the bars in the city's top fashion showrooms; see p.101.

Atomic Via Felice Casati 24. Refreshing spot just north of Porta Venezia where you can have an after-dinner drink and a dance in a cool but relaxed atmosphere – most unMilanese. Closed Mon & Aug.

Bar Bianco Parco Sempione. Right in the heart of the park, this unassuming café becomes a very popular spot on summer nights when it turns into a late-night bar with thumping music. Bus #61, tram #30 or M Moscova. Closed Mon.

Bar Jamaica Via Brera 32. This bar, made famous by the Arte Povera set of the 1950s, is right in the heart of Brera. You can pop in for a coffee or snack during the day or keep drinking well into the early hours. Tables outside in the summer.
M Montenapoleone. Closed Sun in summer.

Bar Magenta Via Carducci 13. An enduringly popular bar with 1920s decor that gets packed to bursting point on Fri nights and weekends with an early-twenty-something crowd. M Cadorna or Cairoli. Closed Mon.

Bhangrabar Corso Sempione 1. Just opposite the Arco della Pace, this Indian-themed bar is a trendy option for happy hour (6.30–9pm) or later, as the evening rolls on and the visiting DJs crank up the latest electronic and world-music sounds. Tram #30 or M Cadorna.

Casablanca Café Corso Como 14. Live DJs spin their tunes in this Baroque-inspired bar-disco, a popular pit stop for those heading on to the club Hollywood. M Pta Garibaldi FS.

Corso Como 10 Corso Como 10. The bar is the best bit of this chi-chi set-up of exhibition space, boutiques, a restaurant and a courtyard café-bar. Prices are extortionate but the atmosphere is very chic and exclusive.
M Pta Garibaldi FS.

Cuore Via G Mora 3. Hidden away down a side street opposite San Lorenzo alle Colonne, this cool, friendly bar is well worth including in your night out. Good music with occasional live bands and DJs set the mixed crowd at their ease. Tram #3.

Diana Garden Sheraton Majestic, Viale Piave 42. Only a couple of years ago this was *the* venue during the Milan Fashion Week, and while the clientele at the Sheraton Majestic is no longer quite so ground-breaking, the garden and bars continue to draw those out on the town and dressed to kill.
M Pta Venezia.

Gattopardo Café Via Piero della Francesca 47 ⊛www.gattopardocafe.com. This ultra-fashionable spot, located in a deconsecrated church, is decked out after Visconti's film *The Leopard*. It opens at 6pm and the door policy gets stricter after 10.30pm when the extensive *aperitivo* buffet is cleared away and the DJ turns up the music. Bus #57 or #43. Closed Mon.

Jazz Café Corso Sempione 8. There's a young, friendly crowd at this café, serving good Milanese food including risotto and cotoletta (count on around €30 for dinner). Once the plates are cleared away the music is turned up and the fun and dancing really begin. Tram #30 or M Cadorna. Closed Sun.

Just Cavelli Café Viale Camoens, Torre Branca. Posturing and preening are *de rigueur* at this popular bar underneath the Torre Branca at the edge of Parco Sempione. M Cadorna or bus #61.

Le Biciclette Conca del Naviglio 10. Smart young things prop up the bar in this swish modern joint in a leafy street near the Navigli. The definitive *aperitivo* bar. M S. Ambrogio, bus #94 or tram #14 or #2.

Lelephante Via Melzo 22. Cocktails are the speciality at this good-time bar popular with a mixed crowd. Hardly a poseur in sight. M Pta Venezia.

Luca's Bar Colonne di San Lorenzo. Unassuming by day, this Ticinese bar kicks into action in the evening, when an unpretentious crowd congregates on the pavement outside. Tram #3 or bus #94. Closed Sun.

Rhabar Alzaia Naviglio Grande 150. Cosy chill-out bar on the canal-side with live DJ sets from happy hour onwards. Prices are reasonable and often a small art exhibition or theatre piece to check out during the week. Bus #3 & #15. Closed Mon & Tues.

Roialto Via Piero della Francesca 55. This huge converted garage on various levels is done out in every conceivable style from 1930s colonial to chill-out lounge. Bus #43 & #57. Closed Mon.

Live music venues and clubs

The city's **clubs** are at their hippest midweek, particularly on Thursdays – at weekends out-of-towners flood in and any self-respecting Milanese trendy either stays at home or hits a bar. Many places have obscure door policies, often dependent on the whim of the bouncer; assuming you get in, you can expect to pay €10–20 entry, which usually includes your first drink. Most clubs don't open until around 11pm, but are likely to carry on through until 4am.

As for **live music**, Milan scores high on jazz, and the pop scene is relatively good by Italian standards: there are regular gigs by local bands, and the city is a stop on the circuit for big-name touring bands.

Blue Note Via Borsieri 37 ⓦwww .bluenotemilano.com. Newish jazz club located in the emerging neighbourhood of Isola, just north of Stazione Garibaldi. Big names and a relaxed atmosphere make this place a top venue. There's a small restaurant, as well as the bar. M Garibaldi FS.

Gasoline Via Bonnet 11a ⓦwww.discogasoline .it. Small, dark, funky club handy for the bars of Brera and Corso Como. On Sun afternoons it hosts a popular gay club called *Bus Stop*. M Garibaldi FS.

Hollywood Corso Como 15 ⓦwww .discotecahollywood.com. Long established as the place to go if you want to be surrounded by beautiful people. Very Milanese but certainly no mould-breaker. M Garibaldi FS.

L'Atlantique Viale Umbria 42 ⓦwww .cafeatlantique.com. Achingly trendy spot where the slickest of Milan's slick meet. Top DJs regularly spin their stuff. Bus #92. Closed Mon & Aug.

Magazzini Generali Via Pietrasanta 14 ☏02.5521.1313. Ex-warehouse that's become a Milan institution with a mixture of popular club nights and live music. Bus #91 or #24.

Plastic Viale Umbria 120 ⓦwww.thisisplastic.com. Historic club that still draws in the crowds to dance to an eclectic mixture of sounds. Very strict door policy. Bus #92.

Rolling Stone Corso XXII Marzo ⓦwww .rollingstone.it. Milan's main venue for rock and pop concerts for years also has club nights at the weekends. The music varies but there's always a choice on the different floors. Bus #73. Closed Mon.

Scimmie Via Ascanio Sforza 49 ⓦwww.scimmie.it. This Ticinese club is one of Milan's most popular venues, with a different band every night and jazz-fusion predominating. Small and intimate, with a restaurant – and a barge on the canal in summer. M Pta Genova FS.

Tunnel Via Sammartini 30 ☏02.6671.1370. With its eye firmly on what's happening abroad this large club and venue located in an old warehouse near the Stazione Centrale is as close as Milan gets to having its finger on the pulse. Closed Mon.

Opera, music, theatre and cinema

For many, Milan is synonymous with **opera**, and the recently refurbished La Scala is unlikely to disappoint, but there is also a good programme of classical music organized throughout the year. Milan's reputation for ground-breaking **theatre** in the 1980s and 90s has waned in recent years, but there are several quality venues. You can also choose from a range of **cinemas**.

Opera

Many of Milan's tourists are in the city for just one reason – **La Scala**, at Via dei Filodrammatici 2 (info ☎02.7200.3744), one of the world's most prestigious opera houses. The opera season runs from 7 December through to July, and there are usually also classical concerts and ballet performances between September and November. The average price of a ticket is about €70 and seats often sell out months in advance. Advance tickets can be bought on the phone or online (☎02.860.775, ⓦ www.teatroallascala.org; the website has a useful seating-plan) two months before the performance, or in person at the Central Box Office, Galleria del Sagrato, underground in the corridors of the Duomo metro station, opposite the ATM office (Sept–July daily noon–6pm), a month before. Ticket collection for reservations is possible from two hours before the start of the performance at the opera house. Some tickets for each performance are set aside for sale on the day; 140 tickets are available for operas and ballets and 80 for concerts, with a maximum purchase of two tickets per person. The system changes frequently, but currently, a list of names is compiled at 1pm, with tickets to be collected at 5.30pm: check the website or ask at the box office for the latest information. Note that some performances, particularly of ballet and classical concerts, are held on the outskirts of the city in the rather less atmospheric Teatro Arcimboldi.

Classical music

Besides opera, Milan offers several good programmes of **classical music** throughout the year. The world-famous Conservatorio Giuseppe Verdi (ⓦ www .consmilano.it) organizes regular concerts in the deconsecrated Santa Maria della Passione next door to the school, just east of San Babila. Musica nelle Chiese, or Music in Churches, is another well-conceived programme of recitals, taking place in the city's atmospheric churches – particularly San Simpliciano and San Marco. Home to the Verdi orchestra, the Auditorium di Milano (ⓦ www.auditoriumdimilano.org), in the Navigli district, offers comfortable modern surroundings for some wonderful concerts, including jazz. Your first port of call should be the tourist office in Piazza Duomo, which has a dedicated desk for information, reservations and ticket sales for all the above venues and many others in the city.

Theatre

The heyday of Milan's **theatre** was in the 1980s, when Giorgio Strehler put the city on the map for contemporary performances of the classics. The Teatro Strehler – named after the director and also known as the Nuovo Piccolo (as it replaced the Piccolo where Strehler had made his name) – at Via Rovello 2 (☎02.4241.1889, ⓦ www.piccoloteatro.org; closed Aug), is a classical theatre with a traditional repertoire and still one of the best in Italy. Teatro del'Elfo, at Via Ciro Menotti 11 (☎02.716.791, ⓦwww.elfo.org), is connected with another famous name, Gabriele Salvatores, the Academy-Award-winning film director of *Mediterraneo*. It has a quality mixed programme offering national and international productions of a more alternative bent.

Cinema

Around the Duomo there are umpteen **cinema** complexes offering all the latest blockbusters, more often than not dubbed into Italian. Sound and Motion Pictures (ⓦwww.spaziocinema.info; €6) organizes the showing of a selection of **original-language films** at the following cinemas: the Anteo, Via Milazzo 9 (☎02.659.7732), the Arcobaleno, Viale Tunisia 11 (☎02.2940.6054; M Pta Venezia), and the Mexico, Via Savona 57 (☎02.4895.1802), on Monday, Tuesday and Thursday nights respectively. In addition, the Odeon Cinema (☎199.757.7505), right in the centre at Via Santa Radegonsa 8, shows original-version films, while the Fondazione Cineteca Italiana, based at the Spazio Oberdan (ⓦwww.cinetecamilano.it), Viale Veneto 2, has a good programme of international art-house movies. In the summer months, **outdoor films** are shown at several venues around the city; see the newspapers for listings.

Gay and lesbian Milan

Milan is one of the country's most gay-friendly cities with little of the religious- and socially-fuelled homophobia of the south. Many of the city's nightspots welcome a mixed crowd, but they often hold specific **gay** nights, too. Naturally, see-and-be-seen venues are Milan's forte, though there is also a choice of more relaxed, as well as more hardcore establishments, as well. The **lesbian** scene is less developed, with just a few dedicated venues. Whatever your taste, Milan's high proportion of would-be models and style-setters certainly means the city has more than its fair share of eye candy.

Central to Italian gay life for decades has been the organization Arcigay (ⓦwww.arcigaymilano.org), and it's worth checking their website to get a handle on any events happening in Milan. The sister organization ArciLesbica (ⓦwww.listalesbica.it) can give you an overview of the lesbian scene in the country. The focus of the Milan scene is the gay bookshop, La Babele, at Via San Nicolao 10 (ⓦwww.libreriababele.it; M Cadorna; closed Mon), which has a gallery alongside a good selection of books and videos. This is also the place to pick up a copy of the *Gay Milan* map, detailing the city's saunas, clubs and cruising areas. In May, the city hosts an international **gay and lesbian film festival** (ⓦwww.cinemagaylesbico.com), which often has fringe activities organized around the same time.

Bars, clubs and saunas

Many of the city's more hardcore gay venues are located on or near Via Sammartini, not far from the Stazione Centrale. There are numerous other establishments around town, although it's not uncommon to have to travel a little out of the centre; we've detailed public transport below. One essential item when visiting Milan's exclusively gay venues is the **ArciUno Club Card**, which most establishments require as a condition of entry. It can be bought (€13 annual membership) on the door at any place that requires it or online through Arcigay (see above).

Billy Club *Amnesia*, Via Gatto cnr with Viale Forlanini ⓦwww.billyclub.it. Prestigious DJs host Sat evenings very popular with a stylish set. Bus #73.

Bus Stop *Gasoline*, Via Bonnet 11 ⓦwww .teadance.it. Fun Sun afternoon date for a mainly mid-twenties crowd. M Garibaldi FS.

Flexo Club Via Orpo 3 ⓦwww.flexoclub.it. Men only at this well-run complex of cabins, dark rooms, bars and a cinema. Closed Sun. M Cimiano.

Lelefante Via Melzo 12. Primarily a lesbian bar, although it attracts a mixed crowd most nights. M Pta Venezia.

Metro Centrale Via Schiapparelli 1 ⓦwww .metroclub.it. Two floors of steam rooms, jacuzzi, saunas and chill-out rooms. M Central FS. Second smaller branch – Sauna Cimiano at Via Oropa 3; M Cimiano.

Papé Satan *Juiss*, Via Canonica 23 ☎02.3361.4453. Sun evenings here are renowned as one of the best gay nights in town, with good music and a cutting-edge crowd. Bus #57.

Popstarz *Plastic*, Viale Umbria 120 ⓦwww .thisisplastic.com. A popular destination for drag queens and flamboyant transvestites on most nights. Thurs has this Milan institution hosting a fun disco for a predominantly gay but mixed crowd. Bus #92.

Ricci Piazza della Repubblica 27. A standard coffee bar by day, this place becomes a stylish bar and club in the evenings. M Repubblica. Closed Mon.

Sottomarino Giallo Via Donatello 2 ⓦwww .sottomarinogiallo.it. Lesbian club with a women-only policy on Sat nights and a mixed crowd on Wed, Fri and Sun. M Loreto.

Listings

Airlines Aer Lingus, Galleria Passarella 2 ☎02.7600.0080; Alitalia, Via Albricci 5 ☎02.2499.2700; Air Canada, Viale Regina Giovanna 8 ☎02.2955.12653; American Airlines, Via Vittor Pisani 19 ☎02.6791.4400; British Airways, Corso Italia 8 ☎02.1478.12266; easyJet ☎899.234.589; Qantas, Corso Italia 8 ☎02.8645.0168. Ryanair ☎899.289.993; Airport enquiries ☎02.7485.2200 (daily 7am–11pm) for both Linate and Malpensa airports.

Car rental Avis (☎02.670.11654), Europcar (☎02.6698.7826), Hertz (☎02.669.0061) and Maggiore (☎02.669.0934) all have desks at the Stazione Centrale, and at both main airports.

Consulates Australia, Via Borgogna 2 ☎02.7770.4217; Canada, Via V. Pisani 19 ☎02.6758.3900; Ireland Piazza San Pietro in Gessate 2 ☎02.5518.8848; UK, Via San Paolo 7 ☎02.723.001; US, Via Principe Amadeo 2/10 ☎02.290.351.

Doctors English-speaking doctors are available at the private International Health Center (☎02.7634.0720, ⓦwww.ihc.it) and The Milan Clinic (☎02.7601.6047, ⓦwww.milanclinic.com).

Exchange Banks usually offer the best rates, but out of normal banking hours you can change money and traveller's cheques at the Stazione Centrale office (daily 7am–11pm), where there's also a 24hr automatic currency-exchange machine. The airports all have exchange facilities.

Hospital There is a 24hr casualty service at the Ospedale Maggiore Policlinico, Via Francesco Sforza 35 (☎02.55.031), a short walk from Piazza Duomo. Emergency ☎118.

Internet There are internet cafés all over town, generally charging around €2 an hour. There are various places along Via Giuseppe Ferrari, the main road immediately to the west of the main station, while the bar in Fnac on Via Torino is a pleasant spot in the centre of town to check your email (€3 per hr).

Left luggage Stazione Centrale (daily 6am–midnight; €3.80 for 5hr, then small increments up to a max of five days). Stazione Nord (Cadorna) also has a few over-subscribed lockers of various sizes for small bags and suitcases (daily 5am–11.30pm; small €3.50, med €4.50, large €6.50 for 2hr 30min).

Pharmacy The Stazione Centrale (☎02.669.0735), which has English-speaking assistants, and Carlo Erba, on Piazza Duomo (☎02.8646.4832); both have 24hr services. Rotas are published in *Corriere della Sera*, and are usually posted on *farmacia* doors.

Police ☎113. Head office at Via Fatebenefratelli 11 (☎02.62.261), near the Pinacoteca di Brera.

Post office Via Cordusio 4, off Piazza Cordusio – not the building marked "Poste", but around the corner (Mon–Fri 8am–7pm, Sat 8.30am–noon).

Telephones International calls can be made at most public telephones, with cards bought from newspaper kiosks (see p.57). If you want somewhere quieter, head for the TelecomItalia offices by the tourist office in the Stazione Centrale (daily 8am–8pm), or any of the hundreds of cheap international call-shops around the stations.

Train enquiries ⓦwww.trenitalia.com; Ferrovie dello Stato ☎848.888.088 (daily 7am–9pm); Ferrovie Milano Nord ☎02.20.222 (daily 9am–6pm).

Lake cuisine

Forget pizzas and tomato sauce: lake cuisine specializes in risotto, polenta, fresh-caught fish and wild mushrooms in butter. The historical emphasis here has been on hearty fare to fuel a day's hard work, making the most of local ingredients, be they fish from the lakes, corn from the fields, or frogs from the marshes.

Rice and pasta

Shortgrain **risotto** rice is grown in paddy fields to the south and east of Milan. Yellow *risotto alla Milanese* is infused with saffron; Pavia's *risotto alla certosina* is made with frogs' legs; in Mantova they favour pumpkin; while on the lakes small prawns (*gamberetti*) and trout (*trota*) are common. In autumn look out for risotto with wild mushrooms. **Pasta** includes stuffed *tortelloni* drizzled with *burro sfuso* (butter melted with sage). Around Bergamo and Brescia you'll find *casoncelli* stuffed with sausage-meat and spinach; while in Mantova *tortelli alla zucca* are filled with sweet pumpkin. Potato *gnocchi* and *bigoli* (thick wheat spaghetti) are typical of Verona, while around Bergamo and Lake Como *pizzocheri*, buckwheat tagliatelle with potatoes, vegetables and cheese, is popular.

Risotto ▲

Salami and hams, Lugano ▼

Meats

Pork, beef and veal dominate, with plenty of offal dishes such as *cervelli* (calf brains). As well as high-quality pork **salami**, there are also salamis made with wild boar (*cinghiale*) in Piemonte, and goose (*oca*) around Pavia. Cured meats include *bresaola*, air-dried beef, and *prosciutto crudo*, Parma ham. Milan is very proud of its *cotoletta alla Milanese*, breadcrumbed veal cutlet lightly fried, Wiener Schnitzel in all but name, brought over by Austrian occupiers. Other dishes include *ossobucco* (braised veal shin), accompanied by risotto; and *bollito misto* (boiled meats), served with *mostarda di Cremona*. *Luganega* is a spicy pork sausage found all over Lombardy and Ticino, while Austrian-influenced goulash and *carne salata* (thin slices of salted, pickled beef) are specialities of Riva del Garda.

Fish

Lake **fish** include tench (*tinca*) and perch (*persico*) – the former a speciality of Lake Iseo when stuffed, baked and served with polenta, the latter filleted and fried in breadcrumbs. One of the region's classic fish specialities is Lake Como's shad (*missoltini*, with various dialect spellings) – small sun-dried fish. Trout (*trota*) is common, often barbecued fresh on lakes Orta and Maggiore. Menus from Como to Verona include pike (*luccio*) – at its best when cooked in local olive oil, with capers and shallots – and lavaret (*lavarello*), baked, steamed or grilled with butter. Another very common lake dish is white fish (*coregone*), a meaty affair, also often grilled, while eels (*anguilla*), chub (*cavedano*) and bleak (*alborelle*) are less ubiquitous staples of lakes Como and Garda.

▲ Fishmongers' sign, Lake Garda

▲ Cheese specialist, Lugano

▼ Char-grilled polenta

Polenta

Lombardy's most famous ingredient is **polenta** (similar to US-style grits) – a slow-cooked porridge of cornmeal served hot topped with cheese or *stufato* (stew), or cooled, sliced into fingers and grilled until crisp. Rabbit (*coniglio*), donkey (*asino*), horse (*cavallo*) or small starling-like birds (*osei*) are the traditional accompaniments.

Cheese

Local **cheeses** are rich. Major names include Gorgonzola, a blue-veined creamy cheese from near Cremona; Taleggio, a soft brie-like cheese from north of Bergamo; and Grana Padano, the local version of Parmesan. There are umpteen other cheeses – one of the most common is *bagoss*, a fragrant yellow cheese from the Brescian mountains.

Café terrace, Bergamo ▲

Mostarda di Cremona ▼

Ten favourite restaurants*

▶▶ **Milan**: *Trattoria Milanese*, Via Santa Marta 11 (p.107). Hearty traditional cooking in an elegant neighbourhood restaurant.

▶▶ **Lake Maggiore**: *Piccolo Lago*, near Verbania (p.135). Award-winning local cuisine in a beautiful, quiet lakefront setting.

▶▶ **Lake Orta**: *Olina*, in Orta San Giulio (p.154). Great service, great atmosphere and delectable local specialities presented with pride.

▶▶ **Lake Como**: *Il Cavatappi*, in Varenna (p.202). Tiny, five-table restaurant where personal attention and perfect home cooking combine to memorable effect.

▶▶ **Lake Lugano**: *La Sorgente*, in Vico Morcote (p.216). Laid-back village restaurant with a beautiful terrace, seasonal specialities and a sense of style.

▶▶ **Bergamo**: *Donizetti*, on Via Gombito (p.238). Sit out in the stone loggia to sample superb local cooking while watching Bergamo pass you by.

▶▶ **Lake Garda (1)**: *Restel de Fer*, in Riva del Garda (p.294). Much-loved rustic tavern, serving rumbustious Trentino home cooking to an appreciative, knowledgeable clientele.

▶▶ **Lake Garda (2)**: *Trattoria agli Olivi*, near Torri del Benaco (p.301). Top-quality Gardesana fare – pasta, lake fish, local wines and oils – on a beautiful hillside terrace.

▶▶ **Verona**: *Enoteca Cangrande*, behind the Liston (p.326). Wonderful array of wines and Veronese nibbles at this welcoming, always-packed eatery off the main square.

▶▶ **Mantova**: *Il Cigno* (*Trattoria dei Martini*), on Piazza d'Arco (p.338). A classy setting in which to enjoy sensational pumpkin ravioli, fresh-caught pike and other local specialities.

*as chosen by this book's authors!

South of Milan: Pavia and the Certosa

Fifty-five kilometres south of Milan and the furthest west of the string of historic towns that spread across the Lombardy plain, **Pavia** is close enough to Milan to be seen on a day-trip, but still retains a clear identity of its own. A comfortable provincial town with an illustrious history, it boasts one of the masterpieces of Italian architecture in the nearby Carthusian monastery, the **Certosa di Pavia**.

Pavia

PAVIA was founded on an easily defendable stretch of land alongside the confluence of the Po and Ticino rivers and was always an important staging post en route to the Alps and beyond. Medieval Pavia was known as the city of a hundred towers, and although only a handful remain – one of the best collapsed in 1989 – the medieval aspect is still strong, with numerous Romanesque and Gothic churches tucked away in a wanderable web of narrow streets and cobbled squares. The town is not, however, stranded in the past – its ancient university continues to thrive, ensuring an animated street life and reasonably lively night-time scene.

Pavia reached its zenith in the Dark Ages when it was capital of the Kingdom of the Lombards. After their downfall it remained a centre of power, and the succession of emperors – including Charlemagne in 774 and Frederick Barbarossa in 1155 – who ruled northern Italy continued to come to the town to receive the Lombards' traditional iron crown. This all came to an end in the fourteenth century when Pavia was handed over to the Visconti and became a satellite of Milan. The Visconti, and later the Sforza, did, however, found the university and provide the town with its prime attraction – the nearby **Certosa di Pavia**. In 1525, the Battle of Pavia, just north of the city, put an end to French domination of the territory (once the Sforza dynasty had died out, the French had taken over) and resulted in the following two hundred years of Spanish rule over Milan and Pavia.

Arrival and information

Regular **trains** make the thirty-minute journey between Pavia and Milan. **Bus** services from Milan Famagosta metro station drop you at the bus station round the corner from the train station in Pavia, on the western edge of the town centre. Buses #3 and #6 connect the train station with the centre, or it's about a ten-minute walk down Corso Cavour to Piazza della Vittoria. The **tourist office** is north off Corso Cavour, at Piazza Petrarca 4 (Mon–Sat 8.30am–12.30pm & 2–5pm; ℡0382.597.001, ⒲www.turismo.provincia.pv .it), in the centre of town.

Accommodation

Pavia's **hotels** are a rather unexciting mix of business hotels and standard three-stars that tend to take the overspill from Milan's commercial fairs, so finding somewhere to stay can be more difficult than you might imagine. Most of the choices are near the station, including the *Aurora*, at Via Vittorio Emanuele 25 (℡0382.23.664, ⒲www.hotel-aurora.eu; ❸), and the three-star *Excelsior*, Piazzale Stazione 25 (℡0382.28.596, ⒲www.excelsiorpavia.com; ❸), both of which are basic, clean and convenient. The four-star *Moderno*, down the road at Via Vittorio Emanuele 41 (℡0382.303.401, ⒲www.hotelmoderno.it; ❻), is the smartest the city has to offer, with a small health centre and bicycles included

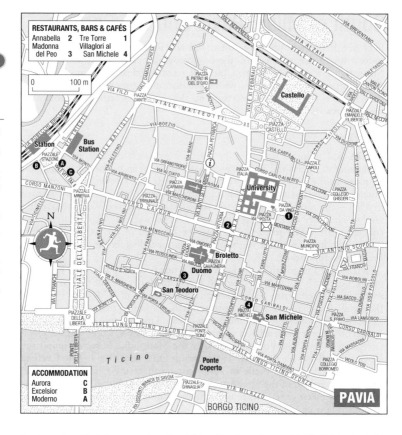

RESTAURANTS, BARS & CAFÉS

Annabella	**2**	Tre Torre	**1**
Madonna del Peo	**3**	Villaglori al San Michele	**4**

ACCOMMODATION

Aurora	**C**
Excelsior	**B**
Moderno	**A**

PAVIA

in the price. Pavia's **campsite**, the *Ticino*, Via Mascherpa 10 (☎0382.527.094; March–Oct), is 3km northwest of town – take bus #4 from the train station.

Pavia

Just wandering around town is the nicest way to spend time here: pick any side street and you're almost bound to stumble on something of interest – a lofty medieval tower, a pretty Romanesque or Gothic church, or just a silent, sleepy piazza. Getting lost is difficult as the town is still based around its Roman axes of the *decumanus* running east–west: Corso Cavour, which becomes Corso Mazzini; and the *cardo* running north–south: Strada Nuova. The River Ticino borders the south of the city centre.

The large cobbled rectangle of **Piazza della Vittoria**, lined with bars, *gelaterie* and restaurants, stands in the centre of the old town. At the square's southern end, the **Broletto**, medieval Pavia's town hall, abuts the rear of the rambling and unwieldy **Duomo**. An early Renaissance sprawl of protruding curves and jutting angles designed by Rocchi and Amadeo, possibly with contributions from Bramante and da Vinci, the cathedral is best known for its huge nineteenth-century cupola, which dominates the skyline of the city. The facade was only added in 1933 and the exterior of the cathedral is still mainly unfinished. Most of the church is closed off for restoration and is not due to reopen until 2010.

Beside the west front of the Duomo, facing **Piazza del Duomo**, are the remnants of the eleventh-century Torre Civica, a campanile that collapsed without warning in March 1989, killing four people.

Southwest of the piazza, the narrow, cobbled streets lead to the neighbourhood church of **San Teodoro** (daily 3–7pm). The twelfth-century basilica was clumsily restored at the end of the nineteenth century, though it's not without charm. The main reason for visiting is to see the fresco on the left-hand side of the nave near the entrance: the *View of Pavia* by Bernardino Lanazani illustrates the city in 1522 with its hundreds of civic towers built by Pavia's noble families in order to show their superiority over their rivals. In the nineteenth century there were still eighty left, but now only three remain.

Also featured in the painting is the **Ponte Coperto**, the covered bridge over the Ticino just to the south of the basilica. The current bridge was rebuilt slightly downriver in the 1940s after the medieval one was bombed; you can still see remnants of the old one jutting out into the water. The bridge leads over to the **Borgo Ticino**, the riverside neighbourhood traditionally inhabited by fishermen and *raniere* (frog catchers); these days there are several restaurants popular with locals. Note the marks on the walls showing the flood levels over the last century. An attractive open park runs along the shore of both banks west of the bridge, a popular sunbathing and picnic spot in summer.

The best of the town's churches is the beautiful Romanesque **San Michele**, a five-minute walk northeast from the bridge along Via Capsoni. This is where the kings of Northern Italy were crowned and Federico I, or Barbarossa, came to receive the title here in 1155. The friezes and capitals on its broad sandstone facade are carved into a menagerie of snake-tailed fish, griffins, dragons and other beasts, some locked in a struggle with humans, representing the fight between good and evil. Sadly, the sandstone is being worn away despite restoration work in the 1960s and some of the figures are being lost for good.

North of here are the attractive courtyards and sandstone buildings of the **University of Pavia**, founded in 1361 by Galeazzo II Visconti, and particularly renowned for its medicine and law faculties. Continuing across busy Piazza Castello, you reach the **Castello Visconteo** (Tues–Sun: July, Aug & Dec–Feb 9am–1.30pm; March–June & Sept–Nov 10am–5.45pm; €6; ⓦ www.museicivici .pavia.it), also initiated by Galeazzo II Visconti in 1360, and added to by the Sforza. The austere-looking building originally housed luxurious apartments, the majority of which were in the wing of the quadrangle destroyed by the French in 1527. The castle was used as a barracks until 1921, and although it's been restored, the rooms that remain are unmemorable. The well-organized **Museo Civico** inside includes an art gallery with a handful of Venetian paintings, an archeology collection with Roman jewellery, pottery and glassware, and a museum of sculpture displaying architectural fragments, mosaics and sculptures rescued from the town's demolished churches.

Eating and drinking

Round the corner from the bus station on Via Fabio Filzi, a branch of the supermarket Esselunga makes a handy place to put together the ingredients for a riverside picnic. Alternatively, the *Punto Bar*, Strada Nuova 9, is a good *paninoteca*, with at least thirty varieties of sandwich and plenty of space to sit down.

The best restaurant in town, with some of the most attractively located outdoor tables in summer, is in an alleyway by the church of San Michele. ⌖ *Villaglori al San Michele*, Viccolo San Michele 4 (☎03.8222.0716; closed Mon & weekday lunchtimes), offers excellent-priced local wines to accompany interesting dishes like rabbit and asparagus lasagne or a mouth-watering selection of cold meats and cheeses in an elegant modern restaurant. Alternatively, across Corso Strada Nuova, the *Osteria della Madonna del Peo*, at Via Cardano 63 (☎0382.302.833; closed Sun), is a good central option serving local specialities, such as risotto with frogs' legs, in a cosy vaulted trattoria.

If you're looking for an alternative to the cafés lining Piazza della Vittoria for your **aperitivo**, the *Tre Torre*, at Piazza Leonardo da Vinci, is a relaxed studenty place with outside tables; or there's *Annabella* on Corso Strada Nuova, which is glitzier and run by the town's infamous fur-coat couturier.

The Certosa di Pavia

Ten kilometres from Pavia, the **Certosa di Pavia** (Charterhouse of Pavia; Tues–Sun: April–Sept 9–11.30am & 2.30–5.30pm; Oct–March closes 4.30pm; free) is one of the most extravagant monasteries in Europe, commissioned by the Duke of Milan, Gian Galeazzo Visconti, in 1396 as the family mausoleum. Visconti intended the church here to resemble Milan's late-Gothic cathedral and the same architects and craftsmen worked on the building throughout its construction. It took a century to build, and by the time it was finished, tastes had changed – and the Visconti had been replaced by the Sforza. As a work of art the monastery is one of the most important testimonies to the transformation from late-Gothic to Renaissance and Mannerist styles, but it also affords a fascinating insight into the lives and beliefs of the Carthusian monks. After the suppression of Catholicism in the latter half of the eighteenth century came the confiscation of ecclesiastical lands by the new secular state of Italy in 1881. It was not until 1968 that a handful of Cistercian monks moved back into the complex and gradually restored it.

You can see the church unaccompanied, but to visit the rest of the monastery you need to join a **guided tour** of just under an hour (free but contributions welcomed), led by one of the monks released from the strict vow of silence. Tours run regularly – basically when enough people have gathered. They're in Italian, but well worth doing – even if you don't understand a word – as it allows you to visit the best parts of the monastery complex.

The church

The monastery lies at the end of a tree-lined avenue, part of a former Visconti hunting range that stretched all the way from Pavia's *castello*. Encircled by a high wall, the complex is entered through a central gateway bearing a motif that recurs throughout the monastery – "GRA-CAR" or "Gratiarum Carthusiae", a reference to the fact that the Carthusian monastery is dedicated to Santa Maria delle Grazie, who appears in numerous works of art in the church. Beyond the gateway is a gracious courtyard, with the seventeenth-century Ducal Palace on the right-hand side and outbuildings along the left. Rising up before you is the fantastical **facade** of the church, festooned with inlaid marble, twisted columns, statues and friezes. Despite more than a century's work by leading architects, the facade remains unfinished: the tympanum was never added, giving the church its stocky, truncated look.

The Milanese architect Guiniforte Solari was the first to work on the facade, starting in 1472 with the medallions of emperors and figures from antiquity around the base. The following layers of reliefs and statues of prophets and saints were created by the Mantegazza brothers, while the richest decorations – in particular the Bible scenes round the two windows – are attributed to Amadeo, who included a self-portrait in the bottom left-hand corner holding a pair of architect's compasses. Lombardo is responsible for the decoration in the upper, slightly simpler, layers.

Inside, the Gothic design of the **church** was a deliberate reference to Milan's Duomo, but it has a lighter, more joyous feel, with its painted ceiling, and light streaming in through the one hundred windows high up in the walls. Halfway down the right-hand aisle, a trompe l'oeil of a Carthusian monk peeping through a window seems to watch visitors as they move around the church. The elaborate seventeenth-century gates to the transept and highly decorated altar, at the far end, are opened when a tour is about to start.

The sculptural highlights of the church lie in the two wings of the transept. In the centre of the north transept lies the stone funerary monument of the greatest of the dukes of Milan, Ludovico il Moro, and his wife Beatrice d'Este, neither of whom are actually buried here. Ludovico commissioned the piece for the church of Santa Maria delle Grazie in Milan, where Beatrice is still buried, but it was moved here in 1564, forty years after his death; Ludovico himself is buried in France, where he died as a prisoner. The exquisite detail of the statue, by another of the ubiquitous Solari clan – Gian Cristoforo – is an important document of sixteenth-century fashions with its tasselled lattice-work dress and glam-rock platform shoes. Many of the church's artworks are by Bergognone, including the fresco behind the funerary monument of the *Crowning of the Virgin* flanked by Francesco Sforza and his son, Ludovico il Moro. The south transept contains the magnificent mausoleum of the founder of the monastery, Gian Galeazzo Visconti, by Cristoforo Romano, including a carving of Gian Galeazzo presenting a model of the Certosa to the Virgin. Both he and his wife, Isabella di Valois, are buried here.

The monastery

Opposite the mausoleum is the door to the delightful **small cloister**, a reminder that the monastery was built for the contemplative Carthusian order rather than simply as a vehicle for wealthy families to buy their salvation. With fine terracotta decoration and a charming geometric garden, this was where monks shared the communal part of their lives, meeting here to pace the courtyard during their weekly ration of talking time. The reliefs around the pleasing terracotta and marble washing area on the far side are early works by Amadeo, showing Christ washing the feet of a leper, and were used by the monks to perform ablutions before entering the nearby **refectory**. Here the monks would eat together on Sundays and holy days and remain in silence while being read Bible passages from the pulpit, accessed via a staircase hidden in the wooden panelling in the middle of the room. The dining room is divided by a blind wall, which allowed the monastery to feed visiting pilgrims and lay agricultural workers without compromising the rules of their closed order. The room was used as the main church of the complex for the first hundred years of existence while the church was completed, and a crude *Madonna and Child* fresco remains on the far wall.

Leading off the side of the small cloister, the breathtaking **great cloister** was the centre of the monks' lives. Lining three sides of the huge green courtyard are the monks' individual houses, each consisting of two rooms, a chapel, a garden and a loggia, with a bedroom above. The hatches to the side of the entrances were for food to be passed through to the monks without any communication.

The final call is the Certosa **shop**, stocked with honey, chocolate, souvenirs and the famous Chartreuse liqueur.

Practicalities

The Certosa is easily reached from both Milan and Pavia, either by bus or by train. **Buses** are more frequent, hourly from Famagosta station (M3) in Milan or from Pavia's bus station, dropping you a fifteen-minute walk from the

Certosa. Arriving by **train**, turn left out of the station and walk around the Certosa walls until you reach the entrance – also a fifteen-minute walk.

If you want something to **eat** while you're here, the café-bar to the left as you look at the main entrance is your best bet for a panino and a drink. There is also a formal restaurant in the old monastery mill, the *Locanda Vecchia Pavia al Molino*, at Via al Monumento 5 (☎0382.925.894), where the cooking is good, but prices high at €60 per head for the *menu di degustazione*.

Travel details

Trains

Milano Lambrate to: Bergamo (hourly; 50min); Brescia (2 daily; 1hr); Certosa di Pavia (9 daily; 20min); Desenzano (2 daily; 1hr); Pavia (every 15min; 25min); Peschiera (2 daily; 1hr 10min); Verona (hourly; 1hr 35min).

Milano Nord Cadorna to: Como (every 30min; 1hr); Varese (hourly; 1hr).

Milano Porta Garibaldi to: Arona (8 daily; 1hr); Bergamo (every 40min; 55min); Chiasso (hourly; 1hr 15min); Como (7 daily; 1hr); Cremona (4 daily; 1hr 40min); Domodossola (8 daily; 2hr); Lecco (hourly; 1hr); Luino (4 daily; 1hr 40min); Stresa (8 daily; 1hr 30min); Varese (hourly; 1hr); Verbania-Pallanza (8 daily; 1hr 35min).

Milano Stazione Centrale to: Bergamo (hourly; 50min); Brescia (every 45min; 1hr 15min); Certosa di Pavia (every 2hr; 30min); Chiasso (hourly; 50min); Como (hourly; 40min); Cremona (7 daily; 1hr 40min); Desenzano (every 30min; 1hr 10min); Domodossola (hourly; 1hr 30min); Lecco (every 2hr; 1hr); Pavia (every 30min; 25min); Peschiera (hourly; 1hr 17min); Stresa (9 daily; 1hr 10min); Varenna (every 2hr; 1hr 10min); Verbania-Pallanza (9 daily; 1hr 20min); Verona (hourly; 1hr 35min).

Pavia to: Certosa di Pavia (14 daily; 10min); Milan Centrale (hourly; 25min).

Buses

Milan (Metro Famagosta) to: Certosa (Mon–Sat 7 daily, Sun 5 daily; 30min).

Pavia to: Certosa (Mon–Sat every 30min, Sun hourly; 20min); Milan Famagosta (Mon–Sat every 30min, Sun 7 daily; 1hr).

2

Lake Maggiore and Lake Orta

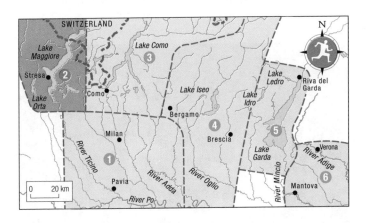

CHAPTER 2 # Highlights

* **Lago Maggiore Express**
A memorable three-stage journey by train and boat through splendid lake and mountain scenery. See p.130

* **Isola Madre** Charming formal gardens, part of the Borromeo islands. See p.134

* **Pallanza** Genial, slow-paced lake resort which beats Stresa for peace and quiet. See p.136

* **Villa Panza** Contemporary art in a fine Baroque villa – well worth the trip to Varese. See p.145

* **Orta San Giulio** Just about the most romantic lake village you could ever hope to find. See p.150

* **Cannóbio** Characterful old town that just wins out over its neighbour Cánnero for lake-appeal. See p.158

* **Ascona** Another beautiful corner, this time facing south from Switzerland. See p.163

* **Locarno-Cardada** Sensational views reached with a futuristic cable car and chairlift. See p.169

▲ Isola San Giulio, Lake Orta

Lake Maggiore and Lake Orta

If it should happen that you possess a heart and a shirt, then sell the shirt and visit Lake Maggiore.

Stendhal, 1817

For generations of overland travellers, **LAKE MAGGIORE** (**Lago Maggiore**) has been a first taste of Italy. Roads and rail lines from Switzerland run between the shores of Maggiore and its minor sidekick **LAKE ORTA** (**Lago d'Orta**); for travellers weary of the cool grandeur of the Alps, the first glimpse of limpid blue waters, green hills and exotic vegetation are evidence of arrival in the warm south. Unmistakeably Mediterranean in atmosphere, with palms and oleanders lining the lakeside promenades and a peaceful, serene air, Maggiore may not be somewhere for thrill-seekers, but it is seductively relaxing. Orange blossom, vines, clear air and the verbena that flourishes on Maggiore's shores – giving rise to the lake's alternative name **Verbano** – continue to draw the tourists, and you'll need to book in advance in peak season. In winter (Nov–Easter) many hotels close down and attractions may be shut.

Maggiore's main sights cluster around the **Golfo Borromeo** in mid-lake; here lie the grand old resorts of **Stresa** and **Pallanza**, with the Baroque

Tourist information

Several administrative boundaries converge on the shores of Lake Maggiore. The northernmost part of the lake is in the Swiss canton of **Ticino** (⊛ www.ticino.ch). On the Italian side, the east bank is in Lombardy's province of **Varese** (⊛ www.turismo .provincia.va.it). The west bank (all of which lies in Piemonte) is divided between the provinces of Novara and Verbano-Cusio-Ossola. The **Distretto Turistico dei Laghi** (⊛ www.distrettolaghi.it) manages tourism for the whole western shore, as well as for Lake Orta and the valleys around Domodossola.

Phone numbers
This chapter covers territory in both Switzerland and Italy. All **phone numbers** prefixed ☏ 091 are **Swiss**; all other numbers (beginning ☏ 03 in this chapter) are **Italian**. For details of international dialling, see p.58.

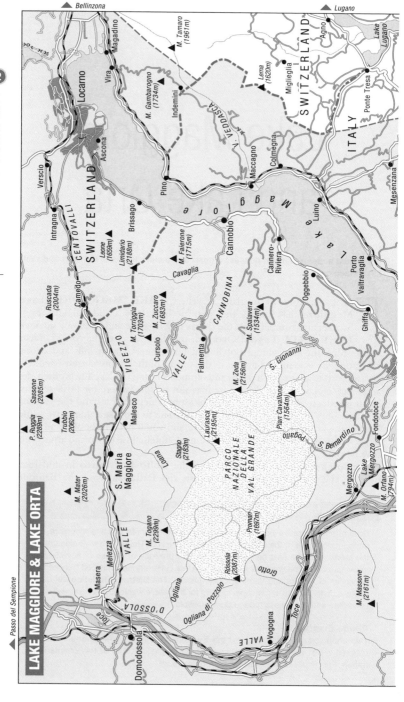

LAKE MAGGIORE & LAKE ORTA

▲ Bellinzona

▲ Lugano

Agno

Lake Lugano

Miglieglia

M. Tamaro (1961m) ▼

Lena (620m) ▼

Ponte Tresa

SWITZERLAND

ITALY

Mesenzana

Locarno

Vira

Magadino

M. Gambarogno (1734m) ▲

Indemini ▼

Maccagno

Colmegna

Luino

Ascona

Pino

Porto Valtravaglia

Verscio

Lake Maggiore

Intragna

Brissago

M. Faierone (1715m) ▼

Cannobio

Cannero Riviera

Oggebbio

Ghiffa

CENTOVALLI

Leone (1659m) ▲

Limidario (2188m) ▲

Cavaglia

SWITZERLAND

Camedo

Ruscada (2004m) ▲

M. Zuccaro (1683m) ▲

M. Torriggia (1703m) ▼

Cursolo

Falmenta

VALLE

CANNOBINA

M. Spalavera (1534m) ▲

VIGEZZO

P. Ruggia (2289m) ▲

Sassone (2085m) ▲

Trubbio (2062m) ▼

Malesco

S. Maria Maggiore

M. Mater (2026m) ▲

M. Zeda (2156m) ▲

S. Gionanni

Pian Cavallone (1564m) ▲

S. Bernardino

Laurasca (2195m) ▼

Stagno (2183m) ▼

Loana

Loana

PARCO NAZIONALE DELLA VAL GRANDE

Pogallo

M. Togano (2299m) ▲

Proman (1697m) ▼

Fondotoce

Mergozzo

Lake Mergozzo

M. Orfano (794m) ▲

Masera

Rossola (2087m) ▼

VALLE

Melezza

M. Massone (2161m) ▲

Grotto

Domodossola

Ogliana

Ogliana di Pozzolo

Vogogna

VALLE

Toce

D'OSSOLA

Toce

Toce

▲ Passo del Sempione

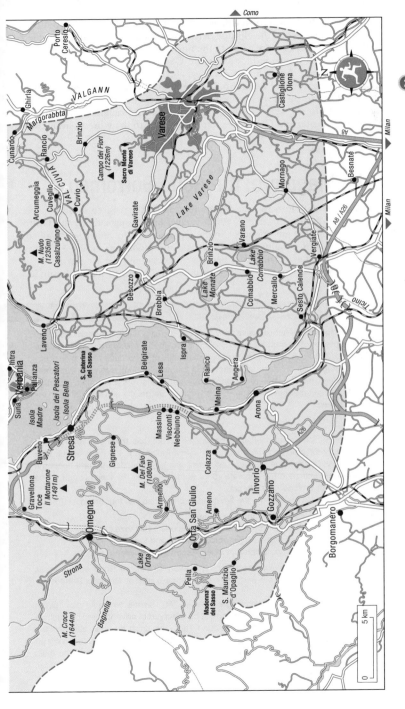

gardens of the **Isole Borromee** floating enticingly just offshore. The southern part of the lake, beyond the cliffside hermitage of **Santa Caterina**, is guarded by the **Rocca Borromeo**, while to the north, the lake narrows between high peaks, sheltering romantic hideaways like **Cánnero**, **Cannóbio** and – across the Swiss border – **Ascona**. The northern end of the lake is dominated by the cultivated Swiss town of **Locarno**. The medieval village of **Orta San Giulio**, on Lake Orta to the west, is a charming counterpoint to its grander neighbours; while to the east the unsung city of **Varese**, caught between lakes Maggiore, Lugano and Como, is a refreshing place to draw breath away from the crowds.

Lake Maggiore: the Golfo Borromeo

The majority of visitors to Lake Maggiore head for the western shore, where a bulging bay disturbs the lake's smooth parallel lines. Long dubbed the **Golfo Borromeo**, for the pre-eminence in the region of the Borromeo – a family of bankers, raised to nobility in the 1450s and still prominent locally – the bay holds some of the Italian Lakes' best-loved attractions. The elegant resort of **Stresa** is the most famous, bearing up under the strains of mass tourism; less

Boats on Lake Maggiore

Lake Maggiore has an extensive ferry network; it's easy (indeed, preferable) to get to most places of interest by boat. Service is provided by **NLM**, Navigazione Lago Maggiore (☎800.551.801, ⊛www.navigazionelaghi.it), who have more than thirty landing-stages, all of which sell tickets (but the smaller booths tend to open only ten or fifteen minutes before a boat is due in). Boats run year-round, although outside the summer season (April–Sept) services are greatly reduced or, on many routes, halted.

Routes

Note that the provincial capital, Verbania (see p.136), has three different landing-stages, none of which has Verbania in its name: **Pallanza** is the most useful; **Villa Táranto** has its own landing-stage; and **Intra** has boats heading up and down the shoreline as well as on a separate route across the lake to **Laveno** (not to be confused with **Baveno** near Stresa).

Because the lake is so long, the timetable is divided up into four broad sectors:

- the lower lake, between **Arona** and **Angera**
- the central area between **Stresa** and **Intra**, including **Pallanza** and the islands
- the northern section around **Cannóbio**, **Cánnero** and **Luino**
- the Swiss basin (*Bacino Svizzero*) around **Ascona** and **Locarno**

Within each sector there is a service roughly every 30 minutes. Boats do run across the sector divisions, but less frequently: quiet corners such as **Ghiffa** or **Ranco** may get just two boats a day.

Most boats are ordinary passenger vessels. "AL" on the timetable denotes an **aliscafo** (hydrofoil) – a faster ride that must be **reserved in advance** and commands a small supplement. Services start around 7am, and finish by 8pm, although the lake's only **traghetto** (car-ferry), which also takes foot passengers, shuttles continuously between Intra and Laveno from 5am to midnight. Supplementing the main timetable, a compact **navetta** shuttles frequently between **Carciano** (near Stresa), Isola Bella and Isola Superiore.

well known, though no less characterful, is **Pallanza**, part of the town of **Verbania**, a boat-ride away across the bay. Between the two lie the sumptuous gardens and villas of the **Isole Borromee**, three tiny islands that include the Baroque **Isola Bella** and the English-style gardens of **Isola Madre**.

The bay is also the focus of lake transport. **Boats** cross frequently between Pallanza, the islands and Stresa, which is also served by fast **trains** from Milan; **buses** north and south along the lake terminate at Verbania; and the lake's only **car-ferry** crosses east–west here, cutting down journey times to Varese and Milan. **Milan-Malpensa airport** is just 45km south.

Stresa

The Maggiore of the tourist brochures begins at **STRESA**, the legendary *grande-dame* of Italian lake resorts. During the nineteenth-century boom in tourism, Stresa remained largely unvisited: boats called in at the Borromeo islands, but bypassed the shoreline. Then, in 1906, the Simplon Tunnel between Switzerland and Italy opened, the final link in a chain of railways that connected Lake Geneva to Milan, and thus northern Europe to the Mediterranean. International trains, including the *Orient Express*, were routed through Stresa, which quickly became a favoured holiday retreat for Europe's nobility and royalty, hosting high society all through the heady 1920s and 1930s.

There are no dedicated sightseeing cruises, although you can easily put together your own itinerary using the widely available timetable leaflets. Check carefully the various symbols and colour-coded notes to identify each route's days of operation: several routes change on **Wednesdays** (to take account of the market at Luino) and some boats run only on *festivi* (Sun and holidays). Services marked with a knife and fork have a **restaurant** on board, serving a set meal (€15).

Fares and passes

Fares are charged on a complicated sliding scale. Each route is assigned a number, according to the distance involved; you then cross-check on the relevant chart for how much that route-number (or *tratta*) costs. Make sure you're checking the chart for individual travellers, marked *individuali* or *singoli* – not the one headlined *comitive e scuole* (groups and school parties). As an example, Stresa to Pallanza is *tratta* 5, which costs €4.20 direct, or €6 if you stop off on the way. Isola Bella to Isola Madre is *tratta* 4 (€3.50/€5.50), while Stresa to Cánnero is *tratta* 8 (€7/€9.50). Just about the most expensive ticket in the Italian basin, *tratta* 9 (Arona to Cannóbio), is €8.30/€10.50. You pay €0.80 extra to use the hydrofoil. Taking an ordinary-sized **car** on the ferry between Intra and Laveno costs €6.60 including the driver, plus €2.80 per passenger.

International tickets cost considerably more: for example, from Stresa or Baveno to any point on the Swiss shore costs €20.50, from Pallanza €18.50, from Cannóbio €15.50. Using the hydrofoil adds €1.60. Don't forget your **passport**.

For all these, a return ticket costs twice the price of a one-way. Children aged 4–12 qualify for a discount.

The **Due Isole** ticket covers unlimited trips between Isola Bella and Isola Superiore; from Arona or Angera it costs €16, from Stresa or Baveno €9.50. The **Tre Isole** ticket adds in Isola Madre; from Arona, Angera or Luino this costs €18, from Stresa, Baveno or Pallanza €11.50. A **Holiday Card** gives unlimited journeys on the whole lake, including Switzerland, for €41 (3 days) or €52 (7 days).

See p.165 for details of fares and passes on the **Swiss** side of the lake.

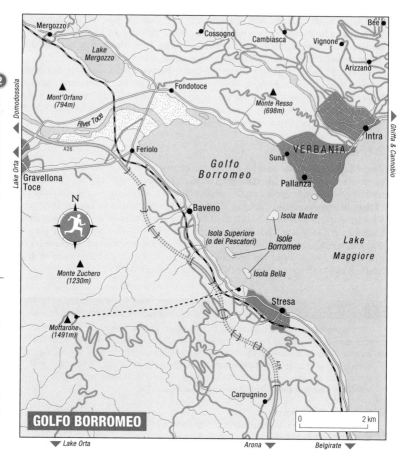

GOLFO BORROMEO

0   2 km

▼ Lake Orta   Arona ▼   Belgirate ▼

Today Stresa is a busy little place, but its greatest days have passed. Apart from the lake views – which are worth coming for – and a rump of grand hotels, the town is rather lacking in character: there are some pleasant spots, but the overall impression, regrettably, is of mundanity rather than sophistication.

Arrival, information and accommodation

Stresa is an hour from Milano Centrale on the high-speed **trains** that continue to Domodossola, Basel and Geneva; slower trains also run from Centrale and Porta Garibaldi. The **train station** is behind the town centre on Via Principe di Piemonte; taxis wait outside, or you could walk right to the crossroads, then left on Via Duchessa di Genova for 200m down to the lakefront. From **Milan-Malpensa airport** (Terminal 1, stop 22), SAF's Alibus runs five times daily (April–Oct only) along the western shore, stopping at Belgirate, Stresa and Baveno (€9; booking essential 48hr ahead by phone or online; ☎0323.552.172, Ⓦwww.safduemila.com). Alibus also runs all year round from Malpensa (Terminal 1, stop 12) to Gravellona Toce (€9), a short bus ride 9km north of Stresa.

Stresa is the linchpin of the dense network of **boat** routes around the islands, as well as a stop for boats heading north from Arona and south from Locarno.

The *imbarcadero* is very central, on Piazza Marconi, and has a large car park alongside, as well as the **tourist office** (daily 10am–12.30pm & 3–6.30pm; Nov–Feb closed Sat & Sun; ℡0323.31.308, ⓦwww.distrettolaghi.it). Additional shuttles to Isola Bella and Isola Superiore depart from Carciano, 750m north.

Hotels

Fiorentino Via A.M. Bolongaro 9 ℡0323.30.254, ⓦwww.hotelfiorentino.com. House-proud two-star hotel tucked away in the town centre, with fourteen comfortable, spacious rooms that are all en suite. ❸

Grand Hotel Bristol Corso Umberto I 73 ℡0323.32.601, ⓦwww.zaccherahotels.com. A Stresa landmark, located on the northern fringe of the town amidst splendid lakeside grounds and renovated in 2007. Interiors are plush, with marble, antique carpets and Tiffany glass – but this is a four-star property, so prices are slightly less astro-nomical than the competition. ❻–❽

Grand Hotel des Iles Borromées Corso Umberto I 67 ℡0323.938.938, ⓦwww.borromees.it. Stresa's grandest hotel, a lakefront palace dating from 1861 that has hosted a good deal of European and international royalty as well as presidents, politicians, celebrities and high society of all kinds. Hemingway was a regular guest, and the hotel features in *A Farewell to Arms*. Today, it's as opulent as ever, with every comfort presented amidst traditional-style luxury. Doubles from €450. ❾

Italie & Suisse Piazza Marconi 1 ℡0323.30.540, ⓦwww.italiesuisse.com. Decent, convenient and well-run three-star hotel opposite the Stresa landing-stage. Most rooms have balconies with lake views – though bear in mind that there is some traffic noise from the lakefront road – and are furnished in fresh, modern style. ❸–❹

Luina Via Garibaldi 21 ℡0323.30.285, ⓔluinastresa@yahoo.it. Friendly little two-star place in the centre of town, with seven rooms (four of them en suite) and a good-value restaurant serving home-made dishes. ❷

Verbano Isola dei Pescatori ℡0323.30.408, ⓦwww.hotelverbano.it. Romantic little three-star hotel occupying the eastern end of the Isola dei Pescatori, off Stresa. The twelve rooms are handsomely furnished, with lake views in one direction or another. In the early morning and evening, once the day-trippers have gone, the island reverts to calm and tranquillity: this is a perfect bolthole in any season. The hotel lays on a private boat service to and from the mainland, on request (free after 7pm). ❻

Villa Dal Pozzo D'Annone Strada del Sempione 5 ℡0322.7255, ⓦwww.villadalpozzo.com. Located 5km south of Stresa on the road to Belgirate, this is a wonderful find – a modestly sized luxury villa hotel, set in quiet hillside grounds with all the requisite lake views but none of the tourist bustle of Stresa itself. The elegant main house, still the family home of the Marquis Dal Pozzo D'Annone, holds six traditionally styled suites, while across the gardens the newer annexe – named *Borgo Ottocentesco* – holds twelve more modern ones; parquet floors, balconies, huge bathrooms and luxury fabrics prevail throughout. With so few guests, the atmosphere is of calm and exclusivity; this is a splendid retreat. Closed Nov–Easter. ❽–❾

The town and around

Stresa's elegant promenade – marred slightly by traffic passing alongside – stretches for over 500m along the lakefront, flanked, for the most part, by pleasant gardens, the best of which form the grounds of the palatial *Grand Hotel des Îles Borromées*. The mellow, chiefly pedestrianized town centre, set back from

Musical events

The **Stresa Festival** (ⓦwww.stresafestival.eu) features prestigious classical music concerts in May, August and September at venues in the town, on all three islands (including piano recitals in the spectacular setting of the Isola Bella *palazzo*), at various medieval churches, including Santa Caterina del Sasso and Lake Orta, and elsewhere. Look out, also, for **Stresa Jazz** (ⓦwww.stresajazz.it), with gigs every two or three weeks from April to October, and late June's classical **Baveno Festival Umberto Giordano** (ⓦwww.festivalgiordano.it). Many other towns around the lake stage their own musical happenings, from church organ music to a celebration of acoustic guitar: ⓦwww.distrettolaghi.it lists the lot.

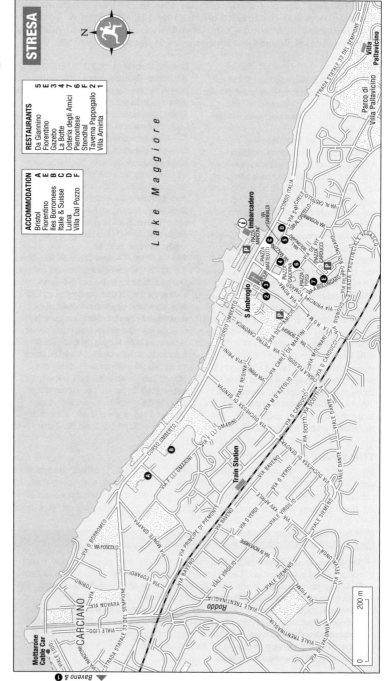

STRESA

ACCOMMODATION
Bristol	A
Fiorentino	E
Iles Borromees	B
Italie & Suisse	C
Luina	D
Villa Dal Pozzo	F

RESTAURANTS
Da Giannino	5
Fiorentino	E
Gazebo	3
La Botte	4
Osteria degli Amici	7
Piemontese	6
Stendhal	F
Taverna Pappagallo	2
Villa Aminta	1

Lake Maggiore

Belgirate & ⑤ ▲

Baveno & ① ▼

Mottarone
Cable Car

CARCIANO

Train Station

S. Ambrogio

Imbarcadero

Aside from the Borromeo islands (see p.131), Stresa's most attractive excursion is to the cliffside church of **Santa Caterina del Sasso** – see p.140 for details.

the *imbarcadero*, comprises half a dozen streets clustered around the little **Piazza Cadorna**, a triangular space filled with café tables dedicated to the mass consumption of outsized ice-cream sundaes. Around 500m south of the centre is the lakeside **Parco della Villa Pallavicino** (March–Oct daily 9am–6pm; €9; Ⓦ www.parcozoopallavicino.it), a patch of green around a fine old house, with a botanic garden and animals such as deer, zebra and wallabies wandering around, safari-park-style.

Separating Stresa from Lake Orta is the **Mottarone** mountain, rising to 1491m. It's hardly the most sensational of peaks, but nonetheless undeserving of the derision heaped upon it by John Ruskin – he referred to it as "the stupidest of mountains" and thought the views dull. Either Ruskin's mood or the weather must have been bad, for in truth the views are impressive, stretching from Monte Rosa on the Swiss border across to the Adamello. Its wooded western slopes are a favourite destination for family outings. The tourist office has leaflets detailing walks in the area. If you're driving up from Stresa, be aware that access is by a private road that was laid by the Borromeo family in the fifteenth century: they charge a **toll** of €4 per car to reach the summit. (The road up from the Orta side is free.) You'd do just as well to take the **cable car** (*funivia*; daily every 20min 9.30am–5.30pm; €8.50 one way, €15 return; Ⓦ www .stresa-mottarone.it), which rises from the Carciano ferry stop, 750m north of Stresa by the lido, and you can rent **mountain bikes** at the base station (€22 per day including cable-car ticket; Ⓦ www.bicico.it). The easy walk up, signposted as path 1, takes four hours. Beside the midway cable-car stop is the lovely **Alpinia Botanic Garden** (April–Oct daily 9.30am–6pm; free with summit cable-car ticket; Ⓦ www.giardinoalpinia.it).

About 5km south of Stresa, the charming old village of **Belgirate** marks a "pretty turn" (*bella girata*), where the road rounds a little headland. From Stresa's waterfront, you could walk the attractive hillside **trail L2** (2hr); this takes in a semi-ruined Roman road to Passera, a stretch of woodland, several country churches and a mule track that heads down to Belgirate's twelfth-century church. The tourist-office leaflet *Trekking alle pendici del Mottarone* has a map and English outline.

Eating and drinking

Stresa's **restaurants** cater well to the town's conservative, generally undemanding clientele – most places serve acceptably decent food, with a few that are truly memorable. Make time for an ice cream or aperitif at one of the cafés on the main Piazza Cadorna.

La Botte Via Mazzini 6 ☎ 0323.30.462. Snug trattoria that is one of the best places to try regional Piemontese cooking; the friendly host serves up local game, polenta and goat's cheeses as well as a variety of tasty pasta dishes. There's no terrace, but the ambience is warm and welcoming. A meal costs around €25. Closed Thurs.

Enoteca Da Giannino Via Garibaldi 32. Sociable little place for light snacks and wine by the glass.

Fiorentino Via A.M. Bolongaro 9. Modest restaurant in the centre of town attached to the hotel of the same name – keenly priced soup, spaghetti and decent *secondi*. Menu €14.

Gazebo At *Hotel Moderno*, Via Cavour 31. Of the cluster of open-air terrace restaurants on this pedestrianized street, *Gazebo* is nicer than most. The food is broadly similar to that of its near-neighbours – soups, pasta and lake fish – but the service is genial and the atmosphere pleasant. Menu around €20. No closing day.

Osteria degli Amici Via A.M. Bolongaro 31. Across the main square, on tiny Piazza Possi, this cosy nook

For its simplicity, diversity and superb scenery, the **Lago Maggiore Express** ticket (ⓦwww.lagomaggioreexpress.com) is one of the best round-trip excursions on the lakes. It comprises three sectors, all of them great journeys in their own right: a long **boat trip** on Maggiore, the stunning **Centovalli railway** between Locarno and Domodossola (for more on this, see p.170), and a **fast train** on the historic Simplon line between Domodossola and Stresa.

The schedules are flexible: you can start and end wherever you like, making your own choice of connections, and you can also do the trip in either direction. The whole thing could take as little as six hours – or you could dawdle over it for a couple of days.

Note that this is not a tour: you are on your own, using **public transport**. You should carry your **passport** (the route crosses into Switzerland) and also check the timetables carefully for the validity of each part of the trip. You must reserve ahead for any **hydrofoil** journeys (and pay a small supplement). On certain boats – marked on the timetables – **lunch** is served for a set price (€15).

Timetables

The journey is possible in spring (mid-March to May Thurs–Sun), summer (June to mid-Sept daily) and autumn (mid-Sept to mid-Oct Sat & Sun). However, because of the big weekly market in Luino (see p.162), different timetables operate on **Wednesdays**, for which either specific itineraries are published (and labelled as Wed only) or specific journeys on a general timetable are coded as Wednesdays only. There are also different itineraries in play depending on whether you're travelling in the **spring/summer** period or the **autumn** period. Double-check that you're consulting the right itinerary for your intended trip.

Fares and itineraries

The complete round-trip in **one day**, in either direction and from any starting-point, costs €30 (from Switzerland, about Fr.48). The **two-day** pass, which allows you to break your journey overnight anywhere on the route and also includes free boat travel on the whole of Lake Maggiore, is €36 (F.r58).

A dizzying sixteen **itineraries** have been devised, starting from different points, running in alternative directions and covering various days of validity – but all that matters is your starting-point. From this key bit of information, the website makes it easy to research your options, or you could leave it until you arrive: local tourist offices have full details of the various routings applicable from their town.

Below, and at relevant points throughout this chapter, we've given **example routings**, which use timetables current at the time of writing; check for up-to-date timings before you set out.

Starting from Stresa

Heading clockwise from **Stresa** (on **Itinerary 7**) involves a train at either 9am or 10.15am. You get a break for coffee in Domodossola before the scenic train ride to Locarno, arriving in time for lunch (or opt for a later train). The boat back departs Locarno at 4.15pm, arriving Stresa 7.10pm. The anticlockwise alternative involves departing by boat at 11.15am (eating lunch on board), taking a couple of hours in Locarno and dinner at Domodossola, arriving back at Stresa at 10.30pm; or, with quicker changes, you could be back in Stresa by 6.45pm.

See the relevant accounts throughout this chapter for outlines of the itineraries from Pallanza, Cánnero/Cannóbio and Locarno. It's easy to put together a trip starting from other points on the lake, too.

is a simple place with an attractive vine-covered terrace, serving tasty *risotti* and fish, plus excellent pizza. Service can be a tad slow. Closed Wed.
Piemontese Via Mazzini 25 ℡ 0323.30.235, ⓦ www.ristorantepiemontese.com. Some of the best cooking Stresa has to offer – light, artfully presented traditional Piedmont dishes, served in an elegant dining room or pleasant garden. Expensive. Closed Mon & Dec–Feb.
Stendhal At *Villa Dal Pozzo*, Belgirate (see p.127) ℡ 0322.7255, ⓦ www.villadalpozzo.com. Drive a few minutes south of Stresa to this exclusive hillside hideaway, for classic Milanese cuisine – *ossobuco*, saffron risotto, and more – served with panache in a splendidly formal setting overlooking the lake. Expect €50 and up. Closed Mon.

Taverna del Pappagallo Via Principessa Margherita 46. Busy, intimate pizzeria with an open wood fire and excellent, low-priced pizzas. Closed Wed.
Villa Aminta Via Sempione Nord 123 ℡ 0323.933.818, ⓦ www.villa-aminta.it. Showy five-star deluxe spa hotel on the lakefront road 1km north of Stresa. Come here less for the rooms than for the terrace restaurant *Le Isole*, which offers the single finest view of Lake Maggiore's islands. Book well in advance for a table at the balustrade: the panorama, gazing over the floodlit palazzo of Isola Bella to the right, Isola dei Pescatori to the left, Isola Madre set back between them, and the lights of Pallanza glittering opposite, is pure lakes romance. The menu of lake staples – with notably good fish – is around €45.

Isole Borromee (Borromeo islands)

However fanciful the Isola Bella may be, it still is beautiful. Anything springing out of that blue water, with that scenery around it, must be.

Charles Dickens, *Pictures from Italy* (1846)

Lake Maggiore's leading attractions are three lush **islands** rising from the waters of the bay between Stresa and Pallanza. All three are often dubbed the **ISOLE BORROMEE**, although, strictly speaking, only two are Borromeo property.

Each island is markedly different. The most celebrated is **Isola Bella**, just offshore at Stresa and taken up by a Baroque *palazzo* and formal terraced gardens that are the epitome of Italian lake beauty. Behind, in open water nearer to Pallanza, is the larger **Isola Madre**, occupied by a modest villa, with gardens that are wilder than its twin. These two were acquired by the Borromeo family in the sixteenth century. A stone's throw northwest of Isola Bella is the slender **Isola Superiore**, also known as **Isola dei Pescatori** – once the residence of fisherfolk and still a characterful little nook, with its narrow lanes and old houses.

Romantics will be knocked for six. The atmospheric journey by boat from Stresa, as the Baroque terraces of Isola Bella rise from the water, is fantasy brought to life. Views of the *palazzo* from different angles, as your boat circles to approach the porticoes and shuttered windows of Isola dei Pescatori, are delightful. The drawback, inevitably, is the **crowds**. All summer long, the islands are crawling with people; boats are packed to the gunwales and the quays are shoulder-to-shoulder. Both Isola Bella (outside the *palazzo* walls) and Isola dei Pescatori are spoiled by ranks of cheap souvenir shops and touristy cafés. Nowhere can you escape company entirely, although you'll have the best chance on Isola Madre, the quietest of the three.

Public **ferries** shuttle frequently in both directions between all three islands, connecting to Stresa, Carciano, Baveno and Pallanza on the mainland. Private boat operators at every village jetty offer negotiable rates for excursions to any or all of the islands.

Members of the British **Royal Horticultural Society** (ⓦ www.rhs.org.uk) can show their membership cards to get free admission to both Isola Bella and Isola Madre.

Isola Bella

The poet Robert Southey reckoned **Isola Bella** "one of the most costly efforts of bad taste in all Italy". Bad taste or good, it is undoubtedly an extravagant display of wealth and power. In the mid-sixteenth century the Borromeo family, who had already acquired Isola Madre, turned their attention to what was a rocky islet of fishermen's houses, known at the time as Isola Inferiore. They bought up land piecemeal, slowly moving residents off the island and renaming it in 1630 "Isola Isabella", after the wife of Carlo III Borromeo – a mouthful that was soon shortened to Isola Bella.

Under Carlo's guidance, the architect Giovanni Angelo Crivelli designed terraces for the gardens and laid foundations for a grand house at the northern end of the island. In 1659, Carlo's son, Vitaliano VI Borromeo, hired a new architect, Francesco Castelli, and the *palazzo* as it stands today began to take shape, with its grand salons, chapels and sumptuous galleries. Andrea Biffi took over in 1671, and it was under his stewardship that the palace and its monumental gardens became imbued with the High Baroque taste. Vitaliano died in 1690 with most of the work completed, although the vast, unfinished Salone dominating the northern wing of the palace, based on the plans of the San Lorenzo basilica in Milan, was redesigned in 1781 and only completed under Vitaliano X Borromeo as late as 1958.

Visiting (mid-March to mid-Oct daily 9am–5.30pm; €11; joint ticket with Isola Madre €16.50; ☏0323.30.556, ⓦwww.borromeoturismo.it) needs a tolerant frame of mind. Even if grand houses and formal gardens are right up your alley, your patience may still be tested by the size and bustle of the crowds. The best advice is to organize your transport so you're already on the island when the *palazzo* opens in the morning; that way, you can have perhaps half an hour before the first of the tour groups arrives. Book online or by phone at least a day ahead for your own **guided tour** of the palace in English (€35; takes 35min), or pick up an **audioguide** (€2.50) at the entrance.

The palazzo

A tour begins at the piazza in front of the picturesque, stepped harbour, enclosed by three wings of the *palazzo*. To the right is the Borromeos' **private chapel**,

▲ Isola dei Pescatori

built in the 1840s and housing the twin-arched tomb of Vitaliano and Giovanni Borromeo carved from Carrara marble. Opposite, past the ticket office, is the **main staircase**, completed in 1680 with a barrel vault and, on the walls, large stucco crests. At the top is the large **Sala delle Medaglie** (room 3), named after ten gilded wooden tondi positioned high on the walls. This was used as a banqueting chamber; a large Murano crystal chandelier (1769) hangs above. On one side is the opulent **Sala del Trono** (Throne Room); on the other is the vast **Salone** (room 5), the largest room in the palace, three storeys high, with pillars supporting the dome vault. The colour scheme is stunning – areas of white stucco interspersed with fields of turquoise – with windows that look out over the water.

Beyond the Sala della Musica is the **Sala di Napoleone** (room 7), where the great man slept with his wife Josephine during a stay in 1797. A sequence of smaller, more intimate rooms extends round to room 12, the **Stanza dello Zuccarelli**, named after the artist who has several landscapes displayed here, alongside three English tapestries dating from the late sixteenth century. Room 14, the grand **Sala da Ballo** (Ballroom), is the last in this section: stairs descend to six remarkable **grottoes** (rooms 15–20), facing north down at the water level, each of which has walls, ceiling and floor covered by decorative patterns and mosaics in coloured stones. They were intended to be cool, informal retreats from the summer heat, and the effect is rather like exploring your way through dark, naturalistic caves – a mirror-image of the formal, furnished rooms above. After the Sixth Grotto, stairs head up again to the final sequence of rooms, ending with the long **Galleria degli Arazzi**, or Tapestry Gallery (room 24), lined with rich, exquisitely detailed sixteenth-century Flemish tapestries.

The gardens

You exit the palace in front of the **Atrio di Diana** (Diana's Atrium), a polygonal structure arranged around a statue of the goddess, with twin staircases leading up to a balustraded terrace. Beyond is the large, open **Piano della Canfora** (Camphor Terrace), which takes its name from a camphor tree planted by Vitaliano IX Borromeo in 1819. Exits to the right deliver you to the remnants of the old village that once occupied the island, but ahead lie the famous Italianate Baroque **gardens**, dotted with fountains and statues, and filled with orange and lemon trees, camellias, magnolias, box trees, laurels, cypresses and much more. The centrepiece, dead ahead, is the **Teatro Massimo**, a three-storey confection of shell-, mirror- and marble-encrusted grottoes, topped with a suitably melodramatic unicorn, mini-obelisks, and various Greek gods and cherubs in attendance. A flight of steps leads up to the topmost **terrace**, where you can stand at the balustrade, 37m above the lake waters, and enjoy uninterrupted views on all sides. Below, the easternmost end of the island is taken up with the suitably named **Giardino d'Amore**, a parterre of four symmetrical beds framed by cone-shaped coniferous yews, with the octagonal Torre della Noria on the south side and Torre dei Venti on the north.

Isola dei Pescatori (Isola Superiore)

Hemingway's favourite island, **Isola dei Pescatori** (or Isola Superiore), lies within spitting distance of Isola Bella and the shore. Despite the invasions of sightseers, there are no sights as such, although the island has kept its cluster of old houses (about fifty people live here year-round) and retains a certain charm. Along with the obligatory trinket stands and cafés there are a few ordinary bars and shops, and it's not hard to find a good spot for a scenic, waterside picnic.

The two most worthwhile **restaurants** are, to the west, the *Belvedere* (℡0323.32.292, ⓦwww.belvedere-isolapescatori.it; April–Oct; no closing day), and to the east the 🏯 *Verbano* (℡0323.30.408, ⓦwww.hotelverbano.it; no closing day). Both are charming, moderately priced places with shaded terraces at the water's edge, serving fresh fish. Booking is essential. Note that no public boats visit the island after about 7.20pm, so to stay for dinner you must arrange private transport with the *Verbano* (free after 7pm).

Isola Madre

Out in the bay is **Isola Madre**, larger but less visited than Isola Bella, with a small, tasteful *palazzo* and extensive gardens (mid-March to mid-Oct 9am–5.30pm; €10; joint ticket with Isola Bella €16.50; ⓦwww.borromeoturismo.it). The island was inhabited as early as 846 AD, when it was known for its olive trees and was dubbed the Isola San Vittore. By 998 it had become Isola Maggiore. It passed to the Borromeo family in the sixteenth century, and works proceeded slowly to build the villa and the azalea-rich, English-style gardens around it. By 1704 the island was being called Isola Madre, most likely after Margherita Trivulzio, mother of Renato I Borromeo.

The original landing-stage is on the north side of the island, from where a long, stepped avenue leads up to the house, but today ferries dock on the south side. Steps rise to a terrace level; to the left is a short walk around to a café-restaurant (where private boats dock), while the ticket office and entrance to the villa grounds are to the right. The free handout map describes a long circuit of the gardens, beginning at the ticket gate with the south-facing **Viale Africa**, lined with tropical exotics including lemons, magnolias and carob trees. Break the route, if you like, and head up the steps to your left to reach the house, or continue ahead along the **Piano delle Camelie** and through the various stages of this lovely garden; don't miss the **Piazzale dei Pappagalli**, home to a colony of parrots and peacocks and a magnificent, thirty-metre-high fragrant magnolia. In front of the house is the **Loggia del Cashmir**, where rises the single largest example of a Kashmir cypress tree in Europe, over two hundred years old.

The Borromeo family have furnished the **villa** with various historical bits and bobs taken from their other houses – a doll collection here, a four-poster bed there; this is much more appealing than Isola Bella, with none of the pomposity and grandeur. Room 6 holds scenery and puppets from the island's eighteenth-century **Teatro delle Marionette**, while room 15 is the beautiful **Salotto Veneziano** (Venetian Drawing-Room), with elaborate Rococo wall decoration imitating a floral canopy.

Turning right on exiting the house brings you to the charming **Piazzale della Cappella**, centred on a pond with pink, red, white and yellow water-lilies and a hibiscus. Coffee, mimosa and banana plants add to the allure, with the little **Mortuary Chapel** on one side, dating from 1858. Steps lead down to the landing-stage past the **Viale delle Palme**, a line of giant palms interspersed with *Ginkgo biloba*.

Baveno

BAVENO, 4km north of Stresa, is a soporific little town, catching some of its bigger neighbour's overspill but not offering a great deal itself. It made – and, to a certain extent, still makes – a living from its **quarries**, which show themselves in stark white gashes in the slopes behind the town. Aside from quartz, the most famous stone to be quarried here is **pink Baveno granite**, used in the building of St Paul's in Rome and the Galleria Vittorio Emanuele in Milan – one of sixty-odd varieties found nearby (including a particular local mineral, bavenite).

Baveno's Art-Nouveau landing-stage is one of the nicest on the lake. Directly opposite, across the main road, in the town hall on Piazza Dante Alighieri, is the **tourist office** (April–Sept Mon–Sat 9am–12.30pm & 3–6pm, Sun 9am–noon; restricted hours in winter; ℡0323.924.632, ⓦwww.distrettolaghi.it). A tight-packed web of picturesque residential alleys surrounds the square. Baveno holds some fine nineteenth-century villas – in 1879 Queen Victoria stayed in what is now called the Villa Branca – and the church, **Santi Gervasio e Protasio**, retains its eleventh-century square facade, with Roman inscriptions adorning many of the re-used stones and a fifth-century baptistry alongside.

Sporty kids will love Baveno's **Adventure Park**, Strada Cavalli 18 (July & Aug daily 10am–11pm; May & June daily 10am–7pm; March, April, Sept & Oct Sat & Sun 10am–7pm; ⓦwww.lagomaggioreadventurepark.com), with a climbing wall, rope walks, a mountain-bike trail and more. An adult and a child together pay from €25 to €50, depending on the number of activities selected.

Lake Mergozzo

Beyond Baveno, Lake Maggiore ends at an expanse of reeds and marshes at the mouth of the River Toce. The main road bends right to hug the shore towards Verbania, while the autostrada and rail line dodge either side of the bulbous **Mont'Orfano** (794m) – named for its orphan status, remote from nearby peaks – on their way north to Domodossola. Omegna, at the head of Lake Orta (see p.156), lies 7km south of **GRAVELLONA TOCE**, the main town hereabouts.

Behind the marshes, and loomed over by Mont'Orfano, is the titchy **Lake Mergozzo** (**Lago di Mergozzo**), which formed part of Maggiore until silt from the Toce built up in the ninth century. It is now a free-standing tarn cut off from its giant neighbour, cool, clean and very deep. A road runs along its eastern shore; the wooded western slopes are steep, but hold the scenic Sentiero Azzurro footpath linking the hamlet of Montorfano in fifteen minutes with **MERGOZZO** at the head of the lake, an attractive old village with some interesting lanes to poke around in. Mergozzo would be a perfect location for a romantic little bistro at the water's edge; hopes rise when you spot terrace tables, but crash when you realize they belong only to the tacky *Birreria Freelance* pub. Mergozzo's hotels are similarly disappointing.

The best **restaurant** is on the lakeshore road, partway between Mergozzo and the village of Fondotoce – the atmospheric ⚜ *Piccolo Lago* (℡0323.586.792, ⓦwww.piccololago.it). It has been in the same family for forty years, now run by chef Marco Sacco and his sommelier brother Carlo. The interior is modern and airy, with picture windows, and service is smooth and discreet; this is a fine spot for a gastronomic seduction. Marco's cuisine combines Piemonte mountain cooking with the more sophisticated flavours of lake cuisine – for example, Mergozzo trout, lightly smoked in-house, or a flan of the local Bettelmatt cheese with a pear mustard. Pasta (such as chestnut-flour tagliatelle) is all home-made. Menus cost upwards of €75.

For now, the brothers are concentrating on the restaurant: across the road, the *Piccolo Lago*'s unrenovated **hotel** rooms (❸) are merely three-star. They're en suite, clean and quiet; free parking, access to the private beach and equal proximity to Stresa and Pallanza are all plus points.

Pallanza (Verbania)

The largest town on this stretch of the lake, **Verbania** is a modern conceit, formed in 1939 in a fit of Fascist zeal by "uniting" the old lakeside neighbours of Pallanza and Intra with nearby Suna, Fondotoce and a few inland villages and giving the project a grandiose title intended to evoke the Roman name for Lake Maggiore, *Lacus Verbanus*. The outcome is that Verbania is a will-o'-the-wisp: despite its appearance on maps and bus timetables, no actual town exists with that name. Pallanza, Intra and the others maintain their own clear identities and territories.

With a characterful old quarter set back from its *imbarcadero*, **Intra** is a bustling commercial town and transport hub, looking east across the lake. By contrast **PALLANZA** is a lovely, placid little resort, facing south over the bay and revelling in some beautiful views, exceptional sunsets and a balmy winter climate. The main road cuts inland, bypassing the centre of Pallanza, which has, as a result, one of the quietest and most attractive waterfronts on the whole of Maggiore. There's very little to do other than relax in the sunshine, sample the local restaurants, take the odd boat-trip and stroll in the lavish gardens of **Villa Táranto** nearby – a perfect Italian Lakes holiday.

Arrival, information and accommodation

From Milan, the most direct route by **car** to Pallanza is the A26 autostrada to Gravellona Toce, 10km west. "Verbania-Pallanza FS" station – on the same **train** line as Stresa, with fast services from Milan (Centrale and Porta Garibaldi) – lies 8km west of town, on the main road between Fondotoce and Gravellona, served by taxis or bus #2 every thirty minutes. From **Milan-Malpensa airport** (Terminal 1, stop 22), SAF's Alibus runs five times daily (April–Oct only) to Suna, Pallanza and Intra (€11.50; booking essential 48hr ahead by phone or online; ☎0323.552.172, ⓦwww.safduemila.com). Alibus also runs all year round from Malpensa (Terminal 1, stop 12) to Gravellona Toce (€9). Pallanza and Intra are served by frequent **boats**, and Intra has the lake's only **car ferry**, shuttling to Laveno, from where Varese (see p.143) is just 22km further. Full details of lake transport are on p.124.

Pallanza's main **tourist office** is by the old harbour at Corso Zanitello 8 (April–Sept daily 9am–1pm & 3–6pm; Oct–March Mon–Fri 9am–1pm, Mon, Tues & Thurs also 3–5.30pm; ☎0323.503.249, ⓦwww.distrettolaghi.it). There are smaller offices at the Pallanza *imbarcadero*, Via delle Magnolie 1 (Mon–Sat 8.30–11.30am & 2–7pm; ☎0323.557.676, ⓦwww.verbania-turismo.it), and the Intra *imbarcadero* (Wed–Sun 9am–12.30pm & 2–5.30pm). All can advise on attractions in the town, as well as walks and excursions in the mountainous Val Grande National Park, which spreads north towards the Swiss border.

> ### Lago Maggiore Express
>
> See p.130 for details of the **Lago Maggiore Express** excursion ticket. Clockwise from **Pallanza** (following **Itinerary 9**), you start at 9.30am with a short boat ride to Baveno, where you pick up the train to Domodossola and then have the choice of the scenic Centovalli railway straight to Locarno, arriving just after 1pm for a leisurely lunch, or a slightly longer time in Domodossola and then an hour's break in the middle of the Centovalli trip at the mountain village of Santa Maria Maggiore (where you can grab a quick bite). Either way, your boat departs Locarno at 4.15pm, arriving back at Pallanza at 6.50pm. The alternative routing anticlockwise involves an 11.35am lunch-boat departure, returning at 6.35pm or 7.40pm, depending on how long you choose to break the journey in Locarno or Domodossola.

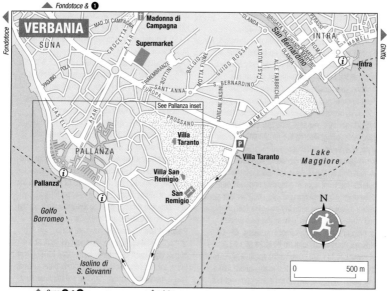

RESTAURANTS

Bolongaro	3
Dam a Traa	2
Il Burchiello	4
Milano	5
Piccolo Lago	1

ACCOMMODATION

Grand Hotel Majestic	E
Novara	C
Ostello Villa Congreve	D
Pallanza	B
Pesce d'Oro	A

Hotels

Grand Hotel Majestic Via V. Veneto 32
℗ 0323.504.305, Ⓦ www.grandhotelmajestic.it. For
once, a grand hotel that lives up to the name. A
traditional establishment of the old school which
ticks all the boxes – magnificent waterfront
location, impressive history (dating from 1870),
Belle Epoque architecture without flummery or
bombast, beautiful English-style grounds, state-of-
the-art facilities and staff who are formal but
accommodating. Rooms are furnished in classic
style, many with balconies, and most with lake
views (either side or front). Most significantly of all,
almost no traffic passes within earshot: the road
outside the front door is a narrow one-way lane
used chiefly by walkers and cyclists. This fact alone
raises it well above similarly styled hotels on this
and other lakes. Come to hear the lake waters
lapping and the parquet floors creaking. ⑥–⑨
Novara Piazza Garibaldi 30 ℗ 0323.503.527,
Ⓦ www.hotelnovara.com. Well-kept little hotel in
the centre of Pallanza, on the main square just a
few steps from the lake. Rooms are compact but
clean and attractive, and the welcome is warm. ②
Ostello Villa Congreve (HI hostel) Via alle Rose
7 ℗ 0323.501.648, Ⓦ www.aighostels.com &
Ⓦ www.ostelloverbania.it. The only hostel on Lake
Maggiore, a short, signposted walk uphill from the
tourist office. It's a friendly place set in an old
hillside villa, with en-suite rooms and small dorms
(€16); the staff also organize activities in the area.
Mid-March to Oct. ①

Pallanza Viale Magnolie 8 ℗ 0323.503.202,
Ⓦ www.pallanzahotels.com. An excellent
four-star hotel, on the Pallanza waterfront just
across from the *imbarcadero*. The building dates
from the early 1900s, but has been entirely
renovated inside – rooms are fresh, airy, characterful and spacious. Make sure you have a lake
view, preferably on a balconied upper floor:
windows face southwest towards Isola Madre and
Baveno, and the late afternoons are sensational, as
the sun, framed in the Toce valley, sinks behind the
peaks of Monte Rosa. Service is cheerful and
efficient, and there is parking available (though the
spaces on the street are free). ④
Pesce d'Oro Via Troubetzkoy 136, Suna
℗ 0323.504.445, Ⓦ www.hotelpescedoro.it. About
10min walk west of Pallanza in the little township of
Suna, this is a decent three-star family hotel in what
was a monastery dating from the sixteenth century.
Rooms are good, if a little generic, but the personal
touch is what marks this place out as special – the
Piazza family have been owners and managers for
30 years, and have created a warm, friendly environment for their guests. ②–③

The Town

Pallanza's pedestrianized waterfront is centred on the dapper **Piazza Garibaldi**:
boats dock here, most hotels are within a short stroll, and both tourist offices
are nearby, the main one overlooking the old harbour, another at the *imbarcadero*.
The broad piazza is flanked by terrace cafés and restaurants. It's a sociable spot:
families and old-timers chat their afternoons away under the trees, while the
kids play in the fountains. As dusk falls, join in the *passeggiata* to and fro along
the lakeside Viale delle Magnolie adjacent.

Attractions are few: nose your way around the alleys, and up Via Ruga to the
Museo del Paesaggio (April–Oct Tues–Sun 10am–noon & 3.30–6.30pm;
€2.50), which holds late nineteenth- and early twentieth-century landscape
paintings of the area, as well as sculpture and some archeological finds. Via
Ruga – and the pedestrian zone – end at **Piazza Gramsci**, site of the post
office and bus stops. Beyond here, well north of the centre on Viale Azari, is
the Renaissance **Madonna di Campagna** (daily 9am–noon & 4–6pm), with
an unusual octagonal arcaded lantern and Romanesque bell-tower and, inside,
sixteenth-century frescoes attributed to the school of Gerolamo Lanino.

Apart from Villa Táranto (see below), Pallanza has two fine **gardens**. Beside
the main tourist office is **Villa Giulia**, built in 1847 and renovated in Art-
Nouveau fashion in 1904; its grounds, landscaped in English style, are open to
the public. Signposted on the slopes above the town is **Villa San Remigio**,
with rhododendron-rich gardens designed in 1916; visits, which include the
fine Romanesque hilltop **oratory** – with its eleventh-century frescoes – are
possible only by booking with the tourist office.

Villa Táranto

Pallanza's major attraction is the garden of **Villa Táranto**. The house, built in 1875, was bought in 1931 by Captain Neil McEacharn, scion of a wealthy Scottish industrial family, who spotted an advert for it in *The Times*. Over decades, McEacharn landscaped and cultivated the grounds of the villa, planting seeds gathered from around the world and establishing an extraordinarily rich and varied botanical garden. He died at Villa Táranto in 1964 and is buried in a mausoleum in the grounds.

The villa has its own landing-stage, a stop for virtually all Stresa–Intra **boats**, though it can also be reached from Pallanza **on foot** on Via Vittorio Veneto (takes about 30min); alternatively, **rent a bike** (€12 per day) from *Gelateria Oasi*, Via Ruga 15. Via Veneto is a narrow, lakefront road which leads from the old harbour around the headland; it is one-way for cars towards Pallanza – but most traffic is diverted elsewhere and virtually no vehicles use it. On the way, you'll pass the tiny **Isolino di San Giovanni**, an offshore islet owned by the Borromeo; its villa, once a favoured haunt of Toscanini, has no public access.

You arrive at Villa Táranto's *imbarcadero*, with a free parking area alongside. The **ticket office** (April–Oct daily 8.30am–6.30pm; €8.50; Ⓦ www.villataranto.it) stands at the entrance gate beside a pleasant terrace **café/restaurant**. There are 7km of paths winding around these beautiful grounds, with the free map leading you past the delightful **Fontana dei Putti** (cherub fountain) to the dahlia garden and the greenhouses holding giant Amazonian lilies. Further round is the **Valletta**, a little valley created in 1935, with a charming arched bridge, and a set of **terraced gardens** with a field of **lotus** flowers. Give yourself at least an hour, if not a half-day, to take it all in. The villa itself – now off-limits at one end of the gardens – is the seat of the Provincia di Verbano-Cusio-Ossola.

Eating and drinking

Pallanza's **eating** options are, on the whole, decent, middle-of-the-road sorts of places, neither sophisticated nor especially noteworthy. The exception is the *Milano*, Corso Zanitello 2 (Ⓣ 0323.556.816; closed Mon eve & Tues), an expensive restaurant in a quiet, romantic setting, with terrace tables overlooking the old harbour. Their small menu of fish and pasta staples is done exceptionally well, but expect a bill of €75 per head and upwards. In the same vein is the nearby *Piccolo Lago* (see p.135), just west of Pallanza on Lake Mergozzo.

Such extravagance aside, the most pleasant of Pallanza's array of waterfront restaurants is the *Bolongaro*, Piazza Garibaldi 9, where you can choose pizza or fairly standard mains from a mid-priced menu. *Il Burchiello*, Corso Zanitello 3 (Ⓦ www.ilburchiello.eu; closed Wed), is a fresh, friendly little spot with a contemporary feel that specializes in fish and seafood – try the fettucine with octopus, or just go for the catch of the day. Their menu is €15, and they host live music on Fridays. In Suna, 1km west of Pallanza, the busy waterfront *Hostaria Dam a Traa*, Via Troubetzkoy 106, is popular with locals, with a chic interior and a sunny terrace. Back in Pallanza, for a sociable drink try *Birreria Stregatto*, Via Cadorna 20 (closed Mon), set around an attractive courtyard and open until after midnight.

For coverage of Lake Maggiore **north** of Verbania, turn to p.156.

Southern Lake Maggiore

The southern reaches of Lake Maggiore peter out bathetically into reedy inlets; the horizons are low and undistinguished, and there are few attractions compared to the natural beauty further north. The highlight of the area is the hermitage of **Santa Caterina del Sasso**, wedged into the rocky cliffs opposite Stresa. On the western shore, the few little communities south of Stresa are pretty enough, but blighted somewhat by the traffic on the lakeside road; the major town of this part of the lake is **Arona**, eminently missable. The eastern shore is notable chiefly for the stout **Rocca Borromeo** castle, which dominates **Angera**.

Santa Caterina del Sasso

Tucked into the cliffs on the eastern, Lombard shore of the lake, and connected by regular boats to Stresa, is the hermitage of **SANTA CATERINA DEL SASSO** (April–Oct daily 8.30am–noon & 2.30–6pm; rest of year 9am–noon & 2–5pm; Nov–Feb closed Mon–Fri; free; Ⓦ www.provincia.va.it/santacaterina). This beautiful little monastic complex – visible only from the water – is well worth a visit for its frescoes and its sense of tranquillity, but make sure you come at opening time: for most of the day crowds swamp the place. Arriving by boat involves climbing **80 steps** from the landing-stage; or there's a parking area on the clifftop road between Leggiuno and Reno, from where **268 steps** lead down to the hermitage.

The site dates back to 1170, when Alberto Besozzi, from nearby Arolo, was shipwrecked in a storm, invoked the help of St Catherine of Alexandria and survived; he subsequently withdrew to a cave here, in the cliff of Sasso Bàllaro, to devote his life to prayer. Local townspeople began construction of a votive chapel shortly afterwards, and the complex grew. By 1620 fourteen monks lived here, but a suppression decree in 1770 forced the last six out. The sanctuary crumbled until it was declared a national monument in 1914 and restored. Today, it is home to a Carmelite monk and seven oblates.

The complex is tiny: you could walk from one end to the other in three minutes. The steps from above and below meet at the lovely **entrance gallery** (1624), with arches looking out over the lake, which leads to the **South Convent**. Inside, opposite the giftshop, is the Gothic **Chapterhouse**, decorated with frescoes including a pristine image from 1439 of St Eligius healing a horse. A door gives onto a small courtyard; ahead, beneath the four Gothic arches of the **Small Convent** (1315) is the **church**, with its stubby Romanesque bell tower and graceful Renaissance porch. Dating from 1587, this is a movingly quiet and holy space. A fresco of *God the Father*, dated 1610, adorns the Baroque vault above the high altar; around the church are other, older examples. A rear chapel, dedicated to the Blessed Alberto, is known as the **Chapel of the Rocks**: five massive boulders fell through the roof around 1700 and became lodged, as if miraculously, above this chapel, supported by the vaulting. They stayed that way for two centuries, finally crashing to the floor in 1910 (and were removed in 1983).

Arona

South of Stresa, the road hugs the lakeshore for 16km to **ARONA**, the major town at the south end of the lake. It's a busy, humdrum place which makes few concessions to tourism. The *imbarcadero* is in the centre, at one end of the main waterfront road **Corso della Repubblica**; at the other, past 300m of car parks, is the **train station**.

There's a **map** of Lake Maggiore on p.122. For details of the **boats**, see p.124.

From the *imbarcadero*, head right onto the old quarter's central shopping street, **Via Cavour** – past upmarket handbag and fashion boutiques. Via Cavour ends at the broad **Piazza del Popolo**, Arona's prettiest square, adorned with the Gothic arches of the fifteenth-century **Casa del Podestà** – but tainted by having traffic channelled along one side. The views from here across the water to the Rocca Borromeo castle above Angera are sensational. On the slopes high above Arona rises a 35-metre-high, hollow, bronze **statue of San Carlo Borromeo** – an archbishop of Milan (1560–1584) who was canonized in 1610 – blessing the town; you can climb steps inside (April–Sept daily 8.30am–12.30pm & 2–6.30pm; shorter hours in winter; €6.50) to look out of his eyes and – bizarrely – his ears and nose too.

From the *imbarcadero*, head up Via Gramsci and turn right to find the **tourist office** (Tues–Sat 9.30am–12.30pm & 3–6pm, Sun 9.30am–12.30pm; ☏0322.243.601), within the *municipio* (town hall) on Piazza De Filippi. *Piccolo*, Via Cavour 30 (closed Thurs), is a modern **café** with music and good coffee; nearby is *Osteria degli Acrobati*, Piazza San Graziano 30, a popular spot for light bites. Arona's top **restaurant** is *Taverna del Pittore*, Piazza del Popolo 39 (☏0322.243.366; closed Mon), a rather stiff place to savour the best of lake cuisine for €50 and up; *Al Cantuccio*, opposite at no. 1 (closed Mon), has good food at half the cost. At the *Florida*, a characterful **hotel** at Piazza del Popolo 32 (☏0322.46.212; ❷), let the genial manager show you to the airy old rooms, some of which have balconies on the square.

Angera: the Rocca Borromeo

Directly opposite Arona, tucked into a creek on the Lombard shore, is the smaller, more characterful town of **ANGERA**. Boats shuttle frequently between the two; the road journey is 16km around the end of the lake, past malls, multiplex cinemas and camping superstores, crossing a bridge over the Ticino at Sesto Calende. Boats dock in Angera at Piazzale della Vittoria, alongside the long Piazza Garibaldi.

Signposted on the hilltop above the town is the **Rocca Borromeo** (mid-March to mid-Oct daily 9am–5.30pm; €7.50; ⓦwww.borromeoturismo.it), a rare example of a medieval fortress totally preserved in its original form. Built in the eleventh century and expanded by the Visconti in the fourteenth, the castle was bought in 1449, along with Angera town, by Vitaliano I Borromeo for the vast sum of 12,800 lire; it became a key point of defence for the Lombards against the Swiss. Extensively refurbished in the seventeenth century, it remains a fine old building, its towers and swallow-tail battlements crowning the wooded hill.

From the car park just below the walls, you walk up to enter the castle; ahead is the café, while under the arch (which forms part of the fifteenth-century **Borromeo Wing**), is the giftshop and steep, cobbled internal courtyard. You climb the slope in front of the **Della Scala Wing**, faced in bleak Angera stone; in the left corner is the mighty **Torre Principale**, dating from the twelfth century. As you come round to the left, you face the **Visconti Wing**, with arched windows and a small double staircase. Left of here, pass through an elegant seventeenth-century triple-arched portico in the Borromeo Wing and turn to the right to climb the staircase into the fortress. At the top of the stairs, ahead lie half a dozen grand rooms filled with Borromeo family portraits, but if you double back on yourself you'll find the stunning **Sala di Giustizia** (Law Court), a large room with two fluted cross-vaults. Its six bays, each with mullioned windows, are covered by a thirteenth-century fresco cycle showing the Visconti success at the Battle of Desio in 1277, with the military exploits related, in the upper registers, to the signs of the zodiac. Wooden stairs at the far end climb to the top of the Torre Principale, for spectacular lake views.

Ground-floor rooms in the Visconti Wing, and a doorway beside the entrance arch in the Borromeo Wing, are given over to the diverting **Museo della Bambola** (Doll Museum), one of the most complete collections in Europe, while the Della Scala Wing holds the **Museo della Moda Infantile** (Children's Fashion).

North to Laveno

A kilometre or two north of Angera on the quiet lakeside road is **RANCO**, just about the sleepiest of all the lake's sleepy little corners. Virtually no traffic passes – Ranco lies 2.5km down a turning off the main lakeside highway – and there are just two boats a day: one in the morning to Stresa, one in the evening to Arona. There is literally nothing to do, other than bask in the sun and stroll through the well-tended waterside gardens. The lovely old **hotel** *Il Sole* (T0331.976.507, Wwww.ilsolediranco.it; ❽) capitalizes fully on this, with a range of traditionally styled suites – luxurious, but a little fussy for some tastes – beautiful grounds and a Michelin-starred gourmet **restaurant** (closed Mon & Tues).

Otherwise, there is little reason to turn off the main road north out of Angera, which passes through placid **Ispra**, headquarters for research institutes attached to the European Commission. At **Leggiuno**, there is a turnoff to a clifftop car park, from where steps lead down to **Santa Caterina del Sasso** (see p.140).

Roughly 22km north of Angera, and 25km south of Luino (see p.162), **LAVENO** is an industrial town and transport hub. **Car ferries** shuttle continuously across to Intra on the western lake shore (see p.136), and the town has two **train stations**: Laveno-Mombello, 1km south of the centre, is on the line between Luino and Gallarate (change at Gallarate for Milano Porta Garibaldi), while Laveno-Mombello Nord, in the town centre, is a terminus for trains from Varese and Milano Cadorna/Nord.

Val Cúvia

From Laveno major roads head south to Varese and Malpensa airport. A good reason to drive this way is to branch off into the pretty **Val Cúvia** that runs parallel to the shore between Monte Nudo (1236m) and the protected area of Campo dei Fiori (1226m). The valley-floor road, flanked by forests of chestnut, connects Laveno with Luino (see p.162).

In **CASALZUIGNO**, 10km from Laveno and 16km from Luino, is the **Villa della Porta Bozzolo** (Wed–Sun 10am–6pm; Oct–Feb closes 5pm; closed late Dec & Jan; €5; free to UK National Trust cardholders; Wwww.fondoambiente.it), a magnificent eighteenth-century Lombard country villa. It's a pleasure to wander freely in the cool rooms of the house and through to the older seventeenth-century wing. Salons to the left of the entrance hold a billiard table and a piano, but the most impressive room is the **library**, with a huge desk on a dais. Upstairs are stone-flagged bedrooms with their original furnishings. The terraced Italian **gardens** are splendid, with an avenue of oaks, a frescoed temple, and more.

Just east of the turnoff to the villa, a minor road climbs for 3km to **ARCUMEGGIA** – a steep, narrow lane which switchbacks dangerously: you'll barely be able to get out of first gear. In the 1950s, the locals invited leading Italian artists of the day to fresco the village's stone cottages; the combination of the mountain setting and the art is an alluring one. Beyond Arcumeggia, mountain roads continue over the ridge and down to Porto Valtravaglia on the lake.

Varese

VARESE gets short shrift from visitors, despite its location plum in the centre of the Lakes region – roughly equidistant from Como, Lugano and Lake Maggiore. The reasons for heading inland to this commercial hub aren't immediately obvious – yet Varese, the so-called "**Città Giardino**" (Garden City), has a good deal more to offer than might be expected.

When the railway arrived from Milan – the State line in 1865, and the Nord line in 1886 – Varese became a favoured spot for wealthy Milanese to build their holiday homes. The fashion coincided with the flowering of Art Nouveau (known in Italy as "**Liberty**"), and to this day Varese's outskirts are filled with superb examples of Liberty architecture, in villas and grand hotels.

And the links with Milan went deeper: for Italians, Varese has long been indelibly associated with high fashion, principally shoes. Although the famous Trolli shoe family sold up to Benetton in 1995, and most of the city's shoe manufacturers have now departed, Varese retains its air of cool, fashion-conscious sophistication. With its gardens, its **Sacro Monte** of hillside chapels, superb contemporary art at **Villa Panza**, and the unexpected wonder of Florentine Renaissance frescoes in **Castiglione Olona**, Varese merits a stopover.

Arrival, information and accommodation

By **car**, Varese is on the A8 autostrada, an easy 45km north of Milan (and only 25km north of Milan-Malpensa airport). It is also 25km west of Como, 22km east of Laveno, and 33km south of Lugano. Varese's two **train** stations stand east of the centre. The **Stazione FS**, on Piazzale Trieste, handles trains from Milan – Porta Garibaldi and Porta Vittoria – with the **bus station** alongside. Just across the tracks, accessed from Viale Casula, is the **Stazione FNM** (listed on timetables as "Varese Nord"), midway on the line between Milano Cadorna Nord and Laveno-Mombello Nord on Lake Maggiore.

Varese's **tourist office** is behind the main square, at Via Carrobbio 2 (June–Sept Mon–Fri 9am–noon & 3–7pm, Sat 9am–noon & 3–6pm; Oct–May Mon–Fri 9am–noon & 3–6pm, Sat 9am–noon; ☏0332.252.412, ⓦwww .turismo.provincia.va.it).

Hotels in town

Bologna Via Broggi 7 ☏0332.234.362, ⓦwww.albergobologna.it. Great little family-run hotel and restaurant on the edge of the pedestrianized centre, set into what was a convent dating from 1550. Frills are few but the rooms are decent enough and there is private parking. ❸

Crystal Via Speroni 10 ☏0332.231.145, ⓦwww.crystal-varese.it. Centrally located four-star business hotel, with comfortable rooms and parking – a safe pair of hands if all else should fail. ❻

Hotels out of town

Borducan Via Beata Caterina Moriggi 43, Santa Maria del Monte ☏0332.222.916, ⓦwww .borducan.com. Quiet Liberty-style villa on the Sacro Monte hillside, with ten traditional, individually styled rooms, often split-level (connected by spiral stairs), some with balconies – but only modestly sized. This is an old building of great character: think creaking staircases, polished woods and welcoming service. See p.148 for some background. ❹–❺

Colonne Via Fincará 37, Santa Maria del Monte ☏0332.222.444, ⓦwww.hotelcolonnevarese.com. Alongside the Sacro Monte funicular top station, a

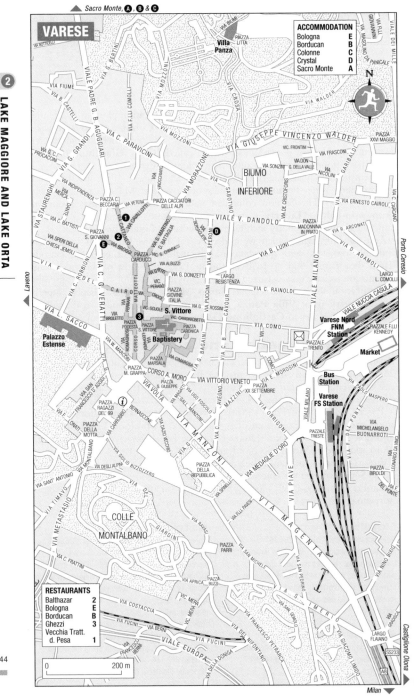

short walk from the *Borducan* (the two have the same owners). Rooms here are airy and very pleasant, especially those with balconies for the view over Varese, but they don't quite share the *Borducan*'s touch of class. ⑥

Sacro Monte Via Bianchi 5, Santa Maria del Monte ☎0332.228.194, ⓦ www.albergosacromonte.com. Superb value three-star hotel just below the Sacro Monte church – freshly modern, very quiet, with great views and excellent facilities. ❸

The City

Varese has a compact and elegant historic centre, comprising a tight cluster of pedestrianized streets spreading north from the main **Piazza Monte Grappa**, a spread of angular Fascist architecture dating from 1927. The stone-paved **Corso Matteotti** leads out of the square, with chic boutiques and cafés crowding beneath its arcades.

To one side is **San Vittore**, built in the late sixteenth century and adorned with a Neoclassical facade; its domed **campanile** is a seventeenth-century addition, and still bears the scars of the 1859 battle for the town, when Garibaldi faced down the Austrian army. Inside the church, the first chapel on the left holds a painting of a topless *Mary Magdalene* by Il Morazzone, painted in 1627 but long hidden from view on the grounds of decency. On the south side of the church, the twelfth-century **baptistry** (unlocked on request) – unusually quadrangular, not octagonal, and with a matroneum above the presbytery – holds a seventh-century font, recessed into the floor beneath a monolithic (and unfinished) tenth-century replacement. The remarkably fresh interior frescoes, dating from around 1325, include, on the south wall, all twelve apostles rendered in artistic style with personalized faces, and a *Crucifixion* on the east wall showing bird-like angels swooping down to an expressively suffering Christ.

A five-minute walk from Piazza Monte Grappa, on Via Marcobi-Via Sacco, stands **Palazzo Estense** (now the town hall), built in the 1760s by Francesco III d'Este, duke of Modena. Its extensive **gardens** are modelled on Vienna's Schönbrunn, with fountains and formal terraces. Adjacent is the wilder, lusher English-style garden of the **Villa Mirabello**, replete with grottoes, arbours and babbling streams. Both are open daily during daylight hours.

Villa Panza

A little north of Varese city centre, set amidst the Liberty villas in the hillside suburb of Biumo Superiore, is one of the region's most original art galleries. The sober, elegant, eighteenth-century Villa Menafoglio-Litta-Panza – or **Villa Panza** for short (Tues–Sun 10am–6pm; closed Jan; €8; free to UK National Trust cardholders; ⓦ www.fondoambiente.it) – donated to the nation in 1996 by its last owner, Count Giuseppe Panza, stands amidst beautiful gardens, with views of the Alps. Adorning its interior is the Count's world-class **contemporary art** collection. Give yourself a couple of hours to take it in.

The villa is well signposted from the centre, and is also served by city bus A from the train station and Piazza Monte Grappa (every 20min); it has free parking and a pleasant café.

The main house

Almost all the paintings in the **main house** are monochrome canvases by postwar American artists, big blocks of purple or silver or green, hanging – at first glance, incongruously – in rooms with ornate stucco ceilings and refined

Como (see p.178), Lugano (p.208), Milan-Malpensa airport (p.67) and Laveno on Lake Maggiore (p.142) are all easily reached from Varese by car or public transport.

Baroque furnishings. It's worth picking up a free **audioguide**: the outstanding English commentary explains works that might otherwise appear meaningless.

The **ground floor** includes a billiard room (room 4), hung with deep monochromes by Californian Phil Sims, and a sumptuous Empire Dining Hall (room 8), designed in 1829, with frescoes, a stucco ceiling, Classical columns and, now, two stunning acrylics – one black, one silver – by David Simpson.

On the **upper floor**, the left-hand wing has been cleared of furniture: one highlight is the Yellow Room (room 18), housing three large-scale works in black, white and yellow by Ford Beckman. The opposite wing retains furnishings from its time as the Panza family home. The most memorable space here is the dining room (room 27), with eight ethereal paintings by David Simpson, a fine sixteenth-century Tuscan table in walnut, and several African and pre-Columbian figurines set on the fifteenth-century Umbrian sideboard. This room, and the drawing room alongside, showcase the Count's remarkable taste for leavening an aristocratic lifestyle with what was, when he started buying it in the 1950s, deeply unfashionable art.

The rustici

The villa's **rustici** (outbuildings) house works that are site-specific – that is, the artists were invited to Villa Panza and created pieces designed to be seen in their specific location. Many are now owned by the Guggenheim Foundation.

Connecting to the villa's upper-floor galleries are rooms showcasing works by **Dan Flavin** (1933–96), the first artist to work exclusively with artificial light, in the form of fluorescent tubes. Off the first corridor (room 32) are rooms suffused with light from pink, red or blue tubes, in different configurations. Beyond is Flavin's *Varese Corridor* (room 36), a striking installation (press the button by the door to turn it on and off), with more rooms to either side. Don't miss works here by the conceptual artist Robert Irwin, notably the ghostly, intriguing *Varese Scrim* (room 43), as well as the extraordinary *Sky Space* by James Turrell (room 47). Room 48 holds a sound sculpture by Michael Brewster.

Stairs lead down to temporary exhibits. Make time for room 56 here, featuring a light installation by German artist Maria Nordman: you wait for a few minutes in a dim chamber before proceeding into the main room – apparently pitch-dark. Allowing your senses to adjust over, perhaps, ten minutes is a fittingly memorable conclusion to the villa's surprises.

Sacro Monte di Varese

On the northern outskirts rises the **Sacro Monte di Varese**, one of several "holy mountains" – comprising a series of hillside shrines dedicated to Mary – that were established across Lombardy and Piedmont during the Counter-Reformation. This hill, thickly wooded and topped by a convent, has been a centre of Christianity since the Dark Ages. In 1604, fourteen chapels were built in a coiling line up the hillside, each filled with frescoes and statuary on the Mystery of the Rosary, beginning with the Annunciation and ending with the Assumption. The route, known as the **Via Sacra**, was designed with enough space between each chapel – so the tale goes – for pilgrims to recite ten *Ave Marias*. These days, the broad, leafy path, still with its original cobbles and boasting fine views, is used as much by Sunday walkers loafing their way up the hill as by devotees who pray at each chapel. The path rises steeply, gaining 260m over a distance of 2.2km. Reckon on an hour to walk it all.

The start of the Via Sacra lies 5km north of Varese, accessed via Viale Aguggiari and marked by the **Primo Arco** (First Arch) and **Prima Cappella** (First Chapel). All the chapels are locked; to see inside press the light switch and peer

Hiking the Via Verde Varesina ("3V")

The mountainous area of the Provincia di Varese, lying between lakes Lugano and Maggiore, is the setting for the **Via Verde Varesina**, or "**3V**", one of the region's best long-distance footpaths. It was conceived to link the European E1 trail, which runs from Norway to Sicily (passing through Porto Ceresio on Lake Lugano), with the Grande Traversata Alpina, which ends on the western shore of Lake Maggiore. The 3V comprises **ten stages** – 134.5km in total – following a looping route from Porto Ceresio to the Sacro Monte di Varese, then on to Laveno, Arcumeggia and Luino, up to Monte Lema and down to Maccagno. All ten stages (complete with English route descriptions), plus five variations, are shown in detail on an excellent 1:35,000 **map** produced by DeAgostini for the Provincia di Varese, available from tourist offices. The ten traditional stages are all graded T (for "Tourist" – that is, easy); some of the variations are slightly harder. More information is at ⓦ www.provincia.va.it/3v.

through the window. At the top, the path ends at a bombastic nineteenth-century **Statue of Moses**, above which rise the blank walls of a convent that has housed a closed community of nuns since 1492. The convent church, **Santuario di Santa Maria del Monte** (daily 8am–noon & 2–6pm) – rebuilt in 1474 over the remnants of a fourth-century original – is accessed from a small piazza bearing a statue of Pope Paul VI. Its ornate Baroque interior holds a revered medieval Black Madonna in wood, purportedly fashioned by St Luke himself, while the adjacent **Cappella delle Beate** houses the shrine of Caterina and Giuliana, two local girls who founded the convent. A concealed upper corridor allows the nuns to pray unseen.

On the other side of the church is **SANTA MARIA DEL MONTE** village, looking out over the valley – a hundred or so people live here. Just below the church, **Museo Baroffio** (March–Oct Thurs, Sat & Sun 9.30am–12.30pm & 3–6.30pm; €3) holds some minor artworks, while **Museo Pogliaghi**, showing antiquities, has been undergoing restoration for years. A short walk down through the alleys brings you to a knot of hotel/restaurants beside the beautiful Liberty-style **funicular** station.

To reach the Sacro Monte, **bus** C (every 20min) runs from Varese city centre to the Prima Cappella; it continues either up the hill into the village (Mon–Fri) or to the base funicular station (Sat & Sun). The **funicular** operates daily in August (10am–7pm), otherwise only at weekends (Sat 2–7pm, Sun 10am–7pm; Nov–March Sun only; €2 return).

Campo dei Fiori

Narrow roads continue past Santa Maria del Monte into the broadleaf forests of the **Parco Regionale del Campo dei Fiori**, a swathe of green mountainside centred on the peak of Campo dei Fiori (1226m) atop which stand an observatory and meteorology station. This is beautiful country for leg-stretching walks and picnics-with-a-view. Partway up, you may notice a turn in the road by a red-and-white barrier alongside a gatekeeper's stone lodge. This marks a private road leading a short way into the forests to the **Albergo Campo dei Fiori**, a grand hillside hotel built in 1912 by the architect Giuseppe Sommaruga and visible from all over Varese. A caretaker family live in one wing, but otherwise this fine building, complete with all its original Art-Nouveau fittings, has been left to crumble since it closed in 1953. Beautiful railings by Sommaruga are covered in rust and grime. The top station of the hotel's funicular nearby and panoramic restaurant above – both disused – are graceful Liberty buildings in utter disrepair amidst the encroaching forest.

The reason for this tragic neglect centres on the thicket of aerials and satellite dishes atop the abandoned hotel. The family which owns the site (along with the prestigious motorcycle firm Cagiva) gain more by renting roof-space to TV and communications companies than they would by refurbishing the hotel and opening it to the public. So they let the place rot, with scandalous impunity.

Eating and drinking

Varese has a good range of high-quality places to eat and drink. A number of **cafés** occupy Piazza del Podestà and its environs – one of the best is *Pasticceria Ghezzi*, Corso Matteotti 36 (closed Sun), a mirrored, chandeliered patisserie dating from 1924. It is renowned for its *Dolce Varese*, a tasty concoction of chopped almonds and dried fruit. Among a cluster of sociable café-bars around Piazza Carducci is the attractive *Balthazar*, Via Cattaneo 3 (closed Sun), with tables spread over an internal courtyard. Like most hereabouts, it stays open until 1 or 2am.

The *Bologna*, Via Broggi 7 (closed Sat), is a cheerful, family-run **restaurant** with excellent food at moderate prices. Nearby, intimate *Vecchia Trattoria della Pesa*, Via Cattaneo 14 (℡0332.287.070; closed Sun eve & Mon), specializes in lake fish; menus are around €35.

Otherwise, head up to the Sacro Monte. Here, the three hotels (see p.143) all have good restaurants, each with a panoramic terrace. Top choice, for character and atmosphere, is the ⚘ *Borducan*, an establishment with a history. The original owner, Davide Bregonzio, accompanied Garibaldi on campaign to Sicily in 1860, sailing on, after the battles, to North Africa. He brought luscious Algerian oranges back to Varese, and after trying out different recipes, in 1872 hit on a mellow liqueur that blended orange oil with the aromatic herbs found on Varese's hillsides. Bregonzio called his creation "**Elixir Al Borducan**" after the Arabic word for orange, and opened a bar to sell it. That bar is the *Borducan* restaurant and hotel, owned today by Bregonzio's great-great-grandniece, and it remains the one place where you can sample the liqueur – which is still made only in Varese, though now from organic Sicilian oranges. It's perfect for a sunset tipple before dinner on the terrace.

The Varesotto

Varese's hinterland, the **Varesotto**, is chiefly worth driving through to get somewhere more interesting, but it has a handful of minor attractions.

West of Varese, down on the plain, lies the small **Lago di Varese** – prettier from a distance than close to – on the northern fringes of the the **Parco Naturale Lombardo della Valle del Ticino**, within which resides Milan-Malpensa airport.

North of Varese, the SS233 road to the Swiss border at Ponte Tresa heads through the deep **Val Ganna**, passing, after 14km, the little **Lago di Ghirla**, which offers plenty of opportunities for good walks. Ponte Tresa, 7km north on Lake Lugano, is covered on p.217.

A different road, the SS344, leads northeast from Varese into the Val Ceresio and on to Porto Ceresio, on another arm of Lake Lugano (see p.217). The main attraction here, just outside Bisuschio, is the Renaissance **Villa Cicogna Mozzoni** (guided tours April–Oct Sun 9.30am–noon & 2.30–7pm), with a splendid formal garden.

Castiglione Olona

Deep in the Olona valley 8km south of Varese, **CASTIGLIONE OLONA** was rebuilt in Tuscan style in the fifteenth century and hosts superb **frescoes** by a master of the Florentine Renaissance, **Masolino**. They are worth going well out of your way to see – but signage is poor. From Varese, head south on the SS233 (towards Saronno) for 8km to the modern part of Castiglione Olona. After passing a church on the right, at the next set of traffic lights turn right onto Via IV Novembre and follow the hill down into the atmospheric old quarter.

Castiglione Olona owes its prominence to local boy **Cardinal Branda Castiglioni** (1350–1443). Branda taught law at Pavia University, was appointed Bishop of Piacenza, travelled to Hungary as legate of Pope John XXIII, and was a major player at the ecumenical councils of Pisa (1409), Constance (1414–18) and Basel (after 1431). From the 1420s onwards, he rebuilt his home town according to Renaissance principles and commissioned art to decorate its churches and mansions.

On the main Piazza Garibaldi stands the **Palazzo Branda Castiglioni** (Tues–Sat 9am–noon & 3–6pm, Sun 10.30am–12.30pm & 3–6pm; Oct–March closed Sun morning; €4), a fourteenth-century house where the cardinal was born and died. Upstairs is the cardinal's bedroom, with allegorical frescoes dating from 1423, and his study, frescoed by Masolino with a Hungarian landscape. Across the square, the **Chiesa di Villa** was built in the 1430s in the style of the great Florentine architect Brunelleschi: it is a cube topped by a cylinder that conceals the dome. Flanking the main door are two enormous statues of St Christopher and St Anthony.

The Collegiata: Masolino's frescoes

Via Branda heads up the hill as a cobbled lane, rising steeply to the **Collegiata** (Tues–Sun 10am–6pm; Nov–March 10am–1pm & 2.30–5pm; €6.50), built by the cardinal in 1422 on the ruins of the old castle. The portal, added later, was originally too tall: you can see where the rose window had to be raised to make space. The presbytery has frescoes by Masolino on the life of Mary, while over the altar hangs an unusual eight-armed Flemish candelabrum from the 1420s, depicting St George killing the dragon.

What lifts a visit out of the ordinary are the frescoes in the adjacent **Baptistry**. Formerly the Castiglioni family chapel, this small building holds what is considered Masolino's masterpiece – a fresco cycle painted in 1435 on the life of John the Baptist. The colours are rich and bright, the texture and detailing wonderfully clear.

The cycle begins to one side of the **west wall**, with two faded scenes of the visitation. The **north wall**, alongside, shows what is probably the birth and naming of John (Zacharias is shown writing the word Johannes). Scenes in the presbytery show John in the desert, talking to Jesus. The top of the **east wall** has a beautiful depiction of Jesus' baptism in the River Jordan. Still on the east wall, to the right of the window is shown John condemning Herod – who summons his guards – and the impatient Herodias. Further round, John languishes in prison. The highlight is the glorious **south wall**. Beneath a Renaissance scene of columns and porticoes, Salome dances. Next, the head of John is brought in to a stone-faced Herodias, seated amongst her frantic daughters. Above, John's companions are shown burying him in a cave.

Other frescoed vignettes include, on the soffit of the arch, St Jerome translating the Bible, while the west wall has an unusual view of fifteenth-century Rome, centred on the Pantheon. Across the cloister from the Baptistry, a little **café** serves as a perfect spot to draw breath.

Lake Orta

The westernmost of the major Italian lakes, lying wholly within Piemonte, **LAKE ORTA** (**Lago d'Orta**) appears an afterthought, a little croissant-shaped tarn that is closer to the Matterhorn than Milan. Perhaps that's why it is relatively quiet, seeing a fraction of the numbers who pile into Stresa nearby.

Dubbed *Lacus Cusius* by the Romans, after the local Usii tribe – and still referred to as **Cusio** – Orta is unique among the subalpine lakes for having no outflow in the south. Only the small Nigoglia stream leaves the lake, and it flows northwards through the town of Omegna, giving the stubborn Omegnesi their motto: "The Nigoglia flows uphill, and we'll do whatever we please!"

Yet Omegna and most of the other lakeside towns are not especially attractive. Aside from the beauty of the lake itself, with its deep blue waters and green fringe of mountains, the main reason to come this way is for **Orta San Giulio**, the single most captivating medieval village on this – or, perhaps, any – Italian lake. Part of the allure is the **Isola San Giulio** just offshore, once a nest of dragons, now adorned with a monastery and eleventh-century church. The romance of the place is unforgettable, with narrow, cobbled lanes running through the town, and the towers and facades of the island suspended in the foreground of a lake-and-mountain view that constantly changes in the clear, shifting sunlight.

Orta San Giulio

ORTA SAN GIULIO is the cat's whiskers. It has everything, this medieval village, well kept but largely unrenovated, where narrow, cobbled streets snake between tall, pastel-washed *palazzi* with elaborate wrought-iron balconies. Life centres on the waterfront **Piazza Motta**, which looks directly across at Orta's prime attraction – the **Isola San Giulio**. This wooded islet, only 400m offshore, shelters a closed community of nuns, their convent built around a beautiful medieval church. The harmonious ensemble of town, piazza and island is pure theatre, especially at night, when floodlights on the island pick out an arch here, a loggia there, rising to a pinnacle of graceful architecture. Charm isn't the half of it: Orta is bewitching.

The town is, inevitably, popular, although – summer Sundays apart, when approach roads can be jammed with traffic – it's rarely crowded. Orta accommodates its visitors with grace and good humour, and retains a small town's easy approach to life, best sampled midweek or out of season (though many businesses close in Jan).

Arrival and information

The whole of the town centre is **closed to traffic**. From the turning on the main road, beside the Oriental-style Villa Crespi, the **Via Panoramica** runs ahead past the tourist office and the left turn for the Sacro Monte; 700m further are big parking garages around **Piazzale Prarondo** and **Piazzale Diania**, on the hillside above Orta. Continue ahead for another 600m, and you end up at the little residents-only car park on Piazza San Bernardino.

You're allowed to drive into the historic centre to unload at a hotel – but only with prior permission: cameras record every vehicle's number plate. The access roads are also extremely narrow in parts: anything much bigger than a Fiat Punto won't get through.

There's a **map** of Lake Maggiore and Lake Orta on p.122.

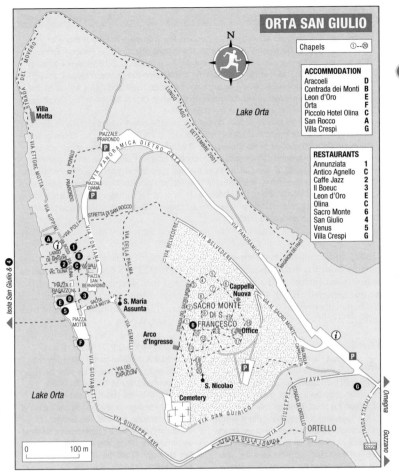

Three **buses** a day arrive from Stresa and Baveno, terminating at Piazzale Prarondo. Orta-Miasino **train station** – on the obscure Novara–Domodossola branch line – is around 3km east: turn left out of the station onto the main road and walk downhill for about twenty minutes to reach the town.

Orta's main **tourist office** (Wed–Sun 9am–1pm & 2–6pm; ☎0322.905.163, ⓦwww.distrettolaghi.it) is bizarrely located in a hut on the Via Panoramica, way up above the town centre 100m from Villa Crespi. In the old town there's an information office within the town hall, Via Bossi 11 (Mon & Wed–Fri 11am–1pm & 2–6pm, Sat & Sun 10am–1pm & 2–6pm) – but they have limited resources. The Consorzio Cusio Turismo (ⓦwww.lagodorta-cusio.com) has good information, as does ⓦwww.orta.net.

Accommodation

Orta's **accommodation** is generally good, but limited: you should always **book in advance**, at any budget. Many places offer free parking on request.

Trenino di Orta

Every day, a motorized tourist train – dubbed the **trenino** – makes a more or less continuous circuit between Piazza Motta, the tourist office on Via Panoramica and the parking garages around Piazzale Prarondo, for a fare of €2.50 one way, €4 return (less for children). This can be invaluable for conquering Orta's steep slopes, though if you want to use it to transport heavy bags between hotel and car it will be at the discretion of the *trenino* driver: officially, that's what Orta's taxis are for. On some runs, the *trenino* also heads out to the train station.

You can use the *trenino* to access one of the most pleasant **walks** in the area. From the dropoff point at the tourist office hut, walk down Via Panoramica for 100m or so, then cut right off the road into the woods. This leads you down to the shore, for the waterside stroll around Orta's peninsula on the scenic **Lungolago 11 Settembre 2001** footpath, past a handful of little houses and some prime spots for quiet sunbathing and swimming. It eventually delivers you (about 30min in total) past the privately owned Villa Motta to the *Hotel San Rocco*, at the northern edge of Orta town centre. You can continue through the town and beyond to complete a circumambulation of the whole peninsula (1hr).

Hotels aside, you can **rent en-suite rooms** or self-catering apartments, most notably from the little office at Via Olina 40 (☎0322.905.656, ⒲www.ortainfo .com): *Casa Vacanze Olina* includes houses and flats sleeping from two to five people (generally €300–400 for 3 nights in high season), while *La Casa sul Lago* is a large villa divided up into several apartments (7-night minimum stay in high season). Another good option is ⒲www.ortalakeflats.com.

Hotels

Aracoeli Piazza Motta 34 ☎0322.905.173, ⒲www.ortainfo.com. Eye-popping little design hotel (pronounced *ara-chaylee*) tucked into one corner of the main square; check-in is at *Hotel Olina* down the street. There are only seven rooms, on four floors (with a lift), each stylishly presented with plain white walls, designer furniture, a/c and huge walk-in showers. Go for the lusciously large "Room of One's Own", up under the eaves, with two double futons on the floor, billowing white drapes and stunning lake views over the rooftops. Breakfast is gourmet. ❹–❺

Contrada dei Monti Via dei Monti 10 ☎0322.905.114, ⒲www.lacontradadeimonti.it. Comfortable, well-kept little hotel in an eighteenth-century house on one of the steep lanes leading off the main drag – and consequently better value than its neighbours. Rooms are fresh and stylish, with soft fabrics and warm colours, many of them overlooking a little internal courtyard where breakfast is served in summer. Closed Jan. ❹

Leon d'Oro Piazza Motta 42 ☎0322.911.991, ⒲www.albergoleondoro.it. Long-standing old *albergo* directly on the waterfront behind the main square, with renovated three-star rooms offering some great lake views. Owned by the same family as the *Contrada dei Monti*. ❹

Orta Piazza Motta 1 ☎0322.90.253, ⒲www .hotelorta.it. A traditional grand hotel in a perfect location on the main square, in the same family today as when it opened in 1864. Nowadays reduced to three-star status, it is still a decent choice. The best rooms face the lake and the island: choose from suites with their own terraces, or doubles with balconies; it's worth booking for these well in advance. Others, with and without balconies, face the piazza. Closed Nov–March. ❸–❹

Piccolo Hotel Olina Via Olina 40 ☎0322.905.532, ⒲www.ortainfo.com. Little hotel alongside the *Olina* restaurant in the historic centre, with twelve contemporary designed rooms of varying sizes – very clean and attractive. Also has an annexe nearby on Via Poli. Closed Nov to mid-Dec. ❷–❸

San Rocco Via Gippini 11 ☎0322.911.977, ⒲www.hotelsanrocco.it. What a disappointment this place is. The delightful building – a seventeenth-century former convent – occupies a prime stretch of central waterfront. Its secluded location, well away from the bustle, offers fine views of the island and the mountains. The lakeside swimming pool is to die for. Inside, however, a rethink is desperately needed. The supposedly four-star rooms are badly dated, and those in the main building are hot, cramped and poky (some in the adjacent *Villa Gippini* wing are bigger, though no less tired). There is one lift, big enough for two people. And absurd rules are in place: despite the presence of a splendid terrace, next to the pool and directly on the west-facing waterfront, guests are not permitted to dine *al fresco* – the restaurant will only serve indoors. To enjoy the evening outside, you must survive on drinks and peanuts. We are including the hotel here for two reasons: its unbeatable location, and in the hope it will improve. ❻–❼

Villa Crespi Via Fava 18 ☎0322.911.902, ⓦ www.hotelvillacrespi.it. Orta's most characterful hotel, located away from the lake in its own grounds up above the town. This extraordinary building, resembling a Moorish palace, dates from 1879, when Cristoforo Crespi, a cotton-trader who made his fortune in Baghdad, returned to Orta and built a palace to remind him of the East. The

reception area is a tall, airy space of Arab arches and a confection of stucco and carved wood, the corridors and rooms still have their elaborate inlaid parquet flooring, and standards in fitting and decor are exceptionally high, with coordinated tones and fabrics, eighteenth- and nineteenth-century furniture, frescoed ceilings and luxurious bathrooms. Service is warm and courteous. With only eight rooms and six suites, an air of exclusivity prevails. Closed Jan to mid-Feb. ❼–❾

Campsite

Camping Orta Via Domodossola 28 ☎0322.90.267, ⓦ www.campingorta.it. Good-quality site about 1km north of Orta, sandwiched between the main road and the lake, with nice facilities and a private beach. Also has bungalows and caravans for weekly rent. Open year-round.

The Town

The pace of life in Orta is slow and civilized, with everything revolving around the main square, **Piazza Motta**, dubbed the *salotto*, or drawing-room – a broad, deep piazza ringed around on three sides by elegant facades and open on the fourth, with the lake and island visible behind a screen of horse-chestnut trees. Orta's Wednesday **market** has been held here since 1228. *Gelaterie*, terrace cafés and restaurants share space under the arcades with art galleries, designer boutiques and fancy shops. On the north side is the **Palazzo della Comunità**, or **Palazzotto**, Orta's titchy town hall, built in 1582 and supported on a portico, with faded frescoes of crests and sundials.

From here, the main street – cobbled, and barely two or three metres wide – heads northwards as **Via Olina**, lined with tall sixteenth- and seventeenth-century buildings. Cafés, restaurants and shops pack the street at ground level; above are many graceful wrought-iron balconies. Orta's oldest street is the quieter **Via Bersani**, running parallel to Via Olina slightly higher up; it is

---

Boats on Lake Orta

Passenger **boats** crisscross the lake, though the main focus of interest is the five-minute voyage between Orta and the Isola San Giulio. At Orta's landing-stage on Piazza Motta, there's no differentiation between the "official" boats of Navigazione Lago d'Orta (☎0322.844.862), which run frequently at weekends but sporadically on weekdays (€2.50 return), and the **motorboats** operated by a consortium of local owners, which scoot across more or less on demand (€4 return; ⓦ www.motoscafisti .com). You can also charter your own motorboat (around €50 for 30min) or **rent a rowing-boat** (roughly €12 per hr for two people).

Elsewhere, the "official" boats run continuously on a circuit around the central part of the lake, crossing from Orta to the island, then to Pella and one or two of its neigh-bours, before returning to Orta: this could comprise a nice little half-hour **sightseeing tour** (€4; ticket valid all day). Otherwise, their schedule is patchy: only two boats a day head north to **Omegna** (€6 return), with extra services on Thursdays, Omegna's market day. A one-day pass for the whole lake costs €7.30.

"Official" boats run daily in **summer** (late March to mid-Oct) and in **winter** on Sundays only (Sat & Sun in late Oct) or not at all (Dec–Feb). The motorboat captains waiting on the quay at Orta, however, will put together any kind of lake tour on request.

accessed from Piazza Motta by the **Salita della Motta**, a broad, stepped lane that climbs steeply east towards the fifteenth-century church of **Santa Maria Assunta**, renovated in Baroque style and dramatically floodlit at night.

Above the town, reached on foot from the church or from its own parking area above the Via Panoramica, is the **Sacro Monte di San Francesco**, a tight little skein of 21 chapels that winds around the hilltop, built from 1590 to 1785. Each chapel holds a tableau of painted terracotta statues acting out a scene from the life of St Francis of Assisi – but artistry takes second place to didactic clarity. The chapels make up a devotional route still followed by pilgrims, though just as many visitors come simply to picnic, admire the views of the lake and inhale the pine-scented air.

The island: Isola San Giulio

The **Isola San Giulio**, a tiny, car-free island just offshore, is dominated by a stern, white convent and the more graceful tower of a medieval basilica. According to legend, the island was the realm of dragons and serpents until 390 AD, when Julius, a Christian from Greece, arrived. He asked to be rowed to the island, but no boatman brave enough came forward. Julius crossed alone, using his staff as a rudder and his cloak as a sail, banished the monsters, founded a sanctuary and thus earned himself a sainthood. He died in 392, and was laid to rest in the church he'd built. In its place now stands a tenth- and eleventh-century successor, with a fine Romanesque bell-tower easily visible from the mainland.

All boats dock at the island's southern point, beside the **Basilica di San Giulio** (April–Sept Mon noon–6.45pm, Tues–Sun 9.30am–6.45pm; Oct–March Mon 2–5pm, Tues–Sun 9.30am–noon & 2–5pm). For a small church, the interior is impressively lofty. Much of the decoration, including the vaulting, dates from a Baroque eighteenth-century refit, but frescoes from as early as the fourteenth century survive all round the walls, many of them naïve in design but remarkably well preserved. The fine **pulpit**, made in the early twelfth century from dark stone quarried nearby at Oira, is covered in symbols of the four evangelists and images of good winning over evil: note the crocodile locked in battle with the phoenix. The saint's remains can be viewed in the crypt.

From the church, the only **street** – a picturesque cobbled lane – leads around the island; it's a twenty-minute walk, past the various buildings which make up the Benedictine convent, home to more than sixty nuns. In an attempt to preserve the tranquillity of the island, the sisters have put up double-sided signs in four languages at regular intervals along the walking route: if you walk clockwise, the path is the **Street of Meditation**; anticlockwise, it is the **Street of Silence**. Needless to say, the rather Buddhic contemplations on each sign are ignored by virtually everyone. Partway round is a pleasant little café-restaurant.

Note that you'll be refused admission to the church if you're wearing shorts or a short skirt, and the municipality (on request from the scandalized nuns) has banned swimming at the island's landing-stage.

Eating and drinking

It's easy to gather **picnic** ingredients and filled panini at the *gastronomia* on and off Piazza Motta. *Enoteca Il Boeuc*, Via Bersani 28, serves tasty **snacks** to accompany well-chosen wine.

Of Orta's **restaurants**, the ⚜ *Olina*, Via Olina 40 (☎0322.905.656; closed Wed), is a fine choice, serving excellent local specialities beautifully cooked and presented, along with thoughtful extras like aperitifs on the house, plus good vegetarian options. *Pizzeria Annunziata*, Via Bossi 2 (closed Thurs), is a fresh, modern place with friendly service and a wide range of pizzas. The smarter

▲ Isola San Giulio

Antico Agnello, Via Olina 18 (☎0322.90.259; closed Tues), offers tasty Lombard and Piemonte dishes, great puddings and congenial service. On Piazza Motta itself, top choice is the *Venus* (☎0322.90.256; closed Mon), which sprawls over the cobbles in front of the landing-stage; its ice cream is excellent, and its inexpensive menu of standard fare is well presented. Tucked around the corner is the terrace of the *Leon d'Oro* (☎0322.911.991), a long line of candlelit tables directly on the water, looking out to the floodlit island. The food is local, served with grace and informality. *Caffè Jazz*, Via Olina 13 (☎333.923.2522; closed Mon), is a romantic little jazz bar – dark wood, ladder-back chairs and candles – that offers a small, moderately priced menu of Piemontese specialities.

Outside the centre, the friendly little restaurant *Sacro Monte* (☎0322.90.220; closed Tues) nestles in the grounds of the Sacro Monte, with a cosy interior and attractive *al fresco* tables, while on the island, the *San Giulio* (☎0322.90.234; closed Mon) has a peaceful waterside terrace and motorboat shuttles in the evenings.

Orta's top choice is the *Villa Crespi* (☎0322.911.902; closed Tues, Wed lunch), which has a glittering, Michelin-starred restaurant. The chef's ten-stage *menù degustazione* starts around €120, including pairings for each course from the cellar's five hundred wines.

Around Lake Orta

The remainder of the lake is disappointingly humdrum. **PETTENASCO**, just north of Orta, hosts a clutch of New-Age retreats; the road up to the Mottarone (see p.129) passes from here through **Armeno**. A few kilometres south, below **Ameno**, in the township of **VACCIAGO**, is the **Collezione Calderara** (mid-May to mid-Oct Tues–Sun 10am–noon & 3–6pm; free), contemporary art shown in the seventeenth-century villa of the painter Antonio Calderara (1903–78) – whose own landscapes of Lake Orta are beautiful.

Otherwise, the lake is largely given over to suburban towns and light industry. Orta has long been a manufacturing centre for bathroom fittings: the multi-national Giacomini tap company, based on the western shore at **SAN MAURIZIO D'OPAGLIO**, is celebrated at the town's Museo del Rubinetto (Tap Museum; check times with tourist office). Nearby on this wooded slope is the Baroque **Madonna del Sasso** church, perched atop a rocky crag and clearly visible from Orta San Giulio. Sleepy **PELLA** is handy for a light lunch on a cross-lake trip: wander back from the lakefront to discover its frescoed church, decorated with strange truncated pilasters in the apse.

At the northern tip of Lake Orta stands the busy little town of **OMEGNA**, with a photogenic old quarter good for window-shopping. Omegna is home to chic cookware firms Bialetti (designers of the iconic Moka Express stovetop espresso-maker), Lagostina and Alessi: alongside the Alessi factory, signposted just north of the centre in **CRUSINALLO**, is the **Alessi Shop** (Mon–Sat 9.30am–6pm; June–Sept also Sun 2.30–6.30pm), an outlet store offering the full designer range, heavily discounted.

Traffic streams through Omegna to join the autostrada 7km north at **Gravellona Toce**. North of Gravellona, the highway – signed for the **Passo del Sempione** (Simplon Pass) – reaches into the Alpine territory of the **Val d'Ossola**, a web of mountain valleys surrounded by walls of sheer peaks marking the Swiss border. On a lakes-based stay, the only reason to venture this far north is for the town of **Domodossola**, 33km north of Gravellona Toce (see p.170).

Northern Lake Maggiore

North of Verbania (see p.136), the lake becomes wilder, narrower, more mountainous – and much less visited. Nonetheless, it pulls off a couple of gems just before the Swiss frontier: **Cánnero** and **Cannóbio** are as charming as anywhere on the lake. **Luino** on the eastern shore is promoted for its huge weekly market, but has little else going for it.

There's a **map** of Lake Maggiore on p.122. For details of the **boats**, see p.124.

Northwards, across the Swiss border (which is abruptly signposted hereabouts as "*confine*" or just "CH"), the enchanting botanical island gardens on the **Isole di Brissago** are a mini version of those on the more famous Isole Borromee at Stresa, while the nearby resort of **Ascona** is characterful, south-facing and picturesque. At the very top of the lake stands **Locarno**, a cultured town of elegant architecture, good food and great shopping.

Buses run from Verbania (Pallanza and Intra) to Ghiffa, Cánnero and Cannóbio. Some continue across the border to Brissago, from where Swiss buses head on to Ascona and Locarno.

Ghiffa

Occupying a small headland 5km north of Intra, **GHIFFA** has some of the lake's longest sightlines, south beyond Stresa, north as far as Maccagno. The former Panizzara hat factory, 500m north of the landing-stage – now largely converted into apartments – contains the diverting **Museo dell'Arte del Cappello** (Hat Museum; April–Oct Sat & Sun 3.30–6.30pm; free). Roads coil up to Ronco, access point for the **Sacro Monte di Ghiffa** (Ⓦwww .sacromonteghiffa.it), a trio of chapels within a nature reserve.

Clocks tick slowly in the *Hotel Ghiffa* (Ⓣ0323.59.285, Ⓦwww.hotelghiffa .com; ❺–❻), an old-fashioned charmer standing on the lake side of the road, with parking. Its public areas retain their nineteenth-century character – parquet floors, high ceilings, picture windows – as do many of the rooms: the best are the spacious corner rooms on the second floor. Some on the first floor have their own terraces with panoramic lake views, while up on the fourth floor, under the eaves, smaller modernized rooms boast compact, private sun-decks facing the lake.

Cánnero

Roughly 9km north of Ghiffa, **CÁNNERO RIVIERA** – it plays on its suffix – is a beautiful little corner, bypassed both by the main road (which keeps to a higher contour, well above shore level) and by most of Maggiore's crowds. It's a leisure resort, for sure, with a large campsite drawing in holidaying families, but also has more than a touch of class about it. This whole stretch of shore – mostly south-facing and shielded by the mountains – is lush with subtropical flora: lemon, orange and olive trees all flourish, as do palms, magnolias, azaleas, mimosa, bougainvillea and camellias. Cánnero's pretty waterfront promenade is idyllic almost to the point of sedation.

The town occupies a little bulge of land, split by the Rio Cánnero, which flows off Monte Spalavera (1534m) behind the town. The **campsite** *Lido* (Ⓣ0323.787.148) and beach occupy the south side of the headland, the landing-stage and promenade the north. The **tourist office** is in the town centre, on Via Lazzaro (Mon–Sat 9.30am–noon & 3–6pm, Sun 9am–noon; mid-Sept to June closed Wed; Ⓣ0323.788.943, Ⓦwww.cannero.it).

Two peaceful lakefront **hotels** are worth coming this way for, both with private parking and a pool. The venerable *Park Italia* (Ⓣ0323.788.488, Ⓦwww .parkhotel-cannero.it; closed Nov–Feb; ❺–❻), set in lush grounds, has good, tile-floored rooms; the double-balconied second-floor corner ones are delightful. A stroll away, opposite the landing-stage, is the refined *Hotel Cánnero*

See p.130 for details of the **Lago Maggiore Express** excursion ticket. At the time of writing, the route was possible from **Cánnero** or **Cannóbio** on certain days only (on **Itinerary 16**); check before travelling. Heading clockwise, set out by boat around 8.30am, changing in Luino to arrive in Baveno at 10am. From here, catch a train to Domodossola, where there's a pause before the switch onto the beautiful Centovalli railway; either treat Domodossola as a coffee stop and dawdle over lunch in Locarno, or the other way round. The boat back departs Locarno at 4.15pm, arriving in Cannóbio at 5.20pm and Cánnero (after changing in Luino) at 6.10pm. The reverse routing (on **Itinerary 3**) only works from Cannóbio, again on certain days. An 8.25am boat gives time for coffee in Locarno before the Centovalli trip to Domodossola. Have lunch in Domodossola, or press on by fast train to Stresa for lunch there. A mid-afternoon boat or hydrofoil from Stresa arrives back in Cannóbio around 5.30pm.

(☎0323.788.046, ⓦwww.hotelcannero.com; closed Nov–Feb; ❺–❻), a posh lake hotel of the old school. It occupies what was a monastery and the linked Casa del Barone alongside, dating from 1700. Its rooms and grand public areas are tasteful and service is outstanding – genial, intelligent and understated. Relaxing over a meal at the hotel's terrace **restaurant**, or at the adjacent *Europa* (☎0323.788.292), is a pleasure.

Just offshore are two islets, on which rise the photogenic **Castelli di Malpàga**, destroyed by the Visconti in 1414 and partially rebuilt by the Borromeo in 1521. Ask around at the landing-stage for a motorboat to take you out, or rent your own at the *Lido* campsite (about €20 per hr).

Cannóbio

Beyond Cánnero, the narrow road skirts Monte Carza (1116m) for 7km to **CANNÓBIO**, one of Lake Maggiore's most appealing places to stay. A centre of lake commerce for over a thousand years, Cannóbio has a beautiful, and very long, promenade of elegant, pastel-washed facades, most now terrace cafés. On Sunday mornings, the local **market** takes over the waterfront, selling anything from fresh produce to leather goods. Behind, stepped and cobbled alleyways climb steeply into a tightly tangled old village of fifteenth- and sixteenth-century architecture, characterized by arcades, frescoes and charming little piazzas. It's a perfect place to spend a relaxed few days nosing around the streets and exploring the high **Val Cannobina** behind the town.

Arrival, information and accommodation

The main SS34 shoreline **road** passes through Cannóbio as Viale Vittorio Veneto, served by **buses** on the route between Verbania and Brissago. **Ferry** service is good, with links up and down the lake, as well as across to Luino. In the town centre, where the main road narrows by the San Vittore church, on one side the cobbled, pedestrianized Via Umberto I heads down into the old quarter, while on the other is the **tourist office**, Via A. Giovanola 25 (Mon–Sat 9am–noon & 4.30–7pm, Sun 9am–noon; ☎0323.71.212, ⓦwww.procannobio .it). Cannóbio's cheapest **accommodation** is offered by the many lakeside campsites to the north of town, most of which rent bungalows and caravans.

There's a **map** of Lake Maggiore on p.122. For details of the **boats**, see p.124.

Hotels

Antica Stallera Via P. Zaccheo 7 ☎0323.71.595, www.anticastallera.com. A friendly hotel occupying a former post-house and stables, built in 1650 within the village, a short way back from the waterfront. The modern rooms – quiet and en suite – are comfortable, there is free parking and the vine-shaded restaurant terrace is lovely. A great three-star choice, run by the same family for over fifty years. ③

Cannóbio Piazza Vittorio Emanuele III 6 ☎0323.739.639, ⓦwww.hotelcannobio.com. Prominent historic hotel on the quiet lakefront piazza, just above the old harbour, completely

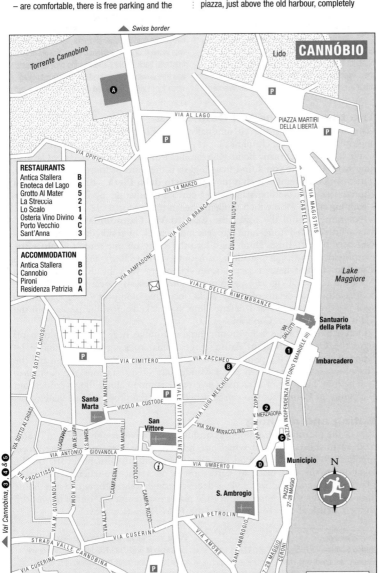

Swiss border

CANNÓBIO

Lido

Torrente Cannobino

A

VIA AL LAGO

PIAZZA MARTIRI DELLA LIBERTÀ

VIA OPIFICI

RESTAURANTS
Antica Stallera	B
Enoteca del Lago	6
Grotto Al Mater	5
La Streccia	2
Lo Scalo	1
Osteria Vino Divino	4
Porto Vecchio	C
Sant'Anna	3

ACCOMMODATION
Antica Stallera	B
Cannobio	C
Pironi	D
Residenza Patrizia	A

VIA 14 MARZO

VIA GIULIO BRANCA

VIA RAMPADONE

VICOLO AL QUARTIERE NUOVO

VIA MAGISTRIS

VIA CASTELLO

Lake Maggiore

VIALE DELLE RIMEMBRANZE

VIA GALLOTTI

Santuario della Pieta

VIA SOTTO I CHIOSI

VIA CIMITERO

VIA ZACCHEO

B

PIAZZA INDIPENDENZA (VITTORIO EMANUELE III)

1

Imbarcadero

VIA MANTELLI

VICOLO A. CUSTODE

Santa Marta

VIA LUIGI MESCHIO

VIALE VITTORIO VENETO

V. MERZAGORA

VIA T. M. ZOPPI

2

San Vittore

VIA MANTELLI

VIA SAN MIRACOLINO

C

VIA SOTTO AI CHIOSI

VIA ANTONIO GIOVANOLA

i

VIA UMBERTO I

D

Municipio

VICOLO LISAGO

VIA DE LUATI

S. MARTA

VIA CROCITISSO

VIA ROMA

VIA GIOVANOLA

VIA ALLA CAMPAGNA

VICOLO CAMPA RIZZO

CAMPA RIZZO

N

S. Ambrogio

PIAZZA 27-28 MAGGIO

VIA PETROLINI

VIA AMORE

SANT'AMBROGIO

VIA 27-28 MAGGIO

CERONI

STRADA VALLE CANNOBINA

VIA CUSERINA

VIA CUSERINA

VIA M. GIOVANOLA

0   100 m

refurbished in 2003. Everything is airy, spacious and kitted out to four-star quality, but lacks that certain something – and you'll have to hold your nose for the cut-out painted headboards and gaudy colour scheme. Nonetheless, the staff are pleasant and attentive, every room has a romantic view (some have balconies, too) and the location can't be bettered. ⑥

Pironi Via Marconi 35 ☏ 0323.70.624, ⓦ www.pironihotel.it. Cannóbio's loveliest hotel – a real charmer, wedged into a narrow fifteenth-century ex-convent on a cobbled lane in the village centre. Rooms are light, bright and attractive – room 12 has its own private frescoed balcony – the staff are friendly, and the atmosphere is fresh and appealing. Member of the Italian *Charme & Relax* group (ⓦ www.charmerelax.com). Closed Dec–Feb. ⑥

Residenza Patrizia Via Veneto ☏ 0323.739.713, ⓦ www.residenzapatrizia.com. A swanky new building north of the centre, with holiday apartments and – on the uppermost floors – eight hotel rooms. Everything is done with flair and style: hi-tech bathrooms with multi-jet showers, spacious rooms with wood floors and designer sofas, balconies to front and back. There's a swimming pool for guests and free private underground parking. Outstanding value for money. Closed Jan & Feb. ⑥

The town and the Val Cannobina

Cannóbio's campsites and an unusually good Lido **beach** (awarded an EU-approved Blue Flag for cleanliness) – as well as Cannóbio's status as the first town inside Italy – attract many holidaying families from the north, especially German and Swiss-German: you'll find that English is the third or fourth language here. The town's only sight as such is the **Santuario della Pietà**, a Bramante-inspired church beside the landing-stage with a curious openwork cupola, built to house a painting of the *Pietà* which suddenly began to bleed in 1522.

Extending behind the town, the wooded **Val Cannobina** offers beautiful views, little-visited stone-built hamlets and a clutch of good countryside restaurants (see below). Buses climb high into the valley, on one route to **Falmenta**, marooned in the jagged shadow of Monte Vadà (1836m), and on another to **Cúrsolo**, from where a scenic seven-kilometre walk heads past Finero to **Malesco** in the Val Vigezzo, a stop on the Domodossola–Locarno train line. The tourist office has details of many walks, including along the Linea Cadorna, a well-preserved World War I defence line that snaked across the peaks from the Val d'Ossola down to Cannóbio.

Only 2.5km into the valley from central Cannóbio, near Traffiume, a turn-off signs the **Orrido di Sant'Anna**, a spectacular rocky gorge surrounded by wooded slopes that is a popular picnic spot. Beside the Roman bridge and the chapel is a small river beach and a wonderfully sited restaurant, the *Sant'Anna* (see below). There is an attractive cycle route running along the riverside from the centre of Cannóbio; you can rent bikes from the shop on Viale Veneto.

Eating and drinking

Part of the pleasure of Cannóbio is noshing your way through the town's **cafés and restaurants**, most of which are relaxed, characterful nooks. The broad, granite-paved Piazza Indipendenza (aka Piazza Vittorio Emanuele III) on the lakefront is the best place to start; most of its terrace restaurants are in the plastic-chairs-and-spaghetti style – decent enough, but nothing to write home about – though some good countryside places may tempt you out of town. Stop in for a **drink** at the cosy bar below the *Hotel Pironi* (see above).

In town

Antica Stallera Via P. Zaccheo 7 ☏ 0323.71.595. Pleasant, enclosed, vine-shaded terrace restaurant attached to this family-run hotel in the village centre. There's no view of the lake, but the food is local and a full meal is unlikely to cost more than €25.

Porto Vecchio At *Hotel Cannóbio*, Piazza Vittorio Emanuele III 6 ☏ 0323.739.998. Although physically part of the hotel, the restaurant is under separate management – which is perhaps why it suffers from occasionally sloppy, over-informal service standards. It is, nonetheless, worth eating

2

here (or just stopping in for an aperitif) simply for the heavenly lakeside terrace, one of the most captivating on all of Maggiore – shaded, quiet, with expansive views. The food is fine, fairly standard, moderately priced north Italian cuisine, but it's a pity they can't stretch beyond plastic chairs and cheap tablecloths. If you can overlook that, book a table by the balustrade for a romantic *tête-à-tête*.

Lo Scalo Piazza Vittorio Emanuele III 32 ☎0323.71.480, ⊛www.loscalo.com. The best and most refined of Cannóbio's restaurants, plum on the waterfront piazza – its white linen tablecloths, crystal flutes and elegant clientele marking it out from its cheaper neighbours. The building is lovely, a fourteenth-century *palazzo* with atmospheric portico, and the cuisine is outstanding, classic Piemonte fare with innovative touches. The fish and seafood *antipasti* are excellent, as are the gnocchi. The menu changes daily, and you can sample a four-course set menu at lunch or dinner. Expect €60 a head and upwards. Closed Mon, Tues lunch.

La Streccia Via Merzagora 5 ☎0323.70.575. Good, typical Piemonte food served in a rustic, low-ceilinged dining room, up one of the steep cobbled alleys leading back from the lakefront (*streccia* is a local word for alley). Local produce – cheese, meats, mushrooms – features strongly, as do regional wines. Prices are moderate; the ambience warm. Closed Tues.

Out of town

Enoteca del Lago Carmine Inferiore, 3km south of Cannóbio ☎0323.70.595, ⊛www.enotecalago .com. Located on the lakeside road, though shielded from road noise, this is a gourmet restaurant, serving top-quality Italian and international cuisine on a fabulous balconied terrace perched above the lake. It doesn't come cheap, though: expect €70 or more per head. Across the road is the pleasant *enoteca*, with wine-tastings and sales. Closed Tues, Wed lunch.

Grotto Al Mater Strada Valle Cannobina 2 ☎0323.77.290. This beautiful little building in an idyllic country setting, 4.8km from central Cannóbio along the road that climbs into the Val Cannobina, was formerly the *Mulini Del Mater*, one of the region's finest gourmet restaurants. It's now a plainer, less ambitious *grotto*, or rustic rural tavern, serving simple fish and pasta dishes in a valley-side setting that remains nothing short of breathtaking. Come for a meal (€20) or just a coffee.

Osteria Vino Divino Strada Valle Cannobina 1 ☎0323.71.919, ⊛www.osteriavinodivino.com. A quiet, shady little spot in the forest down by the river, with a surprisingly hip, urban feel – turn off the Val Cannobina road 2km out of town at a right fork and you're met with designer furniture and trendy haircuts. The specialities are wine, local Alpine cheese, and various kinds of salamis and cured meats, all sampled to the accompaniment of the rushing river. Moderate prices. Open evenings only, plus Sun lunch. Closed Wed & Jan–Feb. No credit cards.

Sant'Anna Via Sant'Anna 30, overlooking the gorge ☎0323.70.682. A perfect little country restaurant, perched spectacularly on a crag above the Orrido di Sant'Anna. Choices like pâté, porcini mushrooms and lamb in a red wine and chestnut sauce make a delicious change from lake fish – and you could easily eat for €25–30 here. Booking essential. Closed Mon (except July & Aug).

North into Switzerland: Brissago

From Cannóbio, the lakeside road continues north on a tight and narrow course around the cliffs that tumble down from Monte Giove (1298m) and the Monte Limidario massif (2187m). After 5km or so, you cross into Switzerland – whereupon the road widens and improves. **BRISSAGO**, 2km further, is a rather soulless little town, determinedly neat and tidy and packed with holiday flats. It's best known for its large **cigar factory** – producer of fine Brissago smokes for over a century. If you're heading on to Ascona or Locarno, you can pick up maps and information at Brissago's **tourist office** on the main street, Via Leoncavallo 25 (March–Oct Mon–Fri 8am–noon & 2–6pm, Sat 8am–noon; July & Aug Sat also 2–6pm; ☎091 791 00 91, ⊛www.maggiore.ch).

The road continues through Porto Ronco (from where boats cross to the **Isole di Brissago**; see p.164) and on for 6km to **Ascona** (see p.163) and **Locarno** (see p.165).

All **phone numbers** in this chapter prefixed ☎091 are **Swiss**; all other numbers (beginning ☎03) are **Italian**. For details of international dialling, see p.58.

The eastern shore: Luino and around

The **eastern shore** of Lake Maggiore has some appealingly quiet hideaways and great opportunities for mountain hikes and drives.

The main centre is the commercial town of **LUINO**, connected by boat to Cánnero and Cannóbio, by bus to Varese and Lugano, and by shoreline trains north to Bellinzona and south to Gallarate (change for Milan Porta Garibaldi). Luino is besieged every **Wednesday** by people pouring in for what is, purportedly, the largest weekly **market** in Europe, a frantically busy emporium seemingly dominated by handbags, clothes, shoes and novelty toys. More interesting stalls, selling homeware or silks and laces, are tucked away, and your nose will lead you to the food section, piled high with cheeses from all over Italy and Switzerland, endless varieties of salami and prosciutto, Sicilian olives and fresh-baked breads. Roads are jam-packed from breakfast-time onwards and parking restrictions are strictly enforced: if you haven't got a space by 8am, don't bother looking. Extra boats and buses serve Luino all day long.

Luino's **tourist office** (daily 9am–noon & 2.30–6.30pm; ☎0332.530.019) is across the road from the landing-stage. One of the most attractive, well-run **hotels** on this shore is the ⚘ *Camin Hotel Colmegna*, 3km north in the hamlet of Colmegna (☎0332.510.855, ⓦwww.caminhotel.com; ❺). The eighteenth-century building has been little altered, and though it's on the busy shoreside road, soundproofing ensures that noise within the hotel is negligible. The ambience is genial, aided by the easygoing outlook of the family running the place; their light, bright three-star rooms all look over the lake. Immediately beyond, the shoreside road enters a tunnel beneath the hill, with the result that the hotel's extensive gardens, which flank the hill, are quiet and peaceful. Wander past the private beach and pergola, with a waterfall and glasshouse on a higher terrace, round to a silent, delightfully secluded path, facing directly west across the water to Cánnero. The hotel's terrace **restaurant** is a delight, with a good, moderately priced menu of local specialities, plus barbecues and buffets on summer evenings; book ahead.

Maccagno and the Gambarogno

MACCAGNO, 5km north of Luino, is a dour working village, split in two by the River Giona. The central **tourist office** is at Via Garibaldi 1 (☎0332.562.009, ⓦwww.prolocomaccagno.it). The **Swiss border** at Zenna lies 9km north; just before, in **PINO**, La Darsena (May–Sept; ⓦwww.ladarsenawindsurf.com) takes advantage of the breezy conditions to offer windsurfing and kitesurfing rental (€15–18 per hr) and courses.

Over the border, the territory extending 13km to the Locarno–Lugano road is known as the **Gambarogno**, a line of shoreside villages backed by rugged mountains. **VIRA** holds the local **tourist office** (July & Aug Mon–Fri 8am–6.30pm, Sat 9am–noon & 3–5pm, Sun 9am–noon; rest of year Mon–Fri 8am–noon & 2–6pm, plus Sat 9am–noon in June, Sept & Oct; ☎091 795 18 66, ⓦwww.gambarognoturismo.ch). On the hillside above Vira is the splendid **Parco Botanico del Gambarogno** (ⓦwww.parcobotanico.ch), showcasing one of Europe's finest collections of magnolias and camellias, alongside azaleas, rhododendrons, peonies and more.

Maccagno and the **Val Veddasca**, which climbs behind the town, are linked to the Gambarogno by testing mountain roads and stiff hiking trails. An improbably steep track leads straight out from Maccagno into the hills, from where there are paths to the dam on little **Lake Delio**. Trails also lead inland from Maccagno to **Curiglia**, beyond which, from Ponte di Piero, a precipitous mule track climbs to picturesque **Monteviasco**, 500m above. There's no road to Monteviasco, and until the recent arrival of a cable car, the mule track was its only link with the world.

For drivers, a road also climbs from Maccagno through the woods to Lake Delio; the views are breathtaking, looking back at Cannóbio, 1000m below on the lake. Beyond the pass at **La Forcora**, this route links up with another that crosses the Swiss border at the isolated hamlet of **INDÉMINI** (930m), 18km from Maccagno. This stone-built village clinging to the valley sides has recently attracted artists and sculptors; workshops are often open, and the simple *Ristorante Indeminese* (☎091 795 12 22) is a great lunch stop. Beyond, it's a drive of 17km over the bleak Alpe di Neggia pass (1395m) – with a mountain inn boasting spectacular views – down to Vira.

An Italian **bus** links Luino and Maccagno with the border village of **Biegno**; walking the 500m of no-man's-land brings you into Indémini, from where a Swiss bus runs down to the ferry at Magadino, beside Vira.

Ascona

On the south-facing side of the Maggia delta, 14km north of Cannóbio and 3km southwest of Locarno, **ASCONA** has been a magnet for idealistic, sun-starved northerners for more than a century. The place was nothing more than a fishing hamlet until the 1890s, but since then it has grown into a cultured, artistically inclined small town, an enticing Swiss blend of character, natural beauty and good shopping.

But the influx of German-speakers, as summer tourists and second-home-owners, has been so great in recent years that Ascona can feel like it has lost its way. Since most of the visitors have, at best, rudimentary Italian, staff in hotels and restaurants are now accustomed to speak to guests in German first. Even the poshest menus are bilingual. Shops frequently advertise special offers in German before Italian, and some cultural activities – readings or gallery openings – take place in German. With general Ticinese disquiet at German-speaking dominance of Swiss affairs, Asconesi are becoming uneasy: voices are being raised for the cantonal government to step in and force Ascona's businesses to use Italian.

The Town

Ascona's *tour de force* is **Piazza Motta**, the cobbled lakefront promenade, south-facing and fully 500m long: the airy views down the lake, flanked by wooded peaks, to the Brissago islands are sensational. There are few better places to watch the day drift by: the morning mists on the water, the clarity of light at midday, the sunsets and peaceful twilight are simply mesmerizing.

Word of Ascona began to spread a century or more ago, when a slow but steady influx began of philosophers, theosophists and spiritualists, most of whom believed that a return to nature was the best remedy for the moral disintegration of Western society. At the turn of the century the artists Henri Oedenkoven and Ida Hofmann established an esoteric, vegetarian artists' colony on the hill of **Monte Verità** beside Ascona. An array of European fringe intellectuals followed: in 1913, Rudolf von Laban set up his nudist School of Natural and Expressive Dance within the Monte Verità community, attracting Isadora Duncan among others. During and after World War I artists and pacifists flocked to Ascona. The buildings atop the peaceful wooded hill are now used mostly for conferences, but a few have been preserved as a **museum** of the movement (Tues–Sun: April–June, Sept & Oct 2.30–6pm; July & Aug 3–7pm; Fr.6; ⓦwww.monteverita.org). It's a short walk up the hill from the bus stop (bus #33) to the **Casa Anatta**, with two floors of the original wooden house given over to papers and photos commemorating the artists' exploits. A walk past the main Bauhaus conference centre and into the woods brings you to the tiny **Casa Selma**, used as the community's retreat, and on further to the **Elisarion**, housing a circular painting by Elisar von Kupffer depicting the spiritual liberations of communal life.

Central Ascona's attractive cobbled lanes leading back from the lakefront are full of artisans' galleries, jewellers and craft shops. The **Museo Comunale d'Arte Moderna**, in a sixteenth-century *palazzo* at Via Borgo 34 (March–Dec Tues–Sat 10am–noon & 3–6pm, Sun 4–6pm; Fr.7; ⓦwww.museoascona.ch), has a high-quality collection focused on Marianne von Werefkin, one of the artists attracted to Ascona in its heyday and joint founder of Munich's expressionist *Blaue Reiter* movement; look out for her terrifying, Munch-like *Il Cenciaiolo* (The Rag-Man, 1920).

Isole di Brissago

Twin islands 4km south of Ascona, the **ISOLE DI BRISSAGO** (April–Oct daily 9am–6pm; Fr.8 in addition to boat ticket; ⓦwww.isolebrissago.ch) are accessible by roughly hourly boats from Locarno and Ascona, and by more regular shuttles from **Porto Ronco**, the nearest point on the mainland. These tiny dots of green in the shimmering lake overflow with luxurian subtropical flora basking in the hot sun. The main island, St Pancras – about ten-minutes' stroll end to end – is given over to a fine botanical garden. At one end is an attractive 1929 villa, now a conference centre and quality restaurant (☎091 791 43 62, ⓦwww.isolebrissago.org): a long lunch here, followed by a siesta under the palms, makes for a most un-Swiss-like afternoon. Note that the signs identifying each plant species lack an English translation. Only groups can stay overnight; everyone else must leave on the last boat (around 6pm). The small island, St Apollinaris, has no public access.

Practicalities

Ascona's **tourist office** is at the top of the old quarter, Viale Papio 5 (Mon–Fri 9am–6pm, Sat 10am–6pm, Sun 2.30–5pm; restricted hours in winter; ☎091 791 00 91, ⓦwww.ascona.ch). The town has literally dozens of **hotels**, with nine on the waterfront piazza alone: a good three-star here is the characterful, family-run *Tamaro* (☎091 785 48 48, ⓦwww.hotel-tamaro.ch; ❺), or a few metres away is the four-star *Castello Seeschloss* (☎091 791 01 61, ⓦwww.castello-seeschloss .ch; ❻), with romantic, tastefully appointed classic interiors. If money's no object, aim for the *Eden Roc*, Via Albarelle 16 (☎091 785 71 71, ⓦwww.edenroc.ch; ❾), one of Switzerland's top luxury hotels, where a south-facing room is a cool Fr.800-plus a night, or the sensuously opulent five-star spa retreat *Albergo Giardino*, Via Segnale 10 (☎091 785 88 88, ⓦwww.giardino.ch; ❾), set in lavish gardens, with similar prices.

Eating, too, is a case of following your nose: every waterfront café lays tables outside. The *Tamaro* offers dining in a pleasant internal atrium, while the *Elvezia* is a good spot for inexpensive pizza and fish dishes; Fr.30 will cover a meal at either. Moving up a price bracket, *Della Carrà* (☎091 791 44 52, ⓦwww .ristorantedellacarra.ch; closed Sun & Mon) has an atmospheric courtyard off the cobbled Via Carrà dei Nasi, serving excellent fish and pasta; *Al Torchio* on Contrada Maggiore (☎091 791 71 26; closed Tues in winter) is strong on local

Boats on Lake Maggiore: the Swiss basin

Boats run by NLM (April–Oct only; ⊛www.navigazionelaghi.it) crisscross the Swiss shores of the lake, as well as continuing down the lake into Italy. See p.124 for full details.

For all but the shortest hops, a **one-day pass** is the most economical choice: unlimited journeys within Zone A (Locarno to Ascona) or Zone B (Ascona to Brissago) costs Fr.15.80, or across Zones A and B Fr.25.50. For reference, a **point-to-point** ticket from Locarno to Ascona is Fr.8.40, Locarno to Isole di Brissago Fr.14.10. Examples of **international** journeys into Italy (and back) include Locarno to Stresa or the islands Fr.37, or Ascona to Cannóbio Fr.22.50. Using the hydrofoil – for which you must **reserve in advance** – adds Fr.3. Various **day-trip excursion** tickets are available, which include boat transport and admission fees for major attractions such as Isola Bella, Isola Madre or Villa Táranto.

Passes

A **Locarno Regional Pass** gives free transport in the Swiss waters of Lake Maggiore for one day, as well as other perks, including free use of buses, trains and cable cars around Locarno and Ascona and discounts on travel around Lake Lugano, for Fr.108 (7 days) or Fr.88 (any 3 days within a week). The combination ticket **Il Lago e la Montagna** (Fr.58; valid 10 days) includes a day-pass for boats on the Swiss sector, admission to the Isole di Brissago, the funicular to Madonna del Sasso and the cable car to Cardada and Cimetta. A **Holiday Card** gives unlimited journeys on the whole lake, including Italy, for Fr.62 (3 days) or Fr.91 (7 days).

Lago Maggiore Express

See p.130 for details of the **Lago Maggiore Express** excursion ticket. Both directions from **Locarno** are well-timed, with enticing stopovers. **Itinerary 14** starts with a morning train through the Centovalli to Domodossola, where a choice of connections bring you on to Stresa for lunch. You could then include a boat trip to Isola Bella and Isola Madre, with two or three hours on the islands, before catching a boat back directly to Locarno, arriving at 6.45pm (earlier on Wed). In reverse, **Itinerary 4** heads directly to Stresa by mid-morning boat or hydrofoil. This allows a decent break for lunch before the 2.30pm train, which gives a brief stop in Domodossola before joining the Centovalli line back to Locarno, arriving at 5.10pm. Variations are also possible from **Ascona**.

specialities; and *Antico Ristorante Borromeo*, Via Collegio 16 (☎091 791 92 81; closed Mon) offers a small, carefully chosen menu, an attractive vaulted interior, a private garden and – best of all – excellent, cheerful service.

The agriturismo *Fattoria l'Amorosa* (see p.220) – with an excellent country restaurant attached – is set amongst vineyards outside Gudo, towards Bellinzona, easily driveable in twenty minutes from Ascona.

Locarno

The characterful Swiss town of **LOCARNO** enjoys a grand location, on the broad sweeping curve of a bay at the top of Lake Maggiore. The arcades and piazzas of the town centre are overlooked by subtropical gardens of palms, camellias, bougainvillea, cypress, oleanders and magnolias, which flourish on the lakeside promenades and cover the wooded slopes which crowd in above the town centre.

Locarno found its feet in the nineteenth century as the most elegant of Swiss resorts. In 1925 its backdrop of *belle époque* hotels and piazza cafés served as the

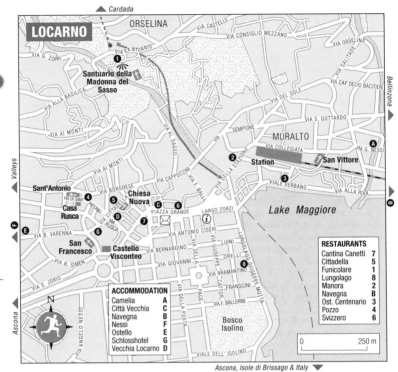

LOCARNO

ORSELINA

Cardada

VIA CASTELLE
VIA CONSIGLIO MEZZANO
VIA ORSELINA
VIA SALTITOE

VIA G. ZOPPI

Santuario della
Madonna del
Sasso

VIA ALLA BASILICA

VIA CAP DECIO BACITIERI

VIA DEL SOLE

VIA S. GOTTARDO

VIA AI MONTI

SEMPIONE

MURALTO

VIA COLLEGIATA

Station   San Vittore

VIA G. NESSI

Valleys

Sant'Antonio

VIA BORGHESE   Chiesa
Nuova

Casa
Rusca

San
Francesco   Castello
Visconteo

VIA DELLA STAZIONE

VIALE VERBANO

VIA ALLA RIVA

LARGO ZORZI

Lake Maggiore

Bellinzona

VIA B. VARENNA

VIA S. JORIO

N

VIA ANGELO NESSI

Ascona

VIA DELLA POSTA

Bosco
Isolino

VIALE DELL' ISOLINO

RESTAURANTS
Cantina Canetti	7
Cittadella	5
Funicolare	1
Lungolago	8
Manora	2
Navegna	B
Ost. Centenario	3
Pozzo	4
Svizzero	6

ACCOMMODATION
Camelia	A
Città Vecchia	C
Navegna	B
Nessi	F
Ostello	E
Schlosshotel	G
Vecchia Locarno	D

0   250 m

Ascona, Isole di Brissago & Italy ▼

setting for the **Treaty of Locarno**, signed by the European powers in a failed effort to secure peace following World War I. These days, Locarno focuses its considerable resources on tourism, and draws in two very different sets of customers: one, from the German-speaking north, arrive to test out their hiking boots, while the other, from fog- and smog-bound Milan, come to test out their sunglasses. The cobbled alleys of Locarno's Old Town, lined with Renaissance facades, can get overrun with the rich and wannabe-famous on summer weekends, yet still – in the midst of the hubbub – the place manages to retain its poise.

Arrival, information and accommodation

Locarno's **train station** is 100m north of the landing-stage and 150m northeast of Piazza Grande; mainline trains depart from ground level, while the local transport company Ferrovie Autolinee Regionali Ticinesi – unfortunately abbreviated to FART – operates trains on the Centovalli line (see p.170) from a separate station below ground.

The **tourist office** is in the Casino complex on Via Largo Zorzi, 100m southwest of the station (Mon–Fri 9am–6pm, Sat 10am–6pm, Sun 10am–1.30pm & 2.30–5pm; ☎091 791 00 91, ⓦwww.maggiore.ch); they can make hotel bookings for you. Locarno's **accommodation** is strongest in the

There's a **map** of Lake Maggiore on p.122.

midrange bracket: if you're after a spot of luxury, head over to Ascona (p.163) or Lugano (p.208).

Hotels

Camelia Via Nessi 9, Muralto ☎091 743 00 21, ⓦwww.camelia.ch. Elegant, eager-to-please family hotel set in fragrant floral gardens offering spacious rooms, some with balcony and lake view. March–Oct. ❹

Città Vecchia Via Torretta 13 ☎091 751 45 54, ⓦwww.cittavecchia.ch. Centrally placed B&B hotel, with dorms (see below) and simple, shared-bath rooms. March–Oct. ❶–❷

Navegna Via alla Riva 2, Minusio ☎091 743 22 22, ⓦwww.navegna.ch. About 1.5km east of the centre, directly on the waterfront, with modern, stylishly renovated rooms, private parking and an excellent restaurant. March–Nov. ❺

Nessi Via Varenna 79 ☎091 751 77 41, ⓦwww .garninessi.ch. Welcoming little family-run place a short way west of the centre, with pool and under-ground parking. Rooms are fresh and decent, with better, bigger ones on higher floors. Closed Jan. ❹

Schlosshotel Via San Francesco 7a ☎091 751 23 61, ⓦwww.schlosshotellocarno.ch. Large,

old-fashioned rooms in a well-kept Old Town pile. March–Nov. ❹

Vecchia Locarno Via Motta 10 ☎091 751 65 02, ⓦwww.hotel-vecchia-locarno.ch. Scruffily characterful Old Town gem, with both shared-bath and en-suite rooms above a courtyard restaurant and wine bar. Dogs charged at Fr.2 per kilogram. March–Dec. ❷–❸

Hostels

Città Vecchia (see "Hotels"). Good Old Town option, with dorms from Fr.35.

Ostello/Jugendherberge Palagiovani (HI hostel) Via Varenna 18 ☎091 756 15 00, ⓦwww.youth hostel.ch. Modern hostel with dorms from Fr.35 and bike rental, but it's in an awkward western location – take bus #31 or #36 to Cinque Vie. March–Nov. ❷

Campsite

Delta ☎091 751 60 81, ⓦwww.campingdelta .com. Quality site, a 15min walk south along the lakeshore. March–Oct.

The Town

The focus of town is **Piazza Grande**, an attractive arcaded square just off the lakefront that is lined with pavement cafés and serves as the town's meeting point, social club and public catwalk. Warm summer nights serve up some great people-watching, as exquisitely groomed locals parade to and fro, all the cafés a-buzz and fragrant breezes bringing in the scent of flowers from the lakeside gardens.

From the west end of Piazza Grande, lanes run up to Via Cittadella in the **Old Town** and the Baroque **Chiesa Nuova**, adorned with a huge statue of St Christopher outside. The quiet arcaded courtyard, reached through a side door, is a charming spot to draw breath away from the bustle. Following the atmospheric Via di Sant'Antonio brings you to the rather sombre church of **Sant'Antonio**, dating from the seventeenth century but rebuilt following

---

Festivals in Locarno and Ascona

Events and festivities run all summer long (see ⓦwww.ticino.ch). The season kicks off in May with Ascona's **Street Artists Festival**, followed in late June by the popular Ascona **New Orleans Jazz Festival**. In July, nearby Magadino holds an **International Organ Festival**, while Locarno hosts **Moon and Stars**, a run of open-air rock and pop gigs by major stars.

The top-class **Locarno International Film Festival** (ⓦwww.pardo.ch), in early August, is rated among the top five film festivals in the world. Catch major offerings on the huge open-air screen in Piazza Grande, playing to 7500 people nightly (Fr.22), or at one of the 12 daily screenings in the city's cinemas (Fr.15).

Over late August and September, Ascona presents its **Settimane Musicali** ("Music Weeks"), a series of prestigious classical concerts staged around the region.

▲ Locarno Film Festival

a fatal roof collapse in 1863. Beside the church, the eighteenth-century **Casa Rusca** (Tues–Sun 10am–noon & 2–5pm; Fr.7) houses a worthwhile art museum focusing on the twentieth-century Swiss artist Jean Arp.

Alleys lead south to the tall **San Francesco**, consecrated as part of a monastery in the fourteenth century. Sixteenth-century renovation added frescoes, most of which are now fading badly. Further down sits the stout thirteenth-century **Castello Visconteo**, now home to the **Museo Archeologico** (April–Oct Tues–Sun 10am–noon & 2–5pm; Fr.7), worth visiting if only for its collection of beautiful Roman glassware and ceramics.

On the other side of town in Muralto, 100m east of the station, is the austere twelfth-century Romanesque basilica of **San Vittore**, built over a church first mentioned in the tenth century and now surrounded by housing developments. Medieval fresco-fragments inside and the Renaissance relief of St Victor on the bell-tower are a diverting contrast to the views over the train station. From here, a pleasant walk along the *lungolago* (lakefront promenade) leads back into town and on south for 1km or so, past beautiful gardens, to the fragrant **Parco delle Camelie**, planted with 900 varieties of camellia.

Madonna del Sasso

Most striking of all Locarno's sights is the **Santuario della Madonna del Sasso** church (daily 6.30am–7pm), an impressive ochre vision floating above the town on a wooded crag – *sasso* means rock – and consecrated in 1487 on the spot where, seven years earlier, the Virgin had appeared to a Franciscan brother. The twenty-minute walk up through the wooded ravine of the Torrente Ramogno and past a handful of decaying shrines is atmospheric enough in itself; or you could take the **funicular** (every 15min) from just west of the train station. The low, Baroque interior of the church features a number of paintings, two of which stand out: Bramantino's emotionally charged *Fuga in Egitto* (Flight to Egypt, 1522) and local artist Antonio Ciseri's *Trasporto di Cristo al Sepolcro* (1870).

Cardada and Cimetta

In high summer, when sweltering Locarno (210m) gets too much, it's easy to escape into the cool, wooded hills above. By the top station of the Madonna del Sasso funicular in Orselina (395m) is the base station of a futuristic cable-car that rises on an ear-poppingly steep course to the plateau of **Cardada** (1350m; Ⓦ www.cardada.ch). A short stroll left from the top station, set amidst fragrant pine woods, is the "Observation Platform", a gracefully designed catwalk suspended off a huge A-frame; a panoramic view takes in Ascona, the lake and the mountains. There are a couple of simple restaurants up here and some easy strolls in the pine forest – many of them wheelchair accessible. Turn right from the top station, and wander for ten minutes or so through the woods to a spectacular chairlift that whisks you even higher, up to the flower-strewn meadows of **Cimetta** (1672m), where there's a restaurant/guesthouse with a terrace view that you won't forget in a hurry.

A return **ticket** from Orselina to Cardada is Fr.27, to Cimetta Fr.33. If you're coming up from Locarno, ask at the base-station of the Madonna del Sasso funicular for a ticket to the top: this discounts the fare and includes half-price car parking in Locarno as well.

Eating and drinking

Piazza Grande is full of cafés and pizzerias buzzing from morning until after midnight, but **eating** and **drinking** is more atmospheric in the Old Town alleys. Fresh fish plucked from the lake is Locarno's speciality – look out for trout (*trota*), perch (*persico*), pike (*luccio*) and whitefish (*coregone*). See p.220 for details of the fine restaurant of the *Fattoria l'Amorosa* agriturismo near Gudo, roughly fifteen-minutes' drive northeast of Locarno.

Cantina Canetti Off Piazza Grande. Plain local cooking (Fr.17) in a noisy diner, with the added bonus of live accordion on Fri and Sat nights. Closed Thurs eve.

Cittadella Via Cittadella 18 ☎091 751 58 85. The popular trattoria at ground level is excellent, serving pizzas, pasta and simple fish dishes for Fr.25 or less, while upstairs the formal restaurant concentrates on fish alone – and does it well (4-course *menú* Fr.75). Closed Mon.

Funicolare Beside funicular top station in Orselina. Quiet, simple place that benefits from a spectacular secluded terrace garden overlooking Madonna del Sasso at which to savour their inexpensive fish specialities. Closed Thurs in winter & Nov–Jan.

Lungolago Via Bramantino 1. Classy pizzeria, *paninoteca* and pub where locals go to flee the invasion of white-knee'd northerners.

Manora Via della Stazione. Good self-service salads and plain cooking in this busy spot across from the train station, open late and Sun.

Navegna (see p.167). A little way east in Minusio, but right on the lakefront and highly acclaimed for its delicately prepared and presented Ticinese cuisine (*menús* Fr.50). Closed Nov–March.

Osteria del Centenario Lungolago 13, Muralto ☎091 743 82 22. One of Locarno's best, serving internationally acclaimed nouvelle cuisine in an appealing blend of French and Italian styles. A lakeside terrace and three-figure bills come as standard. Closed Sun.

Pozzo Piazza Sant'Antonio. Friendly local café-bar on a quiet Old Town square.

Svizzero Piazza Grande. Best of the many pizzerias and diners on the square, with affordable fresh-made pasta, wood-fired pizza and plenty of Italian staples. Bustling from breakfast till the small hours.

Valle Maggia and Val Verzasca

The valleys around Locarno offer exceptional mountain scenery. The wild **VALLE MAGGIA** (⊛www.vallemaggia.ch) comprises a complex valley system stretching north into the high Alps. For a break from the lakes, book well ahead to stay at *Ca' Serafina* (☏091 756 50 60, ⊛www.caserafina.com), an outstanding five-room *pensione* in the rural hamlet of **Lodano**: rooms are spacious and all en suite, and the charming owner, Alexa Thio, speaks English. Dine at *Locanda Poncini*, an excellent local restaurant in neighbouring **Maggia**.

Beyond Lodano, roads divide 30km north of Locarno at **Bignasco** (438m). One route heads northwest into the Val Bavona, hemmed in by sheer scarps and waterfalls. The top station of a cable car rising to the glacial eyrie of **Robiei** (1905m) has a terrace restaurant.

From Bignasco, another road struggles northeast into the Val Lavizzara to **Mogno** (1180m), where you'll spot the tilted circular roof of the church of San Giovanni Battista, designed by Ticinese architect Mario Botta. It's a dazzling achievement – this small building, set on a marble plaza, boasts a supremely elegant interior, bare and silent, encircled in striped marble, with the altar bathed in sunlight. It is worth the journey.

About 3km east of Locarno, the **VAL VERZASCA** above Tenero is blocked by the gigantic **Verzasca Dam**, scene of one of the world's highest bungee-jumps (see ⊛www.trekking.ch): on one side is a dizzying 220-metre drop down to bare rock, on the other a tranquil, blue lake is framed by classic Alpine scenery.

The Centovalli railway

Locarno is the eastern terminus of the scenic **Centovalli railway** (⊛www.centovalli.ch) to the Italian town of Domodossola, known in its Italian section through the Val Vigezzo as the **Ferrovia Vigezzina** (⊛www.vigezzina.com). Little trains run by the FART company depart from beneath Locarno station into the spectacular valley – so named for its "hundred" side valleys – most of the time winding slowly on precarious bridges and viaducts above ravine-like depths. Sit on the left for the best views. The area is renowned for its natural beauty, and, with a walking map from Locarno tourist office, you could get out at any of the villages en route, pick up a trail and head off into the hills. There's no lack of cafés and simple accommodation. One neat way to see the route is with the **Lago Maggiore Express** pass (see p.130).

Tiny **Verscio**, 4km northwest of Locarno, is a lovely stone-built village which houses the **Teatro Dimitri** (⊛www.teatrodimitri.ch), an international mime school founded by the Ascona-born clown Dimitri, protégé of Marcel Marceau. The small theatre stages performances all summer long. Some 3km down the line is **Intragna**, whose graceful seventy-metre bridge was the scene of Switzerland's first-ever bungee jump, and remains a choice spot for leaping.

After the border at **Cámedo** (passport needed), trains roll on through rustic villages of the Italian **Val Vigezzo** to the highest point of the line at **Santa Maria Maggiore** (836m) before easing down into Domodossola.

Domodossola

The busy, characterful Italian town of **DOMODOSSOLA** stands at the fulcrum of three major train routes: Swiss main line trains run west to Bern and Geneva; Italian ones speed south to Stresa and Milan; and little mountain trains depart from underground platforms on a scenic route east through the Val Vigezzo and **Centovalli** to Locarno (see above for details).

Pick up a map at the **tourist office** in the station hall (Mon–Fri 9am–noon & 2.30–6.30pm, Sat 9am–noon; ☎0324.248.265, Ⓦwww.prodomodossola.it), or just walk directly away from the station on Corso Ferraris and Corso Fratelli di Dio, 200m west into the old part of town, set around a series of attractively crumbling arcaded piazzas. **Piazza Mercato** is the finest – conveniently laid with café tables – and also stages the town's Saturday market. From here, pedestrianized Via Briona leads to Piazza Cavour, from where Via Marconi returns to the station.

Strolling on Via Briona leads you past pleasant cafés and **restaurants**. *La Meridiana*, Via Rosmini 11 (☎0324.240.858; closed Mon), offers moderately priced Spanish specialities, as well as fish and pasta dishes. In front of the station, *Piazzetta*, Piazza Matteotti 5, is a cheery, inexpensive joint for good-value pizza, while *Il Giardino*, Via Gramsci 21, serves midpriced fish and risotto on its vine-shaded terrace.

Walk 250m north of Piazza Cavour on Via Binda, then turn right to find *Pasticceria Grandazzi*, Via Castellazzo 23 (Ⓦwww.pasticceriagrandazzi.com; closed Sun pm & Mon), a superb **chocolatier** turning out innovative handmade specialities: munch on their chocolate paintbrushes or take away a chocolate toolbox, complete with delicious spanners and "rusty" nails, dusted with cocoa.

Travel details

Details of routes and timetables for trains, buses and boats in the areas of Piemonte covered in this chapter are at Ⓦwww.vcoinbus.it. Full details of transport in Lombardy – the eastern shore of Lake Maggiore and around Varese – are at Ⓦwww.trasporti.regione.lombardia.it (click "orari"). Timetables for trains, buses, boats and cable cars in Switzerland are searchable at Ⓦwww.rail.ch. Passports are needed for travel between Italy and Switzerland. See p.30 for some guidance on deciphering timetables.

Trains

Locarno to: Bellinzona (every 30min; 20min); Domodossola (every 2hr; 1hr 40min).
Luino to: Milano Porta Garibaldi (hourly; 1hr 40min, change at Gallarate).
Orta-Miasino to: Domodossola (8–10 daily; 1hr); Milano Centrale (7 daily; 1hr 50min, change at Novara).
Pallanza (Verbania) to: Milano Centrale (hourly; 1hr 10min).
Stresa to: Milano Centrale (hourly; 1hr).
Varese to: Milano Porta Garibaldi (hourly; 55min).
Varese Nord to: Milano Nord/Cadorna (hourly; 1hr 5min).

Buses

Ascona to: Brissago (every 30min; 10min); Locarno (every 15min; 15min).
Cánnero to: Brissago (3 daily; 25min); Pallanza (hourly; 25min).
Cannóbio to: Brissago (3 daily; 15min); Pallanza (hourly; 35min).
Locarno to: Ascona (every 15min; 15min); Bellinzona (hourly; 50min); Brissago (every 30min; 30min).
Orta San Giulio to: Stresa (3 daily; 1hr).
Pallanza to: Cánnero (hourly; 25min); Cannóbio (hourly; 35min); Omegna (every 30min; 20min); Stresa (every 30min–1hr; 25min).
Stresa to: Orta San Giulio (3 daily; 1hr); Pallanza & Intra (every 30min–1hr; 25min).

Boats

Following is an outline of summer services; for full information, see Ⓦwww.navigazionelaghi.it.
Arona to: Angera (frequently; 5min); Stresa (approx hourly; 1hr).
Ascona to: Isole di Brissago (frequently; 15min); Locarno (every 50min; 30min).
Cánnero to: Cannóbio (7 daily; 50min); Intra (4 daily; 40min); Luino (7 daily; 10–15min).
Cannóbio to: Cánnero (7 daily; 50min); Luino (7 daily; 10–15min).

Intra to: Laveno (every 30min; 20min); Stresa (every 30min; 55min);

Locarno to: Ascona (every 50min; 30min); Isole di Brissago (every 50min; 45min–1hr); Luino (7 daily; 1hr 40min).

Pallanza to: Isola Bella (every 30min; 30min); Isola dei Pescatori (every 30min; 25min); Isola Madre (every 30min; 10min); Stresa (every 30min; 35min); Villa Táranto (every 30min; 10min).

Stresa to: Arona (approx hourly; 1hr); Intra (every 30min; 55min); Isola Bella (every 30min; 10min); Isola dei Pescatori (every 30min; 15min); Isola Madre (every 30min; 30min); Pallanza (every 30min; 35min); Santa Caterina (hourly; 15min); Villa Táranto (every 30min; 45min).

Lake Como
and Lake Lugano

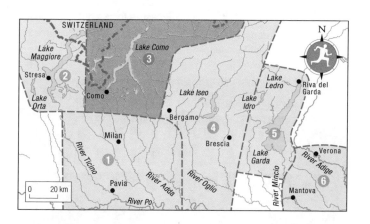

CHAPTER 3 # Highlights

* **Duomo, Como** Italy's most elegant fusion of the Gothic and the Renaissance, towering above Como's old quarter. See p.182

* **Centro Lago** The heart of Lake Como, centred on the enchanting trio of Menaggio, Bellagio and Varenna. See p.189

* **Villa Carlotta** Supremely photogenic lakeside villa, featuring romantic statuary and lush gardens. See p.191

* **Varenna's gardens** Villa Cipressi and Villa Monastero stand beside this lovely lakeside village, amid idyllic subtropical gardens. See p.202

* **Lugano** Elegant Swiss lakefront city, with bags of style, sass and charm. See p.208

* **Monte Generoso** High rocky peak served by rack-railway, with panoramic views from the summit. See p.215

* **Bellinzona** Three medieval castles form a defensive chain above this attractive, little-visited city. See p.218

▲ Villa Carlotta, Lake Como

Lake Como
and Lake Lugano

T he beautiful, neighbouring lakes of **Como** and **Lugano** – the former entirely within Italy, the latter mostly within Switzerland – offer some of the most dramatic mountain views in the region. Both are bound entirely by mountains, giving them, at least in parts, a wilder, less developed feel than lakes Maggiore and Garda, which in their southern reaches touch the populous lowland plains.

Easily reached from Milan in under an hour, Lake Como has been the more famous of the two since Roman times. It remains thoroughly **Italian** (and specifically **Lombard**) in culture, spirit and appeal. On the map, the border between it and Lake Lugano appears an afterthought – yet, in truth, this has been an international frontier for five hundred years and represents a profound cleft of culture and history: Lake Lugano has been **Swiss** since the dukes of Milan lost the surrounding region of **Ticino** to the invading northerners in 1512. Even today, with Switzerland staying out of the European Union, the frontier remains significant.

Crossing and recrossing the border can give fascinating insight into what it is, exactly, that makes Lake Como so unequivocally Italian and Lake Lugano so unequivocally Swiss. The city of Lugano is wealthier, certainly, and lacks the remnants of Fascist and post-Fascist urban design on show in Como. The food on Lake Como is classic Lombard fare – *missoltini* (dried fish), polenta, *pizzocheri*

Tourist information

The western shore of Lake Como, including Bellagio, is in the province of **Como** (ⓦwww.lakecomo.com), while the eastern shore falls within the province of **Lecco** (ⓦwww.turismo.provincia.lecco.it). Lake Lugano – apart from stretches of Italian shoreline around Porlezza in the east and Porto Ceresio in the west – lies entirely within the Swiss canton of **Ticino** (ⓦwww.ticino.ch).

Phone numbers

This chapter covers territory in both Switzerland and Italy. All **phone numbers** prefixed ☏091 are **Swiss**; all other numbers (beginning ☏03 in this chapter) are **Italian**. For details of international dialling, see p.58.

(buckwheat tagliatelle) – whereas Lugano's cooking displays northern influence in its rich dressings, cured meats and Alpine cheeses. In art and architecture, the impact of the Italian Renaissance did seep northwards across the border, but from then to the late eighteenth century, while Europe's nobility were busy putting up opulent villas on Como's shores, Lugano was a backwater, under continuous occupation by a trans-Alpine German-speaking army. Lugano's history is revolutionary, whereas Como's is authoritarian. Today, one way to tell which side of the border you're on is by the extent and type of new building, and by the upkeep of older buildings: Italy crumbles under the weight of history and poor urban planning, while Ticino has gained a reputation for world-class contemporary architecture.

And armies of northerners continue to arrive – though these days as many are English-speaking as German-speaking. Lugano can seem tranquil in comparison with the battalions of tour-buses and camper vans that parade up and down Como's shores all summer long.

To sample the classic images of the lakes – which can be found here in glorious abundance – aim for the best-known names: **Como** itself, **Bellagio** and **Menaggio** on Lake Como, and **Lugano** on Lake Lugano. These are all beautiful places to spend time, as are the quieter, less-visited little corners: **Varenna** on Lake Como, for instance, or **Gandria** on Lake Lugano. **Monte Generoso**, a mountain peak that rises to 1700m plum between both lakes – and is served by a rack-railway from the Swiss side – offers an unparalleled vista across the whole region; while to the north, characterful old towns guard the junction-points of high Alpine valleys: **Chiavenna** on the Italian side, and **Bellinzona** on the Swiss.

Lake Como

This lake exceeds anything I ever beheld in beauty.

Shelley, 1818

Of all the Italian lakes, slender, forked **LAKE COMO** (**Lago di Como**) comes most heavily praised: it is "a treasure which the earth keeps to itself," wrote Wordsworth. This has been the retreat of choice for hard-pressed urbanites for a couple of thousand years at least: Virgil knew of the lake, then called *Lacus Larius* (and still referred to today as **Lario**), while the Roman general Pliny had two villas here, one near Lenno, the other at Bellagio, and wrote in glowing terms of the natural beauty all around. The combination of forested mountains and blue water remains bewitching. The lake came into its own in the Romantic era, when artists, writers, composers and boatfuls of creative wannabes sought inspiration from the magnificence of the surroundings and the simplicity of the working life led by local fisherfolk and craftspeople.

And, in parts, that atmosphere survives: the lake that inspired the poets can still be found – a cobbled piazza here, a romantic view there – but the demands of tourism mean that you should perhaps tone down your expectations. Many parts of the lake are given over to low- and mid-budget holiday-making, with campsites and generic, if serviceable, two- and three-star hotels setting the tone

LAKE COMO

0   5 km

Selma
Lostallo
Chiavenna
Menarola
S. Maria in Calanca
Buseno
Gordona
Moleno
Claro
Castione
Roveredo
Grono
Gorduno
Arbedo
Pizzo Martello (2459m)
(2503m)
Bellinzona
SWITZERLAND
ITALY
Giubiasco
Pianezzo
Péglio
Gera Lário
Sórico
M. Marmontana (2316m)
Liro
Domaso
M. Garzirola (2116m)
Garzeno
Stazzona
Gravedona
Dongo
Abbazia di Piona
Cólico
Pianello Lário
Dório
Bogno
Cavargna
Crémia
Suéglio
M. Legnone (2609m)
Rezzónico
Dérvio
Sonvico
Carlazzo
S. Maria
Tremènico
S. Abbóndio
Pagnona
Valsolda
Porlezza
Plésio
Bellano
Casargo
Ória
S. Mamete
Lago di Piano
Grándola ed Uniti
Vendrogno
Pian d. Betulle (1456m)
Lake Lugano
Menággio
Taceno
Ósteno
VALSASSINA
Varenna
Cortenova
Claino
Cadenábbia
Lanzo d'Intelvi
Laino
Tremezzo
Lenno
Bellágio
Grigna Settentrionale (2409m)
S. Fedele Intelvi
Ossúccio
Sala Comacina
Lierna
Castiglione d'Int
Pigra
Isola Comacina
M. Generoso (1701m)
Argegno
Lézzeno
Civenna
Grigna Meridionale (2177m)
Casasco d'Intelvi
M. S. Primo (1685m)
Ghisallo
Oliveto Lário
Muggio
Brienno
Nesso
Magréglio
Mandello d. Lário
Barni
Abbadia Lariana
Valle di Muggio
M. Bisbino (1325m)
Láglio
Zélbio
Carate Úrio
Pognana Lário
Lambro
Valbrona
Balerna
Moltrásio
Faggeto Lário
Comi di Canzo (1373m)
Laorca
Masliánico
Torno
M. Palanzone (1436m)
Asso
Valmadrera
Malgrate
Cernóbbio
Blévio
Canzo
Lecco
Chiasso
Civíglio
Ponte Lambro
Longone al Ségrino
Civate
S. Fermo d. Batt.
Tavernério
Erba
Cesana Br.
Galbiate
Como
Albavilla
Bosísio Parini
Annone di Br.
Garlate
Lucino
Montórfano

Chiavenna ▶
Chiavenna ▶ Valtellina ▶
Lugano ◀
Gandria & Lugano ◀
Lugano ◀
Milan ▼   Milan ▼   Bergamo ▼
177

Boats on Lake Como

Seeing **Lake Como** from the water is not to be missed – indeed, with heavy traffic clogging the narrow lakefront roads over summer weekends, getting around by boat makes a good deal of sense. Boats are run by the Gestione Navigazione Laghi (☎800.551.801, ⓦwww.navigazionelaghi.it), who have booths for information and tickets at most landing-stages around the lake. Boats run year-round, with the greatest frequency in high season (June–Sept); at other times, services are reduced or, on some routes, halted.

Services and cruise options

It's easy to put together any kind of itinerary, using the widely available timetable leaflets. However, check carefully the various symbols and colour-coded notes to identify each route's days of operation, and be sure to differentiate between timings for the **battello** (ship), which stops everywhere; the **aliscafo/servizio rapido** (hydrofoil/fast service), which stops at major points only; and the **autotraghetto** (car ferry, also for foot passengers), which shuttles across the central part of the lake. Services run between about 7.30am and 8.30pm, though the car ferries start earlier and finish later.

The only genuine **cruises** are dinner-dance excursions from Como on summer Saturdays (9pm–1.30am; €40 including dinner). Otherwise timetables highlight several *Giri Turistici* (tourist trips) which use regular scheduled services as sightseeing voyages: the one-hour journey from Como to Torno or Urio and back (€6.40), for instance, or the two-hour trip from Como to Nesso and back (€10.50). Both these run every thirty minutes. On some routes (marked on the timetable with a knife and fork), you can eat on board – a fixed menu for €15.50.

Fares and passes

Tickets are charged on a complicated sliding scale, set out in a chart at the ticket booths (and online). Each route is assigned a number, according to the distance involved; you then cross-check on the list for how much that route-number (or *tratta*) costs. As an example, Como to Bellagio is given as *tratta* 6, which costs €7.90 (or €11.20 on the hydrofoil). Tremezzo to Cólico is also *tratta* 6, whereas Bellagio to

---

in several places. Halfway up the lake, old-fashioned luxury hotels from the grand old days of tourism preserve an aristocratic air of nostalgia. Making your way in a stately fashion by steamer can still feel wonderfully romantic.

The lake's principal towns – **Como** and **Lecco** – mark the southernmost points of both forks of the lake. The **Ramo di Como** (*ramo* means branch) is the more visited of the two; its twin, the **Ramo di Lecco**, is quieter and wilder. They meet at the **Centro Lago**, the most popular and most beautiful part of the lake, oriented around the trio of **Menaggio** – a pleasant, affordable base for walking and exploring the hinterland – and, for unrepentant romantics, **Varenna** and **Bellagio**.

Como

COMO, it must be said, isn't the prettiest town on the lake. As the nearest resort to Milan and a popular stopoff on the autostrada to and from Switzerland, it's both much visited and, on the outskirts at least, fairly industrialized. The main industry is a rarefied one – Como supplies luxury silk to fashion houses in Milan, Paris and New York – but that doesn't make the suburban factories any more endearing.

Lecco is *tratta* 5, equal to €6.20 (or €9 on the hydrofoil). The most expensive ticket, *tratta* 8 (Como to Cólico, or Lecco to Gravedona), is €9.60/€13.30. The charge for taking an ordinary-sized **car** on the ferry between Cadenabbia, Bellagio, Menaggio and/or Varenna is €6.60 one way, including the driver.

A **return ticket** costs double. EU citizens over 65 get a twenty-percent **discount** (Mon–Fri only). Ask at ticket offices about a **special offer** discounting admission to one of the lake's grand houses if you arrive by boat. You pay a **surcharge** of €1 if you buy your ticket on board, and bags or suitcases over 60cm long may also attract a supplement.

A **pass for unlimited journeys** (*biglietto di libera circolazione*; not valid on hydrofoils) is also priced according to *tratte*. A one-day pass covering six *tratte* (ie anywhere between Como and Bellagio) costs €17, or the whole lake costs €21. The six-day equivalents are €51/€63.

"Two lakes to dream about"

Como e Lugano: Due Laghi per Sognare ("Two lakes to dream about"; April–Oct only; €29) covers a circular trip around both lakes, using boats, buses and trains. It's a great-value way to get a flavour of the landscapes – and the ticket is valid for two days, meaning you can break the journey where you like. Note, though, that that this is not a tour: you are on your own, using **public transport**, as set out in the brochure. The example routings given here follow timetables current at the time of writing; check for up-to-date timings before you set out. From Como heading **anticlockwise** you start at noon with a boat departure to Menaggio (and a scenic lunch on board), then a bus from Menaggio through the hills to Porlezza and a pause before the 4.20pm cruise on the beautiful stretch of water to Lugano. Press on by train and bus back to Como, arriving at either 7.30 or 8.30pm for dinner. The **clockwise** alternative starts with a mid-morning bus and train journey to Lugano for lunch, then a 2.15pm boat to Porlezza, and a break before the 4.15pm bus to Menaggio. From here, a choice of boats, with or without a stop in Bellagio, delivers you back to Como at either 6 or 7pm. Details of timings to/from Menaggio or Lugano are given later in this chapter. Don't forget your **passport**.

Once you penetrate through to the lakeshore, however, things look up. The atmospheric **Città Murata** – Como's old, formerly walled quarter, a dense grid of narrow, pedestrianized lanes – is pleasant for a spot of window-shopping or grabbing a bite to eat. The **Duomo** is a strikingly beautiful and artistically significant building, blending elements of Gothic and Renaissance – well worth the trip to Como on its own. A **funicular** climbs the wooded slopes to offer wonderful views across the water, and there's a smattering of historical interest elsewhere in the town. In the main, though, Como gets on with life quite regardless of the lake on its doorstep or the visitors passing through.

Arrival, information and accommodation

Como San Giovanni station ("Como S.G.") is served by fast **trains** between Milano Centrale and Lugano, and slower trains between Milano Porta Garibaldi and Chiasso. It is on Piazzale San Gottardo, about ten-minutes' walk west of the centre. From the station, head down a grandiose flight of 54 steps through a patch of parkland (poorly lit after dark) to a large sculpture of a splayed hand, from where you cross the two main roads and then continue on Via Garibaldi into the old town. Buses are frequent, and taxis are always available.

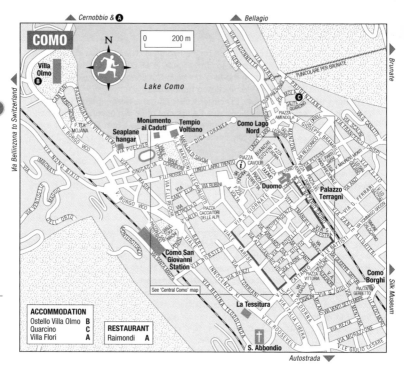

ACCOMMODATION
Ostello Villa Olmo **B**
Quarcino **C**
Villa Flori **A**

RESTAURANT
Raimondi **A**

Trains on the slower FNM line (Ferrovie Nord Milano, or LeNord; ⓦ www
.lenord.it) from Milano Cadorna/Nord pass through **Como Borghi** – located
on Piazzale Gerbetto, five minutes' walk southeast of the Città Murata – and
terminate at **Como Lago** (sometimes called Como Lago Nord), on the
lakefront Piazza Matteotti just across from the **bus station**. From Milan-
Malpensa **airport**, take the Malpensa Express and change at Saronno. **Boats**
dock at one or other of the jetties on Piazza Cavour.

Driving from Milan on the A9 autostrada, the Como Monte Olimpino exit
is most convenient. From Switzerland on the N2 autostrada, just after the
Chiasso border take the Como Nord exit, a narrow sliproad from the left-hand
lane. With the large numbers of *frontalieri* – people who live in Como but drive
to work in Switzerland – you'd do well to avoid trying to cross southwards
during the weekday rush (roughly 4–6pm).

For information on Como – the city and the lake – head to the friendly
tourist office, Piazza Cavour 17 (Mon–Sat 9am–1pm & 2.30–6pm; May–Sept
also Sun 9.30am–12.30pm; ☎031.269.712, ⓦ www.lakecomo.org). A city
information hut stands beside the Duomo on Via Comacini (Mon–Fri
10.30am–12.30pm & 2.30–6pm, Sat & Sun 10am–6pm).

Hotels

Barchetta Excelsior Piazza Cavour 1 ☎031.3221,
ⓦ www.hotelbarchetta.com. Venerable old city-
centre luxury hotel overlooking the main lakefront
square. Many rooms, done up in classic, traditional
style, have balconies. Doubles from around €320. ⑨

Del Duca Piazza Mazzini 12 ☎031.264.859,
ⓦ www.albergodelduca.it. Great little three-
star hotel full of cheery, down-to-earth local
atmosphere, on a picturesque old-town square a
short walk from the lake and the Duomo. Rooms are

small, but made special by windows onto the piazza, windowboxes and, in some rooms, two-person showers. Some less desirable rooms look only onto the titchy internal courtyard. Private parking. 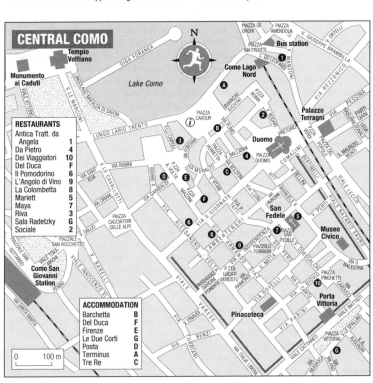❹

🔭 **Le Due Corti** Piazza Vittoria 12 ☎031.328.111, ✉hotelduecorti@virgilio.it. Despite (or perhaps because of) its location well away from the lake – which is 10min walk across town – this is a great place to stay: romantic without being stuffy. Built as a monastery in the seventeenth century, and serving for a time as a post-house, its characterful, rustic-style rooms are arrayed around an internal courtyard, featuring exposed stonework, full-spec bathrooms and old prints on the walls. The *Sala Radetzky* restaurant is excellent. Private parking. ❻

Firenze Piazza Volta 16 ☎031.300.333, ⓦwww .albergofirenze.it. Pleasant mid-range option on the spacious Piazza Volta, just back from the lakefront, with comfortable, smartly modernized rooms set mainly around a quiet internal courtyard. Some have balconies over the square. Private parking. ❹

Posta Via Garibaldi 2 ☎031.266.012, ⓦwww .hotelposta.net. A dour 1930s facade by Como-born Rationalist architect Giuseppe Terragni belies these

good budget rooms in a great central location on Piazza Volta – basic but clean and all en suite. Also some triples and a quad available. Check in at *Hotel Plinius* (Via Garibaldi 33). ❸

Quarcino Salita Quarcino 4 ☎031.303.934, ⓦwww.hotelquarcino.it. A family-run hotel near the funicular on the northeast side of the old town, with quiet rooms, some with their own balconies overlooking the hillside. The family rooms and suites are particularly good value (€110–130) and there is parking available. ❸

Terminus Lungo Lario Trieste 14 ☎031.329.111, ⓦwww.albergoterminus.com. An excellent city-centre hotel, on the lake and just a short stroll from the Duomo. The whole building is done out in Liberty style – the Italian version of Art Nouveau – with rich grained woods and brightly patterned fabrics. Plump for the unique split-level Tower Room, with eagle-eye views over the waterfront. Private parking. ❼

Tre Re Piazza Boldoni 20 ☎031.265.374, ⓦwww .hoteltrere.com. Decent three-star in the centre – modest in both size and ambition, but with spacious rooms, a touch of character, and good value for money. ❹

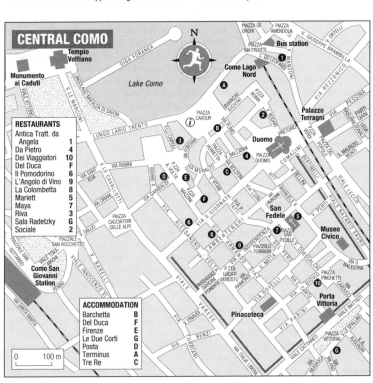

CENTRAL COMO

N

Lake Como

RESTAURANTS

Antica Tratt. da Angela	1
Da Pietro	4
Dei Viaggiatori	10
Del Duca	F
Il Pomodorino	6
L'Angolo di Vino	9
La Colombetta	8
Mariett	5
Maya	7
Riva	3
Sala Radetzky	G
Sociale	2

ACCOMMODATION

Barchetta	B
Del Duca	F
Firenze	E
Le Due Corti	G
Posta	D
Terminus	A
Tre Re	C

0   100 m

Como's new waterfront

At the time of writing, work was under way on **renovations** of Como's cramped waterfront. The lakeside promenade is to be widened, with flood barriers sunk into the pavement that can be raised when water levels rise significantly (two-metre floods, high enough to swamp Piazza Cavour, are not unknown). More trees will be planted, and there is talk of diverting traffic away from the lakeside road. The project is due for completion in 2011 – expect disruption before and after then. In particular, you may find that ferry landing stages have been moved around the bay to allow work to continue.

Villa Flori Via Cernobbio 12 ☏ 031.33.820, ⓦ www.hotelvillaflori.com. Beautiful lakeside villa 2km north of the city centre on the western shore, a little beyond the Villa Olmo gallery. The house dates from the nineteenth century, and has many period fittings and decorations, although the rooms now have all mod cons, as well as balconies looking over the water. The gardens are lovely, with fragrant citrus trees. Private parking. ❼

Hostel

Ostello Villa Olmo (HI hostel) Via Bellinzona 2 ☏ 031.573.800, ⓦ www.aighostels.com. Decent hostel located within the grounds of the Villa Olmo; to get there from San Giovanni station, either take bus #1 or #6, or turn left at the bottom of the long flight of steps in front of the station and walk for about 1.5km along Via Borgo Vico. The hostel serves evening meals, has laundry facilities, rents out bikes and provides a discount on the funicular. Dorms €15. March–Nov.

The City

The obvious place to start an exploration of Como is **Piazza Cavour**, a rather forbidding square on the lakefront bounded by unsightly modern hotels and banks. From here, the rectangular **Città Murata**, or walled town, spreads southeast, in parts bounded by its old walls but frequently with no formal delineation. Northeast of Piazza Cavour, the lakefront road curves around to the **funicular** station below Brunate and on to peaceful **Villa Geno** on the headland. Northwest of Piazza Cavour is a small park where sits a museum commemorating the Como-born inventor of the electric battery, **Alessandro Volta**, but then Como wastes its valuable waterfront with an ugly-looking stadium and seaplane hangar on the way round to the gardens of **Villa Olmo**.

The Duomo

A short walk away from the lake on bustling Via Plinio brings you to Como's architectural set-piece, **Piazza Duomo**. The city's commercial life continues here quite regardless of history or tourism: rather prosaically, men's outfitters and a department store share this modestly sized square with the magnificent west front of the **Duomo**, remarkable for its melding of the Gothic and Renaissance styles. Also facing the piazza, adjacent to the Duomo and connected to it, are the Gothic-Renaissance **Broletto** – the former law courts, prettily striped in pink, white and grey, with a fifteenth-century balcony designed for municipal orators – and the tall, imposing **campanile**, with an angled roof protecting its clock-face.

The current cathedral replaced the ninth-century church of Santa Maria Maggiore, remnants of which survive in the south wall. Work began in the 1390s, while **Gothic** held sway – first with the interior and then, from 1457, the west facade. By 1487, when the side walls were being built and the facade completed (both under the supervision of sculptor Tommaso Rodari), **Renaissance** ideas had taken hold, as shown in the choice of statuary adorning the

▲ The Duomo

facade. The main apse and vestries were begun in the 1510s, at the height of the Renaissance. The south and north apses date from later within the Renaissance – the middle decades of the seventeenth century – while the cathedral was only completed in 1744 with the addition of a **late–Baroque** cupola. Yet, remarkably, the vision for the building remained harmonious throughout; the overriding impression is of cross-stylistic elegance.

The Duomo's west facade

The soaring **west facade** facing the piazza shows the Gothic spirit in its fairytale pinnacles, rose window and buffoonish gargoyles, but it was completed in Renaissance style with rounded rather than pointed arches to the portals. Four vertical lines of saints climb each pilaster on the facade. At top centre is a figure of the resurrected Christ, while occupying small roundels on either side of the main door, below an elegant row of pointed niches, are depictions of Adam (on one side) and Eve (on the other).

The most surprising figures flank the main door: on the left is the Roman author Pliny the Elder, on the right his adoptive son Pliny the Younger – both of them pagans. Associating non-Christians with a house of God would have been unthinkable in 1396, when work on the facade began; yet by the 1480s, when Giovanni Rodari carved these statues – and by 1498, when his sons Tommaso and Jacopo designed their settings on this wall – Christian Renaissance humanists were drawing huge influence from such classical luminaries as the Plinys. The fact that both were also born in Como seems to have secured their inclusion here as honorary saints. The presence of Pliny Junior remains particularly questionable: his principal connection with Christianity was to have tortured two deaconesses in a vain attempt to shed light on what he termed "this depraved superstition".

Como silk

Como is one of the world's great **silk** cities. By the 1500s – a millennium after the secret of sericulture had leaked into Europe from China – silkworm farming was a major industry in and around Como: the city boasted an ideal temperate climate, plenty of fresh water and – crucially – abundant supplies of mulberry leaves (a silkworm's staple diet) from farms in the nearby Po Valley. Como only stopped producing raw silk in the middle of the last century, but it retained its expertise in high-quality finishing of silk items. Today, some eight hundred firms in and around the city – now supplied with Chinese raw silk – are involved in the design, manufacture, printing and dyeing of silk pieces for all the world's big-name fashion houses. Track the history of the industry at Como's excellent **Museo Didattico della Seta** (Educational Silk Museum), by the university on Via Castelnuovo (Tues–Fri 9am–noon & 3–6pm; €8; ⓦ www.museosetacomo.com) – complete with original looms and printing blocks – and then drop by **La Tessitura** outlet store, Viale Roosevelt 2a (daily 10am–10pm; ⓦ www.latessitura.com), crammed with ties, scarves, blouses and home furnishings, alongside a stylish design café (ⓦ www .loomcafe.com). The tourist office can supply a list of the region's other outlet stores; many shops in and around Como stock luxury silk items, or you could aim for the giant Foxtown outlet mall (ⓦ www.foxtown.com), 10km north in the Swiss town of Mendrisio (see p.218).

The Duomo's interior

Just inside the Duomo (daily 7am–noon & 3–7pm; free) are two **holy-water fonts**, placed either side of the main door, supported by splendid Romanesque lions. Alongside is the free-standing Renaissance **Baptistry**, built in 1590 as a small circular temple.

The Gothic-Renaissance fusion of the exterior continues inside. Gothic columns divide the nave and aisles, but the first two intercolumnar spaces have been hung with rich Renaissance **tapestries**, made in the sixteenth and seventeenth centuries, chiefly in Ferrara and Florence. Facing each other across the nave are Guasparri di Bartolomeo Papini's *Sacrifice of Isaac* and *Cain and Abel* (both 1598), while alongside the former is the *Presentation of the Virgin in the Temple*, possibly produced in Brussels in 1569 from figures by Dürer, and featuring striking use of perspective.

Of the cathedral's **paintings**, the south (right) wall features – behind the third column – the gilded St Abbondio altarpiece flanked by a languid *Flight to Egypt* (1526) by Gaudenzio Ferrari, filled with detail and composed on a diagonal axis to emphasize movement, and an absorbing *Adoration of the Magi* (1526) by Bernardino Luini, which includes such exotica as an elephant and a giraffe. Directly opposite, across the church, hangs Luini's *Adoration of the Shepherds* (1526), while a little further along the south wall is his melancholy, heavy-lidded *Madonna* for the St Jerome altarpiece (1521), both works showing the artist's debt to Leonardo.

Where two large **organs** face each other across the nave, the Gothic construction ends: the east end of the cathedral was completed under the influence of the Renaissance, with a distinctive lightness and symmetry of design. The **north apse** holds the colourful Altar of the Crucifixion, while the **south apse** has the Baroque Altar of Our Lady of the Assumption, completed in 1686 with twisting columns in black Varenna marble. The Renaissance **main apse** features the Altar of the Maestri Campionesi, consecrated in 1317 as the main altar of the old Santa Maria Maggiore church, and itself demonstrating another transition in style – from the Romanesque, as seen in the figures of the saints, to the Gothic, exemplified by the flower-ornamented arches which frame them. Overhead soars the spectacular Baroque **cupola**, designed in the 1730s by the master architect Filippo Juvarra, its apparently small lantern illuminating virtually the whole building.

The Duomo's north door, designed by the Rodaris in 1507, is known as the "**Door of the Frog**", for the frog which is carved – coincidentally, alongside the words *Sanctus Paulus* – into the right-hand side of the portal as you emerge into the street. Centuries of curious fingers have rubbed the little beast smooth.

Within the Città Murata

Within the narrow streets of the **Città Murata** – Como's once-walled old quarter – bustling Via Vittorio Emanuele II leads from the Duomo to the rear of the irregularly shaped **Piazza San Fedele**, formerly the city's corn market, on which several medieval frontages survive. Squashed into a corner, its facade and campanile partly obscured by an arcaded building stuck in front, is the church of **San Fedele** (daily 8am–noon & 3.30–7pm; free), once Como's cathedral, dating from 914, though altered since. Its gloomy interior features a pentagonal apse and some eighteenth-century decoration.

Via Vittorio Emanuele II continues to Piazza Medaglie d'Oro. Framing one corner, the elegant Palazzo Giovio and Palazzo Olginati together form the **Museo Civico** (Tues–Sat 9.30am–12.30pm & 2–5pm, Sun 10am–1pm; €3). From the ticket desk, doors open to a peaceful internal courtyard, lined with Roman columns and capitals. Inside, turning left at the top of the stairs brings you past displays of Roman glass, the mummy of Isiuret, a ninth-century BC priestess (with both feet sticking out of her sarcophagus), and Greek vases. Back at the stairs, head the other way for rooms devoted to prehistoric finds. Corridors at two points cross to the adjacent *palazzo*, which displays items related to Garibaldi and the Risorgimento.

From Piazza Medaglie d'Oro, follow Via Giovio to the main street for a view of the towering **Porta Vittoria** city gate, with four storeys of open arches (the internal wooden structure is long gone). Via Giovio continues to Via Diaz and the **Pinacoteca** at no. 84 (Tues–Sat 9.30am–12.30pm & 2–5pm, Sun 10am–1pm; €3), a small collection of medieval painting housed in the dour seventeenth-century Palazzo Volpi.

Outside the Città Murata

Just behind the Duomo, on the other side of the railway tracks, stands the definitive expression of Rationalism by Como-born architect Giuseppe Terragni. Built as the **Casa del Fascio** – a headquarters for the local Fascist party – in the 1930s, it has since been renamed the **Palazzo Terragni** and now houses the Guardia di Finanza. From a distance, the building is almost transparent: you can see right through its loggia to the wooded hills behind. This kind of light, deftly functional architecture broke new ground, yet it stands – by happy coincidence – directly opposite another, equally good example of geometry applied to produce architectural harmony: the apse of the Duomo, 418 years its senior.

Terragni's work can also be seen on the lakeside Piazza Cavour, where the lower storeys of the Hotel Metropole Suisse were reworked by him in 1927. From here, the waterfront promenade curls into a little park designed around a curious temple-like building, the **Tempio Voltiano** (Tues–Sun 10am–noon & 3–6pm; €3). This holds a museum dedicated to Alessandro Volta, a pioneer in electricity who gave his name to the volt – some of the instruments he used to conduct his experiments are displayed inside. Alongside, the **Monumento ai Caduti** is a striking memorial to the dead of World War I. It was designed by Futurist architect Antonio Sant'Elia, another Como native, but built – after Sant'Elia was killed in 1916 at the age of 28 – by Terragni, and stands in stark contrast to its surroundings. The pretty lakeside walk leads on round the bay to **Villa Olmo**, a Neoclassical pile which hosts conferences and exhibitions; whatever is on, its **gardens** (Mon–Sat: summer 8am–11pm; winter 9am–7pm; free) are worth a wander, with lovely waterside promenades and views.

The funicular and Villa Geno

The other way from Piazza Cavour, north along the lakefront to Piazza Matteotti, leads to the **funicular** (every 15–30min daily 6am–10.30pm; June–Aug until midnight; €4.25 return; ⓦwww.funicolarecomo.it). The little carriages take seven minutes to creep up the hillside alongside the gardens of wonderful nineteenth-century villas to **Brunate**, a small hilltop resort that has a few bars and restaurants and great views of the lake. Brunate is also a good starting-point for hikes – the tourist office has free leaflets detailing routes – including a two-day trek through the mountains to Bellagio.

About ten pleasant minutes' stroll further round the lakefront promenade from the funicular is the compact **Villa Geno**, occupying a jutting headland with good views back to Como. The villa's grounds (daily 10am–9pm; winter closes 6pm; free) include a little area to take a dip in the lake.

Sant'Abbondio

On the other side of the centre, a short walk from Piazza Vittoria on Via Muggiasca, is the strikingly attractive Romanesque church of **Sant'Abbondio**, an eleventh-century building erected on the site of a church recorded as early as the fifth century. The exterior has two elegant square campaniles, while the plain, solemn interior of this relatively small church has five soaring aisles divided by columns. The focus of attention is the ornate presbytery, dominated by a cycle of vivid fourteenth-century frescoes on the life of Christ.

Eating and drinking

Como is not renowned for its **culinary** depth, but a little hunting through the old-town lanes will turn up somewhere both affordable and appealing to dine.

For an *aperitif*, or evening **drink**, the atmospheric wine-bar *Osteria del Gallo*, Via Vitani 16 (closed Sun eve), is one of several offering a choice of tasty nibbles with a fine selection of wines. Livelier joints include the noisy *Nova Comum* on Piazza Duomo, packed with drinkers. The waterfront Lungo Lario Trieste, round by the funicular station, hosts a clutch of popular bars.

Day-tripping in Switzerland

Como city centre lies just 5km southeast of the **Swiss border**, and although the tourist office's guidance stops at the border, there's no reason for you to. It's easy to take a day-trip into Switzerland by train or car – perhaps relaxing on the waterfront at Lugano (see p.208), riding the rack-railway to the top of Monte Generoso (see p.215), or exploring pretty Swiss lakeside villages such as Morcote or Gandria. Everything, from an ice cream to a hotel room, can be paid for in euros. For details of the "Two lakes to dream about" ticket, covering a journey by train, bus and boat between Lake Como and Lake Lugano, see p.179.

For **picnic** fare, there's any number of delis scattered around the old town, as well as a mini supermarket (Mon–Sat 8am–1.30pm & 3.30–8pm) on the corner of Via Diaz and Via Natta.

Cafés and snacks

Mariett Via Vittorio Emanuele II 86. Old-fashioned locals' café and meeting-point in this jovial neighbourhood (once Como's Jewish quarter) behind the San Fedele church. Closed Wed.

Maya Via Luini 53. Cool, modern coffee bar, serving a great choice of coffees and delectable hot chocolate from 6.30am. Closed Sun.

Da Pietro Piazza Duomo. Decent café opposite the Duomo, with terrace tables on the square and a quiet *Sala da The* indoors. Simple menus are around €22, or plump for the daily special (*piatto del giorno*) at around €12.

Dei Viaggiatori Via Giovio 13. Easygoing little daytime café at the eastern end of the old town, with tables set out on the adjacent Piazzetta Pinchetti. Closed Sun.

Restaurants

L'Angolo di Vino Via Diaz 69. A good, modern *enoteca* serving typical local cuisine, carefully prepared in a cosy atmosphere with attentive service. Closed Sun.

Antica Trattoria da Angela Via Foscolo 16. Moderately priced restaurant near the Piazza Matteotti bus station, serving inspired regional cuisine using local ingredients. Closed Sun eve & Mon.

La Colombetta Via Diaz 40a ☎031.262.703. A classy, expensive little fish restaurant, with contemporary styling and a small but adventurous menu. The choice starter is the *crudo di pesce* (mixed raw fish) and you could move on to spaghetti *ai ricci di mare* (with sea-urchin) or *rombo al forno* (baked turbot). Fish such as *orata* (gilthead bream) and *branzino* (sea-bass) are common, but you may also see *pescatrice* (monkfish). Mains are around €25; the *menú degustazione* around €50. Open daily until 1am.

 Del Duca Piazza Mazzini 12 ☎031.264.859. A really nice, modestly priced little family-run restaurant on this quiet old-town square, away from the hubbub of Piazza Cavour and the Duomo. Pizzas are especially good, with an extra-long list to choose from, but the quality of all the familiar pasta, salads and meat staples is excellent. Service is warm, courteous and efficient.

Il Pomodorino Via Cinque Giornate 62b, ☎031.240.384. A good branch of the chain of decent, mid-range pizza and pasta restaurants, with pleasant ambience and overlooking an internal courtyard. The grilled meats are excellent, the desserts are home-made, and there are draught beers to accompany. Reckon on €23 or so. Closed Mon.

Raimondi At *Hotel Villa Flori*, Via Cernobbio 12 ☎031.338.233. Romantic restaurant within this nineteenth-century villa hotel on the lakefront 2km north of the centre. Book a terrace table for classic Italian cuisine served with flair and elegance. At least €60 per head. Closed Mon.

Riva Via Cairoli 10. Slick little restaurant just back from the waterfront, with a good selection of pizzas for around €8, lots of grilled meat options (€18 or so), and a range of novelty main-course salads, including American (with rocket and bacon), Norwegian (with cream cheese and smoked fish), Ligurian (with octopus), Jamaican (with prawns), and so on, for about €13. Closed Mon.

Sala Radetzky At *Hotel Le Due Corti*, Piazza Vittoria 8 ☎031.328.111. Formal, expensive restaurant attached to this attractive hotel – once a monastery – just outside the *Città Murata*. The cuisine is classic Lombard fare, and service is excellent – discreet but attentive. Closed Sun.

Sociale Via Rodari 6 ☎031.264.042. Reliable, informal restaurant in a pleasant location just north of the Duomo. The menu is around €16, or you can choose from a broad range of à la carte dishes for around €25 per head. Closed Tues.

The Ramo di Como

The scenic **Ramo di Como** – the Como branch of the lake – is the stuff of tourist brochures. Wooded mountain slopes protect the villages that are crammed onto the narrow shoreline from extremes of temperature, creating perfect conditions for an abundance of subtropical flora. These little communities are almost all pretty, characterful places (or, at least, have pretty, characterful parts to them), and the views of the mountains hemming in the lake are spectacular.

There's a **map** of Lake Como on p.177. For details of the **boats**, see p.178.

On the western side, **Cernobbio** makes for an alluring distraction before you reach the lake's only island, **Isola Comacina**. On the eastern side, a succession of old villages – **Blevio**, **Torno**, **Nesso** – cling to the cliffs on the shore towards Bellagio. Many of the opulent villas that line this stretch of the lake are still privately owned by industrialists and celebrities (George Clooney is a much-celebrated resident of Laglio).

Boats cruising northwards follow a zigzag route. By **car**, you must choose either the western shore to Menaggio or the eastern shore to Bellagio: both are narrow, frequently busy roads that coil along this rocky shoreline – not an easy drive. There is nowhere to cross the lake with a vehicle until you reach the Cadenabbia–Bellagio car ferry. From Como, catch hourly **buses** C10 to Menaggio or C30 to Bellagio (Ⓦ www.sptlinea.it).

Cernobbio and around

Served by frequent boats and buses from Como, **CERNOBBIO** village comprises a compact quarter of old houses just off the lakeside piazza, loomed over by Monte Bisbino (1325m), whose summit marks the Swiss border: a tortuous road reaches to the Rifugio del Bugone, almost at the top.

Cernobbio's opulent **Villa Erba** (Ⓦ www.villaerba.it), dating from 1901, is now a conference centre, closed to the public – though you can book for a private tour of some of the grandest rooms: the film director Luchino Visconti grew up here (and returned in later life).

Nearby stands the palatial **Villa d'Este**, now the grandest of Lake Como's grand hotels (☎ 031.3481, Ⓦ www.villadeste.it; ❾), commissioned in 1568 by Tolomeo Gallio, one of the chief cardinals under Pope Gregory XIII. The villa – converted into a hotel in the nineteenth century – boasts sumptuous gardens and interiors adorned with delicate stucco-work, magnificent frescoes, marble, mirrors and gilding, effortlessly drawing in the super-wealthy. An equally enticing A-list haunt is the *Gatto Nero* **restaurant**, Via Monte Santo 69 (☎ 031.512.042; closed Mon & Tues), a charming hillside trattoria serving hearty, well-presented fare; the terrace views are stunning, but with footballers and fashionistas as regulars, this place is just as much about who's at the next table. Near Cernobbio, in **CARATE URIO**, stop in at chic, contemporary styled *L'Altra Riva* (☎ 031.400.260, Ⓦ www.laltrariva.it; closed Wed) for excellent modern Italian cuisine on the lakefront.

The lake is at its narrowest and deepest by **TORRIGGIA** – just 650m wide, but 410m deep. Caves in the mountainsides on both shores were once home to prehistoric bears. One of the most atmospheric places to stop on this stretch is **BRIENNO**, a medieval hamlet bypassed by the main road: the lake washes up against the old houses, with narrow cobbled walkways winding around and between balconied buildings.

From the next town, **ARGEGNO**, a road branches off into the **Val d'Intelvi**, a high valley system of small, country churches and quiet walks, that ends at **Sighignola** (1300m) on the Swiss border, dubbed the "Balcony of Italy" for its spectacular views over Lake Lugano.

Isola Comacina

A little north of Argegno is **Isola Comacina**, Como's only island. It lies opposite the town of **SALA COMACINA**, across a mirror-calm stretch of water known as the *Conca dell'Olio*, or Basin of Oil. The island is wild and unkempt, dotted with the ruins of nine abandoned churches. Occupied by the Romans, it later attracted an eclectic mix of dethroned monarchs, future saints and the pirate Federico Barbarossa. Eventually it allied with Milan against Como – which prompted Como to sack the island. Abandoned for centuries, it was bought by a local, Auguste Caprini, who outraged Italy by selling it to the King of Belgium after World War I. The island is now administered by a joint Belgian/Italian commission.

Since 1947 the island has been home to an exclusive **restaurant**, *Locanda dell'Isola Comacina* (℡ 0344.55.083, Ⓦ www.comacina.it; June–Aug daily; March–May, Sept & Oct closed Tues; closed Nov–Feb). The owner has made a selling-point of an elaborate "exorcism by fire" at the end of every meal, stemming from a curse supposedly laid on the island in 1169 by the Bishop of Como and involving – essentially – flambéed liqueur coffee. To eat here you pay an all-in price (€60; no credit cards), which covers a set menu with wine – heavily overpriced for what is ordinary fare, but you're paying for the spectacle. Boat transport to and from Sala Comacina adds €6.

The eastern shore: Como to Bellagio

The **eastern shore**, north of Como, is a wilder affair, with rugged cliffs and a narrow road winding between village communities. The boats that zigzag their way up the lake stop at only a handful of points.

TORNO, a medieval rival of Como's, 7km north, retains some fine old buildings, including the Romanesque church of **San Giovanni** and the celebrated sixteenth-century **Villa Pliniana**, viewable only from the water. The villa has hosted a parade of romantic souls, including Byron and Shelley, Ugo Foscolo, Stendhal, Rossini and Bellini, but was named for Pliny's description of the curious intermittent waterfall in its grounds, a natural phenomenon that was studied by Leonardo da Vinci.

Some 10km north, past the cave systems at **Pognana**, is **NESSO**, where gorges cut into the mountains; the **Orrido di Nesso**, an especially high, gloomy example, marks the mouth of the Tuf and Nosè torrents. From Nesso, a narrow branch road twists up into the mountains, eventually joining the Valassina at Asso.

The final 10km stretch into Bellagio is taken up with a series of hamlets wedged into the cliffs; one, **LÉZZENO**, 7km before Bellagio, stands directly opposite the Isola Comacina and is a relatively frequent stop for boats. Coverage of Bellagio starts on p.194.

Centro Lago

As I sit writing in the garden under a magnolia I look across to Varenna in the sun … and the grand jagged line of mountains that bound the lake towards Cólico, almost snowless in August, stand glittering. You never saw anything so calculated to make you drunk.

Matthew Arnold, 1873

Halfway up the lake, where the Como, Lecco and Cólico branches meet, is the **Centro Lago**, the most scenically attractive part of the lake, hosting its three most sought-after destinations. If you have just one day on Lake Como, spend it here.

On the western side, lying north of the sheltered **Tremezzina** shore lies the busy village resort of **Menaggio**, with some great hiking in the surrounding

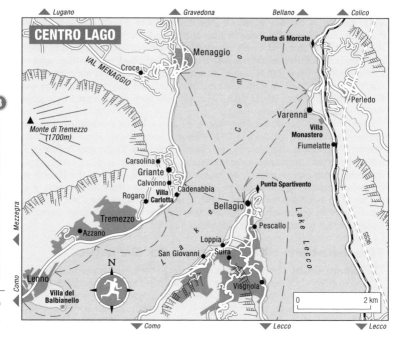

hills above a valley that leads west to Lugano in Switzerland. On the eastern shore, trapped beneath towering cliffs, stands the alluring waterfront village of **Varenna**, while midway between the two, occupying a headland jutting into the lake, nestles **Bellagio**, a picture-perfect village of steps and cobbled alleys.

Although all three are accessible by **road** – andVarenna is also on the **train** line from Milan to Cólico (via Lecco) – the easiest way to get around here is by **boat**: the area is crisscrossed by a dense web of ship, hydrofoil and car-ferry routings that run seemingly continuously in summer, and fairly frequently all year round.

The Tremezzina

Sheltered by a headland, the shore above Isola Comacina, known as the **Tremezzina**, is where Como's climate is at its gentlest, the lake at its most tranquil and the vegetation most lush. Lined with cypresses and palms, it's lovely at any time of year, but unbeatable in spring, awash with colour and heady with the scent of flowering bushes.

Villa del Balbianello

One of Lake Como's most seductive grand houses is the **Villa del Balbianello**, situated on the headland just outside **LENNO** (mid-March to mid-Nov Tues & Thurs–Sun 10am–6pm; house and gardens €11, or €3 to UK National Trust cardholders; gardens only €5, or free to UK National Trust cardholders; ☏0344.56.110, ⓦwww.fondoambiente.it). Access is chiefly by boat (small craft leave frequently from Lenno and Sala Comacina), but on Tuesdays, Saturdays and Sundays you can leave your car either in Lenno or at the gates at the end

There's a **map** of Lake Como on p.177. For details of the **boats**, see p.178.

of the access road (signposted) and walk through the grounds – roughly 800m from Lenno, half that from the gates.

The house is a classic eighteenth-century set piece, built over the remnants of a medieval convent and left to the nation by explorer Guido Monzino, who in 1973 became the first Italian to climb Everest. However, it's the romantic **gardens** that inspire, with their gravel paths between lush foliage (including magnolias, cypresses, plane trees and ilex), and stone urns and arches framing spectacular views across the water. George Lucas filmed parts of *Star Wars Episode II* here.

Tremezzo and around

For more than 150 years, overseas visitors – particularly the British – have been holing up in **TREMEZZO** and neighbouring **CADENABBIA**; the latter's Anglican church was the first in Italy (1891). The tradition continues today, which is a pity, since the area now doesn't represent the best of Lake Como. Many hotels are only average and the lakefront road is busy here, running between the buildings and the water: however good a restaurant may be, eating at terrace tables within metres of passing traffic won't be to everyone's taste. In general, you'll find greater satisfaction elsewhere.

Exceptions include charming *La Darsena* (☎0344.43.166, ⓦwww.hotel ladarsena.it; ❺–❻), a stylish small hotel and restaurant on the lake side of the road near Tremezzo's landing-stage, with spacious, elegant rooms (many with balconies) – or you could always hide away amidst the opulent interiors and tranquil grounds of the five-star *Grand Hotel Tremezzo Palace* (☎0344.42.491, ⓦwww.grandhoteltremezzo.com; ❾) on the lakefront.

The villages in the hills above retain more character. Local tourist offices have details of walks that pass through charming **GRIANTE**, for example – where *Casa Pini*, Via Brentano 12f (☎0344.37.302, ⓦwww.casapini.com; ❷), is a pleasant little B&B, with a lovely garden and home-cooked food – or **ROGARO**, where you'll find the lovely family-run farmhouse restaurant *La Fagurida* (☎0344.40.676; closed Mon), specializing in home-produced *salumi*, polenta and roast rabbit. **Mezzegra** is renowned as the place where, on April 28, 1945, Italy's wartime partisan leader, Walter Audisio, caught up with – and shot – Mussolini, before the dictator could escape into Switzerland. Euphemistic signposts within the pretty village direct you to the site of the "historical event", where, bizarrely, a memorial cross to the Fascist leader stands by a votive shrine to the Virgin Mary.

Villa Carlotta

Located directly on the lakeside road, 100m from the *Grand Hotel Tremezzo Palace*, **Villa Carlotta** (daily: April–Sept 9am–6pm; March & Oct 9am–noon & 2–4.30pm; €8; ⓦwww.villacarlotta.it) is nonetheless best visited by **boat**: views of the house from the water are glorious. The villa is a regular stop for boats plying between Como, Bellagio and Menaggio; alternatively, you could stroll from the landing-stages at Tremezzo (450m south) or Cadenábbia (900m north) – both are pleasant, attractive walks.

Pink, white and exceptionally photogenic, this grand house was built in 1690 by Giorgio Clerici, a banker from Milan. In 1843, it passed to Princess Marianne of Nassau, wife of Albert of Prussia, who gave it to her daughter Carlotta as a wedding present – hence the name.

You approach through the formal terraced gardens in front, and up a distinctive triple-layered scissor staircase. The house displays a collection of eighteenth-century **painting and statuary** beloved of the Sommariva family, owners of the villa at the time of Napoleon. On the ground floor, the rear left-hand room

(Room A) is the one to aim for: here resides the meltingly romantic *Cupid and Psyche*, a copy in marble, done under Canova's direction, of his own original. Elsewhere, as you drift through the rooms, are paintings by Jean-Baptiste Wicar (*Virgil Reading Book VI of the 'Aeneid' Before the Court of Augustus*) and Francesco Hayez (*Romeo and Juliet's Last Kiss*). Room M holds Canova's sculpture *Palamedes*, a fine figure of a man from every angle. Upstairs, rooms have been laid out with original furniture, mostly of the Empire period.

As much as the art or the building itself, though, Villa Carlotta is worth visiting for its expansive, fourteen-acre **gardens**, a beautifully ordered collection of camellias, rhododendrons and azaleas. You can use your ticket to come and go all day.

Menaggio

MENAGGIO, 37km north of Como and 29km east of Lugano, is a bustling village resort with a good deal of character. Busy roads cut into a chunk of the upper town – the lakeshore routes and the road west to Porlezza and Lake Lugano – but below them, around the traffic-free **Piazza Garibaldi** and surrounding alleyways, Menaggio retains much of its poise: it is well-kept, attractive and has a fine view east across the water to Bellagio and Varenna. It also sees more of a mix of tourists than many of its neighbours, with a reputation for sports and activities – notably hiking and cycling in the mountains – as well as sunbathing and swimming.

RESTAURANTS	
Al Paladar de la Memoria	1
Bellavista	C
Di Paolo	B
Il Vapore	4
Osteria Il Pozzo	3
Vecchia Menaggio	2

ACCOMMODATION	
Bellavista	C
Garni Corona	B
Grand Hotel Menaggio	D
Grand Hotel Victoria	A
Ostello La Primula	E

Hiking and adventure sports around Menaggio

There's a good selection of **hikes** in the countryside around Menaggio, ranging from a two-and-a-half-hour walk to the pretty village of Codogna, to the *Sentiero delle 4 Valli*, which leads for 50km through four valleys to Lake Lugano in Switzerland. The tourist office can provide descriptions of the routes in English, including details of how to get to the various starting-points by public transport, but take a map as well.

There's a beach and vast pool at the **Lido** (late June to mid-Sept daily 9am–7pm), as well as **waterskiing** and other activities at the Centro Lago Service on the waterfront.

Arrival and information

Boats and **hydrofoils** shuttle frequently to Menaggio from Tremezzo, Bellagio and Varenna, and there are also **car ferries** from Bellagio and Varenna. The landing-stages are beside each other about five-minutes' walk south of the main lakefront square, **Piazza Garibaldi** – stopping-point for **bus** C10 from Como and C12 from Lugano (@www.sptlinea.it).

The **tourist office**, Piazza Garibaldi 3 (Mon–Sat 9am–12.30pm & 2.30–6pm, Sun 10am–4pm; Nov–March closed Wed & Sun; ☏0344.32.924, @www .menaggio.com), is very well organized, with a wide array of practical information and guidance on local walks.

Accommodation

Bellavista Via IV Novembre 21 ☏0344.32.136, @www.hotel-bellavista.org. Decent, three-star lakefront hotel. Rooms have some style, with drapes and good fabrics, and there's a terrace restaurant, pool and parking. ❹

Garni Corona Largo Cavour 3 ☏0344.32.006, @www.hotelgarnicorona.com. Family-run two-star on the lakefront, with 22 plain but adequately fitted-out rooms, some with lake views and balcony. March–Nov. ❸

Grand Hotel Menaggio Via IV Novembre 69 ☏0344.30.460, @www.grandhotelmenaggio.com. Overlooking the landing-stage, this is one of Menaggio's two historic four-star hotels. Service is remarkably good here and, for such a big place, it has few airs and graces. Rooms are spacious and well-appointed, many with balconies offering wonderful lake views, and there is a pool and private parking. March–Oct. ❽

Grand Hotel Victoria Lungolago Castelli 9 ☏0344.32.003, @www.grandhotelvictoria.it.

Ten-minutes' stroll east from the *Grand Hotel Menaggio*, this splendid old property stands just 150m from the main square, sheltered behind five immense cedar trees. The ambience here is similarly engaging, though quieter: the hotel grounds (with parking) are private and hardly any traffic passes. Old-fashioned standards prevail – in decor, facilities and quality of service – and the genial staff all speak English. March–Oct. ❽

Ostello La Primula Via IV Novembre 86 ☏0344.32.356, @www.menaggiohostel.com. Excellent hostel on the edge of town, with small, clean dorms and a couple of family rooms; reservations are essential. It has its own small beach, bikes for rent and discounts on boat rental. Dorms €15. March–Oct.

Campsite

Europa ☏0344.31.187. Local site just north of town. May–Sept.

Eating and drinking

Menaggio's lakefront square has several **restaurants** serving set menus – and with its holiday atmosphere, it can be lively after dark: restaurants serve late – but for a tad more quality stroll the lanes further back. The town is also handy if you're self-catering, with a couple of supermarkets and some good delicatessens.

For coverage of the lakeshore north of Menaggio, turn to p.204.

Bellavista Via IV Novembre 21 ☏0344.32.136, ⓦ www.hotel-bellavista.org. A good-quality hotel restaurant, with a scenic terrace on the lake and a varied menu ranging from perch with almonds to Chateaubriand steak. Expect around €40.

Osteria Il Pozzo Via Carlo Porta 3 ☏0344.32.333. An attractive small terrace restaurant just back from the lakefront, serving decent local cooking. Closed Wed.

Al Paladar de la Memoria Via Al Lago 23. Modern, lively bar in the lanes behind Piazza Garibaldi, open from breakfast until 2am and also for light meals. Closed Mon.

Il Ristorante di Paolo At Hotel Garni Corona, Largo Cavour 5 ☏0344.32.133, ⓦ www.ilristorantedipaolo.com. A moderately upmarket, white-tablecloth place, serving well-prepared local cuisine – missoltini (dried lake fish), casonsei (meat-filled ravioli) and more – alongside excellent wines. Expect around €35. Closed Tues.

Il Vapore Piazza Grossi 3 ☏0344.32.229. Pleasant little restaurant in a quiet, central location serving local dishes in the modest dining room or on the flower-decked terrace. No credit cards. Closed Wed.

Vecchia Menaggio Via Al Lago 13 ☏0344.32.082, ⓦ www.vecchiamenaggio.it. Simple, good-value meals for around €12 at this central pizzeria/restaurant. Closed Tues.

Val Menaggio and west to Lake Lugano

Menaggio stands at the mouth of a route linking west through the mountains to Lake Lugano. This is a scenic byway, driven easily and quickly, and offers the chance to compare the two lakes: only 11km separate busy Menaggio on Lake Como from **Porlezza**, which faces along the beautiful, little-visited eastern arm of Lake Lugano. Having a meal at **Gandria** (see p.214), or visiting **Lugano** (see p.208) are enticing reasons to head this way.

After climbing out of Menaggio, the road scoots along the floor of the **Val Menaggio** alongside the tiny, reedy **Lago di Piano**, protected as a nature reserve and breeding place for water birds. The Menaggio tourist office has the route description for a pleasant, almost flat two-hour walk in the area that takes in woodlands and a fortified cluster of medieval houses on a peninsula in the lake, known as Castel San Pietro. The **campsite** *OK La Rivetta* occupies a pleasant waterfront site within the reserve, Via Calbiga 30 (☏0344.70.715, ⓦ www.campingoklarivetta.com; Easter–Oct). Porlezza on Lake Lugano (see p.215) is 3km further west.

Bellagio

Cradled by cypress-spiked hills on the tip of the Triangolo Lariano – the triangle of mountainous land between the Como and Lecco branches of the lake – **BELLAGIO** has been called the most beautiful town in Italy. It's not hard to see why. With a promenade planted with oleanders and lime trees, *fin-de-siècle* hotels painted shades of butterscotch, peach and cream, a spectacular

---

Two lakes to dream about

It's possible to start from Menaggio or Bellagio for the round-trip **Como e Lugano: Due Laghi per Sognare** ("Two lakes to dream about"; April–Oct only; details in box, p.211). A boat around 8.10am brings you to Como by 9am for coffee. Press on by bus and train to Lugano for lunch, then a 2.15pm cruise to Porlezza. After a break there, a bus returns you to Menaggio by 4.45pm. Frequent boats make the final hop to Bellagio, if needed.

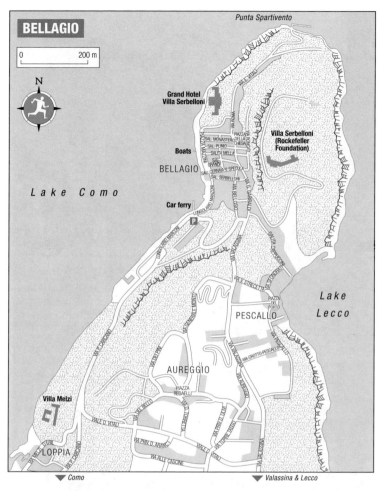

BELLAGIO

0   200 m

N

Punta Spartivento

Grand Hotel
Villa Serbelloni

Villa Serbelloni
(Rockefeller
Foundation)

Boats

BELLAGIO

Lake Como

Car ferry

*Lake
Lecco*

PESCALLO

AUREGGIO

Villa Melzi

LOPPIA

▼ *Como*　　　　　　　　　　▼ *Valassina & Lecco*

mid-lake location and a crumbling core of stepped, cobbled alleyways, Bellagio is the quintessential Italian Lakes town.

This little place has a long history. The Roman statesman **Pliny the Younger** may have had a villa on Bellagio's promontory in the first century AD. The village is first mentioned in 835 as Belasio, and also appears as Bellaxio, Belacius and Bislacus; despite inevitable associations with modern Italian *bella* ("beautiful"), its name derives more prosaically from *bi-lacus*, Latin for "between the lakes". Bellagio's strategic location ensured its success throughout the **medieval** period, and by the early **nineteenth century**, the wealthy families of Lombardy – like their Roman forebears – were coming here simply to relax.

Arrival, information and accommodation

Boats shuttle frequently to Bellagio from Tremezzo, Cadenábbia, Menaggio and Varenna. Passenger ships and hydrofoils dock directly at Piazza Mazzini; **car-ferries** land 150m south by the car park (you're not permitted to drive

▲ Bellagio

through Bellagio unless you're unloading at a hotel). **By road**, Bellagio is 30km from Como and 20km from Lecco, but both are treacherous, narrow roads that coil along the rocky cliffsides: reckon on a slow forty minutes to drive either route, an hour or more if traffic is bad. **Buses** run from both cities, letting you sit back and drink in the views.

The **tourist office** is at the landing-stage, on Piazza Mazzini (Mon–Sat 9am–12.30pm & 1–6.30pm, Sun 9.30am–12.30pm & 1–2.30pm; ☎031.950.204, ⓦwww.bellagiolakecomo.com). Staff have maps and brochures galore, as well as information on activities such as hiking, horse riding, mountain biking and watersports.

Hotels

Bellagio Salita Grandi 6 ☎031.950.424, ⓦwww.bellagio.info. An appealing, modern boutique hotel, in one of Bellagio's tallest buildings. The styling is fresh and contemporary, with huge picture windows, electric blackout shades, wood floors, flat-screen TVs, a/c, spotless en-suite bathrooms. Go for the rooftop vistas from the fourth floor: the corner rooms 401 or 404 are to die for. Cheaper rooms lower down have all the same fittings but less dreamy views. Managed by the family that also runs the *Hotel Du Lac*, with discounts offered at the *Du Lac* restaurant. ❹

Belvedere Via Valassina 31 ☎031.950.410, ⓦwww.belvederebellagio.com. A modern three-star hotel, in the same family since 1880 but now completely refurbished, set in its own parkland at the top of the village, with a swimming pool and wonderful views over the Lecco arm of the lake. April–Nov. ❺

Giardinetto Via Roncati 12 ☎031.950.168. Friendly old one-star place at the top of Bellagio: some of the rooms have lake views and there's a garden where you can picnic. Best of the budget options. No credit cards. March–Oct. ❷

Grand Hotel Villa Serbelloni Via Roma 1 ☎031.950.216, ⓦwww.villaserbelloni.it. Bellagio's most prestigious hotel, and one of Italy's grandest and stuffiest luxury retreats. See p.198 for some history. The opulence of the nineteenth-century interiors is extraordinary, with lavishly ornate ceilings and fittings, original artworks, chandeliers, frescoes and marble, best appreciated to the strains of the hotel orchestra, which plays nightly. The visitors' book reads like an account of

twentieth-century history, from Russian princes through Franklin D. Roosevelt to Churchill, King Farouk of Egypt on honeymoon, JFK and Prince Rainier of Monaco – via Clark Gable, Al Pacino and Michael Schumacher. Amazingly, for such a huge property, there are only 61 rooms (and 20 suites): each is spacious, formal and unique. On-site swimming pool, luxury spa and fitness centre. April–Oct. Doubles from €400. ❾

Du Lac Piazza Mazzini 32 ☎031.950.320, ⓦwww.bellagio.info. Directly opposite the landing-stage, this fine old hotel offers spacious three-star lake-view rooms in classic style. Service – rarely for Bellagio – is excellent, and the atmosphere is one of quiet, informal gentility, aided by the ministrations of the owner-manager Leoni family. March–Oct. ❻

La Pergola Piazza del Porto 4 in Pescallo ☎031.950.263, ⓦwww.lapergolabellagio.it. Stylish, modern en-suite rooms with balconies overlooking the lake and the vine-covered restaurant below, though you'll need your own transport to reach it, since it's away from Bellagio in the neighbouring hamlet of Pescallo. April–Nov. ❹

Silvio Via Carcano 12 ☎031.950.322, ⓦwww.bellagiosilvio.com. Bright two-star rooms with lake views, and an excellent restaurant serving home-made dishes featuring fish freshly caught by the friendly owner. April–Oct. ❸

Campsite

Camping Clarke ☎031.951.325, ⓦwww.bellagio-camping.com. A small, family-run campsite about 10min drive out of town on Via Valassina. May–Sept.

The village and around

Bellagio's first hotel, the *Genazzini*, opened in 1825; its second, the *Florence*, opened in 1852. The two flank Bellagio's scenic **waterfront** to this day, and passenger boats dock midway between them (the *Genazzini* is now the *Metropole*, with a prominent sign commemorating its origins). The **views** from here westwards to the mountains above Cadenábbia are simply lovely; spending an afternoon watching the shadows lengthen, as the ferries parade to and fro across the water, is pure Bellagio.

The central part of town – the **Borgo** – is tiny, laid out on a grid pattern: three streets parallel to the waterfront (Piazza Mazzini at the bottom, Via Centrale in the middle, Via Garibaldi at the top) are connected by seven perpendicular stepped alleyways. **Via Garibaldi**, the main shopping street, is a curious mix of touristy souvenirs, high-class silk and silver outlets, and ordinary delis and pharmacies. Although Bellagio has more than its fair share of fay watercolourists, there is a sense that ordinary life continues here despite the throngs of day-trippers.

At the top of the town is the Romanesque church of **San Giacomo**, built at the end of the eleventh century, alongside a tower (in Piazza della Chiesa) which is all that's left of Bellagio's medieval defences. Across the square, at the head of the Salita Monastero steps, was once a monastic institution attached to the church, occupied since 1919 by the *Bar Sport*.

A short stroll north, only 350m past the *Grand Hotel*, brings you to the **Punta Spartivento**, the "Point Which Divides the Winds", at the very tip of Bellagio's promontory. There's a little harbour here – nice for a cool dip – as well as a pleasant little restaurant (see below) from which to enjoy the unique panoramic vistas out over the lake and mountains. About ten-minutes' walk east of Bellagio on an attractive footpath through vineyards, the enchanting little harbour of **Pescallo**, a fishing port since Roman times, offers a tremendous view of the Grigne mountains looming over the Lecco branch of the lake.

The Serbelloni villas

Confusingly, Bellagio has two grand houses known as **Villa Serbelloni** – one a luxury hotel on the village waterfront, the other a privately owned mansion set amidst lavish gardens on the hilltop above Bellagio. The two are entirely separate today, but once shared a link.

Shielded behind gates at the northern end of Piazza Mazzini is the *Grand Hotel Villa Serbelloni*, built in 1852 as a private house and converted into a hotel twenty years later under the name *Grand Hotel Bellagio*. For the best part of a century, this palatial affair competed with Bellagio's equally grand *Hotel de la Grande-Bretagne* as to which could host the more sophisticated guests amidst the more opulent surroundings, inspiring partisan loyalty among visitors and local residents alike (hundreds of whom were employed as hotel staff). In 1907, the *Grand Hotel Bellagio* acquired as an annexe the seventeenth-century mansion residence of the then-defunct Serbelloni family, which stood on top of the hill above Bellagio – changing its name to *Grand Hotel Villa Serbelloni* in celebration. Barely two decades on, the Wall Street Crash of 1929 forced the hotel to sell its hilltop annexe, although it clung on to the Serbelloni name. Today, with the *Grande-Bretagne* long derelict (despite its beautiful location partway down the Salita Serbelloni steps in town), the *Grand Hotel* offers Bellagio's only five-star accommodation (see p.197).

Meanwhile, in 1959 the real Villa Serbelloni on the hilltop above passed into the hands of the **Rockefeller Foundation**. Although the villa remains off-limits – an exclusive study centre for scholars and politicians – its gorgeous **gardens** are visitable on a guided tour (April–Oct Tues–Sun 11am & 3.30pm; €8; maximum 30 people; cancelled in bad weather; buy tickets 15min in advance from the office at the far end of Piazza della Chiesa). The gardens, formally designed in the nineteenth century on English and Italian lines, offer magnificent **views** over all three branches of the lake, and are liberally sprinkled with evocative grottoes and statuary. It is thought that Pliny's villa stood up here.

Villa Melzi and around

Just beyond Bellagio's lido, the lake promenade continues south for about 500m to **Villa Melzi**, another of Lake Como's great houses, built in 1808 for Francesco Melzi D'Eril, vice president of the Italian Republic. The Neoclassical building is off-limits to the public, but visitors come to stroll in the extensive, luxuriant **gardens** (April–Oct daily 9am–6pm; €6; ⓦ www.giardinidivillamelzi .it), laid out in the English style and crammed with azaleas, rhododendrons, ornamental lemon trees, cypresses, palms, camellias and even a sequoia. Statuary dots the grounds, and you could work out the romantic little pond with Japanese water-lilies, overlooked by cedar and maple.

The gardens extend to the characterful harbourside hamlet of **LÓPPIA**, a relatively quiet retreat after Bellagio, from where you can continue for a further ten minutes' stroll to neighbouring **SAN GIOVANNI**, another attractive little village that hosts the **Museo degli Strumenti per la Navigazione** (Navigational Devices; May–Oct Tues–Sun 10am–1pm; €5), a diverting collection of compasses, telescopes and marine chronometers.

Eating and drinking

Like everything in Bellagio, **restaurants** can be pricey. You'd do best to **book** a table – essential at weekends and in the summer peak period. The best place for **ice cream** is *Il Sorbetto* at the top of Salita Serbelloni. *BellagioPoint.com*, Salita Plinio 8, offers the intriguing combination of internet access and wine tasting.

Barchetta Salita Mella 13 ☏ 031.951.389. A fixture since 1887 in the heart of the old lanes, serving authentic local cuisine: opt for the *pesce del giorno* (€27), or try the *menù gastronomico*, at €46 a head. Closed Tues.

Bilacus Salita Serbelloni ☏ 031.950.480. Opposite the *San Giacomo* (see below), but more formal and slightly more expensive, with an attractive pergola for al fresco dining.

Alle Darsene di Loppia Loppia ☏ 031.952.069, ⓦ www.alledarsenediloppia.com. A quiet, attractive fish restaurant on Loppia harbour, a little south of Bellagio. Closed Mon.

La Grotta Salita Cernaia 14. Decent wood-fired pizza at this cosy place which serves late (until 1am). Credit cards accepted over €25. Closed Mon.

Du Lac Piazza Mazzini 32 ☏ 031.950.320. The restaurant of this fine hotel (see p.197) spreads beneath the arcades directly opposite the landing-stage – surprisingly good for such an obvious location, with carefully prepared daily specials, fair prices (€17–20), and a touch of chic atmosphere after dark.

Mella San Giovanni ☏ 031.950.205, ⓦ www .ristorantemella.it. A family-run trattoria in San Giovanni, near Bellagio – good local cooking, in a genial atmosphere. Menu €26.

Mistral At *Grand Hotel Villa Serbelloni* ☏ 031.956.435, ⓦ www.ristorante-mistral.com. Bellagio's top spot for *haute cuisine*, spreading over a lakeside veranda. It has a Michelin star for its light, creative Italian and Mediterranean food, and they are very proud of their "molecular cuisine", a faddy idea to do with unusual combinations of flavours and ingredients. The dress code is smart-casual.

La Punta Punta Spartivento ☏ 031.951.888. Five minutes' walk north of town, and serving excellent food – especially lake fish – at good prices. Lovely views over the Punta Spartivento.

San Giacomo Salita Serbelloni ☏ 031.950.329. At the top of the Salita Serbelloni steps. A romantic trattoria with tables on the steps outside, serving good local dishes off a small menu with decent wines; a meal is about €25 a head. Closed Tues.

Silvio Via Carcano 12 ☏ 031.950.322, ⓦ www .bellagiosilvio.com. One of Bellagio's most pleasant, attractive dining spots, located just above nearby Lóppia. This is an excellent, modern restaurant attached to an old hotel; the views are beautiful, and the fish – freshly caught by Silvio himself – is superbly prepared (mains around €17). No closing day.

South of Bellagio: Madonna di Ghisallo

The triangle of land south of Bellagio between the two branches of the lake is lush and sunny, busy on the coast but with plenty of quiet inland villages. A little south of Pescallo, a minor road climbs on a twisting course up into the mountains towards Erba, on the Como–Lecco road 28km south of Bellagio. The views over the lake from the peak of **Monte San Primo** (1686m), a steep walk of a couple of hours from the end of its branch road, are much photographed – a breathtaking panorama, with Bellagio on the tip of its triangle down in front. Back on the Erba road, at the top of the ridge behind Bellagio is the church of

Madonna di Ghisallo, patron saint of **cyclists** – a diminutive building but a hugely popular draw for weekend day-trippers; inside, it's packed with trophies, jerseys and cycling memorabilia of all kinds. If you fancy the time-honoured approach (on a bicycle), be prepared for an exceptionally tough climb on slopes of 14 percent – reckon on two hours or more to cover the 12km from Bellagio. Up here, too, is a café, a monument to cyclists (marked "Then God created the bicycle"), a large parking area and even some souvenir stalls.

Beyond Madonna di Ghisallo, the road heads down the gently sloping **Valassína** (or **Vallassína**) – not to be confused with the Valsássina near Lecco – for the final 16km to Erba, passing through the quiet little town of **Asso**, for which the valley was named. Asso is the terminus for stopping trains on a slow line into Milan's Cadorna/Nord station.

Varenna

Halfway up Lake Como's eastern shore, gazing back at Bellagio, is **VARENNA**, perhaps the loveliest spot on the whole lake. Free of through traffic – which is diverted around the village – shaded by pines and planes, and almost completely devoid of souvenir shops, Varenna is set around steep, narrow stepped alleyways, a little cluster of attractive old houses and waterfront cafés. It's an unassuming little place which repays however much time you're prepared to devote to it.

Arrival, information and accommodation

Thanks to this rocky shoreline, Varenna is split into two fragments. **Boats** dock at a northern outpost of the village named Olivedo that also, high up on the landward side of the main road, hosts the **train station** (with regular trains from Milano Centrale via Lecco). Some 300m south via the road or, better, the *passarella*, a scenic walkway which clings to the rocks down at lake level, is the main chunk of the village. Here, on the central square, is Varenna's **tourist office** (April–Sept Tues–Sat 10am–12.30pm & 3–5.30pm, Sun 10am–12.30pm; Oct–March Sat 10am–5pm; ☎0341.830.367, ⓦwww.varennaitaly.com), near the stop for the D20 Lecco-Colico **bus**. If the few (paid) blue **parking** spaces on the square and by the ferry are full, use a (free) white space further out; yellow spaces are residents-only.

Hotels

Albergo del Sole Piazza San Giorgio 21 ☎0341.815.218. Excellent three-star hotel in the village centre. Rooms are light, airy and modern – some with lake views, others overlooking the piazza – and service is warm and courteous. ❹

Albergo Milano Via XX Settembre 29 ☎0341.830.298, ⓦwww.varenna.net. One of Lake Como's friendliest, best-looking small hotels lies tucked away in the narrow lanes between the square and the waterfront. It's justifiably popular, not least for its modern design aesthetic – a breath of fresh air amidst all those fusty old traditional lake hotels. Well run by a charming couple, it has great views from the rooms and breakfast terrace, and an effortless air of cool romance. Evening meals are lovingly prepared. The eight rooms in the main building are supplemented by the Casa Gialla (Yellow House) and Casa Rossa (Red House), two annexes nearby. Closed Dec–Feb. ❺

Beretta Via per Esino 1 ☎0341.830.132, ⓦwww.hotelberetta.it. Welcoming place near the train station that is the best of the cheaper options. It's also the hotel most likely to have room if you haven't booked ahead. ❷–❸

Du Lac Via del Prestino 4 ☎0341.830.238, ⓦwww.albergodulac.com. Varenna's top hotel – a romantic 1823 villa hidden away in a corner of the village right on the waterfront. The renovations have retained much of the old charm: public areas are elegant but not stuffy, rooms are spacious and airy. ❻

Olivedo Piazza Martiri 14 ☎0341.830.115, ⓦwww.olivedo.it. Simple, atmospheric little family-run hotel opposite the landing-stage, stuffed with old prints and knick-knacks. ❺

Royal Victoria Piazza San Giorgio 2 ☎0341.815.111, ⓦwww.royalvictoria.com. Landmark hotel on the main square that ticks the boxes – spacious rooms, stunning lake views, amiable service – but lacks the attention to detail to truly justify its four-star rating: interiors are tired, the breakfast is thin, furniture is make-do. A handy stop-gap if the competition is full. ⑥

Villa Cipressi Via IV Novembre 18 ☎0341.830.113,

ⓦwww.hotelvillacipressi.it. Newly renovated rooms in this wonderful old house offer an enticing blend of romance, grandeur and style – and you get a free run of the lush gardens (see p.202). Book well ahead. ⑥

The village and around

As well as the thirteenth-century **San Giorgio** on the main piazza, Varenna also hosts one of the oldest churches on the lake, the tenth-century **San Giovanni Battista**, almost forgotten on a lower corner of the same square. Barriers at the south door stop you exploring inside, but you can lean over to see well-preserved, if fragmentary, frescoes inside.

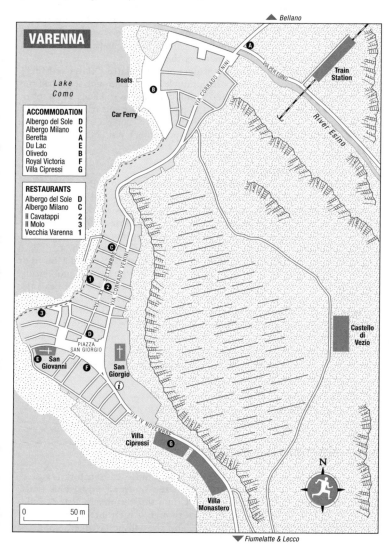

▲ Bellano

VARENNA

Lake Como

Boats Ⓑ

Car Ferry

VIA CORRADO VENINI

VIA PER ESINO

Train Station

River Esino

Ⓐ

ACCOMMODATION	
Albergo del Sole	D
Albergo Milano	C
Beretta	A
Du Lac	E
Olivedo	B
Royal Victoria	F
Villa Cipressi	G

RESTAURANTS	
Albergo del Sole	D
Albergo Milano	C
Il Cavatappi	2
Il Molo	3
Vecchia Varenna	1

VIA SETTEMBRE

VIA CORRADO VENINI

Ⓒ

❶ ❷

❸

Ⓓ

PIAZZA SAN GIORGIO

Ⓔ San Giovanni

Ⓕ San Giorgio ✝

ⓘ

Castello di Vezio

VIA IV NOVEMBRE

Villa Cipressi Ⓖ

N

Villa Monastero

0   50 m

▼ Fiumelatte & Lecco

Varenna's other sights are botanical: now a hotel, the nineteenth-century **Villa Cipressi** (April–Oct daily 9am–7pm; €4), on the southern fringe of the village, has terraced gardens tumbling down to the lake that make a perfect spot to relax with a book in the afternoon sun. The gardens of the adjacent **Villa Monastero** (April–Oct daily 9am–6pm; June–Sept until 7pm; €3; ⓦ www.villamonastero .org) are even more lavish: wandering here feels like a secret discovery. The splendid house, occupying the site of a convent founded in 1200 but dissolved in 1569 because of its nuns' licentious behaviour, is now used as a conference centre, but some of the most beautiful rooms are accessible for visits (April–Oct Sat & Sun 9.30am–1pm & 2–6pm; June–Sept until 7pm; €5). When meetings are on, both house and gardens are closed.

Steep paths creep up the hillside from opposite the landing-stage and Villa Monastero, meeting (after an energetic twenty-minute climb) at the semi-ruined **Castello di Vezio** (April–Oct daily 10am–sunset; free; ⓦ www.castellodivezio .it), allegedly founded by the Lombard Queen Theodolinda in the seventh century and offering spectacular views over the lake.

A short walk south of Varenna, the hamlet of **Fiumelatte** ("River of Milk") is named for the seasonal torrent which tumbles frothily through it for half the year – starting abruptly in March and running dry just as suddenly in October. Leonardo da Vinci was fascinated by the phenomenon, and tried to find out why it occurred; he drew a blank – as, indeed, have modern scientists. This is also the **shortest river in Italy** (and perhaps Europe), just 250m from source to outflow.

Eating and drinking

Varenna's best place to **eat** is also its smallest. Hidden away in the narrow lanes off the main piazza is the tiny ✻ *Il Cavatappi* (ⓣ 0341.815.349, ⓦ www .ilcavatappiwine-food.it; closed Wed), with just five tables. Booking is essential for this delightful little restaurant, where the owner/manager/chef takes the time to discuss the menu with you before turning out simple, beautifully cooked dishes with first-class ingredients. A meal is around €25 a head.

Vecchia Varenna (ⓣ 0341.830.793, ⓦ www.vecchiavarenna.it; closed Mon) is in an unbeatable location, tucked beneath the arcades on the lakeside promenade; book ahead in summer for a table on the terrace – but the location beats the food, which is acceptable but not remarkable (around €30). For snacks, drinks and light meals, *Il Molo*, on the same bay, is very pleasant, with a broad selection of salads and desserts. The pizzeria attached to *Albergo del Sole* (closed Wed), on the main piazza, is another sound choice, with excellent pizza, or hide yourself away on the little terrace of *Albergo Milano* (see p.201) for a romantic dinner of light, tasty Mediterranean cuisine (eves only; closed Tues & Sun); expect a bill around €30.

For coverage of the lakeshore north of Varenna, turn to p.205.

The Ramo di Lecco

Flanked by mountains of scored granite, Lake Como's eastern fork is austere and fjord-like, at its most atmospheric in the morning mists. This is the **Ramo di Lecco** – the branch of Lake Como that terminates at Lecco, also often dubbed the "Lago di Lecco", even though it is an integral part of the whole. It is a quieter part of the lake, and the villages wedged along the shoreline are generally fairly ordinary. Overshadowing it all are the craggy peaks of the **Grigne** range, which rise above the eastern shoreline to 2400m and culminate in the saw-like ridge of **Monte Resegone** above the town of Lecco itself.

South towards Lecco

The road along the **western shore** for the 20km between Bellagio and Lecco is slow and tortuous. Some 8km south of Pescallo, on Bellagio's outskirts, stands **Oliveto**, with a sprinkling of small restaurants and views of the brooding peaks across the water.

The main highway along the **eastern shore** spends most of the 23km between Varenna and Lecco dipping in and out of tunnels, although a quiet minor road dawdles along the waterfront, and **trains** also pass this way on the Colico–Lecco–Milan line. **Lierna**, 6km south of Varenna, is a pretty little place, with its medieval adjunct of Castello occupying a picturesque, beach-girt peninsula, but the main settlement is **MANDELLO DEL LARIO**, an industrial town that has been the production centre of Italy's famous **Moto Guzzi** motorbikes since 1921; there's a **museum** of vintage specimens at Via Parodi 57 (guided tours Mon–Fri 3pm; free; ⓦ www.motoguzzi.it). Just north in Olcio is the *Ricciolo*, Via Provinciale 165 (ⓣ 0341.732.546; closed Sun eve & Mon), a moderately priced **restaurant** with a Michelin star that serves well-received lake cuisine, including a *menú del lago* comprising four courses of local fish. It's a popular spot: book ahead. **Boats** run between Bellagio and Mandello. Just south is the old silk-town of **Abbadia Lariana**, much modernized.

Lecco and around

LECCO, 30km east of Como at the foot of this branch of the lake, is a commercial hub, though prettily spread around its little stretch of waterfront beneath towering mountains. The principal draw for Italians is that Lecco was the childhood home of the novelist **Alessandro Manzoni** (1785–1873), and was the setting for his classic work *I Promessi Sposi* (*The Betrothed*), published in 1827 – the first novel to be written in a pan-national Italian, and the first to paint Italian history in terms of its effect on ordinary individuals. It is required reading in Italian schools to this day. The tourist office and the town oblige with a torrent of Manzoniana: a brochure pinpoints the locations around Lecco of various scenes in the novel, while Piazza Manzoni in the centre holds a grand statue of the author. The **Villa Manzoni**, Via Guanella 7 – where the writer grew up – is open as a museum (Tues–Sun 9.30am–5.30pm; €5).

All this leaves most non-Italian visitors cold, and Lecco has little else to offer. As you stroll the lakefront, past the **Torre Viscontea** – remnant of a medieval castle – you could pop into the **Basilica**, which boasts a set of fourteenth-century Giotto-esque frescoes. The most attractive part of town is **Pescarenico**, an old fishermen's quarter located on the north bank of the River Adda as it flows out of Lake Como on its way into Lake Garlate. It's an atmospheric spot, with narrow alleys and a picturesque, sixteenth-century riverfront piazza.

There's a **map** of Lake Como on p.177. For details of the **boats**, see p.178.

Practicalities

Lecco's **tourist office** is at Via Nazario Sauro 6, off the lakefront Piazza Garibaldi (daily 9am–1pm & 2.30–6.30pm; ☏0341.295.720, ⓦwww.turismo .provincia.lecco.it), with information on hikes in the **Valsássina**, an isolated rural valley that follows a curving course behind the Grigne range. With Como, Bellagio, Varenna and Bergamo all within easy reach, there's no need to **stay**; if you get stuck, aim for *Don Abbondio*, Piazza Era 10 (☏0341.366.315, ⓦwww .donabbondio.com; ❸), a characterful three-star option in Pescarenico, with a moderately priced **restaurant**.

From Lecco, **trains** run north to Varenna, Colico and Tirano, south to Milan (Centrale and Porta Garibaldi) as well as Bergamo and Brescia. The line to Como is poorly served: better to catch a C40 **bus** from the train station. Bus D10 serves Bellagio. **Boats** arrive from Bellagio daily in summer; in spring and autumn there's only a Sunday service, and nothing at all in winter. All timetables are at ⓦwww.trasporti.regione.lombardia.it.

The Ramo di Cólico and northwards

The northern reach of Lake Como – dubbed **Alto Lario**, or the **Ramo di Cólico** – is something of a let-down. Whereas lakes Maggiore and Garda become increasingly attractive the further north you go, the opposite is true on Lake Como. Here, the jagged cliffs and sheer slopes that characterize the lower two-thirds of the lake retreat from the water's edge; instead, the shores comprise marshy plains and reedy inlets, backed by a horizon of peaks. But the main difference is in the towns: there is nowhere here to compare with the charm of a Bellagio or a Varenna. Campsites and caravan parks abound, catering chiefly to holidaying families from northern Europe.

The nicest town to aim for is **Gravedona**, while on the eastern shore there are a couple of diversions between **Bellano** and **Colico**. The dramatic scenery picks up again further north, around the Alpine town of **Chiavenna**.

The west shore: north of Menaggio

On the drive north of Menaggio, fast tunnels tempt you inland. Instead, follow *lungolago* signs onto the slow, narrow lakeside road. That way, you'll stumble across **REZZONICO**, a sleepy hamlet of cobbled lanes woven around a thirteenth-century castle, with a steep path leading down past a trickling stream and grazing sheep to one of the quietest bays on the lake (swimming is banned). *Ristorante Lauro* (☏348.264.6726; ❶) offers simple meals and rooms. Adjacent **PIANELLO** is about as tourist-free as Lake Como gets: there's a small campsite here, but otherwise the pedestrianized waterfront features local families strolling, kids playing and oldtimers soaking up the rays. Ferries stop by the picturesque fifteenth-century campanile of San Martino. Grab lunch at the village pizzeria or just picnic on the shore.

A couple of excellent **restaurants** could tempt you into the hills above the next town, **Dongo**. A tortuous road climbs high to **STAZZONA**, passing first *La Trave* (☏0344.88.688; closed Tues), a friendly little place with its own *salumi* on a €25 house menu. Further up is the terrific *Antica Trattoria Vecchia Pira*

There's a **map** of Lake Como on p.177. For details of the **boats**, see p.178.

(☎0344.88.277; open eves only & Sun lunch; closed Wed), a tumbledown cottage straight out of Central Casting – set above a rushing river, with geraniums in the window box and a scenic terrace. Its menu, also €25, sets dishes such as smoked trout, quiche and artichoke risotto alongside local specialities including polenta and *pizzocheri*.

Gravedona
Nearby **GRAVEDONA**, 17km north of Menaggio, is one of the few towns on the lake as old as Como, with a lazy waterfront set around a curving bay. Wordsworth set off on a moonlight hike from here, got lost and was unable to sleep, "tormented," he wrote, "by the stings of insects". Nowadays it's a pleasant enough town for a stroll, though the main reason to stop is to admire the fine twelfth-century carving of a centaur pursuing a deer – an early Christian symbol for the persecution of the Church – which adorns **Santa Maria del Tiglio**, a handsome, striped church on the lake originally built as a baptistry for the adjacent parish church of San Vincenzo. If it's closed, get the key from the green house on the road nearby.

The east shore: north of Varenna
On the eastern shore, **BELLANO**, 4km north of Varenna, is a workaday town of silk and cotton mills. From the landing-stage follow signs for the three-minute walk up behind Piazza San Giorgio to the **Orrido di Bellano** (April–Sept daily 10am–1pm & 2.30–7pm; Oct–March Sat & Sun 10am–12.30pm & 2.30–5pm; €3.50), a steep gorge with a series of walkways suspended above a roaring river.

About 12km north of Bellano, you'll spot a minor road branching left, signed to Olgiasca. This brings you, 2.6km down a rough cobbled track, to the gates of the **Abbazia di Piona**, perched on a headland that almost encloses a little lagoon. The abbey (daily 9am–12.30pm & 1.30–6.30pm), centred on a Romanesque church dating from the mid-twelfth century, is perfectly tranquil, remote and little visited. A shop (daily 9.30am–noon & 2.30–4.45pm) at the gates sells bottles of the monks' fiery herb liqueur.

From the turning, it's about 5km further north – through Piona itself – to the final stop for Lake Como's boats (and a terminus of some trains from Milan), industrial **CÓLICO**. From here, trains run north over the River Adda and across the **Pian di Spagna**, a marshy plain named for the fortress built in 1603 by the Spanish ruler of Milan as a defence against the Austrians. Their main route into Italy was down the massive **Valtellina**, which stretches east of here to Sondrio and up into the Dolomites. Until Roman times Lake Como extended across this plain; it left behind the **Lago di Mezzola** – not worth stopping for, but a pleasant distraction before you reach the industrial outskirts of Novate. Beyond, the flat Piano di Chiavenna marks the start of the **Valchiavenna**, flanked by the high Alps.

Chiavenna
Lying 26km north of Colico is **CHIAVENNA**, a rather attractive Alpine town. Main roads heading this way are often signposted for the **Spluga Pass** at the head of the Valchiavenna, or for **St Moritz**, which lies beyond the **Maloja Pass**.

It's a short walk from the bus and train stations down Viale Matteotti to **Piazza Bertacchi**, in the pedestrianized old town. Via Dolzino runs to either side, and it's a delight to lose yourself in the characterful old streets, with terrace cafés adorning every piazza. Chiavenna lies at the end of the **train** line from Milan (via Lecco), and also has regular **buses** running between St Moritz and Lugano (via Menaggio) – hence the quantity of Swiss day-trippers.

The **tourist office** (Mon–Sat 9.30am–12.30pm & 2.30–6pm, Sun 9am–12.30pm; ☎0343.33.442, ⓦwww.valtellina.it) is by the bus bays in front of the train station. For a **hotel** try the pleasant little *Flora*, 150m right of the station, Via Don Guanella 10 (☎0343.32.254, ⓦwww.florahotel.com; ❷) – or there's a good **campsite** (☎0343.36.7555) 3km north of town, by the Acquafraggia waterfall.

Chiavenna is known for its *crotti*, natural cellars in the cliffs, which for centuries have been used for maturing wine, salami, cured meats and cheeses. Most are now **restaurants**. The finest is *Crotto al Prato*, Via Picchi 13 (from the station, cross the tracks and follow Via Pratogiano around), where you can sit at outdoor tables by the *boules* pitch with wonderful mountain views. Chiavenna's Saturday **market** spreads over a nearby car park.

North of Chiavenna: the Alpine passes

Chiavenna stands at the junction of two high valleys. To the north, on a steep ascent, are interesting walks to the **Marmitte dei Giganti**, glacial potholes. Beyond, 30km north of Chiavenna, is the **Spluga Pass** (2113m) on the Swiss frontier (see also p.221).

Heading east, buses from Chiavenna quickly reach the Swiss border at Castasegna, which marks the start of the beautiful Val Bregaglia. Just 3km into Switzerland, a narrow road from Promontogno climbs the north wall of the valley to **Soglio**, an eyrie of cobbled alleys and close-set buildings, or you could continue up the valley – past Stampa, birthplace of sculptor Alberto Giacometti – to the **Maloja Pass** (1815m), and on to the legendary Swiss Alpine resort of **St Moritz**. From here, with a bit of advance timetable planning, you can catch the *trenino rosso* (see below) for the scenic journey over the Bernina Pass back into Italy at **Tirano**, from where trains and buses head back to Chiavenna and Lake Como.

The lower Valtellina

Unless you're a keen skier, there's little to draw you to the **Valtellina**, east of Colico – one of Italy's less-appealing Alpine valleys. Cut through by major transport links, it's mined for minerals and is prone to landslides. Busy roads and the train line head up from Lake Como to **SONDRIO**, an undistinguished town 42km east of Colico, known for its wine. In **TIRANO**, 27km further east, the opulent pilgrimage church of **Madonna di Tirano** stands 1km northwest of the centre, commemorating an appearance of the Virgin in 1504, its shrine focused around a statue of Mary dressed in a silk and gold robe donated by local people in 1746.

From Tirano's little station (within which passport control separates the Italian platforms from the Swiss ones), a Swiss train run by the Rhaetian Railway (Rhätische Bahn; ⓦwww.rhb.ch) – dubbed the **trenino rosso** ("little red train"; ⓦwww.treninorosso.it; €18 one way) – heads up the Val Poschiavo on a spectacularly scenic journey to the ice-bound **Bernina Pass** (2328m), terminating (after about 2hr 20min) at the chic Alpine resort of **St Moritz**. Some trains on this line form part of Switzerland's flagship Bernina Express route, served by panoramic carriages, for which seat reservations are obligatory (€5). From St Moritz, Swiss postbuses (June–Oct; ⓦwww.postbus.ch/alps) run back over the Maloja Pass to Chiavenna and Menaggio.

An alternative from Tirano are the Swiss buses (May–Oct; 1 daily) which run down the Valtellina, around Lake Como to Menaggio, and on across the border to **Lugano** (€19.50 one way, plus €8 reservation; Ⓦwww.rhb.ch).

Lake Lugano

Divided from its larger twin – Lake Como – by the international border, **LAKE LUGANO** (**Lago di Lugano**, also often referred to by its old Latin name, **Ceresio**) is, if anything, even prettier. With mountains that are often steeper than those of Como, the lake is noticeably less developed: aside from the stylish city of **Lugano** – which is less than half the size of Como – there are no big towns at all on its shores, which are, in any case, frequently too steep for even the Swiss to be able to build roads. The main part of the lake is in Switzerland, though it twists out into Italy on both sides. Boats, buses and trains pass from one to the other with minimal fuss.

Lugano is the biggest city in the Swiss canton (region) of **Ticino**, whose stunning natural beauty – lush wooded hills rising from azure water, palms swaying against deep-blue skies, red roofs framed by purple bougainvillea – often seems to blind outsiders with romance.

Aside from Lugano itself – and the beauty of the lake – attractions are low-key and largely rural. Jutting out into the lake a stone's throw from the city is the sun-drenched **Ceresio peninsula**, dotted with idyllic country villages and crisscrossed by some lovely walks. The rack-railway up to **Monte Generoso** offers some jaw-dropping panoramic views as well as a host of walking routes

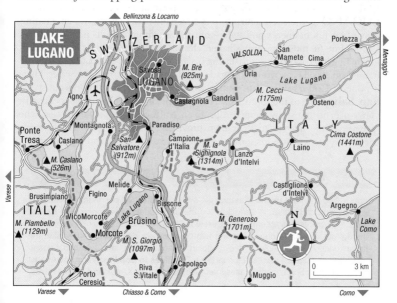

into the nearby valleys, including the idyllic **Valle di Muggio**. And north of Lugano, beyond the Monte Ceneri range (1961m), lies the Ticinese capital **Bellinzona**, a charmingly unfussy city dominated by three well-preserved medieval castles.

Some history

Although linguistically and temperamentally Italian, Ticino has been **Swiss** since the early 1500s, when Uri, Schwyz and Unterwalden – three cantons of Central Switzerland – moved to secure the southern approaches of the Gotthard Pass against the dukes of Milan. For three centuries the Ticinesi remained under the thumb of the tyrannical northerners, until **Napoleon** arrived in 1798 to reorganize the area under his new Cisalpine Republic. But faced with a mere exchange of overlords, the Ticinesi held out for independence, and under the banner *Liberi e Svizzeri!* ("Free and Swiss!"), the **Republic of Ticino** joined Switzerland as a new canton in 1803.

Since then, the Ticinesi – appearances notwithstanding – remain resolutely Swiss, and have little truck with foreigners calling them Italian, although it's almost impossible for an outsider to tell the locals apart from the 36,000 Italian *frontalieri* who cross into Ticino daily to work for salaries well below the Swiss average. A cruel irony of life here is that Ticino suffers Switzerland's highest **unemployment** rates even while its service industries thrive, staffed by Italians and paid for by thousands of German and Swiss-German tourists and second-home owners. As an ethnic and linguistic minority of eight percent in their own country, and nothing more than a quaint irrelevance to the urban hotshots of Milan and Turin next door, the Ticinesi consistently have to struggle to get their voices heard in the corridors of power.

Lugano

With its compact cluster of attractive piazzas and tree-lined promenades, **LUGANO** is the most alluring of Switzerland's lake resorts. It's an exciting, sassy place, full of energy and style – much less famous than its near-neighbour Como, but (it must be said) smaller, cleaner and sexier. While Como looks north, Lugano basks on a south-facing bay of the cerulean blue **Lake Lugano**, framed on all sides by wooded, sugarloaf hills rising sheer from the water. There is none of Como's waterfront clutter. Both **Monte Brè** to the northeast and **San Salvatore** to the south are served by funiculars, and both give spectacular views over to the snow-capped Alps. Even Milanese urban style-junkies, who give very little quarter to their own provincial towns, are prepared to bring friends over to Lugano for some shopping, a lakeside drink and a good meal.

Lugano's festivals

April's two-month **Lugano Festival** (⊛www.luganofestival.ch) features classical soloists and orchestras. In early July are the star-studded free concerts of **Estival Jazz** (⊛www.estivaljazz.ch). The **Ceresio Estate** classical music season runs throughout July and August, flanking two big **firework** displays over the lake: the Italian enclave of Campione throws down the gauntlet in late July and Lugano responds on August 1 (Swiss National Day). The **Blues to Bop Festival** in late August (⊛www.bluestobop.ch) showcases international blues, jazz, rock and gospel artists.

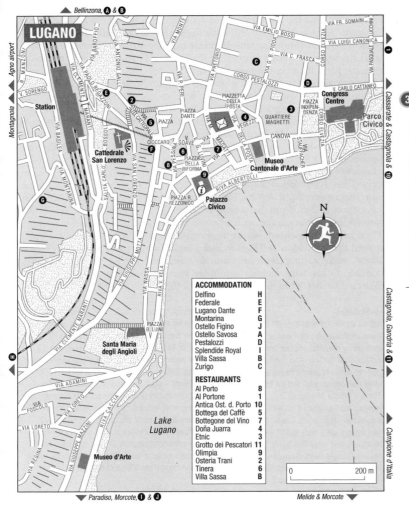

ACCOMMODATION

Delfino	H
Federale	E
Lugano Dante	F
Montarina	G
Ostello Figino	J
Ostello Savosa	A
Pestalozzi	D
Splendide Royal	I
Villa Sassa	B
Zurigo	C

RESTAURANTS

Al Porto	8
Al Portone	1
Antica Ost. d. Porto	10
Bottega del Caffè	5
Bottegone del Vino	7
Doña Juarra	4
Etnic	3
Grotto dei Pescatori	11
Olimpia	9
Osteria Trani	2
Tinera	6
Villa Sassa	B

Lugano stands alongside Zürich and Geneva as a Swiss banking centre, and the city centre reflects this, with none of the *belle époque* stuffiness or lack of direction that blights parts of Lake Como. These old alleys and winding lanes are full of commerce, whether in the form of enticing delicatessens and boutiques or graceful, villa-style hotels and apartment buildings. Explore churches and art galleries, or indulge in the simpler pleasure of a stroll under the lakeside palms. The twilight views over the lake from the summit of Monte Brè, with a warm southerly breeze blowing and the toot and rumble of cars rising from a bed of twinkling lights, could melt the hardest of hearts.

Arrival, information and accommodation

From within Lugano's **train station** a funicular takes two minutes to trundle down to pedestrianized **Piazza Cioccaro** in the centre; if you prefer to walk, follow steps from the station down to Via Cattedrale, which connects to Piazza Cioccaro. Narrow lanes link this with the main **Piazza della Riforma**, one block back from the waterfront. **Parking** is in short supply – make sure your hotel has spaces, or resign yourself to shelling out Fr.25–30 a day at the long-term car parks flanking the train station.

Lugano airport is 4km west of the city in Agno. Shuttle buses wait for flight arrivals; the driver will drop you at your hotel or any point in the centre (Fr.10 one way including luggage). On departure, you must book a pick-up at least one hour in advance (℡079 221 42 43, ⓦwww.shuttle-bus.com). A taxi is around Fr.35. **Milan–Malpensa airport**, 40km southwest of Lugano in Italy, is served by near-hourly shuttles operated by Star Bus (℡091 994 88 78, ⓦwww .starbus.info; Fr.50/€35 return).

Lugano's **tourist office** is opposite the main landing-stage, in the Palazzo Civico on Riva Albertolli (May–Sept Mon–Fri 9am–7pm, Sat 9am–6pm, Sun 10am–6pm; April & Oct Sat & Sun closes 5pm; Nov–March Mon–Fri 9am–noon & 2–5.30pm, Sat 10am–12.30pm & 1.30–5pm; ℡091 913 32 32, ⓦwww.luganotourism.ch), with a branch inside the station (Mon–Sat 2–7pm). They run **free guided walks** in English (mid-March to mid-Oct only) around the city (Mon & Thurs 9.30am) and through parks and gardens (Sun 10am), each starting from the tourist office and lasting two hours thirty minutes. Other trips include a full-day tour of vineyards and wine cellars (March–Dec Sat 10am–6pm; Fr.15; book 24hr ahead on ℡091 641 30 50).

Hotels

Delfino Via Casserinetta 6 ℡091 985 99 99, ⓦwww.delfinolugano.ch. Pleasant, welcoming small family-run hotel, with secure private parking and a pool. Something of an institution, and with a good reputation to uphold; rooms are functional rather than characterful, and the food is of a high standard. Private parking. ❺

Federale Via Regazzoni 8 ℡091 910 08 08, ⓦwww.hotel-federale.ch. Classic old townhouse hotel set in a quiet, leafy district immediately below the station, well away from traffic and with lake views from upper floors; rooms are full of character and good value. Private parking. ❺

Lugano Dante Piazza Cioccaro 5 ℡091 910 57 00, ⓦwww.hotel-luganodante.com. Quality option bang in the heart of the pedestrianized city centre, with good service, comfortable rooms and no trouble from street noise. Private parking. ❻

Montarina Via Montarina 1 ℡091 966 72 72, ⓦwww.montarina.ch. Efficient little place in a nice garden just behind the station, with clean, all-new rooms and helpful management. Closed Jan. ❸

Pestalozzi Piazza Indipendenza 9 ℡091 921 46 46, ⓦwww.pestalozzi-lugano.ch. Very nice, newly renovated two-star, right in the centre, 150m from the lakeshore, some rooms with balconies and lake views. ❸–❹

Splendide Royal Riva Caccia 7 ℡091 985 77 11, ⓦwww.splendide.ch. Lugano's premier city-centre establishment, with traditionally styled public spaces and guest rooms that live up to the hotel's name.

Accept nothing less than one of the vast rooms on the top floor, offering some of the best views in the city. Doubles from Fr.500. Private parking. ❾

Villa Sassa Via Tesserete 10 ℡091 911 41 11, ⓦwww.villasassa.ch. Truly excellent, modern four-star hotel in the hills just north of the city centre. Rooms – which are large, airy, quiet and with contemporary styling – look out onto the gorgeous pool area, with a superb view over the city and lake. Service is cheerily efficient. Private parking. ❽

Zurigo Corso Pestalozzi 13 ℡091 923 43 43, ⓦwww.hotelzurigo.ch. Central, very clean and well-kept three-star, with renovated rooms, private parking and just a trace of style. ❹

Hostels

Montarina (see above). Good low-budget central hotel that also has dorms (Fr.29).

Ostello Figino (HI hostel) Via Casoro 2, Figino ℡091 995 11 51, ⓦwww.youthhostel.ch. A good alternative to the suburban *Savosa* hostel, located in a former fishing village on the Ceresio peninsula, offering dorms for Fr.29.50 and bike rental. Hourly postbuses from outside the Lugano tourist office go to Casoro, a stop beside the hostel (20min). Mid-March to mid-Oct. ❶

Ostello Savosa (HI hostel) Via Cantonale 13, Savosa ℡091 966 27 28, ⓦwww.youthhostel.ch. One of Switzerland's best hostels (complete with swimming pool), with dorms for Fr.43. Take bus #5 to Crocifisso from the stop 200m left out of the train station. March–Nov. ❶

Boats on Lake Lugano

Idyllic **Lake Lugano** merits taking to the water simply for the pleasure of it. SNL (℡091 971 52 23, ⓦwww.lakelugano.ch) name their main landing-stage, opposite the tourist office, **Lugano-Centrale**; some services depart from **Lugano-Giardino** 100m to the east. Within the city, boats also call in at Cassarate and Castagnola further east, and Paradiso to the south.

Between April and October boats run roughly hourly to **Gandria**, while others depart less frequently south to **Campione d'Italia**, **Morcote**, **Porto Ceresio** and on around the peninsula to **Ponte Tresa**, stopping at most places on the way. One boat a day heads east to **Porlezza**, while one morning boat connects at Capolago for the rack-railway up to Monte Generoso. **Cruises** operate around various bays – or the whole lake – throughout the day, some with commentary in English, others offering on-board meals, drinks and/or music. In **winter**, a skeleton service operates to Morcote, with a few boats each week to Campione and Gandria.

Passes

Some short trips cost Fr.20–25, but in general a pass is a good bet: unlimited journeys for one/three/seven days cost Fr.38/58/68.

A **Lugano Regional Pass** gives free travel on Lugano's boats, buses, trains and cable cars, as well as half-price travel on boats in the Swiss part of Lake Maggiore and buses, trains and cable cars around Locarno and Ascona, for Fr.108 (7 days) or Fr.88 (any 3 days within a week).

A great way to combine lakes Lugano and Como is on the round-trip **Como e Lugano: Due Laghi per Sognare** ("Two lakes to dream about"; April–Oct only; Fr.46). Full details are on p.179. A day-trip heading **clockwise** involves a 2.15pm boat to Porlezza, with a stop for coffee before the bus to Menaggio, from where boats head on to Bellagio and/or Como for dinner before the bus and train back to Lugano, arriving at 9 or 10pm. Heading **anticlockwise** is much more civilized: a morning train and bus gives a couple of hours free in Como before a leisurely lunch aboard the noon boat to Menaggio, then a short bus ride to Porlezza for an ice cream and a stroll followed by an afternoon voyage back to Lugano, arriving 5.30pm. On either route, the pass is valid for two days, allowing you to break the journey wherever you like. Don't forget your passport.

The Town

The centre of Lugano is the broad **Piazza della Riforma**, a huge café-lined square perfect for people-watching over a coffee. The lake is a few metres away behind the Neoclassical **Palazzo Civico**, as are the steep lanes of the Old Town on the opposite side of the square. Wandering through the dense maze of shopping alleys northwest of Riforma, you're bound to stumble on the photogenic Gabbani delicatessen – the interior is an Aladdin's cave of fine *salsicce* made especially for the shop, cabinets full of Alpine cheeses from the farmers of Alto Ticino, pastries and foodie delights galore. From bustling Piazza Cioccaro just past the deli, the stepped Via Cattedrale doglegs steeply up to **Cattedrale San Lorenzo**, characterized by an impressive Renaissance portal, fragments of fourteenth- to sixteenth-century interior frescoes, and spectacular views from its terrace.

The narrow **Via Nassa** – one of Switzerland's top addresses for chic, designer-label fashion – heads southwest from Riforma through a string of picturesque little squares to the medieval church of **Santa Maria degli Angioli** on Piazza Luini. This plain little building beside a disused funicular track was founded in 1490 as part of a Franciscan monastery (suppressed in 1848 during Switzerland's

▲ Lugano

civil war). Inside, the wall separating the nave from the chancel is covered by a monumental Leonardo-esque fresco of the Passion and Crucifixion painted in 1529 by **Bernadino Luini**, as well as St Sebastian, graphically pierced by arrows. On the left-hand wall is Luini's fresco of the Last Supper.

Some 100m south on the lakefront is the **Museo d'Arte**, Riva Caccia 5 (Tues–Sun 10am–6pm; Fr.12; ⓦ www.mda.lugano.ch), which stages several major exhibitions a year, while five-minutes' walk east from Piazza Riforma brings you to the **Museo Cantonale d'Arte**, Via Canova 10 (Tues 2–5pm, Wed–Sun 10am–5pm; Fr.7–12; ⓦ www.museo-cantonale-arte.ch), a fine old villa housing paintings by Klee and Renoir amongst work by Swiss and Italian artists.

Monte Brè

From Cassarate, ten-minutes' walk east of the centre, a funicular rises to **Monte Brè** (ⓦ www.montebre.ch), a sheer 660m directly above the city (also accessible by car), offering spectacular views from the summit café over the lake, the curve of Lugano's bay overlooked by San Salvatore, and the snowy Monte Rosa massif. Bracing hikes lead off all over the mountain, while a short walk from the summit is Brè village, dotted with outdoor art installations (ⓦ www.montebre .com): the tourist office runs a **free guided walk** in English through the village (June–Sept Fri 2.30pm; 4hr; meet at funicular base station).

Eating and drinking

Lugano has plenty of pleasant, atmospheric places to **eat**. The many cafés and restaurants around Piazza Riforma all offer good, inexpensive food at lunch and dinner; for more characterful locations, head deeper into the city.

For details of the scenic journey to the top of **San Salvatore**, the sugarloaf mountain rising above Lugano's bay, turn to p.216.

Cafés and snacks

Bottega del Caffè Via Cattedrale 6. Modest café-bar dispensing espresso as it should be. Closed Sun.

Bottegone del Vino Via Magatti 1. Popular old-style wine bar beside the post office, with waiters in aprons and a huge range of wines on offer by the glass or bottle. Closed Sun.

Olimpia Piazza della Riforma. A Lugano landmark, occupying one wing of the Palazzo Civico, and best of the many cafés around the main square for its good, inexpensive food. Meals of Italian staples, steaks or a few more interesting dishes rarely go for more than Fr.30.

Al Porto Via Pessina 3 ⊚www.grand-cafe-lugano .ch. Venerable grand café in the lanes behind Piazza Riforma, built on the site of a medieval convent and boasting Florentine-style frescoes in the old refectory (now used for private parties). The patio, under its cupola, is the perfect place for genteel morning coffee or afternoon tea. Closed eves & Sun.

Restaurants

Antica Osteria del Porto Via Foce 9 ☎091 971 42 00, ⊚www.osteriadelporto.ch. Busy, amiable little riverside terrace restaurant by the marina, serving Ticino-inspired cuisine to a relaxed array of Luganesi families. Menus around Fr.45. Closed Tues.

Doña Juarra Via Vegezzi 4 ☎091 922 03 65. Popular, well-respected evening and late-night bar-restaurant serving good-value, quality Mexican food (*menùs* Fr.30 or so). Closed Mon.

Etnic Quartiere Maghetti, east of the post office. A great, inexpensive bamboo-and-candlelight café/bar/restaurant, tucked away in an unlikely looking mini-shopping centre a few streets back from the lake. The menu is broadly Mediterranean, with Greek and Lebanese light bites alongside tapas and pasta dishes. Eat for around Fr.20, or just plump for a beer or a cocktail from the bar instead. Either way, the atmosphere is cool, friendly and relaxed. Closed Sat lunch & Sun.

Grotto dei Pescatori Caprino ☎091 923 98 67. Alluring little *grotto* (rustic tavern), located near the hamlet of Caprino, across the lake from Lugano – and inaccessible by road. The only way to get here is by boat: a handful head over from Lugano, and smaller craft shuttle across from Gandria. The means of arrival and the isolation are the main attractions, but the atmosphere of the place – and the food – match up: tables are laid out under the shade of the trees, directly on the waterfront. Plump for the succulent perch in butter and sage, or a heartier dish such as beef with polenta. Prices are moderate – around Fr.30. Closed Oct–April.

Osteria Trani Via Cattedrale 12 ☎091 922 05 05. Friendly little local place, tucked away in a quiet corner off the cathedral lane, with a pleasant, sky-lit interior and tables laid out on the steps. Stop in for excellent pasta – including an innovative dish mixing gnocchi, ravioli and lasagne – as well as good perch, bass and vegetarian options. Menus around Fr.50. Closed Sun lunch.

Al Portone Viale Cassarate 3 ☎091 923 55 11. Gourmet restaurant that manages to keep a pleasantly relaxed ambience alongside its inventive new Italian cuisine. This kind of quality commands top prices. Closed Sun & Mon.

Tinera Via dei Gorini 2. Popular rustic *grotto*-style restaurant, specializing in Ticinese and Lombard dishes such as *pollo alla cacciatora* (spicy chicken stew) and home-made pasta, along with an array of excellent local Merlots. Set menus around Fr.22. Closed Sun & Aug.

Villa Sassa Via Tesserete 10 ☎091 911 41 11, ⊚www.villasassa.ch. Outstanding *haute-cuisine* restaurant attached to this luxury hotel in the hills just north of the city centre. The restaurant terrace offers a spectacular view over the city and the lake. The romance is kept up by the service – white-tuxedoed waiters gliding by – and the food, formal European/international cuisine with a North Italian twist: superb lake fish, delicately flavoured filled pastas and the like. Prices are high – rarely less than Fr.50 per head.

Around Lake Lugano

The possibilities for getting out into the countryside around Lugano are plentiful: the tourist office has sheets detailing fifty-odd cycling routes and walking trails out of the city, for all abilities. The best area to head for is the hilly countryside of the **Ceresio peninsula**, extending southwards behind the San Salvatore mountain opposite Lugano, and well served by boats and buses.

There's a **map** of Lake Lugano on p.207. For details of the **boats**, see p.211.

East of Lugano across the Italian border is a cluster of attractive villages on the way to **Porlezza**, beyond which lies Menaggio on Lake Como. West of Lugano in the **Malcantone** district, before the border at Ponte Tresa, there's the memorable attraction of a Swiss chocolate factory at little **Caslano**.

Gandria and east to Lake Como

From Castagnola, just east of Lugano city centre, a pleasant stroll heads east around the base of Monte Brè, joining the Sentiero di Gandria footpath through the **Parco degli Olivi**, a Mediterranean-style lakefront park shaded by olive trees, cypress, laurels and oleander.

After less than an hour's walk from Lugano (or 5min in the car), you come to picturesque **GANDRIA**, rising straight from the water 5km east of the city. There is no road access to the village – the slopes are far too steep. Parking areas are signed off the main road. Wandering down through the narrow alleys, past palm trees growing out of the rocky walls, you come to the landing-stage (served by regular boats from Lugano), around which is crowded a handful of charming terrace **restaurants**: there are few quieter, more alluring corners at which to hole up. Views down this little-explored eastern arm of Lake Lugano frame the pinnacle of Monte dei Pizzoni – and, beside it, Monte Bronzone – sweeping down into the water, with precipitous wooded slopes opposite that are almost completely devoid of habitation. The silence is wonderful. Should you decide to **stay**, *Hotel Moosmann* can oblige with a lake-view room (☏091 971 72 61, ⓦwww.hotel-moosmann-gandria.ch; ➎; April–Oct).

Opposite Gandria, with its own landing-stage served by boats from Gandria as well as Lugano (there are no roads here), is the **Museo delle Dogane Svizzere** (Customs Museum; April–Oct daily 1.30–5.30pm; free), with an interesting collection of smuggler-related bits and bobs.

▲ Gandria

East into Italy: Porlezza

From Gandria, the main road heads east for 1.3km to the international border; after 500m of no-man's-land, you emerge into the **VALSOLDA**, a stretch of Italian lakeside villages headed by **Oria** and **Albogasio**, both of them cheerful little places – thoroughly Italian, and quite unlike Gandria just the other side of the frontier. **San Mamete** is especially picturesque, with its twelfth-century belltower.

A quarter-hour east of Gandria, and 8km from the border, is **PORLEZZA**, the main town on this Italian branch of Lake Lugano – a fairly uninspiring place, with sensational views west over the water but not much else to offer. Take a five-minute stroll through the old quarter, and a three-minute stroll along the lakefront, then settle down with an ice cream. **Menaggio**, on the shores of Lake Como, lies just 11km east (see p.192).

Campione d'Italia

Visible across the lake from Lugano is the enclave of **CAMPIONE D'ITALIA**, which opted out of Ticino's independence campaign in 1798 and so remained Italian when all around it became Swiss. The village – for that's all it is, even though it's very swish – is part of the Provincia di Como; it has Italian police driving around in Swiss-registered cars and uses Swiss francs rather than euros. There is no passport control.

By road, you enter at a modern **arch**: there is a strict one-way system, so you must go right round the town centre before turning back along the lakeshore. Campione's landmark building is its giant **casino** (daily 3.30pm–3.30am or later; ⓦ www.campioneitalia.com). Unlimited stakes apply here, and – despite liberalization of Swiss gaming law – this is still where Lugano's many high rollers come to dally after dark.

Medieval Campione was renowned for its stonemasons, the Maestri Campionesi, whose skills were sought for buildings all over northern Italy; the only example that has survived unscathed in Campione is the little church of **San Pietro** (entirely glassed-in for protection), just off the central **Piazza Roma**. From here, Via Marco da Campione runs south along the lake, back to the arch. About 700m along, and 100m before the arch, is the church of **Santa Maria dei Ghirli** (April–Oct daily 9am–6pm; Nov–March Sat & Sun 9am–4.30pm). *Ghirli* ("swallows") refers to Campione's well-travelled masons, who returned home only rarely. The church – which shows its best side to the lake – is filled with thirteenth-century **frescoes**; especially striking are the scenes on the south wall, showing Salome and Herodias in medieval courtly dress.

Boats dock at Piazza Roma, opposite a row of busy, cheerful and unmistakeably Italian cafés churning out coffees and full meals: *La Taverna* is a good choice (closed Wed, Thurs lunch). Campione's poshest **restaurant** is *Da Candida*, Via Marco 4 (ⓣ091 649 75 41, ⓦ www.dacandida.net; closed Mon, Tues lunch & July); the chef prepares his own foie gras, and imports his own oysters and other seafood from Brittany. Expect a bill well into three figures.

Monte Generoso

From alongside **Capolago** train station (274m) at the southern end of the lake (also accessible by boat from Lugano), a rack-railway climbs on a slow, scenic route up to **MONTE GENEROSO** (1704m; ⓦ www.montegeneroso.ch). For the views alone, this trip is worth taking: from the summit – a short walk above the Vetta (top) station – you can see out across a sizeable part of northern Italy, in an amazing panorama. Milan and Turin are both visible; Bellagio on

Lake Como is in plain sight, as is Arona on Lake Maggiore and the distinctive pyramidal Matterhorn; and you can even see as far as the mountain pass in the Apennines above Genoa. The restaurant by the top station is the starting-point for an array of **walks**, including down to Mendrisio one way (2hr 40min) or Muggio another (2hr 15min); pick up maps and information at the ticket office in Capolago.

San Salvatore and around

From the district of Paradiso, ten-minutes' walk south of central Lugano, a funicular rises to **SAN SALVATORE** (Ⓦ www.montesansalvatore.ch), a rugged rock pinnacle offering especially good 360-degree panoramas from the roof of the little church on the summit, a short climb from the funicular station. This is also the starting point for walks south into the **Ceresio peninsula**: it's about an hour and twenty minutes through Carona village to Morcote (see below) on the tip of the peninsula.

On the top of the Collina d'Oro behind San Salvatore – named 'Hill of Gold' for its sun-drenched tranquillity – sits **MONTAGNOLA** village. The writer Hermann Hesse lived in Montagnola from 1919 until his death in 1962, and wrote most of his classic works here, including *Steppenwolf* and *The Glass Bead Game*. His villa Casa Camuzzi now houses the **Museo Hermann Hesse** (March–Oct daily 10am–6.30pm; Nov–Feb Sat & Sun 10am–5.30pm; Fr.7.50; Ⓦ www.hessemontagnola.ch), an interesting little spot, though the displays – Hesse's umbrella, Hesse's table – are modest. What makes a visit worthwhile is an excellent 45-minute video in English on the writer's life in Montagnola, which the staff can set up for you.

Melide: Swissminiatur

On the eastern side of the peninsula, at the point where the train tracks, main road and autostrada all cross the lake on a low bridge, sits the village of **MELIDE**, home to the kitschy **Swissminiatur** (mid-March to mid-Nov daily 9am–6pm; Fr.15; Ⓦ www.swissminiatur.ch). This small park features 1:25 scale models of just about every attraction in Switzerland, from Geneva's cathedral to Alpine peaks, with moving model boats, trains and cable cars livening up the static displays. A wander past all 113 exhibits could fill a slow hour or two.

Morcote and Vico Morcote

At the peninsula's southern tip, 4km south of Melide, lies the captivating village of **MORCOTE**, once a fishing community and now eking out a living as a lakeside attraction. Its photogenic arcaded houses – and slightly tacky antiques shops – are strung along the shoreline road, where you'll also find the small **Museo del Manifesto Ticinese** (March–Oct Tues–Sat 2–6pm; free), displaying vintage posters, and, nearby, the hillside **Parco Scherrer** (April–Oct daily 10am–5pm, July & Aug until 6pm; Fr.7), a romantic garden of lush flora and exotic follies. A web of stepped lanes leads up the hill behind to **Santa Maria del Sasso** (April–Oct Mon–Fri 8am–6pm, Sat & Sun 9am–6pm; Nov–March Mon–Fri 1.30–6pm, Sat & Sun 9am–6pm), an atmospheric church with sixteenth-century frescoes and great views.

Morcote's waterfront is shoulder-to-shoulder cafés – pleasant enough, but fairly generic (and often crowded). Aim instead for the tinier village of **VICO MORCOTE**, on the hillside above and 1km north: unlike in Morcote, here

There's a **map** of Lake Lugano on p.207. For details of the **boats**, see p.211.

you can stand alone in the cobbled street to absorb the atmosphere. Two restaurants make the trip worthwhile. The rustic, family-run *Osteria Al Böcc* (☎091 980 26 27; closed Tues & Wed) specializes in polenta served seven different ways – expect a bill around Fr.25 – or wander over to the sleek *Ristorante La Sorgente* (☎091 996 23 01, ⓦwww.lasorgente.ch; closed Sun eve & Mon), with stone tables set out on a lovely little terrace and a cool, white-walled interior: lunch on salad and prosciutto (around Fr.25) or sample their handmade pasta alongside dishes such as grilled octopus (*menùs* Fr.50 or more).

Porto Ceresio and around

From Capolago, a minor road cuts west through the medieval village of **RIVA SAN VITALE** and skirts the perimeter of **Monte San Giorgio**, a wooded mountain that is a UNESCO World Natural Heritage Site for its unspoilt environment and fossils. From **BRUSINO ARSIZIO**, an attractive village 5km from Riva, with a handful of lazy terrace cafés, a **cable car** rises to Serpiano on a shoulder of the mountain for lonesome forest rambling. Before you reach Brusino, the road rounds the headland of **Pojana**, occupied by the shady terrace of a simple café-restaurant, offering stunning views north past Lugano to the high Alps.

The Italian border lies 2km beyond Brusino; 1500m further brings you to the genial lakefront town of **PORTO CERESIO**, gazing back at Morcote. In a moment of inspiration, the town built itself a boardwalk on stilts over the water to facilitate the lovely late-afternoon *passeggiata*, which extends either side of the main lakefront **Piazza Bossi**, and takes in several enticing little pockets of west-facing sandy beach. There's not much else to do; boats stop in here two or three times a day from Lugano, but the town is more oriented towards its Italian neighbours – Varese (see p.143) lies just 10km south. The train station is opposite the landing-stage, 300m around the lakeshore from Piazza Bossi.

The Malcantone

Little red trains start from open platforms opposite Lugano's main rail station on a scenic route west through the **Malcantone** district, bound for Ponte Tresa. After circling the pint-sized airport at **AGNO** – above which stands Monte Lema, endpoint of a long, beautiful hiking trail from Monte Tamaro (see p.218) – trains head on to the undistinguished town of **CASLANO**, unlikely home of the **Alprose chocolate factory** (Mon–Fri 9am–5.30pm, Sat & Sun 9am–4.30pm; Fr.3; ⓦwww.alprose.ch), on an industrial estate at Via Rompada 36; from Caslano station, follow the tracks in the direction of Ponte Tresa for about 200m and cut left. As you enter you're greeted, Willy Wonka–like, by a fountain bubbling with fragrant molten chocolate. The museum comprises some old coin-op machines and knick-knacks, plus the chance to watch the mixing machines and production-line conveyor belts in action (Mon–Fri only). The full Alprose range is discounted in the on-site shop.

Caslano is loomed over by the bulbous **Monte Caslano**, which almost chokes this corner of the lake: there is just a narrow, reedy strait between the mountain and the opposite, Italian, shore allowing boats to access **PONTE TRESA**, the rail terminus 3km south of Caslano. This is a schizophrenic little place, divided by the **international border**. The Swiss half of town is placid and neat, but crossing the bridge over the River Tresa for which the town was named throws you into its Italian twin – a mini-maelstrom of cars negotiating a complex one-way system around busy shops.

From Ponte Tresa the main road heads south 25km to **Varese** (see p.143), while minor roads run parallel on both the Swiss and Italian riverbanks for 10km west to **Luino** on Lake Maggiore (see p.162). South around the lakeshore lies **Porto Ceresio** (see p.217).

The Mendrisiotto

South of Lake Lugano, main roads and trains shoot through the hot, dry region known as the **Mendrisiotto**, after **MENDRISIO**, largest town in the area and a major wine-growing centre. There's not a great deal to stop for in the town, although its centre is picturesque; the main draw is the giant **Foxtown outlet mall** (ⓦ www.foxtown.ch), prominently signposted alongside the autostrada, where you can pick up designer-label fashions – Prada, Gucci, Versace, Dolce & Gabbana, and more – at up to seventy percent off.

Near Mendrisio, the village of Morbio Inferiore marks a branch road that climbs into the last valley in Switzerland, the tranquil **Valle di Muggio** (ⓦ www.valledimuggio.ch). Thickly wooded, with seemingly inaccessible hamlets clinging to the steep side opposite the road, this is a lovely, rarely visited backwater; **MUGGIO** (666m), 7km in, has a few taverns where you can grab a bite, and a steep trail leading up to Monte Generoso. 🍴 *Osteria La Montanara* (ⓣ 091 684 14 79; ❷) is a welcoming little inn in **MONTE**, across the valley from Muggio, serving rustic country fare such as venison and other game, home-cured meats, fresh-baked breads and local wines.

Some 6km on, and 23km south of Lugano, the Italian frontier is marked by **CHIASSO**, an unprepossessing border town, with a large train station on the edge of a desultory town centre and swarms of motorized and foot traffic passing through during the morning and evening rush hours. Como's suburbs begin immediately on the other side, trickling on for 5km to the city centre and lakefront (see p.178).

North of Lugano

North of Lugano, the Monte Ceneri range divides Ticino in two. On the northern side, road and rail lines stream down from the Alpine tunnels, funnelling into **Bellinzona**, a quietly elegant city often regrettably passed over in favour of the lakeside resorts.

Monte Tamaro

Just south of the autostrada and rail exit from the Monte Ceneri tunnel, gondolas rise from the town of **RIVERA** (469m) up to **Alpe Foppa** (1530m), located on a shoulder of **Monte Tamaro** (1961m; ⓦ www.montetamaro.ch). By the top gondola station, alongside a little restaurant, is the church of **Santa Maria degli Angeli**, designed by the Ticinese architect Mario Botta in 1990. It's an effortlessly graceful building of porphyry stone, with symmetrical stairs, arches, a long walkway, and extensive views from the belvedere.

The church is worth the journey by itself, but you'll also find plenty of walks up here – not least from Alpe Foppa to the Tamaro summit (1hr 40min) or down to Rivera (2hr 15min) – though the most spectacular heads on an isolated route (4hr 30min) along a ridge west to **Monte Lema** (1624m; ⓦ www.montelema.ch), from where a cable car runs down to Miglieglia, linked by bus to Lugano.

Bellinzona

Few people bother with **BELLINZONA** – their loss, since this graceful old town is the perfect place to draw breath away from the lakeside bustle. A fortress since Roman times, Bellinzona occupies a prime valley-floor position, holding the keys to the great Alpine passes of the Novena, Gottardo, Lucomagno and San Bernardino. In 1242 it was bought by the Visconti family, dukes of Milan, who built a new **castle** atop the hill plum in the middle of the valley, while their allies, the Rusconi family of Como, built another castle slightly up the hillside. In the 1420s the newly independent Swiss confederates north of the Gotthard Pass, who had successfully thrown off Habsburg rule, began a violent campaign against the Milanese forces, which spurred the Sforza dynasty – then in the ascendant in Milan – to reinforce the two castles and build a third, even higher up the hillside. A massive chain of fortifications cut right across the Ticino valley … to no avail, since the Swiss won Bellinzona by treaty in 1503. Three centuries of domination and oppression followed, with Swiss overlords posted to Bellinzona to keep control of the peasantry, until Ticino won its independence in 1803.

Bellinzona lacks a lake, but it also lacks the pace, the crowds and the touristic sheen of its bigger neighbours. This gentle town is blessed with medieval architecture and picturesque churches, with its trio of castles – **Castelgrande**, **Montebello** and **Sasso Corbaro** – listed as a UNESCO World Heritage Site.

It's also worth making a trip here for the weekly **market** of breads, local cheeses, wines, fruit and veg, and handicrafts – one of the best in Ticino (Sat 7.30am–1pm).

The Town

High on Bellinzona's central rock rise the massive towers and walls of **Castelgrande** (Mon 10am–6pm, Tues–Sun 9am–10pm; free), most impressive of the town's three medieval castles. The whole complex has been sympathetically restored by architect Aurelio Galfetti, who added a public **lift**, dramatically recessed deep into the bedrock of the hill behind the central Piazza del Sole, which emerges at a purpose-built modern fortification on an upper terrace of the castle. The castle grounds are serene, overlooked by the slender thirteenth-century **White Tower**, with two upper windows on all four faces, and the fourteenth-century **Black Tower**, with three windows on its longer side. Despite their names, both, like the castle itself, are grey granite, and between them run lines of distinctive Lombard-style **swallow-tail battlements**. Off Castelgrande's central lawns is an entrance to the **Museo Storico** (daily 10am–6pm; Nov–March closes 5pm; Fr.5; joint ticket for museums in all three castles Fr.10), offering a tour through Bellinzona's past, including an excellent audiovisual show (in English).

Steps wind down from Castelgrande to the Renaissance buildings of **Piazza Collegiata** in the Old Town, dominated by the Collegiata church, built by the same architect who worked on Como's cathedral and decorated with Baroque frescoes and stucco. Narrow lanes branch out all around: arcaded **Piazza Nosetto** is just south, with the Cà Rossa house on the way featuring a striking red terracotta facade – a style fashionable in early nineteenth-century Milan. From Nosetto, a gateway leads into the courtyard of the **Palazzo Civico**, a

Locarno (see p.165) and the Swiss shores of **Lake Maggiore** are 15km west of Bellinzona, easily reached by road or a short train journey.

splendid Renaissance building rebuilt in the 1920s along with its loggias, which coil attractively around both upper floors.

Montebello and Sasso Corbaro

Behind the Collegiata, a path rises to the picturesque **Castello di Montebello** (mid-March to Oct daily 10am–6pm; free), some 90m higher in elevation than Castelgrande. From a vantage point on the ramparts, it's easy to trace the line of defensive fortifications which link the two castles across the width of the Ticino valley. The castle itself is impressive, with a fifteenth-century courtyard and residential palace surrounding an older central portion dating from the thirteenth century, the latter now housing a **museum** of Gothic and Renaissance architecture (same hours; Fr.5; joint ticket for museums in all three castles Fr.10).

A stiff 45-minute climb brings you to **Castello di Sasso Corbaro** (mid-March to Oct daily 10am–6pm; free), 230m above Bellinzona, designed and built in six months in 1479 by a military engineer brought in from Florence. It shelters a vine-shaded courtyard *osteria* and has a spectacular rampart panorama; its **museum** (same hours; Fr.5; joint ticket for museums in all three castles Fr.10) includes a gallery showing changing exhibits by contemporary Ticinese artists. Bus #4 runs between the town centre and Artore, near Castello di Sasso Corbaro – a useful alternative to walking both ways.

South of Piazza Indipendenza

Peaceful **Piazza Indipendenza** is 100m south of the tourist office and sports a 1903 obelisk commemorating the first century of Ticinese independence. On the east side of the square is the small church of **San Rocco**, built in 1330 and renovated in 1478. Following Via Lugano south for 600m brings you to Piazza San Biagio, and the gates of the **Villa dei Cedri** art gallery (Tues–Fri 2–6pm, Sat & Sun 11am–6pm; Fr.8; Ⓦwww.villacedri.ch). Explore the beautiful grounds then head in to the museum, which focuses on early modern Swiss and Lombard art. The frescoed church of **San Biagio** beside the villa dates from the twelfth century, while beside a convent 100m west across the tracks is **Santa Maria delle Grazie**, with an enormous, late fifteenth-century interior fresco of the Crucifixion.

Practicalities

Bellinzona's **train station** – with bike rental – is 500m northeast of the Old Town. The well-equipped **tourist office** is in the Palazzo Civico on Piazza Nosetto (Mon–Fri 9am–6.30pm, Sat 9am–noon; ☏091 825 21 31, Ⓦwww .bellinzonaturismo.ch).

Walks around Bellinzona

There are plenty of picturesque **walks** near Bellinzona. One of the best begins in nearby Roveredo (served by postbuses from Bellinzona), from where an old cart track on the "quiet" side of the river heads through tiny San Giulio and into the woods opposite San Vittore, before crossing the river at a little bridge in Lumino and heading on through the forest to Arbedo on the outskirts of Bellinzona. You'll come across plenty of peaceful cafés on the way. Side roads off the main Via San Gottardo lead through Arbedo and under the tracks to the picturesque Chiesa Rossa, an ancient red-washed church sitting lost and forgotten beside industrial warehouses on Via del Carmagnola backing onto the tracks (total 2hr walking). Buses can run you the final 1.5km south into Bellinzona centre.

Bellinzona's **hotels** aren't up to much. You'd do better to head out of town: set amidst hillside vineyards on a minor road between Sementina and Gudo, ten minutes south of Bellinzona, is the charming *Fattoria l'Amorosa* agriturismo (☏091 840 29 50, ⓦwww.amorosa.ch; ❻). Choose between the eight rooms in the main building, presented with taste in a rustic Tuscan style, or the separate cottage 'Isabella', where the kids can sleep on a platform under the eaves, there's a living room, a master bedroom with private panoramic terrace and a basement bathroom featuring a super-size bath sculpted from granite. Balconies and picture windows take advantage of the views.

The *Amorosa's* **restaurant** is a great choice, with menus of refined local cuisine around Fr.50 – plus a choice of top-rated wines (and balsamic vinegars) produced on-site. Within Bellinzona, aim for Castelgrande: you can eat well for Fr.25 at the ⚒ *Grotto San Michele*, which spreads itself over the terrace and also has an interior room; while the formal *Castelgrande* restaurant (☏091 826 23 53, ⓦwww.castelgrande.ch), full of black leather and tubular steel furniture, is a snootier affair – you'll get little change from Fr.60 for its modern, Ticino-inspired cuisine. The atmospheric *Osteria Sasso Corbaro*, in Bellinzona's topmost castle (☏091 825 55 32; closed Mon & Nov–March), serves up authentic Ticinese fare at stone tables in the shady castle courtyard, or in a great hall within; *menùs* are around Fr.25. *Portici*, a pleasant *osteria*/pizzeria in the Old Town on Vicolo Muggiasca (closed Sun lunch & Mon), serves palatable food in its shady courtyard to a young, easy crowd of regulars for Fr.20 or so.

North of Bellinzona: Alto Ticino

Alto Ticino (Upper Ticino), north of Bellinzona, is a haven of wild, lonesome valleys on the approach to the high Alps, dotted with rustic, stone-built hamlets teetering on steep slopes. **Biasca** is the gateway to the region, a small town at the junction of roads from the **Lucomagno**, **Gottardo** and **Novena** passes. Northeast of Bellinzona begins the long drive up to the **San Bernardino Pass** (2065m), on the other side of which is the Zapport glacier, one of the sources of the Rhine. From nearby, a road climbs back into Italy over the **Spluga Pass** to Chiavenna (see p.206).

Travel details

Full details of transport in Lombardy – including trains, buses and boats serving Lake Como – are at ⓦwww.trasporti.regione.lombardia.it (click "orari"). Timetables for trains, buses, boats and cable cars in Switzerland are searchable at at ⓦwww.rail.ch. Passports are needed for travel between Italy and Switzerland. See p.30 for some guidance on deciphering timetables.

Trains

Bellinzona to: Como (hourly; 1hr 15min); Lugano (every 20min; 25min); Milano Centrale (hourly; 1hr 20min).
Como Lago/Nord to: Milano Cadorna/Nord (every 30min; 1hr).
Como San Giovanni to: Lugano (hourly; 40min); Milano Centrale (hourly; 40min).
Lecco to: Bergamo (hourly; 45min); Brescia (hourly; 1hr 35min); Milano Centrale (hourly; 45min); Tirano (every 2hr; 1hr 45min); Varenna (hourly; 35min).
Lugano to: Bellinzona (every 20min; 25min); Caslano (every 20min; 20min); Como (hourly; 40min); Milano Centrale (hourly; 55min).
Varenna to: Lecco (hourly; 35min).

Buses

Bellagio to: Como (hourly; 1hr 10min); Lecco (6 daily; 50min).

Como to: Bellagio (hourly; 1hr 10min); Lecco (hourly; 1hr 10min); Menaggio (every 20min; 1hr 10min); Tremezzo (14 daily; 1hr); Varese (every 20–30min; 1hr 10min).

Lugano to: Melide (approx hourly; 15min); Montagnola (hourly; 20min); Morcote (approx hourly; 30min); Vico Morcote (every 2hr; 35min; change at Olivella).

Menaggio to: Como (every 20min; 1hr 10min); Lugano (9 daily; 1hr).

Boats

These frequencies refer to summer sailings; fuller details are at ⓦ www.navigazionelaghi.it (Lake Como) and ⓦ www.lakelugano.ch.

Cadenábbia to: Bellagio (every 25min; 10min); Varenna (every 25min; 25min).

Como to: Bellagio (6 daily; 2hr 10min); Cernobbio (every 20min; 15min); Cólico (5 daily; 4hr); Menaggio (6 daily; 2hr 25min); Varenna (6 daily; 2hr 40min).

Lugano to: Gandria (hourly; 35min); Melide (every 2hr; 35min); Morcote (every 2hr; 1hr).

Bergamo, Brescia and Cremona

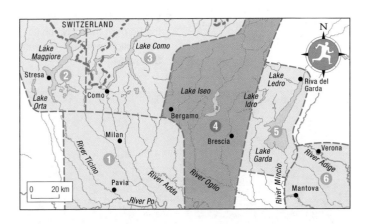

CHAPTER 4   # Highlights

* **Bergamo Alta** Bergamo's historic upper town makes for endlessly fascinating roaming. See p.230

* **Piazza Vecchia** The focal point of Bergamo Alta and one of Italy's great Renaissance squares. See p.232

* **Accademia Carrara** Although Bergamo's gallery is under renovation, works by Botticelli, Titian, Raphael and others remain on display nearby. See p.232

* **Lake Iseo** A sinuous little lake, trapped between mountains – picturesque but over-developed. See p.239

* **Santa Giulia** Brescia's main museum: an absorbing sweep through 2000 years of history. See p.248

* **Pinacoteca Tosio Martinengo** Excellent gallery of Renaissance art in Brescia. See p.250

* **Cremona** Diverting town on the Po plain that plays on its connection with violin-making. See p.254

▲ Bergamo Alta

Bergamo, Brescia and Cremona

The cities of Bergamo and Brescia act as a steadying counterbalance to the fun-loving fripperies of the big lakes. The most important cities on the Lombard plain after Milan, each spent several centuries under Venetian rule, leaving them with art and architecture noticeably different from that elsewhere in Lombardy. Today both are thriving urban centres. **Bergamo** is a city that takes food and fashion seriously; its handsome medieval quarter, high on a hill overlooking the modern city, has a beguiling charm that makes it an essential stop on any journey across the region. Lombardy's second city, hardworking **Brescia**, is frequently cold-shouldered by Italians and visitors alike – inexplicably, since its architecture is attractive, its food unique and its galleries and museums outstanding.

Both cities, too, are in touch with the **mountains**: Bergamo, in particular, is surrounded by wooded slopes that hint at the great Alpine peaks just a few kilometres to the north, where the high valleys draw weekend skiers all winter long.

Midway between Bergamo and Brescia stands the squiggle of **Lake Iseo**, the least celebrated of the big northern Italian lakes. Although prettily enclosed between the hills of the **Franciacorta** wine region to the south and the precipitous mountains flanking the **Val Camónica** to the north, Iseo lacks the romance of Como or magnificence of Garda to temper its commerce and mundanity: it cannot really compete with the big lakes.

South of Brescia, graceful **Cremona**, famous as a violin town since the days of local boy Antonio Stradivari, makes for an easy day-trip from either town, or a diverting stopover as you head east towards Mantova and Verona, or west towards Milan.

Bergamo

Just 50km northeast of Milan, yet much closer to the mountains in look and feel, **BERGAMO** comprises two distinct parts – **Bergamo Bassa**, the modern city centre on the plain, and medieval **Bergamo Alta**, clinging to the rocky slopes 100m higher (the city's name derives from the Celtic *berg-heim*, or "home on the hill").

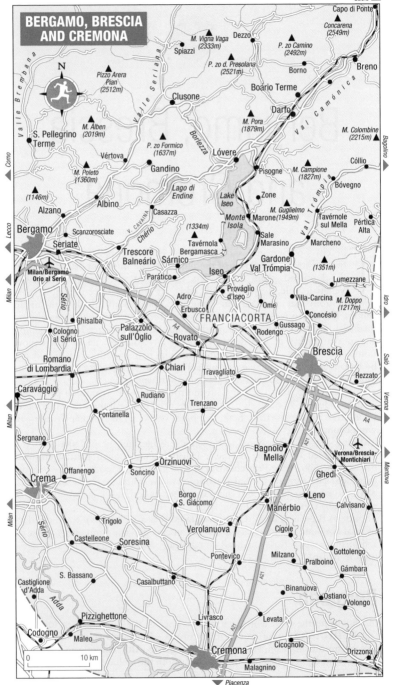

BERGAMO, BRESCIA
AND CREMONA

Edolo

Capo di Ponte

Concarena
(2549m)

M. Vigna Vaga
(2333m)
Spiazzi
Dezzo
P. zo Camino
(2492m)

P. zo d. Presolana
(2521m)
Borno
Breno

Boário Terme

Clusone
Darfo

M. Pora
(1879m)

Pizzo Arera
Pian
(2512m)

M. Colombine
(2215m)

S. Pellegrino
Terme
M. Álben
(2019m)
Vértova
P. zo Formico
(1637m)
Lóvere
Pisogne
M. Campione
(1827m)
Cóllio

Bóvegno

M. Poleto
(1360m)
Gandino
Zone
(1146m)
Albino
Lago di
Endine
Lake
Iseo
Monte
Isola
M. Guglielmo
(1949m)
Tavérnole
sul Mella
Pértica
Alta

Alzano
Casazza
(1334m)
Marone
Sale
Marasino
Marcheno

Bergamo
Scanzorosciate
Tavérnola
Bergamasca
Seriate
Trescore
Balneário
Sárnico
Gardone
Val Trómpia
(1351m)

Milan/Bergamo-
Orio al Serio
Parático
Iseo
Lumezzane

Próváglio
d'Iseo
Villa-Carcina
M. Doppo
(1217m)

Adro
Ome
Concésio

Ghisalba
Erbusco
FRANCIACORTA
Gussago

Cológno
al Sério
Palazzolo
sull'Óglio
Rovato
Rodengo

Romano
di Lombardia
Chiari
Travagliato
Brescia
Rezzato

Caravággio
Rudiano
Trenzano
A4

Fontanella

Sergnano

Bagnolo
Mella
Verona/Brescia-
Montichiari

Offanengo
Órzinuovi
Soncino
Ghedi

Crema
Leno
Calvisano

Borgo
S. Giácomo
Manérbio

Trigolo
Verolanuova
Cígole

Castelleone
Soresina
Milzano
Pralboino
Gottolengo
Gámbara

Pontevico

S. Bassano
Casalbuttano
Binanuova
Ostiano
Volongo

Castiglione
d'Adda
Pizzighettone
Livrasco
Levata
Cicognolo
Drizzona

Codogno
Maleo
Cremona
Malagnino

Piacenza

0   10 km

The Città Bassa is a harmonious mixture of medieval cobbled quarters blending into late nineteenth- and early twentieth-century town planning – but the historic Città Alta is one of northern Italy's loveliest urban centres, a favourite retreat for the work-weary Milanese, who flock here at weekends seeking solace in its fresh mountain air, wanderable lanes and the lively but easygoing pace of its life.

Bergamo owes much of its magic to the **Venetians**, who ruled here for over 350 years, building houses and palaces with fancy Gothic windows and adorning facades and open spaces with the Venetian lion, symbol of the republic. (The *bergamasche* like to say they still look east for their inspiration, conveniently showing their backsides to Milan in the process.) The Venetians' most striking legacy is the ring of gated **walls** that encircles the Città Alta. Now worn, mellow and overgrown with creepers, they kept armies out until the French invaded in 1796 and today enclose a dense network of cobbled alleyways weaving around the set-piece **Piazza Vecchia** and adjacent church of **Santa Maria Maggiore**. Just outside the walls in the Città Bassa, the **Accademia Carrara** holds one of Italy's leading provincial art collections; it is under long-term renovation until 2011, but some of its paintings remain on display in the **Palazzo della Ragione** on Piazza Vecchia.

Arrival and information

By **road**, the A4 autostrada runs from Milan to Bergamo and on to Brescia, while the SS342 is a useful link from Lecco and Lake Como. Bergamo has fast **trains** from Milan (Centrale and Lambrate) and Brescia, and slower ones from Cremona and Lecco. The **train station** is at the southernmost end of the Città Bassa's central avenue, Viale Papa Giovanni XXIII, a long walk from the Città Alta. The **bus station**, opposite the train station to the right, was being rebuilt at the time of writing.

City bus #1 runs frequently between the airport, the train station, the funicular base station and Colle Aperto in the Città Alta – though some services stop short or follow route variations: check timetables carefully. A **funicular** (daily 7am–12.30am) runs every few minutes on the steep route between Viale Vittorio Emanuele II in the Città Bassa (the extension of Viale Papa Giovanni)

Milan-Bergamo (Orio al Serio) airport

Bergamo's **Orio al Serio** airport (airport code **BGY**; ☏035.326.323, ⊛www.orioaeroporto.it) – also called "Milan-Bergamo" – is 4km southeast of Bergamo city centre. Arrivals and departures share one terminal building; arrivals has a well-equipped **tourist office** (daily 8am–11pm; ☏035.320.402, ⊛www.turismo.bergamo.it), with maps, information and free hotel-booking for Bergamo and Milan.

Arrivals also has a huddle of competing bus company kiosks offering rides to **Milano Centrale** station. They boil down to either **Orioshuttle** (☏035.319.366, ⊛www.orioshuttle.com; €8) or **Autostradale** (☏035.318.472, ⊛www.autostradale.it; €8.90; buy two seats and the third is free). Both run daily (approx every 30min 5am–1am) and journey time is about an hour. Autostradale also operates to **Brescia** bus station (5 daily; 1hr; €10).

To reach **Bergamo** take **city bus #1** (daily every 30min 6am–midnight; 15min; ordinary ticket €1.65 or day pass €3.50 or three-day pass €5; ⊛www.atb.bergamo.it). All stop at the train station, with most continuing to the funicular base station and into the Città Alta. A **taxi** (☏035.451.9090) is around €30 into Bergamo, over €100 to Milan.

For journey times to major points from this and other airports, see p.20.

and Piazza Mercato delle Scarpe in the Città Alta. Consult the machines to buy an ordinary **ticket** (valid 75min; €1) or a *biglietto turistico giornaliero* (day-ticket; €2.50) – both usable on buses and funiculars within the city centre (excluding the airport). You can get a *biglietto turistico 3 giorni* (valid 3 days; €5) from outlets listed at every stop (see ⓦ www.atb.bergamo.it for details). The Città Alta is closed to traffic on Sundays.

Information and tours

Tourist information is handled by two organizations. **Turismo Bergamo** (ⓦ www.turismo.bergamo.it) is the more dynamic, but its sole walk-in office is in the airport arrivals hall (daily 8am–11pm; ☎ 035.320.402). Within the city centre, there are two **information offices** (ⓦ www.provincia.bergamo.it /turismo) – in the Città Bassa at the train station (daily 9am–12.30pm & 2–5.30pm; Oct–May closed Sat & Sun; ☎ 035.210.204), and in the Città Alta in the base of the Torre Gombito tower off Piazza Vecchia (daily 9am–12.30pm & 2–5.30pm; ☎ 035.242.226). A **guided walking tour** in English starts from the upper station of the funicular in Piazza Mercato delle Scarpe (April–Oct Wed & Sun 3pm; 2hr; €10), and an **open-top bus** makes a continuous sightseeing tour around town, with recorded commentary (April–Oct Fri–Sun 9am–6pm; 1hr; €13; ⓦ www.city-sightseeing.it).

Accommodation

Bergamo is not somewhere to arrive without a reservation, even out of season: **accommodation** is pricey and, in the centre, fairly limited. There's just a handful of hotels in the Città Alta, with mostly business hotels in the Città Bassa. Tourist offices have details of city B&Bs, including those run by ⓦ www .bedandbergamo.it and ⓦ www.bebilmondoincasa.com.

Hotels in Città Alta

Agnello d'Oro Via Gombito 22 ☎ 035.249.883. In the heart of the upper town, this cosy two-star offers plain, en-suite rooms – a bit small and ordinary when compared to the well-regarded restaurant at ground level, but good value. Some have balconies onto the tiny square below. ❸

Gourmet Via San Vigilio 1 ☎ 035.437.3004, ⓦ www.gourmet-bg.it. Just above the walls of the Città Alta, behind the San Vigilio funicular station, with nine spacious, modern doubles (plus a single and a suite/apartment) boasting wonderful views. The restaurant serves local staples. ❹

Piazza Vecchia Via Colleoni 3 ☎ 035.253.179, ⓦ www.hotelpiazzavecchia.it. Thirteen arty rooms in this three-star hotel occupying a fourteenth-century building on the main 'street' (a pedestrianized alley), a few steps off the central old town square. Rooms feature fresh, contemporary design, great shower rooms and little balconies with views of the hills, but service can be less than forthcoming. Private parking. ❻

San Lorenzo Piazza Mascheroni 9a ☎ 035.237.383, ⓦ www.hotelsanlorenzobg.it. This is a pleasant little spot shoehorned into a historic building, with private parking – rated four stars, but

in truth nearer three. Several rooms benefit from a large balcony facing east over the mountains beyond the walls, but they are small and furnished generically. You're paying for an unbeatable location, in the heart of the old town yet quiet and secluded. In 2002 the hotel dug out its grounds for a much-needed expansion, but work was stopped when Roman ruins came to light. Pending archeological inquiries, this great pit remains open in front of the hotel – ancient walls peeping through an unsightly carpet of weeds. ❺

Sole Via Colleoni 1 ☎ 035.218.238. In a great location steps from the main square, this bright and breezy traditional-style hotel offers simple en-suite two-star rooms with little balconies looking over a back courtyard or the private garden. Although you're in the middle of the bustle, the largish rooms are very quiet, some with a sofa. ❸

Hotels in Città Bassa

Excelsior San Marco Piazzale della Repubblica 6 ☎ 035.366.111, ⓦ www.hotelsanmarco.com. Four-star business hotel near the lower funicular station with good weekend discount rates and parking. The building is ugly, though, and they are only renovating the tired old rooms piecemeal: make

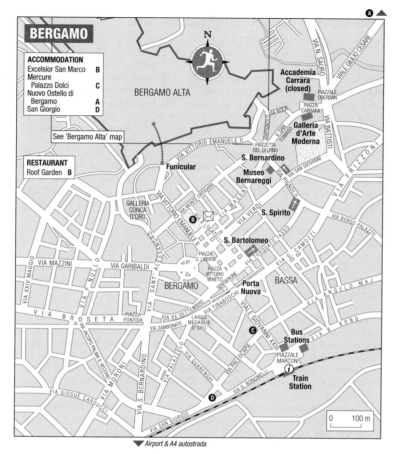

BERGAMO

ACCOMMODATION

Excelsior San Marco	B
Mercure Palazzo Dolci	C
Nuovo Ostello di Bergamo	A
San Giorgio	D

See 'Bergamo Alta' map

RESTAURANT

Roof Garden	B

BERGAMO ALTA

Accademia Carrara (closed)

Galleria d'Arte Moderna

S. Bernardino

Funicular

Museo Bernareggi

S. Spirito

GALLERIA CONCA D'ORO

S. Bartolomeo

BERGAMO BASSA

Porta Nuova

Bus Stations

Train Station

0   100 m

▼ Airport & A4 autostrada

sure you ask for a new one. The roof-terrace restaurant is a highlight (see p.238). **8**

Mercure Palazzo Dolci Viale Papa Giovanni XXIII 100 ☎035.227.411, ⓦwww.mercure .com. Impressive four-star chain hotel a short walk from the station. The soundproofing is excellent: once you're inside, there's no sense that the hotel is bang in the middle of Bergamo's roaring traffic. Everything is very cool and swish and contemporary: rooms have hi-tech bathrooms, plus state-of-the-art satellite TVs, a/c and halogen lighting. It's anonymous but comfortable, convenient and excellent value. Parking at the adjacent underground garage is discounted. **6**

San Giorgio Via San Giorgio 10 ☎035.212.043, ⓦwww.sangiorgioalbergo.it. A friendly, well-run two-star, just 5min walk from the station, often used as temporary digs by short-contract workers. Various sized rooms with or without bathrooms are

available, all spotlessly clean and decently furnished. **2**

Hostel

Nuovo Ostello di Bergamo (HI hostel) Via Galileo Ferraris 1 ☎035.361.724, ⓦwww .ostellodibergamo.it. Excellent hostel which has won awards for being the best in Europe and offers bathrooms and balconies in every room, meals, bicycles for rent, a roof garden and disabled facilities. There's also a great view of the Città Alta. It is a fair distance from the city centre: take bus #6 from Porta Nuova (direction Monterosso/San Colombano), and get off at the stop named Leonardo da Vinci. From here, the hostel is at the top of the steps. Alternatively, reach it on bus #3 from Piazza Mercato delle Scarpe in the Città Alta to the Ostello stop. A bed in a dorm is €17 (breakfast included); there are also singles, doubles, triples and quads. **1**

The upper town: Bergamo Alta

Bergamo's upper town, the **CITTÀ ALTA**, is a remarkably rich urban environment, still enclosed by its sixteenth-century Venetian walls. The appearance of the narrow, steep streets, flanked by high facades, remains largely as it was in the Middle Ages, but the main public spaces – **Piazza Vecchia** and adjacent **Piazza del Duomo** – combine medieval austerity with the grace of Renaissance design. The main street, beginning as **Via Gombito** and continuing as **Via Colleoni**, follows the line of the Roman *decumanus maximus*, topped and tailed by evidence of Bergamo's military past – the **Rocca** to the east, the **Cittadella** to the west.

The best place to start exploring is Piazza Mercato delle Scarpe, at the top station of the nineteenth-century **funicular** that rises from Viale Vittorio Emanuele II (bus #1 serves its lower station). From here, the old town spreads up the hill in front of you. Alternatively, stay on bus #1 to **Colle Aperto**, at the top (western) end of the Città Alta, and then walk back down through the old streets.

The thirty-minute uphill **walk** from the Città Bassa is well worth doing: take bus #2 from the station (or any bus east from Porta Nuova along Via Camozzi), get off at **Via Pignolo** and head left up this attractive street, lined with sixteenth- and seventeeth-century *palazzi*, to Porta Sant'Agostino (see p.236), from where Via Porta Dipinta climbs to Piazza Mercato delle Scarpe.

Piazza Mercato delle Scarpe and Via Gombito

Piazza Mercato delle Scarpe – literally, Shoe Market Square – is an atmospheric introduction to Bergamo's medieval upper town, utterly removed from the bustle of the modern streets below. The funicular station is housed in the fourteenth-century Palazzo Suardi, subsequently the cobblers' guildhall (hence the square's title), faced by a now-disused fountain installed in 1486. Opposite, café tables spread out beneath an attractive medieval portico.

As in antiquity, this square marks a meeting of roads. With the funicular at your back, **Via Porta Dipinta** heads down to the right towards Sant'Agostino, while **Via San Giacomo** descends to the left to another gate in the walls; both of these are broad streets lined with *palazzi*. On the left, the attractive **Via Donizetti** climbs past the former mint (at no. 18) on its way towards Piazza Giuliani behind the Duomo. On the right, **Via Rocca** and, through a passage beside it, **Via Solata** both climb towards the Rocca (see p.235).

Ahead, the main street of the town is **Via Gombito**, undistinguished initially, a dark, narrow lane between five-storey buildings. Shops jostle for attention at street level, an intriguing mixture of down-to-earth delis and butchers, fashion boutiques, bars and places to eat. Look up to the higher floors to catch some beautiful examples of Venetian-influenced architecture – ornate balconies, arched windows and some faded frescoes. On the left, **Piazza Verzeri** is a long, tranquil courtyard, while opposite, to one side of the fifteenth-century church of **San Pancrazio**, three fine medieval tower-houses survive in **Piazza Mercato del Fieno** (Hay Market), near the San Francesco museum (see p.235).

Ahead, by the twelfth-century **Torre Gombito**, which looms to 52m above the main street, **Via San Lorenzo** falls away steeply down to the northern walls and the beautiful **Via Mario Lupo** cuts through a passage up towards Piazza Giuliani, lined with shops dating from the eleventh century. (The wash-house on Via Lupo is a 1930s addition.) A few metres beyond the tower, Piazza Vecchia opens up.

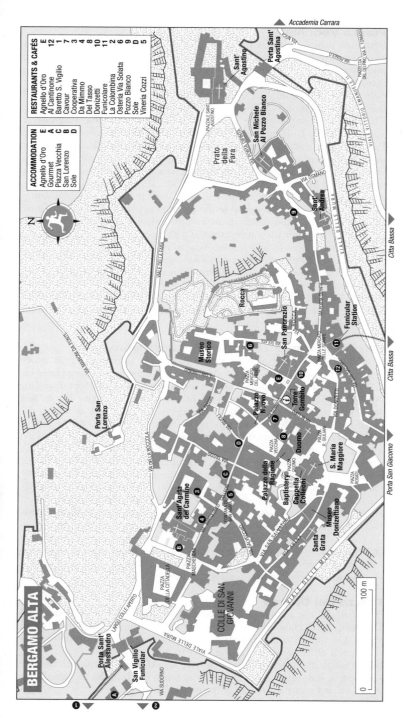

▲ Accademia Carrara

BERGAMO ALTA

ACCOMMODATION
Agnello d'Oro   E
Gourmet   A
Piazza Vecchia   C
San Lorenzo   B
Sole   D

RESTAURANTS & CAFÉS
Agnello d'Oro   E
Al Cantinone   12
Baretto S. Vigilio   1
Cavour   7
Cooperativa   4
Da Mimmo   3
Del Tasso   8
Donizetti   10
Funicolare   11
La Colombina   2
Osteria Via Solata   6
Pozzo Bianco   9
Sole   D
Vineria Cozzi   5

N

100 m

Accademia Carrara

Sant'Agostino

Porta Sant'Agostina

San Michele Al Pozzo Bianco

Prato della Fara

Sant'Andrea

Citta Bassa

Porta San Lorenzo

Rocca

San Pancrazio

Museo Storico

Funicular Station

Citta Bassa

Palazzo Nuovo

Torre Gombito

Sant'Agata del Carmine

Palazzo della Ragione

Baptistery

Cappella Colleoni

Duomo

S. Maria Maggiore

Porta San Giacomo

Santa Grata

Museo Donizettiano

COLLE DI SAN GIOVANNI

Porta Sant'Alessandro

San Vigilio Funicular

Piazza Vecchia

Bergamo's *coup de théâtre* is the magnificent Renaissance **Piazza Vecchia**, a broad, open square enclosed by a harmonious miscellany of buildings, ranging from wrought-iron-balconied houses containing cafés and restaurants to the opulent Palladian-style **Palazzo Nuovo**, now housing the civic library (on the right as you enter from Via Gombito). Stendhal rather enthusiastically dubbed this "the most beautiful square on earth", and certainly it's a striking open space. The most imposing presence is the medieval **Palazzo della Ragione**, a Venetian-Gothic building that stretches across the piazza directly opposite the Palazzo Nuovo, lending a somewhat stagey atmosphere, especially at night when the wrought-iron lamps are switched on. It dates from the mid-twelfth century, though its splendid arched windows over the square were added in 1453. Court cases used to be heard under the open arcades that form the ground floor. A grand covered stairway – the piazza's most eye-catching feature, also dating from 1453 – rises from alongside to the palazzo's upper floor. The piazza itself was the scene of joyous celebrations in 1797, when the French formed the Republic of Bergamo: the square, carpeted with tapestries, was transformed into an open-air ballroom in which – as a symbol of the new democracy – dances were led by an aristocrat partnered by a butcher.

To the right looms the massive **Torre Civica**, or **Campanone**, which you can ascend by lift (April–Oct Tues–Fri 9.30am–7pm, Sat & Sun 9.30am–9.30pm; Nov–March Sat & Sun 9.30am–4.30pm; €3). Its seventeenth-century bell, which narrowly escaped being melted down by the Germans during World War II, still tolls every half-hour.

Temporary exhibition of Accademia Carrara artworks

Until 2011, while Bergamo's prestigious Accademia Carrara gallery is under renovation (see p.237), around a hundred of its masterpieces have been placed on display in the Piazza Vecchia's **Palazzo della Ragione** (June–Sept Tues–Sun 10am–9pm, Sat until 11pm; Oct–May Tues–Fri 9.30am–5.30pm, Sat & Sun 10am–6pm; €5; ⊛www.accademiacarrara.bergamo.it). At the time of writing the layout had not been determined; it seems likely, though, that you will be able to view works such as **Titian**'s remarkable *Virgin and Child*, painted at the age of 27, a touchingly effeminate *St Sebastian* by the young **Raphael** and **Botticelli**'s startlingly modern *Portrait of Giuliano de' Medici*, painted in the 1470s – several hundred years ahead of its time. Look out, too, for a lovely *Devotional Madonna* by the seventeenth-century artist G.B. Salvi (known as **Il Sassoferrato**) – let your eye roam over the textures of cloth and alabaster skin, and the striking use of blue in the Madonna's robe – and a *Portrait of a Young Man* by **Lorenzo Lotto** (only 25 when he painted it in 1505), depicting a subject who, from the expression on his face, thought little of artists. Other noteworthy pieces in the gallery's collection that may or may not be on display include **Mantegna**'s wistful *Virgin and Child*, **Bellini**'s wrenching *Dead Christ Between Mary and St John* and a portrait of a cadaverous *Doge Leonardo Loredan* by **Vittore Carpaccio**.

Piazza del Duomo

Walk beneath the arcades of the Palazzo della Ragione to enter **Piazza del Duomo**, a small, cramped space that was almost certainly the site of the Roman forum. On the left is the incongruous 1886 facade of the **Duomo**, formerly the church of San Vincenzo, dating from well before 1100. It's worth a brief look, though the interior was extensively mucked about with through the seventeenth and eighteenth centuries, from when much of the art dates. It was closed off and under renovation at the time of writing.

The Duomo plays second fiddle on the square to the splendid church of **Santa Maria Maggiore** and its adjacent **Cappella Colleoni**. The twelfth-century church (Mon–Sat 9am–12.30pm & 2.30–6pm, Sun 9am–1pm & 3–6pm; Nov–March closes 5pm), built over an eighth-century predecessor, has a Gothic north portal on the square, decorated with Romanesque lions and, above, an equestrian statue of Alexander, Bergamo's patron saint. It's worth walking round the exterior: this is one of Lombardy's best Romanesque churches, and the apse and minor portals are all beautiful examples of the genre. The rather stubby interior – with a floor-plan that is almost a Greek cross – is a different kettle of fish, dating from a late-sixteenth century makeover. It is extraordinarily elaborate, its ceiling marzipanned with ornament in the finest tradition of Baroque excess, encrusted with gilded stucco, painted vignettes and languishing statues. The confessional (1704), by Andrea Fantoni, displays stunning artistry, festooned with cherubs, saints and prophets and topped by a flaming orb. There's a piece of nineteenth-century kitsch, too – a monument to Bergamo's most famous son, Donizetti (see below), composer of comic opera, who died from syphilis here in 1848: bas-relief putti stamp their feet and smash their lyres in misery. More subtly, the intarsia biblical scenes on the choir stalls – designed by Lorenzo Lotto, and executed by a local craftsman – are remarkable not only for their intricacy but also for the incredible colour range of the natural wood.

Even the glitziness of Santa Maria is overshadowed by the Renaissance decoration of the adjacent **Cappella Colleoni** (Tues–Sun 9am–12.30pm & 2–4.30pm). Built onto Santa Maria in the 1470s, the chapel is an extravagant confection of pastel-coloured marble carved into an abundance of miniature arcades, balustrades and twisted columns, and capped with a mosque-like dome. Commissioned by Bartolomeo Colleoni, a Bergamo mercenary in the pay of Venice, it was designed by the Pavian sculptor Giovanni Amadeo (who was also responsible for the equally excessive Certosa di Pavia). The opulent interior, with a ceiling frescoed in the eighteenth century by Tiepolo, holds Colleoni's sarcophagus, encrusted with reliefs and statuettes and topped with a gleaming gilded equestrian statue. There's also the more modest tomb of his daughter, Medea, who died aged 15. Note Colleoni's coat-of-arms on the gate as you enter; the smoothness of the third "testicle" (supposedly biologically true) bears witness to the local tradition that rubbing it will bring you luck.

Outside on the square is the free-standing **Baptistry** (kept locked), which was removed from the interior of Santa Maria Maggiore in the seventeenth century when christenings were transferred to the Duomo. Behind, at the back of Santa Maria Maggiore, is the bulbous **Tempietto di Santa Croce**, dating from the tenth century.

Museo Donizettiano

From the south door of Santa Maria Maggiore, **Via Arena** climbs towards the west end of the Città Alta, a picturesque, narrow street that skirts, on one side, the Santa Grata monastery; a frescoed doorway into the grounds opens from the street partway up. The sounds of pianos, strings and trumpets drifts down from the windows opposite; behind are the practice rooms of the institute of music which occupies the Palazzo della Misericordia, also the home of the **Museo Donizettiano** (Tues–Fri 9.30am–1pm, Sat & Sun 9.30am–1pm & 2–5.30pm; €3; Ⓦwww.bergamoestoria.org), dedicated to the opera composer Gaetano Donizetti (1797–1848). Donizetti, who was born and died in Bergamo, was, along with Bellini and Rossini, one of the masters of the "bel canto" style, celebrated for his melodramatic lyricism, which reached a peak in *Lucia di*

A €5 **combined ticket** covers admission to the Campanone, the Museo Donizettiano, the Museo Storico in the Rocca and the Museo Storico in the Convento di San Francesco.

Lammermoor. The museum holds display cases of original letters and scores, as well as portraits of the maestro. Other rooms hold his imperial-style bed and a collection of instruments, including a harmonium and a rectangular-cased fortepiano belonging to Donizetti's patron and mentor, Simon Mayr.

Towards the Colle Aperto and San Vigilio

From Piazza Vecchia, the narrow main street continues as **Via Colleoni**, lined with pastry shops selling chocolate and sweet polenta cakes topped with sugar-icing birds. The **Teatro Sociale**, at no. 4, is occasionally open for art exhibitions; it's worth a look for its grandiose interior, designed in 1803. Further on is **Sant'Agata del Carmine**, an attractive single-naved church of the fifteenth century.

Via Colleoni leads into the rectangular, tree-shaded **Piazza Mascheroni**; to the right, views open out over the city and mountains. Passing beneath the **Torre della Campanella** (1355), you enter the **Cittadella**, a military strong-hold built by Barnabo Visconti that originally occupied the entire western chunk of the upper town. The remaining buildings now house a small theatre and two didactic museums, one of archeology, the other of natural history.

Passing through the opposite gateway of the Cittadella brings you out to the **Colle Aperto** – a blast of modernity, with busy traffic and ordinary shops, which still lies within the Venetian walls, though it doesn't feel like it. Just through the **Porta Sant'Alessandro** to one side, a **funicular** rises on a short, steep course to **San Vigilio** – the walk alongside the track is also pleasant, up a steep, narrow road overlooking the gardens of Bergamo's most desirable properties. The view from the summit, topped by the **Castello** and a sprinkling of bars and restaurants, is wonderful.

Returning to the Colle Aperto, you can either walk back through the Città Alta or follow the old **walls** around its circumference – the whole circuit takes a couple of hours. The most picturesque stretch is from the Colle Aperto to Porta San Giacomo, from where a long flight of steps leads back down into the lower city.

The Rocca and down to Sant'Agostino

Returning through the heart of the upper city to Piazza Vecchia, then turning off north on Via San Lorenzo to Piazza Mercato del Fieno, you reach the **Museo Storico** (June–Sept Tues–Fri 9.30am–1pm & 2–5.30pm, Sat & Sun 9am–7pm; Oct–May Tues–Sun 9.30am–1pm & 2–5.30pm; €3; Ⓦwww .bergamoestoria.org). Housed in the ex-convent of **San Francesco**, with a beautiful thirteenth-century cloister, it spans the history of the city from the eighteenth century to 1945.

Following Via Solata from here delivers you after a short, steep haul to the **Rocca**, probably the site of the Roman Capitol, rebuilt and reinforced in the 1330s. The views from its grounds are sensational, out over the eastern parts of the Città Alta: the Gothic frontage of Sant'Agostino is in plain view far below. Within the Rocca is an outpost of the Museo Storico (same timings), devoted to the Risorgimento.

From Piazza Mercato delle Scarpe, at the foot of the Rocca, **Via Porta Dipinta** heads east and down, away from the bustling upper-town lanes. This is an elegant street, lined with seventeenth- and eighteenth-century *palazzi*. Past the church of **Sant'Andrea**, mentioned as early as 785 but rebuilt in 1840 – with a fine altarpiece of the *Madonna and Saints* by Moretto – stands the quiet little church of **San Michele al Pozzo Bianco**, overlooking a junction of streets. The atmospheric interior – with a supporting structure of medieval arches – holds an array of frescoes, including works by Lorenzo Lotto.

Further down, Via Porta Dipinta skirts the open, grassy **Fara**, dominated by the Gothic facade of the deconsecrated **Sant'Agostino**, a beautiful, lofty church founded in 1290 and now used for temporary art exhibitions. The adjacent ex-convent houses the Faculty of Letters and Philosophy of Bergamo University.

Just below, cars and buses line up at traffic lights to shoot the central arch of the stout **Porta Sant'Agostino**. From outside the gate, **Via Pignolo** and the stepped and cobbled **Via della Noca** head down into the twisting streets of the medieval quarter below.

The lower town: Bergamo Bassa

Bergamo's lower town – the **CITTÀ BASSA** – spreads north from the train station in a comfortable blend of Neoclassical ostentation, Fascist severity and leafy elegance. Wandering through the **Sentierone**, an open, tree-lined piazza alongside the central **Porta Nuova**, is the best way to get a feel for the area. From here, it's a pleasant walk east into the medieval quarter of **Borgo Pignolo**, with an atmosphere that presages the Città Alta lanes. At the top of the district, a short walk from the upper town walls, stands the **Accademia Carrara** gallery, under renovation at the time of writing.

Porta Nuova and the Sentierone

At the heart of the busy, traffic-choked lower town, midway along the main Viale Papa Giovanni XXIII, the mock-Doric temples of the **Porta Nuova** mark the **Sentierone**, a spacious piazza with gardens, and a favourite spot for Bergamo's citizens to meet and stroll beneath the trees. The area was laid out by Roman architect Marcello Piacentini in the 1920s with a plan focused on traditional elements – loggias, porticoes and piazzas – that preserved the Sentierone, a Bergamasque rendezvous since the 1620s, and maintained a visual and aesthetic connection between the upper and lower towns. Piacentini's arcades still flank this pleasant spot, along with the eighteenth-century **Teatro Donizetti** and the church of **San Bartolomeo**, which holds a *Madonna with Child* by Lorenzo Lotto (1516). Frowning down on the square is the **Palazzo di Giustizia**, built in the bombastic rectangular style of the Mussolini era, while the rather more elegant **Torre dei Caduti** (1924) rises ahead, above Piazza Veneto. Off to the west is Via XX Settembre, the city's main shopping street, leading to the medieval porticoes of Piazza Pontida at its western end.

Via Pignolo

From the Sentierone, **Via Torquato Tasso** leads east into the oldest part of the Città Bassa. Marking the junction with the old medieval thoroughfare of **Via Pignolo** is the Renaissance church of **Santo Spirito**, originally fourteenth-century, with Lorenzo Lotto's altarpiece of the *Blessed Virgin Enthroned* (1521) and an eight-section polyptych by Ambrogio Bergognone (1507).

The Borgo Pignolo formed in the Middle Ages as overspill from the upper town, and its main artery, Via Pignolo, has a largely unchanged appearance and ambience: narrow, gloomy and atmospheric, with many architectural features – balconies, mullioned windows – surviving. At the junction with Via Verdi is the small, unremarkable church of **San Bernardino**, with Lotto's altarpiece of the *Blessed Virgin*, opposite the **Museo Diocesano Bernareggi** (Tues–Sun 9am–12.30pm & 3–6.30pm; €3; ⓦ www.museobernareggi.it). Among the modernized rooms of ecclesiastical treasures and liturgical vestments nestles the odd gem – a ninth-century Longobard silver crucifix here, a *Christ Resurrected* by Lotto there – culminating with a series of eight ghoulish portraits of skeletons, painted in the eighteenth century for Bergamo's festival of the Dead Souls.

Via Pignolo continues past the marble facade of **Sant'Alessandro della Croce** to the attractive **Piazzetta del Delfino**, occupied by a dolphin fountain built here in 1526. Ahead, Via Pignolo leads to the Porta Sant'Agostino, while **Via San Tomaso** (Ⓦ www.viasantomaso.com), packed with galleries, antiques shops and cool cafés, heads right towards the Accademia Carrara.

Accademia Carrara

Just below the upper town, close to the city walls, stands the **Accademia Carrara**, Piazza Carrara 82 (Ⓦ www.accademiacarrara.bergamo.it) – Bergamo's best art gallery and one of Lombardy's leading collections. At the time of writing, the gallery was closed for a top-to-toe refit, due for completion in 2011. Some of its artworks are temporarily on display in the Palazzo della Ragione in Piazza Vecchia (see p.232).

Galleria d'Arte Moderna e Contemporanea

Opposite the Accademia Carrara is the **Galleria d'Arte Moderna e Contemporanea**, Via San Tomaso 82 (Ⓦ www.gamec.it). Opening hours and admission varies with each temporary exhibition – often of world-class stature – but, in addition to the headline show, there is a small **permanent collection**. Among painting by Kandinsky and Graham Sutherland are bronzes by the twentieth-century Bergamo-born sculptor Giacomo Manzù and a moody *Still Life With Fruit*, surprising for having been painted at the age of 71 by surrealist Giorgio de Chirico.

Eating and drinking

One of the pleasures of Bergamo is its **food and drink**, easily enjoyed whether you assemble picnics from the many *salumerie* and bakeries in the old town, or opt to graze around the city's terrific **osterie**. The town's culinary attractions are headed by game – hunting and devouring the local wildlife is a major pastime – as well as the signature dishes of polenta *taragna* (with butter and cheese) and *casoncelli*, ravioli stuffed with sausage meat, sage and butter. With Bergamo's popularity it's always worth **booking ahead** – essential at weekends. You'll find the best **ice cream** in town under the luxurious balconies of *La Mariana* on Largo Colle Aperto, Bergamo's oldest *pasticceria*.

Cafés and snacks

Caffè Funicolare In the funicular station on Piazza Mercato delle Scarpe. Good-value snacks served on a terrace with a spectacular view over the Città Bassa. Open until 2am. Closed Tues.

Caffè del Tasso Piazza Vecchia Ⓦ www.caffedel tasso.it. Bergamo's oldest café and wine bar, founded in 1476 beside the Palazzo della Ragione. The barrel-vaulted interior was once the city's leading meeting-point for artists and writers –

Treno Blu

A good excursion from Bergamo on summer Sundays (May, June & Sept only) is to take the vintage **Treno Blu**, operated by the **Ferrovia del Basso Sebino** (Ⓦ www .ferrovieturistiche.it), to the rail junction at Palazzolo and then on the short but scenic stretch along the Oglio river to Parático on **Lake Iseo** (see p.242). Boats connect from Sárnico (opposite Parático) to Iseo, Monte Isola and around the lake. A return fare from Bergamo to Parático is €8, while a combi train/boat return fare to Iseo is €12, to Monte Isola €14.50. Twice a year they lay on a steam loco for the run.

with its bookcases and sculptures, it retains its atmosphere today. Tables also spill out onto the square's cobbles.

Cavour Via Gombito 3. A fine *pasticceria* just down from Piazza Vecchia, and one of the most attractive cafés in town – don't miss their hot chocolate.

Cooperativa Città Alta Vicolo Sant'Agata, signposted off Via Colleoni. This cooperative venture – a cheery amalgam of café, restaurant and bar (open until 2am) – boasts a happy hour on Thurs and a pleasant garden where you can idle away your time admiring the distant hills. The food – low-priced local dishes served with informality – is excellent. Closed Wed.

Pozzo Bianco Via Porta Dipinta 30b. An atmospheric *birreria* jammed between houses, just down from Sant'Andrea and well off the tourist routes. Inside is a long, narrow beer hall with high tables and wooden benches where students and arty types gather for the sociable buzz. Menus are €15–25 – good, hearty fare, with pizza, *focacce* and *piadine* to fill things out. Open until 2am.

Restaurants

Agnello d'Oro Via Gombito 22 ☎035.249.883. Cosy little restaurant tucked into a seventeeth-century building on the main street, bedecked in copperware and decorative ceramics, and with every shelf and sill crowded with bottles. Menus of traditional Bergamo cuisine – polenta, rabbit and the like – are €25–30. Closed Sun eve & Mon.

Al Cantinone Via Donizetti 25a ☎035.217.417. A warm and welcoming little trattoria just by the funicular, off Piazza Mercato delle Scarpe, but on a quiet street and so usually not crowded. This is a great place for Bergamasque food, with good takes on the polenta staples. Menu €22. Closed Wed.

Baretto di San Vigilio Via Castello 1 ☎035.252.845, ⓦwww.baretto.it. A quiet, classy restaurant opposite the top station of the San Vigilio funicular, with an unbeatable choice of excellent dishes on an attractive vine-covered terrace with wonderful views. Prices reflect the location: expect around €50 per head for dinner. Closed Mon.

Da Mimmo Via Colleoni 17 ☎035.218.535, ⓦwww.ristorantemimmo.com. Family-run restaurant on the main street, founded in 1956 by the father of the current owners, and housed in a *palazzo* dating back to 1357. The food is as special as the surroundings: perfect, freshly prepared local

cuisine, served with flair in a sumptuous setting, and equally popular with local families as with power-diners out to impress. Don't miss the desserts, hand-prepared by the dedicated pastry chef. Closed Tues.

Donizetti Via Gombito 17a ☎035.242.661, ⓦwww.donizetti.it. Excellent choice on the main street for a slap-up meal or a *degustazione* platter of local meats and cheeses washed down with fine wine: the long list of options takes in goat's cheeses, *prosciutti crudi*, Bresaola, *salumi d'oca* (goose) and more. Genial service and great food mark the place out. Inside is warm and welcoming; in summer tables are laid out in the loggia.

La Colombina Via Borgo Canale 12 ☎035.261.402. A very appealing little trattoria near the Colle Aperto with tasty, good-value traditional food and wonderful views. Book for a table on the balcony. Closed Mon & Tues.

Osteria di Via Solata Via Solata 8 ☎035.271.993, ⓦwww.osteriaviasolata.it. Extremely posh little restaurant, with silver place-settings, flowers and candles on every table – service is formal, the food is exceptional. The five-course *menù degustazione* is around €70, there are various *foie gras* dishes and a long list of desserts. Closed Sun eve & Tues.

Roof Garden At *Hotel Excelsior San Marco*, Piazza della Repubblica 6 ☎035.366.159, ⓦwww .roofgardenrestaurant.it. The top (eighth) floor of this four-star hotel hosts a trendy, expensive *haute cuisine* restaurant – perfect as an escape from the tide of traditional Bergamasque *osterie* in the upper town. Expect a fresh, innovative take on inter-national fine dining, *nouvelle*-style (tiny portions, artfully presented). The surroundings are spectacular, with tasteful, contemporary interiors offset by the floodlit walls of the old town that loom seemingly within reach. An open-air terrace runs around the exterior.

Sole Via Colleoni 1, ☎035.218.238. A justifiably popular restaurant attached to the eponymous small hotel, serving traditional local specialities and fish in an attractive garden in summer. Closed Thurs.

Vineria Cozzi Via Colleoni 22a ☎035.238.836, ⓦwww.vineriacozzi.it. A classy, historic wine bar with around three hundred wines to choose from and excellent local cooking. Dishes include *casoncelli bergamaschi* (ravioli with braised meat) and local polenta. The *menù* is around €30. Closed Wed.

Bergamo's valleys

Industrial development has done a thorough job of ruining much of the countryside around Bergamo, although, traffic permitting – the weekend jams can be appalling – if you push on up the valleys things do improve.

Northwest of Bergamo the **VAL BREMBANA** follows a mountain-fringed route that was well-trodden in the Middle Ages by caravans of mules transporting minerals from the Valtellina down to the cities of the plain. The road is now frequented mostly by weekend skiers heading up to Fóppolo (1508m) at the head of the valley, and by less energetic Italians en route to **San Pellegrino Terme** to take the waters. San Pellegrino (source of the famous bottled water) has been Lombardy's most fashionable spa since the early 1900s; it's from this period that its extravagant main buildings – the grand hotels and casino – date. Redevelopment is under way: a local entrepreneur is planning to relaunch the town as a getaway for Milan's super-rich with a seven-star hotel and luxury spas.

To the east of Bergamo, the **VAL CAVALLINA** has also suffered with factories and generic housing developments. The holiday area around **Lake Endine** isn't bad, but you're more likely simply to pass through on a route to Lake Iseo (see below).

The **VALLE SERIANA**, northeast of Bergamo, is the most developed, with factories and apartment blocks competing for space with forests and mountains, and rivers reduced to streams by hydroelectric schemes. The upper reaches of the valley, an easy bus-ride from Bergamo, are still fairly unspoilt.

Clusone

CLUSONE, a picturesque hilltop town 35km northeast of Bergamo, is the main draw in the Valle Seriana for its **Chiesa dei Disciplini** (a 10min walk uphill from the bus station) – specifically, the church's two fifteenth-century exterior frescoes. The upper fresco, *The Triumph of Death*, portrays three noblemen discovering an open tomb containing the worm-infested corpses of the pope and emperor, overlooked by a huge skeleton, representing Death. *The Dance of Death*, below, contrasts the corrupt nobility with a procession of contented, God-fearing commoners dancing their way happily towards death.

Clusone – with its medieval core and attractive Liberty mansions – is worth a wander, especially on Mondays when the steep curving streets are taken over by a market selling local sausage and cheeses. The **tourist office** (Mon–Sat 10am–noon & 3–5pm, Sun 9am–noon; ☎0346.21.113, ⓦwww .turismoproclusone.it) is on **Piazza dell'Orologio**, named for the sixteenth-century clock on the Palazzo Comunale, which shows the time (backwards), the date, sign of the zodiac, duration of the night and phase of the moon. The cosy **restaurant** *Mas-cì* (☎0346.21.267, ⓦwww.mas-ci.it) – part of *Albergo Commercio*, Piazza Paradiso 1 – serves local specialities like *scarpinocc* (sausage-filled ravioli) and polenta with wild mushrooms on its attractive vine-shaded terrace. From Clusone, buses connect to Lake Iseo.

Lake Iseo and the Val Camónica

However you approach it, **LAKE ISEO** (**Lago d'Iseo**) raises expectations: descending from Clusone (12km), the road passes through steep gorges, thick forests and angular mountains, at the foot of which lies the glittering lake, while the approaches on the opposite side, from Brescia (25km) or

There's a **map** of Lake Iseo on p.226.

Gardone Val Trómpia (20km), are no less dramatic, the former winding through the Franciacorta hills (see p.253), the latter coiling tightly down out of the mountains.

And yet Iseo (also known by its Latin name, **Sebino**) – the least known of the major lakes outside Italy and considerably smaller than its neighbours – has charm best appreciated from afar. The apartment blocks, harbourside boutiques, ice-cream parlours and heavy industry of **Lóvere** on the western, Bergamo shore, and the holiday traffic around **Iseo** on the eastern, Brescia shore put paid to any notion that this remarkably beautiful, S-shaped chip of blue amidst the mountains might have escaped either tourist exploitation or industrialization.

Rising from the water mid-lake is **Monte Isola** (or Mont'Isola), a giant wedge of an island that can offer something of a getaway, while stretching northwards, the broad **Val Camónica**, famous for its Bronze Age rock-carvings, reaches into the high Alps.

Iseo

ISEO town is a busy little holiday centre, attractive and very touristy. The arcades and shops on its linked waterfront squares of Largo Zanardelli, Porto Rosa and **Piazza Garibaldi** bask in the afternoon sun. It's a pleasant enough place for a stroll, along the narrow Via Campo, lined with flower-filled balconies, or into the web of lanes behind Piazza Garibaldi, but there's not a great deal to do – although there's a great deal of people doing it. Even the great man Garibaldi himself, atop a huge chunk of mossy rock in the eponymous piazza,

Boats on Lake Iseo

Boats run by Navigazione Lago d'Iseo (☎035.971.483, ⊛www.navigazionelagoiseo .it) crisscross the lake from late March to late December. Service at **Iseo** is roughly every thirty minutes in each direction – south to **Sárnico**, north to **Monte Isola**, **Lóvere** and **Pisogne**. *Traghetti* (ferries) also shuttle continuously, 24 hours a day, to and from Monte Isola – from **Sulzano** to **Peschiera**, and from **Sale Marasino** to **Carzano**.

Fares
Tickets are charged on a complicated sliding scale. Each route is assigned a number, according to the distance involved; you then cross-check on the published list for how much that route-number (or *tratta*) costs. As an example, Iseo to Peschiera (or anywhere on Monte Isola) is given as *tratta* 2, which costs €2.60. Sárnico to the island is *tratta* 3, equal to €4.10. The most expensive ticket, *tratta* 4 (Iseo to Lóvere), is €5.60. A return costs slightly less than two one-ways. There's a **supplement** of €1.10 for a suitcase, €2.15 for a bulky bag or **bicycle**. A **day pass** is €11.20.

Cruises
Cruises include the **Tour delle Tre Isole** (€5.50), which runs three times on summer Sundays (daily in mid-Aug) from Iseo around Monte Isola and its two minuscule offshoots, Isolino di San Paolo and Isolino Loreto. The romantic **Crociera Notturna** is a serene four-hour glide after dark (June–Sept Sat 8.30pm from Iseo; Aug also Fri; €35, including dinner and drinks on board). Barcaioli Monteisola also runs its own cruises and **water-taxi** service (⊛www.barcaiolimonteisola.it).

Gardens of the lakes

The lakes region of northern Italy and southern Switzerland – renowned for its spectacular natural beauty – also has a reputation for some of the finest gardens in Europe. With a climate that is more Mediterranean than Alpine, the lakes nurture a stunning array of flora, best experienced in the region's many formal gardens, set against backdrops of blue water and high mountain peaks.

Garden design

Villa Táranto, Pallanza ▲

Chinese garden plants, Giardino Botanico André Heller ▲

Isola Bella, Lake Maggiore ▼

Italian garden design had its roots in the gardens of ancient Rome – which, in turn, drew inspiration from older Hellenistic *paradeisoi*, or paradise gardens. The Greek word *paradeisos* comes from an ancient Persian term meaning "enclosed by a wall": Alexander the Great saw walled gardens and royal hunting parks on campaign in Persia, and brought the idea back home. These developed into the Roman concept of countryside estates, landscaped with terraces, trees and abundant planting, and peristyle gardens, small, enclosed open spaces within a town house. Medieval period gardens were inward-looking, focused around cloisters and private, walled retreats, often planted with kitchen herbs and medicinal plants. By the mid-fifteenth century, Renaissance ideas took hold and wealthiest families began, like the ancient Romans, to divide life between a villa – a grand country estate, suitable for leisure – and a palazzo, or noble town house, suitable for business.

Italian garden design focused on the taming of nature, emphasising structure and symmetry, with elaborate geometric designs (imported from France), topiary (originally Dutch) and flat, grass lawns cut across by gravel paths (from the English). These principles – exemplified in Verona's Giardino Giusti and the seventeenth-century Baroque gardens of Isola Bella – held sway throughout Europe for three hundred years.

In the second quarter of the eighteenth century, a new aesthetic emerged in England, based on appreciation of the irregularity of natural forms and landscapes, with rolling lawns, irregularly shaped ponds, meandering streams and patches of woodland. This English style

▲ Isole di Brissago, Lake Maggiore

▼ Lemons, Lake Garda

caught on around Europe: the gardens of Villa Melzi and Isola Madre are both in the English style. With the strong English links to the Italian Lakes from the mid-nineteenth century onwards, the **English style** continued to influence the design of many lakes gardens: in many places (the Borromeo islands of Lake Maggiore, or the Palazzo Estense in Varese), a formal Italian garden is juxtaposed with a wilder English garden alongside.

Planting

There are hundreds, probably thousands, of varieties of plants in the gardens of the Italian Lakes. Lake Garda is especially known for its **lemon** trees, but you'll also find lemons and oranges growing on lakes Maggiore, Lugano and

Parco Giardino Sigurtà, Valeggio ▲

Villa Monastero, Varenna ▼

Como. Many gardens feature mixtures of evergreen and deciduous trees: Villa del Balbianello, for instance, has oaks as well as firs, while Villa Melzi has a promenade of plane trees in addition to exotic pines, Japanese maples and palms. Exotic plants such as lilacs, jasmine and magnolia began to be imported to Italy from the East around the middle of the sixteenth century. Two of the most common flowering plants on the lakes are azaleas and rhododendrons, both cultivated in abundance at Villa Carlotta on Lake Como and Villa Taranto on Lake Maggiore, as well as in many other gardens. The huge Kashmir cypress on Isola Madre is purportedly the largest example in Europe, while this island garden also features such exotics as banana plants, hibiscus and palms. The three lakes which surround Mantova, south of Verona, are fringed by lotus flowers, imported in the 1920s.

Perfect conditions

The **climate** and **topography** of the lakes region are perfect for maintaining gardens. These southern foothills of the Alps catch clear, warm **sunshine** all year round. In addition, the lakes have moderate extremes of **temperature**, since water both heats up and cools down more slowly than land. Maggiore and Garda are big enough to act as giant **solar batteries**, storing up the sun's energy all summer and then releasing it slowly during the winter, keeping their shores balmy and frost-free. In several places – Salò and Gardone on Lake Garda, or Pallanza on Lake Maggiore – a rocky wall of **cliffs** shields a narrow strip of south-facing shore from cold northerly winds, thereby creating a warm, protected **microclimate** in which subtropical exotics can flourish.

looks rather bored with the whole affair. Stop in for a nice lunch, or to take ship for the island, but unless you've booked a week's holiday at one of the many hotels or campsites lining this shore, there's little to keep you.

Practicalities

Iseo is served by **trains** and **buses** from Brescia. From Bergamo, buses run direct to nearby Sárnico, or you could take a train to Palazzolo and switch there to an Iseo-bound bus. Iseo's **train station** lies at the eastern end of Via XX Settembre, 350m inland from the **imbarcadero** at the western end.

The helpful **tourist office** is on the lakefront promenade at Lungolago Marconi 2 (daily 10am–12.30pm & 3.30–6.30pm; shorter hours in winter; ℡030.980.209, Ⓦwww.bresciatourism.it). Websites such as Ⓦwww.lagodiseo .org, Ⓦwww.lagoiseo.it and Ⓦwww.cooptur.it are also useful.

The best **hotel** within the town is *Iseo Lago*, Via Colombera 2 (℡030.98.891, Ⓦwww.iseolagohotel.it; ❺), a bright, airy four star on the southern outskirts, with modern, well-equipped rooms, good service and some stylishness. It shares facilities with the *Sassabanek* tourist centre alongside (Ⓦwww.sassabanek.it), which has a lido, swimming pools, tennis courts, saunas, gyms and shops, as well as **camping** areas, caravans and bike rental (Ⓦwww.iseobike.com). On the town-centre waterfront is the two-star *Milano*, Lungolago Marconi 4 (℡030.980.449, Ⓦwww.hotelmilano.info; ❷), which has pleasant en-suite rooms, some with balconies overlooking the lake.

There are plenty of places to **eat** on and just off the main squares: *Da Rocco*, Via Sambuco 20 (closed Wed), is a traditional, old-fashioned family trattoria, in much the same vein as *Osteria Le Ciacole*, Vicolo Cantine 8 (closed Tues). Head away from the lake down the narrow Vicolo dell'Ombra to the beautiful little Piazza Mazzini, ringed by shuttered stone houses and echoing to the sound of church bells; here you'll find *Il Paiolo* (closed Tues), a lovely, family-run restaurant with good, moderately priced local cooking.

Monte Isola (Mont'Isola or Montisola)

Amidst Lake Iseo looms the traffic-free **MONTE ISOLA**, a huge chunk of mountain that is Italy's – and Europe's – largest lake island, over 3km long and 600m high. As a magnet for local day-trippers in summer and at weekends, it's unlikely to provide much solitude, but a walk or cycle-ride round the perimeter of the island (9km by road, or about 15km following paths above the shore) gives great views.

There are five landing-stages around the island: on the south side are **Peschiera** (nearest to Sulzano on the mainland) and **Sensole**, while on the north side are **Carzano** (opposite Sale Marasino on the mainland), **Paradiso** and **Siviano**. Ferries shuttle over from Iseo and other points frequently (see box opposite).

There's a little **tourist office** at Peschiera (℡030.982.5088, Ⓦwww .tuttomonteisola.it and Ⓦwww.monteisola.com). Staff here, and at the tourist office in Iseo, can direct you to places on the island offering **bike rental**.

The island has a sprinkling of attractive **hotels**, with restaurants serving tasty regional dishes. The *Bellavista* (℡030.988.6106, Ⓦwww.albergo -bellavista.it; restaurant closed Tues; ❶) is in Siviano; the waterfront *La Foresta* (℡030.988.6210; restaurant closed Wed; ❷) stands five-minutes' walk outside Peschiera; with the rather posher *Sensole* at Sensole (℡030.988.6203; ❸). The most alluring of the string of waterside **restaurants** on the hour-long stroll between Peschiera and Sensole is *La Spiaggetta* (℡030.988.6141; closed Tues), a tiny, family-run trattoria that is open for lunch only.

Around Lake Iseo

North of Iseo, past **Marone**, the cliffs close in, dropping sheer to the water; a tortuous road climbs from Marone through chestnut woods to the village of **Zone**, in an area of rocky pyramids topped by granite boulders, a result of the erosion of glacial moraine deposits. Just south of Iseo is an area of marshland known as **Torbiere**, protected as a nature reserve and bird sanctuary.

SÁRNICO, at the southernmost point of the lake, is an attractive old town, linked to its neighbour **Parático** by a bridge over the River Oglio. The broad, waterfront piazzas of the *contrada* (the old quarter) give way to narrow, cobbled lanes climbing the hill behind to the **Museo Civico/Pinacoteca Bellini** (Sat & Sun 10am–noon & 4–7pm; free), displaying local paintings and furniture in the restored fifteenth-century Palazzo Gervasoni. Sárnico's **tourist office** is at Via Lantieri 6 (April–Sept Tues–Sat 9am–12.30pm & 3–6.30pm, Sun 9.30am–12.30pm; June–Aug also Mon 3–6.30pm; ☎035.910.900), and there are some nice places to take a break, including *Café Solair* on the sunny Piazza Besenzoni and friendly *Bar Centrale* on Piazza XX Settembre.

In the hills around Sárnico are a number of Art Nouveau villas designed by the architect Giuseppe Sommaruga, while, 3km west in **CREDARO**, the tiny Cappella di San Rocco – attached to the thirteenth-century church of San Giorgio – was frescoed by Lorenzo Lotto in 1525: look for his ethereal *Nativity with St Sebastian and St Rocco*. The caretaker who lives alongside (☎035.935.355) will unlock the chapel on request.

Lóvere and Pisogne

The scenic route from Sárnico up the western shore (25km) – more scenic still when viewed from the water – passes below towering cliffs that often force the road into tunnels. Beyond **Tavernola Bergamasca** and **Riva di Solto**, both limestone quarrying towns, is **LÓVERE** at the lake's northern tip, once a Venetian textile centre, now making its living from steel. The centre of town is the long **Piazza XIII Martiri**, lined with bars and cafés but also busy with lakefront traffic. Here, too, is the **tourist office** (July & Aug daily 9am–noon & 2–6pm, Sat & Sun until 7pm; reduced opening outside summer peak; ☎035.962.178), alongside the *imbarcadero*. A short walk south is the lakefront **Accademia Tadini** gallery (May–Sept Tues–Sat 3–7pm, Sun 10am–noon & 3–7pm; ⓦwww.accademiatadini.it; €5). The main level – including works by Parmigianino, Crespi and a *Madonna and Child* by Jacopo Bellini – is less engaging than the modern collection upstairs, which runs from a striking self-portrait by Hayez at 90 years old (1881) to thought-provoking portraits by the Loverese artist Giorgio Oprandi (1882–1962).

PISOGNE faces Lóvere across the lake. Signposted on the outskirts is the little fifteenth-century church of **Santa Maria delle Neve** (Tues–Sun 9.30–11.30am & 3–6pm; reduced hours in winter), where the artist **Romanino** painted a fresco cycle in 1534 – beautiful enough to have since been dubbed *La Cappella Sistina dei Poveri* ("the Poor Man's Sistine Chapel"). The basilica's interior walls are covered with Romanino's graceful art, the *Passion* to the west and south and a trompe l'oeil design in the vaults of a sky crowded with prophets. Out here, far from the strictures of urban taste, the artist could let his imagination soar, and the result is a uniquely fresh, original vision. If the church is locked, ask in town at *Bar Romanino* (closed Mon) for the key.

Val Camónica

Like many of the beautiful valleys in this region, the **VAL CAMÓNICA** is tainted by the indiscriminate scattering of light industry through its lower reaches. Factories, warehouses and discount superstores crowd the valley floor through the spa town of **Darfo–Boario Terme** and industrial **Breno** (from where a mountain road crosses east to Bagolino; see p.285).

The main reason to come this way is for the **prehistoric rock carvings** found all the way up the valley, covering a period of several thousand years. The first indications of human habitation date from after the last **Ice Age**: around 8000 BC, people arrived to hunt elk and deer, and drew their achievements on the local smooth-faced sandstone. A second phase of **Neolithic** occupation began around 6000 BC, with hunter-gatherers developing agriculture and art showing figures at prayer. From the fourth century BC, the **Bronze Age** inhabitants – by then known as the Camuni, from which the valley's name derives – drew themselves with possessions such as jewellery, while the last, **Iron Age** phase, up to the Roman conquest, features wheeled carts, houses, and scenes of people working or fighting.

The best place to view the rock art is at **CAPO DI PONTE**, 38km north of Lóvere by bus (and also on the train line from Brescia and Iseo). Pick up a map at the Pro Loco **tourist office** by the main road, Via Briscioli 42 (Mon 9am–noon, Tues–Sat 9am–noon & 2.30–4.30pm, Sun 9.30am–12.30pm; ☎0364.426.619, ⓦwww.proloco.capo-di-ponte.bs.it), or follow the yellow signs across the river and walk up into the **Parco Nazionale delle Incisioni Rupestri** (Tues–Sun 9am–6pm; €4), in the **Naquane** district. This open area contains thousands of carvings, beginning with the **Great Rock** in front of the site's shop, where stick-and-blob figures give a taste of Camuni life over a thousand-year period. There are scenes of hunters, agricultural workers, a religious ceremony presided over by priests, and a Bronze Age burial in which the deceased is surrounded by his weapons and tools. To see how the civilization developed into the Iron Age, head for Rock 35, carved with a blacksmith, and Rock 23, with a four-wheeled wagon transporting an urn. Elsewhere, in **BEDOLINO** outside Cemmo, 2km above Capo di Ponte, a rock in someone's garden is carved with a **Bronze Age map** showing huts, fields, walls, canals and the Rosa Camuna, a stylized flower which has been adopted as the symbol of Lombardy.

Brescia

The road to **BRESCIA** is the road less travelled. To most Italians, Brescia (pronounced *bresha*) means heavy industry or business meetings. To most outsiders, it's somewhere to be bypassed while plotting a route from Lake Como to Lake Garda. But if you've had your fill of picturesque medieval villages, or if the touristy commerce of the lakes is starting to irritate, Brescia might be just the thing.

What Brescia lacks in classic good looks it makes up for in history. Brixia – as it then was – was a major **Roman** city, designated *Colonia Civica Augusta* in 27 BC. Evidence is widespread, from the **Capitoline Temple** overlooking the forum to well-preserved mosaic floors of Roman villas in the **Santa Giulia** museum. Its medieval and Renaissance history under the Venetians left a Brescian school in painting – with many examples viewable in the **Pinacoteca** – and fine architecture in the main **Piazza della Loggia**, while neighbouring **Piazza Vittoria** holds as striking an ensemble of Fascist architecture as anywhere in the region.

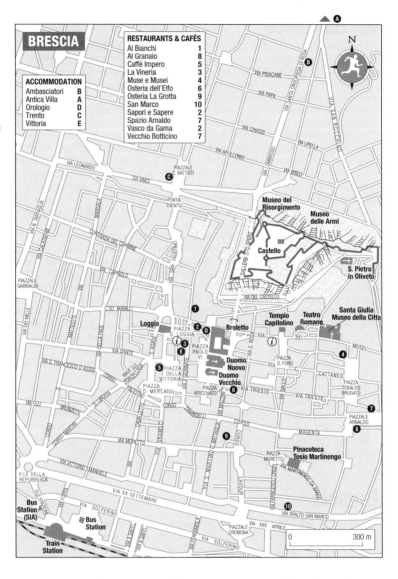

BRESCIA

RESTAURANTS & CAFÉS

Al Bianchi	1
Al Granaio	8
Caffè Impero	5
La Vineria	3
Muse e Musei	4
Osteria dell'Elfo	6
Osteria La Grotta	9
San Marco	10
Sapori e Sapere	2
Spazio Arnaldo	7
Vasco da Gama	2
Vecchio Botticino	7

ACCOMMODATION

Ambasciatori	B
Antica Villa	A
Orologio	D
Trento	C
Vittoria	E

Brescia remained a success into the modern era, moving from silk production through railways to an iron and steel industry. This is chiefly located in the nearby **Val Trómpia**, where the manufacture of cutlery, cookware and firearms helps support the national, as well as the regional, economy. With a population topping 200,000, Brescia today is Lombardy's second-largest city.

Yet it merits barely a footnote in most lakes itineraries: tourism is well down the city's list of priorities. This gives the historic centre a uniquely unpretentious charm: in a region of spectacular natural scenery and legendary urban beauty, Brescia refuses to be pigeon-holed. Other cities may offer themselves up on a platter for visitors' approval, but Brescia doesn't preen. It's just a serious, working city, almost completely free of tourists and with plenty to fill an absorbing couple of days.

Arrival and information

Brescia has three exits off the A4 **autostrada**, Ovest (west), Centro and Est (east). It is served by main-line **trains** from Milano Centrale, Verona and Desenzano/Sirmione, as well as slower trains from Lecco, Bergamo and Cremona. The **train station** is an unattractive fifteen-minute walk from the centre, or you can cross the road for **city bus** #1 (direction Mombello) or #2 (direction Pendolina), which both head into town on Via San Martino della Battaglia and Via Mazzini. A *biglietto ordinario* (valid 75min; €1) or *biglietto giornaliero* (valid 24hr; €2.80) are buyable from the shop by the bus stop or the bus driver. Full details at ⓦwww.bresciamobilita.it.

Flanking the train station are two **bus stations** – the main **Stazione Autolinee**, with buses from Verona, Cremona, Mantova, Iseo, Bergamo-Orio al Serio airport and Brescia-Montichiari airport, and the **SIA bus station**, with buses from Desenzano, Salò, Riva, Idro and Val Trómpia. Information is at ⓦwww.trasportibrescia.it.

The main **tourist office** is at Piazza della Loggia 6 (Mon–Sat 9.30am–6.30pm, Sun 10am–6pm; ℡030.240.0357, ⓦwww.bresciatourism.it). Another office, run by the province, is at Via dei Musei 32 (Mon–Thurs 9am–noon & 2.30–4.30pm, Fri 9am–noon; ℡030.374.9916).

Accommodation

Brescia's **hotels** are a fairly undistinguished bunch, almost universally aimed at business travellers. At the lower end of the market, there's a cluster of rather nasty cheap hotels around the station and adjacent main roads that are best avoided. Book ahead if you're planning to be here in May, when the Mille Miglia vintage car rally – which starts and ends in Brescia – attracts thousands to the city.

Ambasciatori Via Crocefissa di Rosa 90 ℡030.399.114, ⓦwww.ambasciatori.net. A fine, family-run four-star hotel occupying an unattractive modern building 1km north of the centre, with spacious rooms (the interior has been gutted and entirely redeveloped), good facilities, an excellent restaurant and top-quality service. Road noise, especially on higher floors, is minimal; a/c is standard; and bathrooms and furniture are modern and attractive. Children under 10 stay for free in their parents' room. There's free parking, and bus #1 from the station stops outside. The management have offered a discount to readers who mention this Rough Guide when booking. ❹–❺

Antica Villa Via San Rocchino 90 ☎ 030.303.186, ⓦ www.hotelanticavilla.it. Small villa hotel north of the centre below a wooded hill. Its 15 rooms with bathrooms have soundproofing and a/c, and there's a good deal of character to the place, though it is awkwardly far out. Bus #1 stops outside. ❸
Orologio Via Beccaria 17 ☎ 030.375.5411, ⓦ www.albergoorologio.it. Attractive boutique three-star insinuated into an old building beside the Broletto and Piazza Paolo VI. Rooms have been carefully renovated and updated with a good deal of taste, matching the warm welcome and genial service. ❹–❺

Trento Piazza Battisti 31 ☎ 030.380.768. Decent two-star on a busy square just north of the centre – best of the budget options. Bus #7 from the train station. ❷
Vittoria Via X (Dieci) Giornate 20 ☎ 030.280.061, ⓦ www.hotelvittoria.com. Brescia's sole five-star option, built in 1933 in Fascist style, with lots of gleaming marble and chandeliers adorning the lobby. The rooms are similarly grand, done up in traditional style – lots more marble, dark wood, sober drapes, stiffly formal flunkies: the perfect place to live out those Agatha Christie costume-drama fantasies. Good central location. ❼

The City

Brescia's city centre comprises a network of shopping streets enclosing a compact cluster of piazzas. The ancient **Piazza della Loggia** is the heart of the city, though the adjacent Fascist-era **Piazza della Vittoria** is larger. Nearby **Piazza Paolo VI** holds the remarkable **Duomo Vecchio**. Just to the east rise a huge **Roman temple** and **theatre**.

Two outstanding museums add to Brescia's allure: the ex-monastery complex of **Santa Giulia** houses excellent displays on the history of Brescia, and the **Pinacoteca** has a fine Renaissance art collection.

Piazza della Loggia and around

Brescia's main square is also its prettiest – **Piazza della Loggia**, which dates back to 1433, when the city invited Venice in to rule and protect it from Milan's power-hungry Visconti family. The Venetian influence is clearest in the fancy **Palazzo della Loggia** which dominates the west side of the square – and in which both Palladio and Titian had a hand – and in the ornate **Torre dell'Orologio** opposite, modelled on the campanile in Venice's Piazza San Marco. Around 1480, in a gesture of self-aggrandizement, the city authorities set bits of inscribed Roman stonework into the unified frontage of the shops lining the square's south side, later taken over by the **Monte di Pietà**, a kind of municipal pawnbrokers. The Roman chunks survive in the same facade today; part of the building is now the city tourist office. Just nearby, below the Torre dell'Orologio, a **monument** commemorates the Fascist bombing, in 1974, of a trade-union rally here, in which eight people were killed and over a hundred injured. The terrorists left the bomb in a rubbish bin: you can still see the blast damage on the pillar. To the north is the **Porta Bruciata**, a defensive medieval tower-gate giving onto Via dei Musei (see p.248); insinuated into the gate itself is the tiny, conical church of **San Faustino in Riposo**.

Brescia's main shopping streets spread out opposite the tourist office, onto **Corso Mameli**, which cuts west beyond Largo Formentone and Piazza Rovetta – the scene of a rather desultory daily secondhand clothes market – as a narrow, bustling thoroughfare, packed with delis, bars and boutiques. To the north, **Via San Faustino** storms into an amiable neighbourhood of laundrettes and local cafés on its way towards the Contrada del Carmine, the former red-light district.

While Brescia is building itself a new **metro** (ⓦ www.metro.bs.it) – due to open in 2012 – expect roadworks and traffic disruption in and around the city centre.

▲ Piazza della Vittoria

Streets connect south from Piazza della Loggia, behind the tourist office, into the long, Fascist-built **Piazza della Vittoria** under the stern gaze of the monumental post office building, its facade – like much of the square – done in contrasting shades of highly polished marble. The architect Piacentini's clinical arcades march off down the square in rigid formation, and grandiose corner steps struggle to mask the square's uneven topography. The south side of the square leads to **Piazza del Mercato**, a cobbled square of more interest to the stomach than the eye: as well as a supermarket, small shops selling local salamis and cheeses nestle under its dark porticoes.

Piazza Paolo VI

Passages from Piazza della Loggia and Piazza della Vittoria lead east across **Via Dieci Giornate** – lined with arcades – and through to what was once Piazza del Duomo. Renamed **Piazza Paolo VI**, after the Brescian-born Pope Paul VI (1897–1978), this is one of the few squares in Italy to boast two cathedrals, though, frankly, it would have been better off without the chilly **Duomo Nuovo** (Mon–Sat 7.30am–noon & 4–7pm, Sun 8am–1pm & 4–7pm), a heavy Mannerist monument that took over two hundred years to complete, its grim Neoclassical facade concealing a tall cupola. Much more appealing is the adjacent twelfth-century **Duomo Vecchio**, or **Rotonda** (April–Oct Tues–Sun 9am–noon & 3–7pm; Nov–March Tues–Sun 10am–noon & 3–6pm), a unique circular church of local stone. Its fine proportions aren't easily appreciated from outside, as the building is sunk below the current level of the piazza.

You enter at the matroneum, the upper gallery previously reserved for women to pray, looking down over the interior. Here stands the tomb of Berardo Maggi, a thirteenth-century Bishop of Brescia, in red Verona marble. The transept and presbytery were added to the church in 1450, in a very late style of Gothic. As you look down, the chapel to the right holds two paintings by Romanino and four by Moretto, who also has a striking *Assumption* as the main altarpiece. Glass set into the transept pavement reveals the remains of Roman baths (a wall and geometrical mosaics) and the apse of an eighth-century basilica, which burned down in 1097. The crypt is supported on a random array of reused Roman columns.

Alongside the Duomo Nuovo, to the north, stands the **Broletto**, the twelfth-century town hall that was the municipal seat of power before the construction of the Palazzo della Loggia.

The Roman temple and theatre

Adjoining the Broletto to the north, **Via dei Musei** marks the line of the Roman *decumanus maximus*, the main east–west street. It's a narrow, undramatic thoroughfare today, although lined with some historic *palazzi*. A short walk east brings you to what was the centre of Roman Brixia, **Piazza del Foro**, built over the ancient forum (which was substantially larger than the current square). Dominating the area are the tall columns of the **Tempio Capitolino** (daily 11am–4pm; free), a Roman temple built in 73 AD, now partly reconstructed with red brick. Behind are three reconstructed *celle*, probably temples to the Capitoline trinity of Jupiter, Juno and Minerva. Adjacent to the east, reached by dodging around a side-street, is a part-excavated Roman **theatre**; ongoing archeological work has revealed frescoes and remnants of an older temple beneath the current one.

Santa Giulia: Museo della Città

A short walk further east along Via dei Musei brings you to the civic museum of **Santa Giulia** (Tues–Sun: June–Sept 10am–6pm; Oct–May 9.30am–5.30pm; €8; ⓦwww.bresciamusei.com). This is housed in the sprawling ex-Benedictine convent of San Salvatore and Santa Giulia, founded in 753 over what was, during the Roman period, a residential quarter of frescoed villas. The layers of history on show make this a fascinating place to spend a couple of hours; there is a vast amount to get through, so we've focused on specific **highlights**. The museum frequently hosts major modern art exhibitions (see ⓦwww .lineadombra.it for details), which can close certain galleries.

Roman and medieval galleries: the Winged Victory

From the ticket desk, head right and down to the basement for the **prehistory** gallery, dominated, at the end of a long corridor, by the evocative fourth-century BC iron **Daone helmet**, an Etruscan piece found in Daone, above Lake Garda.

Turn right and back on yourself for the first **Roman** gallery: beyond a series of inscribed mileposts, a remnant of Brixia's *cardo maximus* is visible both inside and outside the monastery walls. Head up a short flight of stairs to galleries set out around the ground floor of the monastery's northern cloister. Room 3 holds a model of Brescia's Tempio Capitolino, while a museum highlight is in room 6 – a bronze, life-sized **Winged Victory** discovered in the temple. This was adapted in the second century AD from a pre-existing fourth-century BC statue of Aphrodite admiring herself in a mirror: the artist added a military tunic and wings and changed the goddess's mirror into a shield, on which Victory is inscribing her champion's name. The mirror and shield have long been lost, as has the helmet of Mars beneath the figure's left foot.

Signs lead round to a catwalk that passes through the (covered) excavation area of two **Roman houses** discovered beneath the monastery gardens. The colourful mosaic floors of each villa (known as a *domus*), and the remnants of frescoed walls, are amazingly well preserved; walking this close to them, tracing a path through the rooms they adorned, is a real treat.

Past a gallery of capitals and Roman glassware – and an exit to the cloister, which is lined with Roman funerary inscriptions – a doorway leads to the **early medieval** galleries, displaying Lombard and Carolingian grave goods such as swords, pottery and gold crosses. Further on, the rooms devoted to the **city-states** (**comune and signorie**) begin, on the right, with two fine bronze wolves' heads, of about the twelfth century, taken from the Broletto – a rare example of secular Romanesque work.

San Salvatore: the Nuns' Choir
An exit here leads into the first of the museum's three churches, **San Salvatore**. Follow signs straight through on the right to climb to the upper-level **Coro delle Monache**, or **Nuns' Choir**. This soaring, barrel-vaulted space above the main floor of the San Salvatore church is covered in colourful frescoes, most of them executed in the 1420s by Floriano Ferramola. Overhead is *God the Father*, while the most striking image is a *Crucifixion* against an open landscape on the east wall (which has windows down into the church). Scenes from Christ's childhood adorn the upper panels all round the room. On the west side, moved here in the 1880s, is the dour marble mausoleum of the Martinengo family, excessively encrusted with ornament, beyond which is the church of **Santa Giulia**, now off-limits.

Returning down the stairs delivers you into San Salvatore itself, most of which is early medieval (parts date from the eighth century, visible through grilles in the floor). A circular route leads down to the ancient crypt and up again, to exit the church in the southeast corner.

From here, the itinerary continues to the **Venetian** galleries – with elegant reliefs and statues, as well as re-creations of aristocratic Brescian family homes of the period – and the **Applied Arts** galleries, with majolica and beautiful sixteenth-century Murano glassware.

Santa Maria in Solario
Signs deliver you back to the ticket desk, from where you can head left on the itinerary devoted to the history of the Santa Giulia monastery, and a gallery dominated by a seventeenth-century statue in Carrara marble of St Julia herself. Head outside into the southern cloister and left, to enter **Santa Maria in Solario**, a square twelfth-century church with an octagonal lantern. You arrive in a lower room housing the **Lipsanoteca**, a small, fragile, ivory reliquary casket from the fourth century, covered in superbly detailed carving in three bands: the top and bottom are devoted to stories from the Old Testament, while the central band details scenes from Christ's life.

Stone stairs lead up into the main chamber of the church, extensively frescoed by Ferramola (1513–24). In the three apses of the east wall, Mary is flanked by St Catherine and St Benedict, while the north wall shows scenes from the life of St Julia. Overhead is a spectacular, midnight-blue **frescoed dome**, speckled with gilded brass stars.

Dominating the centre of the room is a glass case holding the **Croce di Desiderio**, an eighth-century wooden cross, covered in sheet metal and studded with more than two hundred gemstones, mostly Roman in origin. Desiderius was king of the Lombards, and this eye-popping item would have represented a significant part of his treasure – spiritual and material.

The exit, in the west wall, leads downstairs into the cloister of San Salvatore, facing the bell tower. Follow signs to the right back to the ticket desk.

The Castello
Behind Santa Giulia, Via Piamarta climbs the **Cydnean Hill**, the core of early Roman Brixia, mentioned by the poet Catullus. Fragments of a Roman gate survive just before you reach the sixteenth-century church of **San Pietro in Oliveto**, named for the olive grove that surrounds it.

The hill is crowned by the **Castello** (daily 8am–8pm; free), begun in the fifteenth century by Lucchino Visconti and added to by the Venetians, French and Austrians. The resulting confusion of towers, ramparts, halls and court-yards is difficult to interpret, though it makes a good place for an atmospheric picnic. Museums here include the large **Museo delle Armi** (Tues–Sun: June–Sept 10.30am–6pm; Oct–May 9.30am–5pm; €5) and **Museo del Risorgimento** (same hours and ticket).

Pinacoteca Tosio Martinengo

Brescia's main art gallery is the **Pinacoteca Tosio Martinengo**, a short walk south of Santa Giulia, entered at Via Martinengo da Barco 1 (Tues–Sun: June–Sept 10.30am–6pm; Oct–May 9.30am–5pm; €5; ®www.bresciamusei.com). The collection – built up separately by two nineteenth-century Brescian noblemen, Paolo Tosio and Leopardo Martinengo (hence the name) – forms a compact, high-quality gallery, well worth an hour or two.

Section 1: Raphael and Lorenzo Lotto

Two of the best paintings come first, at the top of the stairs in **room 1.1** – both by the Renaissance master **Raphael** and both fragments of larger works. On one side is an ethereally beautiful *Angel* (1501), painted as part of a retable for the Umbrian abbey of San Nicolà da Tolentino; after an earthquake destroyed the church, the damaged retable was cut up. Three fragments survived: one is in the Louvre, another is in Naples, and the third – this angel – was discovered for sale in a Florentine market by Paolo Tosio and brought to Brescia. The virtuosity of this small portrait is dazzling – more so when you realize that Raphael was just 17 years old when he painted it. Opposite is another small work by Raphael, a *Risen Christ*, showing – in the accurate rendering of the body's musculature, the movement in the slightly turned stance and details such as a whisper of five o'clock shadow – the debt the young artist owed to Leonardo.

The same room also has a major work by **Alessandro Bonvicino**, one of a trio of artists at the head of the Brescian Renaissance (the others were Moretto and Romanino), who brought techniques of colour and humanistic portraiture learned from Titian and other Venetian masters back to Brescia, blending them with local, Lombard styles. Bonvicino's *Salome* (c.1537) is an insightful portrait of Renaissance courtesan Tullia d'Aragona, whose mother was known for sexual impropriety. In an attempt to recover her own and her family's reputations, Tullia took to writing poetry, and the artist portrays her as a melancholy victim – as Salome was – of her mother's manipulations.

Room 1.2 has a fine *Adoration of the Shepherds* (1530) by **Lorenzo Lotto**, a Venetian who lived in Bergamo and had great influence on the Brescian school. The tenderness of the Christ-child reaching out to a sheep, the bold colouring and the blue sky are all signs of a Venetian style, and here, unusually, the Virgin is shown kneeling in the manger. The artist has shown his two patrons, members of the wealthy Bagnoni family, as shepherds, incongruously dressed in the elegant clothes of noblemen. **Room 1.3** – amongst portraits by non-Italians – has a wonderful *Flautist* by Nicolas Tournier (1625), strikingly lit, showing the beginnings of a Flemish influence.

Section 2: "Great Paintings of the Cinquecento"

Next door in **room 2.1**, near an inscrutable, introspective portrait of a man by one of the leading figures of the Brescian school, **Romanino**, is *Boy with a Flute* by **Giovanni Gerolamo Savoldo** (c.1525). This arresting work shows a proud young musician, complete with a feather in his cap, stopping midway in a tricky passage to glance at the painter, his long fingers still in position on his recorder. Savoldo shows off his skill in handling light by pinning a half-folded sheet of music to the wall behind the flautist, and then expertly depicting the play of shadows. **Room 2.2** holds a double-sided work by Vincenzo Foppa, who painted under the patronage of the Visconti in Milan, Pavia and elsewhere. Foppa met Bramante and Leonardo in Milan, and is credited with introducing Renaissance ideas to Brescia after arriving here as an old man. His *Madonna with Saints* (1514) is backed by *St George, St Sebastian & St Rocco*. Rocco is a popular fixture in country churches around Lombardy: he was the patron saint of plague victims, and is always shown lifting his tunic to show the pustules on his thigh.

In **room 2.3**, Romanino's raw *San Gerolamo Penitente* (c.1536), depicting the hermit-saint mortifying his flesh and his soul, is juxtaposed with a more classical representation of Renaissance ideas – Moretto's *Exaltation of the Holy Cross* (c.1520), where the separation of the sacred from the profane is shown very literally as a horizontal layer of cloud.

The grand, high-ceilinged **room 2.4** houses frescoes removed from the abbey of San Nicola, at Rodengo-Saiano near Brescia. The best is the first – *Dinner in the House of Simon the Pharisee* by Romanino again (1528–31). In a sub-Michelangelesque piece of dramatic theatre, Mary Magdalene is shown cast down at Jesus' feet, about to wash his feet with tears; above, Jesus makes a highly expressive gesture with hands and shoulders to the disdainful male company, as if to say "Let her be." Alongside is the similarly assured *Dinner at Emmaus*, depicting the moment when the disciples see Christ breaking bread and thereby realize that he truly is resurrected; in the background, a boy serving a plate of food has been given an expression of stunned disbelief. Nearby, amongst some huge retables, Romanino shows his skill again in a *Nativity* (1545), painted for Brescia's church of San Giuseppe, with Mary in a gorgeous silver cloak and the Palazzo della Loggia behind.

In **room 2.5**, beyond Savoldo's night-time *Adoration of the Shepherds* (c.1540) – with, in the back, one shepherd giving his pal a leg-up to a high window so that he can lay eyes on the newborn Jesus – hangs Moretto's chilling *Passion* (c.1550). Slouched on a flight of steps is a pale Christ – perhaps before the crucifixion, perhaps already after death – with a terrible, reproachful look in his eyes, a frozen expression that is nonetheless tempered by knowledge of the victory over death that will come. Behind, an angel, his red garment the only splash of colour amongst shades of grey, holds up Christ's robe, his face twisted by angry tears. For all its age, this disturbing work comes across as shockingly modern.

Sections 3 (Giacomo Ceruti) and 4 ("Rediscovered Treasures")

Room 3.1 marks a break, with two rooms of canvases by **Giacomo Ceruti**, known as "Il Pitocchetto" after the first work here, *Due Pitocchi*, or Two Paupers (c.1730–34), epitomizing the eighteenth-century shift into an awareness and depiction of the reality of daily life for ordinary folk. Ceruti's two characters – a bright-eyed chap with a withered arm, seated across from his chum in a ragged old army greatcoat, with a jug of wine and pouch of tobacco on the table between them – are matched by a nearby snapshot of a washerwoman (c.1720) and other paintings of spinsters, cobblers and more. Ceruti's formal portrait of an old man (c.1724), opposite the paupers, demonstrates his maturity: even here, a noble visage unmistakeably shows the vagabond beneath.

Across an upper staircase in the *palazzo* are "Works in Search of an Author", paintings which have been restored and often re-attributed. The best known is *St George and the Dragon* in **room 4.1**. Painted in the 1450s, it hangs alongside an X-ray image that shows how much retouching and overpainting had been done before this final, charming image was achieved. **Room 4.2** has a sequence of the *Four Seasons* by Rasio, done in Arcimboldo style, with fruit and flowers used to compose the figures.

Down at street level, across the *palazzo* courtyard, are two rooms of **drawings**, including a characteristic *Portrait of Lieven van Coppenol* by **Rembrandt** (c.1658), a marvellous *Adam and Eve* by **Dürer** (c.1504) and Venetian scenes by **Canaletto**.

Eating and drinking

Brescia has plenty of reasonably priced **places to eat** in the centre of town, specializing in local dishes such as *casoncei* (large meat-filled ravioli) or game. Many menus feature pasta stuffed with (or polenta smothered in) *bagòss*, a locally produced cheese – rich, spicy and flavourful.

When it comes to *aperitivo* time, head for lively Piazzale Arnaldo to the east of the centre, where a clutch of atmospheric **café–bars** fill up quickly after work and stay buzzing into the small hours.

Cafés and snacks

Caffè Impero Piazza della Vittoria. Grandiose, stylish 1930s café tucked beneath Piazza della Vittoria's marble arcades. Closed Sun.

Muse e Musei Piazza T. Brusato 24 ☎030.45.048. An ideal location just a few steps from the exit of the Santa Giulia museum: sink into a sofa or armchair in this pleasant, modern interior for a drink, or sit up for a light meal. They tag themselves a jazz club, cigar club and wine bar – and do all three with some style. Service is genial and the food is good and moderately priced. Open until 2am. Closed Wed eve & Aug.

Osteria dell'Elfo Piazza Vescovato 1b ☎030.377.4858. Decent little osteria on this central square, with tables spread on the piazza. They cater to the pre- and post-theatre crowd, serving well-presented salads and light meals of pasta and fish. Closed Tues.

Spazio Arnaldo Piazzale Arnaldo 3, ⓦwww.spazio arnaldo.it. Tags itself "bar/food/sound" – a cool, lively hangout in a happening part of town. Closed Mon.

Vecchio Botticino Piazzale Arnaldo 6. A dim, funky little *osteria* and *enoteca*, with a small menu of standard light meals filling out its main function as a wine bar and meeting-point. Service is friendly and the atmosphere is sociable. Open until 1am. Closed Sun.

Restaurants

Al Bianchi Via Gasparo da Salò 30 ☎030.292.328, ⓦwww.osteriaalbianchi.it. Historic restaurant dating from 1880 in a quiet location just off Piazza Loggia. A popular evening spot, serving a variety of tasty, moderately priced local dishes, specializing in Brescian meaty mains, presented with home-made flair. Closed Tues eve & Wed.

Al Granaio Piazzale Arnaldo ☎030.375.9345. A fine *osteria* under the arcades of the old city granary. The covered terrace is an atmospheric place for lunch, and is candlelit after dark, complete with comfy chairs and sofas. The food is competent, moderately priced local fare, with good pasta *primi* and a broad choice of wines.

La Vineria Via X Giornate 4 ☎030.280.543. Acclaimed little trattoria tucked beneath the arcades just off Piazza Loggia. The emphasis is squarely on wines, but this is an *osteria con cucina*, also serving decent meals in its pleasant, contemporary interior. Closed Mon.

Osteria La Grotta Vicolo del Prezzemolo 10 ☎030.44.068, ⓦwww.osterialagrotta.it. Charming little place, dating from the 1920s, with an atmospheric interior and a menu centred on its own, high-quality *salumi* and other local specialities, Expect to pay around €35. Closed Wed.

San Marco Via Spalto San Marco 15 ☎030.45.541. Apparently run-down little dive on a main road south of the centre, with tired, 70s-era furnishings – but nonetheless widely recognized as a great place for authentic, inexpensive Brescian cooking, offering simple dishes prepared with pride. Closed Sun, Mon eve.

Sapori e Sapere Via Beccaria 11 ☎030.40.073, ⓦwww.saporiesapere.eu. Cool, contemporary restaurant between Piazza Loggia and Piazza Paolo, with artfully placed bookcases and designer uplighting. The specialities of the house include all the usuals – fresh lake fish, desserts made in-house – but here the kitchen is open to view and the chic style gives the place a lift. A meal costs around €40.

Vasco da Gama Via dei Musei 4c ☎030.375.4039. Warm, cosy restaurant tucked into the old walls beneath the Porta Bruciata just off Piazza Loggia. The wood-beamed interior is lit by candles, and art adorns the stone walls. Food is excellent, with a wide range of lake fish and a long list of desserts: try the tender ham, either smoked or marinated with thyme, followed by *trofie alla portoghese* (a Genoese pasta with seafood) or *paella valenciana*. Expect to pay €50. Closed Tues.

Around Brescia

On even the speediest journey towards nearby **Lake Iseo** (see p.239), it's worth making time to stop in the **Franciacorta** wine region, and although the mountainous **Val Trómpia** north of Brescia is, in its lower reaches anyway, marred by industry, it does offer a couple of scenic driving detours through the mountains west to Iseo and east to **Lake Idro** (see p.284).

Franciacorta

Between Brescia and Iseo is the **FRANCIACORTA**, a hilly wine-producing district rising from the built-up plain. It got its name from the religious communities which lived there from the eleventh century onwards: they were exempt from tax and known as the Corti Franche, or free courts. Wine producers soon moved in, attracted by the possibility of owning vineyards in a duty-free haven. These days the area is no longer tax free, but the wine continues to flow. The best is the **Franciacorta DOCG** (Denominazione di Origine Controllata e Garantita), Italy's most refined sparkling wine, produced according to Champagne methods. It comes in various types: Not Dosed/Pas Dosé (extremely dry), Extra Brut, Brut Satèn (a silky-smooth mixture of Chardonnay and Pinot Blanc), Sec, Demisec and Rosé. There are non-sparkling **Terre di Franciacorta DOC** – both *bianco* and *rosso* – and a host of lesser **IGT** (Indicazioni Geografiche Tipiche) wines. You'll also find bottles on sale from nearby DOC areas, such as Cellatica, Botticino, Garda Classico and Lugana.

Tourist offices in Brescia and Iseo stock a map of the **Strada del Vino Franciacorta** (W www.stradadelfranciacorta.it), a route which winds for 80km through the area, passing visitable vineyards, hotels and restaurants along the way. **ERBUSCO** is a good choice, at the heart of Franciacorta wine production, boasting four major producers, several wine shops and tasting cellars and the extremely posh Relais & Châteaux hotel *Albereta* (T030.776.0550, W www.albereta.it; 9). Attractions of **RODENGO-SAIANO**, on the Brescia–Iseo road, include not only the **Abbazia Olivetana**, a restored tenth-century abbey, but also the **Franciacorta Outlet Village** (W www.franciacortaoutlet .it), where brand-name stores sell designer-label fashion at up to seventy percent off.

Val Trómpia

Brescia is famous for its arms industry, the impact of which is unavoidable when you pass through the **VAL TRÓMPIA**, north of the city. The industry dates back over four hundred years, started by the Venetians, who were keen to utilize the iron ore deposits of the area. The centre of today's (much diminished) arms industry is **Gardone Val Trómpia**, 20km north of Brescia: James Bond fans should come here to pay homage at the headquarters of **Beretta** (no public access), arms manufacturers since 1400, makers of 007's favourite gun and suppliers of weapons to US police forces to this day.

Before Gardone and beyond, as far as **Lavone**, the valley is crammed with industry; it's only when you reach **Bovegno**, 37km north of Brescia, that nature takes over: paths from this small village lead up to Monte Muffetto (4hr) and the tarns on Monte Crestoso (5hr 30min). The head of the valley is far beyond, at Passo di Croce Domini, but there is a tortuous road, passable in summer, branching off to Bagolino (see p.285), forming a long but scenic route to Lake Idro.

Alternatively, from just below Gardone, another scenic road – a favourite with weekend bikers – branches west for 20km to Iseo (see p.240).

Cremona

An attractive provincial town 55km south of Brescia, on the plain of the River Po, **CREMONA** is known for its **violins**. Ever since Andrea Amati established the first violin workshop here in 1566, followed by his son Nicolò and pupils Guarneri and – most famously – **Antonio Stradivari** (1644–1737), Cremona has been a focus for the instrument. Today the city hosts an internationally famous school of violin-making, as well as frequent classical concerts – not least those dedicated to the city's other famous son, composer **Claudio Monteverdi**.

Cremona has some fine Renaissance and medieval buildings, and its cobbled streets make for some pleasant wandering, but it's a modest sort of place: target it as a half-day trip from Brescia or Milan, on a looping route towards the richer pickings of Mantova (see p.327).

The Town

The centre of Cremona is the splendid **Piazza del Comune**, a narrow space dominated by monumental architecture. The west side is the least dramatic, though its buildings, both thirteenth-century – the red-brick **Loggia dei Militia** (formerly headquarters of the town's soldiery) and the arched **Palazzo del Comune** – are lavish.

▲ Torrazzo and west facade of the Duomo, Cremona

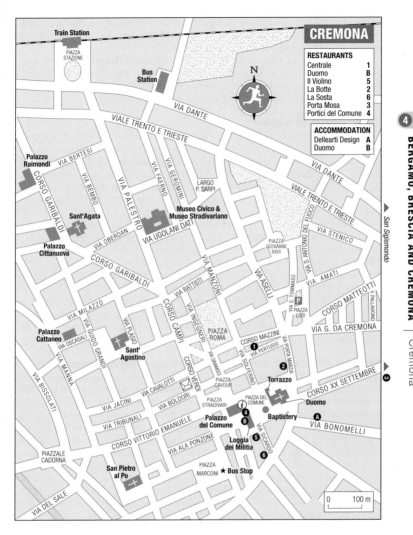

In the northeast corner of the square, visible from far and wide, looms the gawky Romanesque **Torrazzo**, at 112m one of Italy's tallest medieval towers. Built in the mid-thirteenth century and bearing a fine Renaissance clock dating from 1583, it can be climbed for excellent views (Tues–Sun 10am–1pm & 2.30–6pm; €4, joint ticket with Baptistry €5).

Adjacent stands the **Duomo** (Mon–Sat 7.30am–noon & 3.30–7pm, Sun 10.30–11am & 3.30–5.30pm), connected to the Torrazzo by way of a Renaissance loggia. The Duomo's huge facade, made up of classical, Romanesque and fancy Gothic elements, focuses on a rose window from 1274. Originally conceived as a basilica, its transepts were added when the Gothic style became more fashionable, and the interior is rather oppressive – lofty and dim, marked by the dark stone of its piers, and covered by naïve frescoes done in the sixteenth century, including a trompe l'oeil by Pordenone on the west wall showing the *Crucifixion* and *Deposition*. Also of note are the fifteenth-century pulpits, decorated with finely tortured reliefs.

The south side of the square features the octagonal **Baptistry** (Tues–Sun 10am–1pm & 2.30–6pm; €2, joint ticket with Torrazzo €5), dating from the late twelfth century. Its vast bare-brick interior is rather severe, though lightened by the twin columns in each bay and a series of upper balconies.

Collezione di Violini

Directly opposite the Torrazzo, the Palazzo del Comune – which also houses the tourist office – has, on an upper floor, a small museum of historic violins variously dubbed the **Collezione di Violini** or **Sala dei Violini**, or just **Gli Archi di Palazzo Comunale** (Tues–Sat 9am–6pm, Sun 10am–6pm; April–June, Sept & Oct also Mon 9am–6pm; €6, joint ticket with Museo Civico €10). It is only visitable on guided tours, which run continuously; buy tickets from the bookshop in the courtyard.

After climbing the stairs you are ushered past a stone-faced security guard – these violins are worth millions – into a room holding nine individual violins in glass cases. These include a very early example made by Andrea Amati in 1566 for Charles IX of France, and later instruments by Amati's son, Guarneri – plus, of course, Stradivari. The guide gives a spoken history of each violin and plays recordings of the different instruments. However, unless you're a violin nut, this is all rather over-reverent; instead, check with the tourist office in advance to find out when one of the instruments is to be brought out and **played**. This happens at least twice a day, as long as at least fifteen people are in attendance.

Museo Civico, incorporating Museo Stradivariano

The pilastered Palazzo Affaitati, at Via Ugolani Dati 4 – a pleasant ten-minute stroll north of Piazza del Comune – holds the **Museo Civico "Ala Ponzone"** (Tues–Sat 9am–6pm, Sun 10am–6pm; €7, joint ticket with Collezione di Violini €10). The museum is strikingly designed, and forms an excellent setting; it's just a pity the art it holds is so uninspired. The star painting is a *St Francis Meditating* by **Caravaggio**, showing the artist's typically deft handling of light. To find it, head into the *cinquecento* gallery; it's hanging in an alcove in the far left-hand corner. Beyond here, hunt out rooms 18 and 19, holding Chinese porcelain, Japanese ivories, Meissen ware and two little examples of eighteenth-century Wedgwood. From room 15, head upstairs for three rooms of nineteenth- and twentieth-century art, including *Le Nereidi*, a languid, mysterious work painted in 1906 by Cremona-born Emilio Rizzi (1869–1940).

Return to the stairs and head up again into a long hall, where, at the far end, a suite of eighteenth-century rooms – filled with the sound of recorded violin music – holds the **Museo Stradivariano**, displaying models, paper patterns, tools and acoustic diagrams from Stradivari's workshop, a letter to his patron dated 12th August 1708, and more violins, violas, viols and cellos, hanging impotently in glass cases. An informative video helps to unravel the mysteries of the violin-maker's art.

From the ticket desk, separate stairs head up to the **Sezione Archeologica**, displaying Egyptian amulets, rather beautiful Greek vases and delicate Roman glassware.

San Pietro al Po and San Sigismondo

Southwest of Piazza del Comune, on Via Tibaldi, the church of **San Pietro al Po** has better frescoes than the Duomo; its walls are coated with sixteenth-century art and stuccoes. Look for the trompe l'oeil work of Antonio Campi in the transept vaults, and Bernadino Gatti's hearty fresco of *The Feeding of the Five Thousand* in the refectory next door.

If you like that, you'll love **San Sigismondo** on the eastern edge of town (bus #2 from Piazza Cavour). Built by Francesco and Bianca Sforza in 1441 to commemorate their wedding – Cremona was Bianca's dowry – its Mannerist decor is among Italy's best, ranging from Camillo Boccaccino's soaring apse fresco to Giulio Campi's *Pentecost* in the third bay of the nave, plagiarized from Mantegna's Camera degli Sposi ceiling at Mantova. Other highlights include Giulio's *Annunciation* on the entrance wall, in which Gabriel is seemingly suspended in mid-air, and the gory *John the Baptist* in the second left chapel, by Giulio's younger brother Antonio.

Practicalities

Cremona is an easy half- or full-day trip from Brescia: a speedy drive on the A21 **autostrada** (40min), slightly longer by train (50min). Piazza Lodi has the most central parking. The **train station** is on Via Dante, ten-minutes' walk north of Piazza del Comune; bus #1 runs regularly to Piazza Cavour.

The **tourist office** (daily 9am–12.30pm & 3–6pm; June–Aug closed Sun pm; ☎0372.23.233, ⊛www.provincia.cremona.it) is on Piazza del Comune, opposite the Torrazzo, and has details of classical concerts and a list of violin-makers' workshops. **Accommodation** includes *Duomo*, Via Gonfalonieri 13 (☎0372.35.242; ❷), with bright, air-conditioned en-suite rooms; and *Dellearti Design Hotel*, Via Bonomelli 8 (☎0372.23.131, ⊛www.dellearti.com; ❺), aimed at chi-chi urbanite guests who like their contemporary styling. Look out for the Monteverdi festival of Baroque music every May (⊛www.teatroponchielli.it).

Eating and drinking

Numerous cosy *osterie* serve Cremona's excellent **local specialities**, especially *bollito misto* – a mixture of boiled meats, served with *mostarda di frutta* (also known as *mostarda di Cremona*), fruit suspended in a sweet mustard syrup. The excellent *gastronomie* that cluster around Corso Garibaldi and Corso Campi make good places to put together a **picnic**.

Centrale Via Pertusio 4, off Via Solferino. A local institution that keeps the Cremonesi happy with well-priced traditional dishes, served with gusto. Closed Thurs.

Duomo Via Gonfalonieri 13, down the side of the Palazzo Comunale. The tables outside this popular hotel restaurant make a fine, sunny spot to tuck into a crispy pizza. *Menù* around €15. No closing day.

Il Violino Via Sicardo 3 ☎0372.461.010, ⊛www.ilviolino.it. Top choice for a gastronomic experience – a quality restaurant metres from the main piazza specializing in local dishes such as *tortelli* with bass or *risotto alla zucca*, followed by a variety of excellent fish dishes. Book ahead. Closed Mon eve & Tues.

La Botte Via Porta Marzia 5. A youngish, local crowd come to this taverna for plates of *affetati* (cold meats and cheeses) and other regional specialities. Closed Mon.

La Sosta Via Sicardo 9 ☎0372.456.656. By the main piazza, this attractive *osteria* does a great line in Cremonese specialities at reasonable prices. Closed Sun eve & Mon.

Porta Mosa Via Santa Maria Betlem 11. A simple *osteria* serving delicious local dishes, washed down by well-chosen wines. Ten-minutes' walk east of Piazza del Comune. Closed Sun.

Portici del Comune Piazza del Comune 2. Nicest – and best-located – of the many pleasant pavement cafes and *gelaterie* dotted around the main squares, in a plum position under the arches directly opposite the Duomo's facade. Closed Tues.

Travel details

Full details of transport in Lombardy – including the area covered by this chapter – are at ⓦwww.trasporti.regione.lombardia.it (click "orari"). Timetables for all train routes in Italy, including those outside Lombardy, are at ⓦwww .trenitalia.com. Timetables for those bus routes that extend beyond the borders of Lombardy are on the relevant bus company's website; those for Brescia–Verona buses are at ⓦwww.trasportibrescia.it. See p.30 for some guidance on deciphering timetables.

Trains

Bergamo to: Brescia (hourly; 50min); Lecco (hourly; 35min); Milano Centrale or Porta Garibaldi (every 40min; 50min).

Brescia to: Bergamo (hourly; 50min); Capo di Ponte (5 daily; 1hr 55min); Cremona (approx every 2hr; 50min); Desenzano/Sirmione (every 30min; 20min); Iseo (approx hourly; 40min); Milano Centrale (every 30min; 1hr); Verona (every 30min; 45min).

Cremona to: Brescia (approx every 2hr; 50min); Mantova (hourly; 55min); Milano Centrale (6 daily; 1hr 10min).

Iseo to: Brescia (approx hourly; 40min); Capo di Ponte (5 daily; 1hr 15min); Pisogne (7 daily; 30min).

Buses

Bergamo to: Clusone (every 30min; 1hr); Lóvere (every 30min; 1hr 10min); Sárnico (hourly; 55min).

Brescia to: Cremona (hourly; 1hr 15min); Desenzano (at least hourly; 55min); Gargnano (every 30min; 1hr 25min); Iseo (6 daily; 40–50min); Mantova (hourly; 1hr 25min); Salò (at least every 30min; 55min); Verona (hourly; 2hr 20min).

Cremona to: Brescia (hourly; 1hr 15min).

Iseo to: Lóvere (2 daily; 45min); Pisogne (5 daily; 30min).

Lóvere to: Capo di Ponte (2 daily; 1hr).

5

Lake Garda

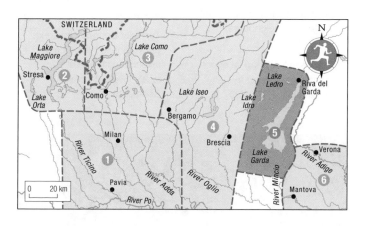

CHAPTER 5 # Highlights

* **Sirmione** Medieval village squeezed onto a narrow peninsula: dodge the crowds and head out to the cliff-edge Roman ruins. See p.268

* **Punta San Vigilio** The quietest spot on Lake Garda, an isolated headland with an exclusive hotel at its tip. See p.275

* **Salò** Dignified old town, more worldly and interesting than its touristy neighbours. See p.277

* **Gargnano** Alluring lakefront village crowded in by mountains. See p.283

* **Lake Idro** Isolated tarn in the mountains behind Gargnano, reached on the scenic "Four Lakes Drive". See p.284

* **Riva del Garda** The lake's top destination, a holiday resort with a unique history and plenty of character. See p.289

* **Lake Ledro** Tiny dot of blue in a high valley above Riva; a perfect place to draw breath. See p.296

* **Torri del Benaco** Gracious old Veronese village on the lakefront with one of the lake's loveliest hotels. See p.300

▲ Torri del Benaco

Lake Garda

I sat and looked at the lake. It was beautiful as paradise, as the first creation.

D.H. Lawrence, *Twilight in Italy* (1916)

LAKE GARDA (**Lago di Garda**, often called by its Latin name **Benaco**) is the largest and cleanest of the Italian lakes, the best-known abroad and also the most popular: something like seven percent of all tourists to Italy head here. A body of water this big alters the local climate, which is milder and – thanks to a complex pattern of lake breezes – sunnier than might be expected, creating Mediterranean conditions well north of the Med itself.

More even than its near-neighbours Como and Maggiore, Garda serves as a bridge between the Alps and the rest of Italy. The north of the lake, narrow and hard to reach, is tightly enclosed by mountains that drop sheer into the water: villages survive where they can, wedged into gaps in the cliffs. Further south, the lake spreads out comfortably, mountains replaced by gentle hills that precede the plain of the River Po: this is a land of commerce and easy communication, a comfortable life in comfortable surroundings. Whereas the north has polenta and Alpine cheeses, the south has olive groves, vineyards and citrus orchards. The north is famous for windsurfing and sailing; the south boasts some of Italy's top luxury spas.

It is this diversity which has fed a tourism industry that is very nearly succeeding in its efforts to devour every last usable bit of shoreline. Every summer, resorts in all corners of the lake are swamped by visitors: northern European holiday-makers tend to head for the northern and eastern resorts (tiny Limone struggles under the weight of a million tourists a year), while Italian families tend to prefer the southern and western shores. Trying to move around on summer weekends is not easy, to say nothing of trying to enjoy the

---

Tourist information and bookings: visitgarda.com

Lake Garda is shared between three different provinces (in fact, three of Italy's twenty regions converge here). The northernmost tip of the lake, around Riva, is in the province of **Trento**, part of the region of Trentino. The western shore, from Limone to Sirmione, is in the province of **Brescia**, part of Lombardy. The eastern shore, from Malcésine to Peschiera, is in the province of **Verona**, part of Véneto. All three collaborate, along with a number of local hotel consortia, on the official tourism portal Ⓦ**www.visitgarda.com**, which offers impartial information and hotel bookings for resorts all round the lake, along with useful extras like airport transfers. Other handy sites include Ⓦ www.lagodigarda.it and Ⓦ www.gardainforma.com.

LAKE GARDA

0 _____ 5 km

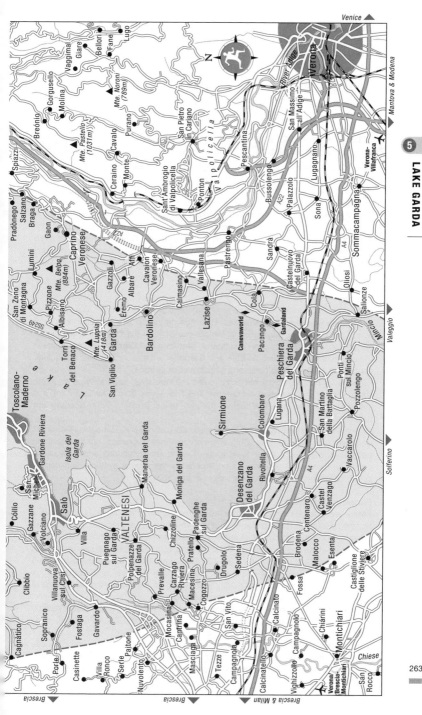

beauty and tranquillity of the lake itself. Visiting slightly out of season – in May to June, or September to October – allows you to appreciate the surroundings in relative peace and quiet.

In the south, the main draw is the spa village of **Sirmione**, though its neighbour **Desenzano** is a cheerier spot and the old village of **Garda** retains much charm. On the western shore, **Salò** is lovely, a historic town on its own bay, while further north, **Gargnano** is one of the lake's best destinations, a small village that remains largely unspoilt.

Boats on Lake Garda

Lake Garda's ferries are run by **Navigazione Lago di Garda** (☏800.551.801, ⓦwww.navigazionelaghi.it). There are almost thirty landing-stages and, since the shoreside roads are often busy with traffic, taking to the water is the easiest – and most scenic – way to get around. Boats run year-round, although outside the summer season (March–Oct) services are greatly reduced or, on some routes, halted.

Most boats are ordinary passenger vessels, marked on the timetable "**Batt**" for *battello*. Some are faster, marked "**Cat**" for *catamarano*. A few, marked with a red "**Sr**", for *servizio rapido*, are extra-quick hydrofoils; these command a small supplement. A blue "**T**" stands for *traghetto*, or car-ferry. Services run daily, roughly 8am to 8pm.

Routes

Several routings make their way along the whole of Lake Garda, but the most frequent services link the lake's busiest resorts. In the north, boats shuttle at least hourly between **Riva**, **Limone** and **Malcésine**, while in the south, there is similar frequency on routes between **Desenzano**, **Sirmione** and **Garda**. Popular resorts in the centre of the lake, such as **Salò** and **Gardone**, are also well served, but quieter spots such as **Gargnano** have long gaps between boats.

The lake's two east–west **car-ferry** routes are timetabled separately as *traghetto veicoli*. These shuttle between **Maderno** and **Torri** (every 35min; takes 25min), and between **Limone** and **Malcésine** (hourly; takes 20min). Both accept foot passengers.

Services marked with a knife and fork generally (but not always) have a **restaurant** on board, serving a set meal (€15). There are no nonstop **cruises**, but timetables at each landing-stage publicize local routings as cruise excursions and it's easy to create an itinerary of your own. Check carefully the various symbols and colour-coded notes to identify each route's days of operation.

Fares and passes

Fares are charged on a complicated sliding scale. Each route is assigned a number, according to the distance involved; you then cross-check on the published chart for how much that route-number (or *tratta*) costs. As an example, Torri to Salò is *tratta* 4, which costs €6.90 by boat or catamaran, or €9.80 on the *servizio rapido*. Desenzano to Sirmione is *tratta* 2 (€3.40/€5.20), while Garda to Malcésine is *tratta* 5 (€8.60/€11.80). The most expensive ticket, *tratta* 7 (Riva to Desenzano), is €10.80/€14.50. Taking a small/medium-sized **car** on either ferry costs €7.50/9.10 including the driver, plus €4.50 for each passenger.

For all these, a **return** costs twice the price of a one-way; the return half is valid on the day after purchase. EU citizens over 65 get a discount (Mon–Fri only), as do children aged 4–12.

A **biglietto di libera circolazione** gives unlimited journeys for one day: choose either the whole lake (*Intera Rete*; €24.80), or the lower lake between Desenzano and Gargnano (*Basso Lago*; €16.80), or the upper lake between Malcésine and Riva (*Alto Lago*; €14.80).

In the northern section of the lake, **Limone** is too busy for comfort, though nearby stands **Riva del Garda**, the lake's best-known holiday spot – a charismatic small town with a long history. On the eastern shore, **Malcésine** is another village that is too popular for its own good, though **Torri del Benaco**, further south, is another highlight – an attractive lakefront village that has avoided the worst of the crowds.

Basso Garda: the lower lake

BASSO GARDA – the southern third of the lake, before the mountains begin – comprises a big, apple-shaped bay, its shores curving to enclose a succession of holiday towns. The topography is gentle: this landscape of low, rolling hills and a lake-influenced Mediterranean climate are ideal for nurturing excellent wines and undemanding tourist resorts.

If you're approaching from Milan or Verona, the lower lake is likely to be your first encounter with Garda; depending on the season it will either reinforce or shatter any romantic preconceptions of what the Italian Lakes should be all about. In winter, and even at the top and tail of the season, this area can be bewitchingly beautiful, with snow on the peaks further north, a balmy climate, few hotels open and a lazy, introspective pace to life. But in midsummer, the lower reaches of Lake Garda can be as crowded as anywhere in northern Italy, with holiday-makers cramming the promenades and traffic clogging every road. The best advice, if you visit at this season, is to find yourself a bolthole-with-a-view and let the lake work its magic.

At the lake's southwestern corner stands **Desenzano**, a thoroughly likeable town with space to absorb the crowds. Nearby, little **Sirmione** occupies a peninsula projecting into the centre of the bay, its old streets heaving with sightseers. Further east, a succession of pretty but often very busy lakefront villages line the shore around to the stylish little resort of **Garda**, beyond which rise the mountain slopes of Alto Garda (see p.276).

Lake Garda's winds

Garda is swept by regular **winds** – so regular, you could virtually set your watch by them. The main wind is the **Pelèr** (also called **Suer** or **Vento**), which blows all year round from the north, starting in the small hours and lasting until midday. It begins gently, but by the time the sun is up, it can be felt across the whole surface, bringing fine weather along with a distinctive sequence of waves (small, large, then three wavelets).

The southerly **Ora** picks up after midday, lasting until dusk; it's felt mainly in the central and northern parts of the lake, often not blowing at all in the south in summer (though when it does, it can leave clouds on the mountain-tops).

Several lesser winds include the **Ponale**, which blows out of the Valle di Ledro, and the **Ander**, which blows from Desenzano towards Garda. If there is calm around Gargnano, a blustery **Vent da Mùt** could be on the way. A southerly **Vinezza** sweeping from Peschiera towards Maderno in the afternoon signals bad weather to follow. The strongest is the **Balì**, a winter northerly gusting from the heights above Riva which causes a heavy chop but usually blows itself out after 24 hours.

Desenzano and around

Lake Garda's largest town, at its southwestern extremity, **DESENZANO DEL GARDA** is an engaging place that bustles with activity most of the year. Behind the attractive lakefront, lined with bars and restaurants, ordinary town life continues in the steep lanes behind the waterfront leading up to the **castle**, from where there are spectacular views. The main square, **Piazza Malvezzi** – its terrace cafés watched over by a statue of St Angela Merici, founder of the Ursuline order – twists out to either side of the old harbour, which is fronted by some beautiful houses. Nearby, the seventeenth-century "**duomo**" (actually just the parish church) holds a crowded, eye-catching *Last Supper* by Giambattista Tiepolo (1743).

A short walk away on Via Crocefisso lurks the entrance to the **Villa Romana** (Tues–Sun 8.30am–7pm; Nov–Feb closes 4.30pm; €2), one of Italy's most important late-Roman villas. As anarchy spread in Rome during the fourth century AD, those who could afford to retreated to grand country estates such as this one. Past the ticket desk and small museum, you come outside to the

excavation area and, first, to Area A. An octagonal vestibule (room 1), with its mosaic floor largely intact, leads into what was a colonnaded porch (room 2), surrounded by mosaics of hunting scenes and chubby cupids and, under a modern brick shelter, through an atrium to the main dining area (room 4), with another decorative floor mosaic. A multitude of other rooms lie off to each side. A walkway leads over the mosaic pavement to Area B, with more elegant geometric mosaics (rooms 39–42). Areas C and D, in the far corner of the site, are still only partially excavated.

Practicalities

Desenzano is a major transport hub, with **boats** arriving from all around the lake and a good **train** service on the fast Milan–Brescia–Verona line. It also has its own exit on the nearby A4 **autostrada**, and **buses** arriving from neighbouring towns. The **tourist office** is just off the main square, Via Porto Vecchio 34 (Mon–Fri 9am–12.30pm & 3–6pm, Sat 9am–12.30pm; ☎030.914.1510, ⓦwww.visitgarda.com). ⓦwww.hotelspromotion.it is also useful. City Sightseeing runs an **open-top bus** (June–Aug daily 9.30am–5pm every 90min; €20; ⓦwww.city-sightseeing.it) on a scenic route around the lakeshore, from Desenzano to Sirmione, Lazise and back (takes 3hr), with recorded commentary in English.

Hotels abound: there are thirty-odd in the vicinity, though many are fairly ordinary. The nicest in the centre is the *Park*, Lungolago C. Battisti 19 (☎030.914.3351, ⓦwww.parkhotelonline.it; ❹–❺), a modern four-star with a range of standard and superior rooms, while the *Tripoli*, Piazza Matteotti 18 (☎030.914.1305, ⓦwww.hotel-tripoli.it; ❸–❹), has decent three-star rooms with good facilities overlooking the busy lakefront square.

Restaurants

Caffè Italia Piazza Malvezzi 19 ☎030.914.1423. Informal seafood restaurant on the main square, with a long bar and terrace tables. Dip into their oddities, such as a raw shellfish platter (if you dare) or a swordfish starter, or plump for mains such as turbot with onion and asparagus. Around €35. Closed Mon.

Cavallino Via Murachette 21 ☎030.912.0217, ⓦwww.ristorantecavallino.it. Top choice in town – an expensive, refined temple to gourmet Gardesana cooking, positioned well back from the lakefront bustle. Innovative takes on lake fish dishes and Mediterranean seafood mark it out as worth a splash. Expect €60 or more. Closed Sun eve & Mon.

La Contrada Via Bagatta 12 ☎030.914.2514, ⓦwww.ristorantelacontrada.com. A rather classy "Slow Food" restaurant hidden away behind the main square, with excellent fish (perch, pike, seabass, whitefish) alongside Milanese classics such as *ossobuco* with saffron risotto. Dine amid paintings and antiques, and expect a bill north of €40 a head. Closed Wed.

Otium Via Roma 3 ☎030.914.3623. Great little "wine restaurant" in the lanes just back from the lakefront, serving moderately priced lake staples alongside an array of local vintages. Closed Thurs.

North of Desenzano: the Valtenesi

A little north of Desenzano the lakefront road detours inland through the rolling hills of the **Valtenesi**, a bucolic region of vineyards and olive groves. The main settlement, **PADENGHE**, is a quiet, prosperous little town, very spick and span, though it's a different story up at the hilltop castle: venture through the gateway and you'll find the interior still crowded with ramshackle, claustrophobic houses. From Padenghe, a minor road detours inland for 6km to **PUEGNAGO**, where you can sample the rosé wines – Garda Classico DOC Groppello and Chiaretto – that the Comincioli vineyard has been producing since the sixteenth century.

The main road out of Padenghe makes a beeline north for Salò (see p.277), bypassing the photogenic harbour village of **MONIGA** and the castle on the headland above the beaches around **MANERBA**. Partway along the main road, you'll spot the rarity of an Italian microbrewery, the **Brewery Manerba**, with its large, bright **pub** (Tues–Thurs 5pm–1am, Fri 5pm–2am, Sat & Sun 4pm–2am; ⓦwww.manerbabrewery.it). Their very palatable house beers – a blond lager, a white beer, a fruity dark beer and a strong, double-malted brew – are around €7.50 a litre, and are also sold bottled to take away.

Isola del Garda

Off the Valtenesi shore north of Manerba, the elongated **ISOLA DEL GARDA** (ⓦwww.isoladelgarda.com) is the lake's largest island, formerly the site of an ancient monastery once visited by St Francis. The old buildings were replaced around 1900 by a fanciful **villa** in Venetian neo-Gothic style. Italianate terraced **gardens** lead down to the lake, lush with lemon and pear trees, persimmons, jujube, pomegranates, bougainvillea and roses, while beyond, much of the island is covered by coniferous **woodland**, alongside Mediterranean shrubs, cypresses, cedars, bay trees and more.

The island remains privately owned – the Cavazza family live there all year round – and is visitable only on a **guided tour**. These run in summer only (June–Sept), as publicized on boat timetables and the website: trips run from several points, most frequently from Salò (6 weekly), but also with direct service from Garda, Desenzano, Sirmione and elsewhere (all 2–3 weekly). The fare (€27–35, depending on where you start from) covers return boat transport and a two-hour guided tour, including a tasting of local products.

Coverage of the western shore continues with **Salò** on p.277.

Sirmione and around

Sirmio, gem of the peninsulas and islands
Which Neptune bears in liquid lakes or the vast sea –
How willingly and happily I visit you!

Catullus, 56 BC

Things have changed since the Roman poet Catullus scribbled a verse to celebrate coming home to his villa at **SIRMIONE**. This narrow promontory, extending 4km into the lake from the southern shore, is now occupied by an attenuated holiday resort, and the tranquillity which Catullus sought is consequently long gone. Little Sirmione – barely more than a village in size – creaks under the pressure of a million overnight stays every year, and is almost suffocated with hotels and touristy commerce. Sirmione has Lake Garda's only mineral spring, rising 300m offshore on the lake bed, and several hotels and **thermal spas** take advantage, with many programmes of therapies for various ailments. Tens of thousands of people come for the traditional twelve-day cure.

Make no mistake: this is a beautiful, unusual spot, well worth a visit for the spectacular **castle** and equally spectacular ruined **Roman villa** on the steep-sided headland – but having to elbow a path through the crowded lanes of the old village to reach them may rapidly try your patience. If you can, pay the extra to enjoy the beauty of the setting while shielded behind the gates of a luxury hotel.

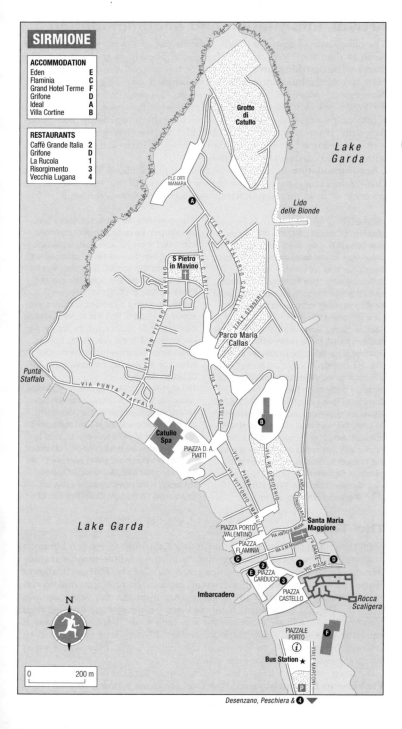

SIRMIONE

ACCOMMODATION
Eden	E
Flaminia	C
Grand Hotel Terme	F
Grifone	D
Ideal	A
Villa Cortine	B

RESTAURANTS
Caffè Grande Italia	2
Grifone	D
La Rucola	1
Risorgimento	3
Vecchia Lugana	4

Grotte di Catullo

Lake Garda

Lido delle Bionde

P.LE ORTI MANARA

A

VIA CAIO VALERIO CATULLO

S Pietro in Mavino

VIA C. CARICI

VIALE GENNARI

VIA SAN PIETRO IN MAVINO

Parco Maria Callas

Punta Staffalo

VIA PUNTA STAFFALO

VIA C. V. CATULLO

B

VIA ANSA

VIA RE DESIDERIO

VIA COMBONI

Catullo Spa

PIAZZA D. A. PIATTI

VIA G. PIANA

VIA VITTORIO EMANUELE

Lake Garda

Santa Maria Maggiore

PIAZZA PORTO VALENTINO

VIA ANTICHE MURA

PIAZZA FLAMINIA

VIA S. M. MAGGIORE

P.V DANTE

C

2

E

PIAZZA CARDUCCI

1

VIC BISSE

D

3

Imbarcadero

PIAZZA CASTELLO

Rocca Scaligera

PIAZZALE PORTO

i

F

VIALE MARCONI

Bus Station ★

N

0   200 m

Desenzano, Peschiera & **4** ▼

Arrival, information and accommodation

The old quarter of Sirmione stands at the far end of a slender peninsula, 4km north of the main Desenzano–Peschiera road. The village is closed to traffic; there's a large **parking area** at the end of the approach road, Viale Marconi. Here, too, are the **bus station** and **tourist office** (Easter–Nov daily 9am–8pm; Nov–Easter Mon–Fri 9am–12.30pm & 3–6pm, Sat 9am–12.30pm; ☏ 030.916.114, ⓦ www.sirmionehotel.com), with the *imbarcadero* on Piazza Carducci, a short stroll away. City Sightseeing runs an **open-top bus** (June–Aug daily 10am–5.30pm every 90min; €20; ⓦ www.city-sightseeing.it) on a scenic route around the lakeshore, from Sirmione to Lazise and back (takes 2hr), with recorded commentary in English.

Accommodation spreads all the way down the peninsula, though the most characterful choices pack the lanes of the old town. All our recommendations are either in quiet locations or have rooms facing away from the bustle.

Hotels

Eden Piazza Carducci ☏ 030.916.481, ⓦ www
.cerinihotels.it. This was where Ezra Pound was staying when he met James Joyce, in 1920. Now a fine four-star hotel, it's a modern, cool and comfortable retreat from the bustle of the village: opt for a lake-view room facing west, and muse on the glittering waters as the ferries come and go below you. Closed Nov–Feb. ❺–❻

Flaminia Piazza Flaminia ☏ 030.916.078, ⓦ www
.hotelflaminia.it. A quality, renovated four star on a central square in the village. Interiors are attractive, done up in contemporary style, and there's a range of rooms, with and without lake views. One of the few hotels to stay open all year round. ❺–❻

Grand Hotel Terme Viale Marconi ☏ 030.916.261, ⓦ www.termedisirmione.com. Located just beside the castle, this is a palatial affair, with most rooms facing east away from the road, across the lake. It comes with a lovely pool and private beach, as well as fitness facilities and discounts on spa treatments. Closed Feb. ❽–❾

🏃 **Grifone** Vicolo Bisse ☏ 030.916.014,
📧 grifonesirmione@gmail.com.

House-proud little two-star, tucked down a quiet alley alongside the castle, with all sixteen rooms looking east across the water. Decor is plain and simple, but there's the warmest of welcomes and this is a great little spot to hole up, away from the bustle, and enjoy the lake. Closed Nov–Feb. ❷

Ideal Via Catullo ☏ 030.990.4245, ⓦ www
.hotelidealsirmione.it. A near-perfect location, well north of the village on the top of the hill overlooking the very tip of the headland, with the lake and the Roman ruins just metres away. Rooms, however, though decent, are uninspired: all the character comes from the views and the surroundings. Closed Nov–March. ❺

Villa Cortine Via Catullo ☏ 030.990.5890, ⓦ www
.hotelvillacortine.com. A fantastical mansion built in 1870 by the Austrian noble Kurt von Koseritz and about as exclusive a retreat as could be imagined. Its grounds spread over a wide area, enclosed by walls, its interiors are lavish to the point of bombast, with frescoes, marble and gilding everywhere – but it offers priceless peace and quiet. Half board is compulsory in high season, pushing a standard double above €600 a night. Closed Nov–Feb. ❾

The Town

From the end of the road by the tourist office, the only access into Sirmione is across a narrow, fortified bridge over an inlet: the whole town is **traffic-free**. Looming beside are the battlemented walls of the **Rocca Scaligera** (Tues–Sun 8.30am–7pm; €4), a fairytale castle with boxy turreted towers almost entirely surrounded by water. It dates from the thirteenth century, when the Della Scala/Scaligeri family of Verona expanded and fortified their territory. You're free to roam around the walls – the enclosed harbour is especially photogenic – and climb the towers: 77 steps lead up to the keep, followed by another 92 to the top of the highest tower, from where views over the rooftops of Sirmione are lovely.

The town spreads out across a few piazzas either side of the narrow main street, **Via Vittorio Emanuele**, packed with cafés, ice-cream parlours, postcard stands

▲ Grotte di Catullo

and a few fashion and jewellery shops. To one side is the fifteenth-century church of **Santa Maria Maggiore**, worth stopping at to admire the pretty seventeenth-century entrance arcade that re-used ancient columns (including a fourth-century milepost), before pressing on to **Piazza Piatti** at the far end of the shopping area. From here, the **trenino elettrico** (little electric train; €1.50) makes short work of the 750m or so along Via Catullo, past the cypresses and olive groves. If you walk, it's worth detouring up to the asymmetrical, hut-like church of **San Pietro**, which has thirteenth-century frescoes and an eleventh-century bell tower; its shady grounds make for a good picnic stop.

Occupying the tip of Sirmione's headland, perched on rocky slopes high above the lake, are the **Grotte di Catullo** (Tues–Sat 8.30am–7pm, Sun until 5pm; Nov–Feb closes 4.30pm; €4), the remains of a large, first-century BC/AD Roman villa (167m by 105m). The connection to Catullus is unsubstantiated: he is known to have had a villa at Sirmione, and the ruins have been dated to the right era, but nothing links this particular house to the poet. Beside the ticket office stands a small museum displaying artefacts and mosaic fragments. From here, you can roam the open-air ruins freely; the setting, among olive trees, with birds singing and bees buzzing in the lavender, is lovely, with superb views across the lake towards the mountains, though – even with the help of maps and signboards – it's not always easy to tell which part of the villa is which.

Sirmione's beach

From partway along Via Catullo, a path heads down to water level and the **Lido delle Bionde** (May–Oct daily 8am–midnight) where you can eat, drink, swim in the lake or sunbathe on the pontoon or nearby rocks. If you continue, you'll reach a fenced-off area at the tip of the peninsula. The signs warn of landslides, but most people press on regardless: the flat rocks are good for sun-soaking. Swimming or paddling is inadvisable, though, since the rocks are slippery below the surface.

Turn to p.266 for an account of Sirmione's western neighbour, **Desenzano**.

Eating and drinking

Sirmione has dozens of **cafés and restaurants**, most of them touristy and pretty uninspired. The *Caffè Grande Italia* on Piazza Carducci stands out for its history: it's been churning out the ice-cream sundaes since 1894, and still does so with a touch more panache than its neighbours.

Top restaurant in town is *La Rucola*, Vicolo Strentelle 5 (☎030.916.326; closed Thurs & Jan–Feb), a sophisticated little spot near the castle, with a refined menu of lake fish and meat specialities along with perfect pizzas from their wood oven. Prices are high: expect more than €80. A classy option in the centre is *Risorgimento*, Piazza Carducci 8 (☎030.916.325; closed Tues in winter), with tables on the square and a good, moderately priced menu of fish dishes, while another excellent choice by the castle is *Grifone*, Vicolo Bisse 5 (☎030.916.097; closed Thurs), boasting a romantic lakefront garden and simple, carefully prepared food served with a smile.

Sirmione's best restaurant lies outside town, by the main road towards Peschiera. The *Vecchia Lugana* (☎030.919.012, ⓦwww.vecchialugana.com; closed Mon) is a very sleek, upmarket restaurant occupying an old building with contemporary styled interiors and a beautiful, private terrace on the lake. Their innovative cuisine mixes classic Gardesana fish dishes with Brescian country staples such as polenta with rabbit, aided by service that is world-class. Book a week or more in advance. As this book went to press, they were about to open six luxury hotel suites on an upper level.

San Martino della Battaglia and Solferino

The landscape of low hills south of Sirmione holds Lake Garda's finest **wine** country: the overlapping DOC areas of **Lugana**, **San Martino della Battaglia** and **Garda Classico** all produce excellent wines, sold widely in the region.

But on June 24, 1859, this quiet farmland experienced death on an appalling scale. In the wars surrounding the Risorgimento, combined Italian and French

Selva Capuzza

Between San Martino and Solferino lies **SELVA CAPUZZA**, a farm hosting the excellent country **restaurant** *Cascina Capuzza* (☎030.991.0279, ⓦwww .selvacapuzza.it; closed Mon–Wed). This is a popular local secret, extended families crowding in to enjoy a slap-up meal in an appealingly rustic setting of converted, ivy-covered farm buildings, all exposed brick and stone-tiled floors. There's no menu: choose from what your waiter describes or go for the set four courses (around €35), washed down with one of the (very) local wines. The atmosphere is informal and easygoing, the food hearty, made with local ingredients and presented with pride.

To find it, start from the roundabout by the A4 tollbooths, around 5km south of Sirmione. Follow the country lane Via Bonata (signed to San Pietro and Centenaro) for 900m through the vineyards. At a fork, turn right, and then, 200m on, turn left at the T-junction. Continue ahead for 1km, ignoring a signpost pointing right to Selva Capuzza. After a zigzag round a farmhouse, at the next sign to Selva Capuzza continue ahead for 100m: the restaurant is on this corner. The *Borgo San Donino* annexe holds simple, roomy **apartments** (❸–❺), with expansive views across the fields, bookable by the day or week.

forces under Napoleon III defeated the Austrian army under Emperor Franz Josef on two fronts. The first victory was won by the Italian King Vittorio Emanuele II near **SAN MARTINO** (subsequently suffixed "**della Battaglia**"), where a circular tower, built in 1893 to the memory of Vittorio Emanuele, now stands 70m high, dominating sightlines for miles around. An ossuary chapel holds the bones of hundreds of the slain, and a small **museum** (March–Sept Mon–Sat 9am–12.30pm & 2.30–7pm, Sun 9am–7pm; Oct–Feb Tues–Sun 9am–12.30pm & 2–5.30pm; €5; Ⓦwww.solferinoesanmartino.it) displays uniforms and weapons.

The campaign's bloodiest battle took place near **SOLFERINO**, 11km south, where over 40,000 men were killed or wounded that day. A travelling businessman from Geneva, Henri Dunant, was shocked at the sight of injured soldiers left to fend for themselves, and subsequently called for the formation of a nursing corps to care for the victims of battle – an idea which evolved into the **Red Cross**. Solferino today is a quiet town, its stout **Rocca** and nearby **museum** (March–Sept Tues–Sun 8.30am–1pm & 2.30–6pm; €3) displaying mementoes of the battle, its church ossuary filled with the bones of soldiers.

Peschiera and around

At the southeastern corner of Lake Garda, the old military town of **PESCHIERA DEL GARDA** guards the outflow of the lake into the River Mincio. Its impressive fortifications ("fair and strong", as Dante wrote in the *Inferno*) were revamped in the 1550s by the Venetians, and subsequently reinforced by the Austrians. The old town lies within them, on an island at the mouth of the river, with the modern town occupying the banks either side. Although it's a characterful place to wander, Peschiera can get extremely busy – not least with spillover from the nearby **theme parks** (see p.274). The **tourist office** on Piazza Betteloni (☎045.755.1673) has maps and information.

Valeggio sul Mincio

A more sedate attraction lies 8km south of Peschiera, signposted near **VALEGGIO SUL MINCIO**. The **Parco Giardino Sigurtà** (March–Oct daily 9am–6pm; €9.50; Ⓦwww.sigurta.it), acclaimed as one of Italy's most beautiful gardens, spreads luxuriantly over 125 acres on the moraine hillsides above the river. Two footpaths (each 50min) wind through the park, or you can rent a bike (€4 per hr), a four-person golf cart (€13–16 per hr) or take the tourist train (€3 for a 30min tour).

Nearby is the *Antica Locanda Mincio* (☎045.795.0059, Ⓦwww.antica locandamincio.it; closed Wed & Thurs), a fine country **restaurant**. Follow signs through Valeggio for the old Borghetto district; cross the fortified Ponte Visconteo and then cut around left to the river-front lane below the bridge. This stout waterside inn dates back several centuries; its location is perfect, shaded by trees alongside an old footbridge over the weir. The grand interior features frescoes and decorated beams in the Sala del Camino (Hearth Room), which is warmed by a roaring fire in winter. The cooking is Mantovan in spirit, with *agnolotti* (a local tortellini) in butter, porcini mushrooms and melt-in-the-mouth *prosciutti* featuring alongside lake fish and country cheeses. Reckon on €35–40 a head.

There's a **map** of Lake Garda on p.262. For details of the **boats**, see p.264.

Theme parks: Gardaland and Canevaworld

If you have kids to amuse, aim for one of the **theme parks** just north of Peschiera. The biggest is **GARDALAND** (daily: mid-March to end Sept 10am–6pm; mid-June to early Sept until midnight; also weekends in Oct & Dec; ☏045.644.9777, ⊛www .gardaland.it; €30, children under 10 €26, children less than 1m tall free; discounts for part-day and multi-day tickets), which includes a walk-through SeaLife aquarium. It's pricey, and you pay extra for some attractions, but the rides are exciting and well presented. Parking costs €5, or take the free shuttle-bus which runs from Peschiera train station, 2km away.

A little north is **CANEVAWORLD** (☏045.696.9900, ⊛www.canevaworld.it), comprising two adjacent parks: **Movieland** (mid-March to mid-Sept daily 10am– 6pm, later opening at weekends and in July & Aug; also weekends in Oct), with fake movie-sets and shows revealing the secrets of special effects; and **AquaParadise** (mid-May to mid-Sept daily 10am–6pm; July & Aug until 7pm), with slides, flumes, pools and a pirate island. One day's admission is €21 for one park (€18 for kids under 1.40m high), or €27/23 for both parks. Both parks in two days costs €34/28. Children under 1m go free. Free buses shuttle every thirty minutes (mornings only) to Caneva-world from Peschiera station.

Valeggio (⊛www.valeggio.com) is renowned for gastronomy: it has around forty restaurants, each of which serves its own variation on the local speciality *nodo d'amore* (love's knot), a delicate tortellino stuffed with meat. The third Tuesday in June sees the **Festa del Nodo d'Amore**, a huge open-air dinner seating four thousand at tables on the Ponte Visconteo.

Lazise and Bardolino

Back on the lake, 9km north of Peschiera, the walled village of **LAZISE** was once a major port and retains a photogenic (but privately owned) **castle** and, on the harbour, an arcaded medieval **customs house**. Originally used for building and repairing boats for the Venetian fleet, it later served as a shelter for sheep, whose urine was a vital ingredient in gunpowder. Nowadays the village is crammed with cafés, pizzerias and holiday-makers, but retains a whiff of character, with some picturesque corners. Out of season, when it reverts to being a sleepy lakeside village, the allure is stronger still.

About 5km north is the spruce resort of **BARDOLINO**, home of light, red Bardolino wine. The town is at its most animated in September during the bibulous Festa dell'Uva; otherwise, strolling the lush palm- and pine-shaded promenade is the main activity. The church of **San Zeno**, just above the main road, was built in the eighth century; its Latin-cross form and high domed ceiling became a prototype for later Romanesque churches. Otherwise, concentrate on sampling Bardolino wine at the unlikely-looking nameless bar – known as *Da Romaldì* – on Via Battisti, just back from the lakefront, or try the delicious ice cream at *Cristallo* by the water. A little south of town is the **Museo dell'Olio di Oliva** (Mon–Sat 9am–12.30pm & 2.30–7pm, Sun 9am–12.30pm; free; ⊛www.museum.it), centred on a shop selling local oils, wines and vinegars. On the hillside above, the **Museo del Vino** (March–Oct daily 9am–1pm & 2–6pm; free; ⊛www.zeni.it) is a similar concern, part of the Zeni winery and supplemented by free tastings and sales.

There's a **map** of Lake Garda on p.262. For details of the **boats**, see p.264.

Garda

The ex-fishing village of **GARDA**, 18km north of Peschiera, is one of the more attractive stops on this shore. An ancient settlement, recorded in the tenth century, it has a tight little historic quarter of narrow alleys squeezed between the main road and the lake, although – as in many of Garda's neighbours – the lanes are now characterized by snack bars and souvenir shops. Look for the **Palazzo Fregoso**, a charming sixteenth-century house on Via Spagna with its original external staircase and a double lancet window over an arched passageway. To one side is the *Taverna Fregoso*, a quiet, inexpensive little restaurant serving standard pizza/pasta dishes. Across town, the church of **Santa Maria Assunta** holds Romanesque columns and a fourteenth-century fresco of the *Madonna Enthroned*.

Garda's chief pleasure, though, is strolling its long, curving lakefront promenade, which has plenty of benches from which to soak up the wonderful views southwest over the water. Busy terrace cafés and restaurants abound here – even the fifteenth-century **Loggia della Losa**, originally a dock for the Palazzo Carlotti behind, is now a *gelateria*. See p.268 for details of the pleasant excursion to the nearby **Isola del Garda**.

The **tourist office** is just above the main road, at Via Don Gnocchi 1 (Mon–Sat 9am–7pm, Sun 10am–4pm; ☎045.725.5824). **Eating** in the town isn't great, with not much to choose between places; for something a bit more authentically local, continue up Via Don Gnocchi for about 1km to the first roundabout; here stands *Hostaria La Cross* (☎045.725.5795), a rumbustious and cheery place with a rustic interior and shaded terrace. Food is hearty, traditional and keenly priced. Book ahead – this is a popular spot, lightyears away from the tourist fare on the lake.

Barely half an hour's drive east of Garda, over the ridge beyond **AFFI** (a junction on the A22 autostrada), you cross the river into the scenic **Valpolicella** wine region, perfect for vineyard walks and country restaurants (see p.324). Alternatively, about 10km north of Affi, on the eastern slopes of Monte Baldo near **PORCINO**, is *Ranch Barlot* (☎348.723.4082, ⊛www.ranchbarlot.com), where you can book ahead for **guided horse-trekking** through the hills.

Punta San Vigilio

PUNTA SAN VIGILIO, 3km north of Garda (and 4km south of Torri del Benaco; see p.300), forms a prominent headland flanked by excellent white-shingle pay beaches. The main road passes well inland, behind a shelter of foliage, meaning that traffic noise down on the waterfront is minimal.

From the parking area, an avenue of cypresses leads to the entrance to the **Parco Baia delle Sirene** (April Sat & Sun 10am–7pm, €5; May to mid-June daily 10am–8pm, €8, or €5 after 3pm; mid-June to mid-Sept daily 9.30am–8pm, €11, or €8 after 2.30pm, or €5 after 4.30pm; ⊛www.parcobaiadellesirene.it). The sunny beach here is lovely, and there are sun loungers and picnic tables scattered on grassy slopes planted with pines and planes. As an alternative, footpaths lead to smaller nearby (free) coves, one of which is unofficially nudist.

If you keep walking down the avenue of cypresses, you arrive at a beautiful sixteenth-century villa, surrounded by peaceful olive and citrus groves at the tip of the headland. It and its outbuildings are now one of Lake Garda's most exclusive luxury **hotels**, the *Locanda San Vigilio* (☎045.725.6688, ⊛www .locanda-sanvigilio.it; ◉), with seven double rooms, plus four suites occupying secluded stone buildings a stroll away from the hotel with their own entrances and private gardens. The whole place is bewitching.

Even if you're not staying, sample the atmosphere at the sixteenth-century *Taverna San Vigilio* (closed Dec–Feb), located on the southern tip of the headland on its own tiny harbour, looking across open water. Tables are laid out under trailing vines for drinks and snacks during the day; this isn't a restaurant, but every Friday and Saturday evening in summer (mid-June to Aug), they lay on a candle-lit buffet supper, for which booking is essential. Prices, as you'd expect, are high.

Coverage of this shore continues with **Torri del Benaco** on p.300.

Alto Garda: the upper lake

ALTO GARDA – the northern two-thirds of the lake – is a different kettle of fish from the south. Where the south has gentle shoreside hills, the north has mountain cliffs closing in, often dropping sheer to the water. Ease of access to the southern resorts such as Desenzano and Sirmione can make them almost suburban in ambience; by contrast, the best of the northern villages – **Gargnano** on the west shore, **Torri del Benaco** on the east – retain an elusive, hard-to-define romantic charm. Wherever you end up, the views are spectacular, with mountains rising on every side, cloud-capped or perhaps dusted with snow, and your eye able to pan effortlessly along miles

The lakeshore road

Garda's lakeshore road – dubbed **La Gardesana Occidentale** (SS45bis) on the west (Salò to Riva 45km), and **La Gardesana Orientale** (SS249) on the east (Tòrbole to Peschiera 61km) – is a narrow, ordinary route with one lane in each direction. It clings to the shoreline, often squeezed into a gap of a few metres between the cliffs and the water. On the southern part of the lake you can quite often detour onto a minor road or choose another way, but here there are no options: the topography dictates that there is only one road to follow. This can lead to unusually **heavy traffic**, with cars, lorries, buses, camper vans, motorbikes and – most dangerously – cyclists jockeying for position. On several stretches, the road passes through **tunnels**, all of them dimly lit, some totally unlit: if you're driving with sunglasses on, beware of being suddenly plunged into pitch blackness. The worst sections are between Gargnano and Limone, and between Tòrbole and Malcésine, where the tunnels are very narrow, sometimes lacking a white line dividing the lanes. This was where, in 2008, car-chase sequences in the James Bond movie *Quantum of Solace* were filmed, stunt drivers topping 200kmh in 007's custom-designed Aston Martin. Fantasy aside, those who lack the licence to kill are bound by a 50kmh speed limit.

Aside from the dangers of driving it, the lakeshore road also impacts on each of the communities it serves. Some, such as Tòrbole, suffer by having the road run directly through the centre, creating **noise** and **traffic** that cuts the village off from its shore. Others, such as Gargnano and Malcésine, benefit by having the road pass 100m or more inland, behind the village, thus leaving the shore traffic-free. This also impacts on visitors: a large proportion of **lake hotels**, up and down Garda, are built on the land side of the road, meaning that their views are tempered by the sight and sound of traffic passing just in front. Whenever possible, we've recommended hotels on the lake side of the road, where traffic doesn't impinge.

of the long, straight shores, blue water below, blue sky above. **Salò**, on its own little bay, is the most dignified of lakeside towns, with Art Nouveau villas nestling discreetly above the shore towards and beyond its neighbour, **Gardone**.

In the north, a distinctive history, a spectacular cliff-girt location and a lived-in old quarter give **Riva del Garda** – the most popular holiday destination on the lake, at its northernmost tip – much to recommend it. Its neighbours, **Limone** and **Malcésine**, are two of the prettiest villages of all, but both have sold their soul to tourism: it can be hard to navigate a path through their crowds of holiday-makers, souvenir shops and mediocre restaurants.

Behind Gargnano, roads climb precipitously to **Lake Idro**, a little smear of blue on the map which we've included in this chapter for its remote, mountain atmosphere.

The western shore: Salò to Limone

Do you know the land where the lemon trees grow?

Goethe, 1786

Garda's **western shore** holds some of the most dramatic scenery in the whole Lakes region. The entire area comprises the Parco Alto Garda Bresciano (ⓦ www.parcoaltogarda.net), a diverse chunk of land that includes steep rock faces perched over the lake, rugged mountains rising to 2000m, hidden valleys and the lush beauty of the lakeshore road, lined with palms, bougainvillea and, further north, citrus trees.

A little north of the old Venetian town of **Salò** – in the hills above the sedate resort of **Gardone Riviera** – stands Lake Garda's most idiosyncratic attraction, the eye-popping **Il Vittoriale** villa, former home of the poet Gabriele D'Annunzio. After **Gargnano** – the most attractive and unspoilt of the lake villages – the narrow road offers up tantalizing glimpses of the sparkling water from between the *gallerie* and the lemon trees on the beautiful approach to the nineteenth-century resort of Riva del Garda, north of **Limone** at the head of the lake. Engaging diversions head across the mountains to **Lake Idro**.

Salò

SALÒ is splendidly sited on its own narrow bay tucked into the western shore, at the foot of Monte San Bartolomeo. Capital of the Magnifica Patria – a grouping of lake communes – for more than four hundred years until the fall of the Venetian Republic in 1797, Salò today retains its old-fashioned hauteur. Gasparo da Salò, inventor of the violin (1540–1609), was born here. It's something of a yachties' town today, with a larger-than-usual marina of bobbing masts, but nonetheless has a less touristy profile than its neighbours, offering everything you'd want from a lakes town – long, quiet waterfront promenade, great views, alluring old quarter – but without the crowds and largely without the tat. Unlike Gardone or Desenzano, Salò feels like an ordinary small town, with ordinary shops and its own everyday concerns, transplanted to an extraordinary location on the lake. It is regularly at or near the top of the classification of Italian municipalities by income and quality of life.

There's a **map** of Lake Garda on p.262. For details of the **boats**, see p.264.

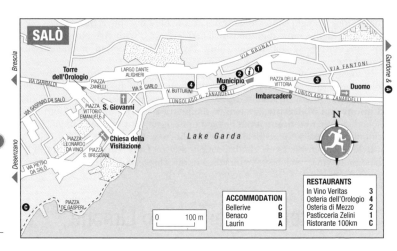

The historic centre is bordered on the west by the sloping, tree-divided **Piazza Vittorio Emanuele II**, busy with traffic and known as the **Fossa** (ditch). At the top, the ancient city gate, dubbed the **Torre dell'Orologio** after renovation works added a clock in 1772, leads through to quiet **Piazza Zanelli**, overlooked by the mullioned windows of the sixteenth-century Casa Bersatti. Pedestrianized **Via San Carlo**, lined by dignified facades, leads down to the grand seventeenth-century town hall, directly on the lake. Alongside is the broad, pleasant **Piazza della Vittoria**, linked by narrow lanes to the unfinished Renaissance facade of the **Duomo** (daily 8.30am–noon & 3.30–7pm), which holds paintings by Romanino and Zenon Veronese, as well as an elaborate Gothic gilded altarpiece. More beautiful old *palazzi* crowd the nearby alleys.

Practicalities

The SS45bis **road** links Salò directly to Brescia, but it has one lane in each direction and is plagued by summer traffic jams: you'd do well to avoid driving this route lake-bound on Fridays and city-bound on Sundays. **Buses** stop on Largo Dante Alighieri. The **tourist office** is behind the town hall on Piazza San Antonio (Mon–Sat 10am–12.30pm & 3–6pm, Sun 10am–1pm & 3.30–6.30pm; ℡0365.21.423, ⓦwww.visitgarda.com).

The Repubblica di Salò

Salò is resonant for Italians for its role in the short-lived *Repubblica Sociale Italiana* (*RSI*), commonly termed the **Repubblica di Salò**, the last-ditch attempt by Mussolini and Hitler to reorganize Italian Fascism. After the Allied invasion of southern Italy and Mussolini's escape northwards, the Nazis annexed the Trentino-Alto Adige region, bringing the Reich's borders down as far as Limone sul Garda. They installed Mussolini as head of a puppet regime in Salò, just 20km away; from September 1943 to April 1945 the town was the nominal capital of Italy. Mussolini established government ministries in several of the Liberty-style villas that dot this shore: Salò's Villa Simonini (now the *Hotel Laurin*) hosted the Foreign Ministry, while Villa Feltrinelli in Gargnano (also now a hotel; see p.286) became the residence of the *Duce* himself. With the Allied liberation the republic collapsed. Mussolini fled, and was executed on April 28, 1945 on Lake Como (see p.191).

One of the best four-star **hotels** on Lake Garda is the 🛏 *Bellerive*, on the edge of the centre, Via Pietro da Salò 11 (☎0365.520.410, 🖥www.hotelbellerive .it; ❻; closed Dec & Jan), offering fresh, tasteful modern rooms with balconies, wood floors and designer bathrooms. Most look over the lake. Service is exceptional – intelligent and warm – and the restaurant is outstanding (see below). An annexe holds apartments for rent (minimum 3-night stay). Otherwise, try the *Benaco*, a decent three-star in the historic centre at Lungolago Zanardelli 44 (☎0365.20.308, 🖥www.benacohotel.com; ❹), with a fine roof terrace. The *Laurin*, behind the town at Viale Landi 9 (☎0365.22.022, 🖥www.laurinsalo .com; ❻–❼; closed Dec–Feb), is lovely, a grand Art Nouveau villa boasting period features in the public areas – the beautiful restaurant has columns, frescoes and Liberty windows – though rather more mundane guest rooms that are comfortable but not exceptional.

For **eating**, *Pasticceria Zelini* (closed Mon) serves snacks, light meals (*menù* €12) and ice cream on its tables spreading over Piazza Vittoria, not far from *In Vino Veritas*, Via Duomo 7 (closed Mon), a genial spot for wine-tasting and light bites. *Osteria di Mezzo*, Via di Mezzo 10, is a cosy, informal place on a quiet lane; more upmarket fish and game specialities are on offer at *Osteria dell'Orologio*, Via Butturini 26a (☎0365.290.158; closed Wed), an atmospheric, old-fashioned tavern that can get very busy. *Ristorante 100km*, in *Hotel Bellerive* (see above), is a classy, contemporary restaurant, the concept being that everything – ingredients, recipes, wines – comes from within a 100km radius of Salò. The menu takes in classic gourmet Brescian cuisine, including exquisite *coregone* (white lake fish), served with flair and priced highly (*menù* around €50).

Gardone Riviera

Just 2km east of Salò, **GARDONE RIVIERA** was once the most fashionable of Lake Garda's resorts and still retains its symbols of sophistication, though the elegant promenade, lush gardens, opulent villas and ritzy hotels now have to compete with more recent – less tasteful – tourist tack. It is famous for the consistency of its climate and the exotic **Giardino Botanico André Heller** (March–Oct daily 9am–7pm; €9; 🖥www.hellergarden.com), laid out above the town in 1912 by Arturo Hruska, dentist to the Russian tsar, and now owned by Heller, an artist. Bamboo, water-lilies, camphor trees, banana plants and more, set amidst artificial cliffs and streams, are interspersed with sculptures and modern artworks.

Gardone Sotto, the old village, comprises a cobbled street and a couple of piazzas sandwiched between the busy Corso Zanardelli road and the lake. Here stands the **tourist office** on Corso Repubblica (July & Aug Mon–Sat 9am–12.30pm & 3.30–6.30pm, Sun 9am–12.30pm; rest of year Mon–Sat 9am–12.30pm & 3–6pm; ☎0365.20.347, 🖥www.visitgarda.com). Of the **hotels** – luxury aside (see box, p.280) – *Diana*, Lungolago D'Annunzio 30 (☎0365.21.815, 🖥www.hoteldianagardone.it; ❸), stands in the old quarter by the *imbarcadero*, some rooms with balconies on the lake. Above the town in Gardone Sopra – the hillside residential quarter beside Il Vittoriale (see p.280) – is the excellent *Locanda Agli Angeli*, Piazza Garibaldi 2 (☎0365.20.832, 🖥www.agliangeli.com; ❺), a family-run place with airy, attractive rooms, a veranda, and peace and quiet.

Gardone Sopra is the best bet for **restaurants**: *La Stalla*, Via dei Colli 14 (☎0365.21.038; closed Tues), signposted off the Via Vittoriale, serves well-priced staples in a tranquil garden; and *Agli Angeli* (see above; closed Mon & Tues) is a good choice for top-quality lake fish and home-cured meats. Down on the lakeside in Gardone Sotto are numerous cafés for coffee or an ice cream, and

Gardone's luxury hotels

Gardone Riviera – once Lake Garda's ritziest resort – specializes in opulent **luxury hotels**, many of which occupy grandiose Art Nouveau villas that went up, often in spacious park-like grounds, in the early years of the last century.

The most famous is **Villa Fiordaliso**, Corso Zanardelli 132 (℡0365.20.158, Ⓦwww .villafiordaliso.it; Ⓘ), since this was where Mussolini installed his mistress, Clara Petacci, during the Repubblica di Salò, and where they spent their last few weeks together in 1945; for around €600 a night you can sleep in their private suite. The villa and grounds are beautiful – and include the separate lakeside Torre San Marco, now a piano bar – but the road is just too close for comfort here, passing within metres of the rear of the building: traffic noise is an irritant.

The largest is the **Grand**, Corso Zanardelli 84 (℡0365.20.261, Ⓦwww.grangardone .it; Ⓘ), which takes up a huge stretch of the waterfront, also on the lake side of the main road. Its public areas remain as glitteringly opulent today as when the hotel opened in 1884, and the rooms – most of which have balconies over the lake – are stylish and pleasant. Churchill holidayed here in 1949, and also stayed at the nearby **Savoy Palace**, Corso Zanardelli 2 (℡0365.290.588, Ⓦwww.savoypalace.it; Ⓘ), renovated from its 1920s heyday in a disappointingly modern style.

Occupying immaculate grounds just above the lakefront road is the **Villa del Sogno**, Corso Zanardelli 107 (℡0365.290.181, Ⓦwww.villadelsogno.it; Ⓘ), an Art Nouveau vision built by a Viennese silk tycoon in 1904 and now a favourite retreat for wealthy Germans and Americans on extended stays. Although everything is in place – interior grandeur, fragrant gardens, tennis courts – you can't shake the feeling that this is luxury-hotel-by-numbers, with little warmth or character.

Perhaps the finest of the lot is the **Grand Hotel Fasano**, Corso Zanardelli 190 (℡0365.290.220, Ⓦwww.ghf.it; Ⓘ), built in the nineteenth century as a hunting lodge for the Austrian imperial family and converted into a hotel around 1900. The interiors are spacious but not extravagant, characterized by a classic, traditionally styled comfort that – unusually for Lake Garda – avoids showiness. In the grounds, the waterfront *Villa Principe* is treated as a separate establishment with its own facilities, including a private beach.

La Taverna, Corso Repubblica 34 (℡0365.20.412; closed Tues), a decent wine-bar with inexpensive plates of typical local fare.

Il Vittoriale

A little way east of Gardone, past the Neoclassical Villa Alba rising above the lakeside road, roadsigns point up the hillside towards one of Italy's most visited museums, **Il Vittoriale degli Italiani**. This is the former home of the poet and nationalist hero Gabriele D'Annunzio, preserved as it was when he died in 1938. It's an excessively grandiose spectacle – D'Annunzio was a shameless egotist and the house is a tribute to his desperate self-obsession – but has nonetheless been declared a national monument. Busloads of visitors (many Italian, and most of them school parties) turn up daily to crowd into the house and walk the garden footpaths.

Vittoriale practicalities

The Vittoriale (Ⓦwww.vittoriale.it) comprises three elements, each with different **opening hours**. The **gardens** are open daily (April–Sept 8.30am–8pm; Oct–March 9am–5pm). D'Annunzio's house, known as the **Prioria**, is closed on Mondays (Tues–Sun 9.30am–7pm; Oct–March 9am–1pm & 2–5pm). The separate **Museo della Guerra** (War Museum) follows the same timetable except that it is closed on Wednesdays.

Weight of numbers means that tickets can be restricted at peak times (Sun, national holidays, some days in July & Aug), when you should arrive an hour or more before the opening time to be sure of entry. Even then, be prepared for a scrum.

Admission is €7 to the gardens only, or €12 including a tour of either the Prioria or the Museo della Guerra, or €16 including tours of both of them. Unless you're devoted to D'Annunzio, touring the house and having a quick poke round the gardens is plenty.

Both the Prioria and the Museo della Guerra can be visited only with a guide, in small groups of 8–10 people. Tours overlap, with guides taking the next lot in every five or ten minutes: there are often several groups working their way through the house at the same time. There's nowhere particular to wait your turn, so just hang around in the courtyard until you get called in. Most guides speak Italian only; ask first for an audioguide in English (free).

Touring the Vittoriale

It's a short but steep walk from the ticket booth up the **main avenue**, with an open-air theatre and gardens to the right offering spectacular lake views. You arrive in the **courtyard** of the house, from where tours depart to explore the interior.

Once D'Annunzio had had the house "de-Germanized", as he put it (the house had been confiscated from the German art critic Henry Thode), it didn't take him long to transform what was a gracious Art Nouveau villa into the showy spectacle it remains today.

D'Annunzio's personality makes itself felt from the start in the two **reception rooms**, one a chilly and formal room for guests he didn't like, the other warm and inviting for those he did. When Mussolini visited in 1925, he was shown to the former (which is the first room on the tour; the latter is one of the last) – where the mirror has an inscription reputedly aimed at him: "Adjust your mask to your face, and remember you are merely glass against steel."

Nor was dining with D'Annunzio a reassuring experience: pride of place in the colourful Art Deco **dining room** was given, as a warning to greedy guests, to a gilded tortoise that had died of overeating. In fact D'Annunzio rarely ate with his guests, retreating instead to the **Sala di Lebbroso** (Lepers' Room), where he would lie on a bier surrounded by leopard skins and contemplate death.

Gabriele D'Annunzio

Born in 1863, Gaetano Rapagnetta – who took the name **Gabriele D'Annunzio** (Gabriel of the Annunciation) – was no ordinary writer, and is often acclaimed as one of Italy's greatest poets. He did pen some exquisite poetry and a number of novels, but he became better known as a soldier and socialite, leading his own private army and indulging in much-publicized affairs with numerous women, including the actress Eleonora Duse. When berated by his friends for treating her cruelly, he simply replied, "I gave her everything, even suffering." He was a fervent supporter of Mussolini, providing the Fascist Party with their (meaningless) war cry *"eia! eia! alalá!"* – though Mussolini eventually found his excessive exhibitionism an embarrassment. In 1921 he presented D'Annunzio with the Vittoriale villa – ostensibly as a reward for his patriotism, in reality to shut him up. D'Annunzio spent the next years expanding the villa and redesigning its interiors. He died in the house in 1938, of a brain haemorrhage while sitting at his desk in the Zambracca room, which remains untouched.

The rest of the house is no less bizarre, characterized by its extreme gloominess: D'Annunzio reportedly had an eye condition which meant daylight was painful to him. Every room has thick, opaque (often coloured) glass in the windows, and the combination of heavy drapes, thick rugs, dark woods and low, narrow passages – D'Annunzio stood just 5'4" tall (1.62m) – makes for a singularly claustrophobic experience. The blue **bathroom** has a tub hemmed in by over nine hundred objects, ranging from Persian ceramic tiles, through Buddhas, to toy animals; and the **Sala del Mappamondo** contains, as well as the huge globe for which it is named, an Austrian machine-gun and books, including an immense version of *The Divine Comedy*. Suspended from the ceiling of the **auditorium** adjoining the house is the biplane that D'Annunzio used in a daring flight over Vienna in World War I.

The adjacent **Museo della Guerra**, reached up an external staircase from the courtyard, has displays on D'Annunzio's military adventures, including medals awarded to him, banners and photographs.

Rammed into the cypress-covered hillside above the house is the prow of the battleship **Puglia**, used in D'Annunzio's so-called "Fiume adventure". Fiume (now Rijeka), on the north Adriatic, had been promised to Italy before they entered World War I, but was eventually handed to Yugoslavia instead. Incensed, D'Annunzio gathered his blackshirted army, occupied Fiume, declared war, surrendered after a naval bombardment and returned home a national hero. Above, in the gardens at the top of the site, stands D'Annunzio's **mausoleum**, a Fascistic array of steps and angular travertine stonework installed in 1955.

Above Gardone: San Michele

In the mountains 500m above Gardone stands the pretty village of **SAN MICHELE**. Three buses (Mon–Sat only) run from Salò and Gardone, but as the views along the road are splendid, you might want to walk the hour or so uphill; the tourist office can advise on short cuts that divert onto hillside tracks. In the village *Hotel Colombér*, Via Val di Sur 111 (☎0365.21.108,

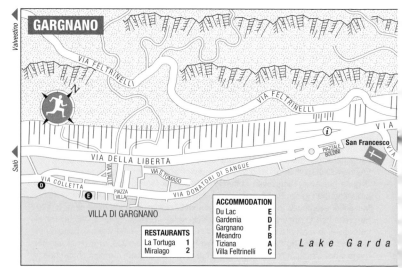

There's a **map** of Lake Garda on p.262. For details of the **boats**, see p.264.

ⓦwww.colomber.com; ❸), has comfortable en-suite rooms (some with balconies), a pool and a decent restaurant serving local specialities and well-chosen wine. It's a good base if you want to do some **walking** to the springs and waterfalls in the surrounding hills; the owners can give suggestions.

Toscolano Maderno

Barely 3km east of Gardone, the road passes through the twin *comune* of **TOSCOLANO MADERNO**, which straddles the delta of the Toscolano river. To the southwest, Maderno has the twelfth-century lakefront church of **Sant'Andrea**, while to the northeast, across the river, Toscolano – which, under the name *Benacum*, was the chief Roman settlement on the lake – has the ancient **Santuario della Madonna di Benaco**, with fifteenth-century frescoes. Between them is a good **beach**, while the valley behind has a tradition of paper-making going back to the fourth century; following the riverside road up into the beautiful, wooded valley brings you past many old **paper mills**, all of them now disused.

Gargnano

A little north of Toscolano, signs announce your arrival in the elongated *comune* of **GARGNANO**, though the road continues on through the outlying villages of **Bogliaco** and **Villa** before reaching Gargnano itself, 15km north of Salò.

This is a lovely spot, perhaps Lake Garda's most pleasant place to stay. Traffic runs a good way inland from the shore here, at a higher contour, leaving the old village itself noise-free. In addition, the narrow, difficult road northwards means tour buses heading south from Riva stop short at Limone and don't bother trying to reach Gargnano. Effectively sealed off by nature from the worse excesses of Garda tourism, Gargnano feels like a haven.

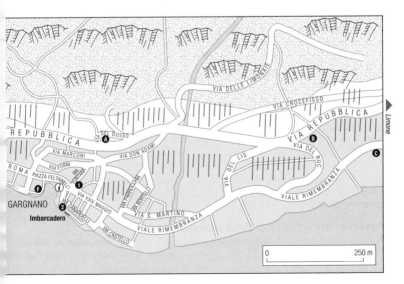

The only road through the lakeside mountains between Salò and Riva climbs from a turn-off at Gargnano. This is a spectacular drive through the hidden mountain scenery of the **Valvestino**, past a dammed lake and on, over a pass, to **Lake Idro**. Idro is utterly removed from the world of Lake Garda, a small, almost Alpine stretch of placid water squeezed between steep, rugged slopes: the dark, stone-built hamlet of **Bagolino**, above the lake, is a bewitching place to draw breath away from Garda's bustle.

This route can be done as the looping "**Four Lakes Drive**" – from Gargnano up past Lake Valvestino to Lake Idro, then down past Lake Ledro to Riva del Garda. It's 89km in total, easily doable as a leisurely day-trip, or split into two or more sections. Alternatively, from Gargnano to Idro then south down the Val Sabbia to Brescia (see p.243) is 84km. These are slow drives, on steep, switchbacking mountain roads, but the views and sense of escape are worth it.

The Valvestino

Above Gargnano, the road concertinas its way up the mountainside in a series of hairpin turns on the way to **Navazzo** and on up to a small **dam** on the River Toscolano. This stretch takes twenty minutes to go 13.5km: you'll rarely be out of second gear. Behind the dam stretches **Lake Valvestino**, a narrow, forked tarn enclosed by the high valley walls. The road crosses the water twice before reaching the isolated inn *Al Mulì* at Molino di Bollone, a junction of roads 5.5km past the dam. Straight ahead lie the villages of the Valvestino – Gargnano tourist office holds maps of a lonesome circular walk (3hr 30min) through the meadows and hamlets above **Turano**, while at **Magasa** is the *Cima Rest* (◉www.cimarest.com), a particularly attractive mountain restaurant (closed Thurs) – but the road continues on the second left (not Bollone) for 6km to **Capovalle**, the main settlement hereabouts, a modern town at 937m above sea level, surrounded by higher peaks. Beyond, over the pass, it's 11km down through the lush, wooded valley to Idro.

Lake Idro

Trapped in the higher reaches of the Val Sabbia above Brescia, the fjord-like **LAKE IDRO** (**Lago d'Idro**, also called by its Latin name **Eridio**) is both the highest of the major Italian lakes (368m above sea level) and the smallest, just 9.5km long by 2km wide. It's a pretty lake on a human scale, with wooded crags reaching down into cool, clear water, but its shores are occupied by rather too many bland little holiday suburbs and clumps of family-oriented campsites to encourage much exploration.

The main town is **IDRO**, a collection of hamlets at the foot of the lake covering both shores. On the western side, amidst shops, bars and hotels, is the **tourist office**, Via Trento 27 (Mon–Wed, Fri & Sat 9am–12.30pm & 1.30–6pm; ☏0365.83.224, ◉www .lagodidro.it). On the quieter, opposite shore, in Crone, *Hotel Alpino*, Lungolago Vittoria 14 (☏0365.83.146, ◉www.hotelalpino.net; ◉), has a bad case of 70s-style brown-itis to go with its grumpy staff, but it has lots of rooms and the views are good. To the north, this road ends 5km on at **VESTA**'s gravel beach, where you can follow trails into the hills or walk the Sentiero dei Contrabbandieri (route 103) around the

For a weekend in early September, the **Centomiglia** sailing event – held annually since 1951 – takes over the village, with hundreds of yachts racing from Bogliaco all round the lake and back.

Arrival, information and accommodation

Buses stop at Piazza Boldini on the main road, opposite the **tourist office** (Mon–Sat 9.30am–12.30pm & 5–7pm, closed Wed pm & Thurs am;

roadless headland. Surfpoint in nearby Vantone (☎339.227.5994, ⓦwww.surfpoint.it; June–Sept) **rents canoes** (€7 per hr). At the lake's northern end is **PONTE CAFFARO**, an unremarkable working town, though crossing its eponymous bridge still has a sense of occasion: until 1918, this marked the international border with Austria. Riva del Garda (see p.289) lies 39km ahead, beyond Lake Ledro.

The area's best restaurant is *Al Poggio Verde* (☎0365.824.591, ⓦwww.alpoggio verde.it), 12km west of Idro: follow the main Brescia road down the valley, then turn right at the big roundabout in **BARGHE** (signposted Preseglie); the ranch-style property is 500m up this road. The **restaurant** (closed Mon) is intimate and elegant; menus (€30–50) combine the local valley cuisine with influences from Lake Garda and further afield: fish arrives fresh daily. Tables on the veranda look out over the fields, and seven airy, pleasant **hotel rooms** (❸) add to the allure.

Bagolino

On the western shore of Lake Idro, near **Anfo**, a turn-off (9km north of Idro, 3km south of Ponte Caffaro) heads steeply up, skirting Monte Breda (1503m) to climb into the Valle di Caffaro, with spectacular views back over the lake. Some 8km up this narrow road lies the captivating mountain village of **BAGOLINO** (ⓦwww.bagolinoinfo .it). Many of its medieval houses are preserved, and 300m beyond the northern end of the village is the church of **San Rocco**, with a startlingly realistic cycle of fifteenth-century frescoes (the priest of San Giorgio in the village keeps the keys).

Al Tempo Perduto (☎0365.99.665, ⓦwww.altempoperduto.it; ❷) is a lovely **hotel** and **restaurant**, in a historic building on the main street, with attractive modern rooms and a warm welcome. Winter sees Bagolino full of skiers, while the village is also famous for its Lenten **carnival**, originating in the sixteenth century and focused on costumed revelry, music and dance.

▲ Bagolino

☎0365.791.243, ⓦwww.visitgarda.com). It's a short walk down through the village to the *imbarcadero*, beside the old harbour, where there's another tourist office (Mon, Tues & Thurs–Sat 2.30–4.30pm). Find more information at ⓦwww.gargnanosulgarda.com. OKSurf, at Parco Fontanella (☎328.471.7777, ⓦwww.oksurf.it), runs windsurfing and kitesurfing courses, and also **rents mountain bikes** (€21 a day). The **campsite** *Rucc*, Via Rimembranza 23 (☎0365.71.805), is near the beach.

Hotels

Du Lac Via Colletta 21, Villa di Gargnano
ⓣ0365.71.107, ⓦwww.hotel-dulac.it. On the
lakefront but 1km south of Gargnano, in the
neighbouring community of Villa. A very pleasant,
old-fashioned hotel, run by the same family as the
Gardenia – standards are high, the welcome is
warm and the rooms are comfortable and unfussy.
Six of them look over the lake, with a balcony or
terrace, and the whole place feels rather like a
much-loved family home. Antique furniture,
en-suite bathrooms and a/c come as standard.
Closed Dec–Feb. ❹

Gardenia Via Colletta 53, Villa di Gargnano
ⓣ0365.71.195, ⓦwww.hotel-gardenia.it.
Perhaps one of the loveliest family-run hotels on
the whole of Lake Garda – rated three stars but
easily worthy of four. The original house dates from
the nineteenth century, bought by the current
owners' great-grandfather (a piano-maker from
Lodi) in 1925, and converted into a hotel in 1957.
The public areas date from that time – featuring
beautifully maintained 1950s decor and fittings –
while the guest rooms have been completely
renovated. With antique furniture, big comfy beds,
well-appointed bathrooms and airy lake views, they
are outstanding value for money, boosted by the
excellent garden restaurant downstairs. Book the
corner room 311 – on the top floor, with two
balconies offering panoramic views of lake and
mountains – and you won't want to check out.
Closed Nov–March. ❺–❻

Gargnano Piazza Feltrinelli 29 ⓣ0365.71.312,
ⓦweb.tiscali.it/h.gar. One-star hotel directly on
Gargnano's old harbour, in business for over a

hundred years; in other villages such a prime piece
of waterfront might have been taken over and
redeveloped. As it is, this remains a frill-free,
house-proud little place, rough round the edges but
clean and tidy. Few budget rooms on Lake Garda
are nicer than the corner room 9 (with a sofa plus
windows over the harbour and the open lake) or
the balconied room 10, where D.H. Lawrence spent
a night. Closed Nov–March. ❷

Meandro Via Repubblica 40 ⓣ0365.71.128,
ⓦwww.hotelmeandro.it. Modern three-star at the
top of the village, just below the main road but with
all rooms facing away, towards the lake: noise isn't
a serious problem. Everything is decent and
serviceable but holiday-hotel generic; just look for
character elsewhere. Closed Dec–Feb. ❹

Tiziana Via Dosso 51 ⓣ0365.71.342, ⓦwww
.albergotiziana.com. Small, friendly two-star,
located slightly above the main road above the
village. Rooms are comfortable, in modern style,
most with lake views. Closed Nov–March. ❷

Villa Feltrinelli Via Rimembranza 38
ⓣ0365.798.000, ⓦwww.villafeltrinelli.com. Built
by a family of lumber magnates in 1892, this
grand lakeside house is set in its own sizeable
grounds just north of the village – an elegant
eleven-roomed villa with an enviable lakeside
position that is acclaimed as the finest hotel on
Lake Garda. Every detail has been considered; it's
worth pawning all your worldly possessions just
for the view from any of the rooms (which can be
enjoyed while soaking in the bath). In high season,
rooms start at a cool €1100 a night; some are
three times that. Minimum two-night stay. Closed
Nov–March. ❾

The village

Gargnano is still more a working village than a resort, its empty lanes tumbling
down the hillside from the main road to a little fishing port. Orange trees line
the lakefront, greeting you off the boat. It's the perfect spot to unwind for a day
or two and wander around the abandoned olive factory or the lakefront villas
with their boathouses, or just to relax with an ice cream or a drink in one of
the waterfront cafés. It was in Villa Igea, just south in the hamlet of Villa, that
D.H. Lawrence stayed while writing *Twilight in Italy*, a work which is beautifully
evocative of Lake Garda's attractions.

Aside from the harbourside ex-**Palazzo Comunale**, which has two cannon-
balls wedged in the wall facing the lake – dating from the naval bombings
suffered in 1866 during the war of independence from the Austrians – the main
sight is the church of **San Francesco**, built in 1289; its cloister has columns
carved with citrus fruits, a reference to the Franciscans' introduction of the crop
to Europe. A stroll along the road which leads north from the harbour takes you
for 3km through olive and lemon groves, past the *Villa Feltrinelli* (see above), to
the eleventh-century chapel of **San Giacomo di Calino**. On the side facing
the lake, under the portico where the fishermen keep their equipment, is a
thirteenth-century fresco of St Christopher, patron saint of travellers.

Lemons – and their rarer cousins, **citrons** – were introduced to Lake Garda from Genoa by Franciscan monks, resident at the monastery in Gargnano, in the thirteenth century. The industry flourished for hundreds of years, at its height exporting fruit as far afield as Poland and Russia. But disease in the 1850s, followed by the 1861 Unification of Italy, gave a lead to Sicily's lemon business, which soon cut into Garda's market. A combination of factors killed the industry off – the production of synthetic citric acid, the requisitioning of agricultural materials during the Great War, and finally a severe frost in the winter of 1928–29.

Its remnants are still visible, embodied in the skeletal remains of the **limonaie** dotted all the way up this coast. These *limonaie* (singular *limonaia*) – or "lemon-houses" – were first built in the seventeenth century to protect the trees from the winter weather: Limone sul Garda was the most northerly point in the world producing lemons on a commercial scale. A *limonaia* comprises a grid of tall stone columns, set in between the trees on the sloping, terraced orchards. In winter, beams and roofs would be placed on the columns to cover the trees, with "walls" of panels and glass panes in between. This would moderate conditions: inside, during the day it could be cooler than outside, but at night it was always much warmer. Lighting fires within the *limonaie* to keep the trees warm was not unknown. When D.H. Lawrence stayed at Gargnano in 1912–13, he recognized an industry on its last legs:

"I went into the lemon-house, where the poor trees seem to mope in the darkness. It is an immense, dark, cold place. Tall lemon trees, heavy with half-visible fruit, crowd together, and rise in the gloom. They look like ghosts in the darkness of the under-world, stately … There is a great host of lemons overhead, half-visible, a swarm of ruddy oranges by the paths, and here and there a fat citron. It is almost like being under the sea …

Looking at his lemons, the Signore sighed. I think he hates them. They are leaving him in the lurch. They are sold retail at a halfpenny each all the year round. 'But that is as dear, or dearer, than in England,' I say. 'Ah, but,' says the maestra, 'that is because your lemons are outdoor fruit from Sicily. One of our lemons is as good as two from elsewhere.'

It is true these lemons have an exquisite fragrance and perfume, but whether their force as lemons is double that of an ordinary fruit is a question. Oranges are sold at fourpence halfpenny the kilo – it comes to about five for twopence, small ones. The citrons are sold also by weight in Salò for the making of that liqueur known as Cedro. One citron fetches sometimes a shilling or more, but then the demand is necessarily small. So it is evident, from these figures, that the Lago di Garda cannot afford to grow its lemons much longer. The gardens are already many of them in ruins, and still more Da Vendere [For Sale]."

Eating and drinking

Gargnano is well served for **places to eat**. For a snack or ice cream there are several cafés to try round the port, as well as the *Osteria del Restauro* (closed Wed), for good, inexpensive local cuisine, and the *Miralago*, next to the tourist office, with excellent food at similarly keen prices.

Just back from the lakefront is the cosy little *La Tortuga*, Via XXIV Maggio 5 (☎0365.71.251; closed Tues, also Mon in winter), a Michelin-starred restaurant offering top food in a formal setting. The €50 menus take in "land" cuisine (innovative takes on meaty Brescian staples, such as breast of duck in balsamic vinegar) or "lake" cuisine (principally fresh fish); add in market-fresh produce, olive oil produced in Gargnano itself and the special chef's menu (€60), and this place is a real treat. With only a half-dozen tables, you need to book well ahead. It's open in the evenings only (also for lunch on Sun).

Tignale and the Tremósine

About 4km north of Gargnano, a narrow road climbs away from the shore, coiling up the steep slopes. This forms a looping detour, roughly 30km of mountain driving through isolated hamlets and deep, wooded valleys before rejoining the main shoreside road at, or just before, Limone. You first reach the hamlets of **TIGNALE**, occupying a plateau some 450m above the lake, with spectacular views – not least from the **Santuario di Montecastello**, accessed up a side-road. The main route then descends into the deep Valle di San Michele before climbing out to cross the even higher plateau of the **TREMÓSINE**; from the main village, **Vesio**, walking trails head out into the nature reserve of Bondo. The main route continues on a reasonable gradient down to Limone, or you can branch off to **Pieve**, perched on the edge of sheer cliffs above the lake, with yet more stunning views, from where a road switchbacks sharply down through a dark ravine to rejoin the shore just north of tiny **CAMPIONE DEL GARDA**, which is set in an amphitheatre of giant cliffs, has some excellent beaches and is one of the lake's main **surfing** and **windsurfing** centres (ⓦwww.vccampione.org).

North of the turn-off to Tignale, where the lakeside road emerges from a tunnel, a headland marks the **Prà de la Fam**, or Field of Hunger, so named after medieval fishermen were stranded here for several days following a storm. Nowadays serving as the harbour for Tignale – and boasting a fine old *limonaia* – it's a pretty little spot for relaxing and swimming alongside the beautiful B&B *Torre degli Ulivi* (ⓣ339.479.9834, ⓦwww.torredegliulivi.it; ❻), set in its own gated grounds, with five modest, airy rooms.

Limone sul Garda

The last town in Lombardy, 20km from Gargnano and 9km from Riva, set among citrus groves on a tongue of land surrounded by rugged mountains, is **LIMONE SUL GARDA** (ⓦwww.visitlimonesulgarda.com). Although it is famous for its lemon cultivation – a commercial concern until the 1920s – its name derives not from the fruit, but from its location at what was the frontier (*limen* in Latin) of Roman control. The coincidence is too much, though, and inevitably almost everyone who visits Limone is under the impression that it is – as one mistaken journalist put it – "a town called lemons".

Limone is undeniably pretty, a stone-built village jammed onto a slender slope between the mountains and the lake, but it is utterly overrun. A million tourists a year stay here, not counting the vast numbers who visit for the day on the boats from Riva and Malcésine; all this in a village with a settled population of just one thousand. The steep, cobbled streets are lined with stalls selling souvenirs, leather jackets and sequined T-shirts; the old stone facades are studded with plastic signs advertising restaurants and hotels; and as you elbow your way through the crowds you'll dig into more German and British ribs than Italian.

The **tourist office** is on the main road, Via IV Novembre 29 (daily 8am–10pm; ⓣ0365.954.720, ⓦwww.limonehotels.com). Most of the fifty-odd **hotels** are generic holiday establishments. Three-star *Bellavista*, Via Marconi 20 (ⓣ0365.954.001, ⓦwww.bellavistalimone.eu; ❸; closed Nov–March), stands out for occupying a Venetian lakeside mansion dating from 1650, though its interiors are blandly modern. More atmospheric is the modest *Monte Baldo*, Via Porto 29 (ⓣ0365.954.021, ⓦwww.montebaldolimone.it; ❹; closed Nov–Feb), a tall, narrow building by the *imbarcadero* renovated in traditional style in 2007. **Restaurants** are similarly uninspiring; the *Monte Baldo* is not a bad option, using home-made pasta and organic meat, but otherwise head for the hills:

Apolipoprotein A-1 Milano

Little Limone, unlikely though it sounds, has made a uniquely valuable contribution to medical science, with far-reaching consequences.

The story began in 1979, when a railwayman, born in Limone but living in Milan for more than twenty years, was hospitalized for a check-up. Doctors discovered that his cholesterol levels were very high, yet he showed no sign of arterial damage or heart disease. They did a further investigation, whereupon Dr Cesare Sirtori discovered an anomalous protein in the patient's blood – dubbed **Apolipoprotein A-1 Milano**. This protein, it transpired, was continuously stripping fat from the patient's arteries, allowing it to be delivered to the liver to be broken down and eliminated: it was, in short, counteracting the effects of smoking and a high-fat diet.

Doctors tested the patient's close family, and discovered that his father and daughter carried the same protein. They then tested every inhabitant of Limone, and found it in dozens of local residents. Archivists set to work, and uncovered the fact that all present-day carriers of the gene are descended from a couple who married in 1644. For centuries many Limonesi – cut off from the outside world – had married close relatives; as is often the case in isolated communities, intermarriage had embedded a genetic anomaly in the local population. In Limone's case, though, the mutation was the beneficial "wonder gene" Apolipoprotein A-1 Milano.

Four major conferences at Limone followed, during the 1980s and 1990s, as scientists grappled with developing a treatment to eliminate heart disease using the protein. In 2000, teams in the US began human trials, and it rapidly became clear that the synthetic version of Limone's protein was highly effective, removing a significant percentage of fatty deposits in the arteries of high-risk coronary patients after just six weeks of treatment. Doctors returned to Limone in 2004 to retest the local population, and discovered that the number of carriers of Apolipoprotein A-1 Milano had grown to 36. Research and human trials are continuing.

Osteria Da Livio, Via Tovo 4 (☎0365.954.203, ⓦwww.osteriadalivio.it; closed Mon) has fine, midpriced local cooking in a friendly ambience among the olive trees high above town.

Riva del Garda

At the northwest tip of the lake, 45km north of Salò, **RIVA DEL GARDA** is the best known of Lake Garda's resorts, and also one of the most rewarding. It is unmistakably a holiday town – windsurfing (or watching others windsurf) is a major preoccupation – but the pedestrianized old quarter, within its ancient walls, is still full of character: its high, narrow lanes are flanked by medieval facades, with the main lakefront square, **Piazza III Novembre**, ringed by late fourteenth-century porticoes and loomed over by the massive cliffs of the Rocchetta.

Recently in Austria, Riva is now Italian, yet it lies within an autonomous Alpine region (Trentino) which is left alone by Rome to set its own laws and conduct its own affairs. Amidst these shifting political loyalties, the only constants are the ever-present lake and mountains. There's a solidity here, and a sense of place that makes Riva an absorbing place to spend time.

Some history

Little survives from Riva's days as a **Roman** settlement. It's the town's strategic importance in **medieval** times that is most evident today. After Riva gained

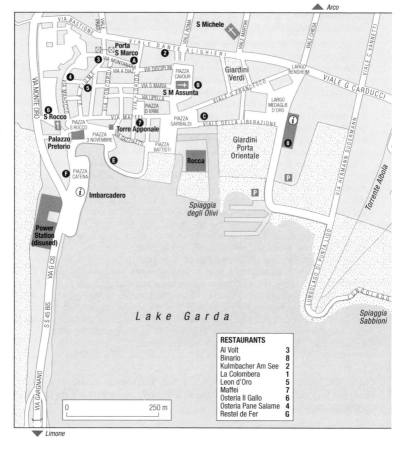

▲ Arco

S Michele

Porta
S Marco

S M Assunta

Giardini
Verdi

S Rocco

Palazzo
Pretorio

Torre Apponale

Giardini
Porta
Orientale

Rocca

Imbarcadero

Power
Station
(disused)

*Spiaggia
degli Olivi*

L a k e   G a r d a

*Spiaggia
Sabbioni*

RESTAURANTS	
Al Volt	3
Binario	8
Kulmbacher Am See	2
La Colombera	1
Leon d'Oro	5
Maffei	7
Osteria Il Gallo	6
Osteria Pane Salame	4
Restel de Fer	G

0   250 m

▼ Limone

autonomy in the twelfth century as a trading port, the Della Scala of Verona, Visconti of Milan and the republic of **Venice** battled for control, all losing out to the Prince-Bishops of **Trento**, who took power in 1509 and kept it until the arrival of Napoleon.

From 1815 to 1918, Riva was part of the **Austro–Hungarian Empire**, serving as a fulcrum for trade between Germany and Italy and taking on a new role as a holiday playground. Archduke Albert, cousin of the emperor Franz Josef, built his winter residence at nearby **Arco** in the 1870s, and high society from all over German-speaking *Mitteleuropa* began flocking to the area, clutching their copies of *Die Italienische Reise* ("Italian Journey") – in which Goethe writes evocatively about his stay, in 1786, in Riva's neighbour, **Tòrbole**.

This Teutonic influence in architecture and culture is what makes Riva different from anywhere else on the lake. The town is full of **tourists** and second-home-owners from across the Alps – turn on the radio and you'll catch news and local ads in German – but whereas other lake destinations find themselves swamped, Riva has enough self-possession, and a large enough area, to emerge fairly unscathed.

ACCOMMODATION
Ancora	A
Bellariva	I
Du Lac et du Parc	H
Europa	F
Feeling Hotel Luise	D
Grand Hotel Riva	C
Ostello Benacus	B
Restel de Fer	G
Sole	E

Torbole ▼

Arrival, information and accommodation

By **car**, it's a slow drive to Riva along either shoreline, 45km from Salò or 65km from Peschiera. From the A22 autostrada, exit at Rovereto Sud and follow the SS240 west for about 18km through the mountains down to Tòrbole. The *imbarcadero* stands beside Piazza III Novembre. Riva's **bus station** is about 1km north of the lakefront, on Viale Trento, but all intercity buses drop off at the *imbarcadero* (if approaching from Limone) or Viale Carducci (if approaching from Tòrbole).

The **tourist office** is on Largo Medaglie d'Oro (daily 9am–7pm; ☏0464.554.444, ⓦwww.gardatrentino.it), with an information kiosk at the *imbarcadero* (May–Sept daily 10am–1pm & 2–5.30pm; closed Wed; ☏0464.550.776).

There's a **map** of Lake Garda on p.262. See p.264 for details of the **boats**.

Hotels

Ancora Via Montanara 2 ⓣ 0464.522.131,
ⓦ www.rivadelgarda.com/ancora. Good-value,
comfortable two-star rooms on an old-town lane.
Service is friendly and there is a good terrace
restaurant. ❸

Bellariva Via Franz Kafka 13 ⓣ 0464.553.620,
ⓦ www.hotelbellariva.com. Modest little holiday
hotel away from the centre with some excellent
features, including free parking and a location
barely 100m from the lakeshore across a lawn:
grab a room on the uppermost floor for a bargain
balcony overlooking the lake and the mountains.
Closed Nov–Feb. ❹–❺

Du Lac et du Parc Viale Rovereto 44
ⓣ 0464.566.600, ⓦ www.dulacetduparc.com.
Riva's grandest hotel, a magnificent building set in
its own lakefront park that was the destination of
choice for German-speaking intellectuals around
the turn of the last century, from Nietzsche and
Freud to Kafka and Thomas Mann. It remains a
high-class, traditionally styled establishment,
modernized but still characterful – and the gardens
are heavenly. Closed Nov–March. ❽

Europa Piazza Catena 9 ⓣ 0464.555.433, ⓦ www
.hoteleuropariva.it. A good mid-range *Best Western*
choice, occupying a tall, historic building on the
main portside square by the *imbarcadero*, with a
pleasant terrace café-restaurant. Rooms are
modern and well-furnished, with lake-view or
town-view options. Closed Nov–March. ❺

Feeling Hotel Luise Viale Rovereto 9
ⓣ 0464.550.858, ⓦ www.hotelluise.com. A chic,
contemporary boutique hotel just out of the centre,
with pristine designer interiors – white sofas,
dark-wood floors, halogen-lit bathrooms – and
good service. Private parking. ❺

Grand Hotel Riva Piazza Garibaldi 10
ⓣ 0464.521.800, ⓦ www.grandhotelriva.it. A noble
fin-de-siècle pile, opposite the Rocca in the heart
of the old town. Rooms are modern, some
balconied ones with lake views and a/c. Open year
round. ❻–❼

🏃 **Restel de Fer** Via Restel de Fer 10
ⓣ 0464.553.481, ⓦ www.resteldefer.com.
A real find, in the quiet backstreets away from the
centre. This was once a farmhouse, out on its own
in the fields (named for the iron gate which still
stands in front); Riva has grown up around it, but
the Meneghelli family are still here, 600 years on.
The restaurant is exceptional (see p.294), and there
are also five simple rooms, comfortably furnished
with individual touches. The owners might request
a three-day minimum stay. ❸

Sole Piazza III Novembre 35 ⓣ 0464.552.686,
ⓦ www.hotelsole.net. Four-star hotel in an unbeatable location, on the main waterfront square; in a
previous incarnation, the hotel hosted the Austrian
Emperor Franz Josef for a night. The exterior is
splendid, and the public areas are full of character,
but the renovated rooms are now rather generic.
Nevertheless, if you can snaffle a room with a
balcony, you get just about the best lake views in
Riva. ❻

Hostel

Ostello Benacus (HI hostel) Piazza Cavour 10
ⓣ 0464.554.911, ⓦ www.ostelloriva.com. Very central
hostel, well run, with renovated two-, four- and multi-
bedded rooms. Closed Nov–Feb. Dorms €16. ❶

The Town

Riva's showpiece main square, **Piazza III Novembre** (named to celebrate the
arrival of Italian forces in 1918), is an attractive, cobbled space, its medieval
Lombard and Venetian facades lined up on three sides below the rugged face of
Monte Rocchetta, the fourth side open to the lake. Its most striking feature is
aural: the noise of footsteps, conversation and laughter bounces off the four-
storey buildings and reverberates down off the high Rocchetta cliffs to make an
enclosed swirl of sound, graphically represented by *Percorsi*, a curious abstract
spiral sculpture in bronze, by Osvaldo Bruschetti, placed on the waterfront.

Prominent on the Rocchetta is the **Bastione** fortress, erected in record time in
1508 – but not quickly enough to save the Venetians from losing Riva the year
after. Even higher, nestled into the crags 585m up, is **Santa Barbara**, a small
white church built in the 1920s that is visible from afar, eerily floodlit at night.

Dominating Piazza III Novembre is the thirteenth-century **Torre Apponale**
(March–Oct Tues–Sun 10am–6pm; June–Aug also Mon; €1), 34m high and
climbable inside for sensational lake views. In the middle of the square are the
Veronese **Palazzo Pretorio**, dating from 1375, and the Venetian **Casa del
Comune**, completed in 1482, while to one side, behind the statue of San

▲ Piazza III Novembre

Giovanni Nepomuceno, co-patron of Riva, and the *imbarcadero* looms a 1920s-era hydroelectric **power station**, complete with its network of pipes that snake, Willy Wonka-like, over the hillside. This was designed to exploit the 500-metre drop in water level from Lake Ledro to this point; today, the generators are hidden within the mountain, and these buildings and pipes are only for show.

Behind Piazza III Novembre, and the adjacent Piazza San Rocco, stretches the **Marocco** quarter, Riva's oldest, named for the *marocche*, or debris, which used to tumble down off the mountain. Via Marocco itself is a long, curving alley of medieval houses, while alongside, **Via Fiume** – once Riva's Jewish quarter – remains a lively street, packed with shops and restaurants, leading to the massive **Porta San Marco** gate, beyond which cars and modern life take over. A trail from here climbs to the Bastione in about thirty minutes and Santa Barbara in a further hour.

A short walk behind the Torre Apponale stands the stout **Rocca**, originally built in 1124 but much altered since, not least by the Austrians, who lopped some height off the main tower in 1852 and turned the fortress into a barracks. It now houses the **Museo Civico** (March–Oct Tues–Sun 10am–12.30pm & 1.30–6pm, June–Aug also Mon; €2; ⓦwww.comune.rivadelgarda.tn.it/museo), with temporary exhibits on the ground floor, a modest *pinacoteca* upstairs and displays of archeology and local history upstairs again.

Eating and drinking

Riva's lakefront is lined with all kinds of **places to eat**, from terrace cafés and *gelaterie* to smarter restaurants. As usual, though, for higher quality it pays to explore a little away from the waterfront.

Restaurants

Al Volt Via Fiume 73 ⓣ0464.552.570, ⓦwww .ristorantealvolt.com. Refined, old-fashioned restaurant in a seventeenth-century *palazzo* beside the Porta San Marco, complete with fancy, gilt-edged mirrors and lace tablecloths. The menu has innovative touches – try the mousse of char with apple purée to start, followed by brochettes of *coregone* in white wine sauce – and service is discreet and formal. Five-course menu €40. Closed Mon.

Binario Largo Medaglie d'Oro ☎0464.520.600, ⓦwww.restaurantcafebinario.it. Very pleasant, large, modern café-restaurant occupying the former train station (long since disused). A perfect, airy spot for a light lunch or just coffee and pastries – the pizzas are excellent, as are salads and grills. Jazz trios play on summer weekends. Closed Tues.

Kulmbacher Am See Viale Dante 39 ☎0464.559.231. Cosy Bavarian restaurant just outside the old quarter, specializing in roast pork, goulash, bratwurst – and, of course, beer. Quality is high: with the number of Bavarian holiday-makers in Riva, it has to be. Closed Wed.

La Colombera Via Rovigo 30 ☎0464.556.033, ⓦwww.lacolombera.it. Make the journey out into the vineyards on the edge of Riva for this excellent, midpriced country restaurant, crowded nightly with locals and others in the know. The menu comprises hearty, straightforward fare – cured meats, filled pastas, steaks and the like – served with gusto in a cheery, unpretentious setting. Closed Wed.

Leon d'Oro Via Fiume 28 ☎0464.552.341. Welcoming restaurant on a busy pedestrianized street, a handy place for good-quality, moderately priced pizza and fish dishes in the heart of the old quarter. No closing day.

Maffei Via Maffei 7, at Piazza delle Erbe. One of Riva's many German-style beer halls, with litres of the amber nectar helped down by stout portions of frankfurters, pâté, pork chops – or you could push the boat out for a pizza (all around €10). Closed Wed.

Osteria Il Gallo Piazza San Rocco 12. Great little eatery under the porticoes just off the main square. There's a short menu of simple local mountain staples and the owner will reel off many more dishes. The good wine list of Trento wines and the relaxed atmosphere make this a fine spot to settle down for the evening. Closed Mon.

Osteria Pane Salame Via Marocco 22 ☎0464.551.954. Tiny place on a back street – a locals' haunt, with no menu: food is cheap and uncomplicated, and there are lots of wines by the glass. Closed Mon.

Restel de Fer Via Restel de Fer 10 ☎0464.553.481, ⓦwww.resteldefer.com. See also "Hotels" p.292. This restaurant, well away from the touristic centre, is outstanding, with real character and charm: eat in the old stone dining hall, or the airy winter garden. The exquisite local cuisine takes in grilled meats, salted freshwater sardines, perch and other lake fish, thick *bigoi* noodles, olive *gnocchi*, Trentino mountain cheeses, wines from the extensive cellar (two of them, a Chardonnay and a Merlot, produced in-house) – everything presented with care and served with panache. Expect high prices, but not astronomical: you're paying for quality. Summer closed Wed; winter closed Mon–Thurs.

Sports and activities at Riva and Tòrbole

The northern shore of Lake Garda around **Riva** – and especially **Tòrbole** – is a hub for sporting activity. All prices below are approximate; check details with local tourist offices. Top of the list is watersports, with a clutch of local outfits offering **windsurfing**: first-timers can get individual tuition (€70 for 3hr) or there are group lessons at various grades (€80 for 3hr). If you're already proficient, you can rent for €50 a day. **Sailing** is also popular, with beginners' courses in a dinghy or catamaran (€135 for 4hr) and rental (€70–130 per day, depending on the size of boat). Shop around: local operators include ⓦwww.pierwindsurf.it, ⓦwww.vascorenna.com, ⓦwww.sailingdulac.com, ⓦwww.surfsegnana.it, ⓦwww.surflb.com and ⓦwww.windsurfconca.com. You can **rent canoes** (€35 a day for two people) at the Sabbioni beach in Riva.

With over a dozen good locations within easy reach of the lake, **canyoning** is a good bet (April–Oct only; half-day €40–60, full-day €75–110; ⓦwww.canyonadv.com & ⓦwww.wetway.it). Several companies offer more traditional **Alpine activities** – ice-climbing, *via ferrata*, trekking and so on; check ⓦwww.alpinguide.com and ⓦwww.guidealpinearco.com for details.

Paragliding – notably off Monte Baldo above Malcésine – is a spectacular way to get an eagle-eye view of the lake. Volo Libero (ⓦwww.timetofly.net) runs tandem paragliding flights for €100, as does ⓦwww.condorfly.com.

Around Riva

There are several good options for exploring beyond Riva. One of the most popular is a gorge and waterfall system 3km north of Riva, the **Parco Grotta Cascata Varone** (May–Aug daily 9am–7pm; April & Sept daily 9am–6pm; March & Oct daily 9am–5pm; Nov–Feb Sun 10am–5pm; €5; ⊛www.cascata -varone.com), where you penetrate the canyon on a series of catwalks, as the waters of the River Magnone thunder down from almost 100m above. The most pleasant approach is on foot (about 45min from Riva waterfront, on Via Ardaro/Marone).

About 5km north of Riva is the old town of **ARCO**, dominated by its twelfth-century **castle**, which teeters dramatically on top of a rocky outcrop, though there's not much to see inside today. Arco, once more favoured as a winter retreat for central European nobility than Riva, has several lovely gardens in the town centre, including a beautiful **public garden** opposite the Casino on Viale delle Palme, filled with hollyhocks, Chinese scented honeysuckle, other exotics and several varieties of palm, cypress and cedar. A short walk to the north is the **Parco Arciducale** (daily: April–Sept 8am–7pm; Oct–March 9am–4pm; free), the arboretum of the Habsburg Archduke Albert's winter palace, built in 1872 and filled with trees from six continents.

Tòrbole

TÒRBOLE, 4km east of Riva at the head of the lake, was thrust into the spotlight during the war between the Milanese Visconti and the Republic of Venice. In 1439, the Venetians organized an army and 240 oxen to drag a fleet of warships from the River Adige over the mountains to Tòrbole, launching them into the lake (and subsequently seizing Riva). These days, though, there's not much left of the town's historical character: the main diversions are **sailing** and **windsurfing**. You'll find Tòrbole's many bars and restaurants packed with toned bodies and suntanned faces: enthusiasts come here from all over Europe,

▲ Tòrbole

attracted by ideal wind conditions. In the mornings, when the wind is gentler, the water is full of wobbling novices attempting to circle their instructors. Although the town is busy with traffic, the view from the waterfront promenade is much better than from Riva, with a direct line of sight due south down the funnel of the lake and west to the formidable cliffs.

The lakefront **tourist office** (Easter–Oct Mon–Sat 9am–noon & 3–6pm; June–Aug also Sun 10am–noon & 3.30–6.30pm; Nov–Easter Mon–Fri 9am–noon & 2.30–5pm; ℡0464.505.177, ⓦwww.gardatrentino.it) stands between the town centre and the landing-stage. There are dozens of **hotels**: *Lido Blu*, Via Foci del Sarca 1 (℡0464.505.180, ⓦwww.lidoblu.com; ❺), on an elongated spit of land at the mouth of the River Sarca, away from the traffic, has some great beaches. It's popular with families on holiday, and has cut-price deals in the low season (open year-round). The modern *Villa Verde*, Via Sarca Vecchio 15 (℡0464.505.274, ⓦwww.hotel-villaverde.it; ❸), is in a peaceful setting also near the river, with its own pool and garden.

Lake Ledro

One of the most pleasant excursions from Riva is up to the little mountain-bound **LAKE LEDRO**, only 3km long – a good bolt-hole where you can escape the crowds on the Garda shore. It's a scenic, sunny spot, flanked by wooded slopes; traffic passes on the northern side, but the southern shore is quiet and there are some good hideaways to be discovered. Several streams fill the lake, but only the Ponale emerges for the short, steep tumble down into Lake Garda: its deep gorge, with a picturesque waterfall, is a spectacular sight from the deck of the boats into or out of Riva. Lake Ledro lies near the end of the long "**Four Lakes Drive**" from Gargnano (see p.284), which can, of course, also be done in reverse.

The old route into the Ponale valley branched off the shoreside road south of Riva. That is now a cycle route and footpath (the walk up from Riva takes about four hours); cars must head north out of Riva on Viale dei Tigli, to be directed into a **tunnel**, 4km long, beneath Monte Rocchetta.

Bronze Age stilt dwellings have been discovered in the lake at **MOLINA DI LEDRO**; reconstructions of them and displays of the site's jewellery and artefacts are at the **Museo delle Palafitte** (March–Nov Tues–Sun 9am–1pm & 2–5pm, July & Aug 10am–6pm; €2.50; ⓦwww.palafitteledro.it). At **PIEVE DI LEDRO**, 3km north at the opposite end of the lake, is the **tourist office**, Via Nuova 9 (Mon–Fri 8.30am–12.30pm & 2.30–6pm, Sat 9am–noon & 3–6pm, Sun 9am–noon; ℡0464.591.222, ⓦwww.vallediledro.com). **Campsites** include the attractive, lakefront *Al Sole* (℡0464.508.496, ⓦwww.campingalsole.it). The **hotel** *Mezzolago* (℡0464.508.181, ⓦwww.hotelmezzolago.it; ❷) in **MEZZOLAGO**, halfway between Pieve and Molina, has pleasant three-star rooms, each with a balcony on the lake.

The eastern shore: Malcésine to Torri

A short way south of Tòrbole, the shoreside road leaves Trentino and enters Verona province, part of the Véneto region. Overlooked by the ridges of Monte Baldo, which tops 2100m – its treeless summit poking baldly out of lushly wooded slopes – the main resorts of Garda's **eastern shore** are heavily touristed and struggle to match the charm of the villages opposite. Holiday hotels and campsites line much of the lakeside road.

The first settlement, **Malcésine**, has an attractive centre but is swamped by holiday-makers: you'll need to work hard to carve out some individuality to a stay here. Heading south, **Brenzone** offers some quieter corners, while **Torri del Benaco** is one of the loveliest places on this shore, an old village with charm and character in spades.

Malcésine

Occupying a headland backed by the slopes of Monte Baldo, the small lakefront village of **MALCÉSINE**, 14km south of Torbole, boasts a pretty, historic core overlooked by the battlements of a medieval castle: it is a picture-perfect backdrop for an Italian Lakes holiday – but that's the trouble. Malcésine is inundated with package holiday-makers (mostly British and German), to such an extent that there is very little local life remaining in the village centre, which is filled with touristy shops and mediocre restaurants. Every boat brings more day-trippers, visiting from Riva or Limone. So many people – and such a lack of local culture – obscure Malcésine's appeal.

If you're booked to stay here, but would prefer to sample somewhere a little more typically Italian, the best advice would be to make full use of boats and buses to explore up and down the shore: trips to Gargnano (see p.283) and Salò (see p.277), for example, are easily done, and can show you a quite different Lake Garda. Verona (see p.306) is an hour-and-three-quarters by bus. And, as always hereabouts, the hillside villages above the lake such as Pai and Crero (see p.300) are where Gardesana life carries on regardless.

Arrival, information and accommodation

Malcésine's **bus station** is on the main lakeside road: the old village spreads out below. From the central square **Piazza Statuto** (now a car park), stepped lanes head down to the *imbarcadero*. Beside the bus station is a **tourist office** (Mon–Sat 9am–7pm, Sun 10am–4pm; ☎045.740.0044, Ⓦwww.visitgarda.com), with a branch near the *imbarcadero* at Via Capitanato 8 (Mon–Sat 9am–1pm & 3–7pm; May–Oct also Sun 9am–1pm; ☎045.740.0837, Ⓦwww.malcesinepiu.it). Many **hotels** in Malcésine are block-booked by tour operators; many others insist on half board and a three-night minimum stay.

Hotels

Aurora Piazza Matteotti 10 ☎045.740.0114, Ⓦwww.aurora-malcesine.com. Good, flexible budget option in the heart of the old lanes, with decent rooms and a touch of character. ❷

Europa Via Gardesana 173 ☎045.740.0022, Ⓦwww.europa-hotel.net. Sleek, contemporary interiors herald this chic four-star hotel just north of town on the lake side of the main road. It has its own gravel beach, pool, parking, spa and an excellent restaurant (see p.298). Closed Nov–Feb. ❼

Majestic Palace Via Navene Vecchia 96 ☎045.740.0383. Excellent four-star holiday hotel in the hills just north of the centre, set amongst olive groves and boasting a large pool, good facilities and welcoming service. Used by many British tour operators. ❻

Maximilan Via Val di Sogno 8 ☎045.740.0317, Ⓦwww.hotelmaximilian.com. Pleasant, upmarket option just south of town in the Val di Sogno district. It's renovated in a fresh, contemporary style: most rooms look south over gardens and the tranquil bay. Closed Nov–Feb. ❼

San Marco Via Capitanato 9 ☎045.740.0115. Basic two-star hotel overlooking the old harbour: expect no frills (and some noise from the promenading crowds), but for cut-price rates it's a fair choice. ❷

There's a **map** of Lake Garda on p.262. See p.264 for details of the **boats**.

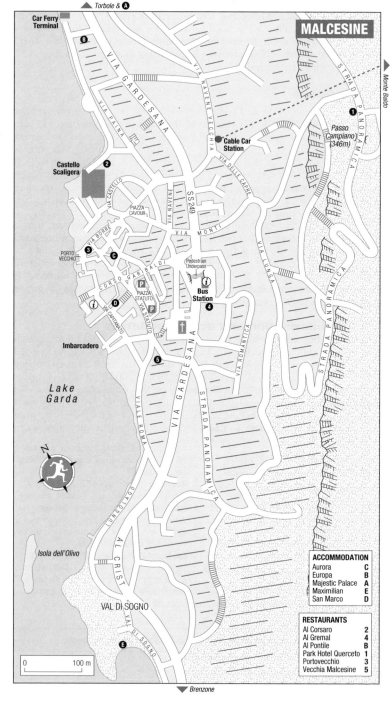

MALCESINE

Car Ferry
Terminal

Ⓑ

VIA GARDESANA

VIA PAINA

VIA NAVENE VECCHIA

▶ Monte Baldo

Passo
Campiano
(346m)

❶

STRADA PANORAMICA

Cable Car
Station

VIA DELLE CARE

Castello
Scaligera

❷

VIA CASTELLO

PIAZZA
CAVOUR

VIA NAVENE

SS 249

VIA MONTI

VIA LUNGA

PORTO
VECCHIO

❸

VIA BORRE

Ⓒ

CORSO GARIBALDI

Pedestrian
Underpass

ⓘ

Bus
Station

❹

P

PIAZZA
STATUTO

ⓘ

Ⓓ

VIA CAPITANATO

VIA STATUTO

P

VIA ROMANTICA

Imbarcadero

✝

❺

VIA GARDESANA

STRADA PANORAMICA

STRADA PANORAMICA

Lake
Garda

VIALE ROMA

N

LUNGOLAGO AL CRIST

Isola dell'Olivo

VAL DI SOGNO

VAL DI SOGNO

Ⓔ

ACCOMMODATION	
Aurora	C
Europa	B
Majestic Palace	A
Maximilian	E
San Marco	D

RESTAURANTS	
Al Corsaro	2
Al Gremal	4
Al Pontile	B
Park Hotel Querceto	1
Portovecchio	3
Vecchia Malcesine	5

0	100 m

The town and Monte Baldo

Malcésine's main sight is the thirteenth-century **Castello Scaligera** (daily 9.30am–8pm; Nov–March closed Mon–Fri; €5), built, like Sirmione's (see p.268), by the Della Scala family of Verona. Goethe was imprisoned here briefly in 1786, having been arrested on suspicion of being a spy: he'd been caught making sketches of the castle's towers, which still loom over the old village.

For more active pursuits you need to head up **Monte Baldo**. There are well-marked trails up the mountain, or you can take the **cable car** (*funivia*; March–Oct daily every 30min 8am–7pm; €11 one way, €17 return; ⓦ www .funiviamalcesine.com), which rises more than 1600m in ten minutes. Be prepared for queues in summer for walkers, and winter for skiers. There are several special trips a day for cyclists to transport their bikes to the top; you can **rent a mountain bike** at G. Furioli in Piazza Matteotti (ⓣ045.740.045) and make a panoramic descent down easy trails to the shore. Footpaths also let you explore the summit ridge.

Eating and drinking

Most of central Malcésine's **restaurants** are awful: the food is rarely too bad, and some locations, right on the waterfront, are lovely – but expect heaving crowds, slapdash service and spag bol on offer almost everywhere you go. But choose carefully, or head further afield, and you'll find some great cooking, service and atmosphere.

Al Corsaro Via Paina 17 ⓣ045.658.4064, ⓦ www .alcorsaro.it. Wonderful restaurant – opened in 2008 – concealed at the base of the castle walls, directly on its own patch of beach and out of sight from anywhere but the water. The cooking is based on freshly caught lake fish, done a thousand different ways: this is a charming, relaxed, modern setting in which to enjoy a refined meal to remember. Prices range either side of €40. Closed Tues.

Al Gremal Via Scoisse ⓣ045.657.0993. For a break from the old town, this attractive, contemporary-styled *enoteca*, perched on a terrace just above the main road, offers wines by the glass and light meals, along with tastings and sales of wines, grappas and oils.

Al Pontile At *Hotel Europa* (see p.297). Stylish, beachfront restaurant attached to this chic, modern hotel, serving innovative modern Italian cooking at moderate prices.

Park Hotel Querceto Via Panoramica 113 ⓣ045.740.0344, ⓦ www.parkhotelquerceto.com. Follow the signposted Strada Panoramica twisting above Malcésine: this four-star hotel is just over the Passo Campiano (346m), high in the hills under the cable-car lines. It occupies a stout Alpine building set in its own park, with stupendous lake views. Inside, the atmosphere is cosy: lots of dark wood, thick beams, traditional styling and big fireplaces. Expect to pay €50 or so for their finely judged regional and local specialities – book ahead for a table on the panoramic terrace.

Portovecchio Porto Vecchio ⓣ045.658.4335. Slightly away from the crush, on this cobbled square in the village centre, serving well-presented Mediterranean cuisine at terrace tables overlooking the water.

Vecchia Malcesine Via Pisort 6 ⓣ045.740.0469, ⓦ www.vecchiamalcesine.com. The best restaurant in town by quite a long chalk, hidden away in its own grounds above Piazza Statuto. Views over the castle and the lake are sensational – as is the cooking, a creative array of sophisticated flavours and artful presentation, *nouvelle*-style. Prices, like the waiters' noses, are high. Closed Wed.

Brenzone and around

South of Malcésine, the elongated community of **BRENZONE** encompasses several lakeside villages dotted along 5km or more of shoreline, as well as a clutch of hamlets clinging to the mountainsides above – high and rugged enough to host decent skiing in winter. Stop in at the **tourist office** (Mon–Fri & Sun 8.30am–12.30pm & 3–7pm, Sat 8.30am–7pm; ⓣ045.742.0076), on the main road as it runs through the waterfront hamlet of **Porto**: they have maps and information about **walking** in the hills – including Path 33, which climbs (in about 2hr 15min) from just above Porto on a steep, scenic forest trail to **Prada Alta**, a village at 1000m.

A short way south of Porto lies the centre of Brenzone, sometimes called by its old village name, **Magugnano**. The main road diverts inland, leaving a little cluster of alleyways by the water free from traffic. Down here, directly opposite the *imbarcadero*, stands the *Hotel Brenzone* (℡045.742.0388, ℗www.hotel brenzone.com; ❺), built in 1911 and still with an appealingly old-fashioned atmosphere to its public rooms; the bedrooms have been tastefully modernized. Its midpriced *Ristorante Al Lago* – specializing in fresh-caught fish, though with some more adventurous dishes including *fegato alla Veneziana* (Venetian-style liver and onions) – is a perfect spot for a quiet meal: gaze across the lake and watch as the ferries glide into dock barely ten metres away.

A kilometre or more south and – still within Brenzone – you come to **Castelletto**. On the lakefront, two more excellent fish restaurants flank the little harbour: *Ristorante Alla Fassa* (℡045.743.3019; closed Tues in winter) is the more formal, with a highly regarded menu of Gardesana cuisine (around €35), while *Osteria Al Pescatore* is a smaller, family-run affair, offering a handful of simple dishes in a cosy, authentic ambience.

Pai and Crero

Castelletto's patch of shoreline is not Garda's most distinguished, the busy road flanked by holiday hotels and scrappy gravel beaches. As always on the lakes, venturing up into the hills pays dividends. From **PAI**, just south of Castelletto, a road squiggles up to **Pai di Sopra** – a beautiful, quiet hamlet with great views, and a bar, a café and the little hotel-restaurant *Locanda San Marco* (℡045.726.0004, ℗www.locandasanmarco.it; ❷) ranged around a square. Similarly alluring is tiny **CRERO**, accessed up an even skinnier turn-off from the lakeshore road a bit further south: signposted from the village square down a scenic footpath stands the the graceful, half-forgotten chapel of **San Siro**, built on these clifftops in the eighteenth century.

Torri del Benaco

TORRI DEL BENACO, 20km south of Malcésine, is one of the prettiest of the villages on this side of the lake. Part of its tenth-century walls still stand, notably the West Tower of the lakefront castle, which was overhauled in 1383 by the Della Scala of Verona. During following centuries, Torri was a financial centre, controlling trade and imposing customs duties.

Although the main shoreside road passes within 100m of the shore here, Torri's old centre – which consists of one long cobbled street, Corso Dante, crisscrossed with tunnelling alleyways and lined with mellow stone *palazzi* – is quiet and appealing. At one end of the street is the **Castello Scaligero** (daily: June–Sept 9.30am–1pm & 4.30–7.30pm; April, May & Oct 9.30am–12.30pm & 2.30–6pm; €3; ℗www.museodelcastelloditorridelbenaco.it), its stout old towers and swallowtail battlements standing guard over the little harbour, illuminated at night to romantic effect. A long *limonaia*, or glasshouse, was built along one side in 1760 to protect the lemon trees inside during cold weather. Outside the castle, the harbourside **Piazza Calderini**, planted with limes and chestnuts, is the focus of the *passeggiata*.

There's a **map** of Lake Garda on p.262. See p.264 for details of the **boats**.

Practicalities

Buses stop on the main road, by the post office; cross the street to Via Lavanda, which leads to the waterfront. If you're **driving**, park by the castle walls: the old centre is off-limits to cars. The **tourist office** is on the harbour (June–Aug daily 9am–1pm & 3–7pm; otherwise restricted hours; ☎045.722.5120, ⓦwww .visitgarda.com).

Budget **hotels** are led by the ⚲ *Garni Onda*, Via per Albisano 28 (☎045.722.5895, ⓦwww.garnionda.com; closed Nov–Feb; ❷), 100m east of the centre. Each spotlessly clean room has its own balcony or terrace and the friendly owners provide a first-rate breakfast.

The top hotel – and one of the loveliest on the whole lake – is the harbourside ⚲ *Gardesana*, Piazza Calderini 20 (☎045.722.5411, ⓦwww.hotel-gardesana .com; ❺–❻). This is a classic old lakes hotel, first recorded in 1452. It has hosted the likes of Churchill, Maria Callas and the Spanish king Juan Carlos I in its time; Laurence Olivier holidayed here with Vivien Leigh in 1954, and the poet Stephen Spender pronounced his visit in 1951 "the happiest two months since the war". It wears its history lightly; there is no sense of pomposity. Service is genial and the rooms, though luxurious, are a bargain – fresh, immaculately kept and thoroughly appealing. Choose between a view of the harbour and castle or the lake (with or without a balcony) – or, in the sensational room 123, relish both: this, dubbed the "Poet's Room", has a large double balcony.

The *Gardesana*'s **restaurant** is equally bewitching, with tables laid out along a balcony above the harbour: you could barely invent a more romantic setting for dinner (book for a table at the railing). Their *menù tipico del Garda* (taking in pike with polenta, chub in butter, fillet of lavaret and dessert) is €45, or you could opt for à-la-carte, including the signature dish of lavaret in a sweet-and-sour sauce (€25). The ambience is refined but not stuffy, with care taken over presentation and service. Many other restaurants crowd Torri's warren of streets. *Trattoria Bell'Arrivo*, on Piazza Calderini, is a cosy little spot with unusually good food: go for the *tortelli al paté di lago in salsa fresca* (€10). For excellent food in unbeatable surroundings, head a couple of kilometres above town towards Albisano; amid hillside olive groves, ⚲ *Trattoria agli Olivi*, Via Valmagra 7 (☎045.722.5483, ⓦwww.agliolivi.it), serves delicious local dishes at bargain prices on a splendid lake-view terrace.

Coverage of this shore continues with **Punta San Vigilio** on p.275.

Travel details

Full details of transport in Lombardy – including buses on the west shore of Lake Garda from Sirmione to Limone, as well as Idro and Bagolino – are at ⓦwww.trasporti.regione.lombardia.it (click "orari"). Local buses for Riva del Garda and Lake Ledro are run by Trentino Trasporti ⓦwww.ttspa.it. Buses from Riva down the eastern shore of Lake Garda are run by APTV ⓦwww .aptv.it; those down the western shore are run by APTV and SIA ⓦwww .trasportibrescia.it. Timetables for all train routes in Italy are at ⓦwww.trenitalia .com. For details of boat services, see p.264 and ⓦwww.navigazionelaghi.it. See p.30 for some guidance on deciphering timetables.

Trains

Desenzano/Sirmione to: Brescia (approx twice hourly; 20min); Milano Centrale (hourly; 1hr 10min); Verona (approx twice hourly; 30min).

Buses

Desenzano to: Riva (5 daily; 1hr 50min); Salò (7 daily; 35min); Sirmione (at least hourly; 20min).
Gardone Riviera to: Brescia (every 30min; 1hr 5min); Limone (3 daily; 1hr); Riva del Garda (5 daily; 1hr 15min).
Gargnano to: Brescia (3 daily; 1hr 10min); Desenzano (5 daily; 1hr); Salò (5 daily; 30min).
Idro to: Bagolino (5 daily; 45min); Brescia (5 daily; 1hr 20min).

Malcésine to: Riva (approx hourly; 25min); Torri del Benaco (approx hourly; 35min); Verona (approx hourly; 1hr 45min).
Riva del Garda to: Brescia (3 daily; 1hr 55min); Desenzano (3 daily; 1hr 50min); Malcésine (approx hourly; 25min); Salò (3 daily; 1hr 15min); Tòrbole (approx every 30min; 5min); Torri del Benaco (approx hourly; 1hr); Verona (approx hourly; 2hr 10min).
Salò to: Brescia (every 30min; 1hr); Desenzano (7 daily; 50min); Gargnano (every 30min; 25min); Milan (3 daily; 2hr 40min); Riva (3 daily; 1hr 15min).
Sirmione to: Brescia (hourly; 1hr 20min); Desenzano (at least hourly; 20min); Verona (hourly; 1hr).
Torri del Benaco to: Malcésine (approx hourly; 35min); Riva (approx hourly; 1hr); Verona (approx hourly; 1hr 15min).

Verona
and Mantova

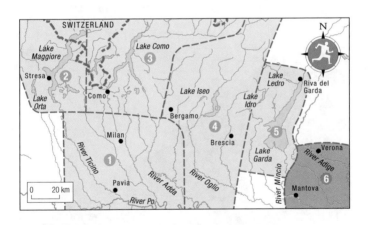

CHAPTER 6

Highlights

* **The Liston** A curve of pavement cafés on Verona's main square – sit back and watch the city pass you by. See p.313

* **Opera in Verona** The historic Arena is a stirring backdrop to world-class opera. See p.314

* **The Arena** Giant Roman amphitheatre, plum in the heart of Verona. See p.314

* **Castelvecchio** Medieval fortress that is now Verona's leading fine-art museum. See p.321

* **San Zeno** Verona's most beautiful Romanesque church. See p.323

* **Palazzo Ducale** The palace of Mantova's Gonzaga dukes, filled with superb Renaissance art. See p.331

* **Palazzo Te** Gonzagan love-nest on the edge of Mantova, replete with vivid, bawdy frescoes. See p.336

▲ The Liston, Verona

Verona
and Mantova

L ying just east of the lakes, the elegant city of **Verona** in western Véneto and its smaller, Lombard neighbour **Mantova** – anglicized to **Mantua** – offer a civilized contrast to the hectic holiday-making of nearby Lake Garda. Replete with fine art, magnificent architecture, good food, great shopping and – in the notable shape of the summer **opera** season at Verona – high culture, too, these are compelling urban destinations in their own right.

We've yoked the two of them together here purely for convenience. Verona's **airport** is a major gateway into the lakes region (along with the city's second airport at Brescia, further west), while Mantova – perfect for an overnight excursion – lies within easy reach of Verona, Brescia and Lake Garda.

Otherwise they share little: Verona is much bigger – the second-largest city in this book – with a reputation within Italy for being a rather hardbitten working town, quite the opposite of its laid-back, romantic tourist persona. Mantova is an altogether more sedate place, known, if at all, for its delectable local culinary speciality, *tortelli alla zucca* (pumpkin ravioli).

Their history is similarly diverse, reflecting Italy's past as a patchwork of independent city states: medieval Verona's ruling family were the **Della Scala** (or **Scaligeri**), warlords and cultivated patrons of the arts who were swept aside early in the fifteenth century by the Venetian Republic, while Mantova's **Gonzaga** dynasty – equally hawkish, equally cultured – retained power for several centuries through the Renaissance. Art and architecture in the two towns are superb, but also quite different.

Verona's Roman **Arena** and medieval streets make for memorable urban roaming, while magnificent frescoes by Mantegna in Mantova's **Palazzo Ducale** and by Giulio Romano at the **Palazzo Te** are worth going far out of your way to see.

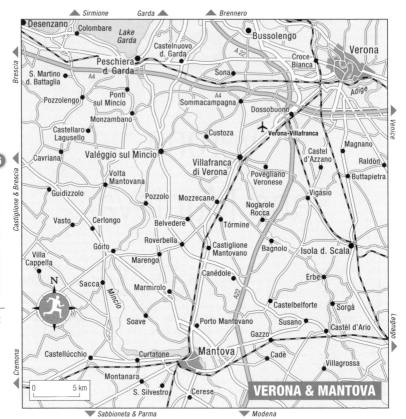

Verona

In fair Verona, where we lay our scene ...
A pair of star-crossed lovers take their life –
Do, with their death, bury their parents' strife.

Shakespeare, *Romeo and Juliet* (Prologue)

With its streets of pink-hued medieval *palazzi*, sublime Renaissance art and architecture, and a longstanding tradition of excellence in food and wine, **VERONA** is a compelling destination. It's a vivacious place, frenetic in parts but always amiable, and is not overwhelmed by the tourist industry, crucial though that is to the local economy. One of the most enjoyable dates in the city's calendar is **Carnevale**, on the Friday before Ash Wednesday: totally unlike its Venetian counterpart, this is a local event, without masks or posing – just lots of people dressing up, amid loud music and confetti.

Verona's economic success – from Roman times onwards – was largely due to its position on the River Adige where major trans-Alpine routes between Austria and central Italy crossed over key east–west roads between Milan and Venice. By the twelfth century it had become a city-state, and in the following century approached its zenith with the rise of the **Della Scala** family (also known as **Scaligeri**). Ruthless in the exercise of power, the Scaligeri were at the same time energetic patrons of the arts, and many of Verona's finest buildings date from their rule, not least the **Castelvecchio** fortress on the Adige. After the fall of the Scaligeri, Verona was governed from Venice from 1405 until the arrival of Napoleon, following which a brief period of Austrian rule was ended by the Unification of Italy in 1866.

But what places Verona squarely on the tourism map is, firstly, its role as the setting for Shakespeare's romantic tragedy *Romeo and Juliet* – doe-eyed couples gather daily at the utterly fake **Casa di Giulietta** to gaze wistfully up at its phoney love-balcony – and, secondly, the huge Roman **Arena** in the heart of the city. This magnificent amphitheatre is impressive enough empty, but every summer it is filled to capacity for a prestigious open-air **opera** festival that has spread Verona's name around the world.

Arrival, information and tours

Two **autostradas** intersect just west of Verona. The north–south A22 (Modena–Brennero) has an exit marked "Verona Nord", 3km north of the intersection. The "Verona Sud" exit lies on the east–west A4 (Milano–Venezia), 4km east of the intersection. You're allowed to drive into the historic centre (which is monitored by cameras) only if you have a booking at a hotel; otherwise, near the Arena are several paid car parks (Cittadella is closest), while parking out by the old city walls is free.

The box below has details of transport links with Verona-Villafranca **airport**; for Verona-Brescia airport, see p.245.

"Verona **Porta Nuova**" is the main **train station**, served by fast trains from Milan, Brescia and Desenzano, and slower ones from Mantova. Inside is a **tourist office** (Mon–Sat 8am–7pm, Sun 9am–3pm; ☎045.800.0861, ⓦ www .tourism.verona.it) as well as left-luggage, with the **bus station** alongside.

During the day (*feriali diurni*), **city buses** (ⓦ www.atv.verona.it) on routes #11, #12, #13 and #72 link Porta Nuova station with Piazza Brà. From 8pm to midnight (*serali*), and all day on Sundays (*festivi*), a completely different timetable operates: at these times, buses #90, #92 #96, #97 and #98 run from Porta Nuova station to Piazza Brà. Buy your ticket (€1; valid 1hr) before boarding, from the machines at bay A or the *tabacchi* in the station hall, and validate it in the machine onboard the bus. A *biglietto giornaliero* is €3.50, though you'd do better to buy a Verona Card (see box, p.313).

Verona-Villafranca airport (Valerio Catullo)

Verona's main **airport** (airport code **VRN**; ☎045.809.5666, ⓦ www.aeroportoverona.it) lies 13km southwest of the city, near the towns of **Villafranca** and **Sommacampagna** (and about 20km southeast of Lake Garda). It is named **Valerio Catullo** after the Roman poet Catullus, and is referred to by any combination of its various names. Be sure not to confuse it with "Verona-Brescia" airport, 52km west at Montichiari (see p.245).

Arrivals and departures share one terminal building. **Buses** head to **Verona**'s Porta Nuova station (daily every 20min 6.30am–11.30pm; takes 15min; €4.50; ⓦ www.aptv .it). A **taxi** (☎045.532.666) into town costs around €30. In Arrivals is a **tourist information desk** (Mon–Sat 9am–6pm; ☎045.861.9163, ⓦ www.tourism.verona.it). For journey times to major points from this and other airports, see p.20.

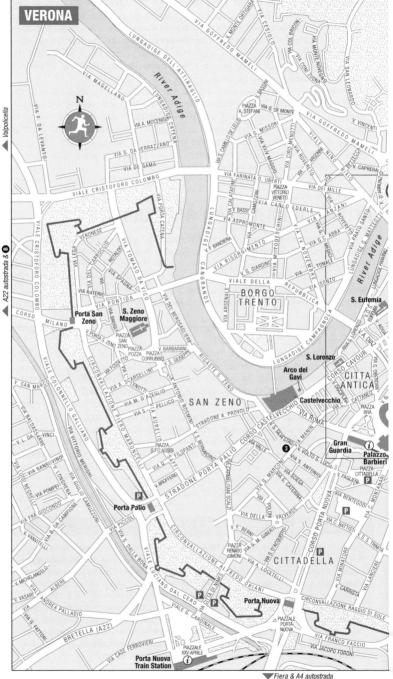

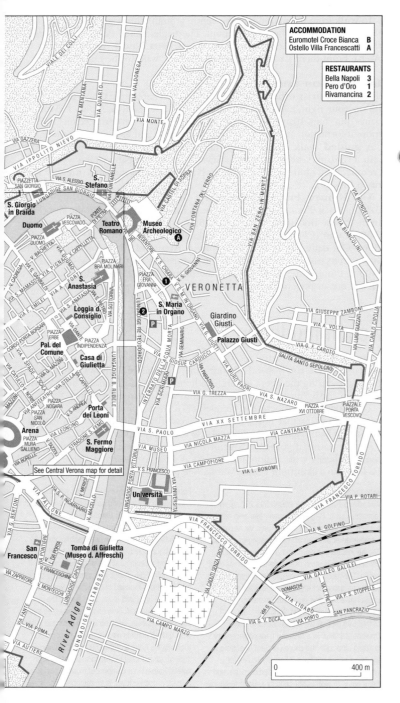

ACCOMMODATION
Euromotel Croce Bianca **B**
Ostello Villa Francescatti **A**

RESTAURANTS
Bella Napoli **3**
Pero d'Oro **1**
Rivamancina **2**

VIALE DEI COLLI

VIA VALDONEGA

VIA MENTANA

VIA QUARTO

VIA MONTE

VIA GAZZERA

VIA IPPOLITO NIEVO

PIAZZETTA
SAN GIORGIO

VIA S. ALESSIO

VIA FONTANELLE

S. Stefano

VIA CASTEL DI SOPRA

VIA FONTANA DEL FERRO

VIA BIONDELLA

VIA BIANCOLINI

LUNGADIGE SAN GIORGIO

PONTE
PIETRA

S. Giorgio in Braida

PIAZZA
VESCOVADO

Duomo

PIAZZA
DUOMO

V. BACHETTA

Teatro Romano

Museo Archeologico

A

VIA FONTANA DEL FERRO

VIA SAN ZENO IN MONTE

RETTORIE

VIA S. CHIUDA

VIA S. GIOVANNI

PIAZZA
FRA
GIOVANNI

1

V. SOTTORIVA

PIAZZA
BRA MOLINARI

V. PIGNA

VIA D. DUOMO

V. ANDREASI

VIA DIETRO DUOMO

V. S. MAMASO

VIA A. FORTI

V. S. ANASTASIA

S. Anastasia

VIA F. EMILEI

Loggia di Consiglio

S. Maria in Organo

2

P

VERONETTA

VIA GIUSEPPE ZAMBONI

VIA A. VOLTA

VIA LUIGI MAZZA

VIA CARLO CIPOLLA

Giardino Giusti

VIA G. GIUSTI

Palazzo Giusti

VIA G. F. CAROTO

SALITA SANTO SEPOLCRO

CORSO PORTA BORSARI

PIAZZA
ERBE

VIA DANTE

PIAZZA
INDIPENDENZA

Pal. del Comune

Casa di Giulietta

VIA CAPPELLO

PIAZZA
NOGARA

LUNGADIGE DI B. RUBELE

INTERRATO DELL'ACQUA MORTA

VIA SCRIMIATURA

VIA SEMINARIO

VIA MURO PADRI

VIA S. NAZARO

PIAZZA
XVI OTTOBRE

PIAZZALE
PORTA
VESCOVO

VIA G. TREZZA

VIA PARADISO

P

VIA CATULLO

VIA STELLA

VIA ANFITEATRO

V. S. ANDREA

PIAZZA
SAN
NICOLÒ

Porta dei Leoni

Arena

PIAZZA
MURA
GALLIENO

VIA LEONCINO

STRADONE S. FERMO

S. Fermo Maggiore

VIA S. PAOLO

VIA S. FERMO

VIA XX SETTEMBRE

VIA CANTARANE

VIA BORELLI

VIA NICOLA MAZZA

VIA CAMPOFIORE

VIA L. BONOMI

LUNGADIGE PORTA VITTORIA

VIA S. FRANCESCO

VIA MUSEO

Università

See Central Verona map for detail

VIA G. BERTONI

VIA S. P. INCARNARO

VIA VALLONE

VIA MACELLO

VIA MERIDI

VIA FRANCESCO TORBIDO

VIA P. ROTARI

VIA N. GOLFINO

VIA FRANCESCO TORBIDO

San Francesco

VIA G. DA PONTIERE

Tomba di Giulietta (Museo d. Affreschi)

V. FRANCESCHINE CAPULETI

VIA ZAPPATORE

V. MONTECCHI

LUNGADIGE CAPULETI

VIA FANTE

VIA POMA

VIA AUTIERE

River Adige

LUNGADIGE GALTAROSSA

VIA CADUTI SENZA CROCE TORBIDO

VIA CAMPO MARZO

VIA GALILEO GALILEI

VIALE PRETO

VIA P. S. STOPPELE

DOMASCHI

VIA LIGABO

VIA G. B.

VIA G. V. DUCA

VIA PORTO

SAN PANCRAZIO

0   400 m

309

To **walk** from the station into the centre (15min), turn right outside and cross the main roads to a busy roundabout. The triple-arched Porta Nuova gate, in the centre of the chaos, faces along Corso Porta Nuova, which leads to the Arena. From there, it's another twenty-minutes' walk to the Duomo.

Information and tours

The main **tourist office** is on Piazza Brà: as you enter from Corso Porta Nuova it's on your right, hidden in the old city walls, at Via degli Alpini 9 (Mon–Sat 9am–7pm, Sun 10am–4pm; ☎045.806.8680, ⓦwww.tourism.verona.it). Find more information at ⓦwww.veronatuttintorno.it and ⓦwww.verona.com.

A **guided walk** departs from the tourist office (daily 5.30pm, Fri–Mon also 11.30am; lasts 75min; €10). Several guide companies (ⓦwww.comune.verona.it/turismo) run bookable **private tours** on demand (roughly €100 or so for 2hr).

The **Romeo bus tour** (June–Sept Tues–Sun 10am, 11.30am, 1pm & 3.30pm; takes 90min; €15; ⓦwww.amt.it) follows a loop around the city centre from Piazza Brà, with a recorded commentary (in English). The Saturday 3.30pm tour (€20) has an English-speaking guide on board. **City Sightseeing** (June–Oct daily hourly 9am–7pm, July & Aug until 10pm; takes 60min; €15; ⓦwww.city-sightseeing.it) has an open-top bus starting from Corso Porta Nuova, though they don't go into the historic centre. For either, buy tickets on the bus or reserve through your hotel.

Accommodation

Verona's **hotels** are pretty good, though options within the historic centre – which is where you'll spend all your time – are limited. Always **book ahead**, especially during the opera season (late June to end Aug) and the huge Vinitaly wine fair (early April), when pressure on rooms is extremely tight.

The Cooperativa Albergatori Veronesi (ⓦwww.cav.vr.it) runs a free **booking service** for its partner hotels from its offices behind the Arena at Via Patuzzi 5 (Mon–Sat 9am–7pm; ☎045.800.9844, ⓦwww.veronapass.com).

An alternative, if you have your own transport, is to stay outside the city in the Valpolicella wine region; hotels such as *Villa del Quar* and *Byblos Art Hotel* lie less than 10km from central Verona (see p.324).

Expensive

Accademia Via Scala 12 ☎045.596.222, ⓦwww.accademiavr.it. Elegant, 95-room, four-star hotel housed in a *palazzo* just off the main Via Mazzini, formerly an equestrian academy dating from 1565. The atmosphere is warm, service is smooth and efficient and it is often used as a business meeting venue. The modernized interiors are lacking in old-world character, but an excellent location and comfortable facilities more than make up. ⑧

Due Torri Baglioni Piazza Sant'Anastasia 4 ☎045.595.044, ⓦwww.baglionihotels.com. Opulent grandeur in a restored thirteenth-century building alongside the church of Sant'Anastasia in the heart of the old town. All ninety rooms (of which eight are suites) are soundproofed, a/c and fitted out with eighteenth-century antique furniture.

Public areas are charming, adorned with frescoes and vaulted ceilings, and an effortless air of wealth and privilege pervades the place. ⑨

Gabbia d'Oro Corso Porta Borsari 4a ☎045.800.3060, ⓦwww.hotelgabbiadoro.it. An admirably expensive, exclusive small hotel, occupying an eighteenth-century *palazzo* just off Piazza delle Erbe. Public areas retain many original features, from exposed brick walls to wood-beamed ceilings and stone-tiled floors. The modernized guest rooms comprise nineteen suites and eight doubles, done up in rich reds and golds, with Turkish carpets and marble bathrooms. ⑨

Victoria Via Adua 8 ☎045.590.566, ⓦwww.hotelvictoria.it. One of Verona's nicer four-star hotels, housed in a complex of older buildings with a snazzy modern foyer. Well-equipped rooms are furnished in romantic style, with especially swanky superior doubles and suites. ❽

Mid-range

Antica Porta Leona Corticella Leoni 3 ☎045.595.499, ⓦ www.anticaportaleona.com. Large three-star hotel close to the Casa di Giulietta, with spacious rooms, some with balconies. Double and twin beds are available, and there are plenty of single rooms. ❺–❻

Aurora Piazza delle Erbe 2 ☎045.594.717, ⓦ www.hotelaurora.biz. Upmarket, central two-star hotel with a warm atmosphere; the staff are friendly and knowledgeable and speak good English, and many of the simple rooms (both en-suite and not) overlook the piazza. An excellent buffet breakfast and a lovely terrace above the square add to the attraction. ❹–❺

Colomba d'Oro Via Cattaneo 10 ☎045.595.300, ⓦ www.colombahotel.com. Formerly a medieval monastery, set on a quiet backstreet behind Piazza Brà, this is an elegant, good-value four-star option, with a variety of rooms displaying tasteful decor and good attention to detail. There is a small bar but no restaurant – though with the Liston just a few steps away, that's no hardship. ❻–❼

Europa Via Roma 8 ☎045.594.744, ⓦ www .veronahoteleuropa.com. Decent three-star hotel round the corner from Piazza Brà. Interiors are a bit tired and some rooms are cramped, but everything is quite serviceable and the convenience of the location makes up for minor deficiencies. Private parking. ❻

Inexpensive

Catullo Via Valerio Catullo 1 ☎045.800.2786, Ⓔⓛ locandacatullo@tiscali.it. The cheapest hotel in the centre, just off the main shopping artery of Via Mazzini, though the family who run it are not very friendly. Large rooms with shabby gentility and plenty of light, some with shared bathrooms. No

breakfast is offered, and they accept cash only in payment. ❷

Ciopeta Vicolo Teatro Filarmonica 2 ☎045.800.6843, ⓦ www.ciopeta.it. An excellent location near Piazza Brà and a family atmosphere make this one-star hotel a bargain, especially if you manage to book room 8, which has a balcony. There is a good, reasonably priced restaurant with pleasant summer terrace. All rooms have shared bathrooms. ❷

Euromotel Croce Bianca Via Bresciana 2 ☎045.890.3890, ⓦ www.euromotel.net. A great option if you're driving but don't want to worry about (or pay for) parking in the centre. Located in a residential suburb 3km west of Porta San Zeno – easily reached from the A22 autostrada, with bus links into the city – this is a cheery, family-run hotel with 67 simple rooms, all en suite with a/c. Service is outstanding: the multilingual staff fall over themselves to be helpful, suggesting excursions, providing maps, bus timetables and more. Free parking. ❸–❹

🏃 **Torcolo** Vicolo Listone 3 ☎045.800.7512, ⓦ www.hoteltorcolo.it. Nicely decorated, house-proud little two-star hotel, with comfy rooms (all en suite) and welcoming owners. With a handy location just behind Piazza Brà it's a favourite with the opera crowd, so book well ahead. ❸–❹

Hostel

Ostello Villa Francescatti (HI hostel) Salita Fontana del Ferro 15 ☎045.590.360, ⓦ www .villafrancescatti.com. Reasonable hostel 3km outside the centre, in a beautiful sixteenth-century villa behind the Teatro Romano (not the Arena!); take bus #73 (bus #91 after 8pm and on Sun) to Piazza Isolo, then walk up the hill. No reservations possible, but with 242 beds, there should be room. There's a midnight curfew, but you can arrange later admission if you've got tickets for the opera. Also does reasonably priced evening meals. The sister hostel *Santa Chiara*, at the bottom of the hill, is used as an overflow. Dorms from €17. ❶

The City

Verona's sixteenth-century Venetian walls enclose a sizeable chunk of the modern city centre. At its heart lies the city's historic core, occupying a peninsula defined by the fast-flowing River Adige. The southern limits of this central area are marked by a stretch of the earlier, fourteenth-century Scaligeri-built walls near **Piazza Brà** and the Roman **Arena**. Just to the west stands the magnificent Scaligeri castle, or **Castelvecchio**, now housing Verona's main art museum.

North of Piazza Brà, the main shopping street, **Via Mazzini**, leads to Verona's other set-piece square, elongated **Piazza delle Erbe**, site of the Roman forum and now dominated by grand medieval architecture. Further

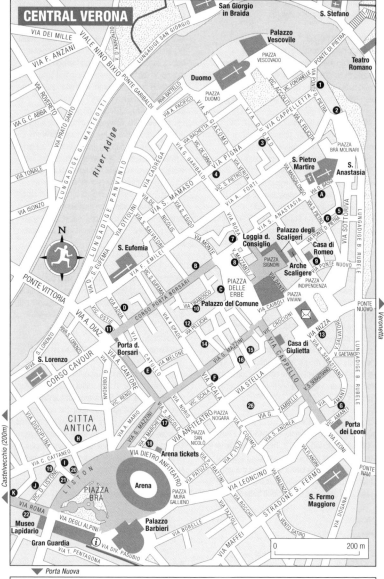

CENTRAL VERONA

VIA DEI MILLE
VIALE NINO BIXIO
VIA F. ANZANI
VIA ROVERETO
VIA G. C. ABBA
VIA PRATO SANTO
VIA TONALE
VIA ISONZO
LUNGADIGE SAN GIORGIO
PONTE GARIBALDI
LUNGADIGE G. MATTEOTTI
River Adige
LUNGADIGE PANVINIO
LUNGADIGE G. B. RE
VIA CADREGA

San Giorgio
in Braida
S. Stefano
Palazzo
Vescovile
PONTE DI PIETRA
Teatro
Romano
PIAZZA
VESCOVADO
Duomo
PIAZZA
DUOMO
VIA A. PACIFICO
VIA S. GIACOMO
VIA PONTE D. PIETRA
VIC. ACQUA
VIC. FONTANELLE
VIA CAPPELLETTA
VIA S. FELICITA
PIAZZA
BRÀ MOLINARI
S. Pietro
Martire
S. Anastasia
VIA DUOMO
VIA SOTTORIVA
VIA G. GARIBALDI
VIA RACHETTA
VIC. DE CANAL
VIA PIGNA
VIC. S. PIETRO
VIA G. MAZZINI
VIA ROSA
VIA S. ANASTASIA
VIA PONTE DI PIETRA
PIAZZA
SIGNORI
Loggia d.
Consiglio
Palazzo degli
Scaligeri
Casa di
Romeo
Arche
Scaligere
S. Eufemia
VIA F. EMILEI
VIA S. EUFEMIA
PIAZZA
DELLE
ERBE
PIAZZA
INDIPENDENZA
PIAZZA
VIVIANI
PONTE
NUOVO
Veronetta
PONTE VITTORIA
CORSO PORTA BORSARI
Palazzo del Comune
VIA CAIROLI
VIA NIZZA
Casa di
Giulietta
PONTE
NUOVO
VIA A. DIAZ
Porta d.
Borsari
S. Lorenzo
CORSO CAVOUR
VIA A. CANTORE
VIA CATULLO
VIA G. MAZZINI
VIA STELLA
VIA S. CAPPELLO
VIA S. SEBASTIANO
Porta
dei Leoni
PONTE
NAVI
CITTA
ANTICA
VIA ANFITEATRO
PIAZZA
NOGARA
VIA LEONCINO
S. Fermo
Maggiore
STRADONE S. FERMO
Arena tickets
VIA DIETRO ANFITEATRO
Arena
PIAZZA
MURA
GALLIENO
Museo
Lapidario
Gran Guardia
VIA ROMA
LISTON
PIAZZA
BRÀ
Palazzo
Barbieri
VIA DEGLI ALPINI
VIA DIV. PASUBIO
VIA T. PENTAGONA
Porta Nuova
Castelvecchio (200m)

0   200 m

The great-value **Verona Card** (ⓦwww.veronacard.it) grants free admission to every church and museum in the city and free transport on all city buses. It comes in two versions – **one day** (€8) or **three days** (€12) – and is on sale at all the museums, monuments and churches and most hotels. Where it grants free admission, we've stated "**free with VC**".

Verona's historic churches

Separately, the **Associazione Chiese Vive** (ⓦwww.chieseverona.it) looks after five historic **churches** – San Zeno, San Lorenzo, Sant'Anastasia, San Fermo and the Duomo. Normal admission to each is €2.50 (though they're all part of the Verona Card scheme), but if you don't have a Verona Card you can buy a pass at any of them granting admission to all five for €5.

north still, past the churches of **Sant'Anastasia** and the **Duomo**, and across the river, stands the impressive bowl of the **Teatro Romano**, with splendid views back over the city. Spread out around the theatre, in the **Veronetta** district, are gardens and more interesting churches. Following the riverfront promenade west from the Castelvecchio leads you to **San Zeno**, one of northern Italy's finest Romanesque churches.

If you're visiting in winter, note that on the first Sunday of the month (Oct–March only) admission to several major sights, including the Arena and Castelvecchio, is reduced to €1.

Piazza Brà

In plain view as you approach from the south, Sanmicheli's impressive **Porta Nuova** gate in the Venetian walls, dating from the 1530s but rebuilt by the Austrians in 1854, is now marooned in the centre of a huge roundabout, encircled by ceaseless flows of traffic. From here the kilometre-long Corso Porta Nuova boulevard charges northwards into the city, ending at the crenellated **Portoni della Brà**.

Just beyond these double arches the mood changes, as traffic is diverted elsewhere and promenading crowds fill the **Piazza Brà**, one of Italy's largest squares, once an outlying meadow (*braida*). Immediately to the right is the **Palazzo Gran Guardia** (1610), a fearsomely blank-featured hulk paired with the equally bombastic Neoclassical **Palazzo Barbieri** (1838) across the way, the latter now housing the municipality. These two look out onto pretty tree-shaded gardens in the centre of the square, which is lightened by the long, gently curving, extra-wide pavement – in red Valpolicella marble – of the **Liston**. This is the focus of the Veronese *passeggiata*, a line of cheek-by-jowl cafés, *gelaterie* and restaurants, all with terrace tables beneath awnings, and all open late into the evening.

At the Via Roma corner, reached through a passage beneath the arcades, is the **Museo Lapidario Maffeiano**, Piazza Brà 28 (Tues–Sat 8.30am–2.30pm, Sun 8.30am–2pm; €4.50; joint ticket with Arena €7; free with VC). Founded in 1714, this is Europe's oldest museum of stone inscriptions, with a varied collection of chiefly Etruscan, Greek and Roman work, including many funerary reliefs.

From Piazza Brà, it's a short walk west to the **Castelvecchio** museum (see p.321).

The Arena

All this serves merely to whet the appetite for Piazza Brà's landmark monument, the superbly preserved **Arena**, the third-largest amphitheatre to have survived since antiquity (after the Colosseum in Rome and the theatre at Cápua, near Naples). Its plan is elliptical, measuring 152m by 123m, and it was built in the first century AD just outside the walls of the Roman city. Earthquakes in 1117, 1118 and 1183 did little damage to the main structure, but effectively destroyed the entire outer encircling wall of the arena, all except for a three-storied section of four arches – now dubbed the "**Ala**", or wing, 31m high – which was left jutting up above the remaining walls at the northern side. With the original outer wall gone, what remains on view is a harmonious, two-storey line of arches, 72 in total, rising 20m above the square.

Inside (daily 8.30am–7.30pm; July & Aug until 5pm; last entry 1hr before closing; €6; joint ticket with Museo Lapidario €7; free with VC) – despite the three earthquakes, floods in 589 and 1239, and fire in 1172 – the Arena has survived more or less unscathed. As you walk out into the dusty pit, 73m long and 44m wide, the thought of what has gone on in this beautiful space, with its 44 tiers in white and pink marble, seating 30,000, is chilling. Aside from the Roman taste for gladiatorial combat, either man-to-man or against wild animals, the Arena has seen duels, public executions, bear-baiting and – an

Opera in Verona

From late June to the end of August, Verona is consumed by its world-famous **opera festival** (the *Stagione Lirica*, or Lyric Season). Over half a million people attend the performances which take place almost nightly in the grand open-air setting of the 15,000-seat Roman **Arena**, in the heart of the city. The festival dates back to 1913, when *Aïda* was staged to celebrate the centenary of Verdi's birth. Since then, the season has always included *Aïda*, along with three or four other, no-expense-spared extravaganzas, invariably chosen from a roster of crowd-pleasers such as *Carmen*, *Tosca*, *La Traviata*, *Nabucco*, *Turandot*, *La Bohème* and *Madame Butterfly*. The stage is vast, stretching across the whole width of the Arena at one end, dominated by colourful scenery: the centrepiece of Franco Zeffirelli's 2002 *Aïda* was a golden pyramid 34m high. The acoustics are excellent (no microphones are used), and choruses hundreds-strong, teams of horses, camels and even elephants on stage make for quite a spectacle.

Seats and prices

Seating is divided into six areas. The best seats (**poltronissime gold**) are the first thirty rows in the front centre of the stalls. One block back and to the sides counts as **poltronissime**, with the furthest blocks to rear and side classed **poltrone**. Numbered places on the first fifteen rows of the Arena's stone steps are **poltroncina numerata di gradinata**; the two blocks flanking the stage are priced lower (**poltroncina numerata di gradinata laterale**). The cheapest seats are unreserved, on the higher rows of stone steps (**gradinata**): blocks D and E are central, blocks C and F are lateral.

Expect to pay around €200 for a *poltronissima gold* seat. Each category costs roughly €20–30 less, down to around €25 for the cheapest seats. Weekend performances (Fri & Sat) cost more. People under 26 or over 60 and people in a wheelchair (plus a companion) are eligible for **discounts**.

Booking tickets

You can book online or by phone (℡045.800.5151, ✆www.arena.it), or in person any time up to the start of the performance at the **Arena Ticket Office**, Via Dietro eighteenth-century attraction – bulls fighting men and dogs. Indeed, the word "arena" derives from the Latin for sand or dust, which was sprinkled liberally after shows to soak up the blood.

By 1890, the taste for public slaughter had eased: the Veronesi packed in, instead, to enjoy the spectacle of Buffalo Bill's touring Wild West Show. Today, rock concerts aside, the Arena is best known for hosting Verona's grand summer **opera** season, the Stagione Lirica – see box below for full details. It's worth clambering to the topmost tier for the panoramic views over Verona's rooftops.

Piazza delle Erbe and around

From the north end of the Arena, the curving Liston plunges into the narrow, traffic-free **Via Mazzini**, past window-displays of Gucci, Versace, Vuitton and Cartier into the heart of Verona's shopping quarter. Several hundred metres of bookshops and wine bars, lingerie shops and pharmacies lead into Verona's second big square, the long, narrow **Piazza delle Erbe** – site of the Roman forum and still the heart of the city today. As the name suggests, the market here formerly sold vegetables, but it has nowadays been largely taken over by souvenirs, knick-knacks and fast food.

Anfiteatro 6b (on performance days 10am–9pm, on non-performance days 10am–5.45pm; rest of year Mon–Fri 9am–noon & 3.15–5.45pm, Sat 9am–noon). In addition, agents around Italy can issue tickets to personal callers – including, in the lakes region, **Brescia**: Tickets Point, Corso Zanardelli 52; **Desenzano**: Easy Lake, Via Mazzini 39; **Garda**: Lagotourist, Piazza Chiesa 20; **Lecco (Lake Como)**: Saltours, Via Volta 10; **Limone**: Limtours, Via Comboni 42; **Malcésine**: Lagotourist, Via Capitanato 2; **Mantova**: Box Office, Corso Libertà 3; **Milan**: Fnac, Via Torino.

On the night

Performances begin at 9pm (in Aug) or 9.15pm (in June & July), and – with long intervals – don't finish until well **after midnight**. Nights can get chilly; you should bring a coat or a shawl. It's a tradition for promenading crowds to fill the streets after the show, and many restaurants stay open until the small hours.

In the stalls seats, **black tie** is not out of place, with jackets and evening dress a minimum. Elsewhere, aim for relaxed **smart casual** – apart from in the cheapest seats, where nobody cares.

If you're in the *gradinata* seats, bring a **cushion** (or rent one inside the Arena; about €4) – four hours on Roman stonework is unforgiving on the *gluteus maximus*. On the higher stone steps, where seating is unreserved, it is fine to come early and bring a **picnic dinner**, but beware that glass bottles, knives and other potential weapons will be confiscated: decant your wine into plastic first. Vendors up here sell ice cream, sandwiches, beer, wine and fizzy drinks. Binoculars to see detail on the stage would be handy.

Even if it's raining, the performance is never **cancelled** before the scheduled start time. If, after a delay of up to two and a half hours, the show is called off before it's begun, you can get a refund by handing your ticket in to the Arena Ticket Office (see above for location) that evening or the following day – or by posting it within ten days (address on website). If the performance is abandoned after it has begun, no refunds will be given.

The Arena has **no cloakrooms** or left-luggage facilities. The **lost property** office is at Gate 5.

▲ Piazza delle Erbe

The buildings framing the square, though, are magnificent. As you emerge from Via Mazzini and look left into the square, at the far end rises the Baroque **Palazzo Maffei**, topped by six statues of Roman gods and goddesses and overlooked on the left by the **Torre del Gardello**, built in 1370. Lining the square's northeast side, to the right of the Palazzo Maffei, is the long **Casa Mazzanti**, its extensive sixteenth-century frescoes seen to best effect floodlit after dark. In front of it stands the **Fontana di Madonna Verona**, of the fourteenth century but incorporating an original Roman statue.

On the square's southwest side, at the corner with Via Mazzini, is the **Domus Mercatorum**, founded in 1301 as a merchants' warehouse and exchange but ruined in an 1878 restoration. The very tall houses – six or seven storeys – at this end of the square formerly comprised part of Verona's Jewish ghetto. Opposite the Domus Mercatorum, the twelfth-century **Palazzo del Comune** (or **Palazzo della Ragione**) is another unfortunate victim of restoration, now sporting a Neoclassical facade which clashes with the **Torre dei Lamberti**, looming above to 84m. Begun in 1172 though not completed until 1463, the tower is climbable (Mon–Thurs 9.30am–8.30pm, Fri–Sun 8.30am–10pm; June–Sept obligatory joint ticket with Arche Scaligere €4, or €6 if you use the lift; Oct–May tower only €2, or €3 with the lift; free with VC) – there are five steps up to the lift, which then bypasses 238 steps. The views from here are splendid, but you can carry on to higher viewpoints: another 125 steps lead to the topmost level.

Beside the Palazzo del Comune is the **Arco della Costa**, named for the whale's rib which hangs overhead. Legend says the rib will fall on the first honest person to walk beneath. It has stayed up there for more than five hundred years.

Piazza dei Signori

The Arco della Costa leads through to the **Piazza dei Signori**, quieter than its crowded neighbour. On the right (southeast) is a side of the Palazzo del Comune that escaped Neoclassical alteration: its Romanesque courtyard survives. Across the entrance to Via Dante, with its stretch of excavated Roman street, is the **Palazzo del Capitano**, while directly ahead, closing the square on its northeast side, the **Palazzo degli Scaligeri** – much restored, and now the prefecture – sports swallow-tail battlements and an incongruous sixteenth-century portal.

To its left (northwest) is a monument to more democratic times: the **Loggia del Consiglio**, Verona's finest Renaissance building, completed in 1493. This was formerly the assembly hall of the city council; its elegant decoration and simplicity of design – eight tall arches at ground level, four mullioned windows above, topped by five statues of Roman notables (including Verona's illustrious native poet, Catullus) – and the warm colouring of its marble facade do much to give this square its sense of harmony.

Arche Scaligere

Passing under the arch that links the Palazzo degli Scaligeri to the Palazzo del Capitano, you come to the little Romanesque church of Santa Maria Antica, used by the rulers of Verona in the thirteenth and fourteenth centuries, the Della Scala/Scaligeri family. In front of the church are ranged the **Arche Scaligere**, some of the most elaborate Gothic funerary monuments in Italy.

Over the side entrance to the church, a fourteenth-century equestrian statue of **Cangrande I** ("Big Dog"; died 1329) gawps down from his tomb's pyramidal roof; this is a copy, the original being displayed in the Castelvecchio (see p.322). The canopied tombs of the rest of the clan are enclosed within a wrought-iron palisade decorated with ladder motifs, the emblem of the family (*scala* means ladder). **Mastino I** ("Mastiff"; died 1277), founder of the dynasty, is buried in the simple tomb against the wall of the church; **Mastino II** (died 1351) is to the left of the entrance, opposite the most florid of the tombs, that of **Cansignorio** ("Top Dog"; died 1375). From June to September, if you hold a ticket for the Torre dei Lamberti (see opposite) you can enter the enclosure to inspect the tombs more closely.

Sant'Anastasia (see p.319) lies 200m north of the Arche Scaligere.

Casa di Giulietta (Juliet's House)

Heaven is here, where Juliet lives …

Shakespeare, *Romeo and Juliet* (III.3)

The Immortal Bard is doubtless clutching his ribs in mirth at the nonsense his poetry has inspired. Leading south from Piazza delle Erbe is Via Cappello, a busy shopping street named after the family that Shakespeare turned into the Capulets. On the left, at no. 23, stands the **Casa di Giulietta** – or, rather, an old, brick house that the municipality pressed into service in the 1930s to satisfy the demand for some visitable locations connected with *Romeo and Juliet*. There is not a shred of evidence to connect Juliet (a fictional creation), nor her family, the Cappelletti (real enough), with this or any other house.

You enter, first, a **courtyard** off the street, dominated by a much-photographed **balcony** that was freshly done up in Gothic style in 1936, to capitalize on the popularity of the "Romeo, Romeo, wherefore art thou, Romeo?" scene in a Hollywood movie of the day. It is, in short, fake – and unreachable from the ground, even for the most passionate Romeo.

Beneath the balcony stands a modern bronze **statue of Juliet**. Legend has it that if you rub Juliet's right breast you'll have a new lover within the year. Her

▲ Casa di Giulietta

gleaming bosom, and the thousands of billets-doux that are stuck and scrawled on the entrance arches and gates (graffiti is now banned within the courtyard itself), testify to the popularity of the pilgrimage here.

The **house** (Mon 1.30–7.30pm, Tues–Sun 8.30am–7.30pm; €6; joint ticket with Juliet's Tomb €7; free with VC) is a plain, much-restored fourteenth-century residence – also, once, an inn – filled out with a jumble of Shakespeariana and a Renaissance-style bed designed in 1968. The only historic items are on the top floor – a few bowls and jugs. Unless you're dedicated to standing on that balcony, save your money.

San Fermo

Via Cappello leads south into Via Leoni with its Roman gate, the **Porta dei Leoni**, and a segment of excavated Roman street, exposed 3m below today's street level. At the end of Via Leoni rises the red-brick **San Fermo** (Mon–Sat 10am–6pm, Sun 1–6pm; €2.50; joint ticket with other churches €5 – see p.313; free with VC), whose inconsistent exterior betrays the fact that it comprises two churches built on top of each other. A church had existed here – where, in 304, saints Fermo and Rustico were martyred – for centuries before the Benedictines built, from 1065 to 1143, a grand upper church for religious ceremonies and a modest lower church to house the saints' remains (which were later transferred upstairs to avoid damage from flooding). Remodelled by the Franciscans in the fourteenth century, the vast Gothic upper church, with its splendid wooden ship's-keel ceiling of 1314, has a fine fresco of the *Annunciation* by Pisanello, while the dampish Romanesque lower church features impressive vaulting and some fragmentary thirteenth-century frescoes.

From San Fermo, it's a quarter-hour's amble south to the Tomba di Giulietta (see p.323), or the same distance (750m) north to Sant'Anastasia.

To the continuing joy of Veronese tourism officials, their city is the setting for the world's greatest love story. Despite the lack of a factual basis to the tale, Verona plays on the association endlessly.

Shakespeare's version wasn't the first. That honour goes to the Vicenza author **Luigi da Porto** (1485–1529). His *La Giulietta*, written a few years before he died, was published in Venice in 1531, to great acclaim. Da Porto claimed he got the story while serving in the Venetian army, when he overheard a Veronese archer telling a tale of two doomed lovers, **Giulietta** (of the **Cappelletti** family) and **Romeo** (of the rival **Montecchi** family), who lived in Verona during the reign of Bartolomeo della Scala (1301–04). Da Porto may have been telling the truth, but the archer probably wasn't: no evidence has been found to authenticate the tale. Although it is known that both families were prominent in Verona at that time, much suggests that they were, in fact, allies rather than enemies.

Several versions appeared in the years following: it was a 1562 English translation of **Matteo Bandello's** retelling which **William Shakespeare** adapted in 1596, retaining the setting in "fair Verona" but anglicizing the family names to **Capulet** and **Montague**. But the version which ultimately brought the legend to a worldwide audience was **George Cukor's** Oscar-winning Hollywood production of 1936, starring Leslie Howard and Norma Shearer alongside stars such as John Barrymore and Basil Rathbone.

It was at this point that the Veronese authorities realized they were sitting on a goldmine. In 1936 they bought up the old house at Via Cappello 23, did it up in Gothic style, "restored" the balcony on the front, and named it the **Casa di Giulietta** – though it's not even sure that the Cappelletti set foot here. They then lit upon a medieval-Gothic house of doubtful ownership at Via delle Arche Scaligere 2: that instantly became the **Casa di Romeo** (now viewable only from the street). The following year, the city polished up an old sarcophagus in red marble at the convent of San Francesco al Corso – which had, for some time past, been co-opted as Juliet's – installed it in a specially adapted subterranean room complete with Gothic accoutrements, and named the site **Tomba di Giulietta** (Juliet's Tomb).

Thus – hey presto! – in the blink of an eye, Verona created for itself a Romeo and Juliet pilgrimage trail. Millions now come to pay homage, most completely unaware of just how loose the links are, either to historical fact or to Shakespeare's tale. Lovelorn thousands even write to Juliet (⊛ www.julietclub.com), the most plangent missives going forward for the "Dear Juliet" prize, awarded annually on St Valentine's Day. It's hard to say where fiction ends and myth begins.

Sant'Anastasia and around

Exiting Piazza delle Erbe at the northern end and turning right takes you onto Via Sant'Anastasia, which leads, in 300m, to Verona's largest church, **Sant'Anastasia** (Mon–Sat 9am–6pm, Sun 1–6pm; €2.50; joint ticket with other churches €5 – see p.313; free with VC). Started in 1290 and completed in 1481, it's mainly Gothic in style, with undertones of the Romanesque in its proportions and design. The fourteenth-century carvings of New Testament scenes around the main doors are the most arresting feature of its bare, unfinished exterior; the soaring interior, with its fifteenth-century marble floor, is spare but elegant, with most of the interior vaulting frescoed. Just inside the main doors are two holy-water stoups, known as the *gobbi*, or hunchbacks: each features a crouched figure supporting the basin on his shoulders. Among the fourteenth- and fifteenth-century artworks around the church, the main highlight is Pisanello's delicately coloured fresco of *St George and the Princess*, high above the chapel to the right of the altar. It is damaged on the left side and placed so far up it's difficult to make out – the normally martial saint appears as something of a dandy.

Out on the little Piazza Sant'Anastasia, to the left of the church's facade rises the eye-catching Gothic **tomb of Guglielmo di Castelbarco**, a podestà of Verona, built in 1320 in a style similar to that of the Arche Scaligere. To its left stands the church of **San Pietro Martire** (rarely open), deconsecrated since its ransacking by Napoleon. Numerous patches of fresco dot the walls, making for an atmospheric interior, though the highlight is the vast lunette fresco on the east wall, an allegorical account of the Assumption, featuring a bemused Madonna amid a bizarre collection of animals.

The Duomo

From Sant'Anastasia, it's a pleasant walk through quiet streets 350m north to the modest Piazza Duomo, overlooked by the red-and-white-striped **Duomo** (Mon–Sat 10am–5.30pm, Sun 1.30–5.30pm; €2.50; joint ticket with other churches €5 – see p.313; free with VC), almost at the tip of Verona's river-girt peninsula. Consecrated in 1187, the Duomo – dedicated to Santa Maria Matricolare – has a facade that is Romanesque in its lower parts, developing into Gothic as it goes up. The two doorways (under restoration at the time of writing) are twelfth-century; look for the story of Jonah and the whale on the south porch. The broad, well-lit interior, with its compound piers, has fascinating architectural details around each chapel and on the columns – particularly fine is the Cappella Mazzanti (last on the right). In the first chapel on the left, an *Assumption* by Titian occupies an architectural frame by Sansovino, who also designed the choir.

Piazza Brà is a good twenty-minute walk (1.5km) south of the Duomo, or you could take the short stroll behind the church, past the beautiful exterior wall of the apse and across Piazza Vescovado to the **Ponte Pietra**, a fixture here since Roman times. The retreating Nazis blew the bridge up on April 24, 1945, but the Veronesi retrieved every stone from the riverbed after the war and faithfully rebuilt it.

Across the river

From the northern side of the Ponte Pietra, it's a short walk left past the twelfth-century church of Santo Stefano and along the embankments to **San Giorgio in Braida** (daily 8–11am & 5–7pm), consecrated in 1447 and, in terms of its works of art, the richest of Verona's churches. The cupola was added in the sixteenth century by Sanmicheli, who also designed the unfinished bell tower. The house beside the church still sports bullet marks from fighting in 1805. Inside, a *Baptism* by Tintoretto hangs over the door, while the main altar, designed by Sanmicheli, incorporates a marvellous *Martyrdom of St George* by Veronese.

Shakespeare in Italian

The **Estate Teatrale Veronese** (ⓦwww.estateteatraleveronese.it) is a season of ballet, jazz and drama (including Shakespeare in Italian) staged chiefly at Verona's atmospheric open-air **Teatro Romano** (not the Arena) in July and August. Buy tickets at the box office in Palazzo Barbieri on Piazza Brà (entrance at Via Leoncino 61; Mon–Sat 10.30am–1pm & 4–7pm; ☎045.806.6485). Seats cost €25–30 in the stalls, €13–18 on the stone steps.

Back at the Ponte Pietra, just to the south stands the first-century-BC **Teatro Romano** (Mon 1.30–7.30pm, Tues–Sun 8.30am–7.30pm; €4.50; free with VC), much restored and now used for concerts and plays. High above it, reached by lift, the **Museo Archeologico** (same hours & ticket) occupies the buildings of an old convent. Its well-arranged collection features a number of Greek, Roman and Etruscan finds, including a magnificent Roman bronze head. From the frescoed chapel at the top the views across Verona are magnificent.

Back down at river level a short way southeast of the Roman theatre is one of the treats of the city – the church of **Santa Maria in Organo** (daily 8am–noon & 2.30–6pm; free), which possesses what Vasari praised as the finest choir stall in Italy. Dating from the 1490s, this marquetry was the work of a Benedictine monk, one Fra Giovanni, and is astonishing in its precision in depicting animals and use of perspective. There's more of his work in the sacristy, while in the crypt you can see reused upside-down Roman columns.

Further south on the same street are the finest formal gardens in Verona, the Renaissance **Giardino Giusti** (daily 9am–8pm; Oct–March closes 5pm; €5), full of fountains and shady corners. It's a short walk from here on Via Carducci down to the Ponte Nuovo and the city centre.

Piazza delle Erbe to Castelvecchio

From the northern side of Piazza delle Erbe, instead of turning right to Sant'Anastasia, if you turn left you enter **Corso Porta Bórsari**, a long, straight, pedestrianized street of fine *palazzi*, built over the Roman *decumanus maximus*. At its southern end – also reached from Piazza Brà on Via Oberdan – stands another of Verona's impressive Roman remnants, the **Porta dei Bórsari**, a gateway that was as great an influence on the city's Renaissance architects as the Arena. Now reduced to a monumental screen straddling the road, it used to be Verona's largest Roman gate; the inscription dates it at 265 AD, but it's almost certainly older than that.

Corso Cavour – a busy traffic street – continues southwest beyond the gateway. Some 200m along is the beautiful twelfth-century church of **San Lorenzo** (Mon–Sat 10am–6pm, Sun 1–6pm; €2.50; joint ticket with other churches €5 – see p.313; free with VC), reached beneath an archway. The lofty interior, in stripes of brick and tufa, is striking, and the church has two towers flanking the facade which hold spiral staircases up to the women's galleries.

Another 250m along Corso Cavour you come to the **Arco dei Gavi**, a first-century Roman triumphal arch that was rebuilt in 1930 after Napoleon's troops tore down the original. This is the best vantage point from which to admire the **Ponte Scaligero**, a fortified bridge with distinctive swallow-tail battlements built by Cangrande II between 1355 and 1375 as a rat-run from the Castelvecchio, at a time when the Della Scala were losing the loyalty of the Veronesi. Like the Ponte Pietra, it survived until 1945, when the retreating Nazis blew it up – but, again, the stones were recovered from the riverbed and the bridge rebuilt. The stretch of shingle on the opposite bank is a popular spot for picnicking and sunbathing.

Castelvecchio

The fortress from which the Ponte Scaligero springs is the **Castelvecchio** (Mon 1.30–7.30pm, Tues–Sun 8.30am–7.30pm; €6; free with VC), also reached on a short walk down Via Roma from Piazza Brà. The building was commissioned by Cangrande II in 1354 and became the stronghold for Verona's subsequent rulers, incorporating part of the city walls along with substantial towers and fortifications.

The castle now holds the civic art museum, whose collection fills a labyrinth of chambers, courtyards and passages that is fascinating to explore in itself. Audioguides (€4) are available at the ticket desk.

Ground floor: rooms 1 to 5

The first set of rooms is devoted to **sculpture**, mostly by unknown artists of the Middle Ages. Room 1 has a twelfth-century sarcophagus showing the graphic martyrdom of saints Sergius (decapitated) and Bacchus (clubbed to death), juxtaposed with a display case holding six pretty little medieval spoons. A fine fourteenth-century St Catherine (room 2) and doleful St Libera (room 3) lead on to two violent, shocking pieces facing each other in **room 4**: a swooning Virgin, full of misery, and a screaming Christ opposite, eyes rolling in agony. The Renaissance panels in room 5 are limp by comparison.

First floor: rooms 6 to 12

The tour continues across the courtyard. Room 6 is the **dungeon** of the Torre del Mastio, now housing various ancient bells. Climb the 33 steps here to enter the residential west wing, known as the Reggia, and turn left for **room 7**, where the frescoes include a flat, Gothic *Nursing Madonna* beside a perspectival, Giotto-esque *Madonna Enthroned*. Giotto himself is reported to have visited Verona in the 1310s.

Room 10 is full of Gothic art, including a beautiful, mystical *Madonna of the Rose Garden* attributed to Stefano da Verona and the ethereal *Madonna of the Quail* by Pisanello. **Jacopo Bellini**'s naturalistic *St Jerome* shows the saint praying in the desert amidst sharp-edged rocks, in Gothic-cum-Cubist style; room 11 – the elongated **Hall of the Reggia** – is dominated by his austere *Crucifixion*, a stark, introspective work.

Room 12, at the back of the hall, holds several Flemish works, including a *Portrait of a Woman* – thought to be the daughter of Philip II of Spain – painted by **Rubens** in Mantova in 1602.

Second floor: rooms 13 to 19

From the hall, climb the 31 steps then double-back and go through the doorway on the right for the Venetian painting of **room 13**. Here, **Giovanni Bellini**'s *Madonna and Child* (1470) is displayed alongside a similar work by his studio assistant; one is wooden and predictable, the other is complex and alive, most notably in the central composition of Mary's crossed hands overlaid by the child's. **Room 14** holds Francesco Morone's *St Bartholomew* in, unusually, bright yellow against a black background.

Head now for small **room 18** at the rear, where hangs **Mantegna**'s superb *Holy Family* (1459), a tight cluster of four classical faces, Jesus as Dionysius, Joseph as an Old Testament prophet. Beside is Mantegna's Piero della Francesca-like *Risen Christ*. Jesus holds a flag of St George, while beneath lurk a sinister cross-eyed Roman soldier and his goitrous pal.

Room 19 holds a collection of **armour and weaponry**; from here, you can walk along the castle walls above the river. At the end, strikingly displayed on a raised plinth, is the equestrian figure of **Cangrande I**, removed from his tomb (see p.317); his expression is disconcerting at close range, a simpleton's grin being difficult to reconcile with the image of the ruthless warlord.

First floor: rooms 20 to 25

Continue down a few steps to **room 20** and a *Passion* by Paolo Morando (known as Il Cavazzola), showing Verona in the background, alongside two portraits by Giovanni Francesco Caroto – a beaming boy holding up a drawing of a stick man (one of the few depictions in medieval painting of a child's work) and, in a rather more sombre vein, a Benedictine novice. Among the showy altarpieces in **room 21**, Caroto's simple, emotional *Pietà* stands out; opposite is an unflattering portrait of Savonarola by the Brescian artist Moretto, showing him as a shifty old sourpuss.

Rooms 22 and 23, with works by **Tintoretto** and a notable *Deposition* by **Veronese**, lead on to a *Portrait of a Man* in **room 24** by the local artist Marcantonio Bassetti (1626), full of insight for the subject's mortality. Room 25 has more seventeenth-century works, including a dark, tumultuous *Expulsion from Eden* by **Bernardo Strozzi**, full of vigorous movement on a sharp diagonal composition.

Stairs lead down to the bookshop and exit.

San Zeno Maggiore

Around 1km northwest of the Castelvecchio – best approached by a pleasant riverside walk (15min) – is the church of **San Zeno Maggiore** (Mon–Sat 8.30am–6pm, Sun 1–6pm; €2.50; joint ticket with other churches €5 – see p.313; free with VC), one of the most significant Romanesque churches in northern Italy and well worth the extra effort to reach.

A church was founded here, above the tomb of Verona's patron saint, as early as the fifth century, but the present building and its campanile were put up in the twelfth century, with additions continuing up to the late fourteenth. Its large **rose window**, depicting the Wheel of Fortune, dates from the early twelfth century, as does the magnificent **portal**, whose lintels bear relief sculptures representing the months – look also for St Zeno trampling the devil. The reliefs to the side of the portal (from the same period) show scenes from the Old Testament on the right and New Testament on the left – except for the bottom two on both sides, devoted to the life of Theodoric. Bronze panels on the doors depict scenes from the Bible and the *Miracles of San Zeno*, their style influenced by Byzantine art; most on the left are from around 1100, most on the right from a century later.

Areas of the lofty and simple **interior** are covered with beautiful frescoes, some superimposed on earlier works, others defaced by ancient graffiti. Diverting though these are, the most compelling image in the church is the high altar's luminous *Madonna and Saints* by Mantegna.

Juliet's Tomb and the Fresco Museum

Roughly 700m southeast of Piazza Brà stands the picturesque ex-Capuchin monastery of San Francesco al Corso, another station on Verona's contrived Juliet pilgrimage trail for its **Tomba di Giulietta** (Juliet's Tomb), with a worthwhile museum of frescoes (**Museo degli Affreschi**) attached. See the box on p.319 for some background.

From the busy road Via Pontiere, duck into a quiet, shaded garden – adorned with a bust of Shakespeare – to approach the old convent (Mon 1.45–7.30pm, Tues–Sun 8.30am–7.30pm; €4.50; joint ticket with Juliet's House €7; free with VC). At the top of the stairs, among the frescoes, are two of the **museum**'s outstanding works – sculptures in marble by the nineteenth-century artist Torquato della Torre: *L'Orgia* shows a reclining nude, radiating post-coital bliss, while *Gaddo* is so lifelike that critics accused della Torre of not sculpting the work but casting it from a living model. Downstairs, the church is now a gallery for large Renaissance and Baroque altarpieces, including a beautiful Mannerist

On the northwestern outskirts of Verona rise the fertile hills of the **Valpolicella** region. The red wines produced here – including Valpolicella itself, Recioto and Amarone – are some of Italy's most famous vintages, exported worldwide. These are not classic landscapes – Valpolicella is a hardworking region of large vineyards and neat, wealthy villages, hemmed in by high valleys – but taking a day or so to draw breath among the vines, cherry trees and olive groves can make for a memorable diversion.

Driving from Verona, follow the SS12 northwest to Parona, from where the minor SP4 road meanders into the heart of the Valpolicella. **Bus** #3 (ⓦ www.aptv.it) runs regularly along the SP4 between Verona (Porta Nuova station) and Domegliara, stopping at every village.

It's around half an hour (15km) to the modest town of **SAN PIETRO IN CARIANO**, where you'll find a **tourist office** on the main road, Via Ingelheim 7 (Mon–Fri 9.30am–1pm & 1.30–5.30pm, Sat 9am–1pm; ⓣ045.770.1920, ⓦ www.valpolicellaweb.it). The **Pieve di San Floriano**, just to the east, is one of the region's most significant Roman-esque churches, or you could head west to the town of **SANT'AMBROGIO DI VALPOLICELLA**, above which – reached by a series of hairpin climbs – stands the beautiful Romanesque **Pieve di San Giorgio**, part of which has been dated to 712 AD. Several walks in the area follow old tracks, including a 3km circular route from **Gargagnano** village dubbed "Percorso delle Quattro Fontane" that passes four restored medieval fountains. From Sant'Ambrogio, it's only a half-hour's drive west through the hills – past **Affi**, a junction on the A22 autostrada – to reach Garda (see p.275) on the shores of Lake Garda.

Signposted near San Giorgio is the charming old *Trattoria Cadelapela* (ⓣ045.680.0245; closed Tues), a great little spot for hearty local cuisine and good wine. Otherwise, in **SAN ROCCO** above San Floriano, aim for *Antica Osteria della Valpolicella* (ⓣ045.775.5010, ⓦ www.anticaosteriavalpolicella.com; closed Mon), serving innovative, midpriced woodland cuisine flavoured with local truffles, nuts and pickles. Close by, near **NEGRAR**, stands the lovely *Locanda '800* (ⓣ045.600.0133, ⓦ www.locanda800.it), a family-run winery with a sleek, highly rated restaurant and four beautifully rustic rooms upstairs (ⓞ).

Alternatively, you could push the boat out at one of the area's luxurious villa hotels. Outside **PEDEMONTE**, *Hotel Villa del Quar* (ⓣ045.680.0681, ⓦ www.hotelvilladel quar.it; ⓞ) occupies a sixteenth-century mansion on an estate producing its own wines; stay in the opulent rooms or book ahead for a table at the two-Michelin-starred *Arquade* restaurant. Close by at **CORRUBIO**, the *Byblos Art Hotel Villa Amistà* (ⓣ045.685.5555, ⓦ www.byblosarthotel.com; ⓞ) represents a complete change: behind its grand, fifteenth-century facade, beautifully restored interiors host outlandish contemporary artworks by the likes of Sol LeWitt, Anish Kapoor and Cindy Sherman. Stroll the grounds with a glass of wine or sample expensive contemporary Italian cuisine at the hotel's chic *Atelier* restaurant.

Many wine estates welcome individuals for **tastings and purchases**; always phone ahead to check opening times. Here's a handful of traditional producers (tourist offices have complete lists): **Accordini** (ⓣ045.770.1985, ⓦ www.accordini .it); **Gamba** (ⓣ045.680.1714, ⓦ www.vini-gamba.it); **Manara** (ⓣ045.770.1086, ⓦ www.maranavini.it); **Recchia** (ⓣ045.750.0584, ⓦ www.recchiavini.it); **San Rustico** (ⓣ045.770.3348, ⓦ www.sanrustico.it).

Archangels by Francesco Caroto and four lusciously coloured semicircular panels by Louis Dorigny. You emerge into the cloister, and follow directions down to the **Tomba di Giulietta**, nothing more than an old sarcophagus, long touted as Juliet's (even though she was a fictional creation), which was installed in this Gothified cellar in 1937.

Eating, drinking and entertainment

One of Verona's great attractions is **eating**: the city takes its food (and wine) seriously, and there are dozens of *osterie* – small, local tavern-like restaurants, almost always excellent – as well as any number of more aristocratic places to eat. The best places are often packed after 9pm, so it's a good idea to either book ahead or eat early; the Veronesi take their time over an evening out, enjoying lengthy pre-dinner drinks.

With the renowned **wine** regions of Valpolicella and Soave on the city's doorstep, not to mention nearby Bardolino and Lugana, almost everywhere serves fine wines – often small amounts in large glasses to release the bouquet. Wine lists can be bafflingly long; if you're in any doubt, order the house wine – frequently a Valpolicella (red) or Soave (white) of some character.

All the main squares have terrace **cafés** and *gelaterie*, with several good places on both Piazza Brà and Piazza delle Erbe. After dark, Piazza San Zeno, out to the west, comes alive with people crowding the nearby cafés and **bars**.

In the week before and after the opera season you may find places close early or shut completely as the city takes a rest. Watch out, too, for the huge Vinitaly wine fair, held every April, when restaurants and wine bars are packed.

Cafés and light meals

Al Ponte Via Ponte Pietra. Sip a glass of wine in the quiet terrace garden while enjoying a splendid view across the river. Stays open as a bar into the small hours. Closed Wed.

Balu Corso Porta Bórsari 57. Verona's best ice cream, just inside the Roman gate. Takeaway only. Closed Mon.

Cappa Piazza Brà Molinari 1a ⊛ www.cappacafe.it. Amiable riverside café in business for forty years, with vaguely Eastern trappings, sofas and floor cushions, a pleasant river-view terrace and live jazz on Sun. Daily till 2am.

Coloniale Piazza Viviani 14c. Best hot chocolate in the city, and good snacks too, in a mock-colonial café setting. Open till midnight. Sept–June closed Mon.

Libreria Via Sant'Anastasia 7. Pleasant little café-bar inside the Libreria Gheduzzi bookshop off Piazza delle Erbe – a real haven from the crowds, and a perfect place to stop with the newspaper for a coffee, fresh-squeezed juice or light meal. The shop stocks English books. Open long hours (Mon–Sat 9am–midnight, Sun 10am–8pm).

Mazzanti Piazza delle Erbe 32. The least touristy of the cafés on this square – also open late as a lively bar. Closed Mon.

Savoia Via Roma 1b. Another favourite *gelateria*, a fixture since 1939 under the arcades just off Piazza Brà – ice cream and *semifreddi* made fresh daily by hand.

Restaurants and wine bars

Expensive

Accademia Via Scala 10 ☎ 045.800.6072, ⊛ www.ristoranteaccademia.com. One of Verona's best addresses, a cool, top-class restaurant renowned especially for its fish and seafood: signature dishes include succulent turbot. *Menù* from €50. Sept–June closed Sun.

Dodici Apostoli Corticella San Marco 3 ☎ 045.596.999, ⊛ www.12apostoli.it. Named after a group of twelve Piazza delle Erbe merchants who used to dine here in the 1750s, this is an atmospheric place to sample Roman- and Renaissance-style cuisine in an old-fashioned setting of tiled floors and frescoed walls. The visitors'

book reads like a *glitterati* history: Bergman, Callas, Garbo, Olivier, Fellini, Mastroianni and others have eaten here; expect a bill to match. Closed Sun eve & Mon, plus two weeks in June/July.

Tre Corone ("Giovanni Rana") Piazza Brà 16 ☎ 045.800.2462, ⊛ www.trattoriagiovannirana.it. Perhaps Verona's most celebrated trattoria, perfectly placed on the Liston opposite the Arena. Giovanni Rana is one of Italy's leading pasta brands, but, that aside, this is a charming, sophisticated place to enjoy excellent Veronese cooking. When the opera's not on, they keep traditional hours. During the opera season, they stay open until 2.30am and present three menus: *Pre-opera* (served until 9pm) and *Dopo Opera* (served from midnight), with a rather more expansive *Tradizionale* menu in between. Expect no less than €50 per head, possibly much more. Closed Mon; Sept–June also closed Sun eve.

Tre Marchetti ("Da Barca") Vicolo Tre Marchetti 19b ☏045.803.0463. Cosy little trattoria a couple of steps north of the Arena, with a classy ambience and a tasteful, old-fashioned interior featuring starched tablecloths and bowtied waiters. The perfect spot for a pre- or post-opera dish of Veronese specialities, but be sure to book. Try the *baccalà alla Vicentina con polenta* (wind-dried cod) or the *fegato di vitello alla Veneziana* (calves' liver) – or classic local *primi* such as *fettucine porcini e tartufo*, with truffles from nearby Lessinia. You might get away with €30, but a bill is more likely to be €50-plus. Closed Sun.

Mid-range

Alla Colonna Largo Pescheria Vecchia 4 ☏045.596.718. Simple but good food and a lively atmosphere in this packed hostelry – much favoured by extended Veronese families out for a slap-up meal. The prices are attractive too (*menù* around €20). Open till 2am. Closed Sun.

🏃 **Bottega dei Vini (aka Antica Bottega del Vino)** Vicolo Scudo di Francia 3a ☏045.800.4535, ⓦwww.bottegavini.it. Illustrious, much-loved wine bar and restaurant, just off Via Mazzini, with a long list of dishes, from fragrant *primi* such as *gnocchetti verdi al pecorino e timo* (spinach gnocchi with sheep's cheese and thyme) or *bigoli con anatra* (thick spaghetti with roast duck) to succulent steaks – horse or Florentine beef. The interior is cosy and always busy with diners or chatty drinkers, and the wine list is one of the longest you'll find in Verona. Open until midnight (3–4am during Vinitaly and the opera). Expect around €35–40. Closed Tues.

Cantina di San Rocchetto Via San Rocchetto 11 ☏045.801.3695. Lively restaurant-cum-wine-bar just off Via Mazzini – perfect for good food, wine and conversation, with tables set out on the (pedestrianized) street in spring and summer. *Primi* are €11–14, *secondi* €18–20 (including such delights as Veronese tripe). The informal *hostaria* section is open 5.30pm–midnight, the downstairs restaurant 7–10.30pm. Closed Mon.

🏃 **Enoteca Cangrande** Via Dietro Listone 19d ☏045.595.022. Attractive, candle-lit wine bar behind Piazza Brà offering a selection of foodie delights – salamis, cheeses, caviar – to accompany its fine wines. Service (which is English-speaking) and quality of fare are highly recommended. Worth booking for a post-opera nosh. No closing day.

Greppia Vicolo Samaritana 3 ☏045.800.4577, ⓦwww.ristorantegreppia.com. Small family-run trattoria near the Piazza delle Erbe that has an excellent reputation and prices around €25–35 a head. Don't be put off by the unprepossessing exterior – inside are columns and vaulted ceilings, and the food and service are superb. Closed Mon.

Osteria alla Pigna Via Pigna 4 ☏045.800.8040, ⓦwww.osteriapigna.it. Elegant, traditional and moderately priced restaurant near the Duomo, where you're given a glass of prosecco to start your meal. The menu includes all the classic Veronese dishes: this is one of the more appealing *osterie* in the city centre. Closed Sun, Mon lunch.

Osteria Le Vecete Via Pelliciai 32a ☏045.594.748, ⓦwww.grupporialto.it. Atmospheric *osteria* a few steps off Piazza delle Erbe that does good food and excellent wines. Crowd in at its wood tables or let the expert (English-speaking) barman recommend some gems from the superb range of local wines. Don't be afraid to check the price on the blackboard behind him: the wines range from cheap to very expensive. The small list of gourmet dishes – including their trademark savoury tartlets – ranges either side of €12.

Inexpensive

Al Carro Armato Vicolo Gatto 2a. One of Verona's most atmospheric old *osterie*, on a narrow street behind Sant'Anastasia, with stone floors, barred windows, lanterns and wooden benches. The menu is small – local-style dishes, very affordable – washed down by excellent wines. Staff are friendly and there's occasional live music on Sun. Open as a bar until midnight or later. Closed Mon.

Bacaro dell'Arena (Pizzeria da Sergio) Vicolo Tre Marchetti 16. Large, canteen-like pizzeria, well located a short walk from Piazza Brà. There's no nameboard: recognize it by the Arena sign overhead. Great for straightforward meals and late-night bites (till 11pm). Closed Mon.

Bella Napoli Via Marconi 14. Great pizzas – the largest in Verona – served in a distinctly Neapolitan atmosphere. Daily till 1am.

Brek Piazza Brà 20 ⓦwww.brek.com. Convenient branch of this national chain of budget-priced self-service restaurants, serving soup and salad, simple hot meals and good desserts for around €10, without the fuss of waiters and menus. No closing day.

🏃 **Osteria al Duomo** Via Duomo 7a. Wonderful, old-fashioned *osteria-bar*, impervious to changing fashion, and enlivened on summer Wednesdays (5–8pm) by live music.

There's a small, inexpensive menu of decent local favourites, including traditional dishes like *bigoli con asino* (thick spaghetti in a bolognese-style sauce of chopped donkey-meat). Open 4pm–midnight. Closed Sun.

Osteria Sottoriva Via Sottoriva 9. Verona's traditional *osterie* don't come much more authentic than this place – rumbustious and full of locals, in a charming residential district near the river. Sit out under the arcades and enjoy a delicious lunch or dinner amid the banter. Closed Wed.

Pero d'Oro Via Ponte Pignolo 25 ☏ 045.594.645. Friendly, family-run trattoria, serving well-priced, authentic Veronese food across the river in Veronetta. *Menù* €18. Closed Mon.

Rivamancina Vicolo Quadrelli 1. Popular late-opening Veronetta bar across the Porta Nuovo bridge that does pasta dishes too. Open till 2am. Closed Sun.

Mantova (Mantua)

Aldous Huxley called it the most romantic city in the world. With a skyline of domes and towers rising above its three encircling lakes, **MANTOVA** (anglicized to **Mantua**) is undeniably evocative. Birthplace of the Roman poet Virgil, this is where Romeo heard of Juliet's supposed death, and where Verdi set *Rigoletto*. Its history is one of equally operatic plots, most of them acted out by the **Gonzaga**, one of Renaissance Italy's richest and most powerful families, who ruled the town for three centuries. Its cobbled squares retain a medieval aspect, and there are two splendid palaces, both of them worth travelling far to see: the **Palazzo Ducale**, containing Mantegna's stunning fresco of the Gonzaga family and court, and **Palazzo Te**, whose frescoes by the flashy Mannerist Giulio Romano have entertained and outraged generations of visitors with their combination of steamy erotica and illusionistic fantasy.

Mantova, for all its attractions, feels like a different world from the lakes. We've included it here as a rewarding one- or two-day addition to an itinerary centred on Verona or Lake Garda: it is easily reached from both of them – and, in many ways, is more alluring than either.

Arrival, information and accommodation

From Verona, it's an easy **drive** south on the A22 autostrada for 30km to the Mantova Nord exit. Mantova also lies on the SS249 road 36km south of Peschiera (via Valeggio; see p.273) and the SS236 road southeast of Desenzano (47km) and Brescia (66km). The **train station** – with good service from Verona, less good from Milano Centrale and Cremona – and nearby **bus station** are a ten-minute walk west of the centre. (Note that buses from Verona drop off first in the more convenient Piazza Sordello.)

Mantova is compact enough to cover **on foot**: even the walk south to Palazzo Te is only twenty minutes. **Bus #1** ("Circolare"; ⓦ www.apam.it) runs frequently from the train and bus stations on a clockwise route east via Piazza d'Arco to the central squares, then south on Corso Garibaldi, west on Viale Risorgimento (stopping near Palazzo Te) and north on Viale Piave back to the train station. Tickets cost €1 (24hr *biglietto giornaliero* €1.90), buyable from *tabacchi*.

Mantova is perfect bike country and has numerous signed **cycle** routes, from a gentle circuit of the lakes (14km) to a six-hour ride up the wooded River

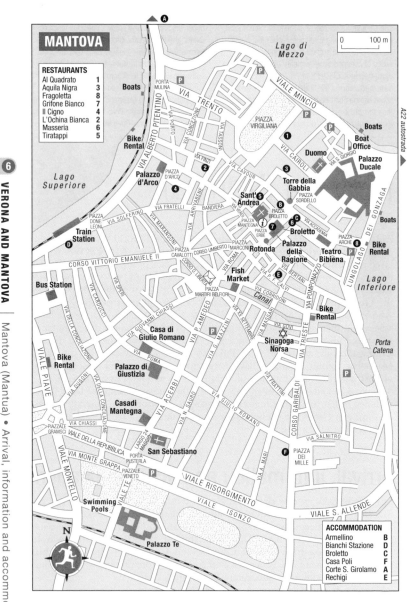

MANTOVA

RESTAURANTS

Al Quadrato	1
Aquila Nigra	3
Fragoletta	8
Grifone Bianco	7
Il Cigno	4
L'Ochina Bianca	2
Masseria	6
Tiratappi	5

ACCOMMODATION

Armellino	B
Bianchi Stazione	D
Broletto	C
Casa Poli	F
Corte S. Girolamo	A
Rechigi	E

Mincio to Peschiera del Garda (43km). You can **rent bikes** (around €9 a day) from Mantua Bike, Viale Piave 22b (℡0376.220.909), and La Rigola on Via Trieste (℡0376.366.677).

The well-organized **tourist office** is at Piazza Mantegna 6 (daily 9.30am–6.30pm; ℡0376.432.432, ⓦwww.turismo.mantova.it).

Hotels

Armellino Via Cavour 67 ☎346.314.8060,
🌐www.bebarmellino.it. Superior B&B with two
attractively furnished double rooms (not en suite)
and a large suite in an eighteenth-century palace
right in the centre of town. There's a pretty garden
for drinks, and breakfast is served in the period
dining room. No credit cards. ❸

Bianchi Stazione Piazza Don Leoni 24
☎0376.326.465, 🌐www.albergobianchi.com.
A pleasant, family-run hotel by the train station
with comfortable rooms and small suites arranged
around an attractive garden. ❹

Broletto Via Accademia 1 ☎0376.326.784,
🌐www.hotelbroletto.com. Small three-star family-
run hotel in the historic centre. Service is cheery
and rooms are adequate (all en suite, with a/c), if a
bit small. ❹

Casa Poli Corso Garibaldi 32 ☎0376.288.170,
🌐www.hotelcasapoli.it. Pristine four-star boutique
hotel on a main road roughly 10min walk south of
the centre. Rooms are done up in a chic, minimalist
style, all wood floors and crisp cotton, aided by
flat-screen TVs and hi-tech accoutrements. The
location is not ideal but they offer good weekend
discounts. ❼

Corte San Girolamo Via San Girolamo 1,
Gambarara ☎0376.391.018, 🌐www.agriturismo
-sangirolamo.it. Occupying a renovated watermill
3km north of town on the cycle route from Mantova
to Lake Garda, this serene agriturismo has en-suite
doubles plus a four-person apartment. Bicycles
available. ❸

Rechigi Via Calvi 30 ☎0376.320.781,
🌐www.rechigi.com. Top-class four-star
hotel in the historic centre. The lobby is a little off-
putting – all gleaming marble and white sofas, with
contemporary art dotted about – but the rooms are
calmer: fresh and modern but decorated with taste.
Excellent service. Private parking. ❻–❼

The City

The centre of Mantova is made up of four attractive squares, each connected to
the next. Lively Piazza Mantegna is overlooked by the massive **Sant'Andrea**
church. Beside it is the lovely **Piazza Erbe**, with fine arcades facing the
medieval **Rotonda** church. To the north, through medieval passageways and
across Piazza Broletto, the long, cobbled slope of Piazza Sordello is dominated
by the **Palazzo Ducale**, the fortress and residence of the Gonzaga, packed with
Renaissance art.

Mantova's other great palace stands in its own gardens 1.5km south of the
historic centre – **Palazzo Te**, adorned with sensational frescoes.

Sant'Andrea

Dominating **Piazza Mantegna** – a wedge-shaped open space at the end of the
arcaded shopping thoroughfares of Corso Umberto and Via Roma – is the
facade of Leon Battista Alberti's church of **Sant'Andrea**, an unfinished basilica
that says a lot about the ego of Lodovico II Gonzaga, who commissioned it in
1470. He felt that the existing medieval church was neither impressive enough
to represent the splendour of his state nor large enough to hold the droves of
people who packed in every Ascension Day to see the holy relic of Christ's
blood which had been found on the site. Lodovico brought in the court
architect, Luca Fancelli, to oversee Alberti's plans. There was a bitchy rivalry
between the two, and when, on one of his many visits, Alberti fell and hurt a
testicle, Fancelli gleefully told him: "God lets men punish themselves in the
place where they sin." Work started in earnest after Alberti's death in 1472, and
took more than two decades to complete.

The Classical facade is focused on an immense triumphal arch supported on
giant pilasters. **Inside** (daily 8am–noon & 3–7pm), the vast, column-free space
is roofed with one immense barrel vault, echoing the facade. The octagonal
balustrade at the crossing stands above the crypt where the holy relic is kept in
two vases, copies of originals designed by Cellini and stolen by the Austrians in

The Jews of Mantova

Jewish settlement in Mantova is recorded as early as 1145. Under the Gonzaga Jews flocked to the city, chiefly from Rome and Germany: the Church had banned Christians from finance, so Jews (who were barred from politics) took on banking and money-lending to the Gonzaga court. By the mid-sixteenth century, two thousand – or over seven percent – of Mantova's population were Jewish. The community produced several notables in the fields of theatre, music, medicine and printing. Later, as in Venice, where the first Jewish ghetto was created in 1516, in Mantova Jews were enclosed within gates and forced to wear a yellow marker on their clothes. Even after emancipation in 1798, Jews remained in the area of the former ghetto, only being forced out around 1900 by the destruction of what was deemed unsanitary housing. Most moved to Milan, many who remained were deported to death camps during World War II, and the community today numbers about seventy.

It is possible to trace the remnants of a Jewish presence in Mantova. Behind the Rotonda, the corner of Piazza Concordia and Via Spagnoli – renamed from **Via degli Orefici Ebrei** (Street of the Jewish Goldsmiths) – marks the re-used site of three adjacent synagogues. The huge **Banca d'Italia** on Via Castiglioni replaced what was the heart of the ghetto, while the **Hotel Rechigi** on Via Scuola Grande is built on the site of the Grand Synagogue, demolished in 1938. A stroll away, at Via Bertani 54, offices now occupy the tall, seventeenth-century **Casa del Rabbino** (House of the Rabbi), its facade decorated with stucco. Where Via Bertani meets Via Pomponazzo, you can see the hinges of the gates that were closed nightly, sealing off the ghetto. A short walk south, behind an anonymous facade at Via Govi 13, is the **Sinagoga Norsa**, the only one of Mantova's six synagogues to have survived: it was removed from its original location on Via Scuola Grande in 1904 and reassembled here. The interior, with its eighteenth-century fittings, is complete and is still used. It can be visited (Mon–Fri 8.30–11.30am) – but ask the tourist office to call ahead for you first.

1846; to see them, ask the sacristan. The painter Mantegna is buried in the first chapel on the left, his tomb topped with a bust of the artist that is said to be a self-portrait. The wall-paintings in the chapel were designed by Mantegna and executed by students, one of whom was Correggio.

Piazza Erbe and around

Beside Sant'Andrea, Piazza Mantegna gives way to **Piazza Erbe**, the town's most distinctive square, with a small daily market and cafés and restaurants sheltering in the arcades below the thirteenth-century **Palazzo della Ragione**, whose impressive wooden-vaulted main hall is viewable during occasional temporary exhibitions. Across from the tourist office is the **Casa del Bianco**, or Casa di Boniforte da Concorezzo, which still has its late-Gothic terracotta decoration and a beautiful portico supported on columns of Verona marble. It has long been occupied by a haberdashery run by the prominent Jewish Norsa family.

Sunk below the present street level is Mantova's oldest church, the eleventh-century **Rotonda di San Lorenzo** (daily 10am–6pm; Mon–Fri closed 1–3pm), which narrowly escaped destruction under Lodovico's city-improvement plans. It lost its roof in the sixteenth century and was effectively turned inside out: houses were built surrounding it and their Jewish occupants (the church lay inside the ghetto boundary) used what is now the interior as an open courtyard. In 1908 the houses were demolished and the church rebuilt; it is now beautifully restored and still contains traces of twelfth- and thirteenth-century frescoes.

At the north end of the square, a passage leads under the red-brick **Broletto**, or medieval town hall, into the smaller **Piazza Broletto**, where you can view two reminders of how "criminals" were treated under the Gonzagas. The bridge to the right has metal rings embedded in its vault, to which victims were chained by the wrists, before being hauled up by a pulley and suspended in mid-air; while on your far left – actually on the corner of Piazza Sordello – the tall medieval **Torre della Gabbia** has a cage attached in which prisoners were displayed. The Broletto itself is dedicated to the city's two most famous sons: the poet Virgil, a statue of whom overlooks the square, and Tazio Nuvolari, Italy's most celebrated racing driver, whose career is mapped in a small **museum** (Tues, Wed & Fri–Sun 10am–1pm & 3.30–6.30pm; March, Nov & Dec Sat & Sun only; Jan & Feb Sun only; €3).

Teatro Bibiena

A short diversion off Via Broletto heads right on Via Accademia, at the end of which stands the **Teatro Bibiena** (Tues–Sun 9.30am–12.30pm & 3–6pm; €2), one of Mantova's last Baroque buildings – the work of Antonio Bibiena, whose brother designed the Bayreuth Opera House. This is a much smaller theatre, at once intimate and splendid, its curved walls lined with four tiers of boxes calculated to make their occupants more conspicuous than the performers. Mozart gave the inaugural concert here on January 16, 1770, a few days before his fourteenth birthday; his impression is unrecorded, but his father was fulsome in his praise for the building, calling it "the most beautiful thing, in its genre, that I have ever seen." Concerts are still staged here (the *Conservatorio* is alongside).

The Duomo

Beyond Piazza Broletto, the cobbled **Piazza Sordello** is a large, sombre space, headed by the Baroque facade of the Duomo and flanked by touristy cafés and grim crenellated palaces built by the Bonacolsi (the Gonzagas' predecessors). The **Duomo**, or Cattedrale San Pietro (daily 7am–noon & 3–7pm), at the top of the square, boasts a rich, light interior, designed by Giulio Romano after the church had been gutted by fire in 1545. Every year on the patron saint's day, March 18, the clothed, uncorrupted corpse of San Anselmo is wheeled out to worshippers.

Palazzo Ducale

Opposite the Duomo on Piazza Sordello, the crenellated Palazzo del Capitano and Magna Domus were taken by Luigi Gonzaga when he seized Mantova from the Bonacolsi in 1328, beginning three hundred years of Gonzaga rule. They now form the core of the **Palazzo Ducale**, an enormous complex that was once the largest palace in Europe. In its heyday it covered 34,000 square metres and had a population of over a thousand; when it was sacked by the Habsburgs in 1630 eighty carriages were needed to carry the two thousand works of art contained in its five hundred rooms.

The main highlight is the **Camera degli Sposi**, frescoed by Andrea Mantegna – but it lies in the farthest corner of the complex: reaching it and heading straight out again will take you through most of the finest rooms. You could easily spend a memorable half-day in here; just seeing the forty-odd rooms currently open involves two hours of nonstop walking. It is, though, very much worth the trek.

Palazzo Ducale practicalities

Admission (Tues–Sun 8.45am–7.15pm, last entry 6.30pm; €6.50; ⓦ www .mantovaducale.it) is from Piazza Sordello, where you can also pick up an **audioguide** (€4, or €5.50 for two). In winter (Nov–March) you must take

At the time of their coup of 1328, the **Gonzaga** family were wealthy local peasants, living outside Mantova on vast estates with an army of retainers. On seizing power in the city **Luigi Gonzaga** nominated himself Captain of the People, a role which quickly became hereditary, eventually growing in grandeur to that of marquis.

Mantova's renaissance began in 1459, when a visiting pope complained that the city was muddy, marshy and riddled with fever. This spurred his host, **Lodovico II Gonzaga**, to give the city a facelift, ranging from paving the squares and repainting the shops to engaging **Andrea Mantegna** as court artist and calling in the prestigious architectural theorist **Leon Battista Alberti** to design the monumental church of Sant'Andrea, one of the most influential buildings of the early Renaissance. Later, Lodovico's grandson, **Francesco II** (1466–1519), swelled the family coffers by hiring himself out as a mercenary – money his wife, **Isabella d'Este**, spent amassing a prestigious collection of paintings, sculpture and *objets d'art*.

Under Isabella's son, **Federico II**, Gonzaga fortunes reached their height; his marriage in 1531 to the heiress of the duchy of Monferrato procured a ducal title for the family, while he continued the policy of self-glorification by commissioning an out-of-town villa – the **Palazzo Te** – for himself and his mistress. Federico's descendants were for the most part less colourful characters, one notable exception being **Vincenzo I**, whose debauchery and corruption provided the inspiration for Verdi's licentious duke in *Rigoletto*. After Vincenzo's death in 1612, the then-bankrupt court was forced to sell many of the family treasures to Charles I of England (many are still in London's Victoria and Albert Museum), just three years before the arrival of the Habsburgs.

a guided tour (free); these start every fifteen minutes, or when twenty people have gathered, and last an hour and a half.

For conservation reasons, only 1500 people a day are allowed to visit the **Camera degli Sposi** (also called the **Camera Picta**). In the peak season for school trips (March 15–June 15 and Sept 1–Oct 15), individuals must book in advance for a timed slot for admission to this room, on ☎041.241.1897 (press 1; English-speaking operators; Mon–Fri 9am–6pm, Sat 9am–2pm). Booking costs €1 extra, payable on arrival.

Areas of the palace usually **closed to the public** – such as the frescoed bridal apartment of Isabella d'Este, the so-called "Summer Quarters", and Duke Guglielmo's apartments, which include a magnificent fretwork-vaulted Coffee House – can be visited as *Percorsi Aggiuntivi* on request (Sat & Sun only), accompanied by a guide (free).

Rooms 1–14: the Corte Vecchia

From the ticket desk, the tour starts in the Corte Vecchia, the oldest wing of the palace. At the top of the Scalone delle Duchesse is the **Sala del Morone** (room 1), where hangs a painting from 1494 by Domenico Morone showing the *Expulsion of the Bonacolsi* from Piazza Sordello, with the Duomo sporting its old, Gothic facade (replaced in the eighteenth century). In the **Sala del Pisanello** (room 3) are the fragments of a half-finished fresco by Pisanello, discovered in 1969 behind two layers of plaster and thought to depict either an episode from an Arthurian romance or the (idealized) military exploits of the first marquis, Gianfrancesco Gonzaga. Whatever its subject, it's a powerful piece of work, charged with energy, in which faces, costumes and landscape are minutely observed.

The **Galleria Nuova** (room 5) is crammed with altarpieces from Mantovan churches suppressed by Napoleon, notably one of *St Francis* by Francesco

Borgani with a view of Mantova behind. At the end, turn left for the splendid **Sala dei Specchi** ("Hall of Mirrors"; room 6), which has a notice outside signed by Monteverdi, who worked as court musician to Vincenzo I: his *L'Orfeo*, the world's first modern opera, was premiered here on February 24, 1607. The room was originally an open loggia, bricked up in 1773; teams of horses are being driven across the barrel-vaulted ceiling from Night to Day.

Vincenzo also employed Rubens, whose *Adoration of the Magi* in the **Sala degli Arcieri**, next door (room 7), shows the Gonzaga family of 1604, seated comfortably in the presence of God; notice Vincenzo with his handlebar moustache. The picture was originally part of a huge triptych, but Napoleonic troops carried off two-thirds of it in 1797 (one part is now in Antwerp, the other in Nancy) and chopped the remaining third into saleable chunks of portraiture; some gaps remain. Opposite is an even larger *Miracle of the Loaves and Fishes* by Domenico Fetti, while on the corbelling above squat nightmarish gargoyle figures. Around the room is a curious frieze of horses, glimpsed behind curtains.

Beyond the **Sala del Labirinto** (room 9), named for the maze on its painted and gilded wooden ceiling, adorned with *forse che si, forse che no* ("perhaps yes, perhaps no"), the **Sala di Amore e Psiche** (room 11) is an intimate and characterful space, with a wooden floor and an eighteenth-century tondo of Cupid and Psyche in the ceiling.

From here, you enter the Corridoio dei Mori, but follow signs immediately right, down the stairs then left along the **Galleria di Santa Barbara**. At the end, more signs point left, down the **Scalone di Enea** staircase (room 14), over a moat and into the fourteenth-century **Castello di San Giorgio** fortress.

Rooms 15–17: the Camera degli Sposi

A spiral ramp (room 15) leads up to a holding chamber, where you may have to wait in order to view the adjacent **Camera degli Sposi** (room 17), which holds the palace's principal treasure: Mantegna's frescoes of the Gonzaga family, done in the period 1465–74 – among the painter's most famous works, splendidly restored. They depict the Marquis Lodovico and his wife Barbara with their family, and are naturalistic pieces of work, giving a vivid impression of real people, and of the relationships between them.

You enter from the south: facing the door, Lodovico discusses a letter with a courtier while his wife looks on; their youngest daughter leans on her mother's lap, about to bite into an apple, while an older son and daughter (possibly Barbarina) look towards the door, where an ambassador from another court is being welcomed – lending credence to the theory that negotiations are about to ensue for Barbarina's marriage.

The other fresco, on the west wall, depicts a landscape of weird rock formations and an imaginary city with the Gonzagan arms above the gate. Divided into three sections by fake pilasters, it shows Gonzagan retainers with dogs and a horse in attendance on Lodovico, who is welcoming his son Francesco back from Rome, where he had just become the first Gonzaga to be made a cardinal. In the background are the Holy Roman Emperor Frederick III and the King of Denmark – a selection which apparently annoyed the Duke of Milan, who was incensed that the "two most wretched men in the world" had been included while he had been omitted. Lodovico's excuse was that he would have included the duke had he not objected so strongly to Mantegna's uncompromising portrait style.

If you have time before the guide sweeps you out, have a look at the ceiling, a beautiful piece of trompe l'oeil, in which two women, peering down from a balustrade, have balanced a tub of plants on a pole and appear to be on the verge of letting it tumble into the room.

You exit to the adjacent **Sala dei Soli** (room 16) and back down the spiral ramp to the Scalone di Enea.

Rooms 18–28: the Corte Nuova

Straight ahead from the top of the Scalone di Enea, you enter the sixteenth-century Corte Nuova wing, designed by Giulio Romano for Federico II Gonzaga. The first rooms are the huge, gloomy **Sala di Manto** (room 18), with a fine coffered ceiling, and the **Sala dei Cavalli** (room 19), whose irregular shape is disguised by a deftly designed ceiling. The **Sala dei Teste** (room 20) once featured eleven busts, all now gone, but its ceiling fresco remains, showing Jupiter in a thoughtful pose holding a thunderbolt. Through the **Sala di Troia** (room 22), with Romano's brilliantly colourful scenes from the *Iliad* and *Aeneid*, is the long **Galleria dei Marmi** (room 23), looking out over the Cortile della Cavallerizza (Courtyard of the Riding School), with its bizarre twisted columns.

Along the courtyard's long side runs the immense **Galleria della Mostra** (room 24), once hung with paintings by Titian, Caravaggio, Breughel and others, all now dispersed; in their place are 64 Roman marble busts of figures such as Virgil, Cicero, Nero and Marcus Aurelius.

Beyond are four small chambers, the **Camera del Fuoco, dell'Aria, dell'Acqua** and **della Terra** (Fire, Air, Water, Earth; rooms 25–28), collectively known as the **Galleria del Passerino**, painted with scenes from Ovid's *Metamorphoses* and formerly filled with displays of natural oddities: crystals, coral, resins, ostrich eggs and even the mummified corpse of Passerino Bonacolsi, pre-Gonzagan lord of Mantova.

Rooms 29–37: back through the Corte Vecchia

A sequence of corridors returns past a suite of miniature rooms long thought to have housed Isabella d'Este's celebrated troupe of dwarf jesters; in fact it is a scaled-down version of the St John Lateran basilica in Rome, built for Vincenzo. Stairs lead up to the **Corridoio dei Mori** (room 29), at the end of which is a sequence of rooms overlooking the unusual **Cortile delle Otto Facce** (Octagonal Courtyard).

Beyond, the stunning **Sala dello Zodiaco** (room 33), whose late sixteenth-century ceiling is spangled with stars and constellations, adjoins the Rococo **Sala dei Fiumi** (room 34), which features an elaborate painted allegory of Mantova's six rivers, flanked at either end by a mock garden complete with painted creepers and two ghastly stucco-and-mosaic fountains. The hanging gardens outside the window are considerably more attractive.

Save some wonder for rooms 35–37, beside the Sala dello Zodiaco. These comprise the **Stanze degli Arazzi**, three rooms (and a small chapel) altered in the eighteenth century to house a set of nine sixteenth-century Flemish tapestries, made from Raphael's cartoons (now in the V&A in London) for the Sistine Chapel depicting stories from the Acts of the Apostles. They are of exceptional virtuosity.

At the end, the Scalone delle Duchesse returns you to the ticket desk.

West of the centre: Palazzo d'Arco

Dominating the compact Piazza d'Arco, 500m west of Piazza Mantegna, is the Neoclassical **Palazzo d'Arco** (Tues–Sun 10am–12.30pm & 2.30–6pm; Nov–Feb Sat & Sun 10am–12.30pm & 2–5pm; €5; ℗www.museodarco.it). It comprises a 1784 rebuilding of the residence of a noble family related to the rulers of Arco, a town near Riva del Garda. The main attraction is a wing of the fifteenth-century *palazzo* which survived in the gardens: its upper **Sala dello Zodiaco** (room 39) has frescoes done by the Veronese artist Falconetto in 1520 – twelve large panels depicting each sign (apart from Libra, which was destroyed when the fireplace was installed). Of the dozen or more rooms open in the main building, all with their original paintings and furniture, look out for room 15, the **Sala Andreas Hofer**, dedicated to a Tyrolean rebel executed in 1810: it features panels of wallpaper printed in 1823 with Italian landscapes, including a smoking Mount Etna.

South of the centre

A twenty-minute walk from the centre of Mantova, at the end of the long spine of Via Principe Amedeo and Via Acerbi, the **Palazzo Te** is the later of the city's two Gonzaga palaces. You can take in a few of Mantova's minor attractions on the walk there.

First is Giulio Romano's **Fish Market**, to the left off Piazza Martiri Belfiori, a short covered bridge over the river which is still used as a market building. Located to the right off Via Principe Amedeo, at Via Poma 18, and overshadowed by the Palazzo di Giustizia, the **Casa di Giulio Romano** was also designed by Giulio; it was meant to impress the sophisticated, who would have found the licence taken with the Classical rules of architecture witty and amusing. A five-minute walk away on busy Via Giovanni Acerbi, the more austere brick **Casa del Mantegna** was designed by Mantegna both as a home and private museum, and is now used as a gallery for contemporary art (hours and admission vary).

Cruises on Mantova's lakes and the River Mincio

Several companies offer **cruises** on Mantova's lakes – bulges in the course of the River Mincio – and on the river itself down to its confluence with the Po. All run daily but must be **booked in advance**: usually a day ahead, but sometimes an hour or so will do. Lago Inferiore, to the east of the city, and Lago di Mezzo to the north are linked, but Lago Superiore upstream to the west is 4m higher, behind a dam built in 1187. The scenery is flat, characte rized by reeds and marshy inlets; lotus flowers abound, introduced in 1921, and you may see herons, egrets and storks.

The leading company is **Motonavi Andes Negrini**, whose ticket office is at Via San Giorgio 2 (☎0376.322.875, ⓦwww.motonaviandes.it), three-minutes' walk from its jetty on Lago Inferiore. Their **Laghi di Mantova** trips meander around Lago di Mezzo, Lago Inferiore and a bit further south to the Vallazza lake – either one hour (€7.50, Sun €8.50) or one hour thirty minutes (€9, Sun €10). An equally scenic cruise on **Lago Superiore** (90min; €9, Sun €10) starts from the jetty by the Porta Mulina; the return journey, as Mantova's towers rise from the water, is a delight. Many other trips are offered, including a day cruise as far as Venice. **Navi Andes** (☎0376.324.506, ⓦwww.naviandes.com), a separate concern, based at its jetty on Lago di Mezzo, runs much the same trips for similar prices.

These can often be busy excursions, on large boats. The difference comes with the **Barcaioli del Mincio** (☎0376.349.292, ⓦwww.fiumemincio.it), local boatmen operating small craft upstream from Mantova on Lago Superiore to Grazie and Rivalta. They run trips on demand for at least ten people (1hr €7; 2hr €9). The *Enigma* is a **solar-powered boat** that follows sightseeing itineraries starting from Rivalta, including full-moon and new-moon trips; check ⓦwww.olympusaquae.it for details. Many of the boats accept **bikes**, so you can create a lazy day-trip – a morning on the boat, a picnic lunch at, say, Rivalta, then a gentle cycle-ride back in the afternoon.

Across the road, the **Tempio di San Sebastiano** (mid-March to mid-Nov Tues–Sun 10.30am–12.30pm & 3–5pm; €1.50) was the work of Alberti, and is famous as the first Renaissance church to be built on a Greek-cross plan, described as "curiously pagan" by Nikolaus Pevsner. Lodovico II's son was less polite: "I could not understand whether it was meant to turn out as a church, a mosque or a synagogue." The bare interior – now deconsecrated – is dedicated to Mantova's war dead; the crypt, its forest of columns adorned with commemorative plaques, is especially atmospheric.

Palazzo Te

6

At the southern end of Via Acerbi, set in its own grounds, stands the **Palazzo Te** (Mon 1–6pm, Tues–Sun 9am–6pm; last entry 5.30pm; €8), also reachable on bus #1 to the stops "Risorgimento 3" or "Repubblica 1", either side of nearby Porta Pusterla.

This grand edifice was designed in the 1520s for playboy **Federico Gonzaga** and his mistress, Isabella Boschetta, by **Giulio Romano**; it's the artist/architect's greatest work and a celebrated Renaissance pleasure-dome. The palace originally formed an island, linked to the mainland only by bridge – an ideal location for an amorous retreat away from Federico's wife and the restrictions of life in the Palazzo Ducale. Although the upstairs rooms hold collections of Mesopotamian and Egyptian antiquities as well as a modest picture gallery, the main reason for visiting is to see Giulio's amazing decorative scheme in the ground floor rooms.

Rooms 1–8: Sala di Amore e Psiche

A tour of the palace is like a voyage around Giulio's imagination, a sumptuous world where very little is what it seems. From the entrance hall, turn left across the Cortile d'Onore to enter the north wing of the palace. The **Camera delle Imprese** (room 3) sets the tone: in the top right corner of the south wall is painted a salamander with the motto *Quod hic deest me torquet*. Salamanders were thought to be asexual, and Federico is saying here "What this lacks, torments me" – a nudge-nudge reference to his own legendary appetites. The salamander pops up with his catchphrase throughout the palace.

In the **Camera del Sole** (room 4), the sun and moon are represented by a pair of horse-drawn chariots viewed from below, giving a fine array of human and equine bottoms on the ceiling. In the **Sala dei Cavalli** (room 7), portraits of prime specimens from the Gonzaga stud-farm (which was also on the island) stand before an illusionistic background in which simulated marble, fake pilasters and mock reliefs surround views of painted landscapes through nonexistent windows.

The function of the **Sala di Amore e Psiche** (room 8) is undocumented, but the graphically erotic frescoes, and the proximity to Federico's private quarters, are powerful clues. The ceiling paintings tell the story of Cupid and Psyche with more dizzying *sotto in su* ("from the bottom up") works by Giulio, amongst other examples clumsily executed by his pupils. The walls are more than a little racy, too, with orgiastic wedding-feast scenes, at which drunken gods in various states of undress are attended by a menagerie of real and mythical beasts. On the north wall, Mars and Venus are climbing out of the bath together, their cave watered by a river-god lounging above who is gushing with deliberately ambiguous liquid flowing from his beard, a vessel he's holding and his genitals. This is either what it seems – a glorying in bodily fluids – or is perhaps a punning reference to Giulio's second name, Pippi (The Pisser), along with encouragement to Federico who, according to his doctors, suffered from "the obstinate retention of urine". Other scenes show Olympia about to be raped by a priapic, half-serpentine Jupiter and Pasiphae disguising herself as a cow in order to seduce a bull – all watched over by the giant Polyphemus, perched above the fireplace, clutching the pan-pipes with which he sang of his love for Galatea before murdering her lover.

Rooms 9–20: Sala dei Giganti

Wander on through the couple of rooms either side of the beautiful **Loggia di Davide** (room 11), with views east across the gardens and west across the Cortile d'Onore, to the extraordinary **Sala dei Giganti** (room 14) at the southeast corner, where revenge is taken on Polyphemus. Its frescoes – "the most fantastic and frightening creation of the whole Renaissance", according to the critic Frederick Hartt – show the destruction of the giants by the gods, in a virtuoso display of artistic skill and imagination. Unusually, there are almost no architectural interruptions to the frescoes: corners have been smoothed into curves, and the images come right down to the floor and go right up across the ceiling, in a sensational, IMAX-like effect. The destruction appears to be all around: cracking pillars, toppling brickwork and screaming giants, crushed by great chunks of masonry that appear to crash down into the room. The fireplace in the eastern wall was removed in the eighteenth century, but Vasari – who visited in 1541 – wrote that "when the fire is lit, the giants burn." That, and the sound of crackling, must have made this room the world's first multimedia fantasy experience, and the effect is little diminished today. Shout or stamp your feet and you'll discover the sound effects that Giulio created by turning the room into an echo chamber.

The remainder of the rooms in the south wing are pretty, but can barely match up. Nearby, signposted in the palace gardens, are the bookshop and café.

Eating and drinking

Mantova has plenty of excellent, reasonably priced **restaurants**, many serving local specialities like *spezzatino di Mantova* (donkey stew), *agnoli in brodo* (pasta stuffed with cheese and sausage in broth) or the delicious *tortelli di zucca* (sweet pumpkin-filled pasta).

Al Quadrato Piazza Virgiliana 49 ☎0376.368.896. A tranquil spot away from the fray, overlooking the Piazza Virgiliana park north of the centre. Serves good pizzas (€7–8) and tasty fish dishes. Expect around €25. Closed Mon.

Aquila Nigra Vicolo Bonacolsi 4 ☎0376.327.180, ⓦwww.aquilanigra.it. A formal restaurant housed in an elegant *palazzo* just off Piazza Sordello, serving delicious seasonal food complemented by an impressive wine list. The fish and, especially, seafood are highly regarded. *Menùs* are €50-plus. Closed Sun & Mon. Closed Aug.

Dal Pescatore Località Runate, Canneto sull'Oglio ☎0376.723.001, ⓦwww.dalpescatore.com. Dedicated foodies should book weeks in advance for this award-winning country restaurant, located some forty-minutes' drive west of Mantova (and currently boasting three Michelin stars). Local ingredients and methods rule, although the husband-and-wife team in charge are famed for their innovative take on classical Italian cuisine. Luxury is the watchword, yet simplicity sets the tone. Make a day-trip of it; it'll be a meal to remember. Closed Mon & Tues. Closed Jan & Aug.

Fragoletta Piazza Arche 5a ☎0376.323.300. Over towards the Lago Inferiore, this is a lively *osteria* shoehorned into a cramped little building. It's been around since 1748 and remains popular with locals for its well-priced regional cuisine. Expect to pay around €30. Closed Mon.

Grifone Bianco Piazza Erbe 6 ☎0376.365.423, ⓦwww.grifonebianco.it. The pick of the restaurants on this square, a welcoming place serving excellent local specialities off a seasonal menu at moderate prices. Closed Tues & lunch on Wed. Closed late June.

Il Cigno (Trattoria dei Martini) Piazza d'Arco 1 ℡0376.327.101. Exceptional restaurant occupying a sixteenth-century mansion in a quiet corner away from the centre. The setting is refinement itself: a civilized, tasteful old dining room, free from music, overlooking a beautiful private garden. And the cooking is out of this world – sweet, delectable *tortelli di zucca* with amaretti, delicately flavoured, melt-in-the-mouth *luccio con salsa* (dressed pike), flavourful local meats (roast guinea-fowl is a signature dish), from a menu which changes seasonally. Service is spot-on – discreet, punctilious, yet welcoming and knowledgeable. There are no prices on the menu: expect well over €60 per head. Closed Mon & Tues, and Aug.

L'Ochina Bianca Via Finzi 2 ℡0376.323.700. Cosy *osteria* where friendly staff serve tasty Mantovan dishes –

this is a mainstay of the Italian "Slow Food" movement, dedicated to promoting quality and conviviality. Five-minutes' walk west from Piazza Erbe. Closed Mon.

Masseria Piazza Broletto 7 ℡0376.365.303, ⓦwww.ristorantemasseria.it. A popular, lively place with good pizzas as well as a wide selection of other moderately priced dishes served at outside tables. Closed Wed & lunch on Thurs.

Tiratappi Piazza Alberti 30 ℡0376.322.366. Atmospheric old wine-bar on this little-visited square, down a concealed passageway beside the Sant'Andrea church. Its terrace tables are a sun-trap – perfect for sampling Mantovan vintages on a slow afternoon. The cuisine is all local as well: mid-priced specialities served with care. Closed Tues lunch & Thurs lunch.

Travel details

Timetables for all train routes in Italy are at ⓦwww.trenitalia.com. Verona's inter-urban buses are run by APTV ⓦwww.aptv.it, Mantova's by APAM ⓦwww.apam.it. See p.30 for guidance on deciphering timetables.

Trains

Mantova to: Cremona (approx hourly; 55min); Milano Centrale (6 daily; 2hr 10min); Verona (approx hourly; 45min).

Verona (Porta Nuova) to: Brescia (2–3hr; 45min); Desenzano/Sirmione (approx twice hourly; 30min); Mantova (approx hourly; 45min); Milano Centrale (2–3hr; 1hr 30min)

Buses

Mantova to: Brescia (approx hourly; 1hr 35min); Peschiera via Valeggio (approx 6 daily; 1hr 10min); Verona (5–6 daily; 1hr 20min).

Verona to: Brescia (hourly; 2hr 20min); Malcésine (approx hourly; 1hr 45min); Mantova (5–6 daily; 1hr 20min); Riva del Garda (approx hourly; 2hr 10min); Sirmione (hourly; 1hr).

Contexts

Contexts

History

A specific Italian **history** is hard to identify – and a northern Italian history even more so. The country wasn't formally united until 1861, and the history of the peninsula after the Romans is one of warring city-states and annexation by foreign powers. Regional and local differences remain strong to this day. What follows is a brief description of key events.

From prehistory to the Romans

Some remains exist from the **Neanderthals** who occupied the Italian peninsula half a million years ago, but the main period of colonization began after the last Ice Age, with evidence of **Paleolithic** and **Neolithic** settlements dating from around 20,000 BC and 4000 BC respectively. Successive inhabitants of the Val Camónica, north of Lake Iseo, left thousands of designs carved into the rocks, giving a unique picture of Neolithic – and, later, **Bronze** and **Iron Age** – life.

Other tribes brought Indo-European languages into Italy. The **Veneti**, in the northeast, and related **Liguri**, in the northwest, developed distinctive cultures and began moving down the peninsula from the north, but the rise of the **Etruscans** in central Italy, mirrored by the colonization of southern Italy by the **Greeks**, halted their progress. Some say the Etruscans arrived in Italy around the ninth century BC from western Anatolia, others that they came from the north, and a third hypothesis places their origins in Etruria. Whatever the case, by the sixth century BC, they were in control of central Italy, edging out the indigenous populations. **Mantova**, on the Po plain, was one of the northernmost Etruscan settlements.

Through the fifth and fourth centuries BC, Gaulish **Celtic** tribes migrated south across the Alps, frequently clashing with the Etruscans and, in 390 BC, almost taking **Rome**. This, though, proved a temporary reversal in the inexorable rise of the city: over the following century virtually the whole peninsula came under Roman domination. The middle decades of the third century BC saw Rome taking Sicily, Sardinia and Corsica, as well as, in 222 BC, what they dubbed "**Cisalpine Gaul**" – that is, Gaul on this side of the Alps, referring chiefly to the area of the lakes and the Po valley.

The Gaulish Celts took a hand in the fightback against Rome, helping the Carthaginian general **Hannibal** cross the Alps in 218 BC (Hannibal continued south, gaining some victories but eventually being overcome by the legions). Their reward was complete subjugation by the Roman military machine, which moved into northern Italy in strength. New **coloniae** were founded, such as Brixia (Brescia) and Cremona, populated with army veterans. Meanwhile, existing Celtic settlements such as Mediolanum (Milan), Como and Verona were Romanized as **municipia**.

Peace and prosperity under **Augustus** and the subsequent first- and second-century AD emperors allowed the northern Italian communities to flourish: agriculture on the Po plain was strong, livestock grazed the hillsides and the cities grew in wealth and sophistication. Rome's moneyed elite established large estates on the lakes – most famously the elder and younger Plinys' villas on Lake Como.

Christianity and the collapse of Rome

In the middle of the third century AD, incursions by **Goths** in Greece and the Balkans, and **Franks** and **Alemanni** in Gaul foreshadowed the collapse of Rome. The persecution of Christians under Emperor **Diocletian** (284–305) produced many of the Church's present-day saints. Plagues had decimated the population, and problems of a huge but static imperial economy were compounded by the doubling in size of the army to half a million men.

To ease administration, Diocletian **divided the empire** into two halves, east and west, basing himself as ruler of the western empire in Mediolanum (Milan). This measure brought about a relative recovery, coinciding with the rise of **Christianity**, which was declared the state religion by **Constantine** at the **Edict of Milan** in 313. Milan's bishop, Ambrose, became a key figure in the spread of the religion, building churches and establishing a theological orthodoxy. Constantinople (now Istanbul), capital of the eastern empire, became a thriving trading and manufacturing city, while Rome itself went into decline, as the enlargement of the senatorial estates and the impoverishment of the lower classes gave rise to something comparable to a primitive feudal system.

By the fifth century, many legions were made up of troops from conquered territories and several posts of high command were held by non-Romans. With little will or loyalty behind it, the empire floundered, and in late 406 **Vandals**, Alans and Sueves crossed the frozen Rhine into Gaul, chased by the Huns. By 408, the imperial government could no longer hold off **Alaric**, who went on to **sack Rome** in 410, causing a crisis of morale in the west. "The whole world perished in one city," wrote St Jerome.

The bitter end of the Roman Empire in the west came after **Valentinian III** was assassinated in 455. It limped on with his eight successors over the next twenty years until the Germanic invaders finally elected their general **Odoacer** as king in Pavia in 476.

During this time the **Christian Church** developed as a more or less independent authority. Continual invasions had led to an uncertain political scene in which the **bishops of Rome** emerged with the strongest voice – justification of their primacy having already been given by Pope Leo I (440–461), who spoke of his right to "rule all who are ruled in the first instance by Christ".

Lombards and Franks

During the chaotic sixth century, the **Lombards**, a Germanic tribe, were driven southwest into Italy, and by the eighth century, when the **Franks** arrived from Gaul, they were extending their power throughout the peninsula from their base at Pavia. The Franks integrated quickly and took over much of the provincial administration. Led by **Pepin the Short**, they saw an advantage in supporting the papacy, giving Rome large endowments and forcibly converting pagans in areas they conquered.

In 753 Pope Stephen II summoned the Frankish army. Pepin forced the Lombards to hand over treasure and 22 cities and castles, which then became the northern part of the **Papal States**. He died in 768, and divided the kingdom between his two sons. One died within three years; the other became known as Charles the Great, or **Charlemagne**.

An intelligent and innovative leader, Charlemagne was proclaimed King of the Franks and the Lombards, and patrician of the Romans, in 773. The treasure of the Lombard king he defeated, Desiderius, is on show in Brescia to this day. On Christmas Day 800, Pope Leo III expressed his gratitude for Charlemagne's political support by crowning him **Holy Roman Emperor**. By the time Charlemagne died, all of Italy from the northern lakes to beyond Rome was part of the huge **Carolingian Empire**.

The task of holding these gains was beyond Charlemagne's successors – who still ruled from Pavia. By the beginning of the tenth century the family was extinct and the rival Italian states had become prizes for which the western (French) and eastern (German) Frankish kingdoms competed. Power switched in 936 to **Otto**, king of the eastern Franks. Political disunity in Italy invited him to intervene, and in 962 he was crowned Emperor; his son and grandson (Otto II and III) set the seal on the renewal of the Holy Roman Empire.

Guelphs and Ghibellines

On the death of **Otto III** in 1002, Italy was again without a recognized ruler. In the north, noblemen jockeyed for power, while in Rome, a series of reforming popes began to strengthen the church. **Gregory VII**, elected in 1073, was the most radical, confronting the emperors and developing the papacy into the most comprehensive and advanced centralized government in Europe in the realms of law and finance. Holy Roman Emperor **Frederick I "Barbarossa"** besieged many northern Italian cities from his base in Germany from 1154; the issue of supremacy – papal or imperial – was to polarize the country for the next two hundred years, almost every part of Italy being torn by struggles between **Guelphs** (supporting the pope) and **Ghibellines** (supporting the emperor).

Meanwhile, trade was flourishing across northern Italy, not least in **Venice**, where a disparate band of refugees from the Lombard invasions had formed themselves into a powerful commercial bloc, trading as far afield as Syria and North Africa. In the eleventh century, revolts in many northern cities, including Pavia, Cremona and Milan, led to the establishment of **communal governments** across the region, many of which – in the face of Barbarossa's attacks – formed themselves into the united **Lombard League**. In 1176, the League defeated Barbarossa in a famous victory at Legnano, and by 1300, a broad belt of some three hundred virtually **independent city-states** stretched from central Italy to the northernmost edge of the peninsula.

In the middle of the century vast numbers died of the **Black Death** but the city-states survived, developing a participatory concept of citizenship quite different from the feudal lord-and-vassal relationship. By 1400 the richer and more influential states had swallowed up the smaller **comune**, leaving four front-runners: Genoa, Florence, Venice and **Milan**, whose sphere of influence included Lombardy and much of central Italy. Smaller principalities, such as Mantova, supported armies of mercenaries, ensuring their security by building impregnable fortress-palaces.

Perpetual vendettas between the propertied classes often induced the citizens to prefer the overall rule of one **signore** to the bloodshed of warring clans. A despotic form of government evolved, sanctioned by official titles from the emperor or pope, and by the fifteenth century most city-states were under princely rather than republican rule: both Mantova and Milan became independent duchies, the former under the **Gonzaga**, the latter under the hugely powerful **Visconti**.

The commercial and secular city-states of late medieval times were the seed-bed for the **Renaissance**, when urban entrepreneurs and autocratic rulers enhanced their status through the financing of architectural projects, paintings and sculpture.

By the mid-fifteenth century the five most powerful states – Naples, the papacy, Milan, and the republics of Venice and Florence – reached a tacit agreement to maintain the new balance of power. Yet though there was equilibrium at home, the history of each of the independent Italian states became inextricably bound up with the power politics of other European countries.

French and Spanish intervention

In 1494, at the request of the Duke of Milan, **Charles VIII of France** marched south to renew the Angevin claim to the Kingdom of Naples. After his success, the kingdom was then acquired by Ferdinand II of Aragon, subsequently ruler of Spain.

Within three years of inheriting the Austrian and Spanish thrones, the Habsburg **Charles V** (1500–58) bribed his way to being elected Holy Roman Emperor. In 1527 his troops sacked Rome, a calamity widely interpreted at the time as God's punishment of the disorganized and dissolute Italians. The **French** remained troublesome opposition despite a defeat at Pavia in 1526, and the **Spanish** – granted the Duchy of Milan under the treaty of Château-Cambrésis in 1559 – were to exert a stranglehold on Italian political life for the next 150 years.

Social and economic troubles were as severe as the political upheavals. While the papacy combated the spread of the **Reformation** – aided, in Lombardy, by the archbishop **Carlo Borromeo** (1538–84), scion of the Borromeo family which remains pre-eminent in the lands around Lake Maggiore – the major manufacturing and trading centres were coming to terms with the opening up of the Atlantic and Indian Ocean trade routes, discoveries which meant that northern Italy would increasingly be bypassed. Mid-sixteenth-century **economic recession** prompted wealthy Venetian merchants to invest in land rather than business.

The seventeenth century was a low point in Italian political life, with little room for manoeuvre between the papacy and colonial powers. The Spanish eventually lost control of their areas at the start of the eighteenth century when, as a result of the War of the Spanish Succession, Lombardy, Mantova and other areas came under Austrian control. The northern states advanced under the intelligent if autocratic rule of Austria's **Maria Theresia** (1740–80) and her son **Joseph II** (1780–92), who prepared the way for early industrialization.

Lightning changes came in 1796, when the French armies of **Napoleon** invaded northern Italy. Within a few years the French had been driven out again, but by 1810 Napoleon was in command of the whole peninsula, crowning himself King of Italy in the Duomo at Milan; his puppet regimes – including a Cisalpine Republic in Lombardy – remained in charge until Waterloo. Napoleonic rule had profound effects, reducing the power of the papacy, reforming feudal land rights and introducing representative government to Italy. Elected assemblies were provided on the French model, giving the emerging middle class a chance for political discussion and action.

The Risorgimento: Italy's unification

The fall of Napoleon led to the Vienna Settlement of 1815, by which the Austrians effectively restored the old ruling class. **Metternich**, the Austrian Chancellor, did all he could to foster any local loyalties that might weaken the appeal of unity, yet the years between 1820 and 1849 became years of

▲ Statue of Garibaldi

revolution. In the north, the oppressive laws enacted by **Vittorio Emanuele I** in the Kingdom of Piemonte sparked off student protests and army mutinies in Turin. Vittorio Emanuele abdicated in favour of his brother, Carlo Felice, and his son, **Carlo Alberto**; the latter initially gave some support to the radicals, but Carlo Felice then called in the Austrians, and thousands of revolutionaries were forced into exile. Carlo Alberto became King of Piemonte in 1831. A secretive, excessively devout and devious character, he did a *volte-face* when he assumed the throne by forming an alliance with the Austrians.

One person profoundly influenced by the growing insurgencies was the radical **Giuseppe Mazzini**, founder in 1830 of the "**Young Italy**" movement, which also attracted **Giuseppe Garibaldi**, soon to play a central role in the **Risorgimento**, as the movement to reform and unite the country was known.

Crop failures in 1846 and 1847 produced widespread **famine** and **cholera outbreaks**, followed by rioting in Sicily, Piemonte and elsewhere. Rulers fled their duchies, and Carlo Alberto altered course again, prompted by Metternich's fall from power in Vienna: he granted his subjects a constitution and declared war on Austria. In Rome, the pope fled from rioting and Mazzini became a member of the city's republican triumvirate in 1849, with Garibaldi organizing the defences.

In Piemonte, Carlo Alberto abdicated in favour of his son **Vittorio Emanuele II**, but one thing that did survive was Piemonte's constitution, which throughout the 1850s attracted political refugees to this cosmopolitan state.

Nine years of radical change began when **Camillo Cavour** became prime minister of Piemonte in 1852. Napoleon III had decided to support Italy in its fight against the Austrians – the only realistic way of achieving unification – as long as resistance was non-revolutionary. The chance to provoke Austria into war came in 1859, when Cavour wrote an emotive anti-Austrian speech for Vittorio Emanuele at the opening of parliament. His battle cry for an end to the **grido di dolore** ("cry of pain") was taken up over Italy. The Austrians ordered the Piemontese to demobilize; the Piemontese did the reverse.

The war was disastrous from the start, and thousands died in 1859 at Magenta and, most notably, **Solferino** near Lake Garda. A truce was quickly signed and, by 1860, following a series of plebiscites, Tuscany and the new state of Emilia (the duchies of Modena and Parma plus the Romagna) had voted for **union with Piemonte**. A secret treaty between Vittorio Emanuele and Napoleon III ceded Savoy and Nice to France, whereupon **Garibaldi** promptly set off for Nice with the aim of causing as much disruption as possible, only to be diverted when he reached Genoa, where he heard of an **uprising in Sicily**. Commandeering two old paddle-steamers and obtaining just enough rifles for his thousand-strong army, the Red Shirts – many of whom were from Lombardy – he headed south. Garibaldi's army outflanked the Neapolitan troops to take the island. After that, they easily occupied Naples, then struck out for Rome. Cavour, anxious that he might lose the initiative, hastily dispatched a Piemontese army to **annexe the Papal States**, except for the Patrimony around Rome. Cavour and Vittorio Emanuele then travelled south to Rome, thanked Garibaldi for his trouble and took command of all territories. In February 1861, the members of the new parliament formally announced the **Kingdom of Italy**.

Cavour died the same year, before the country was completely unified (Rome and Venice were still outside the kingdom). Garibaldi marched unsuccessfully on Rome in 1862, and again five years later, by which time Venice had been subsumed. It wasn't until Napoleon III was defeated by

Prussia in 1870 that the French troops were ousted from Rome. Thus, by 1871 **Unification** was complete.

The world wars

After the Risorgimento, some things still hadn't changed. The ruling class were slow to move towards a broader-based political system, while living standards had worsened in some areas. When Sicilian peasant farmers organized into **fasci** – forerunners of trade unions – the prime minister sent in 30,000 soldiers, closed down newspapers and interned suspected troublemakers without trial. In the 1890s capitalist methods and modern machinery in the Po valley created a new social structure, with rich **agrari** at the top of the pile, a mass of farm labourers at the bottom, and an intervening layer of estate managers.

In the 1880s Italy's **colonial expansion** began, initially concentrated in bloody – and ultimately disastrous – campaigns in Abyssinia and Eritrea in 1886. In 1912 Italy wrested the Dodecanese islands and Libya from Turkey, a development deplored by many, including the radical **Benito Mussolini**.

World War I and the rise of Mussolini

Italy entered **World War I** in 1915 with the chief aims of settling old scores with Austria and furthering its colonial ambitions through French and British support. A badly equipped, poorly commanded army took three years to force Austria into defeat. Some territory was gained – including the Alpine lands north of Lake Garda that became Trentino-Alto Adige – but at the cost of over half a million dead, many more wounded, and a mountainous war debt.

The middle classes, disillusioned with the war's outcome and alarmed by inflation and social unrest, turned to Mussolini, now a figurehead of the Right. In 1921, Mussolini – recently elected to parliament – formed the Partito Nazionale Fascista, whose **squadre** terrorized their opponents by direct personal attacks and the destruction of newspaper offices, printing shops, and socialist and trade union premises. By 1922 the party was in a position to carry out an insurrectionary **March on Rome**. Plans for the march were leaked to Prime Minister Facta, who needed the king's signature on a martial law decree if the army were to meet the march. The king feared civil war and refused. Facta resigned and shortly afterwards Mussolini was handed the prime ministership. Only then did the march take place.

Zealous **squadristi** now urged Mussolini towards **dictatorship**, which he announced early in 1925. Political opposition and trade unions were outlawed, the free press disintegrated under censorship and Fascist takeovers, elected local governments were replaced by appointed officials, powers of arrest and detention were increased, and special courts were established for political crimes. In 1929, Mussolini ended a sixty-year feud between Church and State by reorganizing the **Vatican** as an autonomous Church state within the Kingdom of Italy. By 1939, the motto "Everything within the State; nothing outside the State; nothing against the State" had become fact, with the government controlling the larger part of Italy's steel, iron and ship-building industries, as well as every aspect of political life.

Even today many Italians hark back to Mussolini's dictatorship as an era during which "the trains ran on time". Supporters say he was a great modernizer, draining the malarial swamps in the south, establishing new towns both in Italy and abroad in a confident Neoclassical style, and gradually breaking the Mafia. His racism, social divisiveness, military incompetence and love of authoritarian red tape – legacies which hobble Italy to this day – are conveniently overlooked.

World War II

Mussolini's involvement in the **Spanish Civil War** in 1936 brought about the formation of the "**Axis**" with Nazi Germany. In terms of dress and ceremony Mussolini proved an inspiration to Hitler. **Racial laws** were passed in 1938 discriminating against the Jews, for example banning them from owning more than 100 hectares of land or companies with more than 100 employees. Italy entered **World War II** totally unprepared and with outdated equipment, but in 1941 invaded Yugoslavia to gain control of the Adriatic coast. As well as deporting Jews and other minorities to Nazi death camps in Eastern Europe, Mussolini set up his own **death camps**, including the notorious San Sabba in Trieste.

Before long, though, Mussolini was on the defensive. Tens of thousands of Italian troops were killed on the Russian front in the winter of 1942, and in 1943 the Allied forces gained a first foothold in Europe, when Patton's US Seventh Army and the British Eighth Army under Montgomery landed in Sicily.

In the face of these and other reversals Mussolini was overthrown by his own Grand Council, who bundled him away to the isolated mountain resort of Gran Sasso, and replaced him with the befuddled **Marshal Badoglio**. The Allies wanted Italy's surrender, for which they secretly offered amnesty to the king, Vittorio Emanuele III, who had coexisted with the Fascist regime for 21 years. On September 8 a radio broadcast announced that an **armistice** had been signed, and on the following day the Allies crossed to the mainland. As the Anglo-American army moved up through the peninsula, German divisions moved south to meet them, springing Mussolini from jail to set up the Fascist **Republic of Salò** on Lake Garda. It was a total failure, and increasing numbers of men and women from Communist, Socialist and Catholic parties swelled the opposing **partisan** forces to 450,000. In April 1945 Mussolini fled for his life, but was caught by partisans before reaching Switzerland. He was shot, as was his lover, Claretta Petacci, and both were strung up, feet first, in Milan's Piazzale Loreto.

The postwar years

A popular mandate in 1946 abolished the monarchy, declaring Italy a republic; Alcide de Gasperi's **Democrazia Cristiana** (DC) party formed a government. During the 1950s Italy became a front-rank industrial nation, massive firms such as Fiat and Olivetti helping to double the GDP and triple industrial production. US financial aid – the Marshall Plan – was an important factor in this expansion, as was the availability of a large and compliant workforce, a substantial proportion of which was drawn from southern villages.

The DC at first operated in alliance with other right-wing parties, but in 1963 they were obliged to share power for the first time with the **Partito Socialista Italiano** (PSI). The DC politician responsible for sounding out the socialists was **Aldo Moro**, the dominant figure of Italian politics in the 1960s, and prime minister from 1963 to 1968. The decade ended with the **autunno caldo** ("hot autumn") of 1969, when strikes, occupations and demonstrations paralyzed the country. More extreme forms of unrest broke out, instigated in the first instance by the far right, who were almost certainly behind a bomb that killed sixteen people in **Piazza Fontana**, Milan, in 1969.

The situation continued to worsen through the 1970s. A plethora of left-wing terrorist groups sprang up, many of them led by disaffected intellectuals at the northern universities. The most active of these were the **Brigate Rosse** (Red Brigades), who reached the peak of their notoriety in 1978, when a group kidnapped and killed Aldo Moro. The bombings continued throughout the 1970s, including that of Piazza della Loggia, Brescia in 1974, reaching its hideous climax in 1980, when 84 people were killed and 200 wounded by a bomb planted at Bologna train station by a neo-fascist group.

Inconsistencies and secrecy have beset those trying to clarify the terrorist activities of the 1970s. One Red Brigade member who served eighteen years in jail for his part in the assassination of Aldo Moro recently asserted that spies working for the **Italian secret services** masterminded the operation. A report prepared by the PDS (Italy's party of the democratic left) in 2000 re-iterated the beliefs of many: it alleged that in the 1970s and 1980s the Establishment pursued a "**strategy of tension**" and that indiscriminate bombing of the public and the threat of a right-wing coup were devices to stabilize centre-right political control of the country. Italy was the only European country to consistently give the Communist party around a third of the vote, and there were Establishment fears that it may have become another pawn in the Cold War. The perpetrators of bombing campaigns were rarely caught, said the report, because "those military actions had been organized or promoted or supported by Italian state institutions and US intelligence." Valter Bielli, one of the report's authors, added: "Other bombing campaigns were attributed to the left to prevent the Communist Party from achieving power by democratic means." The report drew furious rebuttals from centre-right groups and the US Embassy.

Scandals and corruption

By whatever means, the DC government clung to power through the 1970s, but the early 1980s saw a series of scandals that severely damaged their reputation, notably when masonic links were discovered between corrupt bankers, senior DC members and fanatical right-wing groups. These events were to set the tone for the next twenty and more years of Italian public life with accusations, investigations and trials of public figures becoming the norm.

Italy's first-ever Socialist prime minister, **Bettino Craxi** – premier from 1983 to 1987 – was at the centre of the powerful Socialist establishment that ran Milan, when in 1992 a minor party official was arrested on corruption charges. This represented the tip of a long-established culture of kickbacks and bribes that went right to the top of the political establishment, not just in Milan – nicknamed **tangentopoli** ("bribesville") – but across Italy. By the end of that year thousands were under arrest in what came to be known as the **Mani Pulite** (Clean Hands) investigation. In 1999, Craxi was convicted, with twenty others, of **corruption**. He was sentenced to five years in prison, but died a year later in exile in Tunisia.

Giulio Andreotti, perhaps the most potent symbol of the sleazy postwar years, seven times prime minister and a senator for life, was also brought to the dock to answer charges of a long-term conspiracy with the Mafia. He denied any association, and was acquitted – partly on technicalities – in 1999 aged 80. In 2002, however, he was charged with complicity in the murder of a journalist suspected to have been blackmailing him, found guilty and sentenced to 24 years in prison – yet after a series of appeals the conviction was quashed, leaving commentators divided about whether justice had been done.

A brave new world

The late 1980s and early 1990s saw the emergence of several new political parties, as many Italians became disillusioned with the old DC-led consensus. One was the right-wing **Lega Nord** (Northern League); its autocratic leader, **Umberto Bossi**, capitalized on a feeling held by many northerners that the state was supporting a corrupt south on the back of the hard-working, law-abiding north. The fascist MSI, renamed the **Alleanza Nazionale** (AN), and a wide coalition of right-wingers, gained ground.

The after-effects of Tangentopoli affected all levels of politics and civil admin-istration almost entirely wiping out the established parties in the municipal elections of 1993. The 1994 national elections saw a new political force emerge: the centre-right **Forza Italia** ("Come On, Italy"), led by the Milan-based media magnate **Silvio Berlusconi**. Berlusconi used the power of his TV stations to build support, and swept to power as prime minister in a populist alliance with Bossi's Lega Nord and the post-fascist Alleanza Nazionale. The fact that Berlusconi was not a politician was perhaps his greatest asset, and most Italians, albeit briefly, saw this as a new beginning – the end of the old, corrupt regime and the birth of a truly modern Italian state. However, as one of the country's top northern industrialists, and a pal of Craxi's, Berlusconi was as bound up with the old ways as anyone. Although he went on to win three elections in the following fourteen years and was head of Italy's **longest-lasting postwar government**, Berlusconi has proved to be no more successful at ruling the country than any of his predecessors. On a personal front not only has he resisted all attempts to reduce the scope of his media business and its conflict of interest with his premiership (see p.43), but his time in the public eye has also been accompanied by a constantly evolving charge-sheet covering money-laundering, corruption, gerrymandering and forcing through backdated legislation to get himself out of sticky court cases.

But, perhaps, more worrying still is the state of the nation: the media-mogul-turned-politician's promises of freedom and prosperity have been shown to be empty. Economic stand-still, social stagnation and stifling bureaucracy have modern-day Italy in a stranglehold. Both Berlusconi's governments and the various left-wing coalitions that have also been in power in the last decade have been too preoccupied by self-promotion and in-fighting to begin to resolve the malaise of the country. Italians, on the whole, have been left bruised, cynical and disillusioned by their leaders.

Books

Below is a selection of books that give a sense of the place, history and culture of northern Italy with particular relevance to the lakes region. As well as novels and travelogues, we've recommended some background texts on art, architecture and history plus a handful of specialist guides. Books marked 🏃 are particularly recommended.

Travel writing and fiction

Anne Calcagno (ed) *Travelers' Tales: Italy* (Group West). Crammed with evocative period detail as well as specifically commissioned contemporary writing by Tim Parks, Lisa St Aubin de Terán and others, this makes a perfect introduction to the richness and variety of Italy.

Ernest Hemingway *A Farewell to Arms* (Scribner). Hemingway's first novel is partly based on his experiences as a teenage ambulance driver on Italy's northeast front during World War I. Some of the scenes are set in Milan and on the lakes.

Henry James *Italian Hours* (Penguin Classics). Urbane travel pieces from

the young James with a couple of pages on Milan and Lake Como; perceptive about monuments and works of art, superb on the different atmospheres of Italy.

D.H. Lawrence *D.H. Lawrence and Italy* (Penguin). Lawrence's three Italian travelogues collected into one volume. *Twilight in Italy* was written on Lake Garda and is infused with the atmosphere of the lake while combining the author's seemingly natural ill-temper when travelling with a genuine sense of regret for a way of life visibly passing away.

🏃 **Tim Parks** *Italian Neighbours* (Vintage), *An Italian Education*

▲ Bookshop in Verona

(Vintage) and *A Season with Verona* (Vintage). Novelist Tim Parks has lived in Italy since 1981. Through deftly told tales of family life, his books examine what it means to be Italian, and how national identity is absorbed. In *A Season with Verona*, Parks spends the 2000–01 football season seeing his beloved team play every game – home and away. The vivid characterizations, backed by highly attuned insight into Italian and Veronese society, make it an engaging page-turner.

Edith Wharton *Italian Backgrounds* (Norton/Ecco Press). Beautiful descriptions of the lakes and the other landscapes Wharton found in her travels. She is at once elegantly enthusiastic and highly informed about the country's art and architecture.

History, society and politics

Baranski and West (ed) *Cambridge Companion to Modern Italian Culture* (Cambridge University Press). Despite the textbook style, this compilation of essays is a useful way to get to grips with contemporary Italian society from fashion or music to politics and identity.

R.J.B. Bosworth *Mussolini* (Oxford University Press). Bosworth paints a vivid picture of *Il Duce* while also explaining the context of Fascism and examines Mussolini's legacy, warning of the strong fascination for him that still exists in Italy today.

John Foot *Milan since the Miracle: City, Culture and Identity* (Berg). Hugely enjoyable and rigorous work that sets out to explore the social questions and sense of identity in this beguilingly complex city.

Paul Ginsborg *A History of Contemporary Italy* (Palgrave Macmillan), *Italy and Its Discontents* (Penguin) and *Silvio Berlusconi: Television, Power and Patrimony* (Verso). The first two are scholarly but very readable accounts of postwar Italian history, illustrating the complexity of contending economic, social and political currents. In his latest book Ginsborg again manages to make the intricacies and contradictions of Italian politics fathomable, this time while tracing the life and career of the country's ineffable politician and his effect on the lives of Italy's citizens.

Tobias Jones *The Dark Heart of Italy* (Faber and Faber/North Point Press). Written during a three-year period in Parma, this interconnected sequence of essays deals with various aspects of modern Italian society, from the legal and political systems to the media and football.

David Lane *Berlusconi's Shadow – Crime, Justice and the Pursuit of Power* (Penguin). Economist writer David Lane continues what has almost become a personal crusade against Berlusconi's corruption, shadowy business dealings and judicial manipulation.

The Longman History of Italy (Addison Wesley Publishing Company). This eight-volume series covers the history of Italy from the end of the Roman Empire to the present, each instalment comprising a range of essays on all aspects of political, social, economic and cultural history. Invaluable if you've developed a special interest in a particular period.

Patrick McCarthy *The Crisis of the Italian State* (St Martin's Press/ Palgrave Macmillan). Subtitled *From the Origins of the Cold War to the Fall* *of Berlusconi and Beyond*, this is a detailed but readable analysis of the root causes and major events of the "Clean Hands" political crisis that was centred on Milan of the 1990s.

Denis Mack Smith *The Making of Italy 1796–1866* (Holmes & Meier); *Italy and Its Monarchy* (Yale University Press). The former is an admirably lucid explanation of the various forces at work in the Unification of Italy, while the latter deals with Italy's short-lived monarchy. The same author has also written a couple of excellent biographies, *Mazzini* and *Mussolini*.

Art and architecture

Milano architectural guide (Umberto Allemandi & Co). A handy volume giving detailed information on the architecture of Milan, with brief descriptions and simple, black-and-white snaps of all the buildings, plus short essays by specialists from the Polytechnic of Milan.

Frederick Hartt *History of Italian Renaissance Art* (Prentice Hall Art). If one book on this vast subject can be said to be indispensable, this is it. A huge, wonderfully illustrated hardback that's something of a bargain in view of its comprehensiveness and acuity.

Elizabeth Helman Minchilli *Villas on the Italian Lakes* (Scriptum). Lavishly illustrated coffee-table book that takes a peek inside the grandest of the private villas that adorn the shores of lakes Garda, Maggiore and Orta. Architecture and decor are examined in detail, and the photography is exquisite.

Peter Murray *The Architecture of the Italian Renaissance* (Schocken Books). Begins with Romanesque buildings and finishes with Palladio – valuable both as a synopsis of the underlying concepts and as a gazetteer of the main monuments in towns including Verona, Mantova and Milan.

Manfredo Tafuri *History of Italian Architecture 1944–1985* (MIT Press). Tafuri analyzes the history, politics and movements that have shaped modern Italian architecture in this seminal work by one of today's leading critics and historians.

Manfredo Tafuri (ed) *Guilio Romano* (Cambridge University Press). This attractive hardback balances beautiful reproductions with insightful essays by Gombrich, Tafuri and others to give a full account of the artist's life and work. A decanted version of the definitive work on the Renaissance master translated from the Italian original.

Italian literature

The following is a selection of Italian writers and works that have a connection with the lakes region.

Catullus *The Poems of Catullus* (Penguin). Although his name is associated primarily with the tortured love poems addressed to Lesbia, Catullus also produced some acerbic satirical verse; this collection does full justice to his range and makes an entertaining companion to a trip to Sirmione, where he had a villa.

Gianni Celati *Voices from the Plains* (Serpent's Tail). A beautifully crafted novel that uses the simple premise of chance encounters on a walk along the Po river to provide the focus for these touching, atmospheric tales.

Gabriele D'Annunzio *The Book of the Virgins* (Hesperus Press). Self-regarding dandy, war hero and worshipper of Mussolini, D'Annunzio – who lived in the extraordinary Il Vittoriale on the shore of Lake Garda – was perhaps the most complex figure of twentieth-century Italian literature. This collection of some of his first works has a foreward by Tim Parks.

Umberto Eco *Foucault's Pendulum* (Ballantine Books). Set in Milan to a backdrop of Masons, Templars and cultural mythology, this rather impenetrable thriller has been described as the forerunner to pop-historical novels like Dan Brown's *The Da Vinci Code*. *The Name of the Rose* (Harvest Books) has some similar themes but is decidedly more readable.

Dario Fo *Plays I* (Methuen Publishing). The Nobel Prize winner fabulously weaves together contemporary politics, surreal farce and the traditions of *commedia dell'arte*. This collection includes a trio of Fo's most famous plays – *Accidental Death of an Anarchist* (inspired by the Piazza Fontana cover-up in Milan), *Mistero Buffo*, and *Trumpets and Raspberries* – along with two previously unpublished short works.

Alessandro Manzoni *The Betrothed* (Penguin). The first modern Italian novel is no pool-side thriller, but a skilful melding of the romance of two young lovers and a sweeping historical drama set in seventeenth-century Milan and Lecco during the plague.

Food and drink

Nicholas Belfrage *Barolo to Valpolicella: Wines of Northern Italy* (Mitchell Beazley). Not as user-friendly as it might be – there are no vintage charts and few maps – this guide nevertheless manages to pack in a wealth of information on the producers and diverse wines of the region.

Elizabeth David *Italian Food* (Penguin). The writer who introduced Italian cuisine – and ingredients – to Britain. Ahead of its time when it was published in the 1950s, and imbued with all the enthusiasm and diversity of Italian cookery. An inspirational book.

Marcella Hazan *The Classic Italian Cookbook* (Ballantine Books). The best Italian cookbook for the novice in the kitchen is a step-by-step guide that draws from all over the peninsula, emphasizing the intrinsically regional nature of Italian food.

Fred Plotkin *Italy for the Gourmet Traveller* (Kyle Cathie Ltd). Comprehensive, region-by-region guide to the best of Italian cuisine, with a foodie's guide to major towns and cities, a gazetteer of restaurants and specialist food and wine shops, plus descriptions of local dishes, with recipes.

Claudia Roden *The Food of Italy* (Steerforth Italia). A culinary classic, this regional guide takes in easy-to-follow local recipes from the people for whom they are second nature. Authentic and accessible.

Specialist guides

Helena Attlee and Alex Ramsay *Italian Gardens* (Ellipsis Arts). Evocatively photographed (by Alex Ramsay), this is a handy pocket-sized guide to more than sixty of the peninsula's most beautiful gardens. It provides histories and descriptions, as well as detailed information on locations, facilities, opening times and accessibility.

Jill Fairchild & Gerri Gallagher *Where to Wear Italy* (Where to Wear). Jaunty, knowledgeable reviews of hundreds of shops and a clear well-organized structure make this fashion guide indispensable to anyone who takes their shopping in Milan seriously.

Penelope Hobhouse *The Garden Lover's Guide to Italy* (Princetown Architectural Press). Large, beautifully illustrated guide taking the reader through the highlights of the best-known and some little-discovered Italian gardens. Well designed with lots of extra features and context on each garden.

Leonardo da Vinci *Notebooks* (Dover Publications). Miscellany of speculation and observation from the universal genius of Renaissance Italy; essential to any understanding of the man.

Passeggiando in bicicletta: Lombardia (Editoriale Eurocamp). A well-organized guide with twenty itineraries for two- to five-hour cycling trips around the lakes region. Some basic Italian is helpful for following the routes and understanding the background info, but you could just take their suggestions and plot the routes on your own map.

Language

Language

Italian

Although you're likely to have few problems finding an English speaker when you need one in the area covered by this book, try a little Italian and your halting efforts will often be rewarded by smiles and appreciation. Regional dialects are still very much in use in Italy today and as the nationalist Lega Nord party has taken hold in the north so the pride in local dialects has increased. Brown-coloured signs bearing the dialect name mark the entrance to towns and villages across the region, especially around Brescia and Bergamo. In the Swiss canton (region) of Ticino, English is generally a third language, behind Italian and German.

As well as some useful **vocabulary** below, we've included a **menu reader** to help you negotiate your way round what's on offer at the table, and a **glossary** of common Italian words.

Pronunciation

Words are spoken as they are written in Italian, and usually enunciated with exaggerated, open-mouthed clarity. The only difficulties you're likely to encounter are the few **consonants** that are different from English:

c before e or i is pronounced as in church, while ch before the same vowels is hard, as in cat.

sci and sce are pronounced as in sheet and shelter respectively.

The same goes with g – soft before e or i, as in geranium; hard before h, as in garlic.

gn has the ni sound of onion.

gl in Italian is softened to something like li in English, as in stallion.

h is not aspirated, as in honour.

Most Italian words are **stressed** on the penultimate syllable. In written Italian, **accents** (either ` or ´) have traditionally been used to denote stress on other syllables, but the acute (´) accent is more rarely used these days. Note that the endings -ia or -ie count as two syllables, hence trattoria is stressed on the **i**.

Italian words and phrases

Basics	
Good morning	Buongiorno
Good afternoon/ evening	Buona sera
Good night	Buona notte
Hello	Salve
Hello/goodbye	Ciao (informal)
Goodbye	Arrivederci
Yes	Si
No	No
Please	Per favore
Thank you (very much)	Grazie (mille)
You're welcome	Prego
All right/that's OK	Va bene
How are you? (informal/formal)	Come stai/sta?

I'm fine	Bene
Do you speak English?	Parla inglese?
I didn't understand	Non ho capito
I don't know	Non lo so
Excuse me	Scusami
Excuse me (in a crowd)	Permesso
I'm sorry	Mi dispiace
I'm here on holiday	Sono qui in vacanza
I'm British/Irish	Sono britannico/a irlandese/a
American	americano/a
Australian	australiano/a
From New Zealand	neozelandese/a
I live in …	Abito a …
Today	Oggi
Tomorrow	Domani
Day after tomorrow	Dopodomani
Yesterday	Ieri
Now	Adesso
Later	Piùtardi
Wait a minute!	Aspetta!
Let's go!	Andiamo!
With/Without	Con/Senza
More/Less	Più/Meno
Enough, no more	Basta
In the morning	Di mattina
In the afternoon	Nel pomeriggio
In the evening	Di sera
Here/There	Quà
Good/Bad	Buono/Cattivo
Big/Small	Grande/Piccolo
Cheap/Expensive	Economico/Caro
Early/Late	Presto/Tardi
Hot/Cold	Caldo/Freddo
Near/Far	Vicino/Lontano
Quickly/Slowly	Velocemente/ Lentamente
Slowly/Quietly	Piano
Mr …	Signor …
Mrs …	Signora …
Miss …	Signorina …
(il Signor, la Signora, la Signorina when speaking about someone else)	

Driving

Left/right	Sinistra/Destra
Go straight ahead	Sempre diritto
Turn left/right	Gira a sinistra/destra
Car park	Parcheggio
No parking	Divieto di sosta/Sosta vietata
One-way street	Senso unico
No entry	Senso vietato
Slow down	Rallentare
Road closed/ under repair	Strada chiusa/lavori in corso
No through road	Vietato il transito
No overtaking	Vietato il sorpasso
Crossroads	Incrocio
Speed limit	Limite di velocità

Some signs

Entrance/Exit	Entrata/Uscita
Free entrance	Ingresso libero
Gentlemen	Signori/Uomini
Ladies	Signore/Donne
WC/Bathroom	Gabinetto/Bagno
Vacant/Engaged	Libero/Occupato
Open/Closed	Aperto/Chiuso
Arrivals/Departures	Arrivi/Partenze
Closed for restoration	Chiuso per restauro
Closed for holidays	Chiuso per ferie
Pull/Push	Tirare/Spingere
Out of order	Guasto
Drinking water	Acqua potabile
Platform	Binario
Cash desk	Cassa
Go/walk	Avanti
Stop/halt	Alt
Customs	Dogana
Do not touch	Non toccare
Danger	Pericolo
Beware	Attenzione
First aid	Pronto soccorso
Ring the bell	Suonare il campanello
No smoking	Vietato fumare

Italian numbers

1	uno
2	due
3	tre
4	quattro
5	cinque
6	sei

7	sette		
8	otto		
9	nove		
10	dieci		
11	undici		
12	dodici		
13	tredici		
14	quattordici		
15	quindici		
16	sedici		
17	diciassette		
18	diciotto		
19	diciannove		
20	venti		
21	ventuno		
22	ventidue		
30	trenta		
40	quaranta		
50	cinquanta		
60	sessanta		
70	settanta		
80	ottanta		
90	novanta		
100	cento		
101	centouno		
110	centodieci		
200	duecento		
500	cinquecento		
1000	mille		

Accommodation

Hotel	Albergo/hotel
Is there a hotel nearby?	C'è un albergo qui vicino?
Do you have a room ...	Ha una camera ...
for one/two/three	per una/due/tre
person/people	persona/e
for one/two	per una/due/ tre
three night/s	notte/i
for one/two week/s	per una/due settimana/e
with a double bed	con un letto matrimoniale
with a shower/bath	con doccia/bagno
with a balcony	con un balcone
hot/cold water	acqua calda/fredda
How much is it?	Quanto costa?

Is breakfast included?	é compresa la prima colazione?
Do you have anything cheaper?	Ha niente che costa meno?
Full/half board	Pensione completa/ mezza pensione
Can I see the room?	Posso vedere la camera?
I'll take it	La prendo
I'd like to book a room	Vorrei prenotare una camera
I have a booking	Ho una prenotazione
Can we camp here?	Possiamo campeggiare qui?
Is there a campsite nearby?	C'è un campeggio qui vicino?
Tent	Tenda
Youth hostel	Ostello della gioventù

Questions and directions

Where? (Where is/ Where are ...?)	Dove? (Dov'è/ Dove sono ...?)
When?	Quando?
What? (What is it?)	Cosa? (Cos'è?)
How much/many?	Quanto/Quanti?
Why?	Perchè?
It is/there is (is it/is there ...?)	C'e ...?
What time is it?	Che ora è/Che ore sono?
How do I get to ...?	Come arrivo a ...?
How far is it to ...?	Quant'è lontano ...?
Can you give me a lift to ...?	Mi può dare un passaggio a ...?
Can you tell me when to get off?	Mi può dire quando devo scendere?
What time does it open?	A che ora apre?
What time does it close?	A che ora chiude?
How much does it cost?	Quanto costa?
(... do they cost?)	(... Quanto costano?)
What's it called in Italian?	Come si dice in italiano?

Travelling

Aeroplane	Aereo
Bus	Autobus/pullman

Train	Treno	bus/train/ferry	pullman/treno/
Car	Macchina/automobile		traghetto
Taxi	Taxi	to ...?	per ...?
Bicycle	Bicicletta	Do I have to change?	Devo cambiare?
Ferry	Traghetto	Where does it leave from?	Da dove parte?
Hitch-hiking	Autostop		
On foot	A piedi	What platform does it leave from?	Da quale binario parte?
Bus station	Stazione degli autobus	How many kilometres is it?	Quanti chilometri sono?
Train station	Stazione ferroviaria		
A ticket to ...	Un biglietto per ...	How long does it take?	Quanto ci vuole?
One-way/return	Solo andata/andata e ritorno	What number bus is it to...?	Che numero di autobus per ...?
Can I book a seat?	Posso prenotare un posto?	Where's the road to ...	Dovè la strada per ...
What time does it leave?	A che ora parte?	Next stop please	La prossima fermata, per favore
When is the next	Quando parte il prossimo		

Menu reader

Local specialities

Bigoli	Local variety of thick spaghetti
Bollito misto	Mixture of boiled meats, usually served with *mostarda*
Burro fuso	Melted butter, usually with sage leaves
Casoela	Pork chop, cabbage and sausage casserole, usually served with polenta
Casoncelli	Ravioli stuffed with sausage-meat
Coregone	White lake fish (lavaret)
Costoletta/Cotoletta alla Milanese	Veal cutlet battered in breadcrumbs and fried in butter
Nervetti con cipolle	Cold starter of calf cartilage and onion dressed with oil and vinegar
Mostarda	Marinated fruit and vegetables with

	mustard, accompanying roasts and *bollito*
Osso buco alla Milanese	Braised veal including bone and its marrow
Pan d'oro	Verona's variation of *panettone*, often in a star shape
Panettone	Dome-shaped egg sponge filled with candied peel and sultanas. Originally from Milan, it is ubiquitous at Christmas time.
Persico fritto	Floured, fried perch
Pizzoccheri	Buckwheat pasta ribbons, usually served with cheese, spinach and potatoes
Polenta	Cornmeal (or grits), served boiled, or boiled and then sliced and grilled
Rane in umido	Steamed frog-meat

Risotto alla Milanese	Saffron risotto
Tortelli alla zucca	Ravioli stuffed with pumpkin

Basics and snacks

Aceto	Vinegar
Aglio	Garlic
Biscotti	Biscuits
Burro	Butter
Caramelle	Sweets
Cioccolato	Chocolate
Formaggio	Cheese
Frittata	Omelette
Grissini	Bread sticks
Maionese	Mayonnaise
Marmellata	Jam
Olio	Oil
Olive	Olives
Pane	Bread
Pane integrale	Wholemeal bread
Panino	Bread roll/sandwich
Patate fritte	Chips (French fries)
Patatine	Crisps (potato chips)
Pepe	Pepper
Riso	Rice
Sale	Salt
Uova/Uove	Egg/eggs
Zucchero	Sugar
Zuppa	Soup

Pizzas

Calzone	Folded pizza, often with cheese, ham and tomato
Capricciosa	Literally "capricious"; topped with whatever they've got in the kitchen, usually including baby artichoke, mushrooms, ham and capers
Frutti di mare	Seafood, usually mussels, prawns, squid and clams
Margherita	Cheese and tomato
Marinara	Tomato and garlic; no cheese

Napoli/Napoletana	Tomato, cheese, anchovy, olive oil and oregano
Quattro formaggi	"Four cheeses", usually including mozzarella, fontina, gruyère and gorgonzola
Quattro stagioni	"Four seasons", usually including ham, pepper, onion, mushrooms, artichokes, olives, etc

Antipasti and starters

Antipasto misto	Selection of starters usually including cold meats, fish or vegetables
Bresaola	Dried, salted beef, sliced thinly
Capponata	Mixed aubergine, olives, tomatoes and anchovies
Caprese	Tomato and mozzarella salad with basil
Insalata russa	Salad of diced vegetables in mayonnaise
Lardo	Paper-thin slices of pork fat
Melanzane alla parmigiana	Aubergine with tomato and parmesan cheese
Peperonata	Green and red peppers stewed in olive oil
Pomodori ripieni	Stuffed tomatoes
Prosciutto cotto/crudo	Boiled ham/dried ham
Salame	Salami
Speck	Smoked ham

The first course (il primo): soups, pasta …

Brodo	Clear broth
Cannelloni	Large tubes of pasta, stuffed

Farfalle	Butterfly-shaped pasta
Fettuccine	Narrow pasta ribbons
Gnocchi	Small potato dumplings
Minestrina/minestra	Clear broth with small pasta shapes
Minestrone	Thick vegetable soup
Pappardelle	Wide, flat pasta ribbons
Pasta al forno	Baked pasta with minced meat, eggs, tomato and cheese
Pasta e fagioli	Pasta and bean soup
Penne	Smaller version of rigatoni
Ravioli	Filled parcels of egg pasta
Rigatoni	Large, grooved tubular pasta
Stracciatella	Broth with egg
Tagliatelle	Pasta ribbons
Tortellini	Small rings of pasta, stuffed with meat or cheese

... and pasta sauce

Amatriciana	Cubed bacon and tomato sauce
Arrabbiata	Spicy tomato sauce, with chillies
Carbonara	Pancetta, pecorino, pepper and beaten egg
Funghi	Mushrooms
Panna	Cream
Parmigiano	Parmesan cheese
Pesto	Sauce with ground basil, garlic and pine nuts
Pomodoro	Tomato sauce
Puttanesca	Spicy tomato, anchovy, olive oil and oregano
Ragù	Meat sauce, known in the UK as Bolognese
Salvia	Sage
Vongole	Clams

The second course (il secondo): meat (carne) ...

Agnello	Lamb
Anatra	Duck
Asino	Donkey
Bistecca	Steak
Carpaccio	Thin slices of raw beef
Cervella	Brain, usually calves'
Cinghiale	Wild boar
Coniglio	Rabbit
Cotecchino	Pork sausage
Costoletta or coteletta	Cutlet, chop
Fegatini	Chicken livers
Fegato	Liver
Involtini	Meat slices, rolled and stuffed
Lepre	Hare
Lingua	Tongue
Maiale	Pork
Manzo	Beef
Osso buco	Shin of veal
Pancetta	Bacon
Pollo	Chicken
Polpette	Meatballs
Rana	Frog
Rognoni	Kidneys
Salsiccia	Sausage
Saltimbocca	Veal with prosciutto and sage
Spezzatino	Stew
Stufato	Stewed meat
Tacchino	Turkey
Trippa	Tripe
Vitello	Veal

... fish (pesce) and shellfish (crostacei)

Acciughe	Anchovies
Anguilla	Eel
Aragosta	Lobster
Baccalà	Dried salted cod
Branzino	Sea Bass
Calamari	Squid
Cefalo	Grey mullet
Coda di rospo	Monkfish
Cozze	Mussels

Dentice	Sea bream	Radicchio	Red salad leaves
Gamberetti	Shrimps	Rosmarino	Rosemary
Gamberi	Prawns	Rucola	Rocket
Granchio	Crab	Salvia	Sage
Laverello	White freshwater lake fish	Spinaci	Spinach
		Zucca	Pumpkin
Luccio	Pike	Zucchine	Courgettes
Merluzzo	Cod		
Ostriche	Oysters		

Some cooking terms

Pesce persico	Perch	Affumicato	Smoked
Pesce spada	Swordfish	Arrosto	Roast
Polpo	Octopus	Ben cotto	Well cooked
Sampiero	John Dory	Bollito/lesso	Boiled
Sardine	Sardines	Alla brace	Barbecued
Sgombro	Mackerel	Brasato	Cooked in wine
Sógliola	Sole	Congelato	Frozen
Tinca	Tench	Cotto	Cooked
Tonno	Tuna	Crudo	Raw
Triglia	Red mullet	Al dente	Firm, not overcooked
Trota	Trout	Ai ferri	Grilled without oil
Vongole	Clams	Al forno	Baked
		Fritto	Fried

Vegetables (contorni), herbs (erbe aromatiche) and salad (insalata)

		Grattuggiato	Grated
		Alla griglia	Grilled
Asparagi	Asparagus	Alla Milanese	Fried in egg and breadcrumbs
Basilico	Basil		
Capperi	Capers	Pizzaiola	Cooked with tomato sauce
Carciofini	Artichoke hearts		
Cavolfiore	Cauliflower	Ripieno	Stuffed
Cavolo	Cabbage	Al sangue	Rare
Ceci	Chickpeas	Allo spiedo	On the spit
Cetriolo	Cucumber	Spiedino	Skewer or kebab
Cipolla	Onion	Stracotto	Braised, stewed
Fagioli	Beans	Surgelato	Frozen
Fagiolini	String beans	In umido	Stewed
Finocchio	Fennel		

Sweets (dolci), fruit (frutta), cheeses (formaggi) and nuts (noci)

Funghi	Mushrooms		
Insalata verde/ mista	Green salad/mixed salad	Amaretti	Macaroons
		Ananas	Pineapple
Lenticchie	Lentils	Anguria/Cocomero	Watermelon
Melanzane	Aubergine or eggplant	Arance	Oranges
Origano	Oregano	Cachi	Persimmons
Patate	Potatoes	Ciliege	Cherries
Peperoni	Peppers	Crostata	Jam tart
Piselli	Peas	Dolcelatte	Creamy blue cheese
Pomodori	Tomatoes	Fichi	Figs
Prezzemolo	Parsley		

Fragole	Strawberries
Gelato	Ice cream
Grana Padana	Local version of Parmesan cheese
Gorgonzola	Soft, strong, blue-veined cheese
Macedonia	Fruit salad
Mandorle	Almonds
Mascarpone	Smooth, rich, soft cheese
Mele	Apples
Parmigiano Reggiano	Parmesan
Pecorino	Strong, hard sheep's cheese
Pesche	Peaches
Pignoli	Pine nuts
Provola/Provolone	Mild cheese made from buffalo or sheep milk, sometimes smoked
Ricotta	Soft, white cheese
Taleggio	Creamy, soft cheese
Tiramisù	Trifle-like dessert
Torta	Cake, tart
Uva	Grapes
Zabaglione	Dessert with eggs, sugar and marsala wine
Zuppa Inglese	Trifle

Drinks

Acqua minerale	Mineral water
gasata	sparkling
naturale	still
Acqua tonica	Tonic water
Bianco	White
Bicchiere	Glass
Birra	Beer
Bottiglia	Bottle
Caffè	Coffee
Caraffa	Carafe
Cioccolata calda	Hot chocolate
Dolce	Sweet
Ghiaccio	Ice
Granita	Iced drink, with coffee or fruit
Latte	Milk
Litro	Litre
Mezzo	Half
Quarto	Quarter
Rosato	Rosé
Rosso	Red
Salute!	Cheers!
Secco	Dry
Spremuta	Fresh fruit juice
Spumante	Sparkling wine
Succo	Concentrated fruit juice with sugar
Tè	Tea
Vino	Wine

Glossary of Italian words

alimentari grocery shops

anfiteatro amphitheatre

autostazione bus station

autostrada motorway

biblioteca library

cappella chapel

castello castle

centro centre

centro storico historic centre/old town

chiesa church

comune an administrative area; also the local council or town hall

corso avenue or boulevard

duomo/cattedrale cathedral

entrata entrance

festa festival, holiday

fiume river

lago lake

largo kind of square

lungolago lakefront road or promenade

mercato market

municipio town hall

paese country village

palazzo palace, mansion, or block of flats

parco park

passeggiata the customary early-evening walk

piazza square

pinacoteca picture gallery

ponte bridge

santuario sanctuary

senso unico one-way street

sottopassaggio subway

spiaggia beach

stazione station

strada road

teatro theatre

tempio temple

torre tower

traghetto ferry

uscita exit

via road (always used with name, eg Via Roma)

Glossary of artistic and architectural terms

ambo A raised pulpit, popular in Italian medieval churches.

apse A vaulted semicircular or polygonal termination of a church, usually eastern.

architrave Lintel or the lowest part of the entablature.

atrium Inner courtyard.

Baroque Exuberant architectural style of the seventeenth century, characterized by ornate decoration, complex spatial arrangements and grand vistas. Also applied to the period's sumptuous style of painting and sculpture.

basilica Originally a Roman administrative building, adapted for early churches; distinguished by lack of transepts.

belvedere A terrace or lookout point.

campanile Bell-tower, sometimes detached, usually of a church.

capital Top of a column.

cella Sanctuary of a temple.

chiaroscuro The balance of light and shade in a painting, and the skill of the artist in depicting the contrast between the two.

chancel Part of a church containing the altar.

cornice The top section of a Classical facade.

cortile Galleried courtyard or cloister.

crypt Burial place in a church, usually under the choir.

decumanus maximus The main street of a Roman town. The second cross-street was known as the *cardo maximus*.

entablature The section above the capital on a Classical building, below the cornice.

ex-voto Painting or object presented in thanksgiving to a saint.

fresco Wall-painting technique in which the artist applies paint to wet plaster for a more permanent finish.

367

Gothic Architectural style of the thirteenth and fourteenth centuries, with an emphasis on verticality, characterized by pointed arches, ribbed vaulting and flying buttresses.

Liberty Italian version of Art Nouveau.

loggia Roofed gallery or balcony.

Mannerism Sixteenth-century style characterized by stylization of Renaissance rules, theatrical motifs and technical skill.

nave Central space in a church, usually flanked by aisles.

Neoclassicism A rigorous architecture of pure geometrical forms based on Classical rules, prevalent in the late eighteenth century.

piano nobile Main floor of a palace, usually the first level above ground.

polyptych Painting on several joined wooden panels.

portico Covered entrance to a building, or porch.

presepio A Christmas crib.

putti Cherubs.

reliquary Receptacle for a saint's relics, usually bones. Often highly decorated.

Renaissance Fifteenth- and sixteenth-century Italian-originated movement in art and architecture, inspired by the rediscovery of Classical ideals.

Romanesque Solid architectural style of the late tenth to mid-thirteenth centuries, characterized by round-headed arches and a penchant for horizontality and geometric precision.

sgraffito Decorative technique whereby one layer of plaster is scratched to reveal a darker-coloured layer beneath.

stucco Plaster made from water, lime, sand and powdered marble, used for decorative work.

thermae Baths, usually elaborate buildings in Roman villas.

triptych Painting on three joined wooden panels.

trompe l'oeil Work of art that deceives the viewer by means of tricks with perspective.

Small print and

Index

A Rough Guide to Rough Guides

Published in 1982, the first Rough Guide – to Greece – was a student scheme that became a publishing phenomenon. Mark Ellingham, a recent graduate in English from Bristol University, had been travelling in Greece the previous summer and couldn't find the right guidebook. With a small group of friends he wrote his own guide, combining a highly contemporary, journalistic style with a thoroughly practical approach to travellers' needs.

The immediate success of the book spawned a series that rapidly covered dozens of destinations. And, in addition to impecunious backpackers, Rough Guides soon acquired a much broader and older readership that relished the guides' wit and inquisitiveness as much as their enthusiastic, critical approach and value-for-money ethos.

These days, Rough Guides include recommendations from shoestring to luxury and cover more than 200 destinations around the globe, including almost every country in the Americas and Europe, more than half of Africa and most of Asia and Australasia. Our ever-growing team of authors and photographers is spread all over the world, particularly in Europe, the USA and Australia.

In the early 1990s, Rough Guides branched out of travel, with the publication of Rough Guides to World Music, Classical Music and the Internet. All three have become benchmark titles in their fields, spearheading the publication of a wide range of books under the Rough Guide name.

Including the travel series, Rough Guides now number more than 350 titles, covering: phrasebooks, waterproof maps, music guides from Opera to Heavy Metal, reference works as diverse as Conspiracy Theories and Shakespeare, and popular culture books from iPods to Poker. Rough Guides also produce a series of more than 120 World Music CDs in partnership with World Music Network.

Visit www.roughguides.com to see our latest publications.

Rough Guide travel images are available for commercial licensing at www.roughguidespictures.com

Rough Guide credits

Text editor: Ros Belford
Layout: Jessica Subramanian
Cartography: Deshpal Dabas
Picture editor: Mark Thomas
Production: Rebecca Short
Proofreader: Elaine Pollard
Cover design: Chloë Roberts
Photographer: Helena Smith
Editorial: London Ruth Blackmore, Andy Turner, Keith Drew, Edward Aves, Alice Park, Lucy White, Jo Kirby, James Smart, Natasha Foges, Róisín Cameron, Emma Traynor, James Rice, Emma Gibbs, Kathryn Lane, Christina Valhouli, Monica Woods, Mani Ramaswamy, Harry Wilson, Alison Roberts, Joe Staines, Peter Buckley, Matthew Milton, Tracy Hopkins, Ruth Tidball; **New York** Andrew Rosenberg, Steven Horak, AnneLise Sorensen, Ella Steim, Anna Owens, Sean Mahoney, Paula Neudorf; **Delhi** Madhavi Singh, Karen D'Souza, Lubna Shaheen
Design & Pictures: London Scott Stickland, Dan May, Diana Jarvis, Chloë Roberts, Nicole Newman, Sarah Cummins, Emily Taylor; **Delhi** Umesh Aggarwal, Ajay Verma, Ankur Guha, Pradeep Thapliyal, Sachin Tanwar, Anita Singh, Nikhil Agarwal

Production: Vicky Baldwin
Cartography: **London** Maxine Repath, Ed Wright, Katie Lloyd-Jones; **Delhi** Rajesh Chhibber, Ashutosh Bharti, Rajesh Mishra, Animesh Pathak, Jasbir Sandhu, Karobi Gogoi, Alakananda Bhattacharya, Swati Handoo
Online: London George Atwell, Faye Hellon, Jeanette Angell, Fergus Day, Justine Bright, Clare Bryson, Áine Fearon, Adrian Low, Ezgi Celebi, Amber Bloomfield; **Delhi** Amit Verma, Rahul Kumar, Narender Kumar, Ravi Yadav, Debojit Borah, Rakesh Kumar, Ganesh Sharma, Shisir Basumatari
Marketing & Publicity: London Liz Statham, Niki Hanmer, Louise Maher, Jess Carter, Vanessa Godden, Vivienne Watton, Anna Paynton, Rachel Sprackett, Libby Jellie, Laura Vipond; **New York** Geoff Colquitt, Nancy Lambert, Katy Ball; **Delhi** Ragini Govind
Manager India: Punita Singh
Reference Director: Andrew Lockett
Operations Manager: Helen Phillips
PA to Publishing Director: Nicola Henderson
Publishing Director: Martin Dunford
Commercial Manager: Gino Magnotta
Managing Director: John Duhigg

Publishing information

This second edition published April 2009 by
Rough Guides Ltd,
80 Strand, London WC2R 0RL
345 Hudson St, 4th Floor,
New York, NY 10014, USA
14 Local Shopping Centre, Panchsheel Park,
New Delhi 110017, India
Distributed by the Penguin Group
Penguin Books Ltd,
80 Strand, London WC2R 0RL
Penguin Group (USA)
375 Hudson Street, NY 10014, USA
Penguin Group (Australia)
250 Camberwell Road, Camberwell,
Victoria 3124, Australia
Penguin Group (Canada)
195 Harry Walker Parkway N, Newmarket, ON,
L3Y 7B3 Canada
Penguin Group (NZ)
67 Apollo Drive, Mairangi Bay, Auckland 1310,
New Zealand

Cover concept by Peter Dyer.

Typeset in Bembo and Helvetica to an original design by Henry Iles.

Printed and bound in China

© Lucy Ratcliffe and Matthew Teller 2009

384pp includes index

A catalogue record for this book is available from the British Library.

ISBN: 978-1-84836-038-9

1   3   5   7   9   8   6   4   2

Help us update

We've gone to a lot of effort to ensure that the second edition of **The Rough Guide to The Italian Lakes** is accurate and up to date. However, things change – places get "discovered", opening hours are notoriously fickle, restaurants and rooms raise prices or lower standards. If you feel we've got it wrong or left something out, we'd like to know, and if you can remember the address, the price, the hours, the phone number, so much the better.

Please send your comments with the subject line "**Rough Guide Italian Lakes Update**" to ®mail@roughguides.com. We'll credit all contributions and send a copy of the next edition (or any other Rough Guide if you prefer) for the very best emails.

Have your questions answered and tell others about your trip at
Ⓦcommunity.roughguides.com

Acknowledgements

The authors would like to thank all those individuals throughout the lakes region who offered help and support with such warmth and generosity. In particular, we'd like to thank the following:

Matthew: LONDON: Alessandra Smith, Adriana Vacca and Stefania Gatta, ENIT; Roland Minder and Evelyn Lafone, Switzerland Tourism; Sarah Belcher at Travel PR and Rosanna Melaragni at Sunvil. TICINO: Patrizia Fransioli and Tosca Zanotta at Ticino Tourism, Bellinzona. LAKE MAGGIORE: Miria Sanzone and Irene Lilla, Distretto dei Laghi, Stresa. LAKE ORTA: Jennifer at the Orta San Giulio tourist office. VARESE: Stella Asciano, VareseHotels.it; LAKE COMO: Giuseppe Pisilli, Provincia di Como; Ester Geraci, Museo Didattico della Seta, Como; Laura Maglia

and Francesca Zuccoli, Provincia di Lecco. BERGAMO: Alessandra Pitocchi, Turismo Bergamo. BRESCIA: Armando Pederzoli and colleagues, Comune di Brescia. LAKE GARDA: Francesca Fiorilli at "Lago di Garda è …"; Patricia, Associazione Albergatori Sirmione; Marta Cobelli, Consorzio Riviera dei Limoni. VERONA: Monica Viviani and Luca Rizzardi, Provincia di Verona.

Lucy: Germana Colombo at the Provincia di Milano for her help; Nicolino for his first few faltering steps; Charlotte for company; and Luca for everything.

At Rough Guides, many thanks to our editor Ros Belford and especially to Monica Woods for all her help in a crisis.

Readers' letters

Many thanks to all those readers who took the time to write, email or contribute to the online forums at ⓦ www.roughguides.com with comments on the previous edition, new discoveries or just an account of their travels. Apologies if we've misspelt or misunderstood anyone's name. Thanks to:

Peter and Elza Barlow, John Barnard, Rev and Mrs R.J. Blakeway-Phillips, Carol Bloomfield, Malcolm Dawson, Susan Deacon, Chris Drayton, Scott Eldridge, Carolyn Grote, Martin Hanney, Jeff Hennessey, M. Jenkins, Mrs Natasha Josephidou,

Bill Munro, Amanda Newman, Tony Nichols and Yves Jatteau, Richard and Sheila Owen, Steven Proud, Diana Sidaway, Susan Stonard, Bill and Carolyn Thomas, Judith Vennix, Miss Lindsey Wignall and Neil Malley.

Photo credits

All photos © Rough Guides except the following:

Title page
Lake Garda © Michael Thomas Photography

Introduction
Thumbnail: Swiss/Italian border at Lugano
  © Travelstock/Alamy
Riva del Garda, Lake Garda © Ian Dagnall/Alamy
Rocca Scaligera, Sirmione, Lake Garda
  © Matthew Teller
Menaggio, Lake Como © Jon Arnold Images/
  Alamy

Things not to miss
02 Watersports, Lake Garda © International
  Photobank/Alamy
04 Bergamo Alta © PCl/Alamy
05 Lago Maggiore Express © Christof
  Sonderegger/swiss-image.ch
07 Bagolino and mountains © Imagebroker/Alamy
08 The Last Supper by Leonardo da Vinci
  © Getty Images
10 Bellinzona's castles © Remy Steinegger/
  swiss-image.ch
14 Monte Generoso © Philipp Giegel/swiss-image
  .ch
15 Opera in Verona © JTB Photo/Alamy

Lake cuisine colour section
Tortelloni © Tim Hill/Alamy

Fishmongers' sign, Lake Garda © Ian Dagnall/
  Alamy
Char-grilled polenta © Food Features/Alamy
Café terrace, Bergamo © Lucy Ratcliffe
Mostarda di Cremona © Eye Ubiquitous/Alamy

Gardens of the lakes colour section
Giardino Giusti Verona © Robert Harding/Alamy
Villa Táranto, Pallanza © CuboImages/Alamy
Chinese garden plants, Giardino Botanico André
  Heller © Avatre Images/Alamy
Isole di Brissago, Lake Maggiore © Christof
  Sonderegger/swiss-image.ch
Lemons, Lake Garda © Natural background/
  Alamy
Parco Giardino Sigurtà © Photo stock/Alamy
Villa Monastero, Varenna © Geoffrey Kirman/
  Alamy

Black and whites
p.174 Villa Carlotta, Lake Como © Russell Kord/
  Alamy
p.183 The Duomo, Como © Matthew Teller
p.196 Bellagio © World Pictures/Alamy
p.224 Bergamo Alta © C Bowman/Axiom
p.233 Cappella Colleoni, Piazza Duomo, Bergamo
  © MB Europe/Alamy

ROUGH GUIDES

SMALL PRINT

Index

Map entries are in colour

C

D

E

F

G

H

I

INDEX

INDEX

Map symbols

maps are listed in the full index in coloured text

▬▬▪	International boundary	↙	View point
▬ ▬ ▬	Chapter division boundary	ⓘ	Tourist office
▬▬▬	Motorway	♦	Place of interest
══	Major road	🏊	Swimming pool
══	Minor road	∴	Ruin
▥▥▥	Steps	♜	Castle
▯▯▯▯	Unpaved road	≍	Bridge
▬▬▬	Pedestrianized street	⊠	Post office
)▥▥▥(	Tunnel	★	Bus stop
▬▬▬	Railway line	✈	Airport
▪▪▪▪▪	Funicular railway	🅿	Parking
--Ⓜ--	Metro line and station	✡	Synagogue
•---•	Cable car	⚓	Monastery
▬▬	River	↑	One way arrow
▬ ▬	Ferry route	↨	Church (regional maps)
▬▬▬	Wall	╪	Church (town maps)
⊠—⊠	Gate	▮	Building
- - - - -	Path	⬯	Stadium
𝍐𝍐	Rocks	+⊹+	Christian cemetery
▲	Peak	▨	Park
/|\	Hill	▨	Beach
Ⓐ	Campsite